MARRIAGE LINES

MARRIAGE LINES

The Richardson Family Letters 1854–1877

edited by

MEG PROBYN

A∫P
Australian Scholarly
PUBLISHING

MELBOURNE

Publication of this book was made possible with assistance from the
Publications Grants Committee of Monash University.

First published 2000 by
Australian Scholarly Publishing Pty Ltd
P. O. Box 299, Kew, Victoria 3101
102/282 Collins Street, Melbourne 3000
Tel: (03) 9817 5208 Fax: (03) 9817 6431

National Cataloguing-in-Publication data:

Marriage lines : the Richardson family letters 1854-1877
Bibliography.
Includes index.
ISBN 1 875606 81 5.

1. Richardson, Mary – Correspondence. 2. Richardson,
Walter Lindesay – Correspondence. 3. Richardson family –
Correspondence. 4. Obstetricians – Australia –
Correspondence. 5. Australia – Biography. I. Probyn, Meg
(Margaret Lilian).

994.0310922

This project has been assisted by the Commonwealth Government through
the Australia Council, its arts funding and advisory body.

Australia Council
for the Arts

for Clive

Contents

Illustrations

Acknowledgements

For permission to publish these previously unpublished letters, I thank Angela and Patrick Neustatter, Margaret A. Capon (executrix of the Henry Handel Richardson estate), and the National Library of Australia (owner of the letters). Without the Manuscript Section of the NLA (particularly Graeme Powell and Greg Wilson), this work would not have been possible. Thanks are due to the late Dorothy Green and to Axel Clark for their pioneering biographical work on Henry Handel Richardson. To the Monash University Library and especially Richard Overell and his staff from the Rare Books Section, I owe my thanks. I am grateful to all the staff who assisted me at the State Library of Victoria, the Public Records Office at Laverton, the Melbourne Archives, the University of Tasmania Library Archives, the Ballarat Public Library, the Geelong Public Library and Historical Society, the Baillieu and the Brownless Libraries at the University of Melbourne, the Mitchell Library and the State Library of New South Wales. On two trips overseas I was greatly assisted by the staff at the Leicestershire Public Records Office at Wigston, the Snaith Public Library, Yorkshire, the Representative Church Body Library and the National Library of Ireland, both in Dublin, the Leith Public Library in Scotland and the British Library in London.

Many hours have been spent in the libraries and research rooms of the Australian Institute of Genealogical Studies at Blackburn and at the Family Centres at the Church of Jesus Christ of Latter-Day Saints at Blackburn, Wantirna and Braeside; each of these organisations is staffed by volunteers whose generosity in time and sharing of knowledge is gratefully acknowledged.

Among the many others who assisted me in the preparation of this work, I wish to thank particularly the Reverend Canon John W. R. Crawford, St Patrick's Cathedral Group of Parishes, who shared documents he had found in his own family research in Ireland. I am grateful to the following persons, each of whom assisted my research: Leigh Hays, Archivist at the Battye Library, Perth; Robin Hocking, at C. J. Ham, estate agents; Robert Ashley and Dianne Campbell, local historians at Ballarat; Rex Fuge and Ian Carlton at the Athenaeum, Chiltern; Mrs Ian Munro, 'Bank House', Lochmaben; Dr John Beattie Wilson, local historian, Lochmaben; Mr and Mrs Albert Laverach and the verger of St James's Parish Church, Rawcliffe; Mrs Una Richards and Mrs Noelene Hoysted.

The members of the team working on the Henry Handel Richardson Research Project at Monash University have been a constant support, discussing and sharing information. My research began when Bruce Steele and Clive Probyn suggested that I might assist them by transcribing the letters for the project. They thought I would enjoy the challenge and they were right. Dr Michael Ackland read the manuscript at an earlier stage and I thank him for his comments and his interest. Special thanks are due to Professor Harold Love, for his scholarly support and his friendship throughout my PhD candidacy.

Zoë, Andrew and Fiona, as always supportive of their mother, enjoyed my research student status. My husband travelled to far-distant places with me, patiently searching through graveyards and peering at microfilms in dusty research offices. To him I owe my thanks and much more.

Preface

There is a fascination in reading personal family letters of another period, for through them so much is revealed of the writers and their society. The distance of time tempers the feeling of intrusion into intimate relationships and private details and yet that distance also necessitates analysis or commentary if we are to understand them fully. The letters in this book are dated from 1854 to 1877 and were written or received by relatives of Henry Handel Richardson, the majority of them by her father and mother.[1] Ethel Florence Lindesay Richardson, the daughter of Mary and Walter Lindesay Richardson, was born in Melbourne on 3 January 1870. She used her married name for her first publications (translations), but when she published her first novel in 1908 she called herself 'Henry Handel Richardson' (HHR), the name of one of her cousins. The primary fascination of the letters for literary scholars has been the extensive use which HHR made of them in the writing of *The Fortunes of Richard Mahony* (1917–1929), for although the trilogy is fiction, HHR borrows extensively from the experiences of her parents, their relatives and friends and from her own early life in Victoria. The letters reveal a different man and woman from Richard Mahony and Mary Turnham; yet Walter and Mary would have recognised something of themselves in the Mahony story. This book contains some cross-referencing to HHR's fiction but its main aim is to explain more about the background of HHR's real families and the social history disclosed and enacted by the writers.

In reply to Mary Kernot,[2] who had sent her a cutting from *The Age* newspaper,[3] HHR wrote:

> I'm getting hardened to having my family history turned up: it was bound to come & I'm not ashamed of it. But the subtle mixture in this article especially noticeable, of truth & fiction will some day have to be put a stop to. It was always our plan that J.G.R. (her deceased husband) shd do this when I was gone. But since he has cruelly left me in the lurch, it will fall to my own (unwilling) pen ... Though I can see that it will be hard work

---

[1] In her diary on Sunday 27 May 1889, Henry Handel Richardson wrote: 'Read a lot of Father's & Mother's letters. It is like reading a love story of 30 years ago. I wonder if any one will ever be as fond of me as he was of her.' NLA MS133/8/7.

[2] Mary Kernot née Robertson (1868–1954), school friend of HHR at the Presbyterian Ladies College, Melbourne, with whom HHR corresponded regularly after the publication of *The Getting of Wisdom*. She was the daughter of John Dickson Robertson (1831–1915), Presbyterian Minister, and his wife, Amelia née Spencer (1833–1911). She married Percy White Kernot, an architect, in 1900.

[3] F. F., 'Eminent Living Australians No. X: Henry Handel Richardson', *The Age*, 14 May 1938.

to make people believe that Mahony is not an exact copy of my father. How cd he be? I was only 9 when he died, & for a year or so had seen nothing of him. And even before that but little. He was middle-aged when we were born, & far more engrossed in his books & studies than in two small children. While later on he was too worried & heart-broken to take much notice of us. I have not one clear picture of him in my mind. J.G.R. always maintained I had drawn Mahony entirely from myself. Fitting this self-portrait into the form of M's material existence. And even into this, other & similar fates were woven. While the figures that surrounded the central figure were one & all imaginary.[4]

HHR never 'put a stop' to the muddle between fact and fiction. Indeed her autobiography, *Myself When Young* (published after her death), contains few real facts about her family background. She either knew very little, or perhaps had forgotten the family stories, or chose to give misleading details.

HHR's parents met in 1854 and married in 1855; they wrote to each other for the next twenty-two years whenever they were apart. Their first child, HHR, was not born until four-teen-and-a-half years after their marriage and her birth was followed fifteen months later by the arrival of their second daughter, Ada Lillian Lindesay Richardson. There are 231 extant letters or parts of letters written or received by Walter and Mary Richardson and these fall into several phases:

- between April 1854 and July 1855, there are eighteen letters—one pre-engagement and seventeen engagement letters—written while Walter was living as a storekeeper in Ballarat and Mary was working as a governess at Bell Post Hill, Geelong;

- between December 1855 and June 1866, there are ninety letters after their marriage when their home   was in Ballarat, Victoria—first a canvas and timber-framed home attached to Walter's shop and later a   more substantial wooden house in Webster Street, built after he had returned to his profession of medical practitioner. Included in this group are seventeen letters (dated 1857 to 1863) from Walter's mother, Lucinda Cheyne, two from his half-brother, John Cheyne, one from the Buninyong Masonic Lodge, and one from his stepfather, Dr Bayne Cheyne, announcing Walter's mother's death in 1866;

- between May 1867 and December 1868, Walter and Mary were living in England where they wrote or received thirty-seven letters: included in this group are six letters from Elizabeth Bailey, Mary's mother, and one from the Ismay Shipping Company;

- between 1869 and 1875, only seventeen letters have survived from a busy period when they returned to live in Melbourne (where their two daughters were born) and then sailed to Europe for a year's trip in 1873 and finally returned to build a new house in Hawthorn in 1875: included in this group are two letters from Elizabeth Bailey written shortly before her death in 1869;

- in 1876, Walter sought another practice in Chiltern and thirty-two letters have survived from this period before Mary, HHR and Lil joined him; another seventeen letters were written by him in the summer of 1877 when he was left in Chiltern while his family took a holiday by the sea;

- the final group of twenty letters were written in August to September 1877 by Walter to his family in Chiltern when he had gone to Queenscliff to find another medical practice.

---

4   ALS: ML MSS45, letter to Mary Kernot dated 20 July 1938.

It was in Queenscliff that Walter's career as a doctor ended in June 1878 and, as his physical and mental condition deteriorated, he was admitted to hospital in Melbourne in September. He died on 1 August 1879, from 'General Paralysis of the Insane'. Mary Richardson outlived him by seventeen years, dying in Munich, Germany, of bowel cancer, with her two daughters beside her, on 26 November 1896, a month before her sixty-first birthday.

Although Mary kept all Walter's letters, Walter only kept hers from their engagement period and a few from the early years of their marriage, for he was concerned about their privacy. He wrote: 'I hope you keep my letters safely from the eyes of the public—'[5]: 'if I thought you burned my letters I would write much longer & fuller ones—'[6]: and when he had written in another letter a particularly loving and passionate sentence about his desire for her, he added: 'for goodness sake <u>burn this letter</u>, or keep it out of sight.'[7] Later he wrote: '<u>If I knew my letters were destroyed I would write differently</u> but you <u>will</u> keep them & I dislike the idea of any other having the chance of reading them. You know my wishes and have known them for years—'[8] Despite his protestations, Mary stored them carefully and although there are gaps in sequences, where letters have probably been destroyed by her daughters or by accident, the letters reflect the development of their life together.

One letter Mary wrote to Walter on 1 July 1855, eight weeks before their marriage, was lost, not by Walter but by the postal or carrier service between Geelong and Ballarat. In it she had answered all his queries about details of her family, including information about her early life in Leicester. She later wrote:

> have you received the missing letter yet? I am so sorry you did not get it there is nothing I dislike so much as my letters to be opened & particularly that one. I feel so vexed about it you cant think.[9]

Her vexation is probably nothing in comparison to that of modern researchers, for it has been surprisingly difficult to uncover facts about her family. Information about Walter's family is equally difficult to obtain although much can be learned from his mother's family gossip.

This book contains more information about the families of Walter and Mary than previously known, including the important pioneer links with Australia that would have been influential in Walter's early life, and corrects some misinformation found in other publications, including HHR's own account in *Myself When Young*. The four family trees (Bailey, Cheyne, Richardson and Sirée) show where HHR fits into the complex relationships, including her link with the writer Iris Murdoch (1919–1999), a fifth cousin of HHR in the Richardson family. The letters are interesting in their own right as an insight into the social issues of nineteenth-century migration to Australia. The single fact that HHR became such an important twentieth-century Australian writer sets them apart from other family letters.

---

5   Letter 65, from WLR to MR, 15 June 1860 (MS133/1/101).

6   Letter 73, from WLR to MR, 28 May 1861 (MS133/1/75).

7   Letter 81, from WLR to MR, 7 February 1862 (MS133/1/77).

8   Letter 152, from WLR to MR, 2 October 1869 (MS133/1/166).

9   Letter 14, from MR to WLR, 22 July 1855 (MS133/1/6).

Introduction

Reading personal correspondence spread over twenty years enables the reader to gain an insight into the writers' personalities and in the development and changes of their relationships. The transcriptions, although inevitably easier to read than the original letters, lose the intimacy of the idiosyncratic styles of the writers—from rushed, large, scrawly writing to the neat, precise hand. Although transcriptions may be second best to the real thing, in many cases the actual letters in this collection are almost illegible. As Dorothy Green wrote:

> A careful examination of Mary Richardson's early letters to her husband would take a long time, longer than I have had time to give to it; they are written, as Richardson says in the novel,[1] in a beautiful minute Italian hand with complicated flourishes, a hand which is almost indecipherable on microfilm since the sentences are written vertically and horizontally on the same sheet, no doubt in order to conserve paper. The originals are almost as illegible.[2]

Once Mary's handwriting is transcribed, her letters are a delight for their spontaneity and their intimate details of the Richardsons' daily life. These transcriptions are as close as possible to the original letters so that the misspelling, punctuation and crossings-out have been included. It is particularly poignant in Walter's case since his handwriting deteriorated as his illness became more pronounced. He admitted in his letter to Mary in September 1877: 'I generally have to write my letters twice over owing to the mistakes, so do not expect so many.'[3] The crossings-out sometimes show only too clearly the state of his health; and his instructions to Mary must have caused her considerable frustration. For example, he wrote to her from Queenscliff in September 1877 when she was trying to sort out the auction for the Chiltern house:

> Sign the cheque <u>yourself</u> & make it payable ~~dont~~ scratch out a bearer ~~but draw your fo~~ & write over or order. that is the safest way to send it nobody can draw but me.[4]

---

[1] 'Mahony discovered three crossed pages, written in a delicately pointed, minute, Italian hand.' *FRM I*, p. 35.
[2] Green 1973, p. 330.
[3] Letter 221, from WLR to MR, 6 September 1877 (MS133/1/232).
[4] Letter 230, from WLR to MR, 20 September 1877 (MS133/1/227).

In contrast to the later deterioration in Walter's handwriting, his early letters are generally clearly written and easy to read, especially when compared to Mary's. Throughout his later letters, particularly those of 1877, Walter added words above the lines, presumably after he had re-read his letters, to clarify the meaning. These additional words have been included in the text without any marks. Characteristics of individual spelling practice have been retained. WLR frequently used non-standard spellings such as 'freind', 'dissapointed', 'xpense' or 'abscence' but there is no difficulty in understanding what he meant so his spelling has been left. Occasionally WLR misspells a word (for example, 'enchancing' instead of 'enchanting' in Letter 118). These have also been left in the text. Abbreviations, which might cause difficulty for the modern reader, have been expanded and missing words or letters have been supplied in square brackets ([ ]).

Many of the writers, but particularly Mary and her mother, use punctuation sparingly. The text is presented without additional punctuation except where essential for the reader's understanding, this additional editorial punctuation being placed in square brackets. Where essential words are missing from the letters, they are inserted within square brackets. There are no editorial additions or emendations apart from those which appear in square brackets in the text.

The Register of Letters (pp. 368–378) lists every letter in chronological order, by sender and recipient, and by manuscript number(s). The documents stored in the National Library of Australia each have a manuscript number, which bears little relationship to the sequential dates of the letters. Where a letter is distributed between two or more documents (which is not infrequent) the other linking document numbers are also indicated. Much of the transcribing time has been taken up by matching odd pages stored in a somewhat haphazard sequence. Very few of the letters written by Walter and Mary are dated: on the other hand Lucinda Cheyne's letters, where they have survived intact, are a model, for she carefully dates every letter and writes her full address. The Walter and Mary letters have been dated and the date (if attributed) placed between square brackets. Dating is sometimes an extremely difficult matter, but references to midwifery cases, external social events and particular issues of newspapers have assisted in achieving accuracy.

The Index to Part I (pp. 379–385) lists all the persons in alphabetical order by page number. The Index to Part II (pp. 386–402) lists persons and vessels mentioned in the letters or endnotes by letter number. If the person appears in the notes to the letters only, the number of the letter is followed by *n*. Where there is a significant biographical note, the letter number is in bold.

While the letters have been reproduced as closely as possible to the original manuscripts, the following editorial style and conventions are used:

Style: In matters of spelling, capitalisation, underlining, deletions, abbreviations and variant signatures, the original manuscript has been reproduced verbatim in order to convey the writer's grammatical and orthographical style. In order to avoid confusion for the reader, however, the following editorial emendations have been made:

• Square brackets enclose editorial supplementation: 'Tell William (Bailey) I was sorry I could not wait for him' [Letter 4]. Where abbreviations are unclear, they are expanded within square brackets: 'I wrote in great annoyance in consequence of the rascality of that unprincipled fellow B[rooke] S[mith]' (Letter 209).

- Where words or phrases have been repeated, these are left unmarked in the text: 'I shall always answer your letters by return return of post ...' (Letter 3).
- An extra space has been inserted between unpunctuated sentences.
- Silent categories:
  a)   partial superscript (or flourish) in dates is standardised: 2^d to 2nd;
  b)   common forms of address (D^r, M^r, M^{rs}, M^{essrs}) and currency superscripts (for example, 6^d) are retained, but points or lines beneath the superscript are omitted;
  c)   marks separating the symbols for pounds, shillings and pence are regularised to en-dashes (£–s–d) instead of a variety of full stops, dashes and slashes;
  d)   dashes indicating end of sentences or phrases are standardised to an em-dash.

Brackets: Parentheses are always authorial; square brackets indicate editorial supplementation, including illegible or missing material due to damage.

Headings: Each letter has been assigned a reference number. A heading within square brackets indicates editorial provision of the names of the writer (and his/her location) and the recipient (and his/her location).

Addresses: When the sender's address has been given in the original, it is recorded immediately beneath the heading of the letter, flush right, lineation designated by vertical lines. Where this has not been provided or has been only partially provided, the information is supplied editorially within square brackets.

Date-lines: Where the sender has indicated the date of writing, this information is set beneath the address, flush right. Where this has not been provided or has been only partially provided, the information is supplied editorially within square brackets. The day of the week, if not provided by the writer, is also added within square brackets. Where the writer ascribes a date and day of the week which do not agree, an endnote clarifies the issue.

Salutation and valediction: The former is given as in the original, but flush left; the latter is reproduced as run-on text, the original lineation signalled by vertical rules. Signatures are set leftwards, double indented. Any additional flourish around the signatures (paraph) is omitted.

Postscripts: These are located flush left and do not represent the lineation of the original.

Texts: Manuscript sources are given as NLA (National Library of Australia) followed by series and manuscript number.

References: Frequently repeated references in endnotes are given in shortened form. See Cue Titles.

Other abbreviations: Frequently repeated references to writers and recipients of letters are given in shortened form. See Abbreviations.

Abbreviations

ABS	Alexander Brooke Smith
ALR	Ada Lillian Lindesay Richardson, Walter and Mary's youngest daughter
BC	Dr Bayne Cheyne, Walter's stepfather
EB	Elizabeth Bailey (née Robinson), Mary's mother
EHB	Edward (Ned) Harold Bailey, Mary's brother
GB	Grace Bailey, Mary's sister
HEB	Harrie Elphinstone Bailey, Mary's nephew
HHR	Henry Handel Richardson (Ethel Florence Lindesay Richardson), Walter and Mary's eldest daughter
JB	John Brett, married to Mary's sister, Lizzie
JC	John Cheyne, Walter's half-brother
JRB	John Robinson Bailey, Mary's brother
LB	Lizzie Brett (née Bailey), Mary's sister
LC	Lucinda Cheyne (née Sirée), formerly Richardson, Walter's mother
LR	Lucinda Richardson, Walter's sister
MR	Mary Richardson (née Bailey)
SAB	Sarah Ann Bailey, Mary's sister
SB	Samuel Bailey, Mary's brother
WB	William Bailey, Mary's brother
WLR	Walter Lindesay Richardson

Cue Titles

A) Manuscript Locations

ADFA	Australian Defence Force Academy, Canberra
NLA	National Library of Australia
PRO	Public Record Office of Victoria, Laverton
SLV	State Library of Victoria
MoU	Monash University

B) Printed Works

ADB Douglas Pike, Bede Nairn and Geoffrey Serle, eds, *Australian Dictionary of Biography.* (Carlton: Melbourne University Press, 1966–1993)

Bowden Keith Macrea Bowden, *Goldrush Doctors at Ballaarat* (Mulgrave: the Author, 1977)

Brothers C. R. D. Brothers, *Early Victorian Psychiatry: 1835–1905* (Melbourne: F. W. Cheshire, 1957)

Brownshill Walter Randolph Brownshill, *History of Geelong and Corio Bay* (Melbourne: Wilke and Co., 1955) with Ian Wynd, *Postscript 1955–1990* (Geelong: Geelong Advertiser, 1990)

Carboni Raffaello Carboni, *The Eureka Stockade* (Carlton: Melbourne University Press, 1980) (first published by the author, 1855)

Case Walter Lindesay Richardson, *Register of Midwifery Cases,* NLA MS133/1/299

Chambers William Geddie and J. Liddell Geddie, eds, *Chambers' Biographical Dictionary,* 2nd edn (London: W. and R. Chambers, 1945)

Clark Axel Clark, *Henry Handel Richardson: Fiction in the Making* (Brookvale, NSW: Simon & Schuster, 1990)

Companion to Australian History Graeme Davison, John Hirst and Stuart Macintyre, eds, *The Oxford Companion to Australian History* (South Melbourne: Oxford University Press, 1998)

Dawbin Lucy Frost, ed., *The Journal of Annie Baxter Dawbin: July 1858 – May 1868* (St Lucia: University of Queensland Press, The Academy Editions of Australian Literature, 1998)

de Serville Paul de Serville, *Pounds and Pedigrees: The Upper Class in Victoria 1859–80* (South Melbourne: Oxford University Press, 1991)

Drosken	G. W. Drosken, ed., *Historical Record of Queenscliffe Borough: 1863–1933* (Queenscliff: Queenscliff Council, 1933)
FRM I	Henry Handel Richardson, *The Fortunes of Richard Mahony, Vol. I, Australia Felix* (London: William Heinemann, 1917)
FRM II	Henry Handel Richardson, *The Fortunes of Richard Mahony, Vol. II, The Way Home* (London: William Heinemann, 1925)
FRM III	Henry Handel Richardson, *The Fortunes of Richard Mahony, Vol. III, Ultima Thule* (London: William Heinemann, 1929)
FS	*The Chiltern Federal Standard*
Garden	Donald S. Garden, Albany: *A Panorama of the Sound from 1827* (West Melbourne: Nelson, 1977)
GW	Henry Handel Richardson, *The Getting of Wisdom* (London: William Heinemann, 1910)
Graham Papers	Microfilm of papers relating to the Cheyne and Graham families (University of Tasmania Archives)
Green, 1986	Dorothy Green, *Henry Handel Richardson and Her Fiction* (North Sydney: Allen & Unwin, 1986).
Haydn's Dictionary	Benjamin Vincent, *Haydn's Dictionary of Dates and Universal Information Relating to all Ages and Nations*, 17th edn (London: Ward, Lock, 1881) (1st edn 1841)
Kelly	William Kelly, *Life in Victoria or Victoria in 1853 & Victoria in 1858*, 2 vols (London: Chapman & Hall, 1860)
Love	Harold Love, *James Edward Neild: Victorian Virtuoso* (Carlton: Melbourne University Press, 1989)
MD	*The Macquarie Dictionary*, 2nd edn (Sydney: The Macquarie Library, 1991)
MWY	Henry Handel Richardson, *Myself When Young* (Kingswood, Surrey: Windmill Press, 1948)
Sadleir	John Sadleir, *Recollections of a Victorian Police Officer* (Melbourne: George Robertson, 1913; facsimile edn, Harmondsworth: Penguin Books, 1973)
Sands	Sands and McDougall, *Melbourne and Suburban Street Directory* (Melbourne: Sands and McDougall, 1863 to 1877)
Serle	Geoffrey Serle, *The Golden Age: A History of the Colony of Victoria 1851–1861* (Carlton: Melbourne University Press, 1963)
Star	*The Ballarat Star*
Stoller	Alan Stoller and R. H. Emmerson, 'Richard Mahony, Walter Lindesay Richardson and the Spirochaete', *Papers presented at a Centenary Seminar on HHR* (Canberra: NLA, 1972) 9–22
Withers	William Bramwell Withers, *The History of Ballarat from the First Pastoral Settlement to the Present Time*, 2nd edn (Ballarat: F. W. Niven and Co., 1887), reproduced as facsimile edn, with Index by Frank Cusack (Carlton: Queensberry Hill Press, 1980) (1st edn 1870)

Chronology

1825–1854

Year		The Bailey/Robinson Family		The Richardson/Cheyne Family
1825	3 May	Elizabeth Robinson marries John Bailey at St Margaret's, Leicester, England		
1826		John Robinson Bailey (JRB) born	Jul–Aug	Walter Lindesay Richardson (WLR) born in Dublin, 4th child of Lucinda née Sirée (4th wife of Alexander Richardson), 14th child of his father
1827			28 May	Alexander Richardson, WLR's father, dies
1828	9 Apr	Edward Harold Bailey (EHB) born; christened at St George's Parish Church, Leicester	8 Apr	Lucinda Richardson marries Dr Bayne Cheyne in Buckinghamshire; after Parisian honeymoon, they move to Bristol
1829	19 Aug	Sarah Ann Bailey (SAB) christened	11 Aug	WLR's half-brother, John Cheyne, christened at Congregational Church, Bristol
1830	17 Nov	Elizabeth Bailey (LB) christened		
1831	12 Jan	Thomas Robinson dies (buried at St George's Church, Leicester	15 May	William Alexander Cheyne, christened
			2 Jun	George Cheyne and his wife Grace arrive aboard *Stirling* in King George Sound, WA
1832				George and Grace Cheyne acquire more land in Albany, WA
1833	9 Jan	Thomas Robinson Burton Bailey christened		John Sirée (brother of Lucinda Cheyne) dies
			10 May	(Rev.) John Cheyne (WLR's step-cousin) marries Anne Levina Forrest in Buckinghamshire
1834	22 Oct	William Bailey christened	Aug	Capt. Alexander Cheyne, (Rev.) John and Anne Cheyne and baby son John St Leger (b. 1834) arrive aboard *James Pattison* in WA
			Nov	George and Grace Cheyne establish home in Albany, WA
1835	9 Aug	William Hester dies	8 Dec	Alexander Cheyne leaves Albany and arrives aboard *Caledonian* in Hobart Town, Tasmania
	28 Dec	Mary Bailey (MR) born		
1836	13 Jan	MR christened	31 Jan	Dr John Cheyne (BC's brother) dies
			24 Feb	Elisabeth Wilkinson (BC's sister) dies
				Baby John St Leger Cheyne dies in Albany
1837	5 Apr	Sarah Robinson marries William Henry Turnham in London		Elizabeth Levina and George (twins) born to John and Anne Cheyne in Albany. George dies
				(Rev.) John Cheyne, wife and daughter leave Albany and sail to New Zealand; stay for a year before sailing to NSW
1838	16 Mar:	Elizabeth Turnham (Bessie) christened	1 Feb	Henry Downing Richardson marries Ellen O'Connor in Dublin
	21 Mar	Samuel Bailey christened		

1839		Grace Bailey (GB) born	20 Nov	Cecilia Wilkinson marries Henry Graham William Henry Graham christened
1840				Lucinda born to Henry D. and Ellen Richardson
1841		William Henry Turnham (Willy) born		
1842			10 Feb 20 Sep	Elizabeth Wilkinson marries Lieut. Fred. Augustus Yorke Lieut.-Col. William Cheyne dies in Edinburgh Henry Handel born to Henry D. and Ellen Richardson
1843		Joseph Turnham emigrates to Hobart Town JRB travels to America (New York and Connecticut)		
1844	12 Jun 12 Oct	Charles Bailey christened Joseph Turnham marries Elizabeth Cutler in Hobart Town		Walter Lindesay born to Henry D. and Ellen Richardson
1845				WLR matriculates as a medical student at Edinburgh University and starts four years of study Alexander born to Henry D. and Ellen Richardson
1846	25 Feb	John Bailey, father of MR, dies JRB returns to England from America and starts work as warehouseman in London	4 Jan	William Alexander Cheyne (aged 14)
1847				Nanny born to Henry D. and Ellen Richardson
1848			24 Jun	Emily Trimmer (George and Grace Cheyne's adopted dau.) marries Andrew Moir, Albany, WA
1849				WLR assistant pathologist in Edinburgh Infirmary (2 mths); awarded degree MD and diploma of Edinburgh College of Surgery; house surgeon for Edinburgh Maternity Hospital (3 mths); resident physician in Cholera Hospital (3 mths); goes to London
			6 May	Henry Downing Richardson dies leaving wife and 5 children (Rev.) John Cheyne and Anne and 5 surviving children leave NSW to live in Victoria
1850				WLR leaves London for Wales where assistant for doctors in Montgomery
			Jul	WLR goes to Kent as assistant to Dr T. H. Smith (father of Alexander Brooke Smith)
1851		JRB (warehouseman) and EHB (mercantile clerk) decide to emigrate	25 Jan	Marmaduke Cheyne born to Caroline and Henry Richardson WLR decides to emigrate
1852	8 Mar	JRB and EHB sail for Australia aboard *Mount Stuart Elphinstone*	2 Jun	WLR sails for Australia aboard *Roxburgh Castle* (on board also Susannah Tyler Nicholson, JRB's fiancée)
	5 Jul	JRB and EHB arrive in Melbourne JRB sets up a softgoods store in Geelong EHB goes to the goldfields (Ballarat)	28 Aug	WLR arrives in Melbourne; goes to the goldfields in Ballarat, first as a digger and then as a storekeeper
1853	29 Jan 25 May	Susannah Tyler Nicholson and JRB marry in Geelong MR, SAB and WB arrive aboard *Anne Cropper* in Melbourne MR becomes governess for children of William and Marion Bradshaw, at Bell Post Hill, near Geelong	May Oct	Alick Cook (WLR's step-cousin) arrives in Melbourne aboard *Wacousta* JC and Mervyn Richardson (Marmaduke's brother) arrive in Melbourne aboard *Goldfinder* Lindesay born to Caroline and Henry Richardson
	7 Dec	Harrie Elphinstone Bailey born in Geelong, son of Susannah and JRB		
1854	April 24 April	MR and WLR meet MR writes the first extant letter to WLR	30 Dec	Lucinda Richardson (LR) arrives aboard *Champion of the Seas* in Melbourne

Chronology
1855–1879

Year		Life of Mary and Walter Lindesay Richardson, Family and Friends
1855	27 Aug	WLR marries MR in Geelong; they live behind the store in Mount Pleasant, Ballarat
		Walter Lindesay Richardson born to Caroline and Henry Richardson
1856	7 Jan	Bruce Cheyne dies in Albany, WA
	13 Feb	Tilly Bradshaw marries Henry Bannester; MR stays at Bell Post Hill for 2 weeks
	13 Sep	Emma (Trotty) born in Geelong to Susannah and JRB
	Dec	WLR registers as a medical practitioner
1857	23 Feb	Charles Cheyne dies in Edinburgh
	Mar	Henry Sirée, his wife and children, Elizabeth (15 years) and Horatio Nelson (13), arrive aboard *Champion of the Seas* in Melbourne to join Alick Cook (Henry's stepson)
	22 Apr	Lucinda Richardson born to Caroline and Henry Richardson
	July	MR has a miscarriage
		WLR attends 14 confinements during year
1858		Henry Sirée takes his children, Elizabeth and Horatio Nelson, back to England/Ireland, but leaves his wife and stepson, Alick Cook, in Victoria
	17 May	WLR is accoucheur at the birth of his niece, Edith Elizabeth, daughter of Susan and JRB, in Ballarat
	6 Jul	Capt. Alexander Cheyne dies in Hobart
		JC arrives in India and joins the Bengal Yeomanry Cavalry
	Aug	William Henry Turnham, MR's cousin, arrives on *Cyclone* in Melbourne; MR visits Melbourne to meet him and stay with friends
		WLR attends 37 confinements during year
1859	Mar–Apr	WLR is very ill with dysentery and takes trip to recuperate in Queenscliff and Collingwood Stockade with the Turnhams
	7 Jun	Elizabeth Bailey marries Capt. John Brett (2nd Rifle Brigade) in Leicester
	30 Jul	Elizabeth Sirée departs on *Yorkshire*, arriving London in October
	13 Aug	Susannah Bailey dies; WLR and MR take care of her and JRB's children, Harrie, Emma (Trotty) and Edith
	29 Oct	JRB is elected to Victorian Legislative Assembly representing Ballarat West; becomes Postmaster General in the Nicholson Ministry (Oct. 1859 to Nov. 1860)
	Dec	MR has gynaecological problems
	15 Dec	JC dies in Assam, India
		WLR attends 53 confinements during year
1860	Jan	MR stays in St Kilda for a holiday to recuperate, taking Trotty (3 years 6 mths) with her in lodgings with Anna Maria Cuthbert, Henry Cuthbert's sister. Harrie (6 years) and baby Edith Elizabeth (18 mths) stay with WLR in Ballarat and become sick
	5 Feb	Edith Elizabeth Bailey dies (aged 18 mths)
	Nov	SB arrives aboard *Result* in Melbourne; stays with MR and WLR
		WLR attends 67 confinements during year
1861	4 Apr	JRB marries 2nd wife, Jane (Jeannie) Rainsford
	May	MR takes Trotty (4 years 7 mths) to live with her father and new stepmother. Harrie was either at a boarding school or staying with the Turnhams at Pentridge
		WLR attends 134 confinements during year

1862	Feb	MR stays in Melbourne with her sister-in-law LR to assist her preparations for her journey to England. WLR joins her prior to LR's farewell
	11 Feb	Gertrude Elizabeth Bailey born in St Kilda, dau. of Jeannie and JRB
	21 Feb	LR departs on *Latona*: arrives at the home of her mother and stepfather, LC and BC, Brighton, England on 16 June
	July	HEB attends Melbourne Grammar School for 6 months
	Sep	Alex Richardson (WLR's nephew) arrives in Melbourne as a midshipman on *Great Australia* for short visit
	15 Nov	Alick Cook departs from Melbourne aboard *True Briton*
		WLR publishes article in *Australian Medical Journal (AMJ)*
1863		WLR appointed an honorary medical officer to the Ballarat District Hospital
	Jan	WLR publishes article in *AMJ*
	1 May	Beatrice Ida Bailey born in St Kilda, dau. of Jeannie and JRB
	Aug	Lucinda Richardson leaves Liverpool on board *Marco Polo*
1864	Apr	MR takes trip with Emily Kabat to visit Murchison family in Kilmore and Broadford, Victoria
	Oct	Lucinda Richardson arrives in Melbourne aboard *Marco Polo*
		WLR publishes article in *Medical and Surgical Review* and another in *AMJ*
1865	Mar	MR stays with relatives in Melbourne
1866	Jan–Feb	MR stays with Jeannie and JRB for the birth of their 3rd child (his 7th)
	7 Feb	Mary Jane Bailey born in East Melbourne, dau. of Jeannie and JRB
	21 Feb	Jeannie Bailey (35) dies in East Melbourne, 2nd wife of JRB
	Feb	HEB enrols at Scotch College (after his stepmother's death)
	20 Mar	MR stays for a month with the Kabats at Hamilton where Leopold is Inspector of Police
	22 Mar	Alex Richardson emigrates to Australia, arriving aboard *Yorkshire*
	7 Apr	WLR graduates at a conferring ceremony at University of Melbourne (degree of Doctor of Medicine)
	1 May	EHB marries Agnes Hablethwaite in Fitzroy, Melbourne
	20 Jun	LC (aged 70) dies in Lochmaben, Scotland
1867	14 Jan	WLR and MR and their nephew, HEB, depart on *Red Jacket*, arriving in London in May
	May	HEB enrols in private school in Tottenham; MR visits her sister and mother and WLR stays in London with MR's sister, SAB, planning a trip to the continent and visiting hospitals
	Jun	WLR and MR visit BC in Lochmaben: MR returns to Leicester and WLR visits Edinburgh
	Jul	WLR and MR take a tour to France (visiting the Great Exhibition in Paris) and Switzerland
	22 Aug	James Harold Bailey is born in N. Melbourne, 1st child of Agnes and EHB
	Sep	MR and WLR rent a house in Eccles, where WLR works on temporary contract for medical practice; HEB transfers to a school in Fairfield, Manchester
	Nov	WLR visits Yorkshire in search of medical practice; finds Rawcliffe, West Riding
		WLR publishes two articles in *AMJ*
1868	25 Jan	WLR arrives in Rawcliffe, leaving MR to pack up house in Eccles (assisted by her mother)
	14 Feb	MR and her mother take train to Rawcliffe. EB returns to Leicester
	2 Aug	BC dies in Lochmaben
	c. 18 Aug	John Walter Brett born, son of LB and Capt. John Brett (JB)
	Sep	WLR and MR decide to return to Australia at the end of the year
	26 Sep	Walter Robinson Bailey born in N. Melbourne, 2nd child of Agnes and EHB
	26 Sep	MR takes train from Rawcliffe to her sister, LB, in Devon, whose baby son, John Walter, is dying
	6 Oct	John Walter Brett dies, son of LB and JB
	30 Oct	WLR joins MR for a short holiday in Devon with the Bretts; they return to Rawcliffe to pack
	28 Nov	MR stays with EB in Leicester while WLR takes train to Manchester and stays with his cousin William Duke Richardson and his wife Caroline; he visits HEB in school in Fairfield
	1 Dec	WLR arrives in Dublin, having sailed from Liverpool; stays with John and Sophie Richardson
	4 Dec	WLR visits Ellen Richardson, his sister-in-law (Henry Downing Richardson's widow) at Mountjoy Prison, where she is Assistant Superintendent
	7 Dec	WLR returns to Leicester, having decided not to visit his sister Caroline in Cork
	26 Dec	WLR and MR in Liverpool about to set sail for Melbourne on *British Prince*
		WLR publishes article in *AMJ*

1869 26 May   WLR and MR arrive in Melbourne; MR discovers she is pregnant soon after arrival
          Jun   WLR visits friends in Ballarat
          5 Jun   George Cheyne dies in Lochmaben
          8 Jul   EB (aged 67) dies in Leicester
          24 Jul   JRB marries 3rd wife, Mary Ringrose Atkins, in South Yarra
          Sep–Oct   MR pays visit to friends in Ballarat

1870 3 Jan   Ethel Florence Lindesay Richardson (HHR) born 139 Blanche Terrace, Victoria Parade, Fitzroy, eldest child of MR
                    and WLR; born probably 4–6 weeks prematurely
          2 Jun   WLR sails from Melbourne to Sydney aboard *Dandenong*
          3–17 June WLR visits Sydney and stays at Parramatta with nephew, Alex Richardson, and Fanny
          17 Jun   WLR sails from Sydney to Melbourne aboard *You Yangs*
          6 Oct   WLR, MR and HHR move to 'Springfield', Chapel Street, St Kilda (Melbourne)
          15 Oct   Edgar Atkins Bailey born in Richmond, son of Mary and JRB
          22 Dec   SB marries Polly (Frances Mary Louisa) Lascelles in Geelong

1871 Mar   HEB returns to Melbourne aboard *Superb*
          28 Apr   Ada Lillian Lindesay Richardson (ALR) born at home, 2nd child of MR and WLR
          6 May   JRB (aged 45) dies in Richmond, son of John and Elizabeth Bailey
          26 Sep   Grace Cheyne (aged 72) dies in Lochmaben
          11 Dec   Edgar Atkins Bailey (aged 14 mths) dies in Williamstown, son of Mary and JRB (deceased)
          18 Dec   Mabel Elizabeth Bailey born in Fitzroy, 3rd child of Agnes and EHB

1872 7 Dec   Edgar Charles Bailey born in Emerald Hill, 4th child of Agnes and EHB

1873 18 Apr   WLR, MR, HHR and ALR depart for London aboard *Atrato*
          11 Jul   *Atrato* arrives in London

1874 1 Jun   Leila Maud Bailey born in Echuca, 1st child of Polly and SB
          June   WLR and MR leave HHR and ALR in Cork with Caroline and Henry Richardson while they holiday in Italy; in Italy
                    they hear news of collapse of banks in Melbourne and WLR returns to Australia from Italy; MR returns to
                    Ireland to collect children and then travels to sister, Sarah, in London
          21 Aug   WLR arrives in Melbourne aboard *Nubia*, having travelled overland from Italy
          17 Sep   MR, HHR, ALR and ASB set sail from Plymouth aboard *Sobraon* on which SAB meets Rev. James Laughton
          3 Nov   Celia Agnes Bailey born in Emerald Hill, 5th child of Agnes and EHB
          12 Dec   *Sobraon* arrives in Melbourne; WLR and family live at Sydney Terrace, Fitzroy Gardens, E. Melbourne

1875 22 Mar   SAB marries the Rev. James Laughton at the Presbyterian Church, Carlton, Melbourne, with WLR and Samuel
                    Bailey as witnesses
          23 Mar   Alexander Richardson marries Elizabeth Frances Watson in the Presbyterian Minister's home, in Carlton,
                    Melbourne. He and his wife visit WLR, MR, HHR and ALR, presenting the children with a doll and a book (*MWY*)
          Aug   WLR and family move to large newly built house near corner of Burwood and Glenferrie roads; WLR works in
                    Hawthorn medical practice; WLR in difficult financial position
          11 Sep: Rev. James Laughton dies of Phthisis and is buried in Melbourne General Cemetery
          30 Sep   HEB marries Leah Harris in Melbourne
          18 Nov   Mary Ringrose Bailey (widow of JRB) marries William Bayles in Malvern
                    MR, HHR and ALR go to Sorrento (Blairgowrie) to stay with Mrs Sydney Graham

1876 23 Mar   Mabel Elizabeth Bailey (aged 4) dies in Emerald Hill, 3rd child of Agnes and EHB
          Jun   WLR leaves Hawthorn to buy practice in Chiltern; rents 'Lake View'
          11 Jul   Sarah Ann Laughton sails from Melbourne to London aboard *Agamemnon*
          27 Jul   MR, HHR and ALR join WLR in Chiltern

1877 Jan   MR, HHR and ALR leave Chiltern for a 3-month holiday in Sorrento and then Queenscliff; while they are away,
                    WLR's health deteriorates
          20 Mar   Walter Robinson Bailey (aged 8) dies Wodonga, 2nd child of Agnes and EHB, buried in Melbourne General
                    Cemetery. WLR goes down to Melbourne for funeral and then on to Queenscliff and discusses possibility of
                    medical practice there
          late April MR, HHR and ALR return to Chiltern
          27 Aug   WLR leaves Chiltern, stays for a few days with Dr Graham in Melbourne and then sails by steamer to Queenscliff;
                    MR is joined by Mrs Sydney Graham in Chiltern and they pack up the house and prepare for an auction. Ned
                    comes down to Chiltern from Wodonga to assist MR
          Oct   The Richardson family is reunited in Queenscliff, at 26 Mercer Street

1878 Jun   WLR is relieved of his official duties
          11 Sep   WLR is admitted to Cremorne Private Hospital, Richmond
          mid-Sep   MR takes up appointment as postmistress at Koroit and she, HHR and ALR live at the post office. JRB's
                    daughter, Gertrude Bailey (aged 16), lives with them, to help MR
          9 Nov   Emma (Trotty) Bailey, working as a governess in Wangaratta, marries Robert B. Hoysted at Wangaratta
          18 Nov   WLR transferred to government asylum at Yarra Bend

1879 1 Jan   Frank Lascelles Bailey born at Sandhurst, 2nd child of Polly and SB
          24 Feb   WLR released from asylum and lives at Koroit with his family
          1 Aug   WLR dies in Koroit
          23 Sep   Percy François Bailey born in Wodonga, 6th and last child of Agnes and EHB

THE RICHARDSON FAMILY TREE

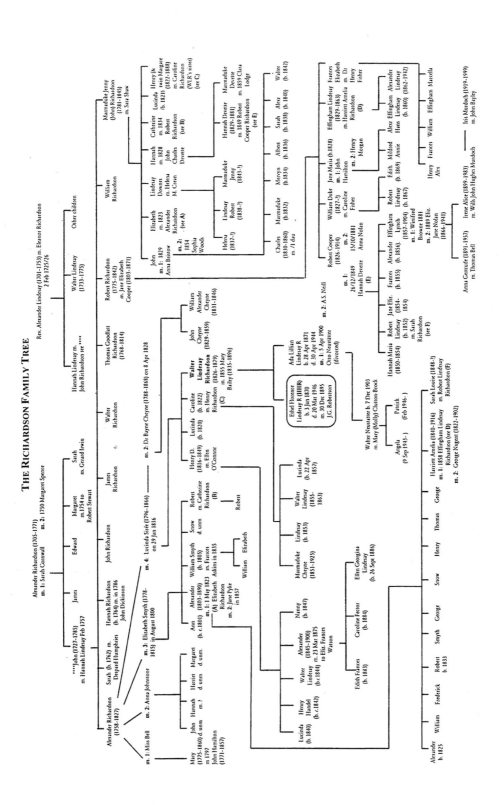

THE BAILEY FAMILY TREE

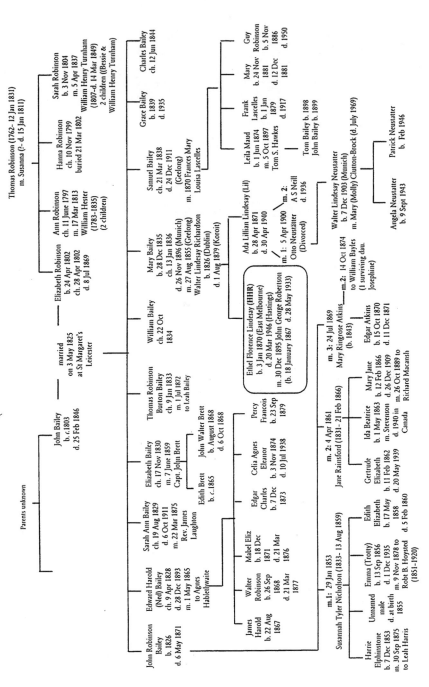

The Cheyne Family Tree

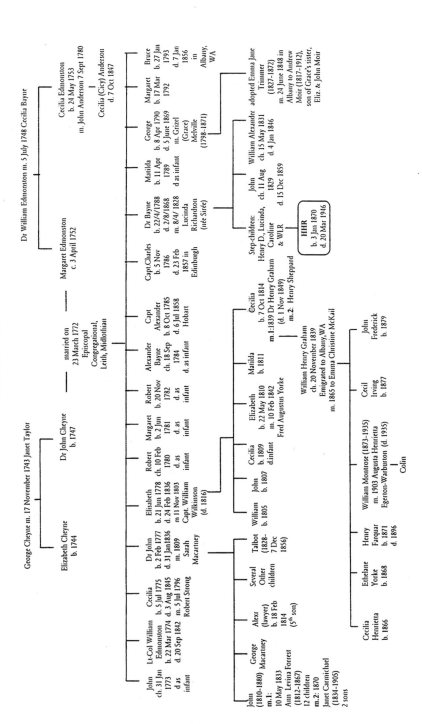

The Sirée Family Tree

Siree?

- Charles Sirée (attorney exchequer Jan 1775 m. Patience)
- Catherine Jane Sirée m. 1794 John Hastings Babington
- Jane Sirée m. 1797 Thomas Harding
- Henry Sirée Attorney — married 1792 — Harriet McCausland

McCausland?
- Harriet McCausland
- Unknown children

Children of Henry Sirée and Harriet McCausland:

- John (Attorney) b. c1793 d. c1833 m. Clementine d. 29 Dec 1858
- Lucinda b. 1796 d. 20 June 1866
  - m.1: 29 Jan 1816 Lieut Colonel Alexander Richardson b. Jan 1758 d. 28 May 1827
  - m.2: 8 Apr 1828 Dr Bayne Cheyne b. 22 April 1788 d. 2 August 1868
- Harriet b. 1798? m. 1823 Daniel Bastable
- Caroline b. c1800 m. 1823 Charles William Osborne
- Amelia b. 1806
- Horatio Nelson b. 1808 m. 1833 Catherine Nelson (Nanny)
- Henry b. c1812 m. 1839 Elizabeth Charlotte Cook née Harricks b. c1810
- Oliver b. c1815

Alexander (Alick Cook) b. c1828 from her previous marriage

Children of Henry b. c1812:
- Elizabeth b. 1842
- Horatio Nelson b. 1844

Children of Lucinda (with Alexander Richardson):
- Henry Downing b. Dec 1816 d. 6 May 1849 m. 1 Feb 1838 Ellen O'Connor
- Lucinda b. 1820
- Caroline b. 1822 m. 1845 Henry Richardson (1822-1888)
- Walter Lindesay Richardson b. 1826 d. 1 Aug 1879 m. Mary Bailey 27 Aug 1855

Children of Lucinda (with Dr Bayne Cheyne):
- John Cheyne b. 1829 d. 15 Dec 1859
- William Alexander Cheyne b. 1831 d. 4 Jan 1846

Children of Henry Downing:
- Lucinda b. 1840
- Henry Handel b. c1842
- Walter Lindesay b. c1844 d. 20 Aug 1900
- Alexander b. Oct 1845 d. 20 Aug 1900 m. 23 Mar 1875 Elizabeth Francis Watson
- Nanny b. 1847

Children of Alexander:
- Edith Frances b. 1883?
- Caroline Fetor b. 1884
- Ellen Georgina Lindesay b. 26 Sept. 1886

Children of Walter Lindesay Richardson and Mary Bailey:
- Marmaduke Cheyne (b. 25 Jan 1851 d. 16 Feb 1925)
- Lindesay b. 1853
- Walter Lindesay (1855-1863)
- Lucinda b. 22 Apr 1857
- Ethel Florence Lindesay R (HHR) b. 3 Jan 1870 d. 20 Mar 1946 m. 30 Dec 1895 J.G. Robertson
- Ada Lillian Lindesay R b. 28 Apr 1871 d. 30 Apr 1944 m.1: 5 Apr 1900 Otto Neustätter (divorced) m.2: A.S. Neill

Walter Neustätter b. 7 Dec 1903 (Munich) m. Mary (Molly) Clutton-Brock
- Angela b. 9 Sept 1943
- Patrick b. Feb 1946

Part I

Biographical Background

I

The Richardson Family

This book is not a biography, but in order to understand the letters it is necessary to reconstruct the lives of the family members. The letters of Lucinda Cheyne, despite the 'obsessively religious, belligerently Protestant'[1] side to her writing, prove to be an invaluable source of family information (and gossip). The Bailey, Cheyne, Richardson and Sirée families are complex, with names and nicknames repeated over generations. The references in Lucinda's letters to 'Alick', 'Alexander' or 'Elizabeth' would easily be understood (and identified) by Walter and Mary, but pose difficulties for the modern reader. As Dorothy Green wrote of one such name: 'The number of Marys in the letters makes for confusion, and needs the concentrated effort of a full-time biographer to clear it up.'[2] The 'Marys' are easier to sort out than the 'Alexs', 'Alecs' and 'Alicks'. There are three generations of Lucindas and endless complications in the stepfamily of Cheynes. References to their friends compound the problem for there are two Cuthbert, two Graham and three Henderson families that require clarification throughout the letters.

Walter Lindesay Richardson's ancestry is difficult to research, for civil registration of births, marriages and deaths began later in Ireland than elsewhere in the British Isles. Compulsory civil registration in Ireland came in two stages: the *1844 Act for Marriages in Ireland: and for Registering Such Marriages* introduced civil registration of Protestant marriages commencing on 1 April 1845; secondly, the registration of births, deaths and all marriages began on 1 January 1864. From the sixteenth to the nineteenth century, the protestant Church of Ireland was the State Church, and although it was always a minority church, its influence on society and government matters was disproportionate to its numerical strength. The records kept by each parish church were the only ones for births, marriages and burials. The Act disestablishing and disendowing the Church of Ireland was passed in 1869, and came into effect on 1 January 1871. After that date it was expected that parish records would be transferred to the Public Record Office. Under a subsequent Act of 1876, all registers of births

---

[1]   See Molly Clutton-Brock, 'The Melancholy Optimist: An Account of Walter Lindesay Richardson and his Family', *Meanjin Quarterly*, June 1970, p. 193.

[2]   Green 1986, p. 357.

and burials up to 31 December 1870 and marriages up to 31 December 1845 were to be
handed over to the Public Record Office, except where the parish could satisfy the Master of
the Rolls that the local parish could provide an adequate and secure location. When the Public
Record Office was severely burnt in 1922 only a tiny number of parish registers survived. In
the aftermath of the fire a search was made for surviving records. It was discovered that 637
registers had survived in local parishes and that 124 parishes had kept copies of the registers
sent to the Public Record Office.[3] Many of these registers are now deposited in the
Representative Church Body Library in Braemor Park, Dublin, but they are in a frail and
dilapidated state, and the shrinkage of the parchment makes research for names and events
very difficult.

   The search for more information about the Richardson family is aided by a publication
by John O'Hart in 1892 on the old Irish families[4] and by the family tree[5] which was drawn up
by Walter's cousin, John Richardson,[6] in 1867 and copied by Walter when he visited Dublin
in 1868. Unfortunately, neither of these is completely accurate. John Richardson included
very few women (and even fewer dates) on the tree. John O'Hart's book does include females
but the daughters are mainly listed separately, so the birth sequence is not clear.

   The Graham Papers held in the archives of the University of Tasmania Library, Hobart,
provide a further source of information on Walter's family. Elisabeth Cheyne,[7] the sister of
Walter Richardson's stepfather, married William Wilkinson,[8] and their daughter, Cecilia
Wilkinson, married Henry Graham, a surgeon in Edinburgh, in 1839. After his death ten

3   Raymond Refaussé, 'The Records of the Church of Ireland', in James G. Ryan ed., *Irish Church Records: Their History, Availability and Use in Family and Local History Research* (Glenageary: Flyleaf Press, 1992), pp. 41–52.
4   John O'Hart, *Irish Pedigrees or the Origin and Stem of the Irish Nation*, 2 vols, 5th edn (Baltimore: Genealogical Publishing Co., 1989) (1st published Dublin 1892), pp. 372–373, 392–393.
5   NLA MS133/1/274.
6   John Richardson was the son of Marmaduke Jenny Richardson (1781–1845) and his wife Sarah née Shaw. A barrister in Dublin, he was the older brother of Henry Richardson, who married WLR's sister, Caroline.
7   Elisabeth (Bess) Wilkinson née Cheyne (1778–1836), the fifth child of John and Margaret Cheyne; she was born on 21 June 1778, married William Wilkinson, of the British Navy, on 11 November 1803, and died on 24 February 1836. Despite his frequent absences at sea, Bess and William Wilkinson had six children before his death on 28 February 1816—William (b. 1805); John (b. 1807); Cecilia (b. 1809 and died as an infant); Elizabeth (b. 1810, married Lieutenant Frederick Augustus Yorke); Matilda (b. 1811); and Cecilia (b. 1814, married Henry Graham)—both Elizabeth and Cecilia remained in touch with their uncles.
8   Captain William Wilkinson (d. 28 February 1816) promoted to Lieutenant on 29 April 1797, Commander on 27 April 1801 and Captain on 21 October 1810. David Syrett and R. L. DiNardo, *The Commissioned Sea Officers of the Royal Navy 1660–1815* (Aldershot: Scholar Press, 1994). He served with Sir Horatio Nelson at the Battle of the Nile (1 August 1798) against the French (after which battle Nelson was created a Baron and William was awarded a gold medal presented by the Prize Agent for Lord Nelson). William was on the *Elephant* under Captain Foley during the bombardment of Copenhagen on 2 April 1801 against the confederacy of Armed Neutrality formed by Russia, Sweden and Denmark. After this battle, Nelson was created a Viscount and William was appointed Captain of the *Holstein* (Danish) which he brought back to England with the wounded. 'Lord Nelson would not let Sir Hyde Parker alone until he had made me [Captain]—I am writing this on board my own ... Lord Nelson says he shall never lose sight of me and Captain Foley has written me the most pressing letters of recommendation to the Lords of the Admiralty of me, that I ever heard, he read to me before he sent it.' Letter from William Wilkinson to his brother Jack, 4 April 1801, Graham Papers, University of Tasmania, Hobart.

years later, Cecilia married Henry Sheppard.[9] Her son by her first marriage, William Henry Graham,[10] emigrated to Western Australia to join his great-uncle, George Cheyne. He married in Albany and sent his sons to be educated in Hobart. Eventually the family moved to Tasmania and lived at 'Cheyne Hall', Browns Road, Hobart. The documents comprising the Graham Papers were sent out from England by William Henry Graham's daughter, Ethelane Yorke Graham, who gave them to her nephew, Colin Graham, the son of her brother, William Montrose Graham. Colin Graham lent the papers to the University of Tasmania. With the aid of these papers, the public records, the family tree, and Lucinda Cheyne's letters, and with the assistance of the great-great-grandson of Alexander Richardson, the Reverend Canon John Crawford, many new facts can now be revealed.

The actual date of Walter Lindesay Richardson's birth has not heretofore been established. Although previous researchers have suggested that Walter was born in late 1825,[11] it is now certain that he was born in 1826 and very probably in late July and before 26 August. This may be deduced from various sources of evidence, including his mother's letters. She wrote on 10 April 1860: 'I shall think of you on your birthday especially, if I am in the body at the time, for every day, at early dawn, and 8 at night, you are remembered on other days, and my daughter Mary is not forgotten'; and on 26 August 1861, she wrote: 'My beloved Walter, I did not forget you on your birth day, your father remembered you also.' The other evidence for his birthday is from Walter himself; he told Mary that his father died when he was nine months old.[12] Alexander Richardson died on 28 May 1827.[13] It is not possible to rely on the accuracy of any of the Australian certificates (marriage, children's birth and death certificates) as ages were not always recorded correctly, but at his death on 1 August 1879 it was stated that Walter was aged fifty-three (which would be consistent with a birth year of 1826 if he had been born on or before 1 August). On his marriage certificate of 27 August 1855, his age was recorded as twenty-nine, which also tallies with a birth year of 1826.

Walter's father, Alexander, was the son of John Richardson of Farlough, County Tyrone, and Hannah Lindesay of Cahoo, County Tyrone. John Richardson became the High Sheriff of County Tyrone and a Captain of the Dungannon Volunteers. John and Hannah produced eight sons, including Alexander the eldest son, born in December 1757 or early January 1758,[14] and two daughters called Sarah and Hannah. Alexander made his career in the army. In January 1779, John Richardson settled £747–19–6, a considerable sum, on Alexander for

9   Cecilia Wilkinson was born on 14 May 1812 according to her Uncle Alexander Cheyne, but christened on 7 October 1814 according to Leith Parish Church records. Her first husband, Henry Graham, died on 1 November 1849 and some years later she married Henry Sheppard.
10 William Henry Graham (christened 20 November 1839) was only ten when his father died. He emigrated to WA to join his great-uncle, George Cheyne. He married Emma Christine McKail in 1865 in Albany and they had the following children: Cecilia Henrietta Augusta (b. 1866), Ethelane Yorke (b. 1868), Henry Farquhar (b. 1871), William Montrose (b. 1873), Cecil Irving (b. 1877), and John Frederick (b. 1879).
11 See, for example, Clark, p. 4.
12 Letter 8, from WLR to MR, 19–25 June 1855.
13 Malahide Parish, County Dublin, gravestone—'Sacred to the memory of Alexander Richardson of Farlough, Co. Tyrone, Summerhill, Dublin and Clairville near this place, esq, obiit May 28 1827 etat 69. This tomb is erected as a tribute of respect by his affectionate wife.' *Journal of the Society for the Preservation of the Memorials of the Dead*, vol. xii, p. 518. The Reverend Canon J. W. R. Crawford drew my attention to this entry.
14 He was baptised on 17 January 1758 according to the Drumglass Parish Records, Dungannon. For the purposes of this book, his birth year is 1758 although he may have been born in the end of December 1757.

'the promotion and advancement of the said Alexander his son in the Army'.[15] At that time Alexander became a Lieutenant—presumably his father's settlement purchased the commission—in the Ninth Regiment of Foot, and served in the American War of Independence.[16] In 1781, he was a Lieutenant in the Ninety-Seventh Regiment of Foot. By 1796 Alexander was a Captain in the Royal Tyrone Regiment of Militia[17] and by 1805, his eldest son, John, was a Lieutenant in the same regiment.[18] At his retirement from the militia Alexander was, according to Walter, a Lieutenant-Colonel.

Although HHR stated that her grandfather Richardson married twice,[19] in fact he appears to have been married four times (three times according to O'Hart). Lucinda clearly knew of his first wife, Miss Bell, daughter of the Surgeon-General of Ireland,[20] whom Alexander must have married when a teenager; for their daughter (according to Lucinda's letter[21] reporting the death of this daughter) was born in 1775 when he was only in his eighteenth year. Alexander's and the former Miss Bell's daughter, Mary Richardson, was married in 1797 to John Hamilton, a relative of the Duke of Hamilton.[22] O'Hart overlooks Miss Bell and states that Alexander's first wife was Anna Johnstone, the daughter of the Honourable George Johnstone, who, according to O'Hart, was Governor of West Florida from 1765 to 1770. By this marriage he had one son, John, and three daughters, Hannah, Harriet and Margaret. Alexander married for a third time shortly before 7 August 1800,[23] this wife being Elizabeth Smyth,[24] by whom he had one daughter and four sons (Ann, Alexander, William Smyth, Snow and Robert). The name 'Snow', which appears on the family tree, comes from Elizabeth's mother—Henrietta, née Snow.

In 1815, Elizabeth died, aged only thirty-seven, and Alexander, a much-widowed man, looked for a new bride, to help him run his household and care for his children. There is no

---

[15]   Deed of Settlement, dated 18 January 1779. Ref: 327/533/220322, Registry of Deeds, Dublin.

[16]   War Office, *A List of all the Officers of the Army: viz The General & Field Officers; The Officers of the Several Troops, Regiments, Independent Companies, and Garrisons: with the Alphabetical Index to the Whole* (London: War Office, 1779), p. 73.

[17]   His status was noted in a deed of Lease of 28 acres to William Pike, dated 20 June 1796. Ref: 503/500/325165, Registry of Deeds, Dublin.

[18]   John Richardson's status was noted in a deed of Lease and Release, in which his father gave him an annuity of £100, dated 28 January 1805. Ref: 566/143 Registry of Deeds, Dublin.

[19]   *MWY*, p. 1.

[20]   No surgeon called Bell is listed in A. Peterkin and William Johnston, *Commissioned Officers in the Medical Services of the British Army 1660–1960*, 2 vols (London: The Wellcome Historical Medical Library, 1968), though on page 61 Archibald Richardson is listed as 'State Surgeon and Surgeon to the Forces in Ireland, 7 January 1784. Died 1787 (before 10 March). He succeeded George Ruxton. His fee was 6s 8d a day.' However, since George Ruxton also is not listed separately, it must be assumed that the surgeons to the forces were not always commissioned officers.

[21]   Letter 67, from LC to WLR, July 1860.

[22]   Marriage License in 1797 for John Hamilton and Mary Richardson. *Index to the Act or Grant Books, And to the Original Wills, of the Diocese of Dublin [c.1638] to the Year 1800 from the Appendix to the twenty-sixth Report of the Deputy Keeper of the Public Records and Keeper of the State Papers in Ireland* (originally published in Dublin, 1895) (Baltimore: Clearfield, 1997).

[23]   Marriage settlement between Alexander Richardson and Elizabeth Smyth, dated 7 August 1800, states that they were already married. Ref: 532/93/348235, Registry of Deeds, Dublin.

[24]   Elizabeth Smyth (1778–1815), the third daughter of Captain William Smyth or Smith (57th Regiment), of Ballinure. Her father had died prior to her marriage. Her mother was Henrietta Snow, the fifth child of Robert Snow, who received the freedom of Waterford in 1737, and his wife Anna Maria née Alcock, who was related to the Viscountess Grandison of Dromana. Her two older sisters had both married Captains and her two younger sisters married Sir N. B. Scottowe and Sir Edmund Scottowe, respectively. Two of her three brothers were in the army: Colonel Snow Smyth and Thomas St George Smyth. O'Hart, p. 393.

portrait or description of Alexander but he must have been an attractive gentleman, for the young and lively Lucinda Sirée[25] soon agreed to the match and in no time their marriage settlement was drawn up and his fourth marriage took place. This wedding was no small affair. Their parish church was St Thomas's but they were granted special permission by the Lord Bishop of Kildare, Dean of Christ Church Cathedral, to allow the Reverend John Armstrong Coghlan, a Minister from St Thomas's, to marry them in the cathedral on 29 January 1816.[26] At the time of their marriage, Alexander was fifty-eight and Lucinda was only in her twentieth year. In their Marriage Settlement, Alexander agreed to settle on Lucinda an annuity of £300 (from houses, lands and tenements owned by him).[27]

Lucinda and Alexander started their married life in Dublin with probably at least five of his youngest children aged between seven and fifteen years still living at home. At the end of their first year of marriage, Henry Downing Richardson was born and baptised on 28 December 1816 at St Thomas's Church, Dublin.[28] The marriage between a couple so disparate in age and experience evidently proved difficult, and in December 1819 Lucinda and Alexander separated, 'reciting that some unhappy differences had arisen between the said Alex. Richardson and the said Lucinda Richardson his wife and that they had eventually agreed finally to separate and live apart from each other'.[29]

The terms of their separation allowed Lucinda to live as if she were a 'femme sole', a free and legally independent woman, and Alexander gave her an annuity of £200. It may have been Alexander's generosity, not only in financial matters but in his liberal acceptance of her independence, which reconciled Lucinda to the marriage, for although it is not known how long they had been parted, they were reunited within three months or so after the separation deed was signed. Lucinda was immediately pregnant again. Their first daughter, Lucinda, was baptised on 31 December 1820 and Caroline in August 1822, both at St Thomas's Parish Church in Dublin, which was close to their home in Summer-hill, north of the River Liffey. Summer-hill was once a street where wealthy families lived, but all the grand eighteenth- and nineteenth-century houses have since been demolished and replaced by public housing. In addition to his house at Summer-hill, Dublin, Alexander Richardson had owned or rented for many years a property at Swords, a small country town seven miles north of Dublin, and still listed his homes as '58 Summer-hill & Swords' up to 1824 in the Directory under the heading 'Nobility and Gentry'.[30] But in 1826 he bought or rented a house at Malahide, a small town on the coast north of Dublin City, where the beautiful scenery and the twelfth-century castle still attract visitors.

[25]　Lucinda Sirée (1796–1868), daughter of Henry Sirée, an Attorney, and his wife, Harriet née McCausland, who married in 1792 (marriage licence for Harriet McCausland and Henry Sirée cited in *Index to the Act or Grant Books, And to the Original Wills, of the Diocese of Dublin [c.1638] to the Year 1800 from the Appendix to the twenty-sixth Report of the Deputy Keeper of the Public Records and Keeper of the State Papers in Ireland* (originally published in Dublin, 1895) (Baltimore: Clearfield, 1997)).

[26]　Raymond Refaussé, with Colm Lennon, eds, *The Registers of Christ Church Cathedral, Dublin* (Dublin: Four Courts Press, 1998), p. 118.

[27]　Marriage Settlement dated 27 January 1816. Ref: 697/628/478673, Registry of Deeds, Dublin.

[28]　The church no longer exists but the fragile parish registers are held at the Representative Church Body Library, Braemor Park, Churchtown, Dublin.

[29]　Deed of Legal Separation, 27 December 1819. Ref: 747/541/508677, Registry of Deeds, Dublin.

[30]　See *Pigot's City of Dublin and Hibernian Provincial Directory for 1824* (London: J. Piggot & Co., 1824).

Walter Lindesay Richardson was born at 'Clairville' in Malahide Parish in the summer of 1826 and may have been baptised privately for there is no record of his baptism in the parish records. 'Clairville' was a medium-sized Victorian mansion in its own grounds, since demolished. After the death of Alexander Richardson on 28 May 1827, the family did not remain in Ireland for long. The recent discovery of a letter[31] from Dr Bayne Cheyne[32] to his oldest surviving brother, Lieutenant-Colonel William Cheyne,[33] dated 28 March 1828, reveals that he and Lucinda Richardson were about to be married. She was living with her three younger children (Henry was at boarding school) at Emberton, Buckinghamshire, where Bayne was staying with his cousin, Cecilia Anderson,[34] recuperating after a debilitating illness in Edinburgh. Bayne also reveals that he had known Lucinda Richardson for some time. Had he visited his brother, John Cheyne, in Dublin[35] and had they met while she was still married? The letter is printed in its entirety as it is previously unknown and unpublished:

To: Lieut. Colonel William Cheyne, at Cheyne St, Stuckbridge, Edinburgh
From: Bayne Cheyne, Emberton, Buckinghamshire

28 March 1828

My Dear William

As I have the prospect soon of quitting the state of celibacy I owe to you as the head of the family a communication on this important subject. I would have sent you one at an earlier period had not the irregular notices conveyed in the usual routine of correspondence between Emberton & your quarter rendered a formal account from me of what was going forward in some degree superfluous. Nothing could be farther from my thoughts when I left Edinburgh than matrimony. & I had known the Lady who means to favor me with her hand for a considerable time before the interest I began to feel for her awakened any idea that I ought to essay the acquiring her good graces. As matters now stand you may conceive perhaps, that I have hit upon the very worst means

[31]   Graham Papers, item 3.
[32]   Dr Bayne Cheyne (1788–1868), born 22 April 1788, the twelfth child and ninth son of sixteen children of John Cheyne, surgeon of Leith, Scotland, and his wife, Margaret née Edmonston. His mother was the daughter of William Edmonston, fellow of the College of Surgeons, and his wife, Cecilia, 'sister to William Bayne who was mortally wounded in Lord Rodney's great battle while in command of the *Alfred*, 74, being the senior of the three Captains to whom a monument was erected in Westminster Abbey: and daughter of Alexander Bayne, Professor of Scots Law in the university of Edinburgh whose life appears in the penny Encyclopaedia & who is noticed in Disraeli's *Calamities of Authors*.' Graham Papers, item 2.
[33]   William Edmonstone Cheyne (1774–1842), born 22 March 1774, the second son of Dr John Cheyne and his wife Margaret née Edmonstone. He was a Lieutenant-Colonel.
[34]   Cicy (Cecilia) Anderson (d. 7 October 1847), the daughter of John Anderson and Cecilia née Edmonstone (Bayne Cheyne's aunt), who married on 7 September 1780. The date of Cicy's death was recorded by Capt. Alexander Cheyne at the front of his *Diary*.
[35]   John Cheyne, MD, FRSE, MRIA (1777–1836), Physician General to the Forces in Ireland, was born on 3 February 1777 at Leith, fourth child and third son of John and Margaret Cheyne. 'In June 1795 he [John Cheyne] obtained his medical degree & immediately joined the Royal Artillery at Woolwich. He was present at the actions with the Irish Rebels at Ross, Vinegar Hill, etc, in 1798. In 1809 he commenced practice in Dublin where he ultimately obtained great professional distinction. In 1820 he was appointed Physician General. In 10 years his practice yielded him an average annual income of £500. In 1825 he became affected with nervous fever & in 1831 retired, and on the 31st January 1836 died at Sherrington, a village near Newport Pagnell in Buckinghamshire.' Graham Papers, item 2.

that could be devised for effecting a cure of the complaint which constrained me to take flight from Edinburgh. Or in other words that a wife & four children is the most inefficacious remedy that could be presented for sleepless nights & the Nervous feelings therewith connected. You will have learned however through the medium of Cicy's letters that my procedure has not been so desperately foolish as it may at first sight appear. The eldest child a very fine boy[36] is at a boarding school. The other three[37] are the quietest & most tractable creatures I have ever seen & are not addicted either to the annoying practice of romping by day, or the still more disagreeable one of screaming by night.

The management of them as far as their wordly affairs are concerned will be so much the less a subject of care to me as a provision has been left for them by their late father. In respect of the improvement of my own finances, the match cannot be considered as improvident in the usual sense of the term. Mrs Richardson besides has the generous intention of placing at my disposal all the money she may possess so as to leave herself entirely dependent on me. Such a behaviour is quite the reverse I understand of what is usually expected to take place, where the circumstances of the Lady are similar to those under which Mrs R is at present situated. It is not for one to institute any comparison between her & John's wife,[38] yet I cannot help expressing my belief, that were you & my other brothers acquainted with her personally, you would see no cause to regret the connection that is about to be formed.

Her health has been for a considerable time delicate & her nerves weak, but her spirits are naturally good & when well she has a great deal of the Irish buoyancy & liveliness presenting in this respect a remarkable contrast to myself. But from Cicy's account of her you will probably have derived a more & better idea of her person & character than I can give you.

In the letter I wrote a day or two ago to Charles[39] I mentioned that we intended to set out for Paris on the 8th of next month the day fixed upon for our marriage. This is a journey I should never have thought of could my intended have lived in London (without the risk of her health suffering) until I had completed some preparatory studies of a professional kind, which I intend to make & which I hope will be carried on in Paris as well if not better than any where else.

By the bye I shall be much obliged to you if you could send me a notice of any tolerable Hotel or boarding house in Paris, where we may be accommodated at a moderate rate. Having been more recently there than I you may recollect some place that may answer better than any of those of which I my self have knowledge. Perhaps also you may be able to direct me whether I ought to get French money in London or in Calais. Mrs R. sends you her kindest regards| Yours affectionately

    B. Cheyne

---

[36]   Henry Downing Richardson (1816–1849), aged eleven.

[37]   Lucinda (aged seven years), Caroline (five years) and Walter Lindesay Richardson (twenty months).

[38]   Sarah Cheyne née Macartney married Dr John Cheyne (1777–1836) in 1809. She was the daughter of the Reverend Dr Macartney, vicar of Antrim.

[39]   Captain Charles Cheyne (1786–1857), eleventh child and eighth son of John and Margaret Cheyne.

P.S. The less that is said of my marriage to the friends of the family the better. Mrs R. for particular reasons being desirous that the time when it is to take place should be kept as discreet as possible.

Lucinda may have wished that news of her second marriage not be broadcast because her first husband had died only ten months before. Bayne's description of Lucinda matches Walter's enthusiastic report of her to Mary during their engagement.[40] They were married on 8 April 1828 and spent their honeymoon in Paris. He was almost forty and she was in her thirty-second year when she embarked on this second marriage.

After their honeymoon, Dr Bayne Cheyne bought a practice in Bristol and the family settled down to life in the genteel suburb of Clifton, with the addition of two more boys, John born in August 1829 and William Alexander born in May 1831. Walter was only twenty months or so old when his mother remarried and only three when the first of his half-brothers was born. John and William Alexander Cheyne were both christened in the Bridge Street Independent or Congregational Church, Bristol.[41] Walter was therefore brought up in England (and not in Dublin as was previously thought), the fourth of six children, by an Irish mother and a Scottish stepfather. Bayne and Lucinda's marriage lasted for forty-two years until Lucinda's death in June 1866 and surviving correspondence indicates that the marriage was a happy one.

Despite the difficulties of Lucinda's first marriage, she appears to have maintained a friendly relationship with Alexander's children by his previous marriages. Her eldest stepdaughter, Mary Hamilton, was married the year after Lucinda was born and was twenty-one years older than her stepmother, but Lucinda was fond of her and her husband and 'was always on good terms with them'.[42] Of her other stepdaughters, Hannah, Harriet and Margaret, we have very little information except that Harriet and Margaret died unmarried (which might mean that one or both of them may have died in infancy). Alexander's eldest son, John, was alive in 1805 but had died unmarried sometime before 1829;[43] probably predeceasing his father. Her other five stepchildren, Ann, Alexander, William Smyth, Snow and Robert, would have still been at home when she married their father.

There are few clues to the success of the reconciliation between Alexander Richardson and Lucinda, except for the phrase 'his affectionate wife' inscribed on Alexander's Malahide gravestone, but in later life she seemed proud of the honour bestowed on her by her marriage to Alexander. She sent a set of little silver salt spoons to Mary and Walter, after having them re-gilded in Brighton, and wrote in February 1861:

I have at last forwarded the little salt spoons, to dear Mary's Mother who undertakes to convey them to you, they are a poor token, but love can be manifested in trifles as well as in larger gifts, when you look on them may they testify of mine for you, dearest daughter Mary, and any who may yet be yours. They are silver, gilt, they will tell you of my young days when your late father placed me at the head of his house and table,—[44]

40   Letter 6, from WLR to MR, 11–17 June 1855.
41   John was christened on 11 August 1829 and William Alexander, on 15 May 1831.
42   Letter 67, from LC to WLR, July 1860.
43   His name is not included in the list of sons of Alexander in the deed of 16 October 1829. Ref: 865/500/576500, Registry of Deeds, Dublin.
44   Letter 69, from LC to WLR and MR, 20 February 1861.

By the time of her second marriage, her stepsons Alexander and William Smyth Richardson (both in their early twenties) were in financial difficulties and in 1829 an annuity from their father's estate had to be used to pay off this debt.[45] How the debt arose is not clear but the story of this profligacy percolated through to HHR and accounts for her comment: 'the wild sons of the first marriage had contrived to run through the family inheritance'.[46] Lucinda's comments (thirty-five years after the death of her first husband) about her stepson Alexander show that he developed into a most respectable member of society.[47] On 1 January 1863, after commenting about Henry, her son-in-law who was a Dublin solicitor, she wrote:

> [Henry] will be a credit to you when you return. So will his brother John, and your brother Alex—in both of whom I take a deep interest—Character is precious and Alex' has established a good one and is now a servant of our Saviour, married to a sensible useful woman [Jane Pyke, his second wife], who is a good mother to his little Sarah, Tommy is in the Army I believe.

Lucinda's second husband, Bayne, was not only devoted to her but also brought his skills as physician to her household. For him this marriage, just days before his fortieth birthday, made a considerable change to his life, but he liked his stepchildren and the birth of his own two sons must have been a special source of pleasure.

Henry Downing Richardson and Walter Lindesay Richardson did not follow their own father's profession into the army. Henry became a naturalist[48] and Walter chose medicine, his stepfather's profession. Although several members of the Cheyne family entered the army (including Lieutenant-Colonel William Cheyne, Captain Charles Cheyne, Captain Alexander Cheyne), the Cheyne name had been made famous by doctors.[49] Bayne's second oldest brother, John, who had worked in Dublin for many years, was the Physician General of the Irish Forces until 1831, when he retired through ill-health to a small village, Sherrington, near Newport Pagnell, in Buckinghamshire. It may have been through him that Lucinda met Bayne.

---

[45]   Deed of 16 October 1829. Ref: 865/500/576500, Registry of Deeds, Dublin.

[46]   *MWY*, p. 1. HHR believed that her grandfather had only been married twice, not four times.

[47]   Alexander Richardson (1803–1890) became an Inspector of the Dublin and Kingston Railway Company. On 1 May 1823 he married his cousin, Elizabeth Richardson, eldest daughter of Marmaduke Jenny (John) Richardson (1781–1845), of the Rothay and Caithness Regiment of Fencibles, and his wife Sarah (née Shaw). Elizabeth bore him twelve children and subsequently died. He then married Jane Margaret Pyke in 1857, the daughter of Captain William Pyke, Royal Navy, Devon.

[48]   'H. D. Richardson, naturalist, 1 Priestfield, Dolphin's Barn.' Henry Shaw, *The Dublin Pictorial Guide & Directory of 1850* (Belfast: The Friar's Bush Press, 1988): compiled in 1849, the year of Henry Downing Richardson's death.

[49]   Dr Bayne Cheyne's father, Dr John Cheyne (b. 1747), 'practiced medicine & surgery & was a man of great cheerfulness, benevolence, good sense & intelligence of mind and who had succeeded his Uncle, John Cheyne, a kindred spirit & one who had acquired the name of friend of the poor. Dr Cheyne's great-grandfather & his family were Episcopalians & devoted to the Stuarts to whose agents they, in 1715, lent considerable sums of money which were never repaid; and his portrait by Sir John Medina (1659–1710), still hangs in the hall of the College of Surgeons in Edinburgh.' Extract from the life of John Cheyne, Graham Papers, University of Tasmania. Medina was a portrait painter, born in Brussels, of Spanish parentage, who settled in Edinburgh in 1688. Dr George Cheyne (1670–1742), friend and doctor of Alexander Pope and author of twelve medical treatises, was also related.

On 1 February 1838, Henry Downing Richardson married Ellen O'Connor (the daughter of Thomas O'Connor of Lucan, Co. Dublin). Their marriage took place at the fashionable (Protestant) St Mary's Church, Dublin. They had five children: Lucinda, Henry Handel (the name borrowed by his cousin for her *nom-de-plume* when she published *Maurice Guest* in 1908), Walter Lindesay, Alexander and Nanny. The story told by his great-niece[50] about Henry Downing Richardson dying in a fire aboard the *Amazon*, is not true. The *Amazon*, a West Indian mail steam ship sailing for the Panama, left Southampton on her first voyage, on Friday 2 January 1852, and two days later on the Sunday morning, 4 January, was destroyed by fire at sea, about 110 miles off Land's End. From Walter's papers it is clear that his brother died prior to 1851 and, after a search of the obituary notices, it can now be confirmed that he died in Dublin on 6 May 1849. His death was announced in *The Freeman's Journal* four days later. Walter wrote about his brother's death in his notebook[51] but the relevant pages have been torn out. Here is the facing note:

> On the sad event recorded upon the opposite pages I undertook the care of one of my late brothers children Walter Lindesay my namesake at that time [blank] years old—he remained with his uncle & aunt from the summer of 1849 to October 5th 1850 when I placed him with T. Wilson, Ockham School, Near Ripley, Surrey, the letters I receive from himself indicate progress in hand writing. The events of the present year 1851 have been of interest to myself—my expenditure has equalled my receipts—but I have spent money in acquiring knowledge and time in acquiring experience in professional matters—

Walter's list of expenses for 1851 show that the school fees cost him £18–9–8. A month after her husband's death, Ellen Richardson had four of her children baptised as Protestants at St James's Church. Her son, Walter Lindesay, was in England at the time and so missed this event. Perhaps the Minister who buried Henry suggested that he would only perform this rite if Henry's children were baptised. Later Ellen, who was either a lapsed Roman Catholic or newly converted, decided she wanted her sons to be educated in Roman Catholic schools. While Walter helped to pay for the school fees of nephew Walter Lindesay, Alick, the youngest of Henry's children, was being assisted by his grandmother, Lucinda Cheyne, who was fervently anti-Roman Catholic. Together with her friend, Miss Caroline Fector, she managed to resist the demands of his mother for his return to Ireland. Alick followed Walter to Australia in his late teens and eventually settled as a travelling auditor for the railways in Parramatta, New South Wales (NSW), where Walter visited him and his wife Fanny in June 1870, six months after the birth of his first daughter, Ethel Florence Lindesay Richardson (HHR). Alexander died of cancer of the pelvis on 20 August 1900, at his home 'Glenthorne', The Boulevard, Petersham, NSW, aged fifty-four. At the time of his death, he was Chairman of the Railway Staff Committee.

Henry Handel Richardson visited his grandmother, Lucinda Cheyne, in February 1863[52] and sometime later sailed to America where he spent the rest of his life.[53] That Walter

---

50   Clutton-Brock, pp. 192–208.
51   NLA MS133/1/292.
52   Letter 90, from LC to WLR, 1 January 1863.
53   Henry H. Richardson listed in 'Register of voters of Pittsfield, Massachusetts 1890 ward 5, Naturalization Data', *Berkshire Genealogist* (Berkshire, Massachusetts) Family History Association,

remained in touch with him is evident, for he reported to Mary when they were living in England in 1867 that he had received a newspaper from Henry Handel in America.[54] In December 1868, when Walter paid a last visit to Dublin before returning to Australia, he wrote to Mary that he had:

> applied at the Castle for an order to go over Mountjoy prison. I presented my order & was shewn by the <u>assistant superintendent</u> over the womens prison I did not tell her who I was for some time. You remember she is Alicks mother my brothers widow.[55] She has still the vestiges of beauty and a subdued quiet manner. I went to her little house & saw her daughter Lucinda & was of course much affected. They are R. Catholics—I am going out with Sophy this morning to buy her a new dress—[56]

Caroline Richardson, Walter's sister, married her cousin Henry Richardson[57] in about 1846, when they were both twenty-four. There is a curious comment in a letter from Lucinda Cheyne to her son Walter about Caroline causing great anguish in the family; Lucinda wrote:

> none of the garbled statements nor <u>unguest</u> like conduct to which you allude give <u>me</u> the least concern, such like matters are not <u>new,</u> they took place 25 years ago; as far as I am concerned they cannot be carried on any more,—calumny and <u>backbiting</u> cannot consist with any measure of Religion, or knowledge of the Most High, and we have no inclination to keep up intercourse unless it proceeds from <u>true</u> love, not the interested semblance of it. I was <u>deeply</u> grieved, at the unworthy treatment I met with both from husband and wife, and that more on their account ~~that~~ than <u>my</u> own, but above all I was in anguish on your father's acc', his well known respectability trampled on, his character assailed and this thro' a child nurtured, watched over helped continually by him, O—it <u>was</u> bitter. I am not careful to justify myself, I leave that to Him—whose unworthy servant I am let those who return evil for good, look to themselves, and what they may bring on their house—Your letter caused your father pain he cannot bear to think of the baseness and wickedness of the treatment I received at a time when my heart was overwhelmed and I was deprived of <u>his</u> sympathy & support. <u>No</u> trial that I ever endured was to be compared with Caroline's conduct.—it appals me even <u>now</u> to think of it.—I have a wretched pen more like a stick than any thing else, and your father is gone to bed, I fear it is a Bronchital attack, the writing these few lines to you, & the bringing to mind so many painful circumstances have brought on him illness that may prove very distressing—[58]

If Lucinda was remembering an event which took place twenty-five years before this letter, that is in 1836, Henry and Caroline would only have been in their fourteenth year, surely too young for an elopement. Bayne Cheyne would probably have been away from home

vol. 12: 1 (Winter 1991), pp. 8–15; vol. 12: 2 (Spring 1991), pp. 44–51; vol. 12: 3 (Summer 1991), pp. 80–87; vol. 12: 4 (Fall 1991), pp. 118–125. Source code 7245.7.

[54] Letter 112, from WLR to MR, 28 September 1867.
[55] Ellen Richardson née O'Connor, widow of Henry Downing Richardson.
[56] Letter 142, from WLR to MR, 3 December 1868.
[57] Henry Richardson (1822–1888), an attorney in Dublin, son of Marmaduke Jenny Richardson (1781–1845) and Sarah née Shaw.
[58] Letter 69, from LC to WLR, 20 February 1861.

in February and March 1836, dealing with Cheyne family matters, as his brother, Dr John Cheyne, died on 31 January 1836 followed less than a month later, on 24 February 1836, by their oldest sister, Elisabeth Wilkinson. The 'husband and wife' castigated in the letter may have been people to whom Caroline had made inappropriate remarks about her parents or home life which, being repreated to Lucinda, greatly grieved her. Notwithstanding her youthful behaviour, Caroline had long been forgiven, for Lucinda's letters contain loving references to her daughter. Through Lucinda's letters, Walter and Mary were *au fait* with all the details of Caroline's gynaecological illness and although no letters from Caroline have survived, it is likely that she and her husband would have corresponded regularly. Caroline and Henry had to wait six years before she had the first of four children born between 1851 and 1857, including a son named after Walter Lindesay.[59]

The extant letters from Lucinda Cheyne are progressively more miserable and more religious in content as the years of separation, particularly from Walter, continued. Her and Bayne's youngest son, William Alexander, had died in 1846 and her oldest son, Henry Downing Richardson, in 1849. Walter's departure to Australia was another severe loss. To compound her misery ten months later, John Cheyne, her other son (and Bayne's only surviving son) decided he would follow Walter. He travelled with Mervyn Richardson,[60] arriving in Melbourne on the *Goldfinder* on 23 October 1853. A year later, on 11 October 1854, her eldest daughter, Lucinda Richardson, also set sail on the first voyage of the *Champion of the Seas* to Australia, arriving on 30 December 1854.[61] Lucinda Cheyne was separated by the Irish Sea from her eldest daughter, Caroline, who, languishing with severe gynaecological problems after the birth of her fourth child in 1857, was not expected to survive. At the same time, Lucinda's favourite brother, Henry Sirée, took his wife and his two children[62] to join his stepson, Alick Cook, in Victoria. Henry Sirée and his family returned (separately) but Lucinda's children remained abroad.

John Cheyne stayed with Walter and Mary for a time in Ballarat. At that time he was probably working as a digger. He was in touch with his uncle, Captain Alexander Cheyne, who lived in Tasmania, for there is an entry in Alexander's diary on 2 January 1855 which

---

[59]   Marmaduke Cheyne (1851–1925), Lindesay (b. 1853), Walter Lindesay (1855–1863) and Lucinda (b. 1857).

[60]   Mervyn Richardson, third son of John Richardson and his first wife, Anna Bristow. He left John Cheyne in Australia and returned before September 1857. (See Letter 26, from LC to WLR, 9 September 1857.)

[61]   At the time of her launch on 19 April 1854 in Boston, the *Champion of the Seas* was the largest sailing ship in trade afloat. Built by Donald McKay, she was a beautiful full-rigged clipper. *The Champion of the Seas Gazette*, printed and published throughout this first voyage to Australia by John Stephen Whitty, is reproduced in Rod Fraser, *The Champion of the Seas* (Glen Waverley: Pilgrim Printing Services, 1999), pp. 114–146. Lucinda travelled in a cabin, with 734 other emigrants on board and with a crew of 120, including Captain Alexander Newlands, the commander.

[62]   Henry Sirée (b. *c*.1812), younger brother of Lucinda Cheyne; an attorney in Dublin; married in 1839 to (Elizabeth) Charlotte Cook née Harricks (b. *c*.1810). In March 1857, Henry, Elizabeth and their children (Elizabeth (Bessie) aged fifteen and Horatio Nelson aged thirteen) arrived in Melbourne on the *Champion of the Seas* in March 1857, where her son, Alick Cook, was already living. After a short stay, Harry decided to return to Ireland and, after leaving Horatio in Ireland and Bessie in England, he travelled round America. His wife remained in Victoria and lived for a time assisting in the housekeeping for Bayne Cheyne's nephew, the Reverend John Cheyne and his wife at Castlemaine, until they helped her to return to England in October 1859 when her husband returned to Dublin. Alick Cook remained in Australia until he sailed home on 15 November 1862 on the *True Briton*.

states: 'I wrote a letter to my nephew John Cheyne in reply to his of the 27 November 1854.'
John then moved to Melbourne, setting up a photographic business with a partner;[63] but this
venture did not last long for his partner decided to return to England in 1856. John then
asked Walter if he would like to join him in the business[64] and, after Walter refused, John left
Melbourne for Hobart and stayed with his uncle, Captain Alexander Cheyne, for a short time.
From Hobart he set off for India without consulting his parents, and was employed by a
company in Calcutta. Becoming bored with the tedium of office life in Calcutta, he
volunteered for the Bombay Yeoman Cavalry and subsequently died of fever in Assam in
December 1859. During the autumn and winter of 1859 and 1860, Europe experienced
severe weather. No sooner had Lucinda recovered from bronchitis than Bayne was prostrate
with bronchial and heart problems. They did not hear of John's death for many months for, in
a letter written in June 1860,[65] Lucinda Cheyne wrote that they had not heard from him since
receiving a letter in March. Her letter to Walter announcing John's death has only survived in
part but she wrote on sheet two:

> Your father has not long since got into the habit of naming you and Mary and all our
> children in prayer—we have been praying for the dead these 7 months, and now the
> omission of that one name shakes me terribly,—[66]

Neither Walter nor Mary mentioned Lucinda Richardson in letters prior to their
marriage although she had arrived in Victoria in December 1854, six months prior to their
engagement. The first glimpse of her in Victoria is in 1857 in Lucinda Cheyne's first surviving
letter,[67] in which she wrote to Walter:

> Lucinda is to leave Kyneton in Oct[br]. I shall be well pleased to have her out of the Bush,
> and away from that family you will preserve any letters for her which I may entrust to
> you, until you know where to remit them—I have had very few from her of late ...

The next month, Lucinda Cheyne wrote yet again to Walter:

> If you can give me any intelligence of Lucinda or John I beg you will do it, I am very
> anxious about her, knowing she was to leave Kyneton last month, her Aunt Mrs Harry
> Sirée I believe had invited her, to pass some time with her until she procured another
> situation, but they may have left Melbourne; I have in my two last letters to you,
> enclosed one in each for Lucinda, according to her wishes, she said you would have
> instructions where to forward them—[68]

Lucinda Richardson was back again in Kyneton in April 1859, working for a
Mrs Thompson[69] but by October that year, she had moved to Daylesford to work for

---

[63]   Business card, Cheyne and Scott, address: 7 Collins Street East, Melbourne. In WLR's Scrapbook,
       NLA MS133/1/293.
[64]   Letter 25, from JC to WLR, undated but probably 1856.
[65]   Letter 62, from LC to WLR, 8 June 1860.
[66]   Letter 67, from LC to WLR, July 1860.
[67]   Letter 26, from LC to WLR, 9 September 1857.
[68]   Letter 27, from LC to WLR, 2 October 1857.
[69]   Letter 43, from WLR to MR, 27 April 1859.

Mrs Doveton.[70] That position may have been found for her through her step-cousin, the Reverend John Cheyne, who was a close friend of Commissioner Francis Crossman Doveton.[71] The only extant letter from Lucinda Cheyne to Lucinda Richardson clearly demonstrates the affection the mother had for her children:

> Write often, I do not care how little; if I know that you are <u>alive,</u> it quickens my prayers for you—.[72]

In February 1862, Lucinda Richardson sailed back to England on the *Latona* and Lucinda Cheyne's letter,[73] written only days after her daughter's arrival in June, is filled with happiness and thanks to Mary and her brothers, particularly Edward Harold Bailey (of whom Lucinda Richardson had become very fond), for all their help to her beloved daughter. When Mary left Walter in Ballarat to assist Lucinda's packing, her patience was sorely tried by her sister-in-law prior to her departure. Lucinda Richardson did not remain very long with her mother and stepfather for the climate in Brighton did not suit her and by August 1862 she had decamped to Ireland to her sister, Caroline. Deciding by 1864 that Victoria was where she wanted to be, this independent woman once more set sail from Liverpool aboard the *Marco Polo*, arriving in Melbourne in October 1864.

Walter matriculated in 1845 as a medical student at Edinburgh University, commencing four years of study. He entered a summary of his career in his notebook[74] in December 1851. This reveals that he worked as Assistant Pathologist in the Edinburgh Infirmary for two months in 1849, taking the degree of MD and the diploma of the Edinburgh College of Surgery. He was subsequently House Surgeon to the Edinburgh Maternity Hospital for three months, then Resident Physician in the Cholera Hospital for another three months. Then he left Edinburgh for London. He remained a short time in London before leaving for Wales in January 1850 where he served as assistant for six months with J. P. Wilding and G. Towns in Montgomery. He returned to London in June 1850 and in July was engaged as an assistant to Dr Thomas Heckstall Smith in St Mary Cray, Kent.

The discovery of gold in Victoria in 1851 had caught the imagination of people throughout the British Isles and America. In 1852 Walter decided to seek his fortune on the goldfields in Victoria. He set sail from Gravesend on 2 June 1852 on the *Roxburgh Castle*, on which was also Susannah Tyler Nicholson, the bride-to-be of his future brother-in-law, John Robinson Bailey. Many young men had gone before him including John Robinson Bailey and Edward Harold Bailey, Mary's older brothers, whose ship lay at anchor off Williamstown four days after Walter set sail from England. Walter's links and interest with Australia, however, were more deep-seated because from his early childhood his stepfather had been receiving letters regularly from Australia. Three of Bayne's brothers (and several nephews) were early pioneers in Australia.

---

[70]   Letter 45, from LC to WLR and MR, 19 October 1859. Mary Ann Doveton née Snell was the second wife of Commissioner Francis Crossman Doveton, who had been ordered to Bunniyong in September 1851 by Governor Charles La Trobe to issue licences to the gold miners in an attempt to limit the number of diggers by charging 30 shillings a month.

[71]   Doveton signed the marriage certificate as witness for John Cheyne's second marriage to Janet Mary Carmichael on 9 November 1870 at All Saints' Church, St Kilda.

[72]   Letter 40, from LC to LR, 6 January 1859.

[73]   Letter 82, from LC to WLR and MR, 19 June 1862.

[74]   NLA MS133/1/292.

2

The Cheyne Family in Australia

George Cheyne[1] became a pioneer in Western Australia (WA) in 1831. He was followed by Captain Alexander Cheyne[2] (to WA in 1834, finally settling in Hobart Town, Van Diemen's Land (VDL), in December 1835) and nephew John Cheyne (to WA in 1834, thence to New Zealand, New South Wales (NSW) and finally settling in Victoria in 1848). The third brother, Bruce Cheyne,[3] emigrated to NSW and thence to WA. George Cheyne and his wife Grace (christened Grizel)[4] sailed for King George Sound, WA, in the *Stirling*, arriving 2 June 1831. The ship had been chartered jointly with Marshall McDermott[5] and his wife, Harriet, who had six children born in WA over the next thirteen years. When they arrived at the Swan River settlement they found that all the best land had been taken and that Sir James Stirling[6] had somewhat exaggerated the quality of the land. A Captain in the Royal Navy (East India Company Squadron), Stirling had sailed to NSW aboard the *Success* in 1827 and then

---

[1] George Cheyne (1790–1869), fourteenth child of John and Margaret Cheyne, born 8 April 1790, two years after Bayne. He married Grizel (Grace) Melville; see endnote 4. He died 5 June 1869 in Lochmaben, Dumfriesshire, Scotland.

[2] Captain Alexander Cheyne (1786–1858), tenth child of John and Margaret Cheyne; born 8 October 1785 and died 6 July 1858 in Hobart, Tasmania.

[3] Bruce Cheyne (1793–1856), sixteenth and youngest child of John and Margaret Cheyne; born 27 January 1793 and died 7 January 1856 in Albany, WA.

[4] Grace Cheyne née Melville (1797–1871), eighth of eleven children (and fifth daughter) of Andrew Melville and Katharine (née Marshall), christened on 3 September 1797 at Markinch in Fife. She died at 'Bank House', Lochmaben, on 26 September 1871.

[5] Marshall MacDermott (b. 1800), Captain of the 3rd Foot Regiment. He married Harriet Birch in 1830 before they set sail for WA in the *Stirling*. They had six children: Caroline (b. 1834. Mid Swan and died in 1855 in Adelaide); Frances Mary (b. 1836, Mid Swan); Harriet Agnes (b. 1839); Henry (b. 1841); Charles (b. 1843). MacDermott applied for large grant of land. He was appointed Cashier of the bank at Swan in 1839 and from 1846 to 1855 made frequent trips to South Australia where he was appointed Bank Manager. In 1834 he owned a pure-bred merino flock in WA, imported from the flock of Joseph Trimmer. See further details on William Trimmer in endnote 13.

[6] Sir James Stirling (1791–1865), first Governor of WA, from 1831 to 1838. He was married to Ellen Mangles. In 1834 he led a bloody raid against a Nyungar group near Pinjarra, with over twenty people killed. His autocratic ways became unpopular with the settlers and in 1839 he resigned and left WA, never to return. He resumed his naval career, becoming an Admiral.

explored the continent's west coast on behalf of the Colonial Office. He was convinced that the west could become a prosperous colony and, on his return to England, persuaded the British government to support colonisation. He sailed with his wife, Ellen (several months pregnant), their first child and a number of artificers and their families on the *Parmelia*. Their escort was HMS *Sulphur*, carrying a garrison from the 63rd Regiment, with their wives and families. The new colony was proclaimed in 1829, with Stirling as Lieutenant-Governor until 1831, when he became a full Governor. The generous terms for grants of land to settlers were printed in *The Times* and reprinted in the form of handbills to attract settlers. As Stirling's capital was tied up in WA—he had been granted 100,000 acres from the Crown—it was imperative to him that the new colony should succeed. The reports he sent home were glowing. The terms for land attracted George Cheyne, who was granted 16,490 acres on arrival, selecting a further 1000 acres in the Plantagenet region in 1832 and another 15,000 acres at Kendenup. With considerable capital to establish George as a merchant, the Cheynes included in their cargo two prefabricated wooden houses from Sweden. In addition, they were accompanied by three Swedish indentured servants. Having acquired a town allotment in Albany, George and Grace sailed in the *Sulphur* around the coast from the Swan settlement to King George Sound settlement at Albany. It was also to this area that the eighteen-year-old John Henty was dispatched by his older brothers, James and Stephen[7] to select some land in November 1831, the Cheynes and the Hentys becoming friends.

In June 1834 the *James Pattison* arrived in Albany, bringing back Sir James Stirling, who had been visiting England to counter the colony's bad reputation and to encourage more settlers. He was accompanied by a number of new settlers (many of whom he knew personally) including George Cheyne's brother, Captain Alexander Cheyne, and nephew John, the son of Dr John Cheyne, their older brother. This nephew John Cheyne[8] travelled with his wife, Annie Levina, and son, John St Leger, and they remained in Albany for two years. Their subsequent story is told later in this chapter. Of the new migrants on the *James Pattison*, only three remained for the long haul—Peter Belches,[9] Thomas Brooker Sherratt[10] and Patrick Taylor.[11] These new settlers were disappointed at the lack of development in the new colony, largely due to the shortage of labour. The settlers met at Cheyne's house in November 1834 to

---

[7]   James Henty (1800–1882), Stephen George (1811–1872) and John (1813–1868) were the sons of Thomas Henty (1775–1839) and his wife, Frances Elizabeth née Hopkins (1777–1848). Sent by their father, a leading merino breeder in Sussex, to take up a selection in the new colony, they arrived on the *Caroline* in October 1829. Disillusioned with WA, they moved to VDL where they were reunited with their parents and other siblings. After Edward Henty (1810–1878) made a trip to Portland Bay in search of suitable land, part of the family settled there (illegally squatting), leaving (in VDL) James as a leading business man, Charles (1807–1864) as a bank manager and William (1808–1881) as a solicitor and politician.

[8]   John Cheyne (1810–1880), son of Dr John Cheyne (1777–1836), Physician General to the Forces in Ireland, and his wife, Sarah née Macartney.

[9]   Captain Peter Belches, RN (1796–1890), had served on the *Success* with Stirling. He was appointed Harbour Master at Albany at £100 per annum, a sinecure since even at its busiest only about one vessel a week came to the port. Garden, p. 52.

[10] Thomas Brooker Sherratt (1791–1859), accompanied by his wife Amelia (1800–1842) and a large family. He built the Sherratt Family Inn, a two-storeyed building in which to house his family and his merchant business. He was the Postmaster until 1842 when he lost the position through his incivility and bad temper. Although his career could have been similar to Cheyne's, he lacked the latter's emotional stability and died a broken man. Garden, p. 52.

[11] Patrick Taylor (1807–1877), a wealthy young man who had not been expected to live through the voyage, married Mary Bussell (1802–1887) and settled in Albany. Garden, p. 53.

draw up a petition to the British government to have convicts sent to WA but their plea was unsuccessful.

In 1835, George and Grace adopted Emily Jane Trimmer,[12] the daughter of William Trimmer,[13] who had drowned in the Swan River on either 31 December 1835 or 3 January 1836. William Trimmer had arrived at the Swan settlement with his daughter and brother, Arthur,[14] in the *Atwick* on 25 April 1831. On board also were Captain James Mangles,[15] a botanist and a cousin of Lady Stirling, and Charlotte Carter, who married James Henty a week later, with Stephen Henty and Arthur Trimmer as witnesses. In 1836 Arthur married Mary Ann Spencer, daughter of Sir Richard Spencer.[16]

George Cheyne is well remembered in WA with Cheyne Beach and Cheyne Bay among the many places named after him.[17] A leader in the small community, he became prosperous because he had all the necessary ingredients to succeed—capital, the ability to work hard and the entrepreneurial skills, which led him to diversify his financial interests. He established himself at first as a merchant and licensed spirits dealer but eventually farmed his land with the help of nephews. He also established a whaling station in the Sound in the late 1830s. At one stage Cheyne was involved in a feud with the Governor Resident at Albany, Sir Richard Spencer, an irascible man, whose temperament may have been in consequence of head injuries suffered during his naval career in the war with France. Spencer was also the father-in-law of Cheyne's adopted daughter's uncle, Arthur Trimmer. Notwithstanding this personal link, Cheyne called for an enquiry into Spencer's administration. The mutual dislike between the two men erupted when Spencer shot and killed a horse of Cheyne's which had strayed on to Spencer's land. Captain Alexander Cheyne wrote in 1835:[18]

> Tuesday 17 Feb^y: George's action against Sir Richard Spencer for destroying his horse was brought on today but given against George from a deficiency of proof. Mr McKay gave Sir R^d a severe lecture for his conduct, the conviction on all parties was Sir R^d guilt.

---

[12] Emily Jane Trimmer (1827–1872) was married on 24 June 1848 to Andrew Moir (1818–1912), the nephew of her adopted mother, Grace Cheyne. Emily and Andrew Moir subsequently had eight children and took over George Cheyne's farms and businesses when George and Grace returned to Scotland in 1860.

[13] William Trimmer (1796–1835/36), Lieutenant of the 17th Foot, the son of Jane and Joseph Trimmer, one of a handful of merino sheep breeders in England. His brother, Spencer Trimmer, had sailed with James Henty on the *Caroline*, arriving at Swan River in October 1829. George Cheyne was William Trimmer's executor, which might explain why he and Grace were able to adopt Emily Jane.

[14] Arthur Trimmer (1807–1877) was married on 18 April 1836 to Mary Ann Spencer (1818–1886), the daughter of Sir Richard Spencer, the Governor Resident at Albany.

[15] Captain James Mangles returned to England and in 1836 wrote to Georgiana Molloy (1805–1843), the wife of Captain John Molloy (1780–1867), to persuade her to collect and send him seeds of the native plants of the region. This she did for over five years. Her meticulously packed seeds were sent by Mangles to various botanical gardens in England, where they were propagated and scientifically classified.

[16] Sir Richard Spencer (1779–1839), the Governor Resident at Albany, arrived in Albany in September 1833.

[17] R. Stevens, 'Builders of Albany: George Macartney Cheyne', *Journal and Proceedings of the Western Australian Historical Society*, IV, 3 (1951), p. 68. This article has some misleading facts (including confusing George Cheyne with his nephew, George Macartney Cheyne, in the title) but contains some useful insights into the conditions facing the colonists and George Cheyne's outstanding personal qualities.

[18] Alexander Cheyne, Diary, Transcripts, Battye Library, Perth.

Cheyne was Chairman of the Albany Road Trust formed in 1838, and in April 1841, although a Presbyterian, he was elected as one of the trustees for the construction of an Anglican church at Albany. He established a trading station at Cape Riche and in 1842 moved his family to the station, which by this time was prospering, as foreign whaling vessels used it to avoid the high port dues at Albany. Several more relatives joined him in WA, including another nephew George Macartney Cheyne[19] and Grace's nephew Andrew Moir,[20] who arrived in 1842 and six years later married the Cheyne's adopted daughter, Emma Jane Trimmer. Another relative of Grace, Andrew Muir (1802–1874), his wife, six children and mother-in-law, arrived in January 1844 in the *Ganges*. Both Andrew Moir and Andrew Muir settled permanently in WA.

During 1858 the Cheynes made their home in a new two-storeyed granite residence (now called 'Norman House'), which George had erected in Stirling Terrace, Albany. Overlooking Princess Royal Harbour, it was built on the site of the original hut where they had first made their home in 1831. The new substantial home was very different from the hut, 'which had only a boat sail for a door, Mrs Cheyne had several unpleasant encounters with natives'.[21] George Cheyne became more and more concerned about his health after his youngest brother, Bruce, died of heart disease in 1856 in Albany. Resolving in 1860 to return to Britain, they first lived at 2 Lansdowne Terrace, West Brighton (near Bayne and Lucinda Cheyne), until they finally made their permanent home in a country residence, 'Bank House', in Lochmaben, near Dumfries. Lucinda and Bayne moved from Brighton in late 1864 or early 1865 to live with them and two years later Lucinda died there, on 20 June 1866. Walter and Mary stayed at 'Bank House' with Bayne, George and Grace the following summer and, while the Richardsons were still in Yorkshire, Bayne died on 2 August 1868. George died less than a year later on 5 June 1869. Grace continued to live at 'Bank House' until her death on 26 September 1871.

While George had become a wealthy man in WA, his brother Alexander fared less well financially but is nevertheless remembered in Tasmania as a prominent pioneer. Captain Alexander Cheyne was born on 8 October 1785, the tenth child and seventh son of John and Margaret Cheyne. He was apprenticed to an iron founder and then joined the Royal Engineers. Having reached the rank of Captain in 1811, he remained with his regiment for five more years, before retiring on half-pay in 1817. Five years later he became Director of the Glasgow Edinburgh Union Canal. In 1833 he sold his commission and sailed for King George Sound, WA, to join his brother George. Alexander worked for the government in WA as the Superintendent of Mounted Police and as a surveyor. He was also appointed as a Justice of the Peace. But in June 1835 he received a private letter from Sir James Stirling 'intimating that the

[19]   George Macartney Cheyne is sometimes confused with his uncle, George Cheyne (see Bassett, p. 165). He was another son of Dr John Cheyne, Bayne's older brother, and his wife Sarah née Macartney. He graduated with a BA from Trinity College, Dublin, in 1830. Captain Alexander Cheyne's diary reveals that he never settled, was sometimes sulky, and that his uncles were not very surprised when he packed up and left for home. He worked for a couple of years in WA as the Government Auctioneer. 'Macartney has no perseverance & not being bred to any business I do not see what he can do at home or America.' Cheyne, 6 April 1835.

[20]   Andrew Moir (1818–1912), the son of John Moir (1792–1868) and Elizabeth née Melville (b. 1795), who was Grace Cheyne's sister. In 1842 his parents and siblings followed him to WA in the *Dido*.

[21]   Letter from George Cheyne to Governor John Hutt in February 1839, quoted in R. Stevens, 'Builders of Albany: George Macartney Cheyne', *Journal and Proceedings of the Western Australian Historical Society*, IV, 3 (1951), pp. 70–71.

situation of Superintendent of Police was done away, a serious disappointment to me.'[22] He had already sent his curriculum vitae to a contact in Van Diemen's Land and in July he received a message advising him that, 'The Governor[23] would embrace the first favourable opportunity to employ me.'[24] In December 1835 he left Albany in the *Caledonian*, reaching Hobart Town on 8 December 1835. After a promising start in Hobart his career became a litigious battle with successive administrations. The following is a previously unpublished letter[25] written by Alexander on 9 October 1852 to his widowed niece, Cecilia Graham (née Wilkinson), before her second marriage. The letter encapsulates his career and misfortunes since he had arrived in Hobart Town:

My dear Cecilia

I was much gratified by the receipt of your letter of the 15th May which reached me on the 16th of last month since then no ship has left this direct for England.

I am under the impression that I answered the only letter I received from you but it is now so long ago that I cannot state positively that I did; but if not, it is very contrary to my usual practice; as I have long been in the habit of replying to every letter which reaches me. Now that you have resumed writing I hope you will continue a regular correspondent.

I have constantly received some accounts of your movements from your uncle Charles[26] or Bayne, so far as they were acquainted with them. You mentioned being easily disheartened; you ought not to be so, in doing what you believe to be right. Perseverance is a most useful qualification to get through the world, and impress this strongly on the mind of your son[27] it is one of the most useful lessons you can teach him.

It gives me much pleasure to learn that your trials have been sanctified to you. They are always inflicted for our spiritual welfare and are continued till they answer the end for which they are imposed. Few persons have suffered more severely than myself, but I have been greatly strengthened to support me under them. My prospects at present are somewhat better

I have been treated with great injustice by the Government of this Colony, but it would occupy many sheets of paper fully to explain all my grievances. My correspondence with the Government has consumed, not quires only, but reams of paper. I have been completely ruined in my pecuniary circumstances. I was removed from the first Government situation I held by Sir John Franklin[28] about whom there is

---

22   Alexander Cheyne's Diary, 3 June 1835.
23   George Arthur (1784–1854), Lieutenant-Governor in VDL from 1824 to 1836. He appointed Cheyne Director General of Roads and Bridges.
24   Alexander Cheyne's Diary, 2 July 1835.
25   Graham Papers, item 6. Minor corrections in spelling and punctuation have been made to assist the reader.
26   Captain Charles Cheyne (1786–1857), living in Edinburgh.
27   William Henry Graham, who was aged thirteen at the time of this letter, emigrated later to WA to join his great-uncle George Cheyne.
28   Sir John Franklin (1786–1847), appointed Lieutenant-Governor of VDL in 1837 as successor to George Arthur. Franklin's lack of administrative experience and personal naivety (coupled with the colony's hostility to government) made him vulnerable to the intrigues and conflicting interests of colonial officers, particularly John Montagu, the Colonial Secretary, and Matthew Forster, the Treasurer. He was recalled in 1843, after suspending Montagu, whose appeal was upheld. He became leader of the ill-fated 1847 expedition to discover the north-west passage to the Arctic. *Companion to Australian History*, p. 266. The search for his expedition began and, after twelve years

such a fuss made in England—and he appointed one of his nephews Mr Kay to my situation. Sir John Franklin was succeeded as Lieut. Governor by Sir Eardsley Wilmot[29] who enquired into my case[30] and gave me a certificate exonerating me from all charges & imputations but I could obtain no redress from the Secretary of State, Earl Grey,[31] who declined to reopen my case on the plea that it had been disposed of by his Predecessor Lord Stanley.[32] I then entered into a contract with Sir John Franklin's Government on losing my situation, to supply water to the Town of Launceston, the 2nd Town in the Colony, but Sir John's successor refused to fulfil the agreement, and I have at present an action pending against the Government for compensation for the loss I sustain by its breach of Contract.[33] The Secretary of State for the Colonies has admitted my claim to be one of strict right and has directed the Lieut. Governor to afford me every facility to bring my claim before a Court of Law for decision but instead of this every obstacles has been raised to prevent my doing so. Had my action been against a private individual, he could not have prevented me bringing an action, but the Government is protected against any action being brought against it, and which can only be done by authority from the Home Government, this has been given me but the Lieut. Gov. has disregarded it, and I have complained against him to the Secretary of State. I do not expect a decision before the end of the year and the change of ministry will probably delay it much longer. The correspondence on this matter has been going on for about ten years, and it is my persevering disposition that has enabled me to carry it through.

Sir Eardley Wilmot appointed me Town Surveyor for Hobart Town in Jan[y] 1846 with a Salary of £150. His successor Mr La Trobe[34] appointed me Director of water works with a salary of £300 a year at the request of the City Commissioners to whom the water works were transferred for which an Act of Council was to be prepared & passed. A dispute arose between the Lieut. Governor Sir Wm Denison[35] & the City

---

and more than twenty different attempts, on 6 May 1859, Lieutenant Hobson found a cairn, a tin case and some human remains.

[29]   Sir John Eardley Eardly-Wilmot (1783–1847) succeeded Sir John Franklin as Lieutenant-Governor of VDL. His wife remained in England but he was accompanied by his three youngest sons, August Hillier, Robert Charles Chester and Charles Octavius, all of whom received public office. The British Prime Minister, William Gladstone, dismissed Eardly-Wilmot in April 1846, supposedly for his failure to suppress homosexuality among convicts.

[30]   Franklin dismissed Cheyne without a hearing when John Montagu, the Colonial Secretary, put the blame on Cheyne when a more expensive tower was commenced at St George's Church, Battery Point, although Cheyne said that he had been instructed by Montagu to proceed with the construction. Two years later a note verifying Cheyne's statement was discovered and, as Franklin was about to leave, it was left to his successor, Eardley-Wilmot, to take proceedings to clear his name. In March 1844 Cheyne was exonerated.

[31]   Earl Charles Grey (1764–1845).

[32]   Edward Geoffrey Smith Stanley, 14th Earl of Derby (1799–1869).

[33]   In 1842 Cheyne had successfully tendered to supply water to Launceston, but government delays over the passing of the necessary legislation bankrupted him. He finally received £3000 compensation in 1853 for the loss of the water contract.

[34]   Charles Joseph La Trobe (1801–1875), Superintendent of the Port Phillip District and subsequently first Governor of that territory, now called Victoria, superseded Eardly-Wilmot on 13 October 1846. During his short stay as 'administrator' he resolved to remove every officer chargeable with incapacity or neglect, and many were dismissed. Sir William Denison arrived to take over as Lieutenant-Governor in January 1847. John West, *History of Tasmania*, vol. 1 (Launceston: Henry Dowling, 1852), p. 261.

[35]   Sir William Thomas Denison (1804–1871), Lieutenant-Governor, arrived at Hobart Town on 25 January 1847. He was a skilled engineer, promoted Lieutenant in the Royal Engineers in 1826.

Commissioners regarding the mode in which the Town was supplied with water when Sir Wm Denison took advantage of the Act of Council not having been passed, and resumed possession of the water works. It was then my duty to endeavour to maintain the rights of the Inhabitants as secured to them by Law; Sir Wm Denison to get rid of my representation removed me from office, and to justify his conduct he resorted to a palpable falsehood but I could obtain no redress from the Secretary of State. It appears to be the practice of the Colonial Office to support the Governors of Colonies whether they are right or wrong. My exertions to defend the rights of the Inhabitants is pretty generally known to them and I hope it will now be of use to me. I have now been five years without employment and all my means being expended I am daily getting deeper into debt. I am however glad to say that through the influence of a friend of mine with Mr Clarke[36] a Lieut. of Royal Engineers & private secretary to the Lieut. Governor Sir Wm Denison who is also an officer of Engineers (a Captain) His Excellency Sir Wm has been induced to offer me a subordinate situation in the road Department for which I was formerly its Head. The Salary will be only £100 a year which in these times is a very poor subsistence and much less than is now paid to a common tradesman. Sir Wm Denison intended to have given me a better one but circumstances have prevented it for the present. It is rather galling to be obliged to accept of it but pride must give way to necessity. Had I declined it I could not expect that any other would be offered to me. I have been told that the very first opportunity which presents itself for elevating me to a situation more suited to my inclination & abilities Mr Clarke will be too happy to embrace it.

I have great hope of getting my former appointment of Director of Water works for Hobart Town.[37] A municipal Bill has just passed which comes into operation on the 1st of November when the Citizens are to elect seven Aldermen who appoint one of themselves Mayor of the City and on the 2nd Nov they appoint their officers. The water works are to be transferred to the Mayor & Aldermen. As no one in the Colony understands the whole question relative to the water works better than myself and

---

He had worked on the Rideau Canal, Canada, and had instructed engineer cadets at Chatham. One of Denison's final official actions (before he left for Sydney to take up his new appointment) was to commend a petition from the Legislative Council of VDL that the island's name be changed to Tasmania. This was approved and took effect from 1 January 1856. He sailed with his family to Sydney on 13 January 1855 and became not only Governor of NSW but also 'Governor-General in and over all our colonies of NSW, Van Diemen's Land, Victoria, South Australia and Western Australia'. He remained as Governor-General until 1861 when he took up his appointment as Governor of the Presidency of Madras. He returned to England in March 1866.

[36] Sir Andrew Clarke (1824–1902), military engineer and public servant. His father, Andrew, was Governor of WA and urged Andrew to join him in Australia. As Lieutenant in command of a detachment of Royal Sappers and Miners, he sailed to Hobart Town with Sir William Denison, the new Lieutenant-Governor, with whom he became the best of friends. The following year he was sent to New Zealand with the Governor-General and then returned in 1848 as private secretary to Denison. In 1853, he was appointed the Surveyor-General of Victoria, replacing Robert Hoddle, at a salary of £1200. He entered the Victorian Legislative Council in 1853 as an official representative. He won the seat of South Melbourne in the first election for the Victorian Legislative Assembly in 1856 and held that seat until he left the colony. He joined the first cabinet under W. C. Haines as Surveyor-General and Commissioner for Lands. His return to England was marked by a farewell banquet in Melbourne by the Freemasons, of whom he was Grand Master. He was a cousin of Marcus Andrew Hislop Clarke (1846–1881).

[37] From January to July 1846 Cheyne acted as Town Surveyor of Hobart and was appointed Director of Waterworks in January 1847, until clashes with private interest brought his dismissal.

certainly no person has so strong a claim to the situation I fully expect that the Mayor &
Aldermen will appoint me Director of Water works. A Mr Reeves is the only person who
has as yet come forward as a Candidate for election as an Alderman and he did so before
the Bill actually passed. In a day or two there will probably be several Candidates. I am of
course very anxious to see the list. The negotiations to obtain a Government
appointment for me commenced above a fortnight ago when it was very doubtful
whether the municipal Bill would pass the Council, and but for these doubts, I should
not probably have acquiesced in my application being made to the Lieut. Governor on
my behalf as it was I did not wish it from the belief that Sir Wm Denison would do
nothing for me, but my friend MacDowell[38] managed it with great tact.

You would probably hear of the severe injury I sustained in July 1844[39] from the
upsetting of a Stage Coach causing a compound fracture to my left leg a few inches
above the ankle & seriously injuring the joint. I was confined to bed five months & two
months more to the house & it was nearly twelve months more that I was obliged to use
crutches. When the Coach overturned the horses were not stopped, my foot & ankle
were dragged under the Coach. I never suffered much from the fractured boned of the
leg. My ankle joint continues weak. On level & smooth ground my lameness is scarcely
perceptible but I shall never recover the full strength of the ankle. If I have not had an
excellent constitution I must have lost my leg. I enjoy very good health.

Your Uncle George is at King George's Sound, Western Australia where he has
been above twenty years. In the first instance he suffered great privations but he has now
one of the best farms in the Colony and all the necessaries of life in great abundance.
Bruce has been residing with George for three or four years. He is in delicate health,
perhaps affected in some degree by his dependent situation as he was not successful in his
speculation in these Colonies. George & his wife do all in their power to make Bruce
comfortable & she is an excellent housewife. George has been very pressing that I should
join him, but I have always been sanguine of getting employment here which would be
hopeless at the Sound.

The Victoria gold fields of which you have heard so much continue to yield very
large quantities of gold. It is impossible to calculate what will be the ultimate
consequences of the discovery. We are here feeling some of the evil consequences in the
necessaries of life are nearly three times the price they were eight months ago. Property of

---

[38]   Edward Macdowell (1798–1860), barrister; called to the Bar at the Middle Temple in 1824, he
served for some years on the Midland circuit before being appointed Solicitor-General of NSW in
1830. Tardy in taking up this position, he lost the post and was subsequently appointed to the less
lucrative position of Solicitor-General in VDL. He remained Solicitor-General from January 1833
to September 1837 when he succeeded Alfred Stephen as Attorney-General. In December 1838 his
brother, Thomas, a journalist, joined him in VDL and began his career in the colony as the editor
of the *Hobart Town Courier*. This paper repeatedly attacked the Solicitor-General, Herbert Jones,
who had quarrelled with Edward and, after a public scandal erupted, both Edward Macdowell and
Jones were forced to resign. Edward then concentrated on his legal practice, which became very
successful and included the defence in 1843 of the bushranger Martin Cash. After the recall of
Franklin in 1843, Edward began to get back in favour with the administration and so was
appointed Commissioner of the Insolvency Court in March 1845 and Acting Crown Solicitor in
1851. Although his tenure in this position was made permanent in 1854, the following year he
resigned and moved to Melbourne with his children, where he practised at the Bar until his death
in 1860.
[39]   At that time he had been appointed supervisor of Launceston swamp draining, but the coach
accident in July made him lame and unable to work outdoors.

every kind has risen very greatly in value. The merchants & shopkeepers are making large profits but persons with small fixed incomes are feeling it very severely. The digging for gold is a mere lottery but all who persevere get some, & there are cases of great success. Three young men who have returned lately had sunk 14 pits with very little success, but in their last pit they got a large quantity of gold which they sold on the spot for £6000. A constable of the name of Flinn who returned about a fortnight ago brought above £4000 with him. These no doubt are rare cases, but one such creates great excitement. There are many of the returned diggers now in Hobart Town who have got from £100 to £500 most of whom are squandering their money in all kinds of dissipation intending to go back to the diggings when their money is expended. There are some of the more prudent ones, purchasing property. Very few return to their former occupations. Most of the free mechanics who have the means, have either left this or are on the point of going, wages are consequently very high.

Notwithstanding my advanced age had it not been for the weakness of my ankle, I should very probably have paid the gold fields a visit myself; and at times even with this disadvantage I feel a great desire to go there. In certain seasons the diggers suffer great privations. In the hot season very many suffer from bad eyes & there is a great deal of sickness from the scarcity of water & of bad quality. In the winter season the roads, or rather tracks, for they are not made but in a state of nature—are impassable for carts which increases the price of provisions & other necessaries to an enormous rate.

I received a letter from your uncle Charles on the 8th July dated 15th March last. I was pleased to learn that his health was somewhat improved & that he had been able to take exercise out of doors for a short time on a few occasions.

I had a letter on the 31st July from your uncle Bayne's wife[40] dated 13th April. Your uncle had been dangerously ill and unable to write me. He had been attacked with influenza which affected his lungs. I am most anxiously expecting another letter either from your uncle or aunt.

Your letter was forwarded to me by the Post, I therefore conclude that Mr Joseph Wyatt to whom you entrusted it had changed his intention to try his fortune at the "Diggings" and he has done right if he has strength and perseverance he must do well. So many have already arrived at Melbourne from England & other parts of the world that there is the greatest difficulty in procuring accommodation, and I understand that several large ships have been converted into lodging houses. It is expected that when the hot weather sets in there will be a great deal of disease & mortality from the crowded state of the houses & Barracks, & wanting of proper drainage.

I was much pleased to hear so favorable an account of your son.[41] I sincerely hope he will turn out to gratify your most sanguine wishes.

We have had a considerable degree of political excitement here for the last two or three weeks owing to the bad feeling which exists between the elected members of the Legislative Council and the Lieut. Governor. The Council has passed resolutions expressing their want of confidence in Sir Wm Denison and have petitioned the Queen to remove him.

---

[40] Lucinda Cheyne, WLR's mother.

[41] William Henry Graham, who was aged thirteen at the time of this letter, later emigrated to WA to join his great-uncle, George Cheyne.

22nd Oct The Mail for England which was advertised to close on the 9th Oct has been altered to the 23rd (tomorrow) & there is some doubt whether the vessel may no be detained a few days longer from want of sailors I shall put my letter in the Post Office tomorrow as it would not be safe to risk the vessel being detained.

I have little more to add. The municipal Act of Council does not come into operation till the first of Jany instead of Novr. This has been a great disappointment to me—prolonging my anxiety as to whether I may get the charge of the waterworks under the Mayor & Aldermen. I have not received any further communication regarding the situation promised me by the Lieut. Gov. The delay has arisen from the Comptroller General of Convicts having been detained at Port Arthur where he was investigating the conduct of 300 convicts on their passage from Norfolk Island to Port Arthur. He has returned, & I called upon him today. He told me some difficulty had arisen in providing Quarters for me in his absence but that I should hear from him in a day or two as business has accumulated in his absence.

I am my dear Cecilia| Your Affectionate Uncle

Alex Cheyne

Continue to direct to me at Hobart Town as in the event of my leaving it I shall leave my address at the Post Office

Alexander Cheyne's problems had arisen following the return in March 1841 of the Colonial Secretary, John Montagu,[42] whose personal dislike of Cheyne led him to misrepresent his every official action to Lieutenant-Governor Sir John Franklin. The construction of the tower at St George's Church, Battery Point, caused an open rupture between Montagu and Franklin, and Cheyne became the scapegoat. In 1852 Lieutenant-Governor Denison gave him another chance as assistant superintendent of road building at Ross and a year later he was made surveyor of the main road between Launceston and Hobart until that position was discontinued. The public testimony to his ability and honest intentions was shown by his election as Alderman of the City of Hobart shortly before his death on 6 July 1858, aged seventy-three.

Alexander Cheyne left his estate to be shared between his brother Bayne Cheyne and his nieces, Cecilia Sheppard and Elisabeth Yorke, daughters of his sister Elisabeth Wilkinson (1778–1836). It was the money from this estate, finally sorted out by the lawyers four years

---

[42] John Montagu (1797–1853), son of Edward Montagu (1755–1799), Lieutenant-Colonel in the Bengal Army and kinsman of the Duke of Manchester. He joined the 52nd Regiment, fought at Waterloo, and was promoted to Lieutenant in 1815. He joined the 64th Regiment but then returned to half-pay as a Captain in 1822. In April 1823 he married Jessy, daughter of Major-General Vaughan Worsley, and niece of George Arthur, Lieutenant-Governor elect of VDL, and in August transferred to the 40th Regiment, companies of which were to be sent to NSW. Montagu and his wife sailed in the *Adrian* with Arthur's party, arriving in Hobart Town in May 1824. He was appointed secretary to the Lieutenant-Governor and took over the work at the Colonial Secretary's office, but, despite support from Arthur, the Colonial Office disallowed his nomination as Colonial Secretary or as Clerk of the Executive and Legislative Councils. Notwithstanding the Colonial Office's decisions, Arthur kept Montagu in office. Hearing that his regiment was about to be sent to India, he hastily applied for retirement, but meantime was ordered to escort military invalids who were being returned to England. While in England he sold his commission and was confirmed by the Colonial Office as Clerk of the Councils. He returned to VDL in January 1831, extending his influence as Acting Colonial Treasurer, and, on the retirement of John Burnett in 1835, was appointed Colonial Secretary. Arthur was recalled in 1836 and the inexperienced administrator Sir John Franklin became Lieutenant-Governor.

after Walter's death,[43] which may have assisted Mary Richardson to pay for the school fees for her two daughters, Ettie (HHR) and Lil. Bayne Cheyne's estate had been left to his stepchildren and Caroline's husband, Henry, an experienced lawyer in the Court of Probate in Cork, was in correspondence with Mary over the Cheyne estates:

> Capt[n] Cheyne's left his affairs so complicated that it was only after the expenditure of considerable time and labor that the solicitors (Mess[rs] Mitchell & Baynter) were able to clear up matters and arrive at something like results. It appears that the Capt[n] left a good deal of heritable property consisting of houses in Cheyne St and Sloan St, Edinburgh, the property has been in the possession of certain Bank holders for many years, and security for their mortgages. It was only in searching the Register of Land Rights in Edinburgh that the solicitors discovered that Charles Cheyne,[44] Bayne Cheyne, Mrs Strong,[45] Mrs Yorke[46] and Mrs Sheppard[47] were also Creditors of Capt[n] Cheyne, and next entitled after these Bankholders should be satisfied, & this is, of course, the property would revert to the kin at law Rev[d] John Cheyne of Melbourne.[48]

John Cheyne[49] was born in Dublin and educated at Trinity College, from which he graduated with a Bachelor of Arts. He emigrated to WA with his wife, Anne Levina,[50] their new baby son, John St Leger Cheyne, and his uncle, Captain Alexander Cheyne, on the *James Pattison*, which arrived in June 1834. They settled near George and Grace Cheyne and in 1837 twins, George and Elizabeth Levina, were born. Baby George and his older brother, John St Leger, died in Albany, so only Elizabeth[51] was left in 1838 to accompany her parents on their next voyage. They sailed to New Zealand[52] where they remained for a year before returning to Australia and settling in Liverpool, NSW. John at this time was teaching. A second daughter, Annie Forest Cheyne,[53] was born in Liverpool on 12 November 1838. The

---

43 See two extant letters from Henry Richardson to his sister-in-law, Mary Richardson, NLA MS133/1/244 (22 February 1883), NLA MS133/1/245 (17 August 1883).

44 Captain Charles Cheyne (1786–1857), eleventh child of John and Margaret Cheyne.

45 Cecilia Strong née Cheyne (1775–1845), eldest daughter of John and Margaret Cheyne, married Robert Strong on 5 July 1796.

46 Elisabeth Yorke née Wilkinson (b. 1811), eldest daughter of Captain William Wilkinson and Elisabeth née Cheyne, married Lieutenant Frederick Augustus Yorke on 10 February 1842.

47 Cecilia Sheppard formerly Graham née Wilkinson (1812–1849), youngest daughter of Captain William Wilkinson and Elisabeth née Cheyne. She married first Henry Graham in 1839, then after his death in 1849, she married Henry Sheppard.

48 MS133/1/245, HR to MR, 17 August 1882.

49 John Cheyne (1810–1880), son of Bayne Cheyne's brother Dr John Cheyne and Sarah Macartney (daughter of Bishop Macartney of Antrim). He married Anne Levina Forest on 10 May 1833, at the village where his father had retired, Sherrington, Buckinghamshire. They had twelve children, four of whom died as infants. After the death of Anne, he married Janet Mary Carmichael in 1870 in Victoria, daughter of James Carmichael and Carol Amelia Campbell. He and Janet had two sons.

50 Anne Levina Cheyne née Forest (c. 1812–1867) born in Deal, Kent, the daughter of Charles Forest, who became the Commanding Officer at Cork, and his wife whose maiden name was St Leger.

51 Elizabeth Levina Cheyne (1837–1916) married George Gibson Harper (1830–1906), a banker. She and her husband lived in Castlemaine from 1852 until they died.

52 This is only known because Anne Levina's death certificate states that she lived in New Zealand for one year.

53 Annie Forest Cheyne (1838–1896) married James Williamson, a commercial traveller, on 10 October 1856 in Castlemaine, where she remained until her death.

family then moved to Gosford, NSW, where three sons were born: John Cheyne,[54] William Leigh Richmond Cheyne[55] and Anthony Butler St Leger Cheyne.[56]

John Cheyne was appointed as a teacher at St James College, Sydney, and a son, Charles, was born on 4 June 1848 and buried the next day at St James, Church of England. Soon after this sad event, the family moved to Victoria, where John Cheyne left the teaching profession to join Christ Church of England, Geelong, as a trainee clergyman. On 9 February 1850 twins, Sarah and Alexander Theophilus Cheyne,[57] were born. Sarah only survived a few weeks and was christened by her father on 24 March 1850, before she died. He was ordained deacon in the Cathedral Church of St James, Melbourne on 23 December 1850 and priest on 15 June 1851. After his ordination the family moved to Burnbank, north-west of Ballarat, where Macartney Cheyne[58] was born in 1853. Anne Levina Cheyne's last child, Cecilia,[59] was born at Castlemaine in 1854.

For most of his clerical career, the Reverend John Cheyne worked on the goldfields, particularly in Castlemaine, living for many years at Muckleford, between Maldon and Castlemaine. The first Anglican Minister at Castlemaine was the Reverend J. H. Gregory, a Bush missionary, who in 1850 had been sent on a roving commission in the north of Victoria.[60] In 1852, regular services were being held on the Camp (the goldfield), alternately by the Reverend John Cheyne (Anglican) and the Reverend James Lowe (Presbyterian). Cheyne was not only concerned about the miners' spiritual health. He was one of three men who initiated the building of the hospital at Castlemaine. With Dr W. F. Preshaw[61] and the Reverend James Lowe, Cheyne organised a public meeting on 17 February 1853 and raised sufficient subscriptions to build the first hospital on any of the Victorian diggings. The hospital opened on the Queen's birthday (24 May 1853) and remained in use until 1868, when a new hospital was opened.

---

[54]   John Cheyne (1842–1897), born 12 April 1842 and christened 15 October 1843 at Brisbane Water, NSW. On 3 January 1865 he married Margaret Teresa Monks at St Mary's Catholic Church. He declared on the marriage register that he was a member of the Church of England and that he was a farmer. His bride, the daughter of a farmer, was a housemaid.

[55]   William Leigh Richmond Cheyne (1844–1897), born 18 July 1844 and christened 6 August 1846. Never married, he died aged sixty-one at the Hotham Benevolent Home, North Melbourne.

[56]   Anthony Butler St Leger Cheyne (1846–1913), born 7 June 1846 and christened 26 July 1846. He was married to Esther Teresa Monks (his brother's sister-in-law) on 5 May 1869 at Trinity Church, Maldon, by the Reverend J. C. T. Stretch, father of the Reverend John Francis (Jack) Stretch, with whom HHR later became infatuated. He was appointed to the postal service in Victoria in 1863 and after working in Maldon he became Postmaster at Wodonga from 1869 to 1882; at Wangaratta from 1882 to 1890; at Beechworth from 1893 to 1894; and then in Kyneton from 1894 until after 1900.

[57]   Alexander Theophilus Cheyne (1850–1897), born 9 February 1850 and christened on 4 April 1853 at Christ Church, Geelong. He married Louisa Reed in 1893 and died in 1897 aged forty-seven, in Sale Hospital.

[58]   Macartney Cheyne (b. 1853) became a butcher and married Ellen Shorten (c.1858–1912) on 18 January 1877 in St Paul's Church, Sale. They lived in Heyfield near Sale until his death. Ellen died in Dandenong.

[59]   Cecilia Cheyne (b. 21 July 1854). She married James Aberdour Emslie, a Captain in the merchant service, on 11 February 1875 at All Saints' Church, St Kilda.

[60]   Raymond Bradfield, *Castlemaine A Golden Harvest* (Kilmore: Lourden Publishing Co., 1972), p. 33.

[61]   Dr William Fisher Preshaw (c.1810–1866), surgeon; born in Plymouth, the son of William Preshaw and his wife, Margaret née Mathers. He was married to Isabella née Ogilvy and lived in Jersey prior to emigrating first to Hobart. They had several children including: Robert Holderness (c.1846–1873); David Ogilvy; George Ogilvy; Margaret (m. George Sevier); Lydia Sanders (m. Francis Wynne Hickling).

Talbot Cheyne,[62] a younger brother of John, arrived in Victoria in 1852. He was a solicitor, born and educated as his brother in Dublin, but was suffering from consumption. Presumably he emigrated in the hope that the warmer climate might provide a cure. He lived with John and Anne and their children and was attended by the surgeon, Dr Preshaw, until his death on 7 December 1856 in Castlemaine.

In 1858, the Reverend John Cheyne was appointed the first Incumbent of Sandridge, but he did not stay there long. The *Church of England Record*, January 1860, announced his resignation. His wife did not move from Muckleford for Mrs Henry Sirée stayed with the Cheyne family after her husband decided to return with their two children, Elizabeth and Horatio Nelson Sirée, in 1858. Mrs Sirée was no relation of John Cheyne except by marriage. She was the wife of the brother of John's uncle's wife, Lucinda Cheyne. And yet she was taken in and eventually helped to get a passage back to England[63] by this generous man and his wife.

When Anne Levina Cheyne died in 1867, the family was still living in Muckleford. Three years after her death, John Cheyne married his second wife, Janet Mary Carmichael,[64] on 9 November 1870 at All Saints' Church, St Kilda. They went to Rhyll, Phillip Island, Victoria where two sons were born: Charles Campbell Cheyne (24 April 1872) and James Carmichael Cheyne (19 July 1875). John was described in the Post Office Directory as 'Schoolmaster at Cowes'.

There are no references to this Cheyne family in Walter and Mary's letters but they may have visited them. Lucinda Richardson arrived in Victoria in December 1854 and must have been in contact with the Cheynes for the communities were small and she worked as a governess in the Castlemaine–Daylesford–Kyneton area until her departure for England in 1862. Whether Walter was in touch with his step-cousin, the Reverend John Cheyne, cannot be proved but it is unlikely that they never met since not only did his aunt Elizabeth Sirée stay with the Cheynes in Castlemaine but Lucinda Richardson was a governess to one of Cheyne's best friends, Commissioner Francis Crossman Doveton (a witness at Cheyne's second marriage). The Richardsons would certainly have known of Anthony Butler St Leger Cheyne. When they were living in Chiltern in 1876 to 1877, Ned and Agnes Bailey were in Wodonga, where Anthony Cheyne was the Postmaster and, as Deputy Registrar, registered the death of Walter Robinson Bailey.[65]

The Reverend John Cheyne died on 11 December 1880, aged sixty-nine, leaving his widow with two sons aged nine and six, and eight adult children by his first wife, Anne Levina née Forest. The estate of Captain Alexander Cheyne, who died in 1858, was still being sorted out in 1883 and it is likely that Mary would have been in touch with Janet Cheyne. But there is no concrete evidence to substantiate this supposition.

---

[62] Talbot Cheyne (1828–1856), son of Dr John Cheyne and Sarah née Macartney.

[63] Elizabeth Sirée (b. *c*.1810) departed from Melbourne on 30 July 1859 aboard the *Yorkshire*, arriving in London in October 1859.

[64] Janet Mary Beamis Cheyne née Carmichael (1836–1905), born in Hobart, VDL; the daughter of James Carmichael, architect, and Caroline née Campbell.

[65] Walter Robinson Bailey (1868–1877), born 26 September 1868 and died 20 March 1877; the son of Ned (Edward Harold) Bailey and his wife Agnes née Hablethwaite.

3

The Bailey Family

Mary Bailey was born on 28 December 1835 in Leicester, at that time a small ancient city in the centre of England. She was the seventh of ten children of John Bailey[1] and his wife Elizabeth.[2] Mary's father, John Bailey, according to the marriage notice, came from the small market town of Hinckley, Leicestershire, where a great many Baileys were born. However, there is no record of a birth of a John Bailey in Hinckley consistent with his age at death. How John met his bride, Elizabeth Robinson, is not known; but they married at St Margaret's Church, Leicester, on 3 May 1825. John was on the register of persons entitled to vote in elections for representatives for the Borough of Leicester since 1833 (on the £10 list) and was elected to the Town Council as a councillor representing East St Mary's Ward in 1843.

Elizabeth was the daughter of widower Thomas Robinson,[3] who had been an inn-keeper at 'The George', Coal-hill, Leicester, from the 1790s and then was a maltster in Rutland Street, Leicester. When Elizabeth's mother, Susanna Robinson, died on 15 January 1811, she left three daughters: Ann, aged thirteen-and-a-half; Elizabeth, aged eight-and-three-quarters; and Sarah, only six. (Another older sister, Hanna, christened on 10 November 1799, had been buried on 21 March 1802.) Two years after their mother's death, the fifteen-year-old Ann married William Hester[4] on 17 March 1813.[5] Elizabeth did not marry John Bailey until she

---

[1]   John Bailey (c.1803–1846), solicitor's clerk. He was also the Secretary of the Agricultural Society (as is noted by John Gilbert, in *Southerly*, vol. 22, no. 1 (1962), p. 45). He died aged forty-two on 25 February 1846.

[2]   Elizabeth Bailey née Robinson (1802–1869), born on 24 April 1802 and baptised four days later at St Margaret's Parish Church; the third of four daughters of Thomas and Susanna Robinson.

[3]   'On Tuesday last at St Margaret's, Mr John Bailey, to Elizabeth, second daughter of Mr T. Robinson, of Rutland-street in this town.' *Leicester Chronicle*, 7 May 1825.

[4]   William Hester (1783–1835), third son of John Hester (1751–1826), victualler at the New Inn, High Cross Street, Leicester, and his first wife, Sarah (1747–1798). His father was the Leicester mace-bearer, billet master and sheriff's officer, and a Freeman of the City. William also became a Freeman (7 May 1807) and was an innkeeper at the Lion and Dolphin, Market Place, Leicester. The spelling of 'Hester' has been standardised throughout Part I and Part II, since that is the spelling in all the directories. In Mrs Elizabeth Bailey's will, however, the name is spelt 'Hestor'. Henry Hartopp, *Register of Freemen of Leicester, 1770–1930* (Leicester: Corporation of City of Leicester, 1933).

[5]   Parish register of St Margaret's Church, Leicester.

was twenty-three and it was another twelve years before Sarah Robinson married at the age of thirty-two. Sarah, who was living in London, married William Henry Turnham[6] on 5 April 1837 at St Martin in the Fields, Westminster. It was the brother of William Henry Turnham, Joseph Turnham[7] and his first wife Elizabeth,[8] whom Walter and Mary and the Bailey family in Victoria visited regularly. Joseph, a prison warden, emigrated from London to Hobart Town prior to October 1844 where he met and married Elizabeth Cutler on 12 October 1844. He may have worked in the prison service on Norfolk Island as there is a record of a 'Mr and Mrs Turnham' returning from Norfolk Island to Hobart Town in September 1849 on the *Maguasha*.[9] In 1853 they moved to Melbourne for Joseph to take up employment in the Victorian prison service (on a salary of £300 per annum plus quarters and fuel). His first appointments were at the Marine Stockade, Williams Town, where he commenced on 5 December 1853 as Warden and Acting Overseer; he was promoted to Overseer on 1 January 1854, and Assistant Superintendent a year later. On 23 March 1855, he moved to the Collingwood Stockade as Chief Warden and on 1 January 1861, in line with all other officers under the public service review, his salary was reduced to £250 per annum plus quarters and fuel. On 1 March 1861, light was added to his allowances. On 1 January 1862, there was a further reduction of his salary to £200 per annum (plus quarters, fuel and light) and his position was classified as 3 in the Civil Service Act. On 1 January 1863, he was promoted to Assistant Superintendent (classification 4) at the Pentridge Stockade and was Acting Superintendent from 26 November 1869 to 13 April 1870. Elizabeth died of cancer of the uterine organs in Pentridge Stockade on 30 November 1868, aged sixty-one, before Mary and Walter had returned to Melbourne from their sojourn in England. Joseph remarried on 12 September 1870—to a widow, Emma Youlden (1823–1906) with seven children—a month after he had been appointed Acting Superintendent of the hulk *Sacramento*, where he remained until his retirement on 20 June 1876.[10]

There are three 'Elizabeth Turnhams' in the letters: Joseph Turnham's wife, Elizabeth née Cutler; William and Joseph's sister, Aunt Bessie; and Sarah and William's daughter, Cousin Bessie. It was with Cousin Bessie that Mary, HHR and Lil stayed when they returned to London in 1888. She was then married to a retired army Major and seemed to HHR 'intolerably dull and stodgy'.[11] Sarah and William had another child, Willie (William Henry) Turnham,[12] who came out to Melbourne, at the age of eighteen, on the *Cyclone*, arriving in Melbourne on 10 August 1858 to join his uncle and aunt. He married Lydia Mary Cole in 1863 and from 1864 to 1881 they had ten children, eight of whom survived into adulthood.

---

6   William Henry Turnham (1807–1849), born 23 August 1807 in Topham, Devon; eldest son of Joseph Turnham, a livery stable keeper, and his wife, Agnes née Nunn. His parents married on 29 March 1807 at St Lawrence, Exeter, Devon, five months before his birth. He was described as a cook on his death certificate.
7   Joseph Turnham (*c.*1812–1880), prison warden; born in London. He was the younger brother of William Henry Turnham, who married Sarah Robinson, Elizabeth Bailey's sister. He was therefore the brother of Mary's uncle rather than her 'real' uncle.
8   Elizabeth Mary Ann Turnham née Cutler (1807–1868), daughter of Thomas Cutler (a cabinet-maker) and Agnes née Blundell.
9   *Maguasha* (Captain Taylor) sailed from Norfolk Island to Hobart Town on September 1849. *Shipping List of Arrivals: 1841–1889*, film 4, p. 282.
10   *Staff Appointments: 1853–1873*, VPRS 538 Vol. 1, PRO, Victoria.
11   Elizabeth Turnham (b. 1838), daughter of William Henry Turnham and Sarah née Robinson; christened on 16 March 1838 at St George's Parish Church, Leicester. See *MWY*, p. 87.
12   William Henry Turnham (1841–1905), son of William Henry Turnham and Sarah née Robinson. He was born in London but christened at St Margaret's Parish Church in Leicester.

The descendants of Willie still live in Australia. He joined his uncle in the prison service but, unlike his uncle, was not suited to the discipline. Walter wrote of him: 'Willie appears to be a nice boy pity he has not got the necessary qualification strict probity.'[13] Walter's assessment of Willie appears to be accurate. Appointed as a warden at Pentridge in February 1860, he had ten years of undistinguished public service before he was discharged on 8 July 1870 on the grounds of 'bodily infirmity with a gratuity and 9 months pay'. Remarks on his employment record at Pentridge reveal fines for 'letting off his gun carelessly', 'disobedience of orders', 'disrespect', 'absent without leave', and 'improper language'.[14] He became a journalist on a Brunswick newspaper, remaining in the Brunswick area until his death.

There are eight letters preserved in the NLA collection (and reproduced in Part II) written by Elizabeth Bailey in the last two years of her life. She appears to have been a commonsensical character with an unblinking attitude to death and was clearly a devoted mother, whom her children would greatly miss. Apart from a photograph, the only description of her was written by Lucinda Cheyne, who met her once in 1861:

> Mrs Bailey has been a beautiful woman, and is now <u>very</u> handsome, I would have known her anywhere from Mary's picture, she interests me <u>greatly,</u> and I felt quite drawn to love her, she is <u>gentle, sorrowful</u> & dignified with a countenance full of benignity and sweetness.[15]

She was widowed before her forty-fourth birthday and left with ten children:[16] John Robinson, Edward Harold, Sarah Ann, Elizabeth, Thomas Robinson Burton, William, Mary, Samuel, Grace and Charles. Of these only three—Elizabeth, Thomas and Grace—remained in England during the period covered by the letters. John, Edward, Sarah, William, Mary and Samuel emigrated to Australia (from whence William went to India); and Charles emigrated to America. Charles is the only name that does not appear in any of the extant letters: presumably he had already left England before Mary and Walter returned in 1867–1868. He was certainly alive at the time of his mother's death in 1869, for in her will, to which she attached a codicil in 1869, she bequeathed all she owned 'to all my ten dear children share and share alike'.[17] From her father and her sister, Ann Hester, Elizabeth Bailey had inherited property. It appears that her father had left Elizabeth the house in which she resided— 58 Rutland Street, in the Parish of St Margaret's, Leicester—and Ann had left Elizabeth the house next door (60 Rutland Street) which was occupied by Samuel Hester,[18] Ann's brother-in-law. The house and stableyard, coachhouse, saddle rooms and three cottages adjoining were to revert to Elizabeth's estate on the death of Samuel Hester. Hester was always referred to in their letters as 'old man'[19] by Elizabeth, 'uncle'[20] by Mary, and 'the old gentleman'[21] by

---

13   Letter 44, from WLR to MR, 30 April 1859.
14   *Staff Appointments*, op. cit.
15   Letter 77, from LC to WLR, 26 August 1861.
16   HHR says there were eleven children but there are only records of ten children in the parish records and EB states ten in her will. EB might have suffered a miscarriage or stillbirth between the last two births where there is a gap of five years. *MWY*, p. 3.
17   Probate Records for 1869, Leicester PRO, pp. 415–417.
18   Samuel Hester (1783–1871), fourth son of John Hester and his wife Sarah. Samuel also became a Freeman as were his father and two older brothers (on 7 May 1807). He started his career as his father and brothers, John and William, as a victualler, but then became an Inspector of Weights and Measures.
19   Letter 132, from EB to LB, 19 October 1868.

Walter. He outlived Elizabeth by two years and there was considerable family concern in 1869 when he was pressuring Grace and Sarah (their mother's joint executrix) to give him possession of the house and land.[22] Despite the three houses, three cottages and attached buildings, and shares in the water works, Elizabeth's probate amounted to less than £1000.

The most successful of Mary's siblings in Australia was her eldest brother, John Robinson Bailey.[23] After he left school, instead of entering any of the professions, he sailed to New York. For a short time he worked for a farmer in Connecticut. It is not clear whether he had intended to make his fortune in the United States, or whether he only returned to England because of his father's death. In his diary written throughout the voyage to Australia in 1852 and preserved in the NLA,[24] he mentions in passing that he returned to Liverpool on board the *Independence* but gives no date. It must have been in 1846 for he states that he had worked for six years in London for Mr Elstob (probably as a warehouseman).[25]

John inherited his father's interest in local politics and in October 1859 was elected as a representative in the Victorian Legislative Assembly for Ballarat West until November 1860. Before this successful short foray into politics he had unsuccessfully contested the election in Geelong for the first Parliament of Victoria in 1856. His obituary read:

> A solicitor's son, educated at Harrow until his father's sudden death, he had worked for a farmer in the USA and in soft goods in London before migrating to Geelong in 1852, at the age of twenty-six, and opening a draper's shop.[26]

It is more likely that he had told friends he was educated 'at the harrow' rather than at Harrow.[27] John and his brother Ned (Edward Harold) Bailey set sail for Melbourne on 8 March 1852 on board the *Mount Stuart Ephinstone*. John's diary provides a vivid description of setting off to Australia, the ship, sailing across the oceans and his theatrical entertainments in which he played the starring roles in *Hamlet* and *Macbeth*. His and Ned's experience would have been similar to those of all his family members and Walter who set off after him. He commenced the log as follows:

> How true it is that we never rightly estimate the value of friends until we part from them. Although for six years I have been in daily contact with those whose parting cheers are still lingering on my ear I knew not that my welfare would ever elicit from them the expressions of interest and the kindly offices which my leaving them has called forth. One and all—from the managing partner of the establishment (Mr Elstob)—to the

---

20   Letter 141, from MR to WLR, 3 December 1868.
21   Letter 142, from WLR to MR, 3 December 1868.
22   Letter 152, from WLR to MR, 2 October 1869.
23   John Robinson Bailey (1826–1871), the eldest son of Elizabeth and John Bailey, born in Leicester but there is no record of his christening.
24   NLA MS133/1/268. Mary used the same book to record her return journey to London aboard the *Ormuz* with HHR and ALR in 1888.
25   His profession is stated on the *Mount Stuart Elphinstone*'s manifesto (British Shipping Passenger List, 1852–1869, PRO Archives, Melbourne).
26   Weston Bate, *Lucky City: The First Generation at Ballarat 1851–1901* (Carlton: Melbourne University Press, 1978), p. 135.
27   The archivist at Harrow School, Rita M. Gibbs, has confirmed that there is no evidence of John Robinson Bailey having attended Harrow.

Juniors in the desk have almost vied with each other in good wishes in counsel and assistance to myself and fellow voyagers.—

That we have appreciated and profited by them, I trust is manifest, for never did a party of young adventurers leave Home and native land with lighter hearts and better spirits, than we do upon so speculative a voyage. It will be an eventful day in the annals of all, as well for the remembrance of the fortunes separated as for the scenes—its witnesses—Never perhaps was Wood St since it became the locale of business it now is so startled from its accustomed propriety as when we left the celebrated Hq. From various quarters our party had assembled, and as the time drew near the hurry bustle and confusion of a start became apparent—myself flying hither and thither—in one place to bid good bye, in another to seize upon some stray article of luggage, or to spur on those that were not ready. When at length all were collected, two cabs were summoned, which with the baggage ourselves and friends, were well filled—the whole establishment in a dense crowd at the doors—our neighbours intentive spectators of the scene—Passers by halting to look on. Within three yards our vehicles were stopped by the obstinacy of a carrier whose cart obstructed our progress through the narrow thoroughfare. Entreaty or force were equally futile and there was no other help for it but to retrace our path and seek exit by the contrary outlet. For time was on the wing, it wanted but a few minutes of the hour fixed for the departure of the Train which we had been told was the latest that would convey us to the ship—ere she sailed. At the London Bridge Station we were joined by other friends. Any fact of honor no sinecure—The last gatherings of the party had resulted in a number of small packages of miscellaneous articles, last thoughts and last gifts and required the eyes of Argus[28] to look after them.

Till all were safely stowed I would not enter the train and save the guard was the last in. It was a long train and carried other of our fellow voyagers beside ourselves. Until it stopped at Gravesend, we knew not who was with us—there we mustered, and numbered some twenty or more. Collecting the Baggage in one spot—which was not done without difficulty the train being stopped again for a missing Filter—much to the annoyance of the officials—and for which they may thank their own over positive negligence. We placed it on two trucks, and duly guarded by my Brother[29] and myself, our party and friends ahead and in the rear, emerged into the street. There we were besieged by a crowd of Boatmen whose active competition considerably reduced our fears of the cost of embarkation. From among them we selected the owners of two ferries—who engaged to take us to the ship for 6^d each—and two shillings for each boat load of luggage.

As we passed along towards the Pier, we seemed the objects of a curious interest to the persons around us, accustomed though they are, to seeing such daily. One last purchase was 2/- worth of Bakers bread as a send off against the anticipated biscuits. After half an hours rowing, we reached the vessel anchored amid stream off Wait's Hotel—deposited the baggage in our respective Cabins, showed our friends the accommodation provided—and finding we would not sail till evening, returned with them to the shore, where we sat down to Dinner and a parting glass of wine, they had

---

28   Argus, in Greek mythology, was Io's guardian, whose hundred eyes Hera transferred to the peacock's tail: a vigilant watcher.

29   Edward Harold Bailey.

generously caused to be provided at Pallister's, from the Dining-room window of which, with the aid of Telescopes, we could see all that transpired around the ship—and thitherward they were often directed to detect the preparations and signal for sailing. We remained til 4 PM—at which hour from the growing conviviality I judged it prudent to depart, and so gave strict command to enter the boats, which we did after a last embrace and the exchange of farewell sentiments—and with three lusty cheers, mutually given, bade adieu to all.

On board, busily employed till dusk, arranging cabins, and making preparations for the night. The bedding provided we found in bundles on the lower deck, which on opening consisted of a cotton Flock mattress & Pillow, Quilts, Blanket & pair of sheets, the last smelling horribly from some preparation used in the dressing. In it also were sundry three utensils all of Tin—with knife fork & spoon.

About 9, after a last look at the Town distinguishable only by the lights and a faint moon, turned in, but did not sleep much, from the strangeness of the place and the confused noises around us. At two o'clock, aroused, by weighing of anchor, which with other matters connected to our sailing lasted an hour ...[30]

The boat sailed to Plymouth where it remained for three days, picking up mining equipment and the final passengers who were miners from the British Australian Mining Company. John's diary gives an insight into the British class system for he clearly saw himself, his brother and friends as belonging to the middle class, superior to the working class through 'task habit and education'.

March 15th ... [Plymouth] On board all hands busy receiving machinery and implements for the use of the British Australian Mining Co a detachment of whose miners are to have passage with us. About 4 PM They came alongside in a Smack[31] with their baggage accompanied by a few of their female relatives—one only of whom will go with them. They appear a clean respectable body of men for their station in life, but by no means so stalwart of limb and sinew or so intelligent looking as one would expect to see in a band of pioneers—for such an enterprise. It is a matter of regret to most of those who embarked at Gravesend that so large a body of persons of such an inferior station in life should have been allowed a passage in a vessel sailing on the uniform principle where from the rate of fare, it is naturally expected that the bulk will consist of those who occupy a middle sphere—Not that these men have not an equal right to enjoy with others what they have paid for—but that for a long voyage but little society and less company is to be expected—when tasks habits and education so widely differ.

While John immediately set up a business in Geelong on arrival in Victoria,[32] Ned went to the goldfields in Ballarat and commenced mining. He continued mining for some years but was not successful. Walter wrote in 1856:

---

[30]   NLA MS133/1/294. Catalogued as Mary Richardson's diary of the voyage from England to Australia, 1874, Mary wrote on the back of JRB's diary.

[31]   A small decked or half-decked coaster or fishing vessel.

[32]   He was auctioneer for the firm of Bailey, Honey and Company, ship produce and merchandise brokers of Little Malop Street, Geelong. Brownshill, p. 240.

Harold's party are compelled to put their pipes in, which will take them a month at least
before they can be at work again! Did you ever hear such confounded luck as our friends
and relations have on this hill—[33]

John prospered (though it is difficult to gauge how well) and Ned returned to his
profession as bookkeeper and accountant. Having political aspirations, John sold his business
in 1855 and bought some land to farm in Germantown, Geelong, for one needed capital or
land (worth £200) to be eligible as a candidate for election. He declared his candidacy for the
election in September 1856 to represent Geelong in the first Victorian Parliament but received
little support from the *Geelong Advertiser*, whose editor preferred at least four of the other six
candidates to John. At one electoral meeting the question, 'When did you become possessed of
your present qualification?' was posed. '"Before I solicited the suffrage of the electors," replied
Mr Bailey.' The editor commented dismissively, 'Ten acres of cabbage garden cannot be
truthfully declared to be of the Annual Value of £200 though rented for ten times that sum.'[34]
John came fifth in the poll.

By this time he had already been married for three years to Susannah Tyler Nicholson,[35]
who had followed him to Melbourne from Leicester on the same voyage as Walter on the
Roxburgh Castle. It has always been assumed that Walter Richardson and Mary Bailey met in
circumstances similar to the fictional account, that Alexander Brooke Smith (Purdy) was the
first to meet the Bradshaw (Beamish) family and then introduced his friend Walter (Richard
Mahony) to Mary (Polly Turnham). This account may be true but Susannah and her sister,
Marianne, may have become friends with Walter on the ship, and it may have been through
Susannah that Walter was first introduced to the Bailey family. John Robinson Bailey and
Susannah Tyler Nicholson were married on 29 January 1853, less than six months after her
arrival in Victoria. Their son, Harrie Elphinstone,[36] was born on 7 December 1853 and, on
13 September 1856, during the Geelong election campaign, their daughter, Emma,[37] arrived.
(Susannah had given birth to a son in 1855 but this child did not survive the birth.)

John's other claim to fame at Geelong is as the father of the Country Fire Authority. On
4 March 1854, his rousing speech to a public meeting prompted the formation of the Geelong
Fire Brigade, Victoria's first volunteer brigade outside Melbourne. He explained to the poorly

---

[33]   Letter 23, from WLR to MR, November 1856.
[34]   *Geelong Advertiser*, 26 September 1856, p. 2.
[35]   Susannah Tyler Nicholson (1833–1859), daughter of Henry Nicholson, a Professor of Music in
       Leicester, and his wife Mary. The Nicholson and Bailey families attended the same church,
       St George's Parish Church. Susannah travelled with her sister, Marianne Tyler Nicholson, who was
       a witness at the wedding of Susannah and John Robinson Bailey on 29 January 1853. The
       marriage ceremony at Christ Church, Geelong, was conducted by Theodore Stretch, who became a
       friend of the Bailey family.
[36]   Harrie Elphinstone Bailey (b. 1853), born 7 December 1853 in Geelong; son of John Robinson
       Bailey and his first wife, Susannah Tyler née Nicholson. That his father and uncle emigrated to
       Victoria on a vessel named after the son of Lord Elphinstone, *Mount Stuart Elphinstone*, appears to
       be the inspiration for his second name. He married Leah Harris on 30 September 1875 in
       Melbourne. He is fictionalised as John or Johnny Turnham in *FRM*.
[37]   Emma Bailey (1856–1935), born 13 September 1856 in Geelong; eldest daughter of John
       Robinson Bailey and his first wife, Susannah Tyler Nicholson. She was a governess in Billabong in
       NSW and married Robert Barton Hoysted (1851–1920) on 9 November 1878 at the Holy Trinity
       Church, Wangaratta. Born in Walterstown, County Kildare, Ireland, he was a horse trainer. See
       Letter 49 endnotes for further details. Emma, nicknamed Trotty, appears with the name Emmy or
       Trotty Turnham throughout the three volumes of *FRM*.

1 A photograph of Mary Richardson née Bailey (1835–1896) dated about 1856. 'I shall be rejoiced to see your dear smiling pretty face once more for to tell you the truth I have been very lonely.' (Walter to Mary, Letter 24, November 1856)

2 Walter Lindesay Richardson (1826–1879) aged about thirty-six, with his long, thick side-whiskers in the 'Dundreary' mode, which became fashionable in 1861, after the comedian Edward Askew Sothern played the part of Lord Dundreary in Tom Taylor's *Our American Cousin*. 'I showed her your likeness & she thinks you very good looking & would so like to know you.' (Mary to Walter, Letter 70, 23 May 1861)

3   Elizabeth Bailey (1802–1869), Mary's mother. On the back of this photograph, her grand-daughter wrote: 'Elizabeth Bailey, born April 25 1802, my grandmother. HHR.' 'Mrs Bailey has been a beautiful woman, and is now *very* handsome, I would have known her anywhere from Mary's picture, she interests me *greatly*, and I felt quite drawn to love her, she is gentle, sorrowful & dignified with a countenance full of benignity and sweetness.' (Lucinda Cheyne to Walter, Letter 77, 26 August 1861)

4   Lucinda Richardson, Walter's oldest sister, in the 1850s. Born in December 1820, she followed Walter to Victoria in December 1854. She was the governess for several families in Victoria, including that of Francis Crossman Doveton, the Commissioner ordered to Buninyong in September 1851 by Governor Charles La Trobe to issue licences to the gold miners in an attempt to limit the number of diggers. 'Write often, I do not care how little; if I know that you are *alive*, it quickens my prayers for you.' (Lucinda Cheyne to Lucinda Richardson, Letter 40, 6 January 1859)

5 Lucinda Cheyne (1796–1866), Walter's mother. 'To please you I endured half dying in a photography sky light a few days ago, that I might at least send you a stupid likeness.' (Lucinda Cheyne to Walter, Letter 90, 1 January 1863)

6 Until 1864, this was the home of Lucinda and her second husband, Dr Bayne Cheyne: 17 Buckingham Place, Brighton, Sussex, now turned into three apartments. It has a spacious basement and attics, and a large garden at the rear.

7 John Robinson Bailey (1826–1871), Mary's eldest brother, was elected in October 1859 as a representative in the Victorian Legislative Assembly for Ballarat West and became the Postmaster-General in Nicholson's Ministry until November 1860. After his stint as a parliamentarian, he became a wealthy businessman until his untimely death at the age of forty-five.

8 Susannah Tyler Bailey née Nicholson (1833–1859), the first of John Robinson Bailey's three wives, photographed before her death aged twenty-six. She was John's sweetheart from Leicester and followed him to Victoria on board the *Roxborough Castle*, on which Walter was also a passenger.

9 Ned (Edward Harold) Bailey (1828–
1893), the second oldest sibling in the Bailey
family.

10 Sarah Ann Laughton née Bailey (1829–
1911), Mary's eldest sister.

11 Samuel Bailey (1838–1911), the second
youngest brother, was Mary's favourite
sibling.

12 Grace Bailey (1839–1935), Mary's
youngest sister.

14   Emma Wilmer Cuthbert (1835–1877)

13   Mary's mother-in-law did not like this photo of her: 'Mary is
disfigured, so unlike her picture, it is all clothes, so stiff & old.'
(Lucinda to Mary and Walter, Letter 90, 1 January 1863)

15   Henry Cuthbert (1829–1907)

16 'Beaufort House', Ballarat, about 1876. HHR wrote on the reverse of the photograph: 'Ocock's house.' Left to right: Henry, Annie (aged eight), Emma and old John Cuthbert in the doorway. At the upstairs window is a figure—perhaps John Headen Cuthbert, aged twelve.

18 Mary Richardson in Devonport, England, October 1868, two months before her thirty-third birthday: 'I shall have half a dozen of the reading & smiling beauty for myself.' (Walter to Mary, Letter 135, 22 October 1868)

17 Deciding to return to England, Walter, Mary and their nephew, Harrie (John Robinson Bailey's eldest son), set sail aboard the *Red Jacket* on 14 January 1867. For a few months they lived in Eccles, near Manchester, where Walter was the locum for a medical practice and Harrie was placed in a school. This photograph of Mary was taken in Manchester in 1867.

19 Mary Richardson in the early 1870s

20 Walter Lindesay Richardson, 1870

21   HHR's birthplace: 1 Blanche Terrace, 139 Victoria Parade, Fitzroy, Melbourne. HHR took this photograph on her visit to Australia in 1912. The house now is renumbered 179.

22 Ethel Florence Lindesay Richardson (HHR) aged five months, June 1870, taken before her father's trip to Sydney and Parramatta.

24 HHR aged about fifteen months, April 1871

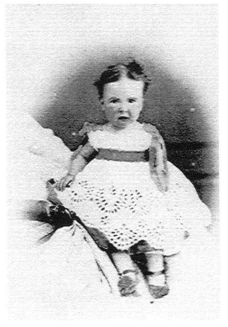

23 HHR aged ten months, October 1870

25 HHR aged about eighteen months, July 1871

26 The photograph of Walter Lindesay Richardson was taken by Hibling and Fields, whose business at 7 Collins Street, Melbourne, operated only in 1872.

27 Ada Lillian Lindesay Richardson (ALR) aged two, April 1873

29 Mary, HHR and ALR, Cork, Ireland, before they returned to Melbourne in 1874

28 HHR aged three, April 1873

30   'Lake View': 'I have just been over a decent house. 6 rooms kitchen stable fowl house pigstye & fine garden with fruit trees—it is the best house in Chiltern.' (Walter to Mary, Letter 175, 28 June 1876)

31   St Paul's Parsonage, Chiltern, visited by His Lordship the Bishop (seated on the horse) and Mrs Moorhouse, 3 May 1877. 'The Bishops visit is postponed until after the 28th [April]—evidently done by the Archdeacon [Tucker] because you are not here.' (Walter to Mary, Letter 211, 14 April 1877)

32   HHR aged seven in Melbourne in 1877. 'I hope dear Ettie has not been reading too much & no London journals or novels.' (Walter to Mary, Letter 231, 21 September 1877)

attended but historically important meeting how fire-fighting was managed in New York City, where a man was stationed at the City Hall day and night to alert the volunteer firemen to any conflagration.[38] He became the first foreman of the Fire Brigade until December 1854.[39] After his electoral defeat in 1856 he changed careers and from January 1857 he became an employee for the Ballarat newspaper, *The Star*, which was owned by Walter's friend, Thomas Drummond Wanliss.[40] How he was appointed is not clear, though he had had some experience writing for the Geelong newspaper. It may be that Walter had introduced him to Wanliss. John and his family moved to Ballarat and joined his siblings—Ned, William and Mary. (Sarah Bailey was a regular visitor to Ballarat in between posts as governess.) Susannah's fourth child, Edith Elizabeth, was born on 17 May 1858 but she and the baby were never well. John's political ambitions were undiminished and two days after Susannah's death on Saturday, 13 August 1859, a letter appeared in the Monday's newspaper from ninety-plus supporters (including Walter), requesting John to nominate for election. Under this letter was his agreement to stand for election and included his platform; this stated that he was:

> in favour of free selection for the *bona fide* occupier after survey; a modified and practicable system of deferred payments; the uniform taxation of all alienated and unimproved lands; ample commonage reserves; the equitable extinction of the squatters' present tenure of occupation, and the more useful employment of the grazing land in the colony: the re-introduction of the system of district councils; the absolute appropriation of at least one half of the revenue derived from the sale of land to the improvement of the roads and bridges of the locality in which it is raised; the ample endowment of municipalities; the establishment of local insolvent courts; the introduction of the South Australian system of registration and conveyance of titles of land; the abolition of State aid, and the adoption of one system of national education; a reform of the Gold Fields Act in every particular which local experience of its working may point out as necessary; the introduction at once of law legalising mining upon private lands; the abolition of the gold export duty; and the reform of the fiscal system of the colony; the establishment of a Victorian mint, and, if practical, of a national bank, for the transaction of the monetary business of the Government and the profitable employment of the savings of the people.[41]

He was elected as a member of the Legislative Assembly,[42] one of the two representatives for Ballarat West, the other being Robert Malachy Serjeant. He became the Postmaster

[38] Murray, Robert and Kate White, *State of Fire: A History of Volunteer Firefighting and the Country Fire Authority in Victoria* (North Melbourne: Hargreen Publishing Co., 1995), p. 26.
[39] Brownshill, pp. 240–242.
[40] Thomas Drummond Wanliss (1830–1923), newspaper proprietor of *The Ballarat Star*, MLA. See endnote to Letter 57 for a short biography.
[41] *Star*, Monday 15 August 1859, p. 2. Note that when HHR visited Ballarat in 1912, she read JRB's platform in the newspaper and used much of it for John Millibank Turnham's rousing address at the hustings. See *FRM I*, p. 269.
[42] Wanliss, a close friend and supporter of JRB, took umbrage when he read the first edition of *The Fortunes of Richard Mahony* (1917), where HHR had conflated the two election experiences of JRB. HHR was forced to change p. 268 and pay twenty guineas to Wanliss for 'imputing to him that after denouncing a candidate for one of the Parliamentary constituencies as an unprincipled scoundrel this charge was withdrawn the next day and the candidate received the support of the *Star*.' Letter from D. M. Mathieson, Edinburgh, solicitor to T. D. Wanliss, 10 December 1919.

General in the Nicholson Ministry from 27 October 1859 to 29 October 1860. He remained as MLA until July 1861. As well as his year as Postmaster General, he was Vice-President of the Board of Land and Works and Commissioner of Public Works (3 September 1860 to 2 October 1860) and Commissioner of Trade and Customs (29 October to 26 November 1860). After he left Parliament he returned to business and became a partner in the firm of Patterson, Ray, Palmer & Co., a well-known drygoods firm in Melbourne.

John was not close to the children of his first marriage and, until he remarried in April 1861, Mary and Walter cared for them. The baby Edith Elizabeth died in February 1860 while Mary and Emma (aged three) were away in Melbourne. Mary and Walter continued to look after Emma but John placed Harrie in a boarding school in Melbourne. Mary was shocked when she saw Harrie three months later in June 1860 and wrote:

> John wishes Harry to return & live with us if you have no objection dear. I said yes for I thought the money would come in useful because he will pay for both now. Harry has quite left school & will stay at Pentridge until I return He looks shockingly ill & John wants to have your advice about him his head is one mass of ringworms Uncle has got the Doctor here to come & see him he has had a bad cough for the last six weeks but that is a little better. I am glad Trotty's quite well & also yourself.[43]

The following year John married Jane (Jeannie) Rainsford.[44] Independent and forthright, she was thought by Mary to be very different from poor Susannah.[45] After John and Jeannie returned from their honeymoon in May 1861, Mary and Emma (not yet four) travelled to St Kilda from Ballarat so that Emma could return to her father and new stepmother. Harrie was already in Melbourne attending school and was staying with the Turnhams in Pentridge Stockade. Jeannie was not too keen on her stepmother role. Mary wrote:

> Jeannie is very anxious to return to Ballarat with me & send Trotty to Pentridge but I want her to let me come first & get the house in order & them to take Harry back.[46]

It is doubtful whether Harrie spent much time with Jeannie for he was staying at Pentridge in February 1862 when Mary visited Melbourne to assist her sister-in-law, Lucinda, pack up for her return to England. Eight months later Harrie's relationship with his stepmother had not improved and Mary wrote in her inimitable unpunctuated style:

> Trotty very thin Harry quite yellow neither improved in look's & according to all accounts very naughty Harry shocking taking <u>improper</u> liberties with Trotty Jeannie will not have him in the house after John comes home—My heart feels sad to think what is to become of them.[47]

There is no way of tracking where Harrie lived from 1862 to 1865, but in July 1865 he attended Melbourne Grammar School for a term. Between 1862 and 1866 John and Jeannie

---

43   Letter 59, from MR to WLR, 5 June 1860.
44   Jeannie (Jane) Bailey née Rainsford (1831–1866), born in Witley, Surrey, third daughter of William Rainsford, a gentleman farmer, and his wife Elizabeth née Taylor. She came to Victoria in October 1860 and she married JRB on 4 April 1861 at Christ Church, St Kilda.
45   Letter 70, from MR to WLR, 23 May 1861.
46   Letter 72, from MR to WLR, 27 May 1861.
47   Letter 84, from MR to WLR, 28 October 1862.

had three daughters: Gertrude Elizabeth,[48] Ida Beatrice[49] and Mary Jane.[50] Unfortunately this third birth proved fatal, and Jeannie died of puerperal fever nine days later, even though the leading obstetrician in Melbourne, Dr Richard Tracy,[51] attended her. John did not part with his daughters this time. After his stepmother's death, Harrie was sent to board at Scotch College. Whether he had continued to be unhappy in school or with his family is not clear, but it was decided that he should accompany Walter and Mary to England in January 1867. The three of them sailed on the *Red Jacket*, arriving in London in March 1867. Harrie was placed first in a school in Tottenham but after a few months, Walter decided to move him to a school in Fairfield, near Eccles, where he settled down and did well. The following year his father wanted him to return to Melbourne and start his career in business but Walter thought Harrie was too young (he was then only fifteen) and John was persuaded to let Harrie stay in England to complete his schooling. Mary and Walter returned to Melbourne in 1869, leaving Harrie still in Eccles, while they arrived in time to attend John's third wedding.

For his third wife John chose Mary Ringrose Atkins,[52] whose father was a barrister and whose brother[53] as 'Dan Barry' became a famous outback theatrical manager. Walter, particularly, enjoyed his connection to this musical family and became close friends with her father. A son, Edgar Atkins Bailey, was born to Mary and John on 15 October 1870, with Dr George Graham[54] as the accoucheur. By this time John was already a very sick man with cancer of the kidneys, liver and spleen and he died six months later on 6 May 1871, aged forty-five. His death at home was witnessed by Dr George Graham, Walter, and Harrie, who had left England in January 1871 on the *Superb* arriving in Melbourne in March. John's baby son Edgar Atkins died (aged fourteen months) on 11 December 1871, seven months after the death of his father. The cause of death was hydrocephalus, after a four-month illness.

[48]   Gertrude Elizabeth Rainsford Bailey (1862–1939), born 11 February 1862 in St Kilda; daughter of John Robinson Bailey and his second wife, Jane née Rainsford. Gertrude never married and worked as Postmistress at Romsey (1883–1886), Wedderburn (1886–1888) and Abbotsford (1888–1900+). She died at Sandringham on 20 May 1939, aged seventy-seven. She appears in *MWY* as the seventeen-year-old cousin who accompanies MR and the children to Koroit (p. 22); she and HHR sailed by sea to save the expense of the move. HHR describes her as 'my forthright, all-knowing cousin' (p. 25). She is probably the model for the fictional Cousin Grace, who met Laura at the station with the godmother: 'a cousin of Laura's, of at least twice Laura's age, who invariably struck awe into the children by her loud and ironic manner of speech. She was an independent, manly person, in spite of her plump roundnesses; she lived by herself in lodgings, and earned her own living as a clerk in an office.' *GW*, p. 26.
[49]   Ida Beatrice Bailey (1863–1940), born 1 May 1863, in St Kilda; daughter of John Robinson Bailey and his second wife, Jane née Rainsford. She married a man called Stevenson and settled in Victoria, Canada, raising at least one daughter.
[50]   Mary Jane (Jeannie) Bailey (1866–1909), born on 12 February 1866 in St Kilda; daughter of John Robinson Bailey and his second wife, Jane née Rainsford. She was only eight days old when her mother died and only five years old when her father died. Brought up by her stepmother, Mary Ringrose Bailey, and a new stepfather, William Bayles, from 1875. She married Richard Macansh on 26 October 1889.
[51]   Richard T. Tracy, MD, LRCSI (*c.*1826–1874), see endnote to Letter 79 for biographical details.
[52]   Mary Ringrose Bailey née Atkins (b. 1843), born in Dublin, daughter of John Robert Atkins, barrister of Toorak and his wife Mary Agnes née Campion. They were married on 24 July 1869 at Christ Church, South Yarra. In 1875 she married her second husband, William Hadzley Bayles, by whom she had a daughter, Josie, who survived into adulthood; two sons died in infancy. She is fictionalised as Miss Lizzie Timms-Kelly in *FRM II*.
[53]   John Ringrose Atkins (1851–1908), see *ADB*.
[54]   George Graham (1829–1893), MD (Melb.), MRCS (Eng.). See Chapter 5: Illness and Death for biographical details.

Like the fictional Turnham, John Robinson Bailey married three times, left six living children (compared to Turnham's five and an expectant third wife) and enjoyed prosperity until his untimely death. The obituary in *The Star* contains some information which is most unlikely (for example, already noted the reference to Harrow), however, the analysis of his personality does tally with many of Walter's comments about his brother-in-law throughout his letters to Mary. It states:

> Mr Bailey was a man of great natural intelligence and force of character. He was a strictly honorable man, and having a long and varied career always commanded the respect of those with whom he came into contact. With him, however, the *suaviter in modo* [gentle in manner] was not so pronounced as the *fortiter in re* [resolute in deed]. This peculiarity of his character caused him to be less liked as a public man than he otherwise would have been, and he was less popular than his considerable ability and thorough honesty of purpose really entitled him to be.[55]

If John Robinson Bailey shared many of the characteristics of John Millibank Turnham, Ned Bailey was very different from his fictional counterpart, Ned Turnham. Edward Harold Bailey[56] was the second oldest in the Bailey family and, having failed to make his fortune as a gold digger, he returned to his profession as bookkeeper and accountant. Ned's first position disclosed in the letters was that of ironmonger and bookkeeper at the Eyres' ironmonger's shop in Ballarat. For many months he lived with Walter and Mary until he finally moved to Melbourne at the end of August 1858, and was employed as a bookkeeper for Bennett Brothers, Grocers and Ironmongers at 154 Brunswick Street, Collingwood, Melbourne. Unlike his older brother, Ned did not marry until he was thirty-eight, in 1866. His bride was Agnes Eleanor Hablethwaite[57] and they had six children from 1867 to 1879. At the start of their marriage, Agnes and Ned lived in 'Palmerston House', Palmerston Street, Carlton where three children were born: James Harold (delivered by Dr James Edward Neild[58] on 22 August 1867), Walter Robinson (26 September 1868) and Mabel Elizabeth (18 December 1871). In 1872, they moved to 163 Albert Road, Emerald Hill where Edgar Charles was born (7 December 1872) and Celia Agnes (3 November 1874). On 23 March 1876, four-year-old Mabel Elizabeth died during a scarlatina and diphtheria epidemic and Ned took his family to Wodonga where he worked as an accountant. At that time, Walter and Mary Richardson moved to Chiltern and Sam Bailey was in Corowa. On 20 March 1877, Walter Robinson, aged eight, died in Wodonga of 'Congestion of the Brain (Effusion on Brain)' after eleven days

---

55   Obituary, *The Star*, Tuesday, 9 May 1871, p. 2.
56   Ned (Edward Harold) Bailey (1828–1893), christened 9 April 1828 at St George's Parish Church, Leicester, England; second son of John and Elizabeth Bailey.
57   Agnes Eleanor Bailey née Hablethwaite (b. 1840), born in Camberwell, Surrey, the daughter of Thomas Hablethwaite, a builder, and his wife Eleanor née Butcher. She was described as a 'Lady' on their marriage certificate.
58   Dr James Edward Neild (1824–1906), medical practitioner and theatre critic; born Doncaster, England, son of James Neild and Sara née Bilton. Having been apprenticed to his uncle for medical training as a surgeon (1842), gained a Licentiate, Society of Apothecaries (1848) and studied at University College, London, he came to Victoria in 1853 and was at the gold fields for a short time. Was employed in Melbourne by the chemist and druggist, David Rutter Long. Married his employer's daughter, Susannah Long (1831–1918), on 26 March 1857. See Harold Love, *James Edward Neild: Victorian Virtuoso* (Carlton: Melbourne University Press, 1989). He and his wife became friends with the Richardsons in 1869, see Letter 152.

of illness. His body was taken to Melbourne General Cemetery where he was interred as his younger sister had been less than a year before by the same undertaker, Joseph Hill. No mention of his death appears in any of Walter and Mary's extant letters but there is a gap in their correspondence and presumably messages would have been sent via telegram for this catastrophic event. The train carrying his body would have travelled through Chiltern and it is most likely that Walter Richardson would have joined the funeral party. His death would have been particularly poignant to Mary and Walter for he was named after his uncle and was the third nephew with the name Walter to die.

Agnes and Ned's final child, Percy François, was born in their home, 'Torrance Villa', Wodonga, on 23 September 1879. By this time, Ned was aged fifty and Agnes, thirty-nine. Staying with them to help Agnes and the three older children was their sixteen-year-old niece, Ida (daughter of John Robinson Bailey), and it was she who registered Percy's birth. When Ned died on 28 December 1893 of 'Epitheliomas of the stomach' in Gipps Ward, City of Melbourne Hospital, his death was registered by the Hall Porter of the hospital. Not surprisingly therefore, the information on this certificate is limited: for example, in the column headed 'If Deceased Was Married' it says 'Not known'. Agnes seems to have left Victoria, probably after her husband's death. Of their children, only Celia Agnes Eleanor died in Victoria—of breast cancer in Chelsea on 10 July 1938, aged sixty-three.

Sarah Ann Bailey,[59] Mary's eldest sister, emigrated with Mary and her brother, William, on the *Anne Cropper*, arriving in Melbourne on 25 May 1853. On the ship's manifesto she is described as a 'lady', whereas Mary is described as a 'Clerk'. Sarah worked as a governess in Victoria and flitted in and out of Mary and Walter's lives until she returned to England in 1861. In 1867 she was living in Victoria Gardens, London, where, it appears from her mother's letters, she looked after a house full of paying guests. When Walter heard the news of his financial ruin in 1874, while on vacation in Italy, he returned immediately overland from Italy to Melbourne. Mary returned to Ireland to collect their two daughters staying with Caroline and Henry Richardson. Whether Sarah had tired of her life in England is not known, but she packed up her belongings and accompanied Mary, Ettie and Lil on the *Sobraon*, which set sail from England in September 1874. On board ship Sarah met the Reverend James Laughton,[60] a Presbyterian Minister, nearly fourteen years her junior and terribly ill with tuberculosis. Notwithstanding these obstacles, when the ship arrived in Melbourne in December, James and Sarah were engaged. They married on 22 March 1875 at the Presbyterian church in Carlton, with Walter and Samuel Bailey as witnesses. Sarah shed three years, claiming to be only forty-two to her groom's thirty-two. Walter became his doctor but there was little he could do, for the tuberculosis was too far advanced. James died less than six months after the marriage, on 11 September 1875, and was buried in the Melbourne General Cemetery. These facts were beautifully entwined into the fictional Zara Turnham's late marriage (in Carlton) to the consumptive Ebenezer Hempel, a Baptist preacher.[61]

Sarah remained in Melbourne until July 1876 when she sailed on the old ship *Agamemnon* to London. Perhaps she wanted to meet her late husband's family, but again she felt unsettled and uncomfortable in her native land. In 1881 she sailed once more for

---

[59] Sarah Ann Bailey (1829–1911), christened 19 August 1829 at St George's Parish Church, Leicester; eldest daughter of John Bailey and Elizabeth née Robinson.

[60] Reverend James Laughton (1843–1875), born in Deptford, Kent, the son of Andrew Laughton, a bootmaker, and his wife, Christina née Dun.

[61] *FRM II*, pp. 138–148.

Melbourne on the *Ellora* and became part of the lives of Mary, Ettie and Lil. Before the marriage of Sarah was discovered, HHR's statement about how her mother afforded the school fees at the Presbyterian Ladies College was not properly understood:

> Just how Mother contrived to meet the expense of my schooling I don't know, I never enquired. Nor would she have wanted me to. That was her business. It may be that the rental drawn from the house at Hawthorn had been put by for the purpose. On the other hand, the authorities of the P.L.C. may have met her half-way. For the College, erected by those true lovers of learning, the Scotch, had been founded with a special eye to the daughters of unmoneyed Presbyterian ministers, and continued, I believe, to accept such girls at the original rates. I couldn't claim to be more than the niece of one; but his widow, my aunt, was a persuasively well-spoken woman, and I seem to have heard that she called on the Principal and laid my case before him.[62]

Sarah remained in Melbourne when her sister and nieces departed for Europe. She kept in contact with HHR and Lil after Mary's death and they continued to send her presents of money, presumably from their mother's estate. In 1911 she was living at the Old Colonist's Home, Rushall Crescent, North Fitzroy, where she died on 6 October 1911 of broncho-pneumonia and cardiac degeneration, aged eighty-two.

William Bailey[63] emigrated to Victoria with Mary and Sarah Bailey on the *Anne Cropper* in 1853 and worked for a time on the goldfields at Ballarat. His chronic asthma made him unfit for the hard labour and he decided to leave Victoria for India. There he worked for the Indian Civil Service until his retirement to Hampstead, London, shortly before Mary, Ettie and Lil visited him on their way to Leipzig, Germany, in 1888. HHR remembers him fondly, for he was kind to his nieces, giving them money for their sightseeing expeditions and taking them to the Savoy Theatre to see Gilbert and Sullivan productions. 'London was "the only place he could breathe in", as he nursed his incurable asthma; and this made him a doubtful companion. One never knew when he was going off, and, did a bad fit seize him, felt sure that he must choke and die.'[64]

Samuel Bailey[65] was Mary's favourite brother and, at the age of twenty-three, he joined his three brothers and two sisters in Victoria arriving in November 1860 on the *Result*. He lived with Walter and Mary in Ballarat from his arrival in Victoria until 1862, working as an accountant at the Bank of New South Wales. He then moved to a new appointment in Melbourne, then Geelong and finally to Sandhurst. In 1870, as a bank clerk at Sandhurst, he married Frances Mary Louisa Lascelles, known as Polly[66] on 22 December 1870 at All Saints' Church, Geelong. They had four children: Leila Maud Bailey (1 June 1874), Frank Lascelles Bailey (1 January 1879), Mary Bailey (who died eight days after her birth on 24 November 1881) and Guy Robinson Bailey (5 November 1886). HHR wrote that her mother on her deathbed said of her brother, Sam, 'He has always been good to me, he'll be good to you

[62] *MWY*, p. 63.
[63] William Bailey was christened on 22 October 1834 at St George's Parish Church, Leicester; fourth son of John Bailey and Elizabeth née Robinson; he never married.
[64] *MWY*, p. 89.
[65] Samuel Bailey (1838–1911), christened 21 March 1838 at St George's Parish Church, Leicester; fifth son of John Bailey and Elizabeth née Robinson.
[66] Frances Mary Louisa Lascelles (Polly) (1855–1934), daughter of Thomas Allen Lascelles, land and stock auctioneer, and Sarah Emma née Atkinson.

too.'[67] HHR visited her aunt Polly and cousin Leila (married to Thomas Henry Southern Hawkes) in Geelong in 1912.

Grace Bailey[68] was only thirteen years old when Mary left home for Australia. The youngest but one in the family, Grace quickly developed a teasing sisterly relationship with Walter when they returned in 1867. He called her 'the Little Indian'[69] and many of his letters contain references to her during their sojourn in England. She worked as a governess and never married. Grace was living in Wansford, Northamptonshire, when HHR renewed her acquaintance in 1888. When she died in 1934, Olga Roncoroni drove HHR in the funeral procession. HHR wrote:

> Mother's youngest sister and on the right side of fifty, she was a vigorous, upstanding woman, plain of face but of an original turn of mind, and full of fun. We took to her at once; and though, on her part, she may have found us rather undisciplined, and, for young girls, too outspoken, we got on well together. Here I may add that she was the sole member of my grandmother's huge family who did not go adventuring overseas. Except for one momentous journey to Leipzig, undertaken in fear and trembling, she was never out of England. She lived for more than seventy years in the same house, and died in it at the ripe age of ninety-five.[70]

Mary's third older brother, Thomas Robinson Burton Bailey,[71] was a terrible worry to his mother. It is not clear what he did for a living but he seems to have spent time in the West End of London, trying to live the life of a man-about-town without the necessary funds at his disposal. He borrowed money from his mother and Walter when the Richardsons were in England in 1867–1868. There is little known about him except that he was not strong and that he suffered from bad feet.[72] His mother said in a letter to Mary and Walter:

> I would not encourage him to Emigrate he could not do a Labourers work and has no idea of Agriculture he has no means nor yet to get an outfit for voyage … I trust something yet may turn up I will ever do a Mothers part but told him I could not continue to find cash as I had invested my capital to bring in an income for <u>my wants</u> but these are Mothers cares and I ought not to trouble you.[73]

Of the four Bailey sisters it was Mary's second oldest sister, Lizzie Brett,[74] who looked most like her. She was five years older than Mary and, when the Richardsons returned to England for their two-year stay in 1867, they spent several weeks together. The Bretts stayed with the Richardsons in Rawcliffe and the Richardsons visited the Bretts in Devonport and Brighton. Walter enjoyed the connection with Lizzie for his brother-in-law, Jack, was a Captain in the Second Battalion of the Prince Consort's Own Rifle Brigade and Walter was

---

67   Diary of the last illness of HHR's mother, 1896. NLA MS133/8/10–21.

68   Grace Bailey (1839–1934), baptised in St George's Parish Church, Leicester; youngest daughter and ninth child of John Bailey and Elizabeth née Robinson.

69   Letter 109, from WLR to MR, dated in this book as 13 May 1867.

70   *MWY*, p. 91.

71   Thomas Robinson Burton Bailey (b. 1832 or 1833), christened 9 January 1833 at St George's Parish Church, Leicester; fifth child and third son of John Bailey and Elizabeth née Robinson.

72   Letter 147, from EB to WLR and MR, 12–14 May 1869.

73   Letter 146, from EB to WLR and MR, 15 April 1869.

74   Elizabeth Brett née Bailey (b. 1830), christened 17 November 1830.

always interested in the activities of the army. Lizzie and Jack Brett were married on 7 June 1859 at St George's Church, Leicester, when he was already a decorated officer. He had joined the Brigade as a young man and served in the Kaffir War of 1846–1847 and that of 1852–1853 (Medal), and was severely wounded at the Battle of Boem Plaats in 1848. He served in the Crimea in 1854–1855, including the battles of Alma and Inkerman (when the English and French defeated the Russians on 20 September 1854 and 5 November 1854, respectively). He was at the siege of Sebastopol (1854–1855, during which he received Medal and Clasps, Knight of the Legion of Honor, and the Turkish Medal).[75] His brigade returned to Aldershot where they were visited by Queen Victoria in 1856. The following year a huge review was held on 26 June 1857 in Hyde Park where sixty-two Victoria Crosses (the first VCs ever to be awarded) were presented by the Queen.[76]

After marrying Lizzie in 1859, Jack was stationed for a time in England, where they had a daughter, Edith,[77] before he was posted to India. He returned with his regiment in November 1867 and was stationed in Brighton and then Devonport. Lizzie became pregnant on his return, and their son, John Walter, was born in August 1868. Unfortunately the baby never thrived and Mary Richardson went back to Devonport, leaving Walter in Rawcliffe, in late September 1868 to be with her sister during the distressing last two weeks of this small baby's life. He died on 6 October 1868, aged seven weeks. In 1874 the regiment was posted to Gibraltar for a time and it is probable that Lizzie and Edith accompanied Jack. He was gazetted Cornet/Ensign on 13 July 1854; Lieutenant on 22 December 1854; Captain on 24 November 1857; Major on 19 October 1872; and Lieutenant-Colonel on 20 February 1873. He retired from the service as Lieutenant-Colonel on full-pay in 1877.

Only Charles remains the complete mystery figure of the Bailey siblings. The activities of all five of Mary's other brothers and three sisters crop up in the extant letters and some facts about their lives have been traceable. During the Victorian period many families sought their fortune and a different life in the colonies and to this extent the Bailey family shares a common history with many Australian families.

---

[75]   Colonel H. G. Hart, *The New Annual Army List, and Militia List, for 1868* (London: John Murray, 1868).

[76]   Brigadier, The Rt Hon. Sir John Smyth, *The Story of the Victoria Cross* (London: Frederick Muller, 1963).

[77]   Edith Brett (b. *c.*1865), daughter of John Brett and Elizabeth née Bailey. She kept in touch with HHR throughout her life and her address can be found in HHR's Address Book. NLA MS133/8/9.

4

Friends and Friendships

'Best friend! Oldest friend! Good heavens, Mary! *do* think what you are saying. How can one continue to be friends with a person one never sees or hears of? ... People don't stand still in this world. They're always changing—up, or down, or off at a tangent ... No, the real friend is one you pick up at certain points in your life, whose way runs along with yours—for a time. A time only. A milestone on your passage—no more. Few or none march together the whole way.'[1]

These words spoken by the fictional Richard Mahony provide an apt starting point for any discussion of the friends of his real-life counterpart, Walter Lindsay Richardson. The letters of Walter and Mary are peppered with the names of friends, some of whom fade from the picture and others remain close for many years. From their very first canvas and timber-framed home to their more capacious homes, they enjoyed entertaining and, over the years, they developed a large network of friends. There were some women with whom Mary formed an immediate bond and although some friendships might falter and change as marriages and children came on the scene, others remained steadfast. From the letters it seems that she always had at least one 'best friend'. Sometimes there would be a tight small circle of women around her, who were all bosom friends. Polly and Tilly Bradshaw, Ellen and Emma Jelfs, Anna Maria Cuthbert, Emily Kabat, Elizabeth Wanliss, Emily Saddler, Anne Ochiltree, Emma Cuthbert and Sydney Graham were all important close friends for Mary in the various stages of her life. Walter and Mary loved evenings spent with friends. They enjoyed music; both played the piano and Walter sang. In Ballarat there were often parties and informal gatherings as well as the more formal balls. Mary enjoyed dancing and he played chess, but his great passion was for whist.

Walter was probably less dependent on intimate friendships, but there was plenty of male company for games or for a chat in the evening while he smoked his meerschaum pipe. His circle of friends included bank managers, stockbrokers, clergymen, lawyers and doctors.

---

[1]   *FRM II,* p. 206.

Of the medical fraternity, he particularly liked old William Wills (the explorer William John Wills's father), Charles Kenworthy, James Stewart and William Heise. One of his closest friends (and professional colleague) at Ballarat was Dr Robert Fawell Hudson, who also became chairman of the Ballarat Gas Company and the Ballarat Banking Company. Whenever Mary was away from Ballarat, Walter was frequently invited to dine out, especially with the Hudsons, the Cuthberts and after 1865, the Saddlers. Whist games are regularly mentioned, with friends such as George Gordon Mackay (Manager of the London Chartered Bank of Australia), William Pooley (Deputy Registrar and first Actuary for the Ballarat Savings Bank), Charles Wale Sherard (Warden of the Ballarat Goldfield) and William Robertson (Manager of the Bank of Victoria). Walter was an active committee member for the hospital and the benevolent asylum and was a busy member of the Freemasons. As part of the 'brotherhood' in Ballarat, he was one of the movers and shakers, though not as influential as friends like Henry Cuthbert. In England for two years from 1867 to 1868, Walter and Mary made friends with their new neighbours and revitalised their relationships with family. Back in Victoria, Melbourne became their home and Ballarat was a place to be visited. They were welcomed warmly, Walter, on his trip alone, staying mainly with the Hudsons and Mary with the Cuthberts, but they had to be careful not to offend their other friends. When Mary went to Ballarat at the end of September 1869, Walter was delayed in joining her because of the severe illness of their servant. Mary wrote to him:

> I am going back to M[rs] Wanlis's to night as she is giving a party on purpose for me but if you only stay such a short time we shall have to go to the Cuthberts on Saturday & the Saddler's on Monday as I have put off going there until you come for I thought you would enjoy that best.[2]

When Mary first arrived in Victoria she became the governess (and nursemaid) for the Bradshaws' young children: Caroline (aged seven), George Frederick (about four), and Emma (two). Her close friendship with the Bradshaw family did not survive long, however. Owned by William and Marian Bradshaw, the Family Hotel on the Batesford Road, Bell Post Hill, Geelong, was situated eight kilometres north-west of Geelong town centre on the main road to Ballarat (the Midland Highway). The family, fictionalised as the Beamish family in *The Fortunes of Richard Mahony*, emigrated from Cambridgeshire, England, to Adelaide with five children in about 1840, where six more children were born (one of whom died). The gold rush in 1851 enticed them to Victoria and the eldest sons became miners, while the parents ran the hotel, conveniently situated for weary travellers to and from the goldfields. The elder daughters, Tilly and Polly,[3] became confidantes of Mary. Polly, though only fourteen, was engaged to Walter's friend, Alexander Brooke Smith. The three girls shared friendships with Emma and Ellen Jelfs, the daughters of a sea captain,[4] and Anna Maria Grundy, the daughter of an architect.[5] The friendship between Mary, Emma, Ellen and Anna survived their marriages and outlasted that of Mary's with the Bradshaws.

---

[2]   Letter 154, 7 October 1869.
[3]   Harriet Matilda Bradshaw (Tilly) (1838–1914) and Marian Buller Bradshaw (Polly) (b. 1842). Their fictional counterparts are Tilly Beamish and Jinny Beamish in *FRM*.
[4]   Thomas Jelfs (1818–1881), from July 1853 to October 1855 the master of the schooner *Bristol* (150 tons), which delivered cargo around the south coast of Australia and across to VDL, particularly between Melbourne, Adelaide, Geelong, Port Albert and Sealers Cove.
[5]   William Grundy and his wife, Anna, lived at Fenwick Street in Geelong.

Six months after the Richardsons married, Mary left Walter in Ballarat to stay for a couple of weeks with the Bradshaws at Bell Post Hill. Tilly's marriage was the reason for the visit and, after ten days of preparation and parties, the wedding finally took place. She married Henry Fisher Bannester, a gold digger from Ballarat, on Wednesday 13 February 1856. Meantime Walter had organised with the bridegroom that he and his new bride would bring Mary home. Mrs Bradshaw, whom Mary affectionately called 'Mother', had other ideas:

> Next <u>Thursday</u> I & Mother are coming up in the four wheel Carriage so you may look out for us love about Tea time for we shall start very early & get through in a day—please dear to tell Ellen to have every thing tidy & comfortable for us but I need not say that for I know darling you will see to that We may be up on Wednesday but cannot say for certain but we shall be sure to be there on Thursday the reason of my not coming sooner is because Mother couldn't leave sooner & she thought I should come up much more comfortable than if I came with anyone else[6]

Mary had resumed her familial relationship with the Bradshaws and 'Mother' evidently enjoyed the company of her 'adopted daughter'. The following year (July 1857) Mary suffered a late miscarriage but there are no letters between Mary and Walter to help trace exactly what happened. It would seem likely that Mrs Bradshaw would have gone to Ballarat to help nurse her and that visit may have been the start of the rupture between her and Walter. From all accounts she was a forthright and domineering woman and one cannot imagine Walter tolerating any interference.

The Bradshaws' eldest son, William Burroughs Bradshaw, was married with three children when, in July 1855, he was made a Justice of the Peace in Ballarat. On first acquaintance Walter liked him and he wrote: 'Tell Mr Bradshaw that Mr W. Bradshaw junior is now <u>a magistrate</u> and a <u>considerable man</u> I saw him on the hustings at the late election here.'[7] However by August 1858 the relationship between the Bradshaws and the Richardsons had deteriorated dramatically. That month William Bradshaw junior and his wife, Rebecca, and five children (including a baby) imposed themselves unexpectedly on the Richardsons' hospitality, and Walter and Mary were obliged to give up their bed for the night. Knowing that Mrs Marian Bradshaw had been making unpleasant comments about them to mutual friends, Walter was not pleased about this intrusion. When the family came back a few days later, requesting another night's accommodation, Walter wrote to Mary:

> I was sitting quietly reading last night about half past seven when I heard a gentle knock at the front door, as Anne [the Richardsons' servant] was laying tea, Ned [Mary's brother] not having come home, I went myself and judge of my <u>surprise</u> to see W. Bradshaw & wife & horror to see the children: I was too <u>irritated</u> by what you said of the slanders of Mrs B. senior and too much in fear of a repetition of squally poor baby <u>all night</u> to submit to the infliction and altho W.B. said they had come to trespass on our hospitality I told them as quietly as I could that I had no accommodation & that you were from home, they went away I have no doubt highly indignant but I owe nothing to them & it is time they were taught manners! A piece of the purest effrontery! and it all arises my dear wife from you turning me out of bed on Sunday night: they thought if we

---

6   Letter 22, 15 February 1856.
7   Letter 13, 17 July 1855.

were silly enough to do that once I would be ass enough to do without any bed for a night.[8]

It wasn't only the Richardsons who had fallen out with the Bradshaws. Mary reported to Walter that Mrs Ellen Darling (née Jelfs) 'has taken her farewell of the Bradshaw's they behaved so badly the last time she was there'.[9] In April 1859 Walter, recovering from a very serious bout of dysentery, passed by the Bradshaw's Family Hotel and saw that it had been sold. He heard in Geelong that the Bradshaw parents were going to live with Polly and her first husband, Henry Allday Alexander, who had been married four months previously on 14 December 1858. (This poor son-in-law, Henry Alexander, died fifteen months later in July 1860.) Walter's cryptic comment to Mary about the failure of the Bradshaws' hotel was: 'very sad is it not, but a punishment for defrauding their governess of her just due!'[10]

Alexander Brooke Smith[11] emigrated to Australia soon after Walter, arriving in Melbourne in October 1852 on board the *Wanata*. He was the son of Caroline and Dr Thomas Heckstall Smith, for whom Walter had worked as an assistant in St Mary Cray, Kent, prior to emigrating. From their letters it is clear that Walter and Mary kept in touch with him throughout Walter's life but whether Mary continued the friendship after her husband's death is not known. Fictionalised as the central character 'Purdy Smith' in *The Fortunes of Richard Mahony*, HHR gave him an Irish background rather than English, and made him a schoolboy friend rather than a friend from Walter's twenties. Despite the changes, there appears to be more than a little of the *real* Brooke Smith in 'Purdy', judging by his behaviour recorded in Annie Baxter Dawbin's *Journals*. She provides a vivid description of Brooke Smith—'that funny little Esquimaux-looking Police Officer'.[12] After a short stint as a miner on the goldfields, Brooke Smith joined the Victorian Police Force. Appointed as a police cadet on 5 November 1852, he worked for the police force in Victoria for the next thirty years. Brooke Smith became engaged to Polly Bradshaw in 1854, but unlike Purdy Smith, he never married. According to Mrs Dawbin, he fancied himself as a ladies' man. She met him when she was living near Portland, where he was based for a time. On 8 April 1859, she danced with him at the home of Mrs Learmonth near Portland and he made her laugh with his mimicry.[13] This certainly reminds one of Purdy Smith's ability to make Polly Mahony laugh, much to the annoyance of her husband: '"It was very stupid of us, I know. But Purdy didn't really mean it unkindly; and he *is* so comical when he starts to imitate people." And Polly was all but off again, at the remembrance.'[14]

In April 1859 Brooke Smith sailed on the *Emu* with a warrant for the arrest of Thomas Chisholm, who had shocked Portland society by his forgery and who had escaped to Europe in the February mail-ship, with £1170 of ill-gotten gains. He arrested Chisholm in County Armagh, Ireland and brought him back to Portland to face charges of forgery and embezzlement. In April 1860, after his return with prisoner Chisholm, Mrs Dawbin complained in her *Journal* that he always wanted to talk about his love-life. She reduced him

[8]   Letter 31, 14 August 1858.
[9]   Letter 38, 28 August 1858.
[10] Letter 42, 21 April 1859.
[11] Alexander Brooke Smith (1834–1882).
[12] *Dawbin*, p. 75.
[13] *Dawbin*, p. 71.
[14] *FRM I*, p. 238

to tears when she told him that everyone thought he was conceited and a 'shocking Flirt'. She considered him self-obsessed: 'I was mightily tired of the Youth & his consummate conceit'.[15] One could almost imagine it was Alexander Brooke Smith's conversation with Walter when Purdy Smith said to Richard Mahony:

> 'Why the woman isn't born I can't get on with. All's fish that comes in my net.—Oh, to be young, Dick, and to love the girls! To see their little waists, and their shoulders, and the dimples in their cheeks! See 'em put up their hands to their bonnets, and how their little feet peep out when the wind blows their petticoats against their legs!'[16]

In 1861 Brooke Smith became a Sub-Inspector at Wangaratta and in February 1863 he was stationed at Chiltern for about a year before leaving for Wood's Point. Between 1870 and 1880 he was posted mainly in the north-east of Victoria and variously described as an 'Inspector at Wangaratta and Beechworth' and 'Officer in Charge of the Ovens District'. It was through Brooke Smith that Walter found the medical practice at Chiltern, and it was there that the friendship began to crumble. In February 1877 Walter was less than complimentary about his old friend in a letter to Mary, describing Brooke Smith's language as 'something dreadful' and reporting that he was 'nearly quite bald & lame still & denounces the world & things in general as usual'.[17] HHR embellished her father's description for Purdy: 'This common, shoddy little man, already pot-bellied and bald; whose language was that of the tap-room and the stable; who sat there bragging of the shady knowledge he had harvested in dark corners, blowing to impress the women; one of life's failures and aware of it, and, just for that this reason, cocksure, bitter, intolerant—a self-lover to the *n*th degree!'[18] There is no evidence that Purdy Smith's fictional fall from grace, when he makes improper advances to Mary Mahony, reflected a real episode in the Richardsons' life.[19] There was a falling-out over a loan in March 1877 when Walter described his great annoyance 'in consequence of the rascality of that unprincipled fellow BS'.[20]

Brooke Smith was severely censored by the Royal Commission on the Police Force of Victoria, 1881, for bungling a chance to catch the Ned Kelly outlaw gang in November 1878. Apparently, on the morning of the 4 or 5 November, four men were seen galloping through Wangaratta and, although there was no positive proof they were the Kelly gang, information was sent immediately to Brooke Smith, who 'was so dilatory in starting and so bungled the whole business that the pursuit, as he conducted it, was hopeless'.[21] Dying in Melbourne on 20 March 1882, Brooke Smith left about £5000 in equal shares to his brothers and sisters.[22]

Another police inspector with whom the Richardsons became close friends was Captain Leopold Kabat.[23] Kabat was born in Galicia (Poland), the son of a landowner, Alexander

---

[15]   *Dawbin*, pp. 161–162.
[16]   *FRM I*, p. 36.
[17]   Letter 206, 24 February 1877.
[18]   *FRM II*, p. 104.
[19]   *FRM I*, pp. 338–342.
[20]   Letter 209, 11 March 1877.
[21]   Sadleir, p. 99.
[22]   Dr Heckstall Smith of Primrose Hill, London, Surgeon; Frederick James Smith in India, Colonel in the Royal Engineers; Horace Malden Smith of Orpington in Kent (stockbroker); Caroline Smith of Orpington (spinster); Emily Malden Alfrey, wife of Dr Henry Alfrey of St Mary Cray, Kent, a surgeon.
[23]   Captain Leopold Kabat (1832–1884).

Kabat, and his wife, Antoinette, née Wagner. When the revolt against Austria broke out in Hungary in 1848, Kabat, with his friend Ladislaus Sylvester Kossak,[24] joined a regiment of lancers in the Polish Legion in support of the uprising. Following the Russian Army's support of the Austrians, the Hungarians were defeated in 1849 and the remnants of the Polish Legion, including Kabat and Kossak, crossed over into Turkey where they were interned. In 1851 Kabat and Kossak were released and made their way to Southampton. They sailed for Melbourne in the steamer *Chusan*, arriving in May 1852. After prospecting for gold without success, they joined the Victoria Police Force as cadets in October 1852. In August 1853 they became naturalised, the first Poles to become British subjects in Victoria.

It was through Alexander Brooke Smith that Walter came to know Kabat, but the deep friendship between Richardsons and Kabats developed through the two wives. Emily Bradley Kabat[25] was the daughter of the squatter John Murchison of Kerrisdale Station, King Parrot Creek. She married Leopold on 5 July 1860 at her parents' home. He was at that time an Inspector of Police. Two of his closest friends and colleagues were the witnesses at the wedding: Alexander Brooke Smith and Charles Hope Nicholson,[26] the latter to become one of the most influential Superintendents of Police in Victoria. Eleven months after their marriage, Leopold and Emily's daughter, Antoinette Emily Favorit known as Dilly,[27] was born on 13 June 1861.

In April 1864 Mary accompanied Emily and Dilly on a trip to visit the Murchisons and stopped off on the way at Kilmore to visit Emily's sister and brother-in-law, Martha and Farquhar MacKenzie.[28] Another sister, Flora Murchison,[29] was a regular visitor to Ballarat and, before she finally married Cuthbert Fetherstonhaugh in 1874, she enjoyed romances with the gentlemen in Richardsons' and Kabats' circle.[30] It is a great pity that Mary's letters from Kerrisdale, near Broadford, have not survived. Only the letter written at Kilmore remains in the collection. How Mary would have enjoyed meeting the Murchison parents at Kerrisdale! Emily's father, John Murchison was the cousin of Robert Impey Murchison (1792–1871), the first geologist to be created a baronet. John was the son of Kenneth Murchison, an officer in the British Army, and Martha (née Urquhart). Both cousins served in the British Army but while Robert returned from the Napoleonic War in 1814 and began his study of geology, John, who was commissioned in the Royal Scots Regiment in 1813, remained in the Army and joined the Scots Fusiliers in 1818. In 1825, while stationed in Nova Scotia, John Murchison had married Mary Ann née Roberts.[31] After serving as quartermaster of the 96th Regiment from 1828 to 1832, he and his family emigrated to New South Wales in 1833, where they lived for eleven years. In 1844 he became a pioneer overlander to Victoria with

24   Ladislaus Sylvester Kossak (1828–1918); see Letter 92.
25   Emily Bradley Kabat née Murchison (1840–1933), daughter of John Murchison (1797–1882) and his wife, Mary Ann née Roberts (1806–1872).
26   Charles Hope Nicholson (c.1830–1898).
27   Antoinette Emily Favorit Kabat (1861–1940).
28   Martha MacKenzie née Murchison (b. 1828), sister of Mrs Kabat, married to Farquhar MacKenzie (1811–1874), the grandson of Sir Alexander Mackenzie of Gairloch, 3rd Bart. For more details of the MacKenzie and Murchison family see the endnotes to Letter 92.
29   Flora Agnes Murchison (1844–1931), youngest daughter of John Murchison. In 1876 Flora married Cuthbert Fetherstonhaugh (1837–1925), pastoralist, clergyman and journalist.
30   'I do not see the use of giving Flora's love if she accepts Mr Pooleys [Deputy Registrar at Ballarat] lock of hair!!' WLR to MR, Letter 94, 22 April 1864.
31   Mary Ann née Roberts (1806–1872).

Farquhar MacKenzie and took up a pastoral run, Kerrisdale, adjacent to the King Parrot Creek, where the family settled.

Through the Kabats, the Richardsons' circle of friends widened and in March the following year Mary went to Melbourne, ostensibly to visit her relatives: but she was also there to farewell three members of the Murchison family. For Flora and her parents, Captain John and Mary Ann Murchison, were sailing to Liverpool on the *Great Britain* for a short visit to England. The Murchisons returned from England at the end of the year, arriving on board the *Royal Standard* in December 1865.

With two close friends involved with the police force in Victoria, the Richardsons could have been well informed about criminal activities, including those of the bushrangers, who plagued the lives of the police. Harry Power[32] had the audacity to bail up their friend Farquhar MacKenzie on 25 February 1870 at 7 p.m. on the Yea road close to King Parrot Creek. Power stole his horse, saddle and bridle. And when Power was finally arrested in the King's River Ranges, near Beechworth, it was Inspector Leopold Kabat who had the pleasure of telegraphing the announcement of his capture to the press. Interestingly, Power, reputed to have been Ned Kelly's tutor in the bushranging business, unwittingly caused Farquhar MacKenzie to become actively involved as a police scout against the Kelly gang. MacKenzie was the Inspector of Sheep, whose job was to administer the Pastoral Scab Act—first for the district known as Benalla and then for Kilmore district and finally, in 1868, for the Echuca area. '[He] had a professional standing in the district that brought him into contact will all classes of people; the talk and family gossip of the place came to him without seeking; he moved about without suspicion even amongst persons who favoured the Kellys.'[33]

In nineteenth-century Victoria 'a policeman's lot was not a happy one': the force was under enormous pressure to bring law and order to unruly bush criminals, larrikin miners and the occasional troublesome squatters. Nor was the police force without its own internal problems. The Inspector of Police at Ballarat, Frederick Winch, and his wife Agnes[34] (also friends of the Richardsons) had as the chief witness at their marriage Captain Frederick Charles Standish,[35] Police Commissioner. Standish was forced to suspend Winch from the police force in 1882 over a scandal. Leopold Kabat, at the age of fifty-two, committed suicide by cutting his throat on 27 September 1884, having arrived only six days earlier in Jerilderie (in NSW) as Superintendent of Police.

Leopold Kabat had been a member of the Yorick Club (formed in 1868), which Alexander Brooke Smith and Walter also joined. Among the other members were friends from the early days in the colony such as John Whiteman,[36] the veterinary surgeon, who became a parliamentarian, and Charles Hope Nicholson, Police Superintendent. There were solicitors and barristers, including John Robert Atkins (John Robinson Bailey's third wife's father), Judge Charles Prendergast Hackett, and Howard Massey Bindon (c.1844–1893) who defended Ned Kelly. Some were politicians, like William Arthur Callander à Beckett

---

[32] Harry Power, alias Henry Johnstone (or Johnson) (1819–1891).
[33] Sadleir, pp. 217–218.
[34] Agnes Winch née Pitman (b. 1829) was married on 15 May 1856 to Frederick Alfred Winch (1827–1892).
[35] Captain Frederick Charles Standish (1824–1883), Police Commissioner, who is described as one of the most aristocratic of the 1850s immigrants.
[36] Only the dates of the members who are not mentioned in the letters or endnotes are given in brackets.

(1833–1901) and his brother Edward à Beckett (1836–1921), Registrar of the University of Melbourne, both sons of Victoria's first Chief Justice, Sir William à Beckett.

Many of Walter's colleagues and friends from the medical associations joined the club, including Joseph Black, John Blair, John Day, William Henry Embling, James Edward Neild and Richard Tracy.[37] Walter would have enjoyed the company of men like Dr John Ignatius Bleasdale, a Catholic priest whose public appointments included membership of the boards of the Melbourne Public Library, Museum and National Gallery, Denominational Schools Board, and the Central Board of Health. Walter met up with him again in Queenscliff in August of 1877 and spent many evenings hearing the gossip about old Melbourne society.[38] The landscape gardener and Director of the Royal Botanical Gardens, William Robert Guilfoyle, was a member, as was Charles Bright, a journalist and lecturer on spiritualism and a member of the Victorian Association of Progressive Spiritualists, of which Walter was President. There were many journalists and newspaper proprietors, including Edward Bateman (1832–1893), editor of *The Ballarat Courier*, Thomas Drummond Wanliss, the editor of *The Ballarat Star* and a close friend of Walter and Mary, and William Bramwell Withers (1823–1913), the journalist and Ballarat historian.

The poet and civil servant George Gordon McCrae (1833–1927) was a member, as were many musicians, actors and theatrical agents, including: George Benjamin Allen (1822–1897), conductor of Lyster's Opera Company; David Lee (1837–1897), organist and conductor of the Melbourne Philharmonic Society; George Selth Coppin, comic actor and entrepreneur; Harold Kyrle Bellew, whose father gave a lecture in Liverpool in November 1868 which Walter attended.[39] John Hennings, the scenic artist, joined, and many other actors from William Lyster's productions.

One actor with whom both Mary and Walter became intimate friends in Ballarat was Miss Julia Harland.[40] She was the wife of William Hoskins,[41] who managed the Theatre Royal in Ballarat from 1860 to 1863. In June 1860 Mary stayed with her brother, John Robinson Bailey, at St Kilda and attended the Governor's Ball. While Mary was absent from Ballarat, Julia helped to entertain the three-year-old Trotty[42] by taking her out every day. An opera singer and actress, she was the daughter of one of the most famous American actors, Henry John Wallack. Marrying in Kent, England, in 1842 (when she was only seventeen), Julia and William Hoskins arrived in Australia in 1856. After three years in Ballarat, he became Manager of the Theatre Royal, Melbourne, and then the Haymarket Theatre, Melbourne in

---

[37]   Short biographies of Dr Richard Tracy and Dr Thomas Embling, the father of Dr William Henry Embling, appear in endnotes to Letters 79 and 105, respectively.

[38]   See Letters 216 onwards.

[39]   John Chippendall Montesquieu Bellew (1823–1874) born at Lancaster; from 1848 to 1868 was an Anglican clergyman in England and Calcutta, for twelve years a most popular London preacher; then turning Catholic, devoted himself to public readings. Walter attended one of his lectures in Liverpool *en route* to Dublin in November 1868. (See Letter 140, 2 December 1868.)

[40]   Julia Harland, stage name of Julia Hoskins née Wallack (1825–1872), born in Washington, DC, daughter of Herny John Wallack and Fanny née Jones.

[41]   William Hoskins (1816–1886), an actor who was born in Derbyshire, studied Law at Cambridge and then began acting in provincial companies in 1839. He was a pupil of Samuel Phelps at Saddler's Wells Theatre, London. After Julia's death in 1872, William married actress Florence Colville and they moved to New Zealand in 1875. She died in 1881 and he returned to Melbourne and married Maude Bowman in 1882. He retired from the stage in 1884 and died in Melbourne in 1886.

[42]   Emma Bailey (1856–1935), born 13 September 1856 in Geelong; eldest daughter of John Robinson Bailey and his first wife, Susannah Tyler Nicholson.

the late 1860s. During 1864 Julia placed an advertisement in the *Star*: 'Mrs William Hoskins (pupil of Manuel Garcia and Signor Schira) gives instruction in the Art of singing and the Piano. Apply Errard St, Sturt St'. She remained in Ballarat for a time and then moved to Hanover Street, Fitzroy, where she died aged forty-seven, on 19 August 1872. The cause of death was 'fatty degeneration of the liver' and it may have been through her health problems that she had first met the Richardsons in 1860. The Bishop of Melbourne, Charles S. Perry, conducted her funeral and she was buried in Melbourne Cemetery.

The Cuthberts and Richardsons were friends from the early days at Ballarat and remained so until Mary left Victoria with her daughters. How they met is not known, but Henry Cuthbert and Walter were both members of the Victorian Lodge of Freemasons. The names of Henry Cuthbert and Richard Ocock, another lawyer and member of the lodge, were combined to create Henry Ocock in *The Fortunes of Richard Mahony*. Born on 29 July 1829 at Boyle, County Roscommon, Henry was the second child and eldest son of John Cuthbert, a landowner and excise officer at Parsonstown, Ireland, and his wife Elizabeth, née Headen. The Cuthbert parents had married on 13 May 1826, and had nine children, three of whom died in infancy (Frances born 1831; James, born 1834 and John, born 1837). Elizabeth Cuthbert died in 1842 when Henry was only thirteen and still at the Drogheda Grammar School. In his final year at school he won the Classics Medal, and went on to study law. He was admitted to the King's Inns in 1848. In 1852 he took his articles, and, after a year's practice in Kilkenny, he was admitted solicitor in the High Court of Chancery of Ireland. In May 1854 he sailed for Melbourne in the *Bloomer* with his younger brother, Kingston.

They were not the first of the Cuthbert family to sail to Australia. In 1849 their cousin Charles Cuthbert, eldest son of Lieutenant Kingston Gore Cuthbert (John Cuthbert's brother), had sailed to Melbourne in 1849, probably for his health, for he died of consumption on 14 December 1858, aged thirty-six. Lieutenant Cuthbert's widow, Mary Cuthbert née Cochrane, followed Charles and sailed to Melbourne with seven children on the *Medway*, arriving in January 1852. Kingston, the second eldest son, was left by his mother and siblings in Ireland, presumably to finish his education. He arrived in Melbourne eighteen months later. Accompanying Mary Cuthbert were Selina (Graham), Maria Amelia (Fullerton), Harriett Georgiana (Hastedt), Henry, Eliza Frances (Yabbicom), Emily (Harding) and Agnes Jane (Stedman), many of whom Mary became acquainted with during her stay in St Kilda and subsequently in Ballarat.[43]

Three months after Henry Cuthbert's arrival, he was admitted solicitor in the Supreme Court of Victoria and soon after he moved to Ballarat to open his practice. Sadly, his younger brother, Kingston, died in 1856 before his father and other siblings joined them. Henry began to build up his network and increase his wealth, at the same time contributing to the development of Ballarat. In his first legal case he established the individual's right to legal representation in the local Miners' Court. He was joint proprietor of *The Ballarat Times* in 1856, and stood as surety for the paper's registration in 1857. The same year, he formed the Ballarat Gas Company and leased forty acres on land held by the Learmonth brothers in Buninyong. (Such leases were not made secure until 1884 when, on Cuthbert's initiative, the Mining on Private Property Act was passed.) He formed the Buninyong Gold Mining Company, which struck gold at Scotchman's lead, and later he was able to buy the Learmonth's 1100 acres for £20,000. He laid the first stone of the Mechanics' Institute was

---

43   See endnotes to Letter 48 for more details on the Cuthbert cousins.

laid, with Masonic honours, on 28 September 1860. He was on the first committee in 1865 of the Ballarat District Orphan Asylum. While the foundation stone of the first portion of the Ballarat Hospital was laid by James Daly, Police Magistrate and Warden, in 1855, the foundation stone of the remainder of the south wing was laid on New Year's Day 1866, by Cuthbert, again with Masonic honours. With his commercial, church and musical interests, he was a director of Permewan Wright & Company, Chancellor of the Diocese of Ballarat, and in 1881 first president of the Liedertafel, the German choral society.

In October 1857 his father John, his older sister Anna Maria, and his brothers Thomas Headen, John and Robert Browne, arrived in Melbourne on board the *Albion*. Anna Maria Cuthbert[44] and Mary Richardson became great friends. They worked together for the church bazaars and they spent a month's holiday in 1860 at St Kilda. Eight years older than Mary, Anna Maria did not marry until she was thirty-seven and her husband, William Nixon, was a stockbroker and close business associate of her brother and friend of Walter.

Henry remained a bachelor until 28 May 1863 when he married the beautiful widow, Emma Wilmer Hepburn, née Kirby. For a wedding present the Richardsons gave them a pair of large, ornate candlesticks, in the form of 'Nubian slaves', still in the possession of the Cuthbert descendants. Emma's first husband was Thomas John Hepburn, son of Captain John Stuart Hepburn,[45] a pioneer overlander and squatter. Hepburn, Joseph Hawdon and John Gardiner crossed overland in 1836 into Port Phillip, driving their cattle until in December 1836 they reached the slopes to the east of Melbourne. Hawdon and Hepburn sold out to Gardiner, who remained in Melbourne, while Hawdon returned to the east coast of NSW and Hepburn returned to Sydney. In 1838, Hepburn set out again from Sydney with his wife and children (including Thomas John, aged two) travelling in a cart and with a flock of 1650 sheep. This time the Hepburns were joined by David Coghill (from whom Hepburn had borrowed money) and William Bowman, who had 2000 and 5000 sheep, respectively. On reaching Mt Alexander, Bowman decided to settle. After three months further travelling, the Hepburns settled at Smeaton Hill, near Creswick, on 15 April 1838. Ten days later, the Coghills settled on two stations, Glendaurel and Glendonald. It took Hepburn ten years to repay Coghill's loan of £2750 and to build a substantial homestead. Hepburn engaged one of the best architects, John Gill from Melbourne, to build him one of the loveliest country

---

44 Anna Maria Cuthbert (1827–1916) married William Nixon (1833–1905) in 1864. They had one son and three daughters, all born in Ballarat: Elizabeth Anna Nixon (1866–1905), William (1867–1901), Helen Lillian (1869–1935) and Emma Florence (1871–1950). Anna Maria died in Ballarat in 1916, aged eighty-nine. Her fictional counterpart is Amelia Ocock, who also married (after her prime) a younger man, who worked for her brother, Henry Ocock.

45 Captain John Stuart Hepburn (1803–1859), born in East Lothian, eldest son of Captain Thomas Hepburn of the Royal Navy, and his first wife Alison Stewart. He was a close relative of the first baronet (created in 1815), Sir George Buchan Hepburn, of Smeaton-Hepburn, East Lothian, Scotland. Hepburn served in the merchant navy. He married Elizabeth née Coombes (d. 1869) and they had ten children born in England, NSW and Victoria. The family emigrated to NSW before finally settling in Victoria. The ten children were: Alice Elizabeth (1831–1865) m. Charles James Murray in 1860; John Stuart (1833–1834); Thomas John (1836–1859) m. Emma Wilmer Kirby (who secondly married Henry Cuthbert in 1863); George Stuart (1838–1903) m. Harriet Frances Wheatley in 1865; Elizabeth (b. 1840) m. Benjamin Butterworth in 1859; Henry (1842–1874); Helen, twin of Mary (b. 1845) m. Arthur Walsh; Mary, twin of Helen (1845–1909) m. Adolphus William Devlin in 1868; Jane (1847–1928) m. Captain Robert Maillard of the 16th Regiment; Annie (b. 1849) m. Charles James Kenworthy (c.1838–1891) in 1869.

houses, 'Smeaton Park'.[46] It was at 'Smeaton Park' that Emma first lived as a bride in 1857. There her first baby died, aged six months, in 1858, and the following year her second son, Thomas John Hepburn, was born in April 1859. Her happiness was short-lived, for two months later her husband died, aged twenty-three, on 21 July 1859. Whether the Richardsons ever visited 'Smeaton Park' is not known but there is a possible family link to the Hepburns. The present owners of the house, the Righetti family, retain John Hepburn's original estate diary, and it includes an intriguing entry on 16 June 1849: 'Reverend Mr Chyne baptised Jane and Annie, also the grocer's child.' This probably refers to the Reverend John Cheyne, Walter's step-cousin, who came to Victoria sometime in early 1849.

At some stage Emma met Henry Cuthbert, who fell very much in love with her. They married in 1863 and she gave birth to John Headen Cuthbert on 11 April 1864, with Walter as the accoucheur.[47] Henry bought twenty-eight acres of land in Ballarat West, near to Lake Wendouree, and there he built a beautiful home, 'Beaufort House', now a student residence. On 16 December 1865 the Cuthbert's second son, Henry Herbert, was born, with Walter again as the accoucheur. Four months later, on 27 April 1866, the baby died. The death certificate confirms that Walter certified the cause of death as 'muco enteritis', that the baby had been ill for ten weeks, and that Walter had attended him on 24 April, three days before his death. How strange that Walter in his letter to Mary on 6 April said that Mrs Cuthbert had called but made no mention of the baby's state of health. It is impossible to know the truth about the baby's death, or whether Emma was as unhappy in her second marriage as the fictional Agnes Ocock. There are Cuthbert family members who believe that she stumbled and dropped the baby on his head because of drink and, whether HHR's account in *FRM* is based on fact or fiction, it has become one of the family's stories. Two years later, on 18 May 1868, Emma and Henry's daughter, Annie Wilmer Cuthbert, was born. Doted on by her father, Annie became a childhood friend of HHR and Lil when they stayed at Queenscliff for part of their summer holidays.

Cuthbert was involved in and won some celebrated legal cases in Victoria, including the Learmonth–Bailey dispute over the Egerton Mine in 1874–1877. His popularity in Ballarat was such that he was petitioned to stand for election to the Legislative Council for the South-Western Province and was returned unopposed in 1874. Mary, HHR and Lil stayed with Emma and Annie Cuthbert at Queenscliff in February 1877, when Walter wrote to Mary:

> I hope this will find you in Queenscliffe & that my last will have comforted you & that you will have a better week with dear Mrs C. Give her my kind love & say I hope her health keeps good—How happy she & Mrs Graham ought to be with no cares on their minds for the future.[48]

Cuthbert was appointed Postmaster General on 3 July 1877 in the Berry administration. Less than one month later, Emma died (1 August 1877). The cause and duration of illness are

---

[46]   'Smeaton Park', completed in 1849, is on the National Trust List A. Comprising eighteen rooms, with basement, ground floor and upper floor all of the same area, the house has a Georgian simplicity considered rare in a large country house in Victoria. See Michael Cantlon, *Homesteads of Victoria: 1836–1900* (Adelaide: The Griffin Press, 1967).

[47]   *Case* 623, 'Mrs H. Cuthbert Solicitors wife, third pregnancy … face towards left thigh.'

[48]   Letter 206, 24 February 1877.

stated on her death certificate as 'Hepatitis—some months; Pulmonary congestion—a fortnight':

> Our obituary notice this morning announces the death of Mrs Cuthbert, wife of the hon. the Postmaster-General, which sad event took place yesterday morning, shortly after one o'clock. The deceased lady had for some time been suffering from disease of the liver, and although favorable symptoms were apparent at intervals, her death was not unexpected. The City Hall and Town Hall flags were yesterday flying at half-mast by way of respect for the deceased, the bereaved hon. gentleman being solicitor to the two corporations. The ensign at Craig's hotel was also lowered half-mast. We understand the funeral will be as private as possible.[49]

The following year, old Mr John Cuthbert died and Walter began his steep decline, culminating in his removal to Cremorne Asylum. Cuthbert used his influence to get Mary a position of postmistress at Koroit. An admired and respected politician, his popularity was enhanced by his stand on 'Black Wednesday', 8 January 1878, when the Legislative Council, dissatisfied with amendments relating to payment of MPs, refused to pass the Appropriations Bill and Premier Berry ordered the dismissal of over two hundred civil servants. Cuthbert refused to dismiss any postal employees. Meantime he secured Mary's position and her daughters' future.[50] He finally resigned office as Postmaster General on 29 July 1878 over the question of council reform. On 11 February 1879 Thomas John Hepburn, Emma's second child by her first husband, died aged nineteen, of 'fatty heart'. And that same year Walter died, on the second anniversary of Emma's death.

Cuthbert continued his distinguished career in public service and managed at the same time to amass a fortune. He held posts of Postmaster General and Commissioner for Trade (1880) and Minister of Justice (1886–1890). His two surviving children were married in 1890. Annie Wilmer married Captain John Wilberforce Stanley-Low on 1 October 1890, and two months later John Headen Cuthbert married Mabel Julia Costin (10 December). Two grandchildren were born in Ballarat the following year: Henry Headen Cuthbert (John and Mabel's baby) was born on 11 November 1891, and fifteen days later, Cuthbert John Stanley-Low was born on 26 November. Meantime Cuthbert and Nicholas Fitzgerald were selected as delegates to the Federal Convention in Sydney in 1891. Henry Cuthbert became Solicitor-General and leader of the council in 1894 until 1899. He was honoured by a knighthood conferred in 1897. Annie Wilmer Stanley-Low died aged only thirty-two on 22 February 1901, followed less than a year later by her husband, who died in Ballarat on 5 February 1902, aged thirty-seven. Their son, Cuthbert John, was left an orphan aged ten. Five years later Henry Cuthbert died aged seventy-seven, on 5 April 1907. A remarkable man, ambitious and clever, he was one of the founding fathers of Ballarat, a staunch Victorian and Australian. He was also someone who did not forget his friends nor past favours.

Members of the Green family, who became friends with the Richardsons during the time spent at Chiltern (1876–1877), were immortalised unflatteringly as the Sheppards in *The Getting of Wisdom* (1910). The Greens and the *real* Sheppards were related and there was an earlier connection with Walter and the Sheppard family revealed by Elizabeth Summons in an

[49]   *The Ballarat Courier*, 2 August 1877, p. 2.
[50]   MR was also helped considerably by the Dod family. See endnote to Letter 44.

article, both fascinating for its gossip and misleading in some of its facts.[51] Summons explains that her great-grandfather, Thomas Sheppard, emigrated with his wife and children from Wiltshire and settled in Buninyong in 1843. It was Sheppard's daughter, Harriet Amy, who became the second wife of the Reverend Samuel Dutton Green. With enough money to buy real estate, Thomas Sheppard soon became a leading figure in Buninyong society and established a profitable brewery. According to Summons, when Walter arrived in the colony nine years later he had a letter of introduction to the Sheppards from their Dublin cousin, Sherborne Sheppard. (It is more likely that the Sheppards knew Walter's stepfather and mother, as Dr Bayne Cheyne had a medical practice for many years in Bristol, Wiltshire, from where the Sheppards came.) No matter how they became reacquainted, Walter shocked the Sheppard family by living off the 'pickings of the goldfield' as a storekeeper and not following his profession. They thought he was 'a loafer and a sponger' and were also convinced that he had a drinking problem. Stanley Sheppard, the great-uncle of Elizabeth Summons, said of Richardson: 'He was a complete bounder—and worse'.[52] Perhaps Walter's behaviour in those early days at Ballarat was the cause of his medical condition twenty years later.

The Reverend Samuel Dutton Green[53] was appointed as the new vicar of St Paul's Church, Chiltern, in May 1876, one month before Walter arrived to take over Dr Rohner's practice. Not long after Walter's arrival, Samuel became seriously ill and was successfully nursed back to health by Walter. Six months later Samuel left Chiltern and, after marrying his second wife, Harriet Sheppard, took up a new post in Colac. Samuel Dutton Green was married for the first time in 1854 to his cousin Eliza Dutton, by whom he had five children: Agnes Maria,[54] Arthur Vincent,[55] two daughters who did not survive infancy (Edith Lizzie and Mabel Dutton), and Florence Emily.[56] Appointed to the Parish of Penwortham and Clare in the Diocese of Adelaide in 1861, the family stayed there a very short time before moving to Oamaru in New Zealand, where Florence Emily was born on 12 April 1862. In June 1872, his first wife Eliza died and Samuel took up an appointment in Kangaroo Ground, Victoria, leaving Florence in New Zealand. It was during this brief time in Victoria that Samuel Green met up with his cousin, Harriet Amy Sheppard. After a short stay in Victoria, Samuel and Arthur Green returned to England, where Arthur was settled in a college. (It is not clear whether the eldest daughter, Agnes Maria, ever left England.) Samuel decided to take up a position in Cape Town, South Africa, where he remained until Arthur joined him in 1875. Arthur matriculated from the College of St Andrew and St Edmund, Salisbury, and completed two years of a law degree at the University of Durham before joining his father in Cape Town. There he worked as a junior master at the Diocesan College, Rondebosch.

In 1876, father and son returned to Victoria, where they were joined by the fourteen-year-old Florence from New Zealand. As she had not completed her schooling, she went to live with Harriet Sheppard's brother, Stanley, and his wife, Mary, in South Yarra, where she attended Mrs Meurisse Haydon's Academy for Girls. After six months in Chiltern, Samuel departed to marry Harriet Sheppard. The wedding took place on 6 February 1877 at Trinity

51   Elizabeth Summons, 'Ethel and Florence and Arthur and Mattie', *Overland*, no. 72, 26, 1978, p. 26.
52   Summons, p. 25.
53   Samuel Dutton Green (1830–1879), born at Baldock, Hertfordshire, England, the son of Job Green and his wife, Martha née Dutton.
54   Agnes Maria Green (b. 1855), a religious of the Community of St Denys in Wiltshire.
55   Arthur Vincent Green (1857–1944), born 31 October 1857 at Albury, Surrey, England.
56   Florence Emily Green (1862–1926), born 12 April 1862 at Oamaru, New Zealand.

Church, East Melbourne. Settling in Colac, Harriet and Samuel had a son, Stanley Dutton, born in July 1878. A year later Samuel died (22 August 1879), aged forty-nine, from peritonitis, in Malvern Road, Prahran, and he was buried in St Kilda Cemetery. After her father's death, Florence continued to live with the Sheppards until after her brother's marriage.

Meantime Arthur continued his studies, matriculating at the University of Melbourne and graduating BA on 4 December 1879 and MA on 31 March 1883. He enrolled for a law degree by correspondence at the University of Sydney, graduating LLB in 1885. Armed with these qualifications he enrolled at the University of Melbourne, graduating LLD on 3 December 1887. The Richardsons still saw Arthur Green at Chiltern for some months after his father's departure, for he had obtained a stipendiary readership under Archdeacon Tucker, his future father-in-law, and took services from Benalla to Yarrawonga while living at Wangaratta and Chiltern. Walter made a few references to Arthur in the January to March 1877 sequence of letters to Mary, but one comment is particularly interesting:

> Arthur Green passed thro to Wodonga & dined & took tea with me on Saturday. He is much improved—[57]

Why Walter made this comment is not clear but it may be that there had been some problem and that Walter was seeking to rehabilitate him in Mary's eyes. When HHR wrote in *FRM III* about the escapade of 'Cousin Emmy' and the curate 'Mr Angus', it is possible that she was remembering a flirtation between her cousin, Emma Bailey, and Arthur Green. Some time later he became engaged to Matilda, daughter of J. K. Tucker, Archdeacon of Beechworth, and they married on 28 December 1880 at Avenel. Florence went to live with her brother and sister-in-law in about 1881 at their residence in East Melbourne. By then she had signed the University of Melbourne's matriculation register, but she did not complete a degree. Instead she gained a diploma from the Australian College of Theology with first class honours. She never married, but devoted her life to religion, her brother and the education of women.

Arthur, his wife Mattie, and his sister Florence were all involved in the early life of HHR. After his marriage, a year in Europe and a curacy at Brighton, Arthur was appointed curate at St Peter's, Eastern Hill Melbourne, the church attended by the girls from the Presbyterian Ladies College. Then in 1885 he was appointed vicar of Maldon where Mary was postmistress. Florence went too, and, encouraged by her brother, she helped to found the Trinity Church High School for Girls, becoming its headmistress. In 1887 Mattie gave birth to Walter Gerard Arthur in Maldon. Then the family moved to Geelong, where Florence founded the Girls' High School, and then to Ballarat, where Arthur was appointed Archdeacon. In 1894 Arthur was elected Bishop of Grafton and Armidale, NSW, the first Victorian-trained clergyman to become an Australian Bishop. Florence accompanied the family and in 1895 she became the first headmistress of the New England Girls' School. When in 1900 Arthur was elected the second Bishop of Ballarat, Florence remained in Armidale as headmistress until 1907 when, the diocese having purchased the school from her, she travelled overseas. Returning to Victoria in 1910, she acted as headmistress of Firbank Church of England Girls' Grammar School, Brighton, for a year until, her health failing, she ended her career. Arthur was a major force in the establishment of the Ballarat Church of England Grammar School for Boys, which opened

57   Letter 209, 11 March 1877.

in 1911. Forced by ill-health to slow down, he decided to resign, which he did in September 1915.

The Sheppard family was upset by HHR's characterisation of Arthur, Mattie and Florence in *The Getting of Wisdom* as the irritable Mr Robbie Sheppard, his downtrodden wife, Maisie, and his unpleasant sister, Miss Isabella. It was particularly hurtful because they believed that Florence, who had been left some money by her mother, had assisted in the boarding and tuition fees of HHR at the Presbyterian Ladies College. This may or may not be true for, as suggested in an earlier chapter, Cheyne family money may have been used for school fees. Notwithstanding the issue of financial help, Mary remained particularly close to Florence and wrote to her, as well as to Sydney Graham, her sister Sarah and brother Sam who were left in Australia, as she sailed along the coast of Australia in 1888 on the final trip to Europe. Telegram blanks belonging to Mary from her Maldon Post Office days[58] include Florence's name and address written on the inside cover in Mary's writing. Florence died of Parkinson's disease on 5 April 1926 at Murrumbeena. Arthur died on 24 September 1944, predeceased by his wife but survived by his son, the Reverend Walter G. A. Green, Vicar of St James's, East St Kilda, at the time of his father's death.

There were many other friends, who appear in the letters, but the most important friendship for the Richardsons in their later days was that of the Grahams. They met Dr George Graham[59] and his wife, Sydney,[60] probably through John Robinson Bailey, who lived near the Grahams in Richmond. As the Bailey's family doctor, George delivered their youngest son, Edgar Atkins Bailey,[61] and was present at John's death on 6 May 1871. For Walter, George was not only a colleague and a fellow lover of fine wines, but also someone with whom he could discuss his most fundamental beliefs. The friendship developed through their involvement with the Victorian Progressive Spiritualist Society. In Sydney Graham, Mary found a truly compatible friend, and a friendship which only death ended.

---

[58] NLA MS133/1/296.

[59] George Graham (1829–1893), MD (Melb.), MRCS (Eng.), medical practitioner and close friend of WLR; born in Cootehill, Cavan, Ireland. See next chapter for more biographical details.

[60] Sydney Graham née Boyd (1835–1923), born on 13 August 1835 in Ahamore, Fermanagh, Ireland; married George Graham, medical practitioner, in 1857 in Cavan, Ireland; died in Clontarf, Dublin, in 1923.

[61] Edgar Atkins Bailey, born 15 October 1870, died 11 December 1871, was the son of John Robinson Bailey and his third wife, Mary Ringrose Bailey (b. c.1843).

5

Illness and Death

Walter died from 'General Paralysis of the Insane', the tertiary stage of syphilis, which is a contagious venereal disease due to infection with the micro-organism *Spirochaeta pallida*. This organic disease of the brain may manifest itself up to forty years after a primary syphilitic infection. It has been suggested that he probably caught syphilis in his youth either in England, or perhaps on board the vessel travelling to Melbourne (on which were several of Lord and Lady Sydney Herbert's former female employees who were emigrating to Australia), or in his carefree days in Ballarat as a gold-digger.[1] The details of what happened in Queenscliff in 1878, when Walter finally became too ill to continue working, are not completely clear. HHR wrote:

> Too frail to carry out the duties of Health Officer, with which he had hoped to supplement his scanty income, my father shrank into himself, and grew more and more peculiar. Patients began to look elsewhere for a doctor. Finally, after a severe illness, he was declared mentally unsound and removed to Melbourne. We saw him again only for a few months at the end of his life—a gentle, broken creature, who might have been a stranger.[2]

It is most likely that their close friends, Dr George Graham and his wife, Sydney, would have gone down from their home in Richmond, Melbourne, to visit the Richardsons in Queenscliff during Walter's increasing incapacitation. The Grahams were very supportive friends and the previous August (1877), while Sydney stayed at Chiltern to help Mary with the move to Queenscliff, Walter had stayed with George at Richmond. Dr Graham would have known only too well what was ailing Walter, for when he first emigrated to Australia in 1858 he had been the medical officer of the Government Lunatic Asylum in Adelaide as well

---

[1]   Alan Stoller and R. H. Emmerson, 'Richard Mahony, Walter Lindesay Richardson and the Spirochaete', *Papers presented at a Centenary Seminar on Henry Handel Richardson 1870–1946* (Canberra: National Library of Australia, 1972), pp. 9–22; and Elizabeth Summons, 'Ethel and Florence and Arthur and Mattie', *Overland*, 72 (1978), pp. 24–30,

[2]   *MWY*, p. 19.

as the Assistant Colonial Surgeon of South Australia; and since his relocation to Richmond, he had been the visiting medical officer for Cremorne Private Hospital, which catered for inebriate and insane private patients.

Dr George Graham first visited Australia as a ship's surgeon in 1853[3] and after his marriage to Sydney Boyd in 1857 they decided to emigrate.[4] Their first child, George Robert Moore Graham,[5] was born in Adelaide in 1860. The following year the family moved to Richmond, Victoria, and they remained in Swan Street until after 1866 when they moved to 'Lyndoch' in Church Street. George Graham was the first medical graduate of the University of Melbourne in 1862. The Grahams had six more children in Richmond between 1862 and 1873: Margaret,[6] Emily Josephine,[7] Luduvina,[8] James,[9] William[10] and Edgar.[11] HHR knew the Graham children well for she and her sister spent many holidays with them at the Grahams' seaside home at Blairgowrie near Sorrento.

George Graham was President of the Medical Society of Victoria in 1878 and President of the Victorian Branch of the British Medical Association in 1883. There is a plaque in the Brownless Library, the University of Melbourne, presented by the Graham children commemorating their parents.[12] The Grahams and the Richardsons became friends after the Richardsons returned from England in 1868 and probably met first through John Robinson Bailey, for George Graham was his doctor. The Grahams also joined the Victorian Association of Progressive Spiritualists, which was formed in 1872 with Walter Richardson as the President.

It was Dr Graham who had advised Walter in August 1877 that the medical practice at Clunes would be too much for him and who insisted that Walter should stay and rest a little longer with him in Richmond before travelling to Queenscliff. Dr Graham would have heard about Walter's symptoms of aphasia and giddiness which had occurred while Mary was staying

[3] Arrived in Perth in June 1853 on board the *Sabrina* (with 320 emigrants).
[4] They arrived in Adelaide in July 1858 on board the *Utopia*.
[5] George Robert Moore Graham (b. 30 June 1860). He passed the matriculation examination for entry into the University of Melbourne in February 1879 but did not complete a degree. He married Fannie Matilda Rosser in 1886.
[6] Margaret Elizabeth Frances Graham (b. 20 March 1862). She was in the first cohort of pupils enrolled at the Presbyterian Ladies College (PLC) in 1875 (enrolment No. 122). Margaret is portrayed as the fictional Georgina in *GW*. On 28 May 1884, she married Dr Charles Beamish Duigan.
[7] Emily Josephine (Josie) Graham (b. 1863) was always an invalid and did not attend school. She was brought from her couch to HHR's wedding breakfast. *MWY*, p. 135.
[8] Luduvina Marion Graham (b. 9 December 1864). She also attended PLC in April 1876, aged eleven (enrolment No. 235). Luduvina is portrayed as the fictional Marina in *GW*.
[9] James Sidney Boyd Graham (1866–1938), born 10 August 1866 and died at Brighton, aged seventy-two.
[10] William Archibald Eyre Graham (1872–1944), born 11 May 1872. He became a surgeon dentist (80 Collins Street, Melbourne) and married Marion Christina Adam on his twenty-fifth birthday in 1897. They had two sons: Henry Boyd Graham (1902) and Boyd Adam (1912). He died at Kew, aged seventy-two. He is portrayed as Marmaduke in *GW*.
[11] Edgar Gerald Hastings Graham (1873–1932) died aged fifty-nine, in Ascot Vale. He is portrayed as Erwin in *GW*.
[12] 'In memory of |George Graham, MD (Melb.) MRCS (Eng.) | Born 1829 Died 1893 | The first medical graduate of the University in 1862 | President of the Medical Society of Victoria in 1878 | President of the Victorian Branch of the British Medical Association in 1883 | and | Sydney Graham | Born 1835 Died 1923| This tablet and a sum of £500 are a gift of their children to the medical school.'

with the Graham family in Sorrento and Walter was in Chiltern in February 1877.[13] During
their discussions in August 1877, Walter and George talked about whether Walter should
invest in the Australasian Insurance Company and Graham had advised him not to because
the Manager, Thomas Jacques Martin, had once been an inmate of Cremorne.[14] Whether the
two men broached the subject of Walter's own medical condition explicitly is not known but
in September it is clear from Walter's letters that Mary stopped insisting on him trying for a
better practice. Maybe Dr Graham had given her or his wife a hint of the true state of Walter's
health.

Dr Graham's long association with Cremorne Private Hospital began prior to 1865 and
ended with its closure in the early 1880s.[15] The care of psychiatric patients had been a problem
in Victoria since its first settlement. The available accommodation was always scarce and,
despite the considerable building programs undertaken from the 1840s, many patients ended
up in prisons unfit for the required nursing. The Yarra Bend Lunatic Asylum had been
established in 1848 on a 620-acre site on the River Yarra. The original buildings were of
bluestone, forming three sides of an elongated square. By 1858 overcrowding necessitated the
building of ten 'cottages', each with six various sized bedrooms, a dayroom, pantry and
storeroom. The cottages were surrounded with flowerbeds and in the centre of the group of
cottages was a building containing a billiard room, reading room, kitchen, storeroom and
apartments for the staff. Surrounding the cottage group was a seven-foot-high fence. This
design, with small groups of secure cottages and a separate large enclosure for the violent
patients, was based on the Devon County Asylum, in England. Visits to the Yarra Bend
Asylum were vividly described by Annie Baxter Dawbin in her journal in 1863 and 1864,
when she was able to gain access through her friend, Dr Edward Barker, who had been on the
Board of Official Visitors since 1853.[16]

Work on a new metropolitan asylum at Kew was commenced in 1857 and, after delays
and controversies, this 'barrack'-style institution finally admitted patients in December 1871.
In 1867, the New Lunacy Statute permitted private asylums to operate openly and to advertise
their facilities. It has been suggested that Dr James Harcourt[17] had been operating a private
asylum in Ascot Vale since 1854, when he first arrived in the colony, and that by 1858 he had
begun to operate Cremorne Private Hospital.[18] By that time, Dr Harcourt had joined the

---

13   'I was up at Maudes posting a letter & I found myself unable to articulate—I could not say what
        I wanted.' Letter 203, from WLR to MR, 17 February 1877.
14   Letter 213, from WLR to MR, 28 August 1877.
15   A Royal Commission was set up in Victoria (the Zox Commission), which lasted from 7 May
        1884 until 29 April 1886, to enquire into and report on the state and condition of asylums for the
        insane and the inebriate, both public and private. Before the Commission completed its most
        comprehensive investigation into the issues, the government closed all private asylums because of
        reports about gross abuses at private asylums in England. Both the Medical Society of Victoria and
        the Victorian Branch of the British Medical Association (of which George Graham was President
        in 1883) urged that this ban on private asylums be revoked. The Zox Commission supported the
        prohibition, stating: 'Now we have a clear field—there being no private asylums in Victoria—to
        avoid the pernicious principle of allowing private speculators to trade on and profit by one of the
        greatest calamities that can afflict humanity.' Brothers, pp. 135–138.
16   Dawbin, 20 June 1863, pp. 332–334 and 25 July 1864, pp. 424–425.
17   James Thomas Harcourt (1813–1893), medical practitioner; prior to his arrival in Melbourne in
        1854, he had been the proprietor of Hunningham and Harbury Hall Lunatic Asylums in
        England.
18   Brothers, p. 79. The advertisement for Cremorne in 1883 reproduced in this book (p. 80) states
        that the private asylum had first been established at Pascoe Vale in 1856.

Board of Commissioners in charge of the administration of the Asylum at Yarra Bend. Controversies about treatment, facilities and costs continually dogged the administration of the Victorian asylums. Dr Richard Bowie's period as superintendent (from 1860 to 1862) came to an end when he was relieved of his position on 25 August 1862 and Harcourt was appointed as the temporary, and unpaid, replacement superintendent until a new appointment could be made. In 1864, the Government of Victoria agreed to a proposal put forward by Dr Harcourt that his Cremorne Private Hospital at Richmond should be used to care for government patients. The following points were agreed: that not fewer than thirty female patients be sent; that this number be guaranteed for not less than twelve months; that an immediate £500 be paid to cover the cost of preparation to be repaid by adjustment of accounts after the first three months; that 30/- be paid per week per head; that all accounts be rendered and paid monthly. Thirty patients were sent by the government in January 1865 and it was Dr George Graham, the local practitioner, who assumed the medical duties and responsibilities for the government patients in the private asylum.[19]

Dr Graham continued to work at his private practice in Richmond, but Cremorne must have been an excellent and reliable source of funds for him. An advertisement for Cremorne in 1883 lists him as the Medical Superintendent.[20] Cremorne had five sitting-rooms and twenty-three bedrooms, and from 1869 to 1885 the charge rose from £3 to £6 per week. On 11 September 1878, Walter was admitted to his friend's care at Cremorne. Why was he moved two months later on 18 November 1878 to Yarra Bend Lunatic Asylum? It is unlikely that it was the expense of Cremorne since there is every reason to assume that the Grahams and other friends and relations would have been more than willing to assist in the medical bills; and, although Mary was fiercely independent and determined to earn her living to support herself and her daughters, it is unlikely that she would have refused help for her husband in his last illness. It is more probable that the accommodation at Cremorne was not suitable for Walter, who may have been at a stage in his illness when he required more secure restraint. There is no doubt that Dr Graham would have placed him at Yarra Bend for good reasons. In 1876, a report on the newer Kew Asylum had revealed that rough treatment was often meted out to patients. The cottage system at Yarra Bend, despite the age of the buildings, permitted comparative freedom of movement within the secure perimeter.

When Walter was admitted into Ward 8, his medical record, which still survives, describes his form of insanity as 'General Paralysis (incipient)' and his condition as regard to 'Marks of violence or other peculiarities' as: 'This patient has normal old scars and marks of injury about his legs—sores on hands.'[21] The next day (19 November), the record states: 'Slept well, takes his food fairly. Is very restless during the day and will give very indirect answers only to questions, continually humming to himself.' On 20 December 1878, he 'had an attack of hemiplegia of the right side' and on 25 January 1879, 'Had another attack of paralysis today while walking about the grounds, fell and scratched his face a little.' Four days later he had improved and was 'able to get up a short time in the morning'. On 17 February, it states 'Somewhat rallied, walks about a good deal.' It was at this time that a decision was made to send him home. Mary and her daughters were by then well established in Koroit where she had become the Postmistress in September 1878, shortly after Walter's admission to hospital.

19   Brothers, p. 79.
20   Brothers, p. 80.
21   NLA MS133/1/271, Yarra Bend Record (copied 2 October 1953), entry for 18 November 1878. The subsequent notes about his condition are taken from this document.

It would have been Dr Graham's advice that was sought by Mary, and the medical staff at Yarra Bend must have agreed that his condition would allow his return to the family. He was 'a gentle, broken creature'[22] when he was sent home on 24 February 1879, 'out on leave for three months'.[23] He never returned to the institution but died just over five months later with his family by his side at Koroit Post Office, on 1 August 1879.

Three months after Walter's death, Dr Graham's expertise in the treatment of psychiatric patients was used when he and eight colleagues (including Drs Gilbee,[24] Cutts,[25] Henry[26] and Neild[27]) were deputed by the Council of the Victorian Branch of the British Medical Association to visit the asylums. Their report once more criticised the newer Kew Lunatic Asylum and stated that it was a disgrace to the community and, although it was under the direct supervision of the Chief Secretary, it was 'the worst managed institution in the colony'.[28]

Despite Mary being so far away from Walter when he was in hospital, it was probably comforting for her to know that their best friends, Sydney and more particularly Dr George Graham, would have been able to visit Walter and monitor his progress. No letters have survived from that period. The Grahams' friendship continued through the years and across the continents; and almost twenty years later in 1895, Sydney Graham, then a widow living in Clontarf, Dublin, came to HHR's rescue over the difficulty of where to be married, when she wrote to HHR in Germany, 'warmly inviting us to have the wedding from her house in Dublin'.[29] From the home of Sydney and her daughters, 4 St Lawrence Road, Clontarf, Dublin, HHR was married to John George Robertson on 30 December 1895. One poignant letter from Sydney Graham has survived;[30] written to Mary in Munich, Germany, a few days prior to Mary's death on 26 November 1896, it shows the deep love and friendship that existed between the two women:

22 *MWY*, p. 19.
23 NLA MS133/1/271.
24 William Gilbee (1825–1885), Honorary Surgeon, Melbourne Hospital and first President of the British Medical Association (Victoria Branch).
25 William Henry Cutts (1828–1897), physician, educated University of Edinburgh; President, Medical Society of Victoria, Victorian Medical Benevolent Society, and the British Medical Association (Victorian Branch); Council, University of Melbourne. *ADB 3*.
26 Louis Hirsch Henry (*c*.1854–1924), physician; a founder and Secretary of the British Medical Association (Victoria Branch). He arrived from England in early 1879 and in May, his name was put forward to the meeting of the Medical Society of Victoria, proposed by Dr George Graham and seconded by Dr Andrew Gray. His application for membership was rejected as he did not get the required three-quarters of the members present at the meeting to support him (with nine votes against and only fourteen for). The Committee meeting later that month made it clear that the rejection was not because of his religion (he was a Jew), but because a relative of his had recently been imprisoned. Henry had come to Victoria with permission from the British Medical Association to establish a Victorian branch. With the support of his colleagues, particularly James Neild, Louis Henry established the branch, which eventually took over the Medical Society. See Love, p. 184.
27 James Edward Neild (1824–1906), forensic pathologist, drama critic, journalist; President and librarian, Medical Society of Victoria; a founder, the British Medical Association (Victorian Branch); President, Melbourne Shakespeare Society.
28 Brothers, p. 101.
29 *MWY*, p. 102.
30 NLA MS133/2/437.

My darling Marie

Do try & take all the nourishment you can. You must try & get better & we shall have such a dear little home together here. I would be ready to go & meet you in Paris. If only your poor mouth was better. I hope you would gain strength

I won't tire you more. Lots of love from all & your own old loving chum

Sydney

Saturday morning

When Mary finally sailed from Australia on the *Ormuz* with her two daughters on 3 August 1888, two days after the ninth anniversary of Walter's death, she not only left her close friends but also an extensive family network including her oldest sister, two brothers and their wives, one widowed and remarried sister-in-law, twelve nephews and nieces, at least five great-nephews, one cousin and his wife with twelve children and an ever-growing number of grandchildren. The letters written and received by Walter and Mary Richardson, spanning the period 1854 to 1877, demonstrate twenty-three years of an intense, loving relationship and a complex family network and, finally, reveal Walter's physical and mental deterioration. The letters are filled with references to friends and relations and events, from international affairs to the local church bazaar. It is no wonder that HHR found her parent's letters an inspirational source for her most famous books, the trilogy, *The Fortunes of Richard Mahony*.

Part II

The Letters

1854–1855

Courtship and Marriage

1854

1   [From MR in Geelong to WLR in Ballarat]

Bell Post Hill [Geelong][1]
April 22nd 1854 [Saturday][2]

Dear D[r] Richardson

    I received your kind note on Thursday & was very glad to hear that you received the key[3] safely. I was rather afraid that it would slip out of the envelope but I endeavoured to fasten it as well as I could. M[r] Candy[4] called upon us on Tuesday as he was returning to Ballaraat so you see that he was not there to teaze us by hiding our thimbles & work. I am very happy to say that Matilda[5] is very much better but M[r] Bradshaw[6] has been very ill owing to a fall he had from the Hay loft he missed his footing & fell, & hurt his back very severely but I am pleased to say he is able to get about a little.

    We are expecting M[r] Smith[7] to see us next Saturday & stay until Monday I am sorry to hear that he is far from being well—

    Miss Jelfs[8] desires to be kindly remembered to you her father[9] has returned so she will have to go on board on Tuesday & I think Matilda will go for a few day's with her as change of air will do her good. I shall only be too happy to render you what assistance I can towards your new Flag[10] if you will only send me word how it is to be done & I will do my best. We had a very pleasant walk before breakfast this morning to the cave[11] to get some green boughs but had a great difficulty in getting up the Hill again & feel very tired from the efforts of it so you must please to excuse this hastily written letter M[r] & M[rs] Bradshaw & Tilly & Polly[12] join me in kindest regards to yourself—in haste

    I remain| Your sincere friend

      Mary Bailey

Text: ALS NLA MS133/1/4

[1] MR was living at the Bradshaws' Family Hotel on the Batesford Road, Bell Post Hill, Geelong, where she was the governess for the Bradshaws' young children, Caroline (aged eight), George Frederick (nearly five) and Emma (three). Bell Post Hill is situated 8 kilometres north-west of Geelong town centre on the main road to Ballarat (the Midland Highway). Bell Post Hill was so named because a laddered spar, on which hung a bell, was erected by the first settlers in the area, John Cowie and David Stead. They landed sheep at Cowies Creek in March 1836 and their run extended from Moorabool River to Corio Bay. The story is told that the bell was used by the partners to inform other settlers about ships sighted in the Bay or to warn settlers about attacks by Aborigines. Ian Wynd, *Geelong—The Pivot* (Melbourne: Cypress Books, 1971), p. 12.

[2] This letter was in response to one from WLR, who reveals in Letter 8 the following year: 'You little puss didn't you suspect I loved you when our eyes first met? Why you refused to come into breakfast the morning after my first visit, I suppose when you received my note about the key you began to suspect I had some little affection of the heart.' See Letter 8. Compare *FRM I*, p. 62.

[3] WLR had left his key behind at the Bradshaw's Hotel and MR had returned it to him.

[4] Possibly Richard Candy (b. *c.*1828), a gold digger, who arrived in Melbourne aboard the *Ajax* in June 1853, having set sail from Liverpool on 15 February 1853.

[5] Harriet Matilda Bradshaw (Tilly) (1838–1914), daughter of William Bradshaw and Marion Buller Bradshaw. Her fictional counterpart is Tilly Beamish in *FRM*; however, unlike Tilly she did not marry Smith.

[6] William Bradshaw and his wife, Marian née Buller, were the employers of MR and ran the Hotel at Bell Post Hill. William's birth and death dates are not known. Marian Buller was the daughter of William and Marian Buller and was christened on 27 October 1805 at the Academy Chapel Independent at Hoxton, London. William Bradshaw and Marian Buller were married in England where they had five children: William Burrows (1827–1915); Charles Feast (1829–1907), born in Ely, Cambridgeshire; Edwin (1831–1901); Edward Buller (b. 1832); Harriet Matilda (Tilly) (1836–1914), born in Sutton, Cambridgeshire, England. The family emigrated to South Australia, where six more children were born: Marian Buller (Polly) (b. 1842); Caroline (b. 1846); a male child who died at birth in 1847; Emma Feast (1848–1851); George Frederick (b. 1849) and Emma (b. 1851). They then moved to Geelong. When MR first met the family, at least three of the sons, William, Charles and Edward, were living in the vicinity of Ballarat.

[7] Alexander Brooke Smith (1834–1881), son of Dr Thomas Heckstall Smith, for whom Walter worked as an assistant in St Mary Cray, Kent, prior to emigrating. ABS sailed to Melbourne on the *Wanata*, arriving in October 1852. On 5 November 1852 he became a police cadet and for the next thirty years worked for the police force in Victoria. His fictional counterpart in *FRM* is the character 'Purdy Smith'. It is believed that he introduced WLR to MR in 1854, having engaged the affections of Polly Bradshaw, then only fourteen years old. He never married.

[8] Ellen Jelfs (1837–1920) born in Birmingham, daughter of Thomas Jelfs and Ann née Beech. She was a friend of Tilly and Polly Bradshaw and became a very close friend of MR.

[9] Thomas Jelfs (1818–1881), from July 1853 to October 1855, was the Master of the schooner *Bristol* (150 tons), which delivered cargo around the south coast of Australia and across to Tasmania, particularly between Melbourne, Adelaide, Geelong, Port Albert and Sealers Cove. He had left Port of Melbourne on 9 February 1854 to sail to Adelaide to pick up ten passengers and a cargo of brandy and sundries, which he delivered to Hobart. He was married to Ann née Beech (1809–1907), with whom he had several children, including Ellen (1837–1920) and Emma (b. 1839). After his stint as Master of the schooner, he became an innkeeper and was landlord until 1859 of the rebuilt and re-licenced Ship Inn, 66 Flinders Lane West, Melbourne. The Ship Inn had been built originally of sawn timber, wattle and daub in 1837 by John Moss, in front of his brewery. It had an unsavoury reputation and its licence was cancelled in 1841 until the inn was rebuilt in 1846. During the 1860s, Jelfs and his wife were living at Schnappers Point, where both WLR and MR visited them. According to Mornington's local historian, Leslie Moorhead, Thomas Jelfs owned ninety-one acres near Schnappers Point and had a butcher's shop on Main Street in Mornington.

[10] 'Every store in Victoria has a flagstaff in front, from the top of which streams the ensign, with its kangaroo, opossum, pick and shovel, or any ingenious device which may suggest itself to the ingenious proprietor.' Kelly, p. 200. See *FRM I*, p. 62 for the fictional account of Polly making the flag.

11 Modern housing development around Bell Post Hill makes the location of the cave impossible to find. However, from the Batesford Road there is a gradual slope, which turns into a steep hill down to the river. See *FRM I*, p. 52.

12 Marian Buller Bradshaw (Polly) (b. 1842), daughter of William Bradshaw and Marion Buller Bradshaw. Her fictional counterpart is Jinny Beamish in *FRM*.

1855

2 [From WLR in Ballarat to MR in Geelong]

Ballaarat

Thursday 2 P.M. [7 June 1855][1]

[No salutation]

I was sorry to leave you my dearest sweetheart as I did the morn of my departure, but delay was dangerous

The sun was just tipping the hills with gold as I ascended the steep of Bates Ford[2] where I took a last look of that spot now so dear to me.

Anon I sat me down on a tuft of grass, and partook of the collation prepared by your dear self—then it rained and I thought of your prediction true prophetess

I have but this moment arrived and I haste to let you know that I arrived safely and that I shall expect you to keep your promises of answering this and enclosing some thing[3] by return of post

I trust your dear self and the family are well, remember me to them individually and kiss me dearest [+ symbol] think on and get mother's consent to shorten the time[4] for I need you at home,

Good bye sweet one| I shall write by Mondays post again| Your fond lover|

W Lindesay Richardson

Text: ALS NLA MS133/1/14[b]

1 WLR proposed marriage to MR on Sunday, 3 June 1855, and she accepted.
2 Four kilometres north from Bell Post Hill where there was a bridge across the River Barwon. In 1853, Batesford was described as 'not much of a stopping place. Being so near to Geelong—four miles and a half—it was too short for a stage.' Kelly, p. 162.
3 MR had promised to send WLR a lock of her hair.
4 MR called Mrs Bradshaw 'Mother'. WLR was anxious for the marriage to take place as early as possible but Mrs Bradshaw did not want MR to leave her employment until later in the year. They married on 27 August 1855 according to the rites and ceremonies of the Wesleyan Church at the bride's home in Hope Town, Geelong, with Isaac Harding the officiating Minister. The 'bride's home' was probably that of the Bradshaws as the same address was given on Tilly Bradshaw's marriage certificate the following year. The Bradshaws were Wesleyan Methodists but MR had been christened in the Church of England. Although there is no record of WLR's baptism, it is likely that he would have been baptised in the Anglican Church at Malahide or perhaps privately at the Richardsons' home, 'Claireville'. From the early years of their marriage, WLR's mother and stepfather (Lucinda and Dr Bayne Cheyne) attended the Independent Congregational Church in Bristol, where their sons, John and William Alexander, were christened in 1829 and 1831, respectively, and presumably WLR attended the same church.

On the wedding certificate, WLR certified that he was a member of the Wesleyan Church. Bristol, the place from which John Wesley had decided to become a field preacher, was the centre for both Wesleyan and other evangelical groups from the 1730s onwards.

3   [From MR in Geelong to WLR in Ballarat]

Bell Post Hill [Geelong]

[Monday, 11 June 1855][1]

My dearest D[r] Richardson

I was never so agreeably surprised as I was yesterday when I returned home from a long walk to the <u>cave</u> (where we had all been to gather mushrooms) to receive a letter from you dear Mother gave it to me I could not imagine for a moment who it could be from but the moment I looked at the address I knew it was from you dear I was very glad to hear that you arrived at home safely how very kind it was of you to write to me so soon for I know you must have been very tired after your long walk. You were not quite out of sight when I came down stairs I could just see you going along the road I thought I should have been in time to see you but I was doomed to disappointment. M[r] Bradshaw returned home that night but he could give us very little information about M[r] Smith he only saw him for a few minutes he said he had been out with the hounds[2] on Tuesday but he could not find time to write to his old Friends at Bell P Hill—I think he is acting rather unkindly to dear Little Polly do you not think so?

I hope you will tell him of it when you write you will for my sake will you not dear? I am sorry to say that we did not get the pictures they were not ready I am afraid they will be lost & that would be a great pity. M[r] B thinks that he has left them in one of the Seargeants[3] houses but Alec has not written to tell us so we do not know what to do for the best

Mother has not answered M[rs] Smiths[4] letter yet I think she feels a little vexed at Alecs neglect. William[5] has gone over to see my Brother Harold[6] to day I do not think he will be back to night I am very glad to tell you that William is very much better. I have enclosed you what I promised & I think it is nothing but right that I should ask for a piece of yours in return. I hope my dear you will not refuse me but I do not think you will. I shall alway's answer your letters by return return of post but I cannot alway's answer for them being in time for the post for the weather is often wet & then no one goes to town.[7] I tell you this in case you should be uneasy at not receiving one. You left the piece of Poetry about "John Brown"[8] on your dressing table I have taken care of it I think I may keep it until you come for it which will be in about three month's we must wait patiently until the time expires & then I will be ready to return <u>home</u> with <u>you</u> I cannot get leave before that. I had to leave off writing my letter last night for my dear Harold came back with William—I was so pleased to see him & he is looking so well I think my happiness is coming on so fast just now that I scarcely know what I shall do there are some letters from dear Old England waiting to be sent for from Melbourne so I hope to get one from my own dearest Mother[9] I shall be so pleased. I wish you were coming down again soon You cannot think how dull & lonely I felt the day you went away. I have again been interrupted in writing by the alarm of fire. I sat talking to Tilly about something when we saw some smoke from the drawing room fire place & there being no fire there made us call M[r] B. when it was discovered that there was some board on fire underneath the Bricks & in the dining room as well it appears to have been burning for a day or two but I am happy to say that it is quite safe now though we might have had the house on fire to night if it had not been discovered in time. I think I have done all you wished me to do since you have been away and as I have nearly filled my paper I must begin to think of leaving off scribbling. Mother Tilly & Polly send their kind love to you & with the same from| Your ever loving & faithful

      Mary

Text: ALS NLA MS133/1/2

1   Reply to Letter 2, posted on Tuesday, 12 June, received by WLR on Saturday, 16 June. MR enclosed a lock of her hair.

2   By the 1850s there were many packs of hounds around the countryside as well as the Melbourne Hunt, supported by the gentlemen settlers. Paul de Serville, *Port Phillip Gentlemen: And Good Society in Melbourne Before the Gold Rush* (South Melbourne, Oxford University Press), 1980, pp. 104–105.

3   Presumably referring to police sergeants.

4   Caroline Smith (1806–1871), wife of Dr Thomas Heckstall Smith and mother of Alexander Brooke Smith. Lived for many years in St Mary Cray, Kent, but died in Brighton, Sussex.

5   William Bailey was christened 22 October 1834 at St George's Parish Church, Leicester; sixth child and fourth son of John Bailey (*c.*1803–1846) and Elizabeth née Robinson (1802–1869). He never married. He emigrated to Victoria with MR and Sarah Bailey on the *Anne Cropper* in 1853 and worked for a time in Ballarat. He went to India where he worked for the Indian Civil Service until his retirement to Hampstead, London.

6   Edward Harold Bailey (1828–1893), christened 9 April 1828 at St George's Parish Church, Leicester; second son of John Bailey (*c.*1803–1846), a solicitor's clerk, and Elizabeth née Robinson (1802–1869). He arrived in Victoria at the age of twenty-four in June 1852 with his older brother, John Robinson Bailey, on the *Mount Stuart Elphinstone*. He worked for a time as a gold digger but then became an ironmonger for Eyres and Co., the hardware and ironmonger's store in Sturt Street, Ballarat. His next position was as bookkeeper and accountant for Bennett Brothers in Melbourne. He was thirty-eight when he married. The wedding took place on 1 May 1866 at the Baptist Church, Brunswick Street, Fitzroy. His bride was Agnes Eleanor Hablethwaite who was born in 1840 in Camberwell, Surrey. They had six children: James Harold (b. 1867), Walter Robinson (1868–1877), Mabel Elizabeth (1871–1876), Edgar Charles (b. 1873), Celia Agnes Eleanor (1874–1938) and Percy François (b. 1879).

7   Geelong town centre.

8   John Brown (1716–1766), essayist, poet and dramatist.

9   Elizabeth Bailey née Robinson (1802–1869), maternal grandmother of HHR; born 24 April and christened 28 April 1802 at St Margaret's Parish Church, Leicester. She was the third daughter of Thomas Robinson and Susannah (d. 1811). She married John Bailey (*c.*1803–1846), a solicitor's clerk. They had ten surviving children and Mary, their seventh child, married Walter Lindesay Richardson. Elizabeth Bailey died on 8 July 1869.

4   [From WLR in Ballarat to MR in Geelong[1]]

                           [Mount Pleasant, Ballarat]

                       Thursday evening. [7 June 1855][2]

D[r] and only sweetheart

    Hurry mother and let us make the day in July instead of August there's a love; what are you blushing about, and what are Tilly & Polly laughing about? My old place looked more comfortable than ever after my return, my little dog "Jily" ran up to me and kissed me, crying like a child, and my other dog "Brandy" evinced equal signs of pleasure; even my old cat came to greet me and I sighed as I thought that there was one want in my establishment: Business is very dull and so I am at a very great expense now, my hope is that you may come and help me to manage better, if you do, tell M[rs] Bradshaw, I promise that you shall go spend some time with her (if we live so long) about the beginning of next year, but if she is heartless & cruel on this point she must expect other people to keep you when they get you—A thousand loves to your dear sisters,[3] I hope you are well my darling, and have no cold; Remember what I told you, and treat yourself as if you are mine entirely—

Tell William [Bailey] I was sorry I could not wait for him on Wednesday morning but I knew that if I saw <u>your</u> face again I should postpone my departure another day, and as travelling and its et ceteras are very ex costly, I thought the more prudent plan was to tear myself from the neighbourhood and fly.

I met two young men at a restaurant 5 miles beyond Meredith[4] & I directed them to M[r] Bradshaws for Thursday night, so you can tell them I did not forget business; The eight miles of floor upon which Miss Tilly purposes to come up for a gallop was very muddy when I passed up it, so much so indeed that I was glad enough to take the bush—

Friday. [8 June] Very high winds indeed today, but the weather pleasant My neighbours all asking me why I did not bring M[rs] Richardson up—A patient who lived near William by the "Prince Albert Hotel"[5] and whom I left doing very well has had a relapse and is now again dangerously ill with Colonial fever[6] We have had a nurse who has been paid 20/- a day for the last month & he is completely knocked up I have been hunting all morning for somebody else, and altho' so many are out of work have not got any one, no one likes the situation—I am afraid there will be hard times both here and in town this winter—

Sunday night [10 June] I went today to the township to deliver your letter to William[7] he asked me very politely to step in to dinner and I saw his lady and family—

Little Charley[8] your favourite is growing and is thin, Billy[9] has a slight cold—M[r] W. Bradshaw has a nice little estate and appears to be very comfortable—

Monday. [11 June] Very stormy. At home all morning send this to the post afternoon and expect a letter from you to be waiting there, you must excuse this, as my cat is in my lap purring furiously insisting on rubbing whiskers with me <u>doubtless suspecting my affections</u> are strayed! Ha! Ha!

Good bye dearest, kiss me x

Love to family by the bye I say [saw] <u>M[r] Bannister</u>[10] yesterday tell <u>Tilly;</u> a very nice gentleman indeed—

Have you heard of my friend Brooke Smith? Good bye once more| Your fondly attached
Walter

Text: ALS NLA MS133/1/13

[1]   WLR had written 'Miss Mary Bailey/ Bradshaws Hotel' on the fold of the letter.
[2]   Written from Thursday, 7 June to Monday, 11 June, posted on 11 June, received by MR on Saturday, 16 June. 1855.
[3]   Tilly and Polly Bradshaw.
[4]   About 40 kilometres north-west of Geelong.
[5]   The Prince Albert Hotel was situated near Gravel Pits lead, an extensive, rich ground discovered in 1853 where the gold mines followed past the Catholic chapel across Bakery Hill and into the bottom of the basin, 'where diggers were gathered like a swarm of bees'. Bate, p. 42. The landlord was Carl Wiesenhavern and his partner was Johan Brandt. The description of their encounter with a gang of ruffians (or 'Vandemonians') during the Eureka Stockade is documented by Carboni, pp. 91–93. The Prince Albert Hotel became the St John's Presbyterian Church. Withers, p. 70.
[6]   Probably typhoid fever.
[7]   William Burrows Bradshaw (1827–1915), a storekeeper at Ballarat; son of William and Marion Bradshaw. He was married to Rebecca née Wells and, at the time of this letter, they had three living children (two had died as infants): Charles Robinson (1850–1880); William

(1854–1933); and Marian Emma (born on 13 March 1855). Another ten children were subsequently born in Ballarat and its vicinity: Alfred Edward (b. 1857), Eugene Matilda (b. 1858), Frederick (b. 1861), Alice (b. 1864), Adelaide Theresa (1866–1867), Ernest Albert (b. 1868), Edwin Burrows (1869–1869), Edwin Burrows (1870–1871), Adelaide Charlotte (b. 1872) and Oswald b. 1874).

8   Charles Robinson Bradshaw (1850–1880) born in Morphett Vale, South Australia; son of William Burrows Bradshaw and Rebecca née Wells. He became a farmer in NSW and drowned while bathing in the River Murray at Gol Gol, on 29 January 1880, at the age of twenty-nine.

9   William (Billy or Willie) Bradshaw (1854–1933) born in Ballarat; son of William Burrows Bradshaw and Rebecca née Wells. He became a house and land agent and was working in Clifton Hill, Melbourne, when he married Minnie Alexandria Holmes (b. 1862) on Christmas Day 1886.

10   Henry Fisher Bannester (b. 1831), a gold digger. He was born in London, the son of Benjamin Bannester, a surgeon. He married Harriet Matilda Bradshaw (Tilly) on 13 February 1856.

5   [From MR in Geelong to WLR in Ballarat]

Bell Post Hill [Geelong]
Sunday Afternoon [17 June 1855][1]

My dearest Walter

I received your Welcome letter last Thursday & was very glad to hear that you were well I am sorry that you would be disappointed in not getting a letter from me on last Monday but it could not be for the weather was so wet that no one went to town but my Brother posted it for me on Tuesday I do not know what day's exactly the Mails leave Geelong & the weather being so unsettled Mr Bradshaw does not go to town but I will write to you every week a Man called here last Saturday & said he had seen Dr Richardson & he sent his love to Mrs Bradshaw & not to her alone but to the Misses Bradshaw—I must thank you for I think you meant some of your love for me at least I took some portion of it. Tilly went to town last Thursday to stay a few day's with Miss Grundy[2] We are expecting her home this Afternoon for Polly has gone with her Father on horseback & she is to stay for a few day's & Tilly to come back. I must thank you very kindly dear Walter for sending the money for my use I hope some day I shall be able to make you some return for it but will you send me word how you wish me to lay it out what I mean is how you wished me to be dressed when I am married I wish you to send me word for I should like to have your opinion. I am afraid I am but a poor hand at writing letters but dear Walter you must take the will for the deed but rest assured I <u>feel</u> more than I can <u>say</u> I often feel that I should say things & then again I do not like to perhaps <u>you</u> know how I feel but you must not laugh at me I shall get the better of it I hope I am sure I shall when I have <u>one kind good</u> face looking at me—

Mother is going to write a few lines to you I expect you will get a good scolding for she thinks you are to impatient & you might wait the three month's but still I do not think she will be quite so strict as to wish to keep me so long however you will see by her letter what she thinks. I was sorry to hear of one of your patients being so ill again I hope he is better The weather has been very fine the last day or two but it threatens rain to night Polly & I had a little walk this morning & got a few Mushrooms. Tilly sends her kind love to you & say's that she will Galop up the 8 miles[3] some day (when <u>we</u> are married) to see us I think Alec is very unkind in not writing to any of us we have never heard from him since he has been away I hope nothing has happened to him Poor fellow I am afraid he is on a dangerous expedition if you should hear from him first I hope you will let us know for Polly is getting very anxious about him—I cannot help thinking how disappointed you would be not to receive my letter before Friday I hope you will not be angry with me for I cannot help it if no one goes to the post. Tilly has come home & is pretty well. I shall be anxiously looking out for a letter next Wednesday I hope I shall not be disappointed William[4] has gone to stay with his Brother John a few day's the change may do him good I shall send a letter by him when he comes to Ballaraat which will be in a week or ten day's. I am glad to say he is getting quite well again—

I was sorry to hear my little favourite Charley was getting so thin if you should see his Father will you tell him I think that Bell Post Hill would do him good & to let him come down the next time M[r] Wells[5] returns. I have not received my English letters at present for Harold has not had time to go to Melbourne for them but I hope he will be able to go next week for I am so anxious to get my own dear Mothers letters it is so long since I heard from her. We have not heard from M[r] Jelfs so I do not think he can have arrived I hope nothing has happened to their vessel.[6] Tilly is very busy hunting for a piece of poetry that would be suitable for you I do not know what it is for she has not shown it to me at present. I tell her that she ought to send it now she has found it but I do not know whether she will or not yet

I have nearly scribbled my paper full I am afraid it is an odd mixture but I do not think you will be tired of reading it will you dear? I know I am never tired of reading yours over & over again so I judge you by myself. You did not send me word how you liked M[rs] W[m] Bradshaw[7] & Ted[8] & all of them will you next time I think I should make a pretty good hand at writing like you for I have been trying & I think a little practice would make perfect I hope dear Walter that your business is improving since you last wrote I can assure you that I will assist you all I can when I come to Ballaraat for I know your expenses must be very great just now I shall be anxiously waiting for answer to this letter for you to tell me what you wish me to lay out the money in I have filled my paper so I must leave off scribbling they all send their kind love to you & hoping you will accept my very very best love & kisses many| I remain dearest Walter| for ever your loving

     Mary

Text: ALS NLA MS133/1/3 and MS133/1/10

[1]   Response to Letter 4: undated but probably written on Sunday, 17 June 1855 and posted Monday, 18 June 1855.

[2]   Anna Maria Grundy (b. 1834) born in Woolwich, the daughter of William Grundy, an architect and his wife, Anna, who lived at Fenwick Street in Geelong. On 15 October 1857 she married George Croll (1828–1893), an engineer, who had been born in Dundee, Scotland. His parents were William Croll (1813–1861), who was an engineer and owner of the Geelong Vulcan Foundry, and Jane née Hutchinson, who lived at Dundee House in Geelong. Anna and George had two children: Anna Isabel (b. 1860) and Cecil Harry (b. 1862).

[3]   The distance from Bell Post Hill to Ballarat is about seventy-nine kilometres.

[4]   Her brother William Bailey.

[5]   Thomas Wells (c. 1813–1884), father of Rebecca and father-in-law of William Burrows Bradshaw, eldest son of William and Marion Bradshaw. Thomas Wells was married to Sarah née Creswell (1814–1876) and they had at least two children living in Victoria—Rebecca and her older brother, Richard (c. 1830–1880), both born in Caen, Normandy, France.

[6]   The *Bristol* arrived in Melbourne on that day (17 June 1855) from Sealers Cove and Launceston, bringing sawn timber, casements, chairs, teapots and four passengers.

[7]   Rebecca Bradshaw née Wells (1833–1877), daughter of Thomas Wells and Sarah née Creswell. When she was seventeen she married William Burrows Bradshaw in South Australia. They moved to Victoria where they lived for twenty-three years and then in 1875 moved to Wentworth, NSW, where she died on 14 September 1877 of a 'wasting palsy'. At her death she left ten living children (six male and four females) and five children had predeceased her.

8   Edward Buller Bradshaw (b. 1832), son of William and Marion Bradshaw; he was the innkeeper at the White Horse Inn, White Horse Gully, Magpie. He married Jane Vincent in 1857 and they had ten children: Edward Buller (1857–1857), Matilda Marian (1859–1871), Alfred Henry (b. 1860), Emma Vincent (b. 1862), Minnie Alexandria (b. 1864), William Edwin (b. 1865), Edith Emily (b. 1868), Marian Alice (b. 1870), Albert George (1872–1872) and Elizabeth Mabel (b. 1876).

6   [From WLR in Ballarat to MR in Geelong]

[Mount Pleasant, Ballarat]
Tuesday. June 11 1855 [Tuesday, 12 June 1855][1]

Dear Love,

I wrote to you and M[rs] Bradshaw yesterday, and I hope you received all safely We have had very severe weather last night and today hail, rain, wind and snow, the last remaining on the ground some time, giving us the rare opportunity of a game at that hearty English pastime snow-balling! I hope you are all well I am making your room comfortable been at it all day, sewing, nailing &c[2]

My poor friend that I left doing so nicely has had a relapse and is I am grieved to say gone to that bourne whence no traveller returns,[3] I called in another medical man to give me the benefit of his advice but medicine is of little avail in that disease;

Think my darling how short and uncertain life is and come and give me the benefit and the pleasure of your company thro' life—Good night dearest kiss me [+symbol] I dreamt of you all last night and did not like to let the day pass without penning a line or two.

Wednesday [13 June]—I went to the Post Office today no letters from you no lock of hair as you promised; I was at the Police Court all day as witness in the case of a dog that had been once mine, and was claimed by somebody who wished to appropriate her Have not yet been able to go to the White Horse Gully but hope to do so tomorrow am very cold so you must excuse my wretched scribble tonight, Good night, dearest love!—

Friday [15 June] I went yesterday to the White Horse Hotel, White Horse Gully M[r] Ed. Bradshaw was not at home, but tho' disappointed in not seeing him I had a very pleasant walk, thro' beautiful scenery wh I long to shew you—it resembles a gentleman's park in England more than any-thing else. I have caught a cold or rather a cold caught me while standing in the Police Court all day on Thursday but colds and Influenza are now quite "a la mode"—How is William? Give him my compliments and ask him if he will be able to attend at our interesting ceremony? I suppose you have perused the service by this time! Ha! Ha! I cant write for laughing!—

But joking apart, seriously, it is an impressive service[4]—

"Wilt thou love her, comfort her, honour, and keep her in sickness, and in health, and forsaking all other keep thee only unto her as long as ye both shall live—Beautiful—

And equally as follows "Then shall the priest say unto the woman."

I gathered some lovely heaths yesterday but tho' exquisite in appearance they want the perfume of English heaths, a great loss to the flowers of the Antipodes!—Goodbye Sweet one [+symbol]

Sunday [17 June] Good morning dearest Mary many thanks for your kind letter and its enclosure which I received safely yesterday. I am confident your pleasure on receiving my letter

was not equal to <u>my joy</u> as I had yours handed me and knowing by a squeeze what it
contained hurried off to devour its contents in private. I suppose M.rs B. dosent see my letters
to you dearest love for altho' there is no harm in love, still one hardly likes to write sweet
nonsense for other eyes than the one next the heart—

Well I was going to say that I hurried off to devour it in private I don't like "My dearest
D.r Richardson", its not kind of you to be afraid to say "<u>Walter</u>", is the name ugly?

And so you all went to the cave did you, pretty place that cave Eh? I prefer the scenery a
little further on, the wooded water course with the gentle slopes and deep precipices, with the
track along the face of the hill, where you gently murmured "<u>Yes</u>"! Of course had the ground
been a little less rough and the season a little milder I should have thrown myself on my left
knee and with one hand on my heart become pathetic but dearest I think we managed it very
well, my feelings prevented me from saying all that I should have done ~~but~~ and I fancied I felt
you tremble on my arm; I had told Brooke the day before in Melbourne that I had a serious
<u>duty to perform</u> and I certainly never expected to see him on the Sunday—With his usual
exuberance of spirits he told me that altho' it undoubtedly was a serious matter he could not
look upon any "popping the question" otherwise than a most ludicrous affair & we both
laughed heartily—

You ask my opinion of his conduct to "dear little Polly"—Now darling I do not see any
thing so very unkind, consider my dear that he has a great deal to do, always knocking about,
doubtless he has written before this, and besides 12 months is a long time and I think he felt
rather hurt himself (<u>as I do</u>) at being treated somewhat cavalierly! put off for so long—Besides
he knows he is safe in the heart of his little betrothed and surely a ride with the hounds was
too tempting and perhaps he expected to be home in time for the post—I know he loves her
dearly and she is his first and only love, and I would as soon doubt my <u>own constancy to you,</u>
as his to his second self⁵—Give the little dear my kind love and sympathise between you,
sighing after two fond hearts that look upon each of you as part of their existence—

I think Brooke has very much improved and rejoice that he encountered the family for
I think the mutual affection has been productive of much benefit to him—

When we love, <u>and feel sure that we are beloved in return,</u> it does and must have a
<u>beneficial influence</u> on <u>our conduct</u>—for as I would not like to have my body disfigured say by
the loss of my fingers or eyes, so I consider now that <u>my mind should be</u> purer and the moral
standard of my actions higher, is it not so? and is not this one of the good effects of love? is not
the state of love one designed for man by an allwise creator for his good! undoubtedly dearest!
and altho' some are not so happy as to encounter a heart that can beat in unison with theirs
every creature on earth loves something—I am not <u>poetical</u> on the contrary (you think rather
<u>prosy</u>) plain matter of sense, I do not like poetry except perhaps on a quiet Sunday morning,
or late of a Saturday night; and I'll tell you why <u>because I love it too much</u>, can you
understand this apparent paradox, at one time of my life I was dosy living in a land of dreams,
of spirits, letting the realities of life glide past almost unheeded, that was when at college (when
all young men go thro' a little studying and a great deal of what they fancy is fun) Late hours
&c impaired my health and it was not until I gave up poetry and nonsense and took to hard
work that I found myself able to cope with the combination of angel and devil in my fellow
mens composition—I cannot read true poetry without feeling my heart beat stronger, I think
you have poetry in your soul I do not mean love that you can scribble verses any ass can do
that, but I think <u>like myself</u> you look beyond <u>the hour, the day</u>: don't you,? the <u>faculty of</u>
<u>looking up</u> as it were, <u>looking to the source of things I mean!</u> Yes I think we shall be happy, of

course dearest, every man and woman have faults, <u>blemishes, imperfections</u> of body and mind, but we must remember that there is <u>no perfect one,</u> and remembering this we must <u>forgive</u>—Are not the following verses pretty?

> The first dear thing that ever I loved
> Was a mother's beaming eye
> That smiled as I woke on my dreamy couch,
> That cradled my infancy.
>
> I never forget the joyous thrill
> That smile in my spirit stirred,
> Nor, how it could charm me against my will
> Till I laughed like a joyous bird.
>
> And the next dear Thing that ever I loved
> Was a bunch of summer flowers,
> With odours and hues, & loveliness
> Fresh as from Eden's bowers.
>
> I never can find such hues again
> Nor smell such sweet perfume,
> And if there be odours as sweet as them,
> Tis I that have lost my bloom.

And so it goes on until it comes to

> And the next dear Thing that ever I loved
> Is tenderer far to tell,
> Twas a voice, and a hand, and a gentle eye
> That dazzled me with its spell.
>
> And the loveliest things I had loved before
> Were but as the landscape now
> On the canvass bright where I pictured her
> In the glow of my early Vow.[6]

And so on finishing with old age—<u>like me</u> as M[rs] B. said! Ha Ha

Well this is a curious letter, but it is amusing and delightful to me to talk to you and this sheet has occupied me as you see many days proving to you that my morning thoughts and my evening sigh has been dear Mary. I have got a little scheme <u>when you come to me;</u> you shall write to <u>my mother</u> and <u>I to yours.</u> I have a dear old mother,[7] that I love dearly, if I were to say that she has been the <u>finest</u> & the <u>cleverest</u> woman of her day I might offend you, sweet one, but she sang as I never heard <u>woman</u> sing, played the piano, harp, flageolet, accordeon, danced in her day played whist and now poor old soul having become old is anxious for me to return home, <u>oh! a letter from you will comfort her old age</u> and shew her that her dear son is happy & does not forget the arms that nursed him—

I am delighted that your happiness is as you say coming fast, I send you what you ask my darling but I am not accustomed to make bows with ribbon so you must take it as it is a token of my love—You say "about three months", now love let it be the beginning of August do there's a dear, I think it wrong, very wrong, to postpone it as if you were afraid of me and as if Mr B. was doubtful of my character—You will find a humble home and will have a poor man for your husband, but there's no queen will be more welcome if you can do without society for a year or two we will go to England & spend many a happy hour in the society of old friends. Kind love to Mrs B. Tilly & dear Polly and a thousand kisses from your dear and attached

        Walter

Text: ALS NLA MS133/1/11, MS133/1/12

[1]   Dated Tuesday, 11 June but probably meant Tuesday, 12 June 1855 and he continued writing on Wednesday (13), Friday (15) and Sunday (17 June). He had received Letter 3 on Saturday, 16 June 1855. Enclosing a lock of his hair, he posted this letter on Monday (18) and Mary received it on Wednesday (20 June).

[2]   Compare *FRM I*, p. 81.

[3]   ' … who would fardels bear,| To grunt and sweat under a weary life;| But that the dread of something after death,| The undiscover'd country from whose bourn| No traveller returns, puzzles the will| And makes us rather bear those ills we have| Than fly to others that we know not of?' *Hamlet*, III, i, 75–81.

[4]   The 'rites and ceremonies of the Wesleyan Church' were based on *The Book of Common Prayer* of the Church of England.

[5]   Annie Baxter Dawbin (1816–1905) painted a rather different picture of Alexander Brooke Smith's faithfulness. 'And on looking out I beheld Mr A. Brooke Smith, coming along, leading 'Sultan' for me. It was really very kind of him; but oh! I did feel selfishly, and thought of all I should have to endure in the way of his love troubles! For I felt certain, somehow, that he had come to confide in my 'tender bosoom'!' She reduced him to tears when she told him that everyone thought he was conceited and a 'shocking Flirt'. *Dawbin*, pp. 161–162.

[6]   Source unknown.

[7]   Lucinda Cheyne, formerly Richardson née Sirée (1796–1866), daughter of Henry Sirée, a lawyer, and his wife, Harriet née McCausland. She married WLR's father, Alexander Richardson (1758–1827), on 29 January 1816 at Christ Church Cathedral, Dublin, when he was aged fifty-eight and she was in her twentieth year. She was his fourth wife and was widowed on 28 May 1827 in Malahide, near Dublin. She remarried on 8 April 1828 in Buckinghamshire, England. Her second husband was Dr Bayne Cheyne (1788–1868), a medical practitioner.

7   [From MR in Geelong to WLR in Ballarat]

                                         Bell Post Hill [Geelong]
                            Sunday Evening [24 June 1855][1]

My dearest Walter

    I have only a little time before retiring for the night to write to you dearest for we have been so busy all day a house full of company that I have not had time to begin to write to you before. I received your dearly prized letter on Wednesday but was sorry to hear that you had caught a cold You must take great care of yourself or you will be ill I think it is my turn to talk to you now. I was thinking of yesterday when we went our walk to the Cave we had a very pleasant one indeed & we all climbed up those high rocks & stood & admired the scenery just where you & I stood but I think I looked more at the scenery to day than when you where with me I could not see that day but I blame you for it. I was sorry you did not see Ted[2] when you went to White Horse Gully but am glad you enjoyed your walk I am sure when you have time (when I come to Ballaraat) I shall only be to delighted to take the same walk with you & then <u>we</u> shall both be able to enjoy it together Harry Bannister[3] is down he is staying here. William will be up at the latter end of next week I will send a short letter by him I have not asked him what you told me at present about being down in August perhaps I may but I don't much like saying it to him do you not think it would be better for you to do it but I will if you wish me particulary

You ask me if I have read the ceremony over indeed dear Walter I have not neither shall I perhaps you will think me superstitious (well I think I am a little though I try to break myself of it) but they say you have 3 years bad luck so I <u>will</u> not read it for fear so please do not ask me. I like those verses very much indeed they are very pretty. I am indeed very fond of poetry though as you say I cannot write them.[4] I will indeed dearest Walter write to your dear Mother if you wish I am sure nothing would give me greater pleasure if you think it would please her I wish I could see her but I can fancy & I am sure I should love her I would do any thing to make her happy if she will but let me & I <u>will</u> do all I can to make you happy dear Walter but as you say we all have our faults & I am afraid mine are very numerous but I will do all I can to become better & <u>you</u> dear Walter must help me I am afraid you will find me rather awkward at first but you must bear with me. You say that if I can do without society &c—indeed & I can I am one that cares very little about [society] & besides who shall I want when I am married but you dear I am sure you will be enough I know no one scarcely but M[rs] Bradshaw's family for I have been here so long that I am known as Miss Bradshaw so there will only be my Brothers & sister Rebecca[5] up at Ballaraat. We all feel very fatigued after our long walk this afternoon so you will excuse me writing this so badly & my headaches dreadful I have not been well all the week I have had an attack of Influenza so I do not feel very well just yet I think it will go round the house I think M[rs] B. has it she seems very poorley. You made a very good excuse for "Brooke" but I do not know what you will say when I tell you that he has not written yet "Now what excuse can you make for him? If you should see or hear from him first you ask him how he would like to see dear Polly wasted ~~sulky~~ & pale fretting about but he must expect it & to see the looks when any one comes from town the anxious have you any letters "No Miss" how would he like it I wonder? I am glad to say that M[rs] Jelfs have returned Ellen has written & ask's whether Mary has had any more letters from D[r] R. & if she <u>answers</u> them if so to give her kind remembrance to him so I send it I have not answered it yet but must to morrow dear Polly & Tilly send their kind love also Mother & hoping dearest that you will excuse this scrawl I must think of saying Good Bye but not before I return you many thanks for what I asked you for the lock of hair I prize it very much I hope I shall hear from you on Wednesday & with very best love & kisses many| Believe me ever dear Walter to remain| Your sincere & loving

Mary

Text: ALS NLA MS133/1/1

1 Response to Letter 6.
2 Edward Bradshaw.
3 Henry Fisher Bannester (b. 1831) married Tilly on 13 February 1856.
4 '*I cannot write poetry myself*,' said Polly, *but I am very fond of it and shall indeed like very much dear Richard to listen when you read.*' FRM I, p. 84.
5 Rebecca Bradshaw née Wells (1833–1877), wife of William Burrows Bradshaw.

8   [From WLR in Ballarat to MR in Geelong]

[Sketch]¹

Ballaaratt Tuesday [19 June 1855]²

My dearest

I posted a letter to you yesterday making the third since I left you, I trust they have all arrived safely, and that the contents pleased you—I have some hesitation about writing thro "Brown Brothers",³ altho I suppose I can depend on none of my letters going astray: we have a splendid morn after a sharp frost and I feel well & happy, how are you love? I am like yourself looking anxiously for letters from my mother & trust the mail will not keep us much longer in suspence—My mother is, or was when I last heard, at Brighton where is yours? when did your father die? I lost mine⁴ when 9 months old,—where were you born? We have lots of questions to ask and answer each other, have we not? Of course I shall take more interest in you and yours than in any one else and all these little minutiae will possess vast importance when we come to hold dear converse, or to speak less a la Johnson,⁵ our cosy chats by our snug fireside—Then I shall want to know what brought you out here tell you where I was living at home, ask you to narrate your adventures since you came here, & tell you gossip about Smith's family &c &c &c &c and so on—

I hope darling you will adopt my plan of jotting down a few minutes converse <u>daily</u> it forms a good sized letter each week, and as you are occupied pretty busily it will not be a tax either upon your time or your love. Moreover you write a charming letter both in regard to penmanship and composition but letter writing improves our style of diction which is much noticed in life—

Thursday [21 June] Your last two letters have made me very happy, my own darling & this last which I received yesterday at 12 oclock commenced so nicely "<u>My dearest Walter</u>", forgive my rude remarks in my last, love, but we men <u>are</u> rough sometimes—I'm so pleased to have a long letter from you so delighted to take it out to the top of a neighbouring hill, and seated on a fallen tree commence a perusal for the hundredth time of the whole series commencing with "Dear Sir" and ending with "your sincere freind" to the last "<u>ever loving</u>"—You little puss didn't you suspect I loved you when our eyes first met? Why you refused to come into breakfast the morning after my first visit, I suppose when you received my note about the key you began to suspect I had some little affection of the heart—

I did send down <u>my love</u> but I sent it down to <u>everybody</u> not liking to particularize to the bearer, altho he was an intelligent man who had been ~~in~~ "butler & steward" in the late Duke of Newcastle's⁶ establishment—he said something about "Mʳ Little's having been very sweet with the tall niece" "Ah!" said I "he ought to have been sweeter;"—

I am happy to hear that Miss Matilda has been enjoying herself[,] present my brotherly love and kind regards, how about the poetry that was to suit me, was it a reproof anent⁷ my style of hat? I am glad to hear that the cheque arrived safely when you get the money love, lay it out as you best like, I hope it will be enough I have known the want of money at <u>critical times</u> and I thought it better to let you have a little fund <u>at your own</u> disposal than to present you with something which tho pretty might not be of real value⁸—Moreover you ought now only to be dependant on <u>me</u>—I was very doubtful for a long time what I should do, for said I to myself "if I do so, and so" she will <u>feel gratitude not love,</u> however I resolved to do what I considered <u>right,</u> and I thought that <u>you would love me for doing so!</u>

As to <u>your dress darling</u>, my taste is simplicity, but do whatever <u>you like</u>, I am quite confident I shall <u>love you</u> in <u>any</u> guise, but remember "Nature's dress is loveliness"; art only spoils—Mother <u>did</u> give rather a severe note on <u>impatience,</u> and <u>your value;</u> why tis the greatest compliment I could have paid <u>to me,</u> that <u>my future</u> wife is so much valued, that her freinds absolutely will not let her go: However cross I may have appeared in my last, (and there is no doubt <u>sometimes</u> I do think it rather hard,) I am at this <u>present moment</u> quite reconciled to defer the happy day <u>until the first week in August.</u> Am I right—I know the ladies privilege of choosing their own time—I have no doubt our worthy mother [Mrs Bradshaw] thinks that wooing-time is the best time of matrimonial life, by her tendency to put it off till 1856 or 1857!

<u>Friday morning</u> [22 June] I hope you will forgive me dearest Mary, but a sad mishap has occurred, I have lost <u>your lock of hair,</u> oh! dear, oh! dear; I always carried your letters and it, and on searching for it this evening I cannot find it! dont be cross, but cut off a <u>wee bit</u> more, do there's a love! and send me it next time—Tell your dear Polly that there is no reason to be uneasy about Brooke, he does not write for many reasons, he is busy and <u>really</u> has now no time, sleeping perhaps one night in the bush, another night in some tent then he does not wish his letters to be seen passing thro' the post, perhaps, as his whereabouts is somewhat secret—I hope he will be able to attend in August, I think he will if <u>he possibly can</u>—I know he would like nothing better, I remember when he asked <u>me</u> to appear at <u>his</u> celebration of the event, we little fancied then that <u>ours</u> would be the first to come off. Time does slip by it is now more than a fortnight since I left you, three weeks ~~tomorrow~~ next Sunday since—our walk to the cave alone—Mr Wm Bradshaw called yesterday and we had a long chat, he is really a <u>very sterling</u> common sense man; one that I like amazingly; I shall not tell you <u>all</u> we said, but this I may say he told me he had heard of <u>some event</u> that was <u>coming off,</u> and he congratulated me—our conversation long as it was, was interrupted not however without his saying that he would see me again & resume the thread of our discourse—I gave him your message about your little favorite Charley and you will see him some day soon He is one of the committee for raising the Patriotic fund[9]—

Business is dead, but I never lay my head on my pillow without thanking Providence for goodness shewn to me, and you may believe me when I say that I think I have <u>now</u> more reason to be thankful than ever I had before—

Hurrah! I've found it the lost lock again, I couldn't rest until I had searched every where, Good night dearest Mary, my own dear love, kiss me.

[Sketches: kiss, arrow through heart and two kissing doves]

Saturday morning [23 June] Glorious morn: up at six, have sent to the Post office altho I <u>do not</u> expect a letter from you dear but I think I shall have one next Wednesday.

Sunday morning [24 June] Good morning dearest! We have a bit of a gale this morning. Going out to dinner today.

Monday [25 June] I had been out yesterday afternoon, and on my return home was seated enjo[y]ing a pipe and a glass of sherry when fancy my surprise to hear a a familiar voice and see the face of your dear Brooke—He was accompanied by Mr Bryce[10] and it seems they came a long distance, and had a long ramble all day after me, the first operation was the preparing a hearty supper at which they distinguished themselves, secondly a little talking, laughing, telling stories, adventures, asking after absent freinds, enquiries as to time past, present, and future, with many other little matters; after a reasonable time we adjourned and retired for the night, where of course there were many little private matters, scraps from letters to be read, locks of hair to be compared and <u>admired,</u> "what a beautiful lock," ["]how I shall blow Polly up," why said I, "why for not giving me one like this"—&c—&c—&c—!

He says he has written—Tell Polly with my love, that he looks better than ever he did before in his life, is all spirits, and has an appetite like a hunter!! So I do not think there is any danger of a decline for 12 months—And now dearest love farewell for the present, Brooke was very much pleased with my <u>little</u> place, and says there is only <u>one want;</u>—There will <u>soon</u> be no need to make that remark I hope, for with your presence near me, I shall indeed be happy; I trust <u>you</u> will be so; if you can put up with the want of <u>many</u> comforts, that you may have been used to, if you can tolerate the rough style of a digger and his freinds, and if you can do without <u>balls</u> for a year or so; You will find a fond heart and a little property at your disposal; farewell my darling, kiss me [+symbol]| Your fond lover

      Walter

The Vignette at the head of the Chapter is a sketch of my place with the exception of the flag staff being 40 feet long which it does not appear—

    Text: ALS NLA MS133/1/15 and MS133/1/16

[1]   Sketch of a wooden hut with flagpole and three animals (two dogs and a cat). See postscript in text above, which was written down the left-hand side of the first page.

[2]   He commenced this letter on Tuesday, 19 June, received Letter 5 on Wednesday (20), and continued the letter until the following Monday (25 June).

[3]   Carriers based in Geelong.

[4]   Alexander Richardson (1758–1827) died on 28 May 1827.

[5]   Samuel Johnson (1709–1784), writer; his conversations, recorded by James Boswell, made him more famous than his books and displayed his erudition, wit, humour and commonsense. WLR was suggesting that their conversations would not be like Johnson's ponderous, antithetic style, but would be intimate chats.

[6]   The late Duke of Newcastle, Henry Pelham, 4th Duke, KG, DCL (1785–1851), lord-lieutenant and custos-rotulorum of Nottinghamshire, steward and keeper of Sherwood Forest, and high steward of Retford. The Pelham dynasty was one of the most powerful political forces in England during the eighteenth and nineteenth centuries. See *FRM I*, p. 82, 'People took to dropping in of an evening—old Ocock; the postmaster; a fellow store-keeper, ex-steward to the Duke of Newcastle—to comment on his alterations and improvements.' HHR wrote to her friend, Mary Kernot, on 11 May 1932, that she had received a letter 'nailing me down on a point in the first Mahony volume. Richard writes to Mary that he has had a visit from the ex-Steward of the Duke of Newcastle, & it turns out that my correspondent actually *had* a brother in Ballarat in the early days, who had filled that post. She wants to know was it a fact that Mahony saw him, or a coincidence! How *can* I possibly tell her, after all these years? I got hold at the time of many old letters & diaries, but whether I cribbed the detail from one of them, or invented it, it's now beyond my power to say.' In fact the fictional Richard did not write to his Mary about the ex-steward, but WLR did write to his real Mary.

[7]   Scottish term meaning 'concerning' or 'in regard to'.

[8]   'That night, into his reply, he slipped four five-pound notes. *Just to buy yourself any little thing you fancy, dearest. If I chose a gift, I might send what would not be acceptable to you.' FRM I*, p. 84.

[9]   It is not clear whether WLR was referring to the 'Friendly Subscriptions' which appear in Carboni's final chapter under the heading—'Friendly Subscriptions, Five shillings, or Ten Shillings from those who can afford it, are solicited to defray expenses. Received by'—a list follows with 'Bradshaw, Esq., J.P.' under the area 'Magpie Gully'. These subscriptions were to assist the miners in their legal and political actions after the Eureka Stockade. Carboni, p. 174.

[10]   Mr Bryce not identified.

9   [From MR in Geelong to WLR in Ballarat]

Bell Post Hill [Geelong]
Thursday Morning [5 July 1855][1]

My dearest Walter

I have received your kind letter & was pleased to hear that you had recovered of your cold As William[2] was starting to day I thought I would send a few lines by him I was very sorry that you kept dinner waiting for him last Monday he has been trying to get a seat in one of the coaches for several mornings but has alway's been disappointed owing to their being full. Ted came down last Monday evening he took us quite by surprise for we had never heard a word about his coming to see us we have had some very wet weather this last week & it is so misty this morning that we can scarcely see five yards I am afraid it will terminate in rain I hope it will hold fine for a few day's as we are busy washing & that must be my excuse for writing only a short note this morning. I am very glad to tell you that dear Polly is recovering her looks very rapidly since she received Alecs letter & she is anxiously looking out for another one

You would laugh to see me going about this morning I think for I have a bad foot I broke a needle in last Friday I thought I had taken it all out but the last day or two it is so painful that Mother has made me put a large poultice on so my foot looks very funny this morning I am very happy to say that Mr Bradshaw's arm is a little better though still far from well. We are very busy indeed this morning but I will write you a long letter on Sunday I wish to write a few lines to Alec if I can possibly get time if I should not give my best love to him Mother Tilly & Polly all send their love to you & with <u>very best love</u> dearest & kisses many I remain | as ever | Your loving

Mary

I am very glad to say that Mr Jelfs have arrived safely in port Ellen sends her love to you You need not have asked me whether you might send your love to her for I like Ellen to well not to wish it but I think you are all getting alike for Polly just asked me whether she might send her love to Dr Richardson. I would say more dear but I really have not time I have written a few lines to Alec he must excuse them for I have not time we are so busy | Good Bye dear

Text: ALS NLA MS133/1/9

[1]   Response to Letter 8. It was delivered to WLR by William Bailey by hand on Sunday, 8 July 1855.
[2]   Her brother, William Bailey.

10   [From MR in Geelong to WLR in Ballarat]

Bell Post Hill [Geelong]
July 1855 [Sunday, 8]

My dearest Walter

Sunday evening has again arrived. I have great pleasure dear in answering your last kind letter I was almost ashamed to send that scrawl by William but as I had promised to write a few lines I sent them but we were so very busy I hardly knew how to spare the time for we had a large wash about at the time I was sorry to hear that you were so dull last Sunday dear I hope that it did not last long

I do not know whether you are the same as me but when I feel dull it generally lasts a day or two. You say I did not tell you who my companion was when we went to the cave. Why if I must tell you it was Polly we left Tilly to walk with the single young man the rest were married & had their wives to walk with so Polly & I clambered to the High rock's we did not take the pathway until we got to the Brow of the Hill. Do you know Mʳ Parson's¹ that kept the Queens Head in Geelong? he has met with a severe accident—he was thrown from his horse last Friday night & it is supposed the horse dragged him along & stamped on his chest & side he has five Ribs broken & his heart hurt they hold out very little hope for his recovery—I think last week was nothing but a chapter of accidents they were two other carriages upset but I do not know to whom they belong

Business is dreadful dull nothing doing scarcely & such a quantity of Poor men on the road begging for a bit of something to eat I am afraid this place will soon get as bad as England. I was sorry you did not get any letters from England but I think dear we can condole with one another for I have not received mine yet & I know there are some waiting for me but Harold has not been for them yet. I have been expecting him up all the week but am disappointed I intend to write to him if he does not come soon. Mother sends her love to you & say's she will write to you next time but I think <u>dear</u> Walter we better let it be somewhere about the middle of August instead of the beginning do you not think so? I hope Brooke came to see you & cheer you up a little you will bring him down with you when you come will you not dear The weather has been nice & fine the last three days I hope it will keep so for a short time for wet weather makes you feel so dull Ted left us yesterday morning to return to the diggings

I suppose you will have seen William before you receive this Poor Boy he would have a wet walk but perhaps it might do him good & get some of his strength back ready for work I daresay he would tell you that I had a bad Foot I am very glad to say that I got a large piece of the needle out to day but it still feels as though there was some left in so I am going to have another poultice on to night.

I am going to have a plain White Muslin dress to be married in I think that will look neater than anything. You have no objection to that have you? You said you liked anything neat so I thought that would please you best.

They are all sitting round the table busy reading but they send their kind love to you dear Walter. We have not had an answer to the last letter that was written to Ellen Jelfs—at present—but I expect we shall soon for we expect her Sister Emma down to see us this week I think I sent you word that she sent her kind regards to Dʳ Richardson—I hope dear that you have got quite well of your cold dear I am afraid you will put yourself to to much trouble about making your home comfortable for me for you know dear that I do not wish it for what will do for you will I am quite sure do for me. One thing I forgot to mention that is you told me if I ever felt to tired to write to you I was not to mind I am sure you need not dearest be afraid of that for it is to great a pleasure to me to write to those I <u>love</u> I must now say Good Bye & with kindest love & kisses Believe me dearest Walter Your true &| loving

    Mary

Text: ALS NLA MS133/1/8

¹   Edward William Parson (1820–1855), landlord of the Queen's Head Hotel, Geelong.

11 [From WLR in Ballarat to MR in Geelong][1]

[Mount Pleasant,] Ballaaratt
Tuesday [10 July 1855]

My dearest

William called last Sunday accompanied by Mr Edward Bradshaw, and handed me your last. I trust your foot is better and that M^r B's treatment has been effectual.

I suppose all lovers are more or less unreasonable for I confess, I felt when last Wednesday passed without any letter and that too the first time since I left—However I am glad it was business that prevented you—William looked in during the morning and I am almost ashamed to say we were so much occupied that I had hardly time to say two words, the place moreover was in one vast heterogeneous confusion my man Friday[2] not having the gift of <u>order;</u> I think if I remember rightly I was making a plum pudding in the intervals of business it <u>took me two hours,</u> but it was much relished in the evening and pronounced unequalled that day at least; in the afternoon of the same day we were visited by some "coloured gentlemen" (who at some former period in the worlds history may have been monkeys[3]) I mean the natives or more properly aboriginals—They exhibited their performances which consisted of throwing the boomerang and asking for brandy—

Brooke has not made his appearance since and I now hardly expect him, I <u>half suspect</u> he is arranging matters so that he may [be] at <u>Bell Post Hill</u> in <u>August,</u> tell my little freind Polly with my love (if you will allow me) Ha! Ha! that she must not delude herself with any such hopes however as it is merely a vague suspicion of mine founded upon nothing—I hope I shall have a long letter from you tomorrow my dear Mary.

Thursday. Tomorrow now my darling, and with it came your nice letter. I did think the one by William was shorter than was absolutely necessary, but I know what a busy place you have of it sometimes—Mr Edward Bradshaw was telling me of some accident that happened to his father and your letter contains a very sad account of your own self going about with a needle in your foot, pon my word, my dear sweetheart, you must have a med^c. man or Surgeon, to live at Bradshaws Family Hotel, and the house should either be called an Hospital or "<u>The Accidental Hotel</u>"—

What in the name of reason induced all the people in Geelong to upset their carriages in one week? Surely they might have arranged it better!—

Your account of your ramble to the cave makes me fancy you must have spent rather a quiet walk a little different from the time my freind Brooke was cutting his antics and Polly was chastening him with her parasol![4]

Business is very quiet in Ballaaratt, and as you say this country is getting almost as bad as England for the poor man—People do not beg here I am sorry to say they do worse, they steal—

You must not have any more low spirits now that you have fixed a day! or at least got so near as to say the <u>middle of August</u> you are not going to keep gradually putting it to next Xmas are you? Bravo one month [missing word(s)] Every-thing is ready here, and her ladyship is anxiously look[ed] for; I heard a gentleman the other night [missing word(s)] "So I hear you are going to be [married] <u>Somebody on the flat?</u> (meaning B[allarat] [missing word(s)] from Geelong" Oh! <u>who is she?</u> I [missing word(s)]

No appearance of Mr Smith yet [missing word(s)] I may be able to bring him down as you request but I fear [you] must not depend upon it—

88MARRIAGE LINES

My kind regards and love to Mrs Bradshaw [Tilly] and Polly, Remember me to the invalid Mr Bradshaw [missing word(s)] that as most probable I shall be down some time next month he had [missing word(s)] defer [missing word(s)] next accident until then—

Mrs Smiths address is

Rowlands

S. Mary Cray, Kent, England.

Ask Mrs Bradshaw to remember me kindly to the family.

I am sure I shall admire you my dear Mary in your white muslin or any dress you may select, allow me to suggest the propriety of a travelling dress of good warmth, for we shall be a good many hours ~~coming up to Ballarat~~ on the road and we must provide against it either being wet or cold—

Tis a desperate morning on Ballaaratt, I dont know how you are down there. Ice last night. I have just been out sawing and splitting wood tis no use sitting over a fire!

This is not so long as my letters are generally but as I have got to go to the post office on the township a mile and a half off and as I have no more news to tell you and as you know very well that all I could say would only amount to the three little words that the birds say to one another, "I love you" you can hardly blame me for saying farewell dearest, take care of yourself the last month you are to be Miss Bailey and oblige my dear Mary| Ever your

Walter

Text: ALS NLA MS133/1/21 and MS133/1/22 [Damaged]

[1] Letter was folded and sealed with red wax. The address is written on the folded letter: 'Brown Brothers & Co., Malop St, Geelong', and in the left-hand bottom corner appears 'Miss Bailey, Mrs Bradshaws'. Postmark is 'Ballarat JY 12 1855'.

[2] The name of WLR's assistant is not revealed in the letters. In *FRM*, Mahony had two assistants: Long Jim, whose mate in the *Proem* is buried alive down a shaft and who joins Mahony after falling into a mine shaft and breaking his collar bone; and Hempel, a strict Baptist and a consumptive, who found that the diggings proved too hard on his physique. Hempel marries Zara Turnham. *FRM I*, pp. 3, 31 and 67.

[3] James Burnett, Lord Monboddo (1714–1799), Scottish lawyer, writer, philosopher, who wrote *Origin and Progress of Language* (six volumes written between 1773 and 1792), in which he theorised man's affinity with monkeys, particularly the orang-outang. Charles Darwin's *Origin of Species* was not published until 1859. There are no other references to Aborigines in the letters.

[4] 'and Tilly hit Purdy over the back with her parasol.' *FRM I*, p. 52.

12 [From MR in Geelong to WLR in Ballarat]

[Bell Post Hill, Geelong]
Sunday Evening [15 July 1855]

My dearest Walter

I received your kind but long expected letter yesterday Afternoon I think I never was so disappointed as last Wednesday as to receive no letter from you I had written you a very long letter[1] answering all your questions about my dear Mother & every thing I could think of & was waiting very anxiously for an answer so much so that although the roads were wet in a very bad state & the day very showery Polly & I persuaded Mother to let us go into town for the letters for she expected one she had written a short note to you & one for Alec enclosed in mine. I thought by my being somehow so over anxious I should be disappointed & indeed

I was it would be impossible to tell you all I imagined nor the reason but the only one that had my hope in it was that you were coming down & intended surprising us. I cannot think how William could have forgotten it for he posted the letter on the Monday & he then started in the afternoon for Ballarat but meeting Ted & all of them he came back & did not start until Thursday & that was partly the reason that I wrote such a short note for I had scarcely any news left to tell but Mr Bradshaw is going to enquire at the Post office in Geelong about it & if it is not to be found there I will send you word and perhaps then you can enquire at the Ballarat Post Office if it has been detained. I should say it was because there was not enough postage paid for the letter I believe was over wait & when William came back I asked him if he had had it weighed & "he said "No he put a sixpenny stamp on & he said he was sure it would be all right so I expected it would if it should be laying at the Post Mr B. will pay the difference & send it to you—

I think it was the longest letter I have written to you I endeavoured to answer all your questions I am sure I can always's have plenty of time to write to you for Mother has sent me on purpose to have my letters posted & for me to get your's I thought dearest in the first part of your letter that you were a <u>little bit cross</u> but you will see by my explanation I was not to blame but the latter part was kind I could not help laughing to think you were two hours making a pudding you must have been interrupted or very busy—You tell me to provide against cold thank you kindly dear for your thoughtful care of me I shall attend to what you say but you have not as yet told me exactly what you mean to do if it is not asking to much I should like to know your intentions & how we shall go to Ballarat I should like to know dearest because I can then arrange things accordingly. I know you said we should go away after we were married but I think it would be such an expense dear to go to the Heads[2] but you know best so please yourself I have no right to interfere but I was only giving you my humble opinion. Polly had a letter from Brooke on Friday—she said he was quite well & is now on the Adelaide leads[3]—Maryboro—he does not think he will be able to come but I mean to write & ask him & I know dear you will do the same Many thanks for Mrs Smiths address Mother will remember you to her: The weather the last day or two has been very fine but looks to night as though we should soon have rain I should think the weather up at the diggings is more like the English Climate than it is down here for you have had snow & we have not. The destitution now prevailing in Collingwood[4] is distressing there were thirteen cases in yesterday's Argus all respectable honest & industrious people that spoke of the people as actually starving it is shocking to read them. I do not know whether I mentioned to you in my last letter that Mr Parsons of the Queens Head in Geelong was thrown from his horse & some of his ribs broken & his heart injured & that he was lying dangerously ill at the Separation[5] "Poor Fellow" he has gone to his last home—he passed here on Friday in the hearse there was a Coroners Inquest[6] held over him the same day & he was buried on Saturday I am happy to say that Mr Bradshaw's arm is better though he is not able to move it at present I told him what you said & he hopes he will not have the misfortune to meet with another accident I have got one piece of needle out of my Foot but am afraid there is a piece still left in for whenever I attempt to walk or touch that side of my Foot it pricks me dreadfully I have had poultices on ever since so I hope in time that it will be brought out I think if the Hotel was called either of the names you mention[7] that we should not have much custom for the house dear do you? I am wondering whether I shall have a letter on Wednesday I half expect I shall not like Saturday you will be having this on Wednesday & poor me will have to go without "Ah if you had only felt half so disappointed as me I pity you I was so struck that I

could hardly believe M[r] Brown[8] for you had always been so regular before I did not know
what to think could be the reason. We have been very quiet to day we had a run round the
Paddock & Garden because the ground was to damp & cold for us to go to the cave. So you
think ours must have been a very quiet walk that Sunday do you but then you must remember
that we enjoyed it for most of our conversation was about you & Alec & they say talking
about the one you love best is the best consolation to not having him with you I very often get
teazed & asked who it is that is going to be married & pretty well teazed where it is know[n]
but when people come & tell me that it is me I say indeed people seem to know my business
better than they do their own & then I run away for I will not satisfy there curiosity. What
interesting things we shall have dearest to talk over when we are together so many questions to
ask one another—I do not think we shall finish for a long time Mother will write to you
when she can answer your letter about different things. My letter love does not look so long
perhaps as it generally is but I think it is only I have written it smaller & closer together
Mother Tilly & Polly send their kind love & hoping my ever dear Walter that this may find
you in good health accept the best wishes with love & kisses many from your ever| true &
loving
     Mary
Good night God Bless & Protect you dear Walter is my prayer.
    Text: ALS NLA MS133/1/7

[1]   This letter, written on Sunday, 1 July 1855, was unfortunately never found.

[2]   Port Phillip Heads (Point Lonsdale and Queenscliff on the east and Sorrento on the west) are
about three kilometres wide with an effective navigable width of about one kilometre. WLR
probably intended for them to stay at Queenscliff.

[3]   The gold rush to Maryborough, Victoria, had begun in late 1854, with an influx of 11,000
miners by December 1854. By the time of this letter, the population had trebled (Serle, pp. 218
and 388). Before the police force was detailed to each new rush, ex-convicts and bushrangers
looted and plundered the mining communities. Alarmed at the lack of protection from police,
the Maryborough miners set up a Mutual Protection Society in May 1855 with the object, 'To
protect the honest and industrious inhabitants of the Maryborough diggings'. Their rules stated
that, 'it be clearly understood by all members, that this Society does not advocate "LYNCHING"'.
In June 1855, it was reported that at Adelaide Lead the 6000 miners were in a very agitated state
because of the presence of a large number of lawless characters including the notorious
bushranger Black Douglas and his gang. In April, Governor Charles Hotham had ordered the
Assistant Commissioner of Police, Captain Charles MacMahon, to send eight more constables
immediately to Maryborough; but the shortage of police due to resignations over the reduction
of pay gave MacMahon no capacity to obey the order. After some further correspondence
between the two, Hotham amended the order to five constables. Betty Osborn and Trenear
DuBorg, *Maryborough: A Social History* (Maryborough: City Council, 1985), pp. 36–43.

[4]   An editorial, 'The Destitution in the Suburbs', appeared in *The Argus* on Saturday,
14 July 1855, following an earlier article on Thursday, 12 July, which listed seventeen cases, 'In
none of these lamentable cases, does the misfortune endured seem to be the result of vice, folly,
or improvidence.' The article listed the primary reason for the problem as want of employment;
and noted that most cases involved artisans rather than labourers and that their pride and silent
endurance worsened their situation. Collingwood had been investigated because of its nearness
to the centre of Melbourne, but it was noted that people in other suburbs were suffering equally.

[5]   Separation Inn on the Ballarat Road., Geelong.

[6]   'An inquest was held yesterday, at the Queen's Head Hotel, before Forster Shaw Esq, Coroner,
and a respectable jury, on the body of Edward William Parsons, late landlord of the Queen's
Head Hotel, whose death was caused by a fall from his horse, when about a mile from the
Separation Inn, Ballarat Road ... The Verdict: That Edward William Parsons accidentally,
casually, and by misfortune came by his death, and not otherwise.' *Geelong Advertiser and
Intelligencer*, 14 July 1855, p. 4.

13   [From WLR in Ballarat to MR in Geelong]

Mount Pleasant
Tuesday [17 July 1855]¹

My darling Mary,

It seems quite an age since I heard from you and as I trust there is a letter to me coming from you today I commenced to you—How is the foot, and how are all the family? Any newsI have not heard of Mᵣ Smith since I wrote last and your letter (and <u>its enclosure!?</u>) are quite safe, I suppose I had better bring them down when I come about <u>the end of the year</u>—Mᵣ Candy paid me a visit on Sunday last and enquired kindly after yourself and the family, he desired his kind remembrances—William² paid me a visit ~~again~~ last week I expected to have seen him on Sunday again, but did not, he appeared in very low spirits: but I accounted for that by the fact of his not being employed at any definite work, as soon as he gets into a shaft he will doubtless be all right: Tell Mᵣ Bradshaw that Mᵣ W. Bradshaw junior is now <u>a magistrate</u>³ and a <u>considerable man</u> I saw him on the hustings at the late election here⁴ There has been a little more gold turned up at the mines lately and this is a very important point as it affects every one here directly and every one in the colony indirectly—I have not got my English letters but expect them by the next mail "The Donald McKay" <u>due</u> since the 11ᵗʰ of this month⁵—

Have you heard from your freinds yet?—

Tis delightful weather, and reminds one of the joke of Currans when asked by a freind if he "had ever seen such a winter" Yes" he replied "last Summer" meaning thereby that the season equalled summer—Tis true our frosts remind us that it is not Summer and on that account perhaps, I often think it is as well <u>you</u> are not here until the mild warm weather comes!—

Thursday [19 July] No letter from you yesterday! Business I suppose—

I was a little dissapointed but dont want to be unreasonable

William came to see me last night, it was very wet and dark, and I insisted upon his staying until morning; I had had a splendid puppy given to me in the morning, and was anxious to rear it if possible, the consequence was that we <u>got no sleep</u> as I had to get up two or three times to quiet the little rascal—

He insisted upon leaving before breakfast as he was in a great hurry to get to work—Add to this that there was no supper cooked, as my assistant was out and I fear he left us with a poor opinion of our hospitality!—

I am happy to tell you that his prospects now are very good, he has got into a party again who have one or two shafts or mines that are expected to do well!—

I hope all are well? Remember me very kindly to all and to your little freind Miss Jelfs— I shall not write a very long letter as I have to go up today to the Post Office, and tis a long dirty walk, so you will excuse this and taking the will for the deed imagine a thousand <u>loves and kisses;</u>

I sen[t Mrs] Smith's address, when I wrote last, did y[ou get] the letter?

I trust the foot is all right, and that you will be more cautious my dear in future.

I am sorry to hear poor Parsons whose accident you told me of in your last is dead, it is very sad to think of the number of persons who kill themselves. | Loves inumerable again my darling and believe me as ever| Your very affect lover

       Walter

Text: ALS NLA MS133/1/17 and MS133/1/18

1   Letter folded, sealed with red sealing wax and stamped with two 2d stamps. The address is written on the folded letter: 'Brown Brothers & Co., Malop St, Geelong', and in the left-hand bottom corner appears 'Miss Bailey, Mrs Bradshaws'. Postmark 'Ballarat JY 19 1855', 'Geelong JY 20 1855'.

2   William Bailey.

3   William Bradshaw, John Victor and Samuel Irwin were made Justices of the Peace in July 1855 (Withers, p. 166). John Victor owned the house in Webster Street, which JRB rented when he and his family moved to Ballarat in early 1857. Victor founded, and was first principal of, Grenville College, Ballarat. In 1856 Samuel Irwin became the first editor of *The Ballarat Star*, for which John Robinson Bailey (JRB) started to work in January 1857.

4   After the events at Eureka in December 1854 and the following Government Commission, the government of Victoria introduced three important bills in the Council, including the enlargement of the Council by twelve members (eight for the goldfields and four nominees). The Commission had advised that the diggers be selected to form local courts. The government went further in legislating that the members of the court be elected every six months by those holding the miner's right. These elections took place in July 1855. These local courts were given complete control of the industry in their localities and were empowered to make regulations on all aspects of the working conditions. The senior administrative officers were to be known as wardens.

5   The *Donald Mackay*, the Royal Mail ship from Liverpool under the command of Henry Warner, finally arrived at Port Phillip Heads on 26 August 1855. 'Arrival of the *Donald MacKay* puts us in possession of intelligence from England to the 5th June. Although the news of the war [in the Crimea] do not amount to confirmation of the report of the decisive successes which reached Melbourne via the Cape, they are of great importance, and of a very cheering character- of such character, indeed, as to render it highly probable that, by the 11th June, intelligence should have been received in London of successes as great and decisive as those the report of which has excited so strongly the expectation of the people of Melbourne'. *The Argus*, 27 August 1855 (WLR and MR's wedding day), p. 4. Peace was proclaimed in April 1856.

14   [From MR in Geelong to WLR in Ballarat]

                             [Bell Post Hotel, Geelong]

                         Sunday evening [22 July 1855]

My dearest Walter

    No letter all this week but I must not be impatient for you had to wait last week but do you not think that you ought to write two this next week to make up for it. I cannot write a long letter this time for several reasons first because I have not heard from you all the week—Secondly I told you most of the news in my last & Thirdly it is getting very late

    I have enclosed this in one to Mr Wm Bradshaw. I was greatly pleased last Thursday night to see my Brother Harold walk in he went to Melbourne next day to get a parcel that was laying there waiting to be fetched. I had a few lines from Mother saying they had not heard from me lately but letters had been sent to me at Melbourne but I have not received them at present "Ah is it not pleasant to receive letters from <u>those </u>that we love & particulary when we are so far separated—

We are expecting Mr Bradshaw & his family all down next week so could you not contrive dear to write a few lines by him if you have time. We are expecting Ellen Jelfs down to morrow to stay with us she sends her love to you. I have been reading all day it has been very dull all day & rainy to night although the last week [h]as been very fine we thought of going to Church this morning but forgot about it until it was too late so shall have to defer it until another Sunday I have been reading a little of the "Comic History of England["]^1 to night I never thought of reading it before but happening to read a sentence or two I was surprised to find how very amusing it was there is something in almost every line How do you like Ted Bradshaw—you did not tell me—we have not heard from Alec since I last wrote I expect I shall get a letter from you dearest on Wednesday have you received the missing letter yet? I am so sorry you did not get it there is nothing I dislike so much as my letters to be opened & particularly that one I feel so vexed about it you cant think I must dear think of saying good night Mother Tilly & Polly send their love & hoping dearest that you will accept my best love & kisses Believe as ever| Your loving

    Mary

Text: ALS NLA MS133/1/6

1 Gilbert Abbott à Beckett, *The Comic History of England: with 20 Coloured Etchings and 200 Woodcuts* by John Leech (London: Bradbury, Evans & Co., 1848). Gilbert à Beckett (1811–1856), one of the founders of the satirical weekly publication, *Punch*, was the brother of Thomas Turner à Beckett (1808–1892), solicitor and politician in Victoria, and Sir William à Beckett (1806–1869), the first Chief Justice of the Supreme Court of Victoria. William's knighthood was secured somewhat irregularly through the agency of his brother, Gilbert, rather than through the request coming through the Governor of Victoria. Gilbert, based in London, wrote directly to the Secretary of State and, after some amusing, if impertinent, correspondence, Sir John Pakenham, the Secretary of State, directed that 'the knighthood should be conceded'. See de Serville 1991, pp. 208–209.

15 [From WLR in Ballarat to MR in Geelong]

        [Mount Pleasant,] Ballaratt
        Monday July 23 [1855]^1

My dearest love

    Not getting any word from you last Wednesday and not receiving your letter on Saturday altho' I sent (owing to the crowd) I determined to go today myself, and ascertain what was really the matter—To my great joy I received yours of Sunday week my darling; so that it could not have been posted to reach me last Wednesday, for I sent my assistant last Wednesday and he declares it was not here, altho' I got some business letters by that mail: I tell you all this because I see there must be one of your letters to me missing somewhere, as you yourself know; now my dearest Mary, your last letter to me, was the best, the longest and the kindest and the dearest you have sent me, and I am going to write you as long and as kind a one if I can—Firstly my dear, I must tell you that business has been very good lately, so that I am in good spirits; it is not very usual I suppose to talk about business in love letters, but still you may excuse this, as I work at it as much for the sake of the future Mrs Richardson, as for myself. The people around me are beginning to be civil, and altho' I have got an awful riff raff set of Irish, still there are one or two decent people that will be delighted to see you. Secondly my health is excellent, (and while I grieve to hear of your bad foot and wish I was there to advise you and <u>to take the needle out)</u> I am counting the days to the middle of next month, & this also puts me in good spirits!—and so you and dear Polly actually walked into town to get no letter from me, now darling what shall I say by way of excuse or apology, let me see I think the real fact is that the missing letter not reaching me by last Wednesday week mail I waited and waited and now you will see that since I received the letter from you <u>before this,</u> I had written two <u>to you</u> without getting any at all <u>from</u> you. You say darling, you thought I was coming down well it all rests with you to say when—

Tis strange about this letter of yours missing for only about a month ago a merchant in town sent me some goods to order, and the bill or invoice usually coming by the next mail, I was surprised not to get it; so when he came up soon after I began to blow him up about the unbusiness way of not letting me have the prices of the goods, he <u>declared</u> it had been sent, had been posted and yet it was not at Ballaratt—Tis very kind of Mr B. to take the trouble of endeavouring to get our letters transmitted punctually to one another, but you see with all the care all of us can take, as Burn's says

"The best laid schemes of mice and men,
    Gang off agie."[2]

and as you fancied the first part of one of my letters <u>was cross,</u> now I consider that <u>very</u> unkind Mary! and shall punish you for it when I see you! The reason why I was two hours making a plum pudding was because I was so busy, and moreover when you come to consider how it was admired! but I shall be happy to take a lesson from you in many little things; gentlemen who have lived in the <u>bush</u> are always more handy at any of the domestic pail of life's drama! but I promise you, you shall have sole management of the cooking department; the great matter is to have <u>plenty to cook,</u> plenty of materials—

I think I will talk over our plans when we meet, I had intended going down to "the heads" and dont know whether I shall not still, but as you say twill be costly! and perhaps the money might be better laid out—I know your aversion to the <u>conveyance</u>[3] and will provide one for <u>ourselves</u>—But all these matters can be organised next <u>month</u>—

Time certainly does fly, tis but the other day since <u>I saw you</u> for the <u>first time;</u> I do trust my own dear darling that your foot is well, and do let me impress upon you the necessity of acting like <u>an old woman,</u> (I mean as regards care and prudence) for the remaining few weeks, not that I mean that you are not after that to take as much care of yourself, but then you know my dear you will have an <u>elderly medical gentleman</u> for <u>your adviser!</u> Love to Mrs Bradshaw and Miss Tilly, not forgetting the future Mrs Smith! Kind remembrances to Mr B. no more accidents I hope—You ask me to write to Brooke how can I darling when I do not know his address, besides where he is today he may not be tomorrow; Oh! I think we'll see him! Your little freind Ellen quite well? and happy? I suppose as the weather is so unfavorable and the walk so long that you have never been in the vineyard since; that was really a pleasant walk, and I enjoyed it very much, tho' not so much as [our] last, and which we are bound to bear in our memory [missing word(s)] I was much amused today, a freind [missing word(s)], sent me word he had a case or two of very [missing word(s)] which he begged to recommend to <u>my</u> notice! This [missing word(s)] the Post office <u>no letters,</u> so you see we are [missing word(s)] turns—

Thursday morning [26 July 1855] Good morning my dear, hope to receive a letter from you on Saturday—You must excuse the commencement of this epistle there was something amiss with the ink I hear there is news from England and I hope a mail

Good bye dearest love, and with every kind wish and prayer for your health and happiness believe me as ever and for ever not only "your sincere freind" but "nearer and dearer" than that| Your ardent love

Walter

I forgot to send you a kiss in my last; [+ symbol] accept a thousand this time—& forgive me

Text: ALS NLA MS133/1/19 and MS133/1/20 [Damaged]

1   Reply to Letter 12. Letter was folded and sealed with red sealing wax. The address is written: 'Brown Brothers & Co., Malop St, Geelong', and in the left hand bottom corner appears 'Miss Bailey, Mrs Bradshaws'. Postmark 'Ballarat JY 26 1855', 'Geelong JY 27 1855'.

2   'The best-laid schemes o' mice an' men,/ Gang aft a-gley./ And lea'e us nought but grief and pain,/ For promised joy.' *To a Mouse*, Stanza 7, Robert Burns (1759–1796).

3   A coach, which ran daily between Geelong and Ballarat on terrible roads. In 1856 the proprietors of the Estafette Line of Coaches, George Hotel, Ballarat, advertised that 'they have spared no expense to secure the most comfortable and commodious coaches in the colony; their horses are selected by the best judges; and they have none but the most skilful drivers in their employment.' *The Ballarat Times*, 20 March 1856, p. 1.

16   **[From WLR in Ballarat to MR in Geelong]**

[Mount Pleasant, Ballarat]
Saturday evening [28 July 1855]

[No salutation]

I have this moment my <u>own darling</u> received yours dated last Sunday,[1] now, do not blame me as you do! I have written constantly and regularly you ought to have had one <u>today</u> and another <u>this day last week</u> I went to the Post Office this morning and after waiting two long hours got nothing from the person I wished—However I make all allowance, I know there <u>must</u> be some little mistake now and then, and believing that I am <u>your own dear</u> Walter and that you love me as well as I do you, I fully believe we shall make it all right when we see one another—Cheer up, August is very near now! I have never heard any word of the missing letter, but am convinced it never came to Ballaaratt for two reasons 1ˢᵗ Because there is no other Dʳ R— here, and secondly because I am well known at the office—

Mʳ B looked very well today, your brother dropped in at the same moment and is looking very well tho' not in such good spirits as when I saw him last—

I hope all are well give my very kind love to all to Mʳˢ B. Miss Tilly and Miss Polly as well as your charming little freind Miss Ellen Jelfs—

I suppose you will have such a nice walk tomorrow, how I wish I were there!

Be sure and enjoy yourself my darling Mary for this is the last week or two that you will have them around you, remember you will be in an awfully dismal place, no pretty faces around you! but in their stead a lot of grumbling Irish, and poor people with occasionally a tipsy man or two! Ha! Ha! He! a pretty picture I've drawn of the future Mʳˢ Richardson's prospects! You must excuse this because I've been interruppted in almost every line until I forget how to spell and because I expect your brother William back every moment and he is to take it down to the White Horse to W.B. [William Bradshaw]—

Now do let me hear from you <u>dear sweetheart</u> this coming week and give me a good long letter, I know you will have <u>a house full</u> and I suppose be very busy but do find time <u>my own</u> love for a letter by next <u>Saturday</u> if you have not written by Wednesday—I got your last kind

nice letter on Monday and it consoled me during the week and I suppose this last note will
have to do this week. Ballaaratt is very dull weather fine; Brooke has not written to me since
dont forget your promise to write and ask him to come down in August, any more accidents?
This will make my second letter this week and redeem my character in your eyes. I wrote to
your brother Harold when I came up last time but I have never received any reply;

And so you all forgot to go to Church did you?

I have never seen Ted Bradshaw! Oh! for I have I was thinking of Charles![2] They appear
very nice, sensible, commonsense young men—Make all enquiries about the missing letters
my darling Mary, and believe me with every wish for your happiness (until you join me as
partner of my joys and sorrows in life)| Your very dear and fond and loving

      Walter

Text: ALS NLA MS133/1/111

[1]   WLR had received Letter 14 written by MR on Sunday, 22 July 1855.
[2]   Charles Feast Bradshaw (1829–1907), a miner at Ballarat, second son of William and Marion
    Bradshaw. He was christened on 18 August 1829 at St Mary Wesleyan Church, Ely,
    Cambridgeshire. He married Euphemia Gibson (c.1837–1887) in 1854 and they had eleven
    children: Mary McFarlane (b. 1855), Euphemia (1856–1857), Matilda Jane (b. 1858), Emma
    Buller (b. 1860), Euphemia (b. 1862), Janet Gibson (1865–1866), Charles (1867–1867),
    George Coates (b. 1868), Harriet Agnes (b. 1870), Florence Marion (b. 1873) and Elizabeth
    Janet (b. 1876). Charles's wife, Euphemia, died on 9 January 1887 from a curious combination
    of 'Shock from fire and Enlargement of the Liver'. She had been born in Paisley, Scotland,
    daughter of a contractor, David Gibson and his wife Mary née McFarlane (c.1810–1883).
    Emigrating to NSW in 1844–45, after eight years in Sydney, the family moved to Ballarat,
    Victoria, where she married Charles two years later.

17   [**From WLR in Ballarat to MR in Geelong**]

                                         [Mount Pleasant, Ballarat]
                          Thursday afternoon [2 August 1855]

[No salutation]

I wrote you my darling, by M^r W Bradshaw last Saturday and altho' I have not much to
say today I am anxious not to dissapoint you of a letter next Saturday, as you seem like myself
to look for one regularly—

Your last dear note told me by its tone that you were well and happy, altho' I fancy that
neither of us will be sorry when the time expires that separates us: the days moreover are daily
growing longer, and spring that most delightful of our seasons in our adopted home
approaches apace—Business I am glad to say continues good, and I am making preparations
for my final trip—I have two very amusing incidents to relate which may afford you as hearty
a laugh as they did me: I received yesterday along with yours of last Sunday[1] a very suspicious
letter addressed Mr Richardson and wh the Post-master doubted was for me; on opening it
I found it a little account from a medical gentleman in Melbourne to wit Mr Richardson
&c—For attendance on Mrs Richardson £20–0–0

The second is that I dream as of course every body does and that I dream of her I think
most of during the day is not to be wondered at but I had a dream the other night when all
around was still, that somehow or other business had managed to go all wrong, and that I was
ruined and compelled to fly; I remember distinctly saying to a freind for I had one left "But
my dear fellow, the worst of it is, that I was on the point of being married"—

I was much relieved when I awoke and found myself all right—

I do get considerably quizzed at ~~about~~ my being about to change my bachelors life—every one has to undergo these little matters, and I do not suppose we suffer more than others, in fact I rather enjoy it, for people seem to think me a lucky fellow!—

You must have waited a long time on Sunday evening if you sat up for your expected guests as I presume they did not arrive until Monday or Tuesday: Mʳ W. Bradshaw is very full of some philanthropic schemes and I fear thinks rather indifferently of me because I dont join, the fact is I have been so robbed and have had so many impositions practised upon me, that I think more hardly of the diggers than I did—

William was not quite well when I saw him last Saturday but I invited him to pay me another visit soon and if I did not find some improvement I told him I should make him have some other medical mans opinion[2]—

My little puppy is alive but sick, if I can rear it twill be a beauty—

I have no English letters, the May mail by which I expect letters from my mother and Smiths family has not arrived—

Strange to say altho' I do not practice I have now (just about when I am going down to see you again) a patient for whose life I have great doubts—His wife is the nicest person among all my neighbours and will be so glad of your company and society—If he lives we will have many a merry party—

I understand matters are very bad in town with the laboring classes, there is an influx of unemployed here which has the effect of reducing wages and making all grumble except the employers—

Mʳ Hydes, & Mʳˢ Hydes,[3] Mʳˢ Young[4] and the Geelong theatrical stars are coming here, also I believe Mʳˢ Catherine Hayes[5] ~~which~~ whom I promise you we shall go and hear if spared, as well as Mʳ G. V. Brooke[6] should he come here—

Give my kind love to the family circle, I will attend to Miss Polly's request about the letter I thought there was an enclosure—

I am glad to hear that Miss Tilly continues to make you laugh occasionally I half guess what it was about when you were writing me last! I hope the children[7] have afforded amusement and that now the fine weather has returned you enjoy many a nice walk, I shall expect to be shown all the pretty spots in the neighbourhood

No news from Brooke!—

I shall not fail to remember all to Mʳ Candy who I am happy to say is now likely to be a rich man, having managed to get an interest in a rich claim—

Once more darling, adieu! a thousand kisses! and my best wishes, with every kind thought until we meet to part no more in life,| Your loving

Walter

Text: ALS NLA MS133/1/112 and MS133/1/113

1 Presumably MR had written a letter on 29 July 1855, which has not survived.
2 William Bailey suffered from asthma.
3 John Proctor Hydes (*c.*1825–1882) was Charles Young's partner at the Queen's Theatre, Melbourne, before leasing the Theatre Royal, Geelong. His wife was Augusta Margaret née Huttmann. Alec Bagot, *Coppin the Great: Father of the Australian Theatre* (Carlton: Melbourne University Press, 1965), pp. 179–190.
4 Jane Eliza Young née Thomson (1827–1902) married to actor, Charles Young. She was born in Bath, daughter of English actress Martha Mary Thomson, who trained her as a dancer and actress; came to Tasmania with her parents and elder sister in 1837. She married Charles Young

(1819–1874) in Launceston, Tasmania, on 6 June 1845 and that year they joined George
Coppin's Company in Melbourne. From 1849, while Jane continued to perform under the
name of Mrs Charles Young, her husband worked mainly as manager and later lessee of Queen's
Theatre Royal. They became members of G.V. Brooke's company. They left for America and
England in 1857 (at her mother's insistence, since she believed that the English audiences would
be more appreciative of the talents of her daughter) and performed in Philadelphia in September
1857. Appearing opposite Jane Eliza was Hermann Vezin (1829–1910), an American actor,
who had trained for the stage in England. The Youngs returned to London and joined the
Saddler's Wells Company, where she was billed as Eliza Young. Although Charles achieved
considerable success as a burlesque actor, Eliza became even more famous. Vezin followed them
and by 1859 he and Eliza were appearing together in Shakespeare's plays. She moved to the
Haymarket Theatre and played Portia to Edwin Booth's Shylock. Charles Young returned to
Australia and Eliza divorced him in 1862, marrying Hermann Vezin the following year. She
then performed under the name of Mrs Hermann Vezin with continuing success.

5   Catherine Hayes (1825–1861), Irish operatic and ballad soprano; born in Limerick. She
appeared at Covent Garden in 1849 and was the first great world artist to visit Melbourne. She
sang at the Queen's Theatre in 1854.

6   Gustavus Vaughan Brooke (1818–1866), Dublin-born actor, made his debut at the Theatre
Royal, Dublin in 1833. He toured USA from 1851 to 1853 and signed an agreement to go to
Australia for George Coppin in Dublin on 13 September 1854. He arrived in Melbourne in
1855, opening George Coppin's new Olympic Theatre, Melbourne, on 30 July 1855. A partner
of Coppin from 1857 to 1859, they operated the Theatre Royal, the Olympic Theatre, Astley's
Amphitheatre, the Cremorne Gardens and four large hotels. He brought a company to the
Theatre Royal, Ballarat in 1860. He became infatuated with a young American actress and
returned with her to England in 1861. He died in the wreck of the steamer *London* on
11 January 1866 in the Bay of Biscay, while *en route* to Melbourne. See *FRM I*, p. 266.

7   Charles William and Marian Emma, the children of William Burrows and Rebecca Bradshaw,
who were visiting Bell Post Hill.

18   [From MR in Geelong to WLR in Ballarat]

Bell Post Hotel [Geelong]
Sunday evening [12 August 1855][1]

My dearest Walter

I am afraid you would think my last letter very short but I was so busy just at that time
& M[r] B. going off that I could not write more so I will try & write a long one this time to
make up for it   first thing, I must say, I was rather disappointed at not receiving any letter
from you yesterday   I quite expected one   how came you to forget to write? I am quite
disappointed but the time is drawing so near that there will not be reason to write many more.
I suppose I must now make up my mind but you must not be angry at my not being quite
ready to be married by the middle of the month but I think if you were to come down about
Wednesday Week—that will be about the 22nd I cannot possibly be ready before but you can
come thence & then you shall say when we shall be married but you must write again & tell
me whether that will do—We had a nice walk to the cave again to day the weather is
Beautiful—I hope it will continue so. We have had letters from Ellen Jelfs I think it is very
likely she may be down   I hope so   I begin almost to despair of seeing Brooke   we have had no
letters from him so we do not know where to write to poor fellow. I hope he is safe—I wish
you knew where he was but you are like us left in the dark as regards [h]is whereabouts   I was
sorry to hear from you dear such a poor account of William   I sincerely hope he is better   his
strength is not equal   I am afraid for the work he has to do   give my kind love to him. I am
sorry to say that M[rs] Bradshaw's two youngest children[2] have been very poorley all the week so

we have had to nurse them I think little Willie is very delicate I sent you a letter Harold left here by Mr Wells. I daresay you have received it before this. I am very glad to hear that Business is pretty good with you every thing down here is very dull little or nothing doing. I hope that your friend will have quite recovered before you leave Ballaraat. I should think that you did have a very good laugh when you received the Doctors Bill for attendance on Mrs Richardson & also at your dream. I did! it just amused me but perhaps not more than you I hope dear that you are quite well & that you have received letters from home I think I have been very fortunate lately I was a long time without any & now I get them all at once I received three more English letters on Thursday night—I have a great many to answer they are all angry with me because I had not written home for 12 months but wrote a long one about three months back & another about a month since So they will be getting them very soon. We have all got Bad colds but I suppose we are only in the Fashion but it is one fashion that we do not admire I hope dearest that you are free from one I am going to answer Ellens letter to night so shall have to be quick for it is getting late & we feel <u>tired</u> after our <u>long</u> walk I shall hope to receive a letter from you on Wednesday & then the next I shall see you down but <u>do not</u> walk it is too far & the roads to bad. Ellen desired her love to you & I shall send yours to her when I write to night. I cannot find any more news to tell you dear so you must excuse more to night—Mother Tilly & Polly send their kind love to you & with best love & kisses dearest Walter| as ever| your loving

    Mary

Text: ALS NLA MS133/1/5

Mary and Walter were married on 25 August 1855 and settled down to married life in Ballarat. Mary's sister, Sarah, was staying with them when the floods occurred on Sunday evening, 16 December 1855.

---

1   Response to Letter 17.
2   Rebecca Bradshaw's two youngest children: William (about eighteen months old) and baby Marian Emma (five months old), who were visiting their grandparents.

19   [From MR in Ballarat to Grace Bailey^1 in Leicester, England]

Miss G Bailey
[December 1855]

My dear Grace

    Walter has just done this^2 to please me to give you an idea of how ridiculous we all looked the night of the Flood.^{3} This is for Grace she must write to me—I have a Nugget^4 for all of you when I come home wishing you all a happy New Year| with love & kisses I remain| Your loving Sister

    Mary

Text: ALS NLA MS133/1/266

1   Grace Bailey (1839–1935), MR's youngest sister.
2   On the reverse of the letter is a sketch of the people—'Mary, Ellen (the Richardson's servant), Mrs Winterbottom, Alfred, Sarah, Walter at the door'—shop and house with the words 'a little idea of what occurred one night'; each person has a bubble of words—Mary, 'Oh! I'm so hot';

Ellen, 'Oh dear me look at the poor fowls'; Mrs Winterbottom (and Alfred), 'I'm afraid our tent
is carried away and listen to the cries of those women'; Sarah, 'Mary how do you feel? I am
shivering and fear the waters will rise higher'; Walter, 'Now then keep yourselves warm'.
Although at the time of the flood WLR was still a storekeeper and unregistered as a doctor, he
had always been known as a doctor and had occasional patients. He had drawn the words
'Dr Richardson' and 'Surgeon' on the roof of the building.

3   The floods occurred on Sunday evening, 16 December 1855. The Ballarat correspondent of *The
Geelong Advertiser* reported to *The Age* under the heading, 'Floods at Ballarat—Immense Loss of
Property' as follows: 'December is a fatal month for Ballarat—last year the sword [Eureka], and
this year fire and flood are the agents. On Sunday towards the evening it began to lighten and
thunder, and immediately the rain and hail followed. I have never in the colony seen such heavy
rain; it came down in literal torrents.' *The Age*, 19 December 1855, p. 5.

4   A lump of gold.

The Ballarat Years

1856

20   [From MR in Geelong to WLR in Ballarat]

[Bell Post Hotel, Geelong][1]
Sunday Even [3 February 1856]

My dear dear Walter

I thought you would like to hear from me by the remittance though I have no news to tell you. I do hope darling I shall soon hear from you Yesterday Polly & I went into Town on Horseback—I enjoyed it very much—I had Tilly's Hat & Habit we went quite early in the Morning & staid all day so I saw all my old friends they enquired very kindly after you dear to day the Frenchman[2] fetched us in a new Spring Cart to the Vineyards from whence we have just returned. I am so sorry darling that I cannot send you any grapes but there are none ripe I am so sorry I met my Brother John[3] yesterday he wanted Polly & I to go & have some dinner with him at Germans Town but we were expecting Mother[4] in Town but I said perhaps we would go another day. Give my love to Harold[5] & tell him that John say's his things are worth a great deal more than 20 £ & he better pay it for M[r] Marsh[6] is going to leave & wishes to know what is to be done about them to morrow evening we are expecting a few friends up to spend the evening so I suppose we shall be very merry "Ah! I do so wish my own darling that you were here I am afraid you will be very much worried whilst I am away but I must take the more care of you when I return

I hope Sarah[7] will arrive safely they all join me in kind love to her & not forgetting my dear Husband

Good bye darling with many kisses Your ever loving wife

Mary

God bless you take care of yourself| MR

Text: ALS NLA MS133/1/49

1 MR was staying with the Bradshaw family for Tilly's wedding.
2 Probably Samuel Perrottet (1827–1907), a French-speaking Swiss, born on 3 January 1827. He
   arrived in Victoria from Switzerland in 1847 and leased a property known as 'Barwondale' in
   the Barrabool Hills near Geelong and planted grapevines. He left his property in the care of a
   friend and went to the gold fields for a time. In a report in *The Age* on 28 September 1869,
   under the heading 'New Insolvents' he was listed as vigneron of Barrabool Hills with a deficit of
   £322–19–4. He became a wine merchant and ran the hotel at Glenormiston, near Terang. He
   married Catherine Craven in Mount Morack, Victoria in 1870 and they had nine children, one
   of whom predeceased his father. Information about the Perrottet family in Geelong and the
   Western District supplied by Mrs Jan Ross, great-grand-daughter, and Michael Sturmfels,
   Western District Historian. After twenty-five years in Victoria, Perrottet moved to NSW where
   he spent the last thirty-three years of his life as a grazier. He died on 17 August 1907 at Trangie,
   NSW. See *GW*, III, 18.
3 John Robinson Bailey (1826–1871), MR's oldest brother.
4 Marian Bradshaw.
5 Edward Harold Bailey (1828–1893), MR's second oldest brother.
6 Not identified.
7 Sarah Ann Bailey (1829–1911), MR's oldest sister.

21   [From WLR in Ballarat to MR in Geelong][1]

[Mount Pleasant, Ballarat]
Thursday. [7 February 1856]

My dear wife,

Sarah has I am sure told you of her hurried departure, and how I had no time to write a
longer epistle, we had heard the night before that he[2] was going to Ballaaratt & did not expect
him—However Sarah was soon ready tho' she did not breakfast here nor wd. she take a glass
of wine, I did prevail on her to take half a doz. biscuits of wh. I am sure she felt the benefit.

I was very sorry to part with her especially at such a time as the present, she behaved in
such a lady-like way during the whole time she was here, that I do not for a moment wonder
at M\r Michaelson's feeling a blank in his household during her abscence: I trust she will get
comfortably settled as she deserves.

I am so glad to hear that you are enjoying yourself my dearest do not hurry to return on
my account for I am sure this place will be so dull for you after the gaieties of Bell Post Hill: I
manage as best I can, and will get on pretty well, it is only a return to my old life, when I had
no one to love & to cuddle me at night; I quite forgot to send you down the other £5 by
Sarah, & indeed I had not got it I send it now by Harry.[3]

M\r Norman[4] told me he thought he saw you in town, William is all right again, I gave
your message to Harold and am so glad that you are reconciled to your brother John:[5] The
weather upon which so much of our comfort here depends, has been very sultry since your
departure, Thunder for 2 or 3 days with showers, today however the rain appears to have set in
steadily and the atmosphere is delightfully cool & pleasant. Had you a Thunder storm last
Monday night I want to know this, because I saw sheet lightening in the South: Sarah awoke
me in the night saying (she had called me a doz times) that she heard the creek rising, I got up
& went out but it was the wind this time. I returned Alick's[6] letter. I am sorry you sent it to
me: especially as I had just had one from his father[7] who poor man fancies he is earning a
name & saving money & who actually sends him out £100 to commence housekeeping! Dont

you think it is about time the wedding day was fixed I suppose it will be either the Thursday or the Monday I hope you have given the bride the benefit of your experience—

Good bye dear wife for today—

Friday [8 February]

It had rained all day yesterday, & at dusk the ~~creek~~ water came tearing over the dam as it did before, making nearly as much noise all night, the creek rose three or four feet and very few slept soundly; Ellen[8] says she ~~did~~ was awake until day-light: I am rather glad Sarah & you were from home, altho' last night I did feel lonely at the prospect of having to get out at the back window again. Thank God nothing unusual occurred and this day tho showery is bearable. The women miss you, and not a few have asked after you: we had every thing off the floors, and all your things on the shelves, matting & carpets up and we both slept in our clothes. Ballaaratt flat was under water but owing to the creek here being clear the water was not kept back: I shall I think move, as soon as you come back: You may give my love to all, I should so like to be present but I suppose matters will be managed just about as ours was

You need not come up with Harry unless you like, that is if he asks you and if Tilly would like it.

He told me he would bring you up, without my asking it so do not be uneasy about doing it, unless you would like to stay longer and provided you have some other means of coming back: do not come in the conveyance if you can avoid it. I have been compelled into reading Lucky[9] for want of something better & I like it very much: Ellen is a good girl and manages very well—

Saturday [9 February]

I do hope Harry will call for this—I have just been out splitting wood and cross cutting it with Ellen. I am going to have company to morrow to dinner M[r] Reynolds[10] & his brother. I trust you are still enjoying yourself and well. I dreamt of you last night also the night you first left: I am getting used to the big bed now altho at first I did feel it a leetle[11] strange.

The people are enquiring after Sarah, she promised one woman to cut out a baby's dress! I miss her very much—I suppose my dearest I may reckon on a letter from you on Monday, you must tell me when to expect you home, so that I may have things comfortable

This is an awfully cold day: but I have got a splendid fire: Business has been a little better since you left—I drew a tooth this morning & charged 10/. I have no objection to as many patients as like to come at that rate.

I hope you have been well, & that you have not required the services of D[r] Gunn.[12] M[r] Anderson[13] from Malop St called here yesterday & M[r] Thom:[14] I was saying that Miss Bradshaw was going to be united in the holy bonds of matrimony, when Mr Thom let out that he had once called there and they played the piano very nicely, & says he "there was a governess there then" Yes I said that was my wife:

M[r] Vineyards[15] has just called, and as he is going down tomorrow I take the opportunity of sending this by him. He says something about a piano: I hope you have got your eye on one under a hundred pounds, you had better not purchase it or engage for its removal until we get removed. He gave me a very sad account of Sarah on her journey! She was nearly fainting by his account for want of food—This not like her good sense.

Good bye dearest, God bless you, my love; I shall send Ellen up on Monday to the Post Office| Your fond husband

W Lindesay Richardson

Text: ALS NLA MS133/1/99 and MS133/1/100

1 The letter had been folded and sealed and on the back WLR wrote MR's address as follows: 'M⁺ W. Lindesay Richardson/ 'Bradshaw's Family Hotel'/ Bell Post Hill/ near Geelong'.

2 Mr Michaelson was Sarah's employer.

3 Henry Fisher Bannester.

4 Not identified.

5 It is not clear why Mary and John had quarrelled but he had a reputation as a forthright and opinionated man and it is likely that she would not allow him to treat her as a young girl once she became married.

6 Alick Cook (b. c.1828), WLR's step-cousin, stepson of Henry Sirée, Lucinda Cheyne's brother. Alick arrived in Melbourne on the *Wacousta* in May 1853 and stayed until November 1862. In 1839 Henry Sirée married a widow, who was listed in the *Index to the Act or Grant Books, And to the Original Wills, of the Diocese of Dublin 1800–1853 from the Appendix to the Thirtieth Report of the Deputy Keeper of the Public Records and Keeper of the State Papers in Ireland* (Dublin: 1899) as Charlotte Cook (alias Harricks). They had two children, Elizabeth and Horatio Nelson. Alick was the son by her first marriage. Lucinda Cheyne writes in Letter 45 (19 October 1859), 'Your Uncle Harry's wife has arrived but her dear boy has remains at Melbourne in a situation.' There is still some mystery about her first name, for on the passenger list of the *Champion of the Seas*, when she came to Victoria with her husband and two youngest children in 1857, she was called 'Elizabeth Siree', and she was always referred to by Lucinda Cheyne as 'Elizabeth' not 'Charlotte'.

7 Henry Sirée (b. c.1812), solicitor in Dublin, WLR's uncle and younger brother of WLR's mother. He graduated with a BA in 1831 from the University of Dublin.

8 The Richardsons' servant.

9 Not identified.

10 Not identified.

11 Little.

12 Dr Ronald Gunn, medical practitioner at Geelong.

13 Mr Anderson's shop was situated in the same street as John Robinson Bailey's old shop.

14 Probably the partner in Thom, Gray & Co; they set up a Wholesale & Retail Drapery & Clothiers on Sturt Street, Ballarat.

15 Samuel Perrottet, a French-speaking Swiss.

22 [From MR in Geelong to WLR in Ballarat]

Bell Post Hill
[Friday, 15 February 1856]

My own darling Husband

I have just time to write a little to you before going into Town[1] for Father[2] is going to take Polly & I in on Horseback because I expect a letter from you in return to the one I wrote last Friday so I shall finish this in Town The Wedding[3] came off on Wednesday morn—every thing past off very nicely but they did not leave here until yesterday morning on account of the weather being rather inclined to be stormy we had a very nice agreeable party in the evening & kept the wedding up untill 6 oclock next morning I did enjoy myself so much but all day we felt tired so I did not write to you. Next Thursday I & Mother are coming up in the four wheel Carriage so you may look out for us love about Tea time for we shall start very early & get through in a day—please dear to tell Ellen to have every thing tidy & comfortable for us but I need not say that for I know darling you will see to that We may be up on Wednesday but cannot say for certain but we shall be sure to ~~leave~~ be there on Thursday the reason of my not coming sooner is because Mother couldn't leave sooner & she thought I should come up much more comfortable than if I came with anyone else Many thanks love for the five pounds which I received safely by the Frenchman.[4] I was sorry to hear about the heavy rains again but we did not have the Thunder here until the Tuesday night & then not much but it rained here all Thursday & part of Friday

all the news I have to tell dearest I shall leave until I see you I hope I shall have a letter to day Mother Father & Polly all send their love & with love & kisses to your own dear self from| Your truly loving wife

Mary

P.S. I shall finish this at Browns if I get a letter & it wants answering I shall not get any piano—

Text: ALS NLA MS133/1/53

1   Geelong town centre.
2   William Bradshaw.
3   Harriet Matilda Bradshaw (Tilly) (1836–1914) married Henry Fisher Bannester on Wednesday, 13 February 1856 at the residence of the Mr Bradshaw Senior, Hope Town, near Geelong (Register 922). The officiating Minister was Isaac Harding and the ceremony was conducted according to the rites and ceremonies of the Wesleyan Church. Henry Bannester, who was twenty-five years old, was described on the marriage certificate as a 'Gold Digger' and Tilly, who was twenty years old, was described as a 'Lady'. The witnesses were the bride's father, William Bradshaw, and the bride's brother, Edward Bradshaw.
4   Samuel Perrottet.

23   [From WLR in Ballarat to MR at Collingwood Stockade]

[Mount Pleasant]
Wednesday [November 1856]

My darling Mary

I have just been out taking a walk round; No xii have knocked off entirely, are not working, and have ceased working up for want of water, they think it will be best to let the paddock remain until next winter!!!!!!

Harold's[1] party are compelled to put their pipes in, which will take them a month at least before they can be at work again! Did you ever hear such confounded luck as our freinds and relations have on this hill—

Vales hole "The 12 apostles"[2] will turn out 4 lbs weight per man, I saw him this morning, digging puddling clay; he had heard from Mrs Vale, you can tell her he is looking very well—He has not paid me a 6^d of his account yet—

Yesterday was very sultry, a little rain in the night & this morning, rendering it pleasantly cool but there is every indication of a hot and dry summer—

I cannot sleep at nights, last night altho' my walk fatigued me so much that I went to bed at 8, I could not get to sleep until 12 oclock; the night before I was just as bad—what is the cause I hardly know, but I can guess—I think I have made up my mind to follow my profession when we move, build a comfortable house for you, and confine myself entirely to that.[3] Times are so altered now and storekeeping so knocked up that I think it will be best to make a start; so when you come back we will choose a site and commence moving as soon as I can raise the money. You can ask Sarah to come up if you like, or we can advertise for a companion, or you might look out for <u>one now</u> as you are just on the spot to choose, also look out for a little parrott[4] in a little cage to hang in your parlour—

You must write me longer letters for your last was very short, commencing with not having heard from me and ending as usual by saying somebody was waiting for you and therefore there was not time to devote to me!—

Not independently of the pleasure your letters afford me, the occupation of letter writing is very improving altho' it may be a troublesome one—

Have you heard of Alick?[5] or seen him? Did you go to Church last Sunday, I think M[r] Vale get longer letters, and more news that I do, so he told me John took M[rs] Vale and M[rs] Whiteman[6] to the Theatre[7] on Tuesday, and set off on Wednesday last. I hope the poor fellow will be more successful in his new career![8]

I have packed up nearly all the goods there are two cartloads, and think I have pretty well exhausted all topics of news. The piano is as bad as ever it was, the sultry weather of yesterday has had a ruinous effect on it! I am very sorry for I was getting on capitally, could play the two first pages!

Umpelby[9] has just passed: poor little chap is complaining fearfully of hard times.

Vale & Sheppard[10] do not come, they have taken to playing at a public house and formed a whist club so that our evenings are rather lonely. You know Allen,[11] he was attacked one night lately while crossing the flat from the Whitehorse Hotel to the Punt by two men one of whom presented a pistol demanding his money—

No xii's shaft horses &c are to be sold by auction on Friday next—

With kind regards to M[r] & M[rs] Turnham[12] love to Sarah I remain my dearest wife with best love & a hundred thousand kisses and hugs for your darling self| Your fond husband

     Walter

Text: ALS NLA MS133/1/14(a)

1   Edward Harold Bailey (Ned), MR's brother.
2   'The Twelve Apostles' was the name of Mr Vale's goldmine.
3   WLR registered with the Medical Board of Victoria on 1 December 1856, when he was listed as No. 467. Prior to his registration, he delivered two babies in Sebastopol in 1856 for Dr Charles S. Kenworthy. *Cases* 121 (21 October 1856) and 122 (17 November), a girl and a boy respectively. His first case after his registration was *Case* 123: Mrs Davis from Magpie on 9 March 1857 ('in consultation with Dr Kenworthy') where he operated to remove a dead foetus ('child dead 7 months').
4   'And a cage with a little parrot in it, hanging at the window!' *FRM I*, p. 179.
5   Alick Cook.
6   Elizabeth Whiteman née Pierse (1833–1874), a governess before her marriage on 15 November 1854 to John Whiteman (1820–1892), whose card for his Veterinary, Shoeing and Forge business is preserved in WLR's Scrapbook (NLA MS133/1/293). Elizabeth was born in London, the daughter of William Fitzmaurice Pierce (superintendent of police at Hobart) and Elizabeth née Dede. John Whiteman, a farrier, auctioneer and veterinary surgeon, became a Member of the Victorian Legislative Assembly, representing Emerald Hill (February 1866 to December 1867). He was born in Dunchurch, Warwickshire, the son of a blacksmith, and educated at the local schools. He moved to London in 1844 and assisted a veterinary surgeon until he migrated to Sydney in 1850, arriving in Victoria in 1852; after a career as a vet and farrier and then parliamentarian, he set up as an auctioneer in partnership with J. D. Mahon. He was a licensee of the Clarence Hotel; councillor of Emerald Hill (1862–1874) and mayor (1864–1865). He wrote *Sparks and Sounds from a Colonial Anvil* (1873). He was a member of the Yorick and Athenaeum Clubs. He married a second time in 1875 to Alice Anne Cornwell.
7   The Geelong Theatre Royal, with G. V. Brooke's company, commenced its summer season on Monday, 20 October 1856.
8   JRB became an editor of *The Ballarat Star* in early 1857. He had sold his business and had been farming some land in Germantown, Geelong, and, at the same time, had been helping to edit a Geelong newspaper. He had recently (September 1856) unsuccessfully contested the election in Geelong for the first Victorian Parliament.

9 Edward William Umpelby or Umphelby (1783–1871) ran the Letter and Commission Office at Sebastopol. He was born in London, (the son of William Umphelby, a farmer, and Elizabeth née Williams) where he married Sarah Letts before emigrating first to Tasmania in about 1851–52 and then to Victoria in 1855. He and Sarah had nine children. He died aged eighty-eight in George Street, South Melbourne, on 2 October 1871 and his death certificate describes his profession as 'Gentleman'. His eldest son, Lieutenant-Colonel Charles Edward Ernest Umphelby (1853–1900), born Richmond, Victoria, was the first Australian to command the Victoria Regiment of Royal Australian Artillery (based at Queenscliff) in 1891. Lieutenant Umphelby died on 12 March 1900 from a wound received during the battle of Dreifontein, Orange Free State.

10 William Horder Sheppard (b. 1830), a druggist, born in Fordingbridge, Hampshire. The following year, he married Elizabeth Roberts on 16 August 1857.

11 Not identified.

12 Joseph Turnham (c.1812–1880), prison warden; born in London. At the time of this letter Joseph was the chief warden of the Collingwood Stockade (appointed 23 March 1855). He was a younger brother of William Henry Turnham, who had married Sarah Robinson, sister of Elizabeth Bailey. He was therefore the brother of Mary's uncle rather than her 'real' uncle.

24 [From WLR in Ballarat to MR at the Turnhams]

[Mount Pleasant, Ballarat]
Friday evening [November 1856]

My dear wife

I received yours of Tuesday this day and as you are as anxious to see me to take you home perhaps I may come next Monday if matters progress favourably.

There has been a sale today lot No xii the proceeds came to upwards of £300–0–0 so that I shall have £20 to bring with me if that will suffice for our expenses I propose / God willing/ setting out on Monday morning by the Geelong coach so you can meet the Geelong steamer wh. lands passengers I think at ~~Geel~~ Sandridge, should you be able to meet me at the wharf or at the railway station I shall be rejoiced to see your dear smiling pretty face once more for to tell you the truth I have been very lonely. I am anxious that this letter should be in time for Umpelby so you will I know excuse brevity;

Kind love to Uncle & Aunt[1] until I see them in person to thank them for their kindness to my dearest Mary.| God bless you dearest love| Your loving husband

Walter

Text: ALS NLA MS133/1/56

1 Joseph and Elizabeth Turnham.

25 [From John Cheyne[1] in Melbourne to WLR in Ballarat]

[Melbourne]
[1856[2]]

[Opening page(s) missing]

had to push him on altho—from real ill health I had thought it would have been all the other way—everything belongs to me—Cameras Chemicals—Furniture—properties & all.—He[3] brought nothing but himself into the concern & had I had but someone with the same as myself I should be doing twice as well—He was to have put in £40—but by his own account got swindled by his employer. I do not think I am unjust to him but I gave him more credit for energy & artistic ability I belie than he deserved as to photography he knew less than I did—& he managed to alienate McGlashon[4] from his liking & interest in my affairs in a great measure,—to my sorrow—altho the old boy still, & latterly particularly is very kind—how I wish I could buy—an instantaneous Camera of his—& certain genuine chemicals his partner has lately sent him out.—& now I fear it will be impossible to have them. It is the sudden death of his partner that determines him to return at once without waiting for the money he was to receive from Government—

Thursday. Nothing cd be done by Thursday.—

I have made an arrangement with a Mr Knight[5] to release my lanterns on condition we apply photography for likenesses & views for them & he to share the profits—so I hope after this week I will lose one drain upon my receipts. On no week you see have we failed to pay rent & boardinghouses from our receipts—even at the worst so the game even in winter is a safe one—& in spring & summer an excellent paying one. Did you join me the rooms wd form an ample dwelling home, for you & yr wife & are in a capital central situation for medical practice.

The Furniture is I may say yr own & wd want but little additions & you might depend that now at least you would find me a steady & docile partner for I am weary of factitious excitement—an independent living is all the object of my hopes—if I can be said to have hopes at all—Well I have worked night & day at this business & have mastered the process & the elements of it—but it is a most fascinating [process?] & where it will stop none can tell I only wish I had been bred a Chemist. Dr Kenworthy[6] called—& spoke of buying a camera—I was busy when he came & could not give him the reception or attention I wished He did not stay long & seemed surprised at my altered appearance I certainly was not well that day but I am gradually

[MS133/1/264] at home. I have been asked to lecture on photography & show photographs by the oxy hydrogen gas[7] at the Atheneum[8]—& as soon as I can get a sufficient number of specimens I will accept it—Well it is now 9 oclock & I will home to my Lodging

Write quickly & say if there is any intention on yr part of joining me A great deal of money might be made by a tour through the Country—taking Likenesses & acquiring at the same time a series of Views of the Country for transmission home & exhibition.—

If I have anything more to say tomorrow I will add

Good   night—Love   to   Mary   &   Miss   Bailey[9]—I   would   never   mislead you—remember—|Yrs affectionately—

Jack

Text: ALS NLA MS/1/263 and MS133/1/264

1   John Cheyne (1829–1859), WLR's half-brother. He came to Victoria with WLR's second cousin, Mervyn Richardson (b. 1834), aboard the *Goldfinder*, which arrived in Melbourne on 23 October 1853.
2   Very difficult to date, but prior to his departure from Victoria for Hobart and thence India. Probably late 1856.
3   Scott, John Cheyne's partner in a photographic business. An advertising card for Cheyne and Scott, 7 Collins Street East is preserved in WLR's Scrapbook. (NLA MS133/1/293).
4   Photo of 'Old Mcglashon' is in WLR's scrapbook (NLA MS133/1/293). 'A. Mcglashon' is listed as a photographer in 1856 in Melbourne (with no address) in Alan Davies and Peter Stanbury, *The Mechanical Eye in Australia: Photography 1841–1900* (Melbourne: Oxford University Press, 1985) p. 195.

5   William Knight, 43 Victoria Parade, Collingwood was listed in the Sands & Kenny's *Directory for 1859* under 'Daguerrean and Photographic Artists'. In 1861 he moved to Brisbane as the employee of Thomas Ham, the engraver and lithographic draftsman. Alan Davies and Peter Stanbury, pp. 46–47.

6   Dr Charles Kenworthy (b. *c*.1824) was educated in Pennsylvania (MD, Penn. 1848). Arriving in Ballarat eighteen months prior to December 1854, he was at the Stockade on the day of the uprising, having offered his services as a surgeon in case there were any armed clash with the military. But after the affray, Kenworthy disappeared from the Stockade and was with the officials in the Camp when the prisoners were marched in. As all the American agitators were subsequently released through Kenworthy's endeavours, he was considered by Carboni to have been a spy. Kenworthy had accompanied one of the mortally ill insurgents, the Canadian Lieutenant Ross, to the Star Hotel. Despite the rumours and insinuations by Carboni, Kenworthy was highly regarded in Sebastopol where he continued to practise until 1864. He was honorary surgeon at Ballarat Hospital in 1857 and 1861, and President of the Horticultural Society in 1859 and 1860, with WLR as Vice-President. (See Letter 44.) He returned to the USA in 1864. Bowden, p. 114.

7   Illumination was produced by burning a small piece of lime or marble in a stream of oxyhydrogen gas, by which means a most brilliant light was given out.

8   The Athenaeum Hall, not the Athenaeum Club which was not founded until 1868.

9   Sarah Ann Bailey (1829–1911), eldest sister of Mary Richardson.

1857

26   [From LC in Brighton, England, to WLR in Ballarat]

17 Buckingham Place,[1] West Cliff Brighton| Sussex, England
Sep[tbr] 9th 1857

My dearest Walter

Altho' in your letter to your father[2] received a few days ago, you only mention having received <u>one</u> of mine, and that one not very much to your taste, I write to say that [I] trust long before this reaches you, you will have received several others, which together with <u>many</u> newspapers, may prove more acceptable Since the commencement of the horrors in India,[3] unprecedented in the history of nations I have sent you and John[4] many newspapers "Times"—"Witness",[5] "Herald", "Chronicle" &c—Brighton Guardian to John, and others, from him I have never had a line since he left Cap[tn] Cheyne,[6] altho' I have written to <u>him</u> repeatedly—this I confess has grieved me not a little, especially <u>now</u> when my health declines so rapidly, and my sight is failing with blindness of <u>one</u> eye threatened.—

I mentioned to you I think in a former letter, the decline of your Sister Caroline's[7] health after and caused by the birth of a daughter[8] She has not rallied—nor is she likely to do so, we caused a consultation to be held, last week between her present medical adviser D[r] Adams and her former attendant D[r] Durham—

Uterine derangement to some extent is present and a complete overthrow of the system, affords little hope if <u>any</u>, of a reestablishment—emaciation to an alarming extent, want of power to take any sustenance, haemorrhage almost always present, intense pain, sleeplessness, sickness, faintness, are the prevailing symptoms, and I am unable to go to her, your father says he could not answer for the consequences of such a journey, in my present broken down condition of constitution—The Summer here has been the most intensely hot, ever remembered in Europe,—it has told severely on us as well as on many others—and we are now old, and not able to bear up under the constant drain of great perspirations—

Mervyn Richardson[9] has returned home!—Henry[10] has seen him—he says John is doing well, he has never written to me, nor yet his father since he left Hobart Town!—

I am sorry my daughter Mary[11] has had a "fausse couche"[12]—yet I am sure it is a mercy both for her and you, I trust by care and quiet, she will recover her strength, and be saved the wear, tear, and anxiety of a family, for some years to come—she is very young yet, and will be better able by and bye, for bringing up children—you are so companionable, she cannot need them—[13]

Lucinda[14] is to leave Kyneton[15] in Oct^br I shall be well pleased to have her out of the Bush, and away from that family you will preserve any letters for her which I may entrust to you, until you know where to remit them—I have had very few from her of late, I fear she does not know her Sister's danger, nor our anxiety respecting her—

Miss F—[16] is pretty well travelling about, in order to keep dear little Alex^r[17] from the Priests—now desirous to seize on every soul they can, as their influence is on the wane in my dear native land,[18] a desire for the Scriptures having spread, with the ability to read.

Your Uncle Charles's[19] death was rather a distressing one, your father when he wrote to you did not know all the particulars, which he afterwards learned from two very full and explicit letters of Dr Christison;[20] this is the summary; In Nov^br Charles had an acute attack of Bronchitis; he managed himself, and on its removal was reduced to great weakness, he caught cold in Jany and the disease returned, was again subdued, but increasing weakness supervening, on the 20th Feby he sent for Dr Christison, who finding him with a thready pulse which on his attempting to get out of bed fluttered and intermitted in such an alarming manner, that Dr C. insisted on administering to him some brandy and water, counselled him to get a nurse instantly who should never leave him a moment, and who would constantly administer great nourishment,—this advice he would not follow, but agreed to get a medical man in the immediate neighbourhood, as D^r C was too far for an emergency—he saw him again however on the [21st] found he had not followed any of his directions, and urged him to remain in bed. as he thought him too weak to rise which he proposed doing as he thought himself well: nothing more of that his last day's history on earth is known, beyond the statement of his housekeeper who about 8 oc. in the evening "heard some odd kind of fumbling on the floor of the room, above her and thinking he wanted something, went up"—

Charles was on the floor in the last gasp, and as she approached him, the struggle ended and life was over!—it is supposed he got out of bed for some purpose, that faintness came on, and for want of help, proved just what Dr C. had apprehended fatal! so the obstinacy he manifested thro' life, caused its termination—Your father was ill in bed when the news came recovering from the very same complaint but under my care; I opened the letter containing the intelligence, and thus saved him the shock by receiving it myself—he left all his money

[Page(s) missing]

Text: AL NLA MS133/1/25

[1]   Lucinda and Bayne Cheyne were living in a substantial but moderately sized single-fronted three-storey terraced house, with basement kitchen. The house, which is the second house from the eastern end of the row, still stands today, but has been turned into three apartments. The ground floor front room has two large casement windows. Over the front door and ground floor

windows is an elegantly curved iron and glass verandah, which continues along the row of houses. Buckingham Road runs parallel with the seashore, at the top of a hill, and is a good fifteen minutes walk from the promenade. At the front there is only a very small garden with an attractive tiled path and three tiled steps to the front door, but at the rear there is a large walled garden.

2 WLR's stepfather, Dr Bayne Cheyne (1788–1868).

3 News of the Indian Mutiny, which started at Meerut on 10 May 1857, reached England in June. Meerut was the largest British military station and widespread discontent among the Indian troops at the overbearing attitude of the East India Company had been growing. The final spark was lit when some Indian soldiers had been gaoled for refusing to use rifle cartridges supposedly lubricated with pigs' and cows' fat, which were taboo substances to both Muslims and Hindus. The remaining troops mutinied, releasing eighty-five of their gaoled friends. Several British officers and their families were killed during the melee. The Indian soldiers escaped to Delhi, where they proclaimed the King of Delhi as the Emperor of India. The conflict spread rapidly, continuing until 1859. The East India Company was abolished in 1858.

4 John Cheyne (1829–1859).

5 *The Witness*, a bi-weekly newspaper published in Edinburgh, had been founded in 1840 by the leaders of the Free Church of Scotland movement. See endnote to Letter 33 on Hugh Miller, who was the first editor.

6 Captain Alexander Cheyne (1785–1858), brother of Dr Bayne Cheyne. He emigrated first to WA on the *James Pattison*, arriving 1834 and after a year, he sailed on the *Caledonian* to Hobart Town where he spent the next twenty-three years and was at one time director of public works. He died 6 July 1858.

7 Caroline Richardson (b. 1822), daughter of Lucinda Cheyne and her first husband, Alexander Richardson; younger sister of Walter. She was married to her cousin Henry Richardson (1822–1888) and they had four children: Marmaduke Cheyne (1851–1925), Lindesay (b. 1853), Walter Lindesay (1855–1863) and Lucinda (b. 22 April 1857). Caroline outlived her husband, Henry. In late 1888, MR, Ettie (HHR) and Lil visited her and her son, Marmaduke Cheyne Richardson, in Cambridge, where he held a curacy and was tutor to the sons of a titled personage. See *MWY*, pp. 91–92. MR visited her in England again as she travelled back (after the marriage of HHR in Dublin on 30 December 1895) from Dublin to Germany in January 1896.

8 Lucinda Richardson, born 22 April 1857.

9 Mervyn Richardson (b. 1834), third son of WLR's cousin, John Richardson (oldest son of Marmaduke Jenny Richardson) and Anna née Bristow. He sailed with John Cheyne (WLR's half-brother) to Melbourne on the *Goldfinder*, arriving in Melbourne on 23 October 1853.

10 Henry Richardson (1822–1888), youngest son of Marmaduke Jenny Richardson; cousin and husband of Caroline Richardson and uncle of Mervyn.

11 MR (Mary Richardson) (1835–1896), her daughter-in-law.

12 A miscarriage (French). There is an intriguing entry in WLR's *Registry of Midwifery Cases*; Case 129 reads: 'Mary R., 21 [under the heading 'Age'], 1 ['Number of Pregnancy'], Dec' 28 ['Date when last Menstruation ceased'], ? ['Supposed Period of Conception'], preceded by a sudden shock, haemorrhage at once.' WLR did not date this entry but it appears after one dated 9 July 1857; if he had then written to his stepfather immediately after this event, Lucinda Cheyne would have known about this miscarriage. The facts seem to fit Mary Richardson: it was her first pregnancy; she was twenty-one; she would remember the date of her last period as 28 December was her birthday (many of the entries for other women under this heading are rather vague).

13 See *FRM II*, p. 60.

14 Lucinda Richardson (b. 1820), eldest daughter of Lucinda Cheyne and 1st husband, Alexander Richardson; sister of Walter. She had arrived in Melbourne on the *Champion of the Seas* on 30 December 1854.

15 Kyneton, where Lucinda was working as a governess, is situated approximately eighty kilometres north-west of Melbourne.

16 Caroline Fector, christened 26 May 1804 at St Mary the Virgin, Dover, Kent, youngest daughter of John Minet Fector and his wife Ann Wortley Montagu, who was related to Lady Mary Wortley Montagu (1689–1762); Caroline had two older sisters and a younger brother: Ann Judith Laurie Fector, born 21 October and christened on 30 November 1799, who married Henry Pringle Bruyeres on 4 December 1822; Charlotte Mary, christened 27 March 1801, who married Sir John Bayley, 2nd Bart and whose son Lyttleton Bayley (1827–1910) (see Letter 40

endnotes for short biography) emigrated to Australia in 1858; and John Minet, christened on 7 April 1812. Caroline was the close friend of Lucinda Cheyne and assisted her in the scheme to prevent Alick Richardson, grandson of Lucinda Cheyne and nephew of Walter, from being brought up a Catholic. An additional note to Miss Fector's family background should include a coincidental reference in a letter written by Mrs Elizabeth Montagu (1762–1800), first cousin of Lady Mary Wortley Montagu's husband, Edward. She wrote to her friend, the poet Elizabeth Carter, from Calais on 23 June 1776, after a trip across the Channel from Dover: 'If any English pass to Calais of yr acquaintance recommend Mr. Fectors [Caroline's grandfather] packets and Capt. Osborne, the civilest best conductor of Ladies in a high wind for he is all attentions and honestly told me before I embarkd that there was rather too fresh a gale, but as ye passage is perfectly safe I wd not loiter at Dover.'

[17] Alexander Richardson (1845–1900), third son of WLR's brother Henry D. Richardson (1816–1849) and his wife, Ellen née O'Connor.

[18] Ireland.

[19] Captain Charles Cheyne (1786–1857), brother of Bayne Cheyne, died on 23 February 1857 in Edinburgh, Scotland.

[20] Sir Robert Christison (1797–1882), physician and toxicologist; son of Alexander Christison, professor of the humanities at the University of Edinburgh (1806–1820). After graduating at Edinburgh in 1819, he proceeded to London and then to Paris where he studied toxicology under Mathieu Orfila (1787–1853), the founder of toxicology. In 1822 he was appointed Professor of Medical Jurisprudence at the University of Edinburgh, and from 1832 to 1877 held the chair of Materia Medica. He became physician to Queen Victoria (1848), president of the Edinburgh Royal Society (1868–1873), and a baronet (1871). He contributed to many journals and wrote the standard *Treatise on Poisons* in 1829. Four of his nephews emigrated to Australia. His namesake, Robert Christison (1837–1915), became the most prominent (see *ADB*) as a pastoralist and a founder of the Queensland Meat Export Company at Townsville. This nephew's elder daughter, Mary Montgomerie (Mimi) Bennett (1881–1961) (see *ADB*), is described by Henry Reynolds as probably the most important Australian humanitarian activist of the 1930s and 1940s. Her allegations at a British Commonwealth League Conference in London in June 1933, that Australia was condoning slavery in the treatment of Aboriginal people, was her first of many forays into Australian politics. Henry Reynolds, *This Whispering in Our Hearts* (St Leonards: Allen & Unwin, 1998), pp. 200, 220.

27   [From LC in Brighton, England, to WLR in Ballarat]

17 Buckingham Place, West Cliff, Brighton, |Sussex, |England
Oct[br] 2nd 1857

My dear Walter

If you get all the letters I write, I do not think you can call me a bad correspondent, for an old woman!—I cannot tell how many newspapers I have sent you these last 3 months, three at least every mail, and sometimes four—all full of this most disastrous India Rebellion, giving accounts the most terrible of the massacres there, 5000 christians have been butchered, with cruelties unprecedented amongst the most barbarous savages: The King of Eternity only knows how it will all end,—

I have my own anxieties about you all; I should like to hear from you a little more frequently; of John I know nothing, a letter I wrote to him a year ago has been returned to me, and his Uncle says he has not had any answers to several letters he had written to him for many months. I fear he has gone off again to the diggings, having got tired of Photography: when Lucinda wrote last she mentioned that he was in bad health; it is now many months since she wrote to me, and Henry has not heard either. Poor Caroline still languishes, there is no change in her symptoms, strength at the lowest ebb, cannot sit up, cannot even bear the being carried in her husband's arms to be laid on a sofa in a tent your Uncle Nelson[1] put up in a field they have beyond the garden looking upon the beautiful bay of Dublin—her little girl[2] will be 6 months old, on the 22nd Inst.—Henry is well, so are the children <u>their</u> little Walter Lindsay, is a very beautiful boy, it was my particular request that he should be named after <u>you</u>, do you ever write to Caroline?

If you can give me any intelligence of Lucinda or John I beg you will do it, I am very anxious about <u>her</u>, knowing she was to leave Kyneton last month, her Aunt Mrs Harry Sirée[3] I believe had invited her, to pass some time with her until she procured another situation, but they may have left Melbourne; I have in my two last letters to you, enclosed one in each for Lucinda, according to her wishes, she ~~had~~ said you would have instructions where to forward them—John's neglect of his father and myself is painful—your father especially feels it acutely, he received yours of June 15th and felt grateful for your remembrance [missing word(s)] he is wonderfully well considering everything [missing word(s)] not forgetting his age(!)

I have a nice garden and cultivate flowers with some success and he begins to take a great interest in the [garden], and even <u>delight</u>—

We are at present rather anxious about his brother George,[4] he has been very desirous of returning to England, but now we learn with no little distress, that he has <u>heart</u> ~~complaint~~ disease (the Aorta) being affected in the same way your Uncle Bruce[5] was—<u>this</u> tries your father—deeply—

You must excuse bad writing, my eyes no longer allow me to be particular, I am forbidden to use them, except as little as possible, and told I am in danger of being blind if I transgress the injunction—I shall send with this two Newspapers, do inform me whether you receive all I send or not—and let me hear from you, as I am anxious about your Rheumatism. Give my best love to my daughter Mary, in which your Father cordially joins, and believe me my very dear Walter| with much love| Your attached and anxious| Mother

     Lucinda Cheyne

I send 3 Newspapers [Torn corner]

19th September, 23rd

stamped, indepen

in the paper.

May God bless you my beloved Son, and your dearest Mary [until] I may meet with you in His Kingdom, where no parting nor tears will be—Amen—

    Text: ALS NLA MS133/1/26 [Damaged]

1   Horatio Nelson Sirée (b. 1808), brother of Lucinda Cheyne, married a widow, Catherine Nelson née Wiley in 1833 as listed in the *Index to the Act or Grant Books, And to the Original Wills, of the Diocese of Dublin 1800–1853 from the Appendix to the Thirtieth Report of the Deputy Keeper of the Public Records and Keeper of the State Papers in Ireland* (Dublin: 1899). Whether she was called 'Nan' as a nickname or whether he had remarried, it is not clear. He was a medical doctor and later lived in Dalkey where Walter visited him in 1867 and 1868. See Letter 144.

2   Also called Lucinda Richardson (b. 22 April 1857).

3   Elizabeth or Charlotte Sirée (b. *c.*1810), wife of Henry (Harry) Sirée, brother of Lucinda Cheyne. In March 1857, she, Henry, and their two children (Elizabeth aged fifteen and Horatio Nelson aged thirteen) arrived in Melbourne on the *Champion of the Seas*. Her son, Alick Cook, was already living in Melbourne. After a short stay, Harry decided to return to Ireland and, after leaving Horatio in Ireland and Bessie in England, he travelled round America. Mrs Sirée remained in Melbourne with her son before moving to Castlemaine to live with Bayne Cheyne's nephew, the Reverend John Cheyne and his wife. They helped her to return to England on the *Yorkshire*, which departed Melbourne on 30 July 1859 and arrived in London in October 1859. Her husband returned to Dublin from the States at the same time. Alick Cook remained in

Australia until he set sail for England on board the *True Briton*, which left Melbourne on
15 November 1862. (See Letters 84, 86 and 87.)

4   George Cheyne (1790–1869), brother of Bayne Cheyne. He and his wife, Grace, were pioneers
     in Albany, WA, arriving there in June 1831 on the *Stirling*. They returned to England and
     finally Scotland in 1860.

5   Bruce Cheyne (1793–1856), youngest brother of Bayne Cheyne. He emigrated to Sydney in the
     1840s, was then in Melbourne prior to 1853, and finally went to WA to join his brother,
     George. He died of heart disease in Albany on 7 January 1856.

1858

28   [From LC in Brighton, England, to WLR and MR in Ballarat]

17 Buckingham Place |West Cliff, Brighton| Sussex.

July 10th 1858

My beloved Walter and Mary

I have been consistently ill since I wrote last and have suffered a great deal—Your Father
has been ill, owing I think to his anxiety about me being obliged to attend to me during the
night he is now threatened with Lumbago and cannot write a few lines without pain, and '
going to bed immediately. I think we told you of your Uncle George's[1] precarious condition
owing to heart disease; the 21st last month we had a letter from him, announcing the
dangerous illness of Capt Cheyne,[2] and a letter from his physician stating that he had no hope
of his recovery; Capt C. had some beautiful King Charles dogs, in walking out with them one
day, on arriving home, he missed <u>one,</u> and dreading the loss of it, he set out again and walked
a great way in search of it, continuing the exertion for 3 or 4 hours, on his return the little
animal was at home, Capt C. felt extreme fatigue became ill, took to bed, and <u>vomitted blood</u>
the discharge, becoming daily larger, in fact he was we think dying of weakness, when the Dr
wrote—I need not say how your father and I felt <u>this,</u> John having forsaken him, who ought
to have been a comfort and a son to him—I have deferred writing you these few lines, hoping
this months mail would enable us to convey whatever intelligence we might receive to you—it
has not however yet arrived—Caroline has been severely ill since I last wrote, and is ordered
away from the sea, two of her fine boys have also been very ill, there is a bad throat complaint
going here called Diphtherite,[3] it has cut off several people and one eminent medical man, it
has also prevailed in Dublin. I had a letter from my brother Harry[4] the day before yesterday
telling me that his daughter Bessie was seriously ill, she has been since Xmas with her Mother's
Sister, at Woolwich, who is married to a Dr Halahan,[5] physician to the R.A.[6] Hospital, that
ague has prostrated her, that lung disease has set in also, and change of air urgently
advised—he asked me to take her, but my state of weakness is such, I am wholly unable to
comply, to move from one room to another being at times more than I can accomplish
without being ready to faint—poor Harry I feel for him, for without <u>God,</u> how <u>can</u> sorrow be
borne?—It is a bitter cup even with a Redeemers breast to lie on, and His loving arms around
us but without Him! I cannot conceive how it can be endured.—I wrote to poor Bessie, whom

I knew, having passed some days at Gathrim Glebe when I last visited Ireland, and having been greatly interested in <u>her</u> and her brother little Nelson I gave them some excellent books & spoke to them of Him who was precious to me, her Mother grasped the truth and wrote to me afterwards that she hesitated no longer, but had cast herself on Christ,—she is now a housekeeper in the house of the Revd John Cheyne[7] at Castlemaine, who loves His Saviour, & preaches Him—

I have heard from our John, a few days ago: he suffered months to elapse before telling us that he arrived safely at Calcutta after a disagreeable voyage of two months,—he found my letters, and the recommendation we had succeeded in getting for him, and had obtained a <u>good</u> clerkship to begin with, but the moist heat of the climate so different from Australia rendered it impossible for him to follow a sedentary occupation, and he had enrolled himself in a corps of Yeomanry Cavalry then being formed to scour the country, & protect the army from the predatory attacks of the roving Sepoys!—thus has he again chosen his own way, rejected our council, and acted in opposition to our wishes. The letter was heartless and ungodly in a peculiar degree, we must now leave him to the Lord, in whose hands are the issues of life and death—

I know nothing of poor Henry and Walter, they are not allowed to communicate with me, the Mother demands Alick,[8] that she may place him at a Romish School, we have consulted counsel, and trust in God to be able to save <u>him</u> at least from the man of sin—secrecy and hiding are enjoined until he enter his 14th year, now not far off—he will be 13 in October. What happiness to have a living loving friend on whose wisdom we can rely, and leave <u>all</u> our concerns in his hands, believing that all things shall work together for our good" according to His promise Romans viii 28![9] My beloved Mary you must study this promise and read the history of Rachel, as recorded in the book of Genesis—do not desire a family, be thankful that you have none. You little know the wear and tear of rearing even <u>one</u> child—your Sister Caroline after being quiet and comfortable for <u>six</u> years became impatient as her husband altho' a God fearing man regretted the want of little one's, they fretted, and prayed, God often gives us what we wish for to prove to us that we had better leave our concerns to Him. Caroline got children but has never recovered the rearing of the <u>first,</u> and an incurable disease has marked her for its victim under which she will before long sink, & leave the poor things alone in a world of misery—believe me in such a climate as Australia it is a peculiar mark of God's goodness to you that you have none; wait <u>His</u> time, your dear husband will love you none the less, ~~and~~ endeavour to invent amusing employment, write and read, with a view to the improvement of your mind, and <u>study</u> the Scriptures—I dread now seeing any one desirous of having what God has denied, so many instances having come within my own knowledge of the fatal results—I send you my dear Son 4 newspapers, 2 Witnesses, 1 Standard, 1 Telegraph, and a little weekly paper, The Christian Cabinet, the article I have marked is written by Aunt Nanny's[10] young brother I have not had a line from Lucinda since Nov^{br} and think it strange—With much love from your father and myself to you and our dear daughter Mary and hoping you get all my letters and Newspapers. I am entreating God to bless you both abundantly above all that I can ask or think according to the riches of his grace|
Your fondly devoted and attached Mother
   Lucinda Cheyne
Miss Fector sends <u>love</u> to both.—I have written with difficulty because of weakness—
   Text: ALS NLA MS133/1/27

1   George Cheyne in Albany, WA.
2   Captain Alexander Cheyne (1785–1858) had died on 6 July 1858, four days before Lucinda
     wrote this letter.
3   Diphtheria (from the Greek *diphthéra*, leather), a febrile infectious disease resembling croup but
     characterised by the formation of a false membrane on the mucous membrane connected with
     the throat. It was named *diphtheritis* by Dr Brétonneau of Tours in 1820. At the beginning of
     1858, there was an epidemic throughout Great Britain when many people were affected and
     died. *Haydn's Dictionary*, p. 242.
4   Henry Sirée.
5   Possibly son of Dr John Halahan, a surgeon in Dublin, and his wife Mary née Handy.
6   Royal Artillery at Woolwich.
7   Rev. John Cheyne (1810–1880) born in Dublin, the son of Bayne Cheyne's brother, John
     Cheyne MD, and Sarah née Macartney.
8   Alick, Henry Handel and Walter were the sons of WLR's older brother, Henry D. Richardson
     (1816–1849), who was the eldest son of Lucinda and Alexander Richardson.
9   'And we know that all things work together for good to them that love God, to them who are
     the called according to his purpose.' Romans 8, verse 28.
10   Probably the wife of Dr Horatio Nelson Sirée, Lucinda Cheyne's brother.

29   [From John Cheyne in Gorruckpore, India, to WLR in Ballarat]

                                        Gorruckpore 550 <u>miles</u> north |west of Calcutta
                                                                              18 July 1858

My dear Walter

        I suppose you got my last: since writing, finding a sedentary life in Calcutta in this
excessively hot climate did not agree with me   I wrote to The Commander of the Bengal
Yeomanry Calvalry[1] & requested he would allow me to join his Reg[t]: I got a favorable reply
but saying the Corps was at such a distance from Calcutta & the roads so unsafe that I must
proceed up at my own risk. I was sworn in in Calcutta by the Town Major along with a friend
of mine a M[r] Lloyd[2] of Limerick of a very good Irish family, a fine tall fellow 6 feet 4 in: We
passed a Surgical examination: & the very next day were ordered up by Rail to Rancegunge
120 miles there to join a detachment proceeding up the country. I would not have thrown up
my engagement with Thacker Spink & Co.[3] had not the pay been no more than that I am
now receiving & had I not been afraid of my health. In the B.Y.C. Corps I get 100 Rupees a
month & a suit of Clothes, arms & accoutrements[4] I have to pay for the keep of my horse &
myself—if I am killed my nearest relation gets a pension of £70 per ann:—Well on reaching
Rancegunge we were duly attached to the party under command of Lieut. Troup,[5] a gallant,
kind young officer (who had had a brother in the Yeomanry cavalry killed but a few weeks
before) & who was very attentive to me & Lloyd. We marched up to Benares in about
8 days—losing a good many men by Sun strokes, black Cholera, & fever on the road,—I
never saw men die so easily before a few hours sufficed to settle a healthy man for ever.
        Most of the men who died belonged to the 6th & 1st Reg[t] who have come from Africa.
Neither I nor Lloyd were taken ill on the way but arrived in Benares the Hindoo's "Holy City"
in excellent health. Here we found the roads so unsafe that we were peremptorily told to
remain till we could proceed with a strong party & there we remained for 5 mortal weeks
living in a large palace called the Mint once the residence of the Rajah of Benares in grand
style with only an officer besides & sundry Wild animals Tiger, leopard, &c to keep us
company. It was reported unsafe to wander about the city, but we were so tired of doing

nothing that we went in one night (you cannot walk during the day) & saw a number of wonders amongst others a Brahmin's observatory, & a grand procession by torch light Gigantic elephants, horses, banners armed men—in silver & gold &c &c &c.

We were the only two Englishmen there & were surrounded by thousands of scowling dark faces but had the utmost civility, & servility shown us.

By the way the Yeomanry Cavalry have inspired the Sepoys with a great deal of wholesome terror. At first they called them The Reg^t of Clerks but after the very first battle they met them in they called them the Devils Regiment. The Cavalry dash at them quite regardless of guns or numbers. They have more than once been publickly thanked on the field of battle. Benares is now the richest city in India There is massive gold upon many of the temples & mosques & of an evening it would do your heart good to hear the rattle of the gold makers Rupees going through the city. The women at Benares are if anything hansomer than in Calcutta—You have a good opportunity of judging of an evening along the Banks of the Ganges where they go to bathe. Both I & Lloyd were attacked with fever at Benares & I afterwards with dysentery—I was much reduced. At Benares, Lloyd received letters from home with a Commission in H.M. 56 Reg^t at Bombay & so he had to retrace his steps & bid me adieu. I leave Goruckpore for Bustic this evening where the main body of my Reg^t are stationed. The road is still unsafe altho' the rebels have been beaten all round & are much disheartened. I believe I shall have a hard time of it but it will only be for a year & if I can come across some loot (i.e. plunder) I may make some money. I have a great deal to say but this letter is already long & I have not too much money at present from travelling about to pay double postage. Many districts we passed through in India are Gold districts, I wrote to the "Englishman" of Calcutta about it & they published a long letter from me. If you see that paper in yr reading room look over the files for June & you will see it. Will you enclose this letter to Lucinda that she may see how I am getting on. I send her my kindest love & will write to her next. I hope Mary is well I will not forget her easily & hope when I am more settled I shall be able to send her some Indian rarities.

I trust you are sleeping well & doing well & that you sometimes think of me. I am now all alone. I have had kind letters sent from home wanting me to come home, oh how kind, but I had no money & now I am tied for a year at least. This is a dreadfully hot climate. I would not like to remain more than a year in it except something very good turned up—address to me| Trooper Bengal Yeomanry Cavalry| Bustic| or else where| known

Give me plenty of news mind & believe me ever your affect. brother

John Cheyne

Text: ALS NLA MS133/1/243 and MS133/1/253

1   Bengal Yeoman Cavalry (1857–1858), a volunteer unit raised in Calcutta, recruited from local Europeans. It was sent to Amorah on the Oudh–Behar border in October 1857 and had several encounters with 'Pandis', disaffected Sepoys.

2   Thomas Francis Lloyd (1839–1921), born 21 April 1839 to Thomas Lloyd, J.P. (b. 1798) of Beechmount, County Limerick, Ireland and his second wife, Julia Palmer (d. 1901), eldest daughter of Captain Francis Tipping Hall. (The elder Thomas Lloyd's first wife, whom he married in 1825, was Anne, daughter of General Edmund Burke.) Thomas Francis Lloyd was educated at Cheltenham. He became an Ensign on 22 June 1855 in 98th Regiment (Prince of Wales's). He served in NW Frontier Campaign, attached to 6th Punjab Infantry against the Mahood Wuzerees during March, April and May 1860 and was present at the action of Polusean. He was awarded Medal with Clasps. On 15 May 1857, he became Lieutenant; 10 May 1861, Captain; 18 November 1868, Major and sometime commander of the 2nd Regimental District; 2 April 1873 promoted to Lieutenant-Colonel commanding the

98th Regiment. In 1911 he was Colonel-in-Chief of North Staffordshire Regiment. On 26 May 1870 he married Mary Henrietta (d. 1937), fifth daughter of Christian Augustus Henry Allhusen, of Elswick Hall, Newcastle-upon-Tyne, and Stoke Court, Bucks. They had one son, Thomas Henry Eyre (1871–1901), Captain of Coldstream Guards, who served in South African War and was killed in action at Brakenlagter, East Transvaal on 25 October 1910. His letters to his mother during the war were later published. Hugh Montgomery-Massingberd, ed., *Burke's Irish Family Records* (London: Burke's Peerage Ltd, 1976), pp. 726–728. H .G. Hart, ed., *The New Annual Army List, Militia List and Indian Civil Service List for 1882* (London: John Murray, 1882), p. 57.

3   Colin John Troup (d. 1876), who appears in the 1856 Army Lists with Robert Henry W. Troup, presumably his brother. Colin Troup joined the 52nd Oxfordshire Regiment of Foot (Light Infantry), which had embarked for India on 30 June 1853 and had its headquarters at Meerut. By 1864 he was a Major General of the Bengal Infantry. The announcement of his death in the 1877 Army List reveals his rank as Lieutenant-General.

4   Garb, dress (French); soldiers' equipment, other than clothes and arms.

5   Not identified.

30   [From WLR in Ballarat to MR in Melbourne]

Webster St [Ballarat]
Wednesday [11 August 1858]

My dearest Mary

I hope that you arrived safely and that M[r] Foster[1] was waiting for you. We had a terrific storm all Tuesday morning so I expect that you did not cross the water until this morning. I see the Cyclone arrived yesterday Tuesday

You will doubtless have seen your cousin[2] & your trip will thus be very "apropos". We have had wet weather ever since you left: we get on pretty well: Ned[3] has given Eyre[4] notice of his intention to leave: Brooke[5] called yesterday evening & stayed an hour and then Shanklin[6] came in & played two games ~~with~~ of chess—

I payed O'Connor[7] £5. this morning for the deed & I enclose you all I have left I will send more next week if spared

M[r] Barry[8] wrote me & said he could not pay post the enclosed to him: I am doing nothing & no money coming in—

W. Bradshaw & wife left about noon on Monday.[9]

Remember me kindly to Mrs Darling[10] & believe me my darling| Your loving husband
Walter

Put it in an envelope & address to Mr Barry or leave it at Mr Brown 59 Flinders St East.

Text: ALS NLA MS133/1/84

1   William Lawrence Foster (b. *c*.1829) was born in Bermondsay, London. Married to Isabel Jane née Brittan (b. *c*.1832) in Dalston, near Shoreditch, they emigrated to Victoria in 1853 on the *Anne Cropper*, on which they met Mary, Sarah and William Bailey. They settled in Geelong and had three children: twins born in 1854, William Morris and George Frederick (the latter died aged five months), and Thomas Brittan born on 8 January 1856. William described himself as a 'gentleman' on Thomas's birth certificate but he had business interests in Geelong and a store on the Melbourne Road in Ballarat. In a letter to the Editor of *The Ballarat Courier* on 5 December 1904, Mrs E. Rowlands wrote that she and her husband pitched their tent in 1853 near to where the old Charles Napier Theatre was afterwards built and near to 'a little store called "The Whaler's Flag", kept by a man named William Foster': *Eureka Reminiscences*, ed. Ballarat Heritage Services (Ballarat: Ballarat Heritage Services, 1998), p. 60.

2   William Henry Turnham (1841–1905), son of William Henry Turnham and Sarah née Robinson. Born in London, he emigrated to Victoria (to join his aunt and uncle) on the *Cyclone*, which arrived in Melbourne on 10 August 1858.

3   Edward Harold Bailey (1828–1893).

4   William Eyres and Co., Wholesale Ironmongers, 70 Sturt Street, Ballarat, for whom Ned worked. William Eyres was born in 1831 at Melkstone, Wiltshire, where his father was an engineer, iron founder and ironmonger. Eyres worked in Dorchester in a hardware business until August 1852, when he and his brother, Thomas, embarked on the ship *Velore*, arriving in Melbourne in January 1853. They spent a month at Emerald Hill (South Melbourne) and, after hearing about the discovery of a massive, quartz-encrusted piece of gold, near Canadian Gully (136 lbs) in February 1853, they loaded up a cart with provisions and set off for the Eureka lead. They mined successfully (sending their father a 28-ounce gold nugget) and by 1855 had enough funds to open a hardware business at Main Road, Ballarat. In 1857 they opened a branch business at Sturt Street, which in 1863 became their only business. William remained in Ballarat and became a leading member of the community as a member of the Ballarat Hospital Committee, the Art Gallery Committee and the Ballarat Saving Bank. Thomas Eyres retired from Ballarat to Adelaide in 1879 and became a partner and manager of McLean Bros and Rigg, which subsequently became Eyres, Black and Co.

5   Alexander Brooke Smith.

6   Robert Shanklin (b. *c.*1820), a chemist at Ballarat.

7   Daniel O'Connor (1809–1884), originally a shopkeeper at Golden Point, Ballarat, he developed and sold explosives for the diggers. He is mentioned in Carboni's account of the Eureka uprising when four miners entered his store and asked in the name of the Committee for powder and shot. Seeing his fine Yorkshire hams, they ransacked his entire store and took his cash box. (Carboni, p. 73.) He was a founder committee member of the Ballarat Fire Brigade. His name crops up throughout WLR's letters as a friend. He is listed in the 1868 Baillière's *Directory* as Inspector of Weights and Measures at Ballarat. In September 1877 (Letter 225), WLR noted the report of the inquiry by the British Wreck Commissioner into the disappearance of the vessel on which a large order of powder for O'Connor was being transported; it was thought to have blown up in July 1876 in the English Channel.

8   Mr Barry not identified.

9   William Burrows Bradshaw, his wife Rebecca (née Wells) and five children had spent Sunday night at the Richardsons (see Letter 31) and Mary must have left Ballarat by the early morning coach bound for Geelong and thence Melbourne.

10 Ellen Darling née Jelfs (1837–1920) married on 29 January 1857 to John Darling (1831–1878), who was born in Glasgow and was working as a ship's carpenter on the *Emu* steamboat. It is noted on their marriage certificate that his father (George Darling) was an architect. For information about her father, Thomas Jelfs, see endnote to Letter 1. The Darlings had two daughters: Jean Emma was born in South Yarra in 1858 and Ellen Annie was born in Moorabbin in 1865. Ellen Darling was listed in the 1868 Baillière's *Directory* as a shopkeeper in Emerald Hill.

31   [From WLR in Ballarat to MR in Melbourne]

Webster St. [Ballarat]
Saturday [14 August 1858]

My dearest wife

I received yours safely and sent the note accompanying it to Miss Cuthbert:[1] I enclose you another £1. and will send another by the end of next week:

What very unpleasant weather you have had dear, it has rained daily here until today. Ned had a letter from Bennett Brothers[2] & I think it very probable he will leave Eyre this month

I was sitting quietly reading last night about half past seven when I heard a gentle knock at the front door, as Anne[3] was laying tea Ned not having come home I went myself and judge of my <u>surprise</u> to see W. Bradshaw & wife & horror to see the children: I was too <u>irritated</u> by what you said of the slanders of M[rs] B. senior and too much in fear of a repetition of squally poor baby[4] <u>all night</u> to submit to the infliction and altho W.B. said they had come to trespass on our hospitality I told them as quietly as I could that I had no accommodation & that you were from home, they went away I have no doubt highly indignant but I owe nothing to them & it is time they were taught manners! A piece of the porest [purest] effrontery! and it all arises my dear wife from you turning me out of bed on Sunday night: they thought if we were silly enough to do that once I would be ass enough to do without any bed for a night—

I presume by this you have seen Turnham & your cousin:

Your letter was very nice and welcome: Anne is <u>improving</u> tho <u>very</u> stupid, I have to see after every thing: No sickness and no money coming in: I went to poor Mc nee's funeral[5] on Thursday Saw MacKie[6] & all the farmers from about Learmonth: Ned paid me £5. but as I have to pay £1. every monday besides butcher & baker & Anne's wages I have not sent more I have not expended 6[d] this week on myself. I will send you down £1. in each letter I dont know whether it is safe to send them to the Hotel but as you have only put Melbourne on yours I am unable to send it to your house

I have not had any letters this morning: from home: The house has not been burnt down yet—I am glad to learn that Ellen welcomed you cordially in spite of the malignant & base slanders circulated by the Bradshaws. I hope you will see poor M[rs] Croll[7] if you stay in Geelong as you return, she knows such lies are false—The weather seems clearing up today & I do hope we may have a fine week next for your sake—

Susan & all[8] are much as usual.

Do you know where my old white knife is?—I enclose Miss Cuthberts answer I think she means that if both lustres & China exceed £8. she will send the balance. Have a <u>distinct bill</u> of what the carriage is to be and say it will be paid on delivery take Sarah or Uncle with you as a witness or else your cousin—Susan says she would like her parcel sent up if it is a large parcel send it by carrier if a small one by coach address it to J. R. Bailey Star Office.

With love dear wife & kisses oh! so many to yourself, as well as kind regards to your host & hostess. I am as you know| Your devoted husband
        Walter
    Text: ALS NLA MS133/1/85

1   Anna Maria Cuthbert (1827–1916) born in Ireland, the eldest child and only surviving daughter of John Cuthbert (1793–1878) and Elizabeth née Headen (c.1795–1842). Her brothers, Henry Cuthbert (1829–1907) and Kingston Cuthbert (1837–1856), emigrated to Victoria, arriving in Melbourne in August 1854 on board the *Bloomer*. Anna Maria, her father and remaining brothers, Thomas Headen (1832–1915), John (1838–1886) and Robert Browne (1841–1880) followed them, arriving in Melbourne aboard the *Albion* in October 1857. She married William Nixon (1833–1905) in 1864 when she was thirty-seven. They had one son and three daughters all born in Ballarat: Elizabeth Anna Nixon (1866–1905), William (1867–1901), Helen Lillian (1869–1935) and Emma Florence (1871–1950). Anna Maria died in Ballarat in 1916 aged eighty-nine. Her fictional counterpart is Amelia Ocock, who also married (after her prime) a younger man. See *FRM I*, pp. 231, 295, 301–302.
2   Bennett Brothers (W. and A.), Grocers and Ironmongers, 154, Brunswick Street, Collingwood.
3   The Richardson's servant.
4   Eugene Matilda Bradshaw born earlier that year, the fifth surviving child of Rebecca and William Burrows Bradshaw.
5   On Thursday, 5 August 1858, James McNee of the Mount Blowhard Hotel (and formerly of the Crow Hotel, Main Road) had an accident when returning home on horseback from Ballarat. He was carrying a heavy parcel and his horse stumbled, throwing McNee on his head. *The*

Ballarat Star reported his accident and death on Tuesday, 10 August, only to retract the death notice on Wednesday as Dr Henry Paul Leman told them after their publication on Tuesday that he was still alive. However, on Thursday it was sadly reported that he had succumbed to his injuries and died on Tuesday night, leaving a widow and children.

6 The Reverend George Mackie (1823–1871), the Presbyterian Minister at Learmonth; born Kincardine, Fife. He came from Scotland to NSW in 1847, then joined the Church of Victoria in 1857 and settled first at Lake Learmonth and Burrembeet and 'being a man of great practical energy he visited other districts, doing evangelistic work and organising congregations. He next went to Horsham and from thence to South Yarra. He was elected Moderator [of the Presbyterian Church Victoria] in 1871, but died within a few weeks.' D. Macrae Stewart, *The Presbyterian Church of Victoria: Growth in Fifty Years 1859–1909* (Melbourne: D.W. Paterson Co., n.d., *c.*1909), p. 118.

7 Anna Maria Croll née Grundy.

8 Susannah Tyler Bailey née Nicholson (1833–1859), first wife of John Robinson Bailey, whom she married on 29 January 1853, Christ Church, Geelong. She emigrated to Victoria in 1852 aboard the same ship as WLR, the *Roxburgh Castle*, with her sister Marianne. She and John had four children: Harrie Elphinstone born 7 December 1853, an unnamed male who died at birth in 1855, Emma (Trotty) born 13 September 1856, and Edith Elizabeth born 17 May 1858. WLR was the accoucheur for Susannah's last confinement (Edith): Case 141—'Mrs Bailey, Webster St, age 26, 4th pregnancy, quickened 5 Dec', duration of pregnancy 276 days, Presentation Head . . . Everything nicely, cord round neck once ... Puer peritonitis.'

32 [From WLR in Ballarat to MR in Melbourne]

Webster St [Ballarat]
Monday [16 August 1858]

My ever dear wife

Two and three letters to your one! I dont know that I ought to write again this week, but as I have had a letter from your mother wh contains enclosures for Sarah & William Henry, why I suppose I had better send them as soon as possible—

I enclose you another £1. wh with the other two makes three sent to the Sir C. Hotham Hotel.[1]

I hope you are enjoying yourself and that you went to Church yesterday, you have been away a week today & you have not said a word about your Uncle, the Webbs,[2] your cousin, the box: I hope you have the likenesses of all the family. Are you still with Ellen or has Turnham invited you, or the Webbs, do you intend staying anytime in Geelong. What wretched dreary weather you must have had if it has been similar to ours rain & drizzle & mud. I do not know that I have any thing to tell

I hope the contents of "the box" have pleased you

Was Uncle kind? Did you find out from Aunt what it was all about. I am very lonely and it is quite disagreeable to go to bed in fact I think I shall sit up tonight—

Croll's foundry[3] is taken: Ned dined at Johns yesterday. I sent down the two umbrellas by the carrier Binney & somebody[4] I will tell you the address tomorrow: a miserably small attendance at church last night—None of the three Accouchement's off yet—

Your poor old mother is very anxious that Ned should go home, it will be a great pity if he does just as he is remaking a footing for himself: he has given Eyre notice in writing to leave next Monday: and I think he will too: I have written today to Lucinda and to Bill[5]—I had no letters from my mother this mail—I do not suppose she has sent anything in the box or they would have told us of it before this—

Monday This day is a little fairer and promises to herald in a fine week which I sincerely hope for your sake my dear Mary—

I think I will postpone finishing this until tomorrow as it is too late for todays post and you would receive one today from me written on Saturday: You did not say how you got on going down <u>alone</u> in the Coach—Was the Jehu[6] civil and did any of the passengers prove troublesome; I was glad to see you had a woman opposite you!—I returned home & awoke Anne & felt very lonely—Was it not cool impudence of W. Bradshaw to try the trick twice of turning me out of bed:

Mrs Paul had the doctor, Paul intended to have had me if anything went wrong[7]— Mrs Sheppard has had a son[8]—I think I shall have the brewers mans wife & another a freind of his—

Wednesday. I did not get any letter from you yesterday but the nice long one this morning dispelled all my clouds & made me happy; it does indeed seem an age dear since that nasty dark morning that separated us—

I am so pleased to hear of your enjoyments, get out as much as possible my darling! Last night Ned & I went to bed about ten, and at ½ past 12 I was awoke by John at the window asking for Ned: he came round to Ned's door came in & told us that there had been a fire at Eyres place, nearly burnt down, with difficulty saved, insured on the 5th August for £2000[9]—What a lovely morning, had my hair cut—

Your arrangement with poor Mrs Barry is the best that could have been made, she ought to have sent an order to her sister to pay £1. however I will send Anne tomorrow—My evenings are so lonely and I cannot go out as I so three ladies in daily expectation! it is very annoying that they are so long—I have sent the umbrellas by Binney & Broadbent office corner of Flinders Lane & Eliz St. try & get the best one mended it will save £1—My darling wife, I will be so happy to see you again—God bless you and protect you and bring you safely home to me, for if anything were to happen to you it would kill me| Your loving

       Walter

Text: ALS NLA MS133/1/98

[1]   Sir Charles Hotham Hotel, situated on the eastern corner of Flinders and Spencers streets, was a three-storey brick construction built in 1854–55 to commemorate the arrival of the new Governor. Later rebuilt.

[2]   George Henry Frederick Webb (1828–1891), son of Samuel Oddie Webb and Isabella Sweet; born in London and died in Caulfield; journalist, barrister, judge. At the time of this letter, he was married to his first wife, Matilda Sarah née Field (1831–1860). They had one surviving daughter, Isabella Elizabeth Webb, born 1856 in St Kilda. Matilda Webb died in Concord, NSW, on 22 October 1860 and on 10 April 1862 he remarried. His second wife was Sophia Sarah Agg (1819–1895), daughter of George Agg, a landed proprietor, and his wife Sophia Euphemia née Cheek. Her siblings were William Henry, Alfred and Clara Agg. George and Sophia, who was already forty-three when they married, had one child, a daughter, Sophie Sarah Ann, born in 1863. Note: both de Serville (1991) and the *ADB* state that George Webb was the government shorthand writer and considered the father of law reporting in Victorian Supreme Court. His older brother, James Hemming Webb (1814–1881), was also a government shorthand reporter.

[3]   Owned by William Croll (1813–1861), father-in-law of MR's friend Anne Maria Croll née Grundy. The Geelong Vulcan Foundry advertised steam engines for sale in his yard for the gold mining industry.

[4]   'Harry Stainland Binney and Thomas Broadbent, general carriers, 43 Flinders st-west.' Sands, Kenny and Co., *Commercial and General Melbourne Directory* (Melbourne: Sands, Kenny and Co., 1858).

[5]   William Bailey.

6   A fast and furious driver; a coachman; allusion to Kings ix, v. 20.
7   James Melvin Paul (1858–1859), first son of the Reverend James Melvin Paul and Anna Maria
      née Sibley.
8   William Poynton Sheppard (1858–1869), son of William Horder Sheppard and Elizabeth
      Roberts.
9   On Wednesday, 18 August 1858, *The Ballarat Star* reported that at 'about quarter to ten o'clock
      last night (Tuesday) a few people passing the street' saw bright flames emerging from William
      Eyre's store as well as from Messrs Nicol, Scott & Co.'s wine store. 'We are informed by
      Mr R. B. Gibbs, that Mr Eyre had, on or about the 5th of the present month effected an
      insurance on the stock, &c, to the amount of £2000, in the Colonial Insurance Office. We
      understand, that according to the terms of the New Act authority the holding of inquests on
      fires, an enquiry will be made into the cause of the present fire, which is at present wrapped in
      mystery.'

33   [From WLR in Ballarat to MR in Melbourne]

                                                                 Webster St [Ballarat]
                                                        Thursday [19 August 1858]

My dear wife Mary
      You will be surprised at my writing another letter to you to day after posting one to you
yesterday but I want you particularly to get your cousin to find out from Cobbs[1] offices where
"Luther"[2] is and where he lives: M[r] Cuthbert[3] has not succeeded in getting the summons
served he says his agent wrote to say he lived in Melbourne. Do this at once like a dear
      We had a lovely day yesterday and to day & all night there has been a continued
pour—What a trip you must have had it seems as if the heavens and the stars conspired
together to make it as unpleasant as possible—I am rather glad of the heavy rain for I know it
cannot last:
      There was an enquiry all yesterday in the fire at Eyre a Coroner's inquest.[4] Ned was
examined every body suspects Eyres of doing it: and half the people say so:
      I look forward with great delight to seeing you again altho I am getting used to sleep
without you: do not think of returning until the weather fines—If you return to Geelong ask
M[r] Foster to enquire at "Cobbs" or the mail office where Jerry lives and when he can be found
at home:
      I am so glad you have bought Hugh Miller's[5] book. Brown asked me 15/- for it—
      Send me up word in your next about Luther and good bye, my own darling be careful of
yourself until we meet I enclosed £1. in yesterdays letter and will send another on Saturday so
as to let you get in [it] on Monday. Good bye ever dearest| Your devoted husband
            Walter
Susan has been in & says she received the parcel & two Bibles last night but as usual there is
something wrong Her mother wrote to say she had sent in the box something for her & she
has not got anything from her family: pray write particularly & let us know if there was any
parcel or letters addressed to her—
      Your sister Lizzie[6] has sent her likeness to John you did not say if you had one from her,
she is very like you indeed:
      Text: ALS NLA MS133/1/86

1   Cobb and Co. was formed by a group of Americans in Melbourne in 1853 after the initial gold
      rushes. The name was provided by Freeman Cobb, one of the founders, and the company was

set up to provide a coach transport system in Victoria similar to that in the USA. The American-designed coaches (using leather strips to act as a cradle for the body of the coach) were hardier than the English coaches and therefore more suitable for the rough roads and tracks. The company expanded through Victoria, New South Wales and Queensland, where it survived until 1924 when the last horse-drawn Cobb coach was withdrawn from service.

² Jeremiah (Jerry) Luther (c.1833–1868) was involved in a law-suit brought by WLR for non-payment of an account. The details of this have not yet been discovered.

³ Henry Cuthbert (Later Sir Henry) (1829–1907), lawyer, later politician.

⁴ The inquest was reported in detail and Ned, who told the Coroner, 'I am an ironmonger in the employment of Mr Eyres', was required to explain what had happened on that particular evening when he had left the store before Eyres locked up. *Star*, 18 August 1858, p. 2.

⁵ Hugh Miller (1802–1856), Scottish man of letters, lay theologian and geologist. He was considered one of the finest writers on geology in the nineteenth century and his writings were widely acclaimed by the public in general. Apprenticed to a stonemason at seventeen, he studied the geology of the quarries and countryside and, inspired by his interest in nature and science coupled with his religious temperament, he began writing. In 1829, while working as a journeyman mason, he published *Poems written in the Leisure Hours of a Journeyman Mason*. At thirty-two he was appointed accountant to the bank in his home-town (Cromarty), where he published in 1835, *Stones and Legends of the North of Scotland*. He was intensely interested in the Church of Scotland's struggles with the law of patronage and argued in two widely distributed pamphlets (in 1839) that ecclesiastical reform was required: 'A Letter to Lord Brougham' and 'The Whiggism of the Old School'. In 1840 Miller went to Edinburgh as editor of the newly founded newspaper, *The Witness*, which opposed patronage in the Church of Scotland. The newspaper gained a wide reputation through Miller's leading articles and also through his brilliant geological series, part of which was published in 1841 as a book, *The Old Red Sandstone*. Of his remaining works on geology, *Footprints of the Creator* (1849) was the most highly regarded. It is not clear which book MR had bought for WLR but it might have been *The Testimony of Rocks* (published in 1857 after his death), which dealt with the borderland between science and religion. See *FRM I*, pp. 189–193, on the influence of the 'development theory' on Mahony.

⁶ Elizabeth (Lizzie) Brett née Bailey, MR's older sister, christened 17 November 1830 at St George's Parish Church, Leicester; second daughter of Elizabeth and John Bailey. She married Captain John Brett, of the Prince Consort's Own Rifle Brigade, on 7 June 1859. They had two children, Edith born about 1865 and John Walter, who died aged seven weeks on 6 October 1868.

34   [From WLR in Ballarat to MR in Melbourne]

Webster St [Ballarat]

Monday 23 [August 1858]

My own darling Mary

Your kind letter of Saturday reached me this morning. I do not think Miss Cuthbert wishes anything done about the furniture she has not sent over and we had better not appear too meddlesome:

I hope you will have a pleasant day today at Collingwood it is fine here but a strong N. wind as usual. Give them my kind love if you see them again: I would rather that your cousin enquired about Luther:

It is astounding that you have had such fine weather while we have had constant rain, so wet that nobody could get out except those compelled by business. I told Susan this morning that you said you had sent everything and read her your letter where you said so, she said "well it is very strange that ~~Mrs~~ my mother in June letter written six weeks after the box started says she sent me a parcel"—

We must have ~~the~~ the boxes sent separate in future She has sent me in your mother's letter to read dated <u>April 7th</u> in wh your mother says she sends a handkerchief for John wh she has possessed for 40 years "Your own mother encloses a parcel & has dropped a trifle in Harry's box"—This letter is dated April 7th.

Very strange is it not and very unpleasant—

You had better enclose a note to John in your next telling him all that came in the box and assure him that his were sent safely & take no notice of what Susan says but we wont have it happen again!—Ned & I dined there yesterday in consequence of a pressing invitation from John himself.

Eyre has been imprisoned all Friday night all Saturday & night, & was only released yesterday on bail of £500[1] John & Burton[2] going surety: Ned remains ~~in~~ till Thursday. He has been paid in full—Imagine poor Mrs Eyre's state:[3] Nothing new: I enclose another £1–0–0. I would like you to go to "Robertson Bookseller"[4] near opposite I think "Argus" office & <u>buy</u> me a copy of the last edition of <u>Taylors "Medical Jurisprudence"</u>[5] price about 15/- and ask him to write down the price of "Churchills Midwifery"[6] Ramsbothams "ditto,[7] and "<u>Parerina Materia Medica</u>"[8]—write & let me know when you start for Geelong and I will send you another £1. You have been very economical my darling heart—It is a fortnight today and you may imagine how slowly the time has past it appears a month at least

Give my kind regards to M^r & Mrs Darling & thank them for their kind treatment of you: assure M^{rs} D how happy we will be to see her when she can come next summer: I do not think it at all likely that Ned will go to Melbourne just now: But he appears to think of going to England next year: Your mother writes so anxiously for him strange with other sons at home:[9] Tis a pity as I tell him, to blight his rising prospects here—He is a good son: Susan children & John have all had influenza colds: I hope dear that yours is better and that you take care of yourself. I look for your arrival now daily, and trust that nothing may befall you:

I went to Church myself yesterday morning alone: Ned went at night also Anne: she has given over picking & stealing, for I locked the safe when I caught her at it and she has the making of a good servant she can make plain suet pudding herself now: Be sure to call on Mrs Croll in Geelong

I shall expect another letter on Thursday at latest and my next will be addressed to Geelong: I fear you have already trespassed on Mrs Darling's hospitality but we can return it: I believe Mrs Potter[10] has lost her baby: She was in deep mourning yesterday:

Remember me kindly to Sarah; find out her prospects and mention Curtaynes[11] name:

I expect Brooke tomorrow: and possibly Curtayne with him: Have got a few eggs for you when you come back altho all have stopped again:

I am very pleased you have managed so well about the cards—I was obliged to give Ann a good talking to this morning she will <u>not</u> do what I tell her, but will persist in having her own way—However you can see what you think of her and if she will do what <u>she is told</u> you can keep her if not she must be told to go home: I pay her regularly—have paid off all debts to this day and am better off than we have been since we came into the house: I have been bespoken today to attend Mrs Hudson[12] next "Tam o' Shanter".

Good bye my love good bye| Your affectionate Husband

Walter

Text: ALS NLA MS133/1/80

1   Eyres had been arrested on Saturday, 21 August, after it was reported by the Coroner that there
     was 'Weight of evidence against him'. The Warden, James Daly, fixed bail at £1500 but refused
     the offers of bail from friends of Eyres on Saturday.
2   When John Robinson Bailey and Evan Burton (both residents of Webster Street) offered bail on
     Sunday, it was accepted by the Warden.
3   Amelia Eyres.
4   George Robertson (1825–1898), publisher and bookseller, opened his bookshop at 85 & 87
     Collins Street East, Melbourne, in 1853.
5   Alfred Swaine Taylor, *Medical Jurisprudence*, 5th edn (London: Churchill, 1854).
6   Fleetwood Churchill, *On the Theory and Practice of Midwifery*, 3rd edn (London: H. Renshaw,
     1855).
7   F. H. Ramsbotham, *The Principles and Practice of Obstetric Medicine and Surgery, in Reference to
     the Process of Parturition*, 3rd edn (London: Churchill, 1851).
8   Not identified.
9   Thomas Burton Bailey (aged twenty-five), Samuel Bailey (aged twenty) and Charles Bailey (aged
     fourteen).
10   Herbert John Potter, born and died in 1858, son of Reverend John Potter and Sarah Anne
     Potter (née Mathews).
11   Probably Thomas W. Curtayne, medical practitioner at Hard Hills, Ballarat.
12   *Case* 148, Mrs Hudson, Creswick Road, 2 September 1858, her sixth pregnancy. The labour
     commenced at 8 a.m. but the baby girl was not delivered until 5 p.m. 'Pain in side ... flooding
     after. Cold water.'

35   [From MR in Melbourne to WLR in Ballarat]

Melbourne

August 25th [Wednesday, 1858]

My dear darling

You see by the commencement of this I have not yet left Melbourne but I have just finished writing to M[rs] Foster to ask her to meet me to morrow by the Steamer & I would stay a few day's with her

I am going this morning to get the book you mention. I was not able to go yesterday I have such a bad headache I did not go to the Webbs I must write to them when I come home. I have got the Cards they are very nicely done. M[r] Harris[1] has been several times to Sarah's enquiring for me but I cannot find him. I think I shall be obliged to make up a small box & send by the carrier for I have no one to carry the thing's backwards & forwards for me & they are too heavy for me so I shall take the things out of the Tin box from home & leave it with Sarah & put some of my things with them into a small box & send them by Binney & Broadbent I will put inside of this how much it will cost you can send Ann & the money with it Susan's parcel shall be at the top it was not my fault the thing's were not in the box & I heard nothing about them until I went down there last week also the Silk pocket handkerchief it was forgotten but you will find it all right I will try to day if I can get any second hand medical book's that you mention but I will be sure to bring the one you want particularly I shall be so glad to see you again my dear I feel so lonely sometimes I am so glad you do not think I have been extravagant I bought a trifle & gave to Ellen for her kindness I could not afford much. Money seems to fly in Melbourne.

I am delighted to hear you are doing so well I hope it will continue I have not felt quite well this last day or two but I can guess what is coming soon

I will write to you from Foster's & tell you when to meet me M^r & Mrs Darling desire to be kindly remembered to you

Sarah will go to Mrs Barry's every week. I have written out 4 receipt's for her to give as she receives the money & then she will send it up. I must say good bye now Sweetheart for I must go out I do so long to see you again with all my love & kisses ever dear Walter| Your loving wife

Mary

PS I have been to Robertsons the bookseller & bought you Taylor's Medical Jurisprudence the price was 17/6 they had not either Ramsbotham or Churchill on Midwifery I will try in Geelong

Send Ann Monday or Tuesday to Binneys for a box addressed to you pay for it. They do not take the money until delivered—in haste God bless you darling| MR

Text: ALS NLA MS133/1/48

[1]   Probably WLR's friend Henry Harris, who was the Worshipful Master of the Victoria Lodge.

36   [From WLR in Ballarat to MR at the Fosters in Geelong]

Webster St [Ballarat]
Wednesday [25 August 1858]

My dear Mary

I received yours this morning & feel much surprised at your not having got a letter I wrote to you and posted myself last Monday it contained £1: I went at once on receipt of yours to the Post Office & found that it was not there so it must be in Melbourne: But I trust before this reaches you you have received it safely. I have sent £1. in every letter I have written to you and enclose one in this—You say you paid carriage on the umbrellas—now I told you distinctly in my letter of last Friday that I had paid all demands 2/6 and I wrote across the address twice /carriage paid in full and it is too bad if they have defrauded you. I enclose the receipt from the office—also a note to Luther,[1] send it to the office and get an answer next day: John has gone down to Geelong today and we thought you would be there as I understood you were going across to day.

I am very lonely and dull and have no news. Ned is out all day and unfortunately I cannot go out on acct of those precious labours wh. do not come off.

A. Brooke Smith called in passing and handed me some letters to read among them was one from Mrs Bradshaw in wh. amidst of lot of rubbish, she spits out her venom at me. God forgive her she has evidently maligned me before to some extent: Drop the acquaintance with the whole family—

I wonder if she remembers the command "thou shalt not bear false witness against thy neighbour" I certainly fear that you are trespassing upon Mrs Darling's kindness I never dreamt you intended staying there so long, you know, my dear one must not render oneself obnoxious or a burden; especially as she appears to be a freind of the Bradshaws and I look now with suspicion upon all ~~know~~ associating with them| Your devoted husband

Walter

Susan & the family are all ill John is coming up again next Saturday he is staying at Skarratts Great Western he would take you to a grand ball on the opening of the Railway works[2]

Ask for Mrs Skarratt[3] if you go over—

I do not know what to do for the best in sending this letter as there has always been a delay in your getting letters sent to the <u>Hotham Hotel</u> as I suppose you have got my last by this I think it will be best to send it to Geelong where I hope you are—as if you sailed on Thursday morning you wd not get it and it would be left behind in Melbourne

   Text: ALS NLA MS133/1/89

[1]   MR must have located Jerry Luther.

[2]   The Ceremony for the Cutting of the First Turf for the Geelong to Ballarat Railway took place on 26 August 1856. The program of events was reported in *The Argus* and included: '9 am couple of guns firing a salute of indefinite duration: 10 am procession from market square will form: 10.30 am procession will move; 11.30 am procession will reach the railway station and await arrival of His Excellency the Governor; 12.30 pm games on railway ground; 1 pm lunch al fresco from whole ox; 2 pm ceremony of cutting the turf; 7 pm display of fireworks; 9.30 pm Ball.' Twelve thousand people turned up in Geelong: 'The usually sedate, quiet and—some people say—dull, has this day gone completely wild with excitement, and has accomplished a holiday such as is rarely witnessed anywhere. The ordinary routine of business has been completely stopped for the nonce.' *The Argus*, 27 August 1858, p. 2.

[3]   It could be the same Mrs Skarrett who ran the Victoria Restaurant near Eureka Stockade in 1854. On the night of the riot she was reported to have drawn a revolver from her bosom and threatened to shoot three men who came to take her horse on the orders of the 'commander-in-chief'. She also tried to assist Peter Lalor by swearing that he was in bed at the time of the riot. Withers, pp. 118–119.

37   [From WLR in Ballarat to MR at the Fosters in Geelong]

Webster St [Ballarat]

Friday 8½ am [27 August 1858]

My darling,

   As Ned will see you this day I send this by him. I sent one the day before yesterday to you at Mr Fosters—Geelong and as I fear you have not received my previous one or letter addressed to you at the Sir C. Hotham Hotel posted on Monday I enclosed a £1. in the last & one in this: I hope that letter has not gone astray but I did not get one from you yesterday. I fear it must have been lost owing to the carelessness of the Hotel people

   Lonely day. how I long to see you and kiss you again

   Have you seen John?

   I was up all night[1] so you must forgive this short scrawl but I cannot write well.

   God bless you until I embrace you my dear dear wife

   John returns tomorrow and Ned on Monday Good bye| Your loving husband

         Walter

P.S. King [Kind] regards to the Fosters

   Text: ALS NLA MS133/1/109

[1]   *Case* 147, 27 August 1858, Mrs Griffiths, Swamp, aged thirty-six, eighth pregnancy, 'Discharge of blood 17 days before birth'. WLR was called out at midnight and the baby girl was born at 3 a.m.

38   [From MR in Geelong to WLR in Ballarat]

Geelong
August 28 [Saturday 1858]

My dearest husband

I write to tell you that I arrived here safely last Night & found a letter waiting for me from you dear Harold called to see me in the Evening & told me he forgot to bring the letter you wrote to me I am so glad to hear you are well darling

Ned went to Melbourne by the first train this Morning I sent the letter to Luther by him he said he would find him also to the Carriers they would not let me leave their until I paid for it was not endorsed paid in the book I had to sign it so Ned said he would make it all right.

I did not send the box by them for they would not take it for less than 12 shillings & I would not pay them so I brought it in the Steamer with me & luckily Mr Foster was sending a dray load of things to there place on the Melbourne road so sent my box free so if you send Ann about Wednesday to carry it I have not seen John I suppose he has returned home by this I hope to hear from you on Monday darling & send me word if there is anything you want. Mrs Darling was very sorry I would not stay longer she has taken her farewell of the Bradshaw's they behaved so badly the last time she was there I intend going to see Mrs Croll if I can find her out I shall return home next Wednesday but I will send you word on Monday what coach I come by & what time it will arrive yesterday darling was the anniversary of our third Wedding day I was thinking of you all day I am afraid you will feel very lonely dear

Ned return's on Monday by the Melbourne Coach M^r & Mrs Foster met me at the Steamer & Captain McLean[1] was very kind in seeing after my things It is very warm—more like Summer weather it thundered last night I shall be so glad to see you again dearest & with all love & kisses I remain| Your loving wife

Mary

Text: ALS NLA MS133/1/52

[1]   Probably Captain Hugh McLean, an early settler of Williamstown, who had kept a boat and two men ready to carry passengers from Sandridge (Port Melbourne) to Williamstown at 2s (20c) per head, with a minimum of 5s (50c) per trip. This service was essential as the two separate settlements of Melbourne and Williamstown, divided by the River Yarra, developed. A wooden paddle steamer *Comet* was the pioneer vessel in the Port Melbourne to Williamstown ferry service in 1854. This service ran from 1854 to 1914 and resumed in 1920 until it finally ceased operation in 1930. Jack Loney, *Bay Steamers and Coastal Ferries* (Frenchs Forest, NSW: A. H. & A. W. Reed, 1982), pp. 10–11.

39   [From WLR in Ballarat to MR in Geelong]

Webster St. [Ballarat]
Monday. [30 August 1858]

My own darling wife

I did not write on Saturday because you had not answered my last, & I did not know if you might go to Geelong after all: I got yours of Sat. this morning, and am delighted to hear you are coming back on Wednesday; I will meet you without fail, I suppose you will come by the 10 oclock coach, so as not to inconvenience Mrs Foster by getting up so early as six: I enclose another £1. as Harold forgot it

I did not find the letter until Saturday night or I might have posted it.

John came home on Saturday; you missed a great treat in Geelong! John went to the Ball,[1] and wanted to find you to take you: I am so sorry you were not there:

I too, thought of our wedding day, yet we do not look back with regret, for we are happier now than ever we were. I have been very lonely, but I felt it more the first week than I have done since, I suppose like every thing else habit accustoms to every thing. I think you have enjoyed yourself, and will have many things to tell us all: Bill[2] is staying at Johns—I have a very bad case, was called out two nights three times at night last week: Susan & children been very ill, and not well yet. Incessant rain all night, & yesterday & the night before—I shall be so glad to see you! how I long to kiss you! and to hear of your adventures:

Anne has very much improved, and does not do any of her bad tricks—but I have never enjoyed my meals since you left, consequently your return will be joyfully welcomed.

I went to church yesterday for the third time by myself, a gentleman from St. Kilda preached, & a collection was made for the roof—

I sent Anne to Mrs Barrys sister & she said she had sent down the money to Mrs Barry. I am afraid Anne cannot carry the box from Fosters but I will send her for it on Wednesday so as to have it by the time you come back—

And now my darling, as this is the last letter I will write Good bye, and may God who has so providentially watched over you keep you for me until you return to my arms, is the prayer of your dear

    Walter

Text: ALS NLA MS133/1/31

[1]   The Ball was held in Geelong at 9.30 p.m. on 26 August 1856 to end the day's celebrations after the Cutting of the First Turf for the Geelong and Ballarat Railway.

[2]   William Bailey.

1859

40   [From LC in Brighton, England, to her daughter LR
     in Kyneton, Victoria]

                     17 Buckingham Place, |West Cliff |Brighton |England.
                                   6th Jany 1859

My beloved Lucinda

You may be certain you were remembered, and often spoken of this Christmas season by us all, I went back 13 years and saw you and the dead[1] and the far away beside me,—Weak, infirm and aged as I am since my fever, I remembered you much before a Throne of grace, and asked for the best blessings for you—and, that we might meet to rejoice together.

My inability to write without suffering, is a great trial, I would fain have power to pour out my heart on paper as in former times, but at times can scarcely hold a pen, and when I would hope to make some way, head ache sets in, and I am compelled to leave off.—I am however better since I last attempted to write, I go out a little in a bath chair[2] drawn by a Donkey, but return sore broken & exhausted I am urged to persevere, and obey, because it is my duty—but it is depressing work.—

I have to announce the death of Clementine,[3] who departed on the 29th last month without my ever hearing that she was unwell—her surviving your Uncle John 25 years is wonderful, as she was older than <u>he</u>—Your Uncle Harry is still in America, we know not what he is about—

dear Caroline is better, but has had a bad attack recently, the dear children and H.[4] well.

Your Father wonderful for him. I have not heard from Walter except by letters to his father for a long time, nor from John since Nov[br] when he was <u>well,</u> and in favor with his commanding Officer & his companions. Your Uncle Alex[r5] was mindful of us, he left all his property to be divided equally between your father, Elisabeth and Cecilia,[6] share and share <u>alike,</u> but he has ordered the term of six years to expire before his affairs are wound up, to prevent <u>loss</u> by the premature sale of his interest in Gas companies &c &c—if ever we get any of it you shall please God get John's debt <u>in full,</u> the payment of which would make me supremely happy. We had M[rs] Monk Mason[7] and one of her children at dinner here a fortnight ago, she is a <u>very</u> handsome woman, she was friendly, and is pleasing, has very little to live on, and has 5 children to bring up—

We hear from Elisabeth very often her husband is now <u>full</u> Colonel,[8] besides having some appointment inspecting the Cadets I think, at Woolwich—we heard from Cecilia to day, relative to the Tasmania affairs, she and her husband are at Stockport, Cheshire, where he has a curacy, did I tell you M[rs] Henry Grey was dead, of Edinburgh,—he[9] is living still—D[r] Duke has lately had £10,000, left him by an Uncle who died here lately, a cause of great joy, as it will provide for his large family. Miss Fectors nephew Lyttleton Bayley,[10] has arrived safely at Sydney with his wife and three children servants &c—better in health <u>all,</u> than when they sailed from London. The passage was made in 84 days. Scarlet fever which has cut off hundreds here, thousands in London is raging in Sydney, they are afraid to go into the Town—Miss F— has had a constant continuance of coughs colds, catarrhs &c all the summer, and her sight grows <u>worse</u>—

Jan[y] 13th I am glad I waited, for I got yours of Nov[br] last night, the sight of your writing rejoiced me. I am concerned to hear of your gum boil, <u>lancing</u> or rather <u>scarification</u> of the gums all round, is the remedy, if you have any medical man near you, get it done. The death of the man who swallowed his teeth was truly horrible. I have left off wearing mine since my fever, and feel <u>much</u> relieved; in any little illness even, they were intolerable! and then the dread of being caught without them, the hiding in consequence from visitors was odd, during my fever I could not wear them, and I cared not for the medical men, I believ[d] I was going <u>home,</u> and only thought of "our Father" now I see everybody, I have always a <u>clean</u> cap, and clean hands, and plenty of visitors.—M[rs] Monck Mason's brother Charles Cheyne was married last Saturday The Bride sent me cards, Harriet Maria Murphy! an Irish lady, his second wife.

Your Uncle Alex[r] divided all his property, but this I am concerned to find out on looking back I have mentioned before, but the will is not to be acted upon for <u>six</u> years! so we are not likely to benefit by his bequest, as we are not likely to live so long. Poor Elisabeth! my heart aches for her, my brother[11] has been very cruel, Bessie broke her heart at being separated from her Mother & brother, and Ireland! She imagines if she could get back to there she would be well, she complained of the <u>smoke</u> of Woolwich, and want of air, if I knew where your Aunt was I would write to her, I have regretted not being acquainted with her address, if you communicate with her, tell her this, with my <u>love</u> and sympathy; I am happy to tell you that dear Caroline is much very much better, the children and Henry all well.

Your Uncle Harry still wandering thro' the United States, Nelson & Nan pretty well. now that my wrist is stronger if my head aches get better I shall write more frequently, I wish I may be able to continue the rides in the Donkey chair, but every thing is so dear here, we are <u>pinched</u> a little—

Write often, I do not care how little; if I know that you are <u>alive,</u> it quickens my prayers for you—It is a long time since I heard from Walter—farewell! Ever your fondly attached Mother while life remains

     Lucinda Cheyne

Text: ALS NLA MS133/1/28

[1] The Christmas thirteen years before (1845), Lucinda and Bayne Cheyne's youngest son William Alexander, would still have been alive. He died on 4 January 1846, aged fourteen. John Cheyne and Henry D. Richardson (LC's oldest son) would also have been alive.

[2] Large wheeled chairs, so called because they were long used in the city of Bath, where invalids were taken to benefit from the mineral waters.

[3] Clementine Sirée (c.1792–1858), widow of John Sirée, Lucinda Cheyne's brother and eldest son of Henry Sirée and Harriet née McCausland.

[4] Henry Richardson.

[5] Captain Alexander Cheyne (1785–1858), brother of Bayne Cheyne.

[6] Elisabeth and Cecilia were the names of Alexander and Bayne's older sisters but they were also the names of his nieces and it is the nieces to whom Alexander was referring in his will. Alexander's oldest sister, Cecilia Cheyne (born in 1775), married Robert Strong on 5 July 1796 and died on 3 August 1845, as noted in Alexander Cheyne's diary. Alexander's second oldest sister, Elisabeth Cheyne (born in 1778), married William Wilkinson on 11 November 1803 and she died 24 February 1836. The Wilkinsons had several children (including Elisabeth and Cecilia) and in his diary, Alexander Cheyne mentions Elisabeth and Cecilia Wilkinson. Cecilia Wilkinson married Henry Graham on 2 January 1839. Elisabeth Wilkinson married Lieutenant Frederick Augustus Yorke of the Royal Engineers (Alexander Cheyne's old Regiment) on 10 February 1842.

[7] Sarah Louise Monck Mason née Cheyne (b. 1828), daughter of Henry Cheyne, born Dargle, Dublin. The relationship of Henry Cheyne to Bayne Cheyne is not known. Henry may have been the son of Dr John Cheyne, Bayne's elder brother. She was the widow of George Henry Monck Mason, relative, perhaps son or grandson, of either Henry J. Monck Mason, LLD, Librarian of the Hon. Society of King's Inns (listed in *Thom's Irish Almanack* for 1816) or William Monck Mason, author of *The History and Antiquities of the Collegiate and Cathedral Church of St Patrick near Dublin* (Dublin: 1820).

[8] Colonel Fred Augustus Yorke.

[9] Dr Henry Grey died in Edinburgh later in the year (1859). He was the Minister of Buccleuch and Greyfriars Free Church, Edinburgh, which Lucinda and Bayne Cheyne and their children may well have attended when they moved to Edinburgh from Bristol. Dr Grey had a long career in the Church from his first appointment in 1813 to Kirk O'Field. In 1821 he was appointed Minister to Marchmont St Giles from St Cuthbert's Chapel and was the first Minister at Bellevue (St Mary's) in 1825. In 1843 differences arose within the Church on the question of the right of patrons to nominate to livings. At the General Assembly, 400 Ministers (nearly half of the body), led by Dr Thomas Chalmers, seceded from the Church and formed the Free Church, which advocated the rights of the parishioners to veto any Minister's appointment. Dr Grey left his ministry at St Mary's to join the Free Church, and, followed by many of his congregation, the Buccleuth Free Church was formed, later joining with the Greyfriars Free Church.

[10] (Sir) Lyttleton Holyoake Bayley (1827–1910), barrister, MP, and judge; son of Sir John Edward George Bayley, 2nd Baronet, and his first wife, Charlotte Mary née Fector, who was the sister of Lucinda Cheyne's friend, Caroline Fector. After his education at Eton, he studied law and was called to the Bar of the Middle Temple on 3 May 1850. He married Isabella née Mactier on 12 May 1852. He and his wife arrived in Sydney in late 1858

accompanied by their two daughters (Ella and Isabella Constance) and one son (Stanhope Lyttleton Fector). Claiming to have a large capital for investment, he quickly settled into the Sydney social scene and was nominated to the Legislative Council of NSW on 19 January 1859. The next month the legal fraternity in Sydney was outraged when, on the retirement A. J. P. Lutwyche, Bayley was appointed Attorney-General. D. H. Deniehy's motion to the Legislative Assembly that such appointments should only be conferred upon persons whose residence in the territory had been of sufficient length to 'afford the country satisfactory guarantees for fitness and propriety' was lost and Bayley took office on 1 March. He stood for the Mudgee electorate in the Legislative Assembly elections and was elected June 1859, with an overwhelming majority. Deniehy immortalised Bayley's appointment in the satirical publication, *How I Became Attorney-General of New Barataria* (Sydney, 1860). In October 1859 the government fell and Bayley resigned on 26 November. In December 1859 he left for Melbourne, where his wife died at St Kilda on 9 April 1860 after the birth of second son, Vernon Batthyring Fector. A month later, he attended the Governor's levee, as did MR with her brother JRB, held on 24 May 1860, in honour of Queen Victoria's birthday (see Letter 57). Bayley's name was listed in *The Age* (25 May 1860) as one of the gentlemen holding private cards of entrée who were presented to the Governor, and he stood on the daïs beside His Excellency. It is not known whether he ever met MR or WLR. Bayley practised in Melbourne as a barrister, with chambers in Temple Court, Collins Street, but within a year returned to England. From April 1862, when he was appointed to the government of Bombay, he spent the next thirty-three years serving in India. His first appointment was as Under-Secretary and in 1866 he became the Advocate-General with a seat in the Legislative Council. He was elevated to the bench of the High Court of Judicature in June 1869 and during the next twenty-five years acted as Chief Justice five times. A Lieutenant-Colonel in the Volunteer Bombay Rifle Corps, he acted briefly as aide-de-camp to the viceroy of India. When the Chief Justice in India retired, Bayley was not appointed to that position and he resigned in disappointment. He returned to England and was created KB. He died on 4 August 1910 at Parkstone, Dorset.

11   Henry Sirée had left his wife (with her son, Alick Cook) in Victoria, his daughter Bessie with her aunt in Woolwich and his son Horatio Nelson in Dublin, and had then gone off to travel around America.

Walter was very ill at the end of March and the beginning of April in 1859 with dysentery. He received the following letter a few days before he took a coach trip to Queenscliff via Geelong to recuperate for a week by the sea. He then sailed across Port Phillip Bay from Queenscliff to Melbourne to visit the Turnhams.

41   [From Masonic Lodge at Buninyong to WLR in Ballarat]

Lodge Room, Buninyong
15th April 1859

Worshipful Sir and Brother

We the W.M. officers and Brethren of the Buninyong Lodge[1] having heard with regret of your recent severe attack of illness, hasten to take advantage of the first opportunity afforded us, collectively, of giving expression to our sympathy with your sufferings; and at the same time to perform the more pleasing duty of conveying to you our sincere congratulations on the prospect of your speedy recovery.

Accept Worshipful Sir and Brother this testimony of our regard and be assured that we are much concerned for your welfare, and that we appreciate the anxious solicitude which you have always shown for the advancement of the craft, as well as that rectitude of conduct which entitles you to the respect and esteem of your brethren in freemasonry.

We are| Worshipful Sir and Brother| Fraternally Yours

[List of 16 signatures[2]]

Text: ALS NLA MS133/1/248

[1]   Buninyong Masonic Lodge met at the Nugget Hotel, Buninyong, and was linked to the Irish Provincial Grand Lodge of Victoria (by patent from the Duke of Leinster, Most Worshipful Grand Master of Ireland).

[2]   F. D. Monfort, J. H. Stanfield, Edward Osborne, John A. Norris, Jas. Mulholland, H. A. Corngold, Wm Whitton Davies, Abr. Taylor, Wm Bailey Rankin, Robt Maddocks, Ralph Ward, James Spring, J. W. Kennedy, John Bilson, John Sheffield, Isedor Yde.

42   [From WLR in Geelong to MR in Ballarat]

Bennetts Hotel, Geelong
Thursday evening [21 April 1859]

My dear M.

Seeing a nice covered waggon passing about 2 P.M. I sent Mary out & got in, starting at once. We got thro' the Main Road pretty well the only person I saw I knew was Robert Cuthbert:[1] after passing thro' Buninyong the driver found it was getting late & put his horses into a trot on a very bad road, it was very bad at first until I got used to it. We arrived safely at the Corduroy Hotel 7 o'clock, where I was moved for the first time—had tea of ham & one egg, and a glass of Brandy, to bed at nine, twice up in the night & three times before starting, which we did at 6 AM, fancy my getting up at 6. and washing in cold water, then turning out and not getting breakfast for 6 miles—which however we did at 8. on liver & bacon & hash. Moved again: then drove on to the Clyde to dinner at 2 moved again: hearty dinner soup, fish, roast mutton, potatoes, cheese, ale—then drove in to this by 7. to tea off curry & chops—

So you see my dear I am already getting better: no pain whatever: and I feel I may eat what I fancy Tomorrow Good Friday is a great day crowds going down to Queenscliffe[2]—The Williamsons[3] were very civil indeed—gave me a letter of introduction to the officer of Customs at Queenscliffe—

And now I am going to astonish you! The Bradshaws of the Family Hotel were sold off yesterday, Furniture House Land & every thing, by Nantes & Brown, the house bought, & when I passed today the blinds all down. They are all going to live with Alexander[4]—very sad is it not, but a punishment for defrauding their governess of her just due!

And now darling I think I have told you all about myself and my doings I hope you will let me have a letter soon from you, you had better draw money from savings bank, & pay John £4 at once on those shares of the Clunes—

Off this morning not quite so well—in some pain. Will write again tomorrow| Good bye darling

     WLR

Text: ALS NLA MS133/1/168

1   Robert Browne Cuthbert (1841–1880), youngest son of John Cuthbert and Elizabeth née Headen. He became a sheep farmer. He married Emma Argyle Campbell (1845–1936) in 1871 and they had five children: Jessie Headen (b. 1872), Henry (1874–1940), Robert Campbell (1876–1893), Emma Argyle (1878–1963) and Anna Nixon (1880–1951).

2   The Borough of Queenscliffe (with an 'e') includes Point Lonsdale. The town of Queenscliff (without an 'e') was created on 12 May 1863.

3   The Williamsons not identified.

4   Not Alexander Brooke Smith, as suggested by Dorothy Green (Green, 1986, p. 367) but Henry Allday Alexander (1835–1860), who had married Marian Buller Bradshaw (Polly) (b. 1842) four months previously on 14 December 1858. He was described on the marriage certificate as residing in Geelong and employed as a 'pound keeper' and she was given no rank or profession. Henry Alexander died in July 1860 and Polly married Robert Jones on 9 October 1867. Jones had been divorced from his first wife the previous July.

43   [From WLR in Queenscliff to MR in Ballarat]

Queenscliffe

~~Thursday 8 AM~~ Wednesday evening [27 April 1859]

My darling Mary

I got your letter again tonight the 2ⁿᵈ, and as I find it will cost me 15/- to get from this to Geelong I have resolved to run up to Melbourne until Monday next—So if you have written one to Geelong P.B. why it will only lie there until I get it thats all—the enclosure all right—pretty well today not moved from 10 to 3 and took a fine walk to gather shells & sea weed—my cer[tain]ty the bazaar[1] will realize £500 or more!

Weather colder difficulty in getting proper food here for me—and I am tired of the place—wish I had stayed at Geelong! I am so grieved for poor Susan[2] give her my love tell her how I feel for her and caution her against solid food—she ought to have had medical advice a month ago I hope to God John wont allow them to <u>do to her what they did to me</u>—Dr H.[3] ought to be cautioned that she is like me <u>highly nervous temperament</u> with a pulse in health often 100. tell him this—

I am better this morning than I have been yet a better night no motion from ½ past 11 till 6—I spent last evening at one of the pilots[4] where we had a game at whist, his lady taking a hand—I took a glass of burnt brandy wh. I think did me good—Remember me to Shanks.[5] I suppose Mʳˢ S is home by this

I wrote Lucinda[6] a long letter addressed to Mʳˢ Thompson's Kyneton was that right?

I leave this tomorrow morning 8 A.M. for Melbourne getting there about 1 or ½ past if you write by tomorrows post I will get it Saturday—& I think of leaving Monday morning—unless they are very pressing & then I may stay a day or two longer.

I am going out for a drive this afternoon 4 miles to Point Lonsdale which you will see on my map—I hope you enjoyed the ball?[7] & that you went—The clergyman[8] called on me. I hope dear the house is not burned down, have you got the garden done? I suppose not! Rather unfortunate that Mʳˢ Jeffery[9] shd be confined of a still born child—Will write again Saturday next—

Good bye loved one| Your own
        Walter

Text: ALS NLA MS133/1/226

1   The Ladies Bazaar in aid of the funds of the Benevolent Asylum was held in the Council
    Chambers, Sturt Street, throughout Easter week, opening on Monday, 25 April 1859. The
    ladies of Ballarat had been preparing for the bazaar for two or three months and they made a
    profit of over £520. The reporter from *The Ballarat Star*, who may well have been JRB, was
    fulsome in his praise: 'The approach to the Chambers was beneath an arch of evergreens, and
    within there were evergreens too, and banners with mottos, and banners without mottos, and
    multicolored hangings, and flowers natural and artificial both very beautiful … But besides
    these outer flourishes about the series of stalls, there were the stalls themselves, laden—yes, that
    is the word—laden with a perfect wilderness of inscrutable beauties in a thousand shapes and
    hues.' The reporter named the lady stall-holders of each stall. 'Last of all, or first of all we have
    the stall presided over by Mesdames Richardson and Drury, and the Misses B. Lynn, Cuthbert
    and Wynne; under whose administration also, in the absence of Dr Evans [the Hon George
    Samuel Evans, LLD, MLA, Victorian Government Postmaster-General] or Mr Paine [postmaster
    at Ballarat] (and verily, we believe, in their absence just as well), the 'Post Office' is placed and
    everybody visited with a letter by a mail that never fails to arrive … let the Peninsula and
    Oriental Company, or any other company's steamers play what vagaries they please.' *Star*,
    25 April 1859, p. 2. What this 'post office' was is not known but it obviously added to the
    coffers of the bazaar. Twenty years later MR became a professional postmistress with the
    assistance of her fellow stall-holder and close friend's brother, Henry Cuthbert, then Postmaster-
    General.
2   Susannah Tyler Bailey née Nicholson died four months later on 13 August 1859 of 'Chronic
    Dysentry and Marasmus'. She was under the care of her brother-in-law, WLR. 'At her residence,
    Sturt St, at 1.25 am on Saturday 13 August after a long and painful illness, in the 27th year of
    her age, Susannah Tyler, the beloved wife of Mr John Robinson Bailey.' *Star*, Saturday,
    13 August 1859, p. 2.
3   Dr Robert Fawell Hudson (1834–1898), physician; son of Robert Hudson, builder, and Mary
    née Fawell. In 1865 he married Elizabeth Ann Bath (1846–1883), daughter of Malachi Bath
    and Elizabeth née Bews. Hudson was born in Salford and educated at University of St Andrews.
    He became Chairman of Ballarat Gas Co. and Ballarat Banking Co. He owned Terawynia
    Station, NSW, in partnership with Agar Wynne and others. He died in Ballarat in 1898.
4   Port Phillip Sea Pilots organisation is one of the oldest in the state. George Tobin started
    piloting ships through the Heads in November 1838 and was granted the first licence by
    Governor Gipps of NSW on 26 June 1839. Eleven pilots were operating privately on a co-
    operative basis by the time of the gold rush. In 1859 the pilots included: Thomas Sutton
    (operating 1839–1859), J. G. Caught (1850–1880) and M. Taylor (1851–1873).
5   Henry Shanks (c.1826–1879), an engineer from Drummond Street, Ballarat.
6   Lucinda Richardson.
7   The Benevolent Asylum Ball was held at Bath's Hotel on Thursday evening, 5 May 1859 and
    tickets were two guineas each. WLR had mistaken the date.
8   There were no churches built prior to 1863 but visiting clergymen came to Queenscliff from
    Geelong.
9   Probably Maria Jefferies née Cuthbert (b. c.1831), born in Stowmarket, Suffolk, England. She
    was married to James Jefferies (c.1824–1874), who arrived in Melbourne in 1852 on the *Severn*.
    They had two living sons: James Julius (b. 1855) and John Charles (b. 1857). Their first son,
    Robert, died aged seven days in 1854 and now their fourth son was stillborn. Nine months later
    a daughter, Alice Florence, was born on 20 January 1860, followed by one more son, George
    Edward (1862–1882), and two daughters, Ada Blanche (b 1864) and Elizabeth Maud, who died
    aged eleven months in 1871.

44   [From WLR in Collingwood to MR in Ballarat]

Collingwood [Stockade, Melbourne]
Saturday morning [30 April 1859]

[No salutation]

I wrote you last my dearest from Queenscliffe Wednesday night, and I sailed to
Melbourne yesterday morning at 8 oclock:—I had not been improving in <u>my worst respect,</u>

altho' I found my legs stronger; I took leave of the place with no regret, for the monotony was rather engendering ennui—I advised Dod[1] the P. Master to telegraph[2] the English news up to John provided it came <u>in any night before 12,</u> so that they might have it in the <u>next</u> mornings <u>issue, without waiting for an answer to his letter.</u> I do not know whether John will consider that I was overstepping my legitimate business at Queenscliffe, by making arrangements for the Star, but I take some credit for what I did, whether he accept the terms or not—

You can read him that: well I took no breakfast before starting xcept bread & butter & cold milk & on board some biscuits & a bottle of porter, no disturbance from 7. to 2. Cab from Station to here found Uncle out at Randles[3] funeral & Aunt delighted to see me & so kind

I live on the plainest food: Kangaroo soup twice after coming here yesterday & not moved <u>all night,</u> for wh. I am very thankful, <u>the first time since the beginning of my illness!</u> so you see dear I began to improve as soon as I started for this really—Everything much improved about the house & so hospitable, all so sorry you are <u>not</u> with me, & so am I but we must learn to do what is right.

I am so anxious about you, no letter now since Tuesday last enclosing £2–0–0. How have you been, & Susan is she better & the bazaar & the ball & every body? Xpect me back Monday night or Tuesday night as I suppose they will not let me start before Tuesday, & they really are so kind it is a pleasure & a happiness to be here. Willie[4] appears to be a nice boy pity he has not got the necessary qualification strict probity[5]—Ned has written here, he has got a situation 15/- per day at Malmesbury, he say date 23rd he has written me—Have you got it?

We are going in today with Uncle & Willie to see the Museum[6] & D[r] McKirdy[7]—I breakfasted off two eggs & a cup of milk, they keep a cow & make their own butter—

Lots of ducks, & turkeys, & fowls & rabbits. We must really see if we cant do something of the sort or else have a jolly good garden to amuse us,[8]

Good bye dearest| I am in a hurry| Your loving husband

Walter

Aunt & Uncles kind love & pressing invitation for you for next summer promised

Text: ALS NLA MS133/1/169

[1]   Charles Dod (*c.*1806–1868), son of Henry and Susan née Dill, born in Taunton, Devon. He was appointed in 1849 as the first permanent officer to take charge of the Registration of Births and Deaths in Queenscliffe and also the Electoral Registrar. Postmaster at Queenscliff from 1853 until his death in 1868, his widow, Anna Maria Dod, succeeded him as postmistress 1869. Her fictional counterpart is Mrs Spence, called Granny by Cuffy and Lucie, see *FRM III*, p. 253. His son, Henry Charles Dod, born 23 July 1854, was appointed to the Postal and Telegraphic service on 24 June 1869 but was not made postmaster of Queenscliff until 1875 to 1884. Two more of the Dod children were appointed to the service: Susan Emily Dod was appointed on 24 February 1870 and worked until her marriage to Richard Holdsworth Mcfarlane in 1876; and Elizabeth Mary (Bessie) Dod (1856–1938), born 23 March 1856, was appointed on 1 April 1876 to assist her brother at Queenscliff. It was Henry and Bessie who, in 1877, taught MR the skills necessary to run a post office (especially Morse code) when WLR's health made him unfit for work. Henry moved to Colac post office in 1884 until 1890, when he was transferred to Kew (1890–1892); then Hawthorn (1892–1894); and finally to Warrnambool, where he remained until after the turn of the century. On 5 September 1881, at All Saints Church in Queenscliff, Bessie married James Lambert Baillieu (1855–1890), the eldest son of James George Baillieu and his wife, Emma Lawrence née Pow. It was Bessie's brother-in-law, William Lawrence Baillieu (1859–1936) who was the 'pivot around whom the family fortune was made' (see *ADB*). Whether WLR knew the Baillieu family at this time is not clear, but he delivered their last baby, Norman Horace, on 17 June 1878, shortly before his breakdown. John F. Waghorn, *Index of Victoria's Postmasters and Postmistresses: 1839 to 1901*

(Thomastown, Victoria: the Author, 1987) and John F. Waghorn, *Index of Victoria Postal and Telegraph Department Staff Who Commenced Duty Between 1839 and 1901* (Thomastown, Victoria: the Author, 1989). Also letter from D.O.D., in *Geelong Advertiser*, 3 February 1929, p. 4, and reply from Mary L. Bailey (Polly, widow of Samuel Bailey), 6 February 1929, p. 4.

2   Queenscliff was the first place in Victoria (outside Melbourne and Geelong) to be supplied with telegraphic communications. The telegraph office (situated with the post office on the site of the present fort) was established in 1856. The first telegraphic officer was Mr Vivian.

3   Detective Walter Rendell (*c*.1826–1859) had died on Tuesday, 26 April 1859 between 7 and 8 o'clock at the wharf, after arresting a man for stealing goods from a lighter (a flat-bottomed barge used for loading vessels). He had fallen between the lighter and the wharf, and drowned. As he was a powerful man and a strong swimmer, it was thought that he must have sustained an injury prior to landing in the water. His body was recovered by the captain of the lighter and taken to the Sir Charles Hotham Hotel. The arrested man escaped during the confusion, but was recaptured as, according to *The Argus*, he was 'well known to police'. Detective Rendell was one of fifty constables drafted from the London Police force and sent out with Superintendent Freeman in 1853, at the request of the Victorian government. He left a wife and three children. His funeral took place on Friday, 29 April 1853 and was an impressive affair, with a hearse decorated with six plumes, drawn by four horses with plumes, escorted by six pall-bearers, followed by two mourning coaches, two lines of all the police who were not on duty, mounted police and finally thirty carriages of friends. A full report of the funeral, including all the names of the senior police and magistrates in attendance, appeared in *The Argus* on Saturday, 30 April 1857.

4   William Henry Turnham (*c*.1841–1905), MR's cousin, son of William Henry Turnham and Sarah née Robinson, the sister of Elizabeth Bailey. His parents married on 5 April 1837 at St Martins in the Field, Westminster. He had one sister, Elizabeth, christened 16 March 1838 at St George's Parish Church, Leicester (referred to as Cousin Bessie by Mary Richardson). He came to Victoria to join his aunt and uncle (Joseph and Elizabeth Turnham) in 1858.

5   WLR's assessment of Willie appears to be accurate. Appointed as a Warden at Pentridge on 3 February 1860, he had ten years of undistinguished public service before he was discharged on 8 July 1870 on the grounds of 'bodily infirmity with a gratuity and 9 months pay'. Remarks on his employment record at Pentridge reveal fines for 'letting off his gun carelessly', 'disobedience of orders', 'disrespect', 'absent without leave', and 'improper language'. *Staff Appointments: 1854–1873*, VPRS 538 Vol. 1, PRO, Victoria. He married Lydia Mary Cole in 1863 and they had ten children from 1864 to 1881. He became a journalist and worked for a Brunswick newspaper and remained in the Pentridge–Coburg area until his death. His widow, Lydia, remarried in 1906 to William Henry Frederick Heberle, who was born in Germany and died in East Melbourne in 1916 aged sixty-eight.

6   Museum of Natural History, Geology, Agriculture and Mining, at the University, Parkville.

7   Not identified. Professor Frederick McCoy (1817–1899) was the Director of the Museum.

8   Five months later at a meeting in Bath's Hotel on 11 October 1859, WLR was elected Vice-President of the Ballarat Horticultural Society, with Dr Charles Kenworthy as President. The chairman of the meeting was Richard Ocock, Solicitor.

45   [From LC in Brighton, England, to WLR and MR in Ballarat]

17 Buckingham Place West Cliff. Brighton| Sussex.| England
do not put Surrey instead of Sussex
Oc^{tbr} 19th /59

My beloved Walter & darling Mary

I have been greatly grieved to find from your last letter[1] dated August 17th that my many letters have not reached you, I know that in reply to dear Mary's communication in regard to your severe illness in April last, I was too late for the mails both I believe, but I thought that there would surely be some vessel going which would convey them, this place is so different from London or the other great seaports, that there are many hindrances and obstructions to the forwarding of letters, notwithstanding its gigantic size: it is but a country Town—we have no Son, brother or nephew to transact business for us. I <u>never</u> go out, and your father has been so long ill, and is now so feeble, I am often at a loss, what to do—or <u>how</u> to get even a common letter posted—you ought to have received 3 letters at least from me since June, telling of my love and sympathy and your father's dangerous illness,—I grieve to think of what Mary has been going thro', while I am thankful that you had the blessed privilege of bringing the glad tidings of the Saviour to any soul, and especially to one of your near Kindred: a death scene reveals to us the unspeakable value of the Gospel, and the emptyness of earth and its shadows—Christ & He only at such a period is the sole stay, the alone resting place for the suffering frame of the distressed spirit, having Him we want <u>no more</u> one little <u>point</u> I venture to mention as differing from, it is "asking <u>her</u> to pray for you all"—a <u>creature</u> cannot intercede <u>in Heaven</u> on earth we <u>may</u> intercede for one another, but before the Throne Jesus is the <u>only</u> advocate, mediator and intercessor, <u>He</u> is our High Priest as well as our Redeemer or nearest <u>of Kin,</u>—

I bless God for not only restoring your health but giving you back your practice, trust Him my beloved Walter, He <u>will</u> provide—I greatly fear dear Mary will suffer from all the fatigue, especially if she have the charge of the dear infant for any length of time, I sent off your letter to M[rs] Bailey,[2] the acc[t] was so full, and interesting, I thought she w[d] like to see it—I had a letter from Lucinda along with yours, she has left Kyneton, and is with M[rs] Doveton[3] at Dagglesford,[4] but where that is I know not, and she does not say, she had not received my letters, consequently, I suppose they are at Kyneton, Your Uncle Harry's wife has arrived[5] but her dear boy[6] remains at Melbourne in a situation, she was to go to her Sister at Woolwich, our present abode is so small we can receive no one even if we were inclined so we shall not see her, your Uncle is staying in Dublin much shaken in health, but a changed man, I trust a <u>new creature,</u> but he has not written me a line, so I am a stranger to his plans and purposes. M[rs] Osborne[7] is in a very critical state of health, <u>worse</u> rather than better D[r] Duke was called in to hold a consultation with her own medical adviser, and Henry[8] tells me he thinks her condition very serious—Your Uncle N—[9] is living in Co Wicklow somewhere, <u>he</u> scarcely <u>ever</u> writes

Caroline has been again <u>very</u> ill, her internal disease going on, her children not yet recovered from the effects of the whooping cough—The cold east winds which set in after the intense heat, have laid many low, your father has rallied again surprisingly, but I dread the winter, he needs so much heat, and our nights are so cold. Such a Summer as the past I <u>never</u> remember the heat was tropical, Ther. 99 in the shade 120 to 130 in the sun.

Oc[tbr] 20th My beloved Walter, I have been seized with an attack of bronchitis, owing as we suppose to the sudden change of the weather great rain having succeeded the heat & drought the dampness consequently considerable—

I hope you receive all my newspapers, I send many and Miss Fector it is that posts them she writes every mail to her nephew Littleton Bayley who is at Sydney, I trust my letters will have turned up, as she <u>herself</u> posted them latterly we often speak of you, she is still active altho' not very strong, M[r] Sinclair[10] still a sort of travelling missionary at Gretna employed by M[r] Cunningham[11] of Edinburgh,—

M[r] Bagot[12] is married again to a Baronets daughter, the wedding took place at Edinburgh,—Pray let me hear <u>soon,</u> and tell me particularly how dearest Mary is, and that poor baby,[13] and as much of <u>yourself</u> and progress in grace as you can—at <u>times</u> I feel the separation trying, prayer for you <u>both</u> is my remedy,—a short letter from John, written sailing

on the Ganges when on his way to <u>Assam</u> desiring us to direct to the post office there, is all
that we have heard since.—the Reg^t is disbanded no pay, but a medal to each—with <u>thanks</u> &
commendations!—do not forget <u>me</u> nor think I can ever cease to love or think of you, but
with life ceasing, assure Mary of my love and constant remembrance, and with your father's
love and blessing to both and my own earnest prayers for your happiness temporal & Eternal
believe me my very dear Son your| attached Mother

      Lucinda Cheyne

Text: ALS NLA MS133/1/29

[1] The letter announced the death of Susannah Tyler Bailey on 13 August 1859, aged twenty-six
years, of 'Chronic dysentery Marasmus'. WLR had been attending her from the beginning of
May 1859 (as soon as he had returned from his trip to Queenscliff and Collingwood). On her
death certificate, her parents were named as Henry and Mary Nicholson and her father's
occupation was described as 'Artist', although he was a professor of music according to the
Leicester *Directories*. She came to Victoria in 1852 and married JRB on 29 January 1853 in
Geelong. She was buried in Ballarat on 15 August 1859 and left three children and her husband,
who was then editor of *The Ballarat Star*.

[2] Elizabeth Bailey (1802–1869), mother of MR, living in Leicester.

[3] Mary Ann Doveton née Snell (1838–1901) married on 14 July 1855 at Castlemaine to Captain
Francis Crossman Doveton (b. 1817), who was the Warden and Justice of the Peace. He had
been previously married to Margaret née Bostock, who died of dysentery in Castlemaine in
January 1853 at the same time as one of their children. By his first wife Francis had several
children including: Margaret Elizabeth and Rachel Emily (1847–1928), both born in Tasmania;
and Annie (b. 1848), Fran (b. 1850) and John Frederick (b. 1852), all born in Victoria. It was
for these children, presumably, that Lucinda Richardson had been engaged as governess. At this
time Mary Ann Doveton had the first of eight children: Thomas Frederick (b. 1857). The other
subsequent seven children were: Honora Maria Mary (1861–1935), Florence Lucy
(1865–1923), Otto Guy William (b. 1868), Henry Albert (1870–1875), Charlotte Ella Alice
(1873–1875), Catherine Josephine (1876–1946) and Bazette (1880–1880). F. C. Doveton
(a close friend of the Reverend John Cheyne) was the Commissioner of Crown Lands when gold
was discovered in 1851. He was ordered by Governor Charles La Trobe to proceed to
Buninyong to bring order to the chaotic diggings with the imposition of a gold field licence tax
of 30 shillings per month. Bate, pp. 12–14, 16.

[4] Daylesford, a small town seventy kilometres north-west of Melbourne.

[5] Mrs Sirée departed from Melbourne on 30 July 1859 on the *Yorkshire*, arriving in London in
October 1859.

[6] Alick Cook.

[7] Caroline Osborne née Sirée (b. 1800), sister of Lucinda Cheyne. She married Charles William
Osborne in 1823. Despite Lucinda's concern about her health, Caroline Osborne was still alive
when WLR visited her in Dublin in December 1868. See Letter 140.

[8] Henry Richardson, LC's son-in-law.

[9] Dr Horatio Nelson Sirée.

[10] Not identified.

[11] Not identified.

[12] Not identified.

[13] Edith Elizabeth Bailey (1858–1860) died when she was eighteen months old on 5 February
1860. She and her two older siblings (Harrie and Emma) were cared for by MR and WLR after
the death of their mother.

46 [From LC in Brighton, England, to WLR in Ballarat]

17 Buckingham Place| West Cliff Brighton| <u>Sussex</u>. | England.

Nov^{br} 9th 1859

My beloved Walter

I made up and your father posted 6 newspapers for you this morg and as I have sore eyes, I can only write a very few lines to tell you how grieved I was to learn that you had not received my letters as writing to you has formed one of my chiefest pleasures, you and my dearest daughter Mary being seldom absent from my thoughts—I wrote last month by the "<u>White Star</u>" there being some change in the Mail packets, and a week afterwards I was concerned to find, that owing to the severity of the weather she was lying by in some port, being afraid to venture out, in consequence of the fearful catastrophe which occurred on the 25th Oc^{tbr} to the Royal Charter[1] by which ~~470~~ four hundred & 70 human beings were hurried into eternity, at Moelfre Bay[2] on the Welch coast, just opposite Beaumaris, almost in sight of Liverpool, after a short and most favorable passage from Melbourne.

The Gales have indeed been fearful, the loss of life <u>terrible,</u> at every port the accts most distressing, both of men and shipping—since Nov^{br} set in nothing but lightning Thunder and hurricanes devastation every where—and this after a summer which for tropical heat and drought was quite unprecedented in this favored country—

This too at a time when War & its horrors were impending over the land, when our navy was depopulated, and men not to be had to man our ships,—With these judgments coming and danger in view God has sent down a gale of the Holy Ghost, and on all sides hundreds have been crying, what must we do to be saved? This took place <u>first </u>in the provence of Ulster, and has extended over Wales Scotland and in this country, manifesting the most blessed results—Prayers & prayer meetings every where for the more extended enlargement of the Church of God, and quickening of the Holy Ghost—I have been wholly shut up these nine months, from weakness, and infirmity, I have had bronchitis these last few months and more lately a fall by which I hurt my ~~knees~~ knee, and from which I have not yet recovered—Your father I am most thankful to say is better, able to go about a little and to nurse me—Lucinda wrote me in August, telling me she was with a Mrs Doveton, but giving me <u>no </u>address, I have a letter for her ready but know not where to send it—Mrs Harry arrived last month from Australia, having been most kindly taken care of and sent home by Revd John Cheyne and wife[3]—Harry arrived from America about the same time—<u>he </u>is a <u>changed </u>man, he is in very bad health but if he live he will I trust preach Christ crucified.—Caroline is still suffering, her children delicate—Miss F.[4]— wonderfully well, Mrs Osborne, still laid up with that fearful complaint, I had <u>one </u>letter from John he is well, his Reg^t disbanded, his address is now Post Office Assam.—I have been longing to hear from you, and hope no letter of yours was sent by the Royal Charter—it is long since I had one, but trust and pray that you are going on from strength to strength <u>body</u> & <u>soul</u> night and morn^g my prayers ascend for this, and for my dear Mary's health & growth in grace also—so that altho' parted here below we may be united in that blessed world where parting and grief are unknown—To my God and Father I commend you believing His promise I will be a God to <u>Thee</u> and to Thy seed after thee—Amen, beloved children, farewell! The time is short, may every blessing attend you both,| Ever your fondly attached| Mother

Lucinda Cheyne

You should receive <u>6</u> Newspapers with this <u>all</u> duly stamped & directed by my own hands.

Dʳ Walter Lindsay Richardson
  Webster St
    Ballarat
      Victoria

Your father sends much love to Mary and yourself—Novᵇʳ 10ᵗʰ I add another Newspaper, giving an accᵗ of Lord Brougham's[5] reception & speeches in Edinburgh which we think will interest you and praying our God to bless & keep you and Mary amid all the trials of this mortal life we are with unchanging love yrs—

Text: ALS NLA MS133/1/30

[1] The *Royal Charter*, built in 1855 by the Gibbs, Bright and Co, was a companion vessel to the *Great Britain*. The disaster happened in the night. (LC dates it as 25 October and *The Age* as 26 October 1859.) Thirteen passengers having disembarked at Queenstown, Ireland, the *Royal Charter* then set off on 23 October 1859 for its final stage of the journey from Melbourne to Liverpool. In the terrible storm and wreck only thirty-nine passengers were saved from 495. *The Age*, 9 January 1860.

[2] Moelfre is on north-east coast of Anglesey, forty-five miles west from Liverpool.

[3] Reverend John Cheyne and his first wife, Anne Levina née Forest. See note to Letter 28.

[4] Caroline Fector.

[5] Henry Brougham, Lord Brougham and Vaux (1778–1868), born in Edinburgh; educated at High School and University of Edinburgh; admitted to Scottish bar (1800). In 1802 he helped to found the *Edinburgh Review* to which he contributed eighty articles expounding his liberal views. He moved to London and was called to the English bar in 1808. Entering Parliament in 1810, he carried an Act making participation in slave trade a felony. His eloquence and boldness gained him huge popular support but not that of the establishment. In 1830 the aristocratic Whigs would, had they dared, have excluded him from the Reform ministry but found him indispensable. In 1830 he was persuaded to accept a peerage and the chancellorship. Having assisted materially in carrying the Reform Bill, he went out with the Whig government in 1834. Founder of Social Science Association (1857), he is best remembered as a law reformer. When not engaged in Parliament, he resided at Cannes where he died on 7 May 1868.

47   [From LC in Brighton, England, to WLR in Ballarat]

17 Buckingham Place| West Cliff| Brighton Sussex.| England
Decᵇʳ 7ᵗʰ 1859[1]

My beloved Walter

It is now within a few days of four months since I heard from you[2] and I am becoming anxious, I have written regularly and sent many newspapers, being desirous you should know the critical state of Europe, and the involvements likely to be occasioned to this country in consequence, but as you will have learned all from the papers which I trust you have received, I need not take up my time by saying any thing of Political matters—but proceed at once to home news—Your Father has been nearly two months ill, and is still confined to the house, but the cough is much abated altho' pretty severe yet, especially in the Evgs he has lost much strength, but is cheerful & contented, indeed we have great reason to be thankful, for notwithstanding the trial from our bodily ailments, and the infirmities of old age your father being 72, we have such boundless source of ever increasing joy in our Jesus, that we are supremely happy and longing for the day when we shall be done with sin and mortality for Ever—I got over my Influenza which it was feared would end in Bronchitis very easily, by putting on a flannel shift which I wore until I nearly tore off all my skin, when I laid it aside, & replaced it by a calico one, which I changed every day, and I am wonderfully well, considering, that I have had great fatigue with attending your father, doing every thing myself—I never go out, except into my garden which was really lovely this last year, there in fine weather I can work for many hours freed from all care about personal appearance communing with God in Christ thro' His works, the flowers and birds, and ever varying clouds, I have six Toads, and one Lizard, I like to watch their habits and gaze on their beautiful eyes, I cannot think them disgusting animals as many do, they are useful in a garden, they destroy vermin.—

14ᵗʰ Decᵇʳ My dearest Walter, an increase of illness on your father's part and fatigue and anxiety consequent on mine stopped my letter—your father is down stairs again but not able to be out, and our mild relaxing weather has given place to fearful N.E. Gales which have brought on hard frost—

Caroline's second boy Lindsay has had an attack of Jaundice, she herself still suffers from her internal complaint, she is patient and resigned, growing in grace, happy and contented—Mʳˢ Osborne's sufferings have been severe, but she is better, and likely to hold on some time longer—The Religious revivals, or more properly awakenings go on, they are no longer confined to Ireland but proceed both in Scotland & England to great lengths, 1500 in Newcastle last week greater numbers in Glasgow, Edinburgh Bristol, and indeed in all our large and populous Towns—I hope you got all the Newspapers; I sent you 6 duly stamped and posted, postage on Newspapers is to be increased next month, I miss your father sadly as I have no one to do any little business for me now, but a stupid Sussex girl, who knows nothing.—I never go out for we cannot afford carriage hire—I am sending you a book for a New Years gift & trust you may like it as much as I do, your father & I read it lately together and found it truly profitable; I am becoming anxious at your long silence but continue to hope notwithstanding my disappointment every mail that comes in. I sent you two Newspapers giving account of the fearful catastrophe of the Royal Charter, many other terrible ship-wrecks have taken place, but none so awful as that one from the unusual circumstance of an Iron Screw Streamer falling to pieces like a pack of card Houses—and all going into Eternity, when they were expecting to walk on shore—I have not heard from John since.[3]

We are expecting Alick home for the holidays he is now 14, and safe from his Mother and the Priests, for which we desire to Praise God. We know nothing of the other poor children;

I trust dearest Mary is well, and not the worse for taking care of the poor little baby[4] assure her of my love, I hope the little book reached her safely—and that she will read it for my sake—Your Father sends much love and many blessings to her and you. God Bless you my beloved Son, and grant us a happy meeting when the Trump of the Arch-angel sounds; then you will know how much I have loved you!—| Ever your attached & anxious Mother

Lucinda Cheyne

Text: ALS NLA MS133/1/32

[1]   Lucinda commenced this letter exactly one week before the death of her son, John Cheyne, in Assam. The news of his death did not reach her for many months.

[2]   She means that it is nearly four months since WLR had written his letter on 17 August 1859 announcing the death of his sister-in-law, Susannah Bailey. She received that letter on or before 19 October 1859.

[3]   John Cheyne died the next day (15 December 1859) in Suddyah in Upper Assam, India, of fever (probably dysentery).

[4]   Edith Elizabeth Bailey (1858–1860), daughter of Susannah (deceased) and John Robinson Bailey.

1860

48   [From MR in St Kilda to WLR in Ballarat]

Heathville House| Alma Road East [St Kilda][1]

[Friday, 6 January 1860]

My dearest Walter

I cannot let the day pass without writing to you as well as Lucinda tho' you have not written to me as yet. I am glad to hear[2] darling that you are so busy & that you are well do you miss me very much. We[3] are very comfortably settled here & live remarkably well. Breakfast at ½ past 8 oclock Lunch at 1 Dinner at six & Tea at 8 we generally walk over to South Yarra after dinner to Miss Cuthberts cousins[4] she has a great number all living in nice houses—with pianos & we pass the evening very pleasantly—there are three of them widows[5] & the finest & prettiest set of ladies I have seen since my arrival here—the oldest[6] is only 27 year's John[7] came to see us last evening & walked over with us I never saw him so agreeable & enjoy himself so much · walked with Miss C all the way chatting but I fancy was rather taken with the pretty widow—walked with me to make enquiries about her & whether she had any family I told him one little girl but this is only imagination on my part so do not breathe a word he is very kind & I fancy will take these lodgings when we leave them & have Harry[8] with him. Yesterday we went to Pentridge[9] saw them all very pleased to see me Uncle apologised for not writing but his hand is not any better It is very expensive to go there being such a distance cost me 7 shillings & so in proportion for every place you want to go to—

Will you send me down a prescription for some ointment for a place that look's vastly like ringworm this shape [sketch of ring of small circles] very red like tiny blisters round the edge also for some blistering liquid as I suffered a deal of pain this last few day's and some ointment that will take away the place quickly as it look's nasty—The weather is terrifically hot not one cool day since here we've been I am going into Melbourne to seek something for Lucinda. I am so glad darling to hear that you are quite well & that the children[10] are good I hope they do not teaze you too much. I hear that Mrs Bradley had a son.[11] How I wish it was mine. There's to be grand doings at the christening. Go to Miss Newham's Wedding[12] & send me all the News—do write to me darling I long to see your handwriting though I cannot see your face—God bless & protect you darling is the prayer of| Your loving wife

Mary

Miss Cuthbert send's her love & so do I with plenty of kisses

Text: ALS NLA MS133/1/61

1   'Nearly all the leading members of the Bar, and lawyers, have houses here, which they have built, or taken a lease. In Alma Road, and its vicinity, may be found attorney-generals, past, present, and future, scattered in profusion.' Clara Aspinall, *Three Years in Melbourne* (London: L. Booth, 1862), p. 305.

2   MR had received a letter from Lucinda Richardson, who was staying in Ballarat with WLR, requesting MR's assistance in finding a new governess position.

3   MR, probably convalescing after a miscarriage, was staying at a boarding house with Anna Maria Cuthbert and Robert Cuthbert. She had taken with her Emma (Trotty), the three-year-old daughter of John Robinson Bailey. John had left his three children in MR and WLR's care since their mother's death the previous August.

4   Anna Maria Cuthbert's cousins were the siblings of Kingston Cuthbert (1832–1913), whose short biography appears in endnote 11, Letter 53. Their father was Lieutenant Kingston Gore Cuthbert (b. *c.*1805), the son of Patrick Cuthbert (b. *c.*1770) of Gowran, Kilkenny, Ireland and his wife Mary née Edgar (b. *c.*1775). Their mother, Mary Cuthbert née Cochrane (1801–1891) sailed to Melbourne with seven children on the *Medway*, arriving January 1852. They were joining Charles Cuthbert (1822–1858), the eldest son, who had sailed to Melbourne in 1849, probably for his health for he died of consumption on 14 December 1858, aged thirty-six. Kingston, the second eldest son, was left by his mother and sisters in Ireland, presumably to finish his education. He arrived in Melbourne eighteen months later. Accompanying their mother were: Selina, Maria Amelia, Harriett Georgiana, Henry, Eliza Frances, Emily and Agnes Jane. Selina (b. *c.*1832) married Saul or Samuel Graham in 1852, with whom she had two daughters and a son before her husband died prior to January 1860. Maria Amelia (b. *c.*1834) married a fellow passenger on the *Medway*, Duncan Fullerton (1824–1854), on 21 June 1853 in the Scots Church, Melbourne. Harriett Georgiana (b. *c.*1835) married George John Hastedt in 1855 and had a son, Kingston Frederick Hastedt, born in 1856 in St Kilda. Henry died aged twenty-two in 1858. Eliza Frances (1837–1881) married first John Yabbicom (1829–1858) in 1855, with whom she had a son, John Henry (1857–1858); secondly she married David Christy in 1863 and their children, born in Ballarat, were: Andrew Patterson (1864–1887), Herbert Cuthbert (b. 1864), Arthur William (b. 1866), David (b. 1869) and Mary Eliza (b. 1874). Emily Eva (1840–1902) married Frederick Harding in 1856 and they had eight children from 1857 to 1872, two of whom died in infancy. Agnes Jane (b. *c.*1842) married Charles Edward Stedman in 1858 and they had five sons and one daughter born between 1859 and 1876.

5   Selina Graham, Maria Amelia Fullerton and Eliza Frances Yabbicom.

6   Selina Graham née Cuthbert (b. *c.*1832).

7   Her recently widowed brother, the Hon. John Robinson Bailey, who had been elected as a member of the Legislative Assembly, representing Ballarat West with Robert Malachy Serjeant. The writ issued by His Excellency the Governor, Sir Harry Barkly, announcing the election of members was dated 13 October 1859. William Nicholson was the Chief Secretary of the Executive Council (see Letter 60 for biographical details). JRB served as Postmaster-General in the Nicholson ministry. His name appears on the foundation stone for the new Ballarat Council Chamber, which he laid on 16 August 1860. This building now forms the eastern part of the City Hall.

8   Harrie Elphinstone Bailey, JRB's eldest son, who had turned six the previous month.

9   Joseph Turnham was Chief Warden at the Stockade and his nephew, William Henry Turnham, was appointed as Warden on 3 February 1860.

10   WLR was looking after JRB's children, Harrie (aged six) and Edith Elizabeth (eighteen months old).

11   Edward Robert Middleton Bradley, born 2 January 1860 at Ballarat West; son of Edward Bradley (b. 1821), a banker at the City of London Bank, and his wife, Phoebe Ann née Warry (b. 1839).

12   Hannah Newnham (*c.*1841–1877), daughter of Thomas Newnham and Mary Parker. In 1860 she married James Spencer Quelch (*c.*1830–1879), born in London, son of Charles Quelch. They had seven children between 1861 to 1875.

49   [From MR in St Kilda to WLR in Ballarat]

Heathville House| Alma Road East [St Kilda]

[Sunday, 8 January 1860]

My dear dear Walter

    I did not get your letter until I returned home last night & had staid at home till eleven expecting to hear from you the enclosure was all right I went to Melbourne yesterday & posted a letter to you also to Lucinda I went to M[rs] Harris & I paid five shillings to have her name put down[1] & M[rs] Horn[2] was to write to her about a situation at St Kilda which I thought would suit her however I must now go & tell her that she is engaged. John took me to see M[rs] Henderson[3] & M[rs] Marsh at Richmond yesterday I like them very well & grand

Houses most magnificent They drove me home in the evening—I have not been to church I felt very poorly but shall go this evening if I feel better the weather has been most oppressive but last night we had a storm which has laid the dust & cooled the air.

I hope baby is quite well again Trotty[4] is a good girl only I am afraid she will be spoilt whilst here I cannot get her to do what I tell her sometimes already John made me a present of a very handsome Table Cloth to match my furniture I shall have to buy another pair of boots walking about so much soon wear's them out[5] I have not been to see the Webbs[6] yet people live such distances from one another that it requires a small fortune to go & see them Miss Cuthbert will leave on Monday week I think the change has done Robert good though he is very thin I was weighed by Uncle & am 7 stones 10 lbs—Miss Cuthbert 7 stones 7 lbs not much difference & her dresses fit me better than my own. We are very comfortable got in just for ourselves 8 bottles of Ale 2 of Port wine & 2 of sherry I pay a third of all expenses we agree remarkably very pleasant to live with

I am glad darling you keep so busy & that you go to the Theatre: it will cheer you up & do you good you surprised me about Nicholson[7] You are getting on famously with Stewart[8] & Heise[9] It is as I have often thought that when you were well known you would be appreciated there are not many so gentlemanly & upright as yourself

I was glad to know Lucinda has got the situation she wished so much for give my love to her & I will write when I return home—you would like the Sea bathing so much I wish you could come & enjoy it, it would do you so much good I will send the neck ties by Miss Cuthbert send me word dear if there is anything else I can do for you any medical book or anything I can get. I long to get a real long letter from you I have not had a whole one yet but I hope I shall on Tuesday I am afraid you will miss Lucy when she goes—

How does Mary[10] get on I hope she does not leave the House—Servants seem to be just as scarce here as in Ballaarat Uncle & Aunt promised to come & see us this week & go down to Brighton with us Have you heard from Ned? What a dreadful thing the loss of the Royal Charter[11] is it seem's to have thrown a complete sadness over Melbourne Please send me any English letter's that come to hand I cannot think of any more news so with love & kisses many I am dear Walter| Your loving wife

     Mary

Love to Lucy & children write soon

    Text: ALS NLA MS133/1/62

[1]   MR had been helping LR to find a new position. Mrs Harris is possibly the woman who ran a general store at 13 Little Latrobe Street East.

[2]   Mrs Horn ran the Registry Office at 79 Collins Street East.

[3]   Elizabeth Henderson née Hogg, wife of John Henderson, a brewer, and mother of Eliza Wanliss.

[4]   Emma Bailey (1856–1935), born 13 September 1856 in Geelong; eldest daughter of John Robinson Bailey and his first wife, Susannah Tyler Nicholson. She was a governess in NSW before she married Robert Barton Hoysted (1851–1920) on 9 November 1878 at the Holy Trinity Church, Wangaratta. Born in Walterstown, County Kildare, Ireland, the son of Frederick William Hoysted and his wife Susanna née Barton, Robert was a horse trainer, a member of the well-known horse-training family. Robert's mother was a first cousin of Sir Edmund Barton (1849–1920), first Prime Minister of Australia. They had nine children, of whom all but the youngest survived infancy: John Robert Bailey (1879–1965), Harrie James (1881–1916), William Arthur Nicholson (1883–1967), Bertie Valentine (1884–1960), Reginald Frederick (1887–1963), Gertrude Edith (b. 1894), Percy Charles (Duck) (1895–1962), Dorothy Ailsa (b. 1896) and Cecil (1899–1901). Emma died in Glen Huntly, Victoria, on 1 December 1935 aged seventy-nine.

5   Pedestrians had a difficult time in the streets of Melbourne, with few pavements, deep gutters and water channels. In winter the conditions were much worse, when the dusty roads became a sea of mud. See Andrew Brown-May, *Melbourne Street Life: The Itinerary of Our Days* (Kew: Australian Scholarly Publishing, 1998), pp. 31–36.

6   George and Matilda Webb and their four-year-old daughter, Isabella. Matilda died later that year in Longbottom, NSW, on 22 October of 'Pulmonary Phithisis', aged twenty-nine years. She was buried in Melbourne New Cemetery on 27 October 1860.

7   Dr George Nicholson (*c.*1816–1880) born in Berehaven, Cork, Ireland, the son of John Nicholson and Margaret née Topham. MRCS England 1854. He arrived in Melbourne as the medical officer aboard the *Ravenscraig* in June 1854. Registered in Victoria in 1856, he was the Honorary Medial Officer at Ballarat Hospital in 1859 and 1861. A keen military enthusiast, he was with the Ballarat rangers from 1857 onwards. Bowden, p. 116.

8   Dr James Stewart (*c.*1829–1906) born in County Tyrone, Ireland, the son of Robert Stewart, a farmer, and his wife Mary née Patton. LRCS, Ireland 1852; FRCS and LKQP, Ireland 1864. He arrived in Melbourne from Liverpool as a surgeon on board the *Rip Van Winkle* in November 1852. Registered as a doctor in Victoria before November 1853, he set up his practice in Ballarat. He was appointed Honorary Secretary of the Ballarat Medico-Chirurgical Society in 1856. He and his partner, Dr James Sutherland, were the proprietors of the Ballarat Hospital, at Bakery Hill. Stewart was a prominent leader in Ballarat during the 1850s as Chairman of the Ballarat West Municipality in 1858–1859. He became a trustee of the Mechanics Institute, and a Director of the Gas Company and the Bank of Victoria. Returning to Ireland with his wife for a few months of further study, they sailed back on the *Great Victoria* in November 1864. After five further years in Ballarat, he and his wife returned to England in 1869.

9   Dr William Augustus Heise (*c.*1814–1885), MB, Dublin; MRCS, England, 1838. He arrived in Melbourne on 14 February 1853 as Surgeon-Superintendent on the *Arabian*. In an advertisement four years before to solicit votes for the office of Honorary Surgeon at the Ballarat Hospital, he stated that he was a physician of Trinity College, Dublin and a retired army surgeon 'of ten years service in Her Majesty's 35th Royal Sussex Regt and in the 26th Cameronians. My colonial appointments have been those of Government Surgeon and Coroner for the District of Ballarat, where I have resided for the past three years & upward.' *Star*, 16 July 1856, p. 1. He was appointed Assistant Colonial Surgeon on 6 April 1853 (salary, £300 a year) and Coroner at Ballarat on 6 May 1853 (£100 a year). He lived at the Camp until 1854, when he was succeeded by Dr David J. Williams (see Letter 218). He worked in private practice in Ballarat and was on the staff of the Ballarat Hospital in 1859, continuing there until 1870. He was Honorary Medical Officer at the Benevolent Asylum in 1862. Bowden, p. 112.

10   The Richardsons' servant.

11   On the night of 25 October 1859, the ship *Royal Charter* went down at Moelfris Bay on the coast of Wales, just opposite Beaumaris, with the loss of 456 lives. 'On the same day … came also the overwhelming intelligence of the wreck of the Royal Charter steam-ship, bringing desolation to many families, and throwing a gloom over the whole country, for how many of us had known & esteemed some of those who had on that awful morning had—Sunk beneath the wave/ Fast By their native shore!' Aspinall, p. 48. See also Letter 46 from LC.

50   [From MR in St Kilda to WLR in Ballarat]

Heathville House| Alma Road [St Kilda]

[Wednesday, 11 January 1860]

My dear Walter

I have just received your dear dear letter I was so disappointed yesterday I was in bad spirits all day I fancied you were ill or at some bad case I am glad you are well & doing such a good practice—I wish it would continue we could soon afford for you to take a country trip with me.—also hope this will do me good & that I shall not be any more trouble to you though I am thinner through bathing than when I came down. Now I will answer a few of your questions I wrote about our journey down there were no <u>gentlemen</u> in the coach they would not assist us in the slightest degree only thought of making themselves comfortable but that did not trouble me much for I am too old a hand to mind those things now—Mr Rowe[1] was very kind when we got in the Railway Carriage at the Werribee: got us cakes & nice hot coffee & would insist upon paying for them himself he keeps a store on the Main Road OConnor's friend. It was bitter cold till we came to Batesford when the air seemed quite different & by the time we arrived in Melbourne we were in a perfect fever—I feel the weather much warmer than when on Ballaraat & yet I think it agrees with me I have only the constant pain in my side.

Our weather must have been very like your's for we had a storm on Saturday & a wet Sunday. I am glad to hear that Lucy wear's the Hoop's[2] I am obliged to get a new set for mine are all broken I am having my silk dress made ready to go to the Houses of Parliament 35 shillings for making & 10s for trimming's but I thought that such a good dress I had better have it made fashionably & then it would serve me for a pattern for the next year—I hope darling that I will please you when I come back I will try & see all that lay's within the power of my purse—but the money goes so fast in going from one place to the other.

Miss Cuthbert leaves for Ballaraat on Monday I hope you will go & see them she takes her cousin Mrs Steadman[3] up with her her husband is a lawyer she is only 18 & very much admired by gentlemen especially so go & give me your opinion she has been most kind & friendly with me spent nearly every evening at her house in fact all Miss Cuthberts relations have treated me like one of themselves move in the best society

I will give this letter to John I have not seen him since Monday Miss Cuthbert say's you are to go & see them on Monday evening & she will bring you a letter from me & give you the latest intelligence respecting my health I shall send your neck ties up by her—Tell Lucinda I will write her a long letter full of news as soon as I return home give her my love & I hope she will be happy & comfortable—I enclose the checque—Anna Maria sends her love & will be sure to have the dog tied up—go & see her she is so very kind I expect M^r & Mrs Marsh to see me today tomorrow I intend going shopping—in Melbourne to buy your neck ties & if I see anything else I will send it I received the 2£'s safely today—do not be long before you write darling & now darling take care of yourself with love & kisses many ever your| loving wife

      Mary

I hope Harry will not be very bad now—did he get the nasty pox. Kiss baby for me love to Lucy tell her to write & send me all the news| God bless you

    Text: ALS NLA MS133/1/63

---

[1]   Richard Rowe had a wheelwright shop on Great Main Road East, Ballarat.

[2]   'As usual, Zara was attired in the height of fashion. She brought a set of "the hoops" with her—the first to be seen on Ballarat—and, once more, Polly was torn between an honest admiration of her sister's daring, and an equally honest embarrassment at the notice she attracted.' *FRM I*, 234. See also Letter 90, in which LC expostulates on the dangers of the crinoline fashion.

[3]   Agnes Jane Stedman née Cuthbert (b. *c.*1843), married to Charles Edward Stedman.

51   [From MR in St Kilda to WLR in Ballarat]

Heathville House| Alma Road [St Kilda]
Monday Jany 16th| 1860

My darling Walter

I received your kind letter this morning I thought you were never going to write me any more & I fancied you were forgetting that you had a wife who loved you in Melbourne. I might not have felt your silence so much had I been well but being ill I felt very lowspirited

When I last wrote to you I was feeling so much better but Wednesday night the pain in my side got so bad that I had to send Robert out for a bottle of blistering liquid & which I applied to my side. Thursday I felt better & Friday morning I told Miss Cuthbert I had not felt so well for months I thought I should enjoy the day so much for we had made a party to go into Melbourne & see the Library & in the evening we were to go to the House of Parliament[1] & hear them speak about ½ past 12 just as we were going into lunch I turned quite sick & faint but it passed off though I could not eat anything but while I was dressing I felt so ill I did not know what to do A dull heavy pain in the womb I imagine left side low down with unwell pains came on all the time I was in Melbourne it was misery to walk about but I did not like to miss the opportunity of going to the House because it was the only opportunity Miss C had of going Well I went but was obliged to leave very soon John was watching me very anxiously for fear I would faint I got safely home & to my horror was saturated with blood the pain still continuing. However lying in the bed eased me: next morning I walked to Dr Evans[2] he said let Nature take its course there was nothing to be alarmed about I have seen nothing since & the pain is going away he say's I am suffering from pure weakness, he was to come & see me to day but has not done so as yet I am anxious for this to be in time for the post so have not time to write a very long letter. Miss C started this morning I could not get the neck ties in Melbourne they are not to be had I will try St Kilda

I sent you two Songs for you to learn by the time I return I am alway's thinking of you darling & what you are doing I am glad to hear you are still busy I hope Poor Harry & Baby are better do you think you will be able to come & fetch me home the Sea would delight you also the Public Library I do hope at the end of the month you will commence to think about it Anna Maria will take charge of Harry

Bye the bye she expects you up there to night do go her friends have all shown me such kindness one of her cousins a Mrs Fullerton[3] is staying with me whilst I write this she thought I would be lonely so came to take me a walk. John was down yesterday he is very attentive

I intend going into Town tomorrow to try & find Mrs Darling & tell John about Harry—write my dear as soon as you can I feel lowspirited & your letter's do cheer me so much I know them by heart reading them so often I called on the Webbs[4] they want me to go & see Clara Agg[5]—it is only 7/6 a return ticket & I can go on a Saturday & return on the Monday

I received the money all safely & was very glad of it for I wanted a pair of boots I find the washing comes most expensive I will send you a list of how the money goes in my next. God bless & prosper you is the nightly prayer on [of] your loving wife| With kisses many I am| Your

Mary

I was dreaming of you this morning I scarcely sleep at all at nights—Good bye dearest

Text: ALS NLA MS133/1/59

1   Fourth item on the Legislative Assembly's agenda concerned Major- General Macarthur CB.
     'Mr Nicholson, Chairman of the Committee to which it was referred to prepare an Address to
     Major-General Macarthur on relinquishing the command of Her Majesty's Land Forces in this
     Colony.' *Votes & Proceedings of the Legislative Assembly Session 1859–60*, No. 24, Friday,
     13 January 1860.
2   Dr John Evans, Robe-st, St Kilda. *Directory 1860*.
3   Maria Amelia Fullerton née Cuthbert, the widow of Duncan Fullerton.
4   George Henry Frederick Webb (c.1828–1891) and his first wife, Matilda Sarah née Field
     (c.1831–1860).
5   Clara Agg, the sister of William Henry, Alfred and Sophia Sarah Agg. George Webb's sister,
     Elizabeth Clara Webb, had married William Henry Agg in 1859. Alfred John Agg (1830–1886)
     was a prominent Victorian civil servant and member of the Melbourne Club. Sophia Sarah Agg
     (1819–1895) became the second wife of George Webb on 10 April 1862. Clara Agg was living
     at Sunbury in 1860.

52   [From MR in St Kilda to WLR in Ballarat]

[Alma Road East, St Kilda]

Thursday morning [19 January 1860]

My own darling Walty

I have just received your dear kind long letter I really think it is the nicest you have
written me since I have been down—I am happy to say that I feel a little better since I last
wrote & am trying all I can to get well I take regularly the medicine D[r] Evans sends me & I
think it is doing good he is very kind & I have changed my opinion of him. M[rs] Evans could
not be kinder if I was her own daughter makes me go there after bathing & gives me
delightful hot coffee & you know darling my partiality for that beverage—she has also offered
me her riding habit & Pony if I can but get a gentleman to take me out as she alway's rides
alone—So last night I heard from M[r] Harriman[1] that Brooke Smith is at Richmond Barracks
on sick leave so I sent word for him to come & see me & then if you have no objection dear
I will ask him to get a horse & take me a ride. I hope his being here will induce you to come
down you need not mind the expense for John told me when I left here he would pay me
back what I had paid M[rs] Hughes[2] as he could afford to pay for my lodgings better than you
could so if I stay here ten five weeks he will give me a checque for 10£s—so you might draw
the money from the bank & I will pay it in when I come up He is very kind—bought me two
nets for my Hair & a fashionable Blue large parasol they are like small umbrella's but not so
large or heavy as my white one.

I have been to D[r] Evans this morning & he examined my chest & said you were right
my lungs are very delicate but he will write to you & tell you all about me he drove me back
in his dog cart.

He thinks change of air & moving about from place to place will be better for me & to
walk as little as I can. So on Saturday I take a return ticket for 10[s]/ & go to Sunbury & return
on Monday afternoon the next day I am going to Richmond and stay with M[rs] Browne[3] thats
Ellen Darlings sister & then the following Saturday Ellen wants me to go with her to
Schnapper Point & stay a week at her Mothers who has a farm down there

D[r] Evan's advises me to go—for the air is so good for invalids he is not quite sure that
the sea-bathing is good for me for my fingers & toes die away & I am a long time before the
blood returns to them but only one hand did today so I think it is passing away—I thought on

my return from Schnapper Point it would be time for me to return & that you would come &
fetch me do try darling you could have a bathe in the Sea & such a long talk to Smith about
old times—it would do you a world of good & me too ~~for~~ I spent this evening with the
Webbs last night I went to Mrs Harrimans I should have gone to Mr Steadman's had I
received an invitation in time but I did not get it until this morning. I am going to see the
Baby[4] & Mrs Cuthbert to day read the enclosed then give it to Anne Maria it will amuse her
& tell Mrs Steadman I wrote an answer to correspond I quite regretted not being there to
inform her how the Bachelor party went off—I am very glad to hear the children are better
Mrs Hughes hopes she will have the pleasure of seeing my husband before I leave. Her
daughter married a gentleman who lived opposite to us at Leicester—

Tell Anne Maria I have not touched the Piano since she left I get no chance.—You
would hear such nice singing if you were to come down—do if it is at all possible. I received
1£ quite safely many thanks dear darling Husband God bless & prosper you I do not sleep
much but very singular when I do I dream of you & home. I do not think I have had one
dream in which you have not appeared—I do long to see your face & have a few kisses it
seem's wretched not to have any. Good bye darling love |Your loving wife

Mary

Let me get a letter on Monday & tell me do you approve of my plans

Text: ALS NLA MS133/1/57

1   Benjamin Cosway Harriman (b. 1831), a clerk in the civil service. In 1858 he married Isabella
    Ellen Webb (b. 1839), daughter of James Hemming Webb, the government shorthand writer
    and brother of George Webb. They had six children: Ellen Elizabeth (b. 1859), Amy Phillipps
    (b. 1861), Clara May (b. 1863), Benjamin John (1866-1951), Norman James (1870-1927) and
    George Henry (b. 1873). Harriman provided surety for *The Australasian Phonographic News* in
    1861. In 1894 he was living at 'Ellendale', Mornington and he provided surety for the
    Mornington Standard and the *Mentone and Moorabbin Chronicle*. T. A. Darragh, *Printer and
    Newspaper Registration in Victoria: 1838–1924* (Wellington: Elibank, 1997), p. 19.
2   Wife of Edward Hughes, contractor, listed in the 1860 *Directory* at Alma Street East, south side.
3   Emma Jelfs married John Browne in 1858.
4   Charles Edward Cuthbert was born on 20 March 1859 at Rosslyn Street, North Melbourne. No
    relation to Henry Cuthbert, his parents were George John Cuthbert (1828–1911), from
    London, whose profession on Charles's birth certificate was described as 'Law Stationer', and
    Agnes Annie née Gaffney. George Cuthbert had arrived in Melbourne on the *Voyager* in January
    1854. Agnes and George were married at the Cathedral Church of St James, Melbourne on
    15 July 1854. According to the Ballarat Rate Book, they lived in Ballarat 1857 to 1859, where
    MR and WLR met them.

53   [From WLR in Ballarat to MR in St Kilda]

Webster St [Ballarat]
Saturday Jany 21, 1860

My dear darling Mary

Yours of Thursday reached me safely and I was so glad to hear that you were better; and
that you were taking the medicines prescribed for you by Dr Evans: Ah! you have changed
your opinion of him have you, well his first impression is not so favorable as is the one formed
after a time: I trust you will enjoy your riding; I am much surprised at Brooke Smith being on
sick leave, again, so soon too after his voyage home.[1] he has never answered my last letter, nor
yours written when I was on the sofa last April:[2] Perhaps he is offended with me for telling his

father, I did not consider his illnesses very alarming, at least what I had seen of them: I am sure I would come down dear love to bring you back, but really I think it would be very unwise—It is true I have been busy for the last month, but I look forward with dread & apprehension to next winter: the healthy season when there is no sickness; & I have not yet saved anything: I have paid Bogle[3] & Thom Gray:[4] & part of Neds & sent you money, but I ought to have £50 in the Bank:[5] However we will see, I will not definitely say "no", neither can I promise "yes": I am very glad you are running about, I quite approve of it & pray that it may restore you & give you flesh, & a color once more in your dear cheeks! I am going to dine at Cuthbert's tomorrow, Sunday: It is very handsome of John to pay for your Lodging & you must thank him very cordially for me from my heart, it certainly comes very apropos & will enable you to get a new carpet & curtains for the bed when you come back: you might perhaps buy them cheaper in Melbourne—

The size of the front room is 12 feet 6 by 12 feet it would require 17 or 18 yards which would do it well, you could get the best tapestry for 4/6 £3–12.[6] & it might be sent up by Reynolds & English. The present carpet is very shabby & will require drugget all thro' to the door of the back room & across thus [small sketch] if we do not get a new carpet: I have delayed it until you come back but the carpet in the back room is entirely gone, the children have torn sad holes with their little feet—They are both better, Baby[7] has had the same low fever that Harry had for some days—Yesterday Friday was our hottest day of the season, this day however exceeds it there being a hot wind:

And so you dream of me nightly my darling? I am beginning to <u>count the days </u>& to feel <u>your abscence</u> God bless you: ~~ye~~ this will be the longest separation we have ever had: Anna Maria tells me M[rs] Graham[8] has gone down, that will be agreeable company; sad thing that losing the two children: Ah <u>I have only lost one child</u>:[9] I am not as busy now, but most likely this weather will set us running about next week; I went to the theatre last night,[10] I felt so dull, with Kingston Cuthbert;[11] was not home till 1. brought home D[r] Wills[12] & we smoked till 2—up at 7. Could eat no breakfast owing to the intense heat & dread going out in the sun!

You need not have sent me a list of your expenses I am perfectly satisfied my dear wife that you would never be wasteful: Mary has been trying her hand at breaking, just to keep in practice until you come back[13]

4 P.M This has been a terrific day Ther 105° in our parlor Harry & I bathed at 12 & after dinner I lay on the floor & so did the children: we bathed again at 4—

All enquire for you very kindly M[rs] Winch,[14] M[rs] Haywood,[15] M[rs] Park[16] & M[rs] Searle[17] called the investigation into Searles[18] conduct has taken place result not made public

Gaol Foster married[19]—Adieu my love| Your

    Walter

Text: ALS NLA MS133/1/54

[1]   Alexander Brooke Smith arrived back in Melbourne in November 1859 on the *Wellesley* with his prisoner, Thomas Chisholm, whom Brooke Smith had arrested in Co. Armagh, Ireland, and returned to Portland, Victoria, where Chisholm faced charges of forgery and embezzlement. See *Dawbin*, pp. 64–65, 126.

[2]   i.e. when WLR was ill.

[3]   Not identified.

[4]   Thom, Gray & Co., advertised their business in *The Ballarat Star* as 'Wholesale & Retail Drapery & Clothiers, opposite the Council Chambers, Sturt St, Ballarat'.

[5]   See *FRM I*, p. 244.

[6]   Seventeen yards at 4/6 per yard costs £3–16–6.

7   Edith Elizabeth Bailey.
8   Charlotte Sophia Graham née Oxenham (1834–1881) married Frederick Graham in 1856.
9   In the winter of 1857, Mary suffered a still birth or a late miscarriage, according to Letter 25 from Lucinda Cheyne, dated 9 September 1857. Charlotte and Frederick Graham's second son, Arthur Carruther, had died on 8 January 1860 aged fifteen months. Their first son, Arthur Frederick, had been born and died in 1857 in Ballarat. They subsequently had two daughters, Ada Charlotte (b. 1862) and Florence Adelaide (b. 1868), and one son Frederick Arthur (b. 1864), all of whom survived to adulthood. Their last son, Arthur Elliott (b. 1871), died aged five years in 1876.
10 At the Theatre Royal 'under distinguished patronage, Mr W. M. Brown will take a farewell benefit ... previous to retiring from Theatre Management'. The first part of the evening's entertainment was a revival of Douglas Jerrold's *Time Works Wonders*, followed by the new burlesque, *Once Upon A Time There Were Two Kings*. (A new season was to commence at the Theatre Royal on 23 January 1860 with William Hoskins' company.) It is more likely that WLR went to the Charlie Napier Theatre to see the fifth night of the 'Eminent Tragedian, Mr G. V. Brooke' in Barrett's comedy, *The Serious Family*, with Brooke and Miss E. Melville, followed by a favourite ballad sung by Miss Melville and a 'Medley Dance' by Miss Josephine. *Star*, 20 January 1860, p. 4.
11 Kingston Cuthbert (1832–1913), civil engineer, born at Gowran, County Kilkenny, Ireland, the son of Lieutenant Kingston Gore Cuthbert and Mary née Cochrane. Kingston arrived in Melbourne in August 1853 on the *Hempsyke*, eighteen months after his mother and siblings and a year before his cousins, Henry and Kingston Cuthbert. He married Eleanor Moore on 14 August 1862 and had five children. Cuthbert commenced work in Victoria's civil service in March 1855 when he was appointed as an engineer and surveyor for the Railway Department. During the next twenty-three years, he and his family moved from one construction site to another. He was promoted through the ranks of the Railway Department until he had almost reached the top. Then came 'Black Wednesday', 8 January 1878, when the Legislative Council, dissatisfied with amendments relating to payment of MPs, refused to pass the Appropriations Bill and the Premier Berry ordered the dismissal of over 200 civil servants. Kingston was dismissed and although many civil servants were reappointed by April 1878, he was not. He practised as an independent civil engineer but turned to alcohol. In January 1885 he was brought before Prahran Court accused of threatening his wife and daughters. He died, aged eighty-one, at Pakenham, estranged from his family, with the Salvation Army left to arrange his funeral. Ian C. McKellar, 'The Cuthbert families of Ballarat', *Ballarat Mechanics Institute Magazine*, 1, 9 (May 1992).
12 Dr William Wills (c.1809–1899), father of the explorer, William John Wills (1834–1861), who set off on the first expedition to cross the Australian continent from south to north with Robert O'Hara Burke (1821–1861) later that year (August 1860). Dr Wills studied medicine at Grainger's Anatomical School, Guy's Hospital and Thomas's and became a MRCS in 1827. He was married to Sarah Mary Elizabeth, née Calley, and they had two sons, William John and Thomas. In 1852 Dr Wills bought a share in a Melbourne gold-mining company and he and his sons planned to travel to Victoria. His wife prevented him from sailing, but their two sons decided to go alone, arriving at Williamstown on 3 January 1853 on the *Janet Mitchell*. Dr Wills followed them later, arriving in Victoria on the *Lady Kennaway* in August 1853. He started his practice in Ballarat the following year. He was one of the founding members of the Medico-Chirurgical Society in Ballarat in 1854. À propos of the Burke and Wills exploration, John Sadleir, who had served with Burke in the police force at Beechworth and had wanted to accompany him on the expedition, wrote that although he acknowledged all Burke's good personal qualities, 'he had no knowledge whatever of the resources by which an experienced bushman might find a living in an Australian desert. If there is any such thing as the "bump of locality", it was not developed in him, for he was continually losing his way in his short trips about Beechworth ... It is a curious fact, too, that his companion, Wills, was deficient in the same respect. Yet was a marvellous journey was that from Cooper's Creek to Carpentaria and back! It was a rash undertaking, perhaps, but with what splendid courage and endurance it was accomplished!' Sadleir, p. 80. Dr Wills returned to England in 1862, where he edited his son's journal. He continued practising in the south of England, where he died on 2 October 1899, aged ninety years. Dr Wills' younger son, Thomas Wills, became a railway station master at Gisborne. His appointment was reported in the *Star*, 9 May 1864.
13 An ironic reference to MR's propensity to break dishes.

[14] Agnes Winch née Pitman (b. 1829), married on 15 May 1856 to Frederick Alfred Winch (1827–1892), Inspector of Police. The chief witness at their marriage was Captain Frederick Charles Standish (1824–1883), Police Commissioner, who is described as one of the most aristocratic of the 1850s immigrants. Winch was a close friend of Standish and they led a congenial social life in the Melbourne Club. Standish was forced to suspend Winch from the police force in 1882 over a scandal. See de Serville 1991, pp. 42–76.

[15] Charlotte Mitford Haywood née Bunce (1844–1926) was born in Adelaide, South Australia. She married Robert Haywood (b. 1834), Ballarat's Receiver and Paymaster, on 14 October 1859 in Ballarat's Church of England by the Reverend John Potter. She was probably the niece of Dr Richard Bunce (both she and Richard had fathers called James). Her mother's name was Charlotte Chappel. Dr Richard Bunce was a witness at her marriage.

[16] Margaret Park née Rickie (1824–1871), married to Adam Steele Park, Manager of the Ballarat branch of the Colonial Bank of Australasia. (He was also Honorary Treasurer of the first committee of the Ballarat Visiting and Benevolent Association. Withers, p. 260.)

[17] Elizabeth Searle née Cooper (b. 1819) married the Reverend Cooper Searle (b. 1819), a widower with two children, on 13 March 1857. She was the cousin of the Reverend David Seddon (see Letter 140) and had migrated with him.

[18] Reverend Cooper Searle, Minister St Paul's Church of England, Ballarat East, was in dispute with the Trustees of the Church, but the nature of the dispute was not made public. It was reported that, 'Yesterday (Tuesday) the Venerable Archdeacon Stretch and Mr Bland, who had been deputed by the Bishop of Melbourne to hold a commission of inquiry into the points in dispute between the Rev. Mr Searle and the Trustees of St Paul's Church, met in the Schoolroom, on Bakery Hill … The Rev. Mr Searle was represented by Mr Cuthbert, solicitor, but that gentleman was not allowed to cross-examine the witnesses; he therefore confined himself to watching the proceedings. Dr George Clendinning [c.1806–1876] represented the Trustees and Church Committee.' *Star*, 18 January 1860, p. 2. Two weeks later, the paper announced that it had received a communication from Bishop Charles Perry stating that Searle had resigned as incumbent of St Paul's Church and that his 'functions in connection with the church will cease on the 21st instant.' *Star*, 4 February 1860, p. 2. One contentious issue at St Paul's Church the previous November (1859), reported in the Ballarat papers, concerned the sale of alcohol at a bazaar in aid of funds for the erection of a parsonage. A couple of letters were published from 'Anti Sly Grog' and 'An Unpledged Teetotaller', expressing disapproval about raising money by the 'direct sale of those drinks which do more to hinder the progress of the Gospel, than all of the other instruments of Satan combined'. *Star*, 7 November 1859. The persons in charge of the refreshment booth were 'Mrs Dr Richardson, Miss Cuthbert and Mrs Searle' and they were selling spiders (brandy mixed with lemonade or ginger beer). The bazaar raised £310. Searle had also resigned as Hon. Secretary of the Ballarat committee of the Chinese Mission in December 1859 after receiving a letter from the Bishop of Melbourne, complaining about 'the tampering with the spiritual opinions of Lo Sam Yuen, the Chinese Missionary by other denominations of Christians'. *Star*, 2 December 1859. The reports are brief and the issues involved are not clear but the end result was a divided Church community and the departure of the Minister. (Reference to Lo Sam Yuen, Weston Bate, *Lucky City: The First Generation at Ballarat 1851–1901* (Carlton: Melbourne University Press, 1978), pp. 155–156.)

[19] 'On the 14th inst, at St Paul's Church by Rev. C. Searle, Charles Forster, Esq., the Governor of H.M. Gaol, to Eliza, eldest daughter of Benjamin Wilmer, Esq., late of Caxton, Cambridgeshire.' *Star*, 16 January 1860. Eliza Hannah Howe née Wilmer (1828–1884), was the widow of George Howe (1818–1859), hotelkeeper, who died on 4 June 1859 of disease of the heart and lungs, leaving two daughters aged nine and three. Howe was one of the very first gold diggers at Golden Point, arriving on 1 September 1851. Withers, p. 33.

54 [From MR in St Kilda to WLR in Ballarat]

Heathville House [Alma Road East, St Kilda]

Tuesday [24 January 1860]

My dear darling Husband

I received your kind letter when I arrived home last night I am so glad you are well love. The weather here has been worse than Black Thursday[1]—I do not know what the Thermometer stood at on Saturday but Sunday was 130° in the Shade & 160° in the Sun.[2]

I was up at Sunbury[3] but not able to move about on Monday when I came home—I was quite fatigued not able to sleep all night on account of one of my old attacks at the chest & stomach so I have been to Dr Evans about it he told me he had been too busy to write to you but would do so at the first opportunity The Graham's came here last Saturday & took apartments here for a fortnight & to day an immense sale of the most exquisite things I ever saw took place in St Kilda at Mr Powell[4] who has made his fortune & returning to England the street was lined with carriages for it is the fashion here for ladies to go to Auctions I could have got some splendid bargains had I had the money to spend—I only bought 1 doz spoons washed in silver for 1£ & they ask three in the shops so every one thinks I made a good bargain I tried for a carpet for they were all velvet pile but the worst one sold for over 6£s so I let them alone The G[rahams] spent over 16£'s well to be them. I was to poorly & tired to go to Richmond to day so am going tomorrow—I do hope my darling Walter will come for the change will do you a world of good Smith comes to take me a ride on Thursday I had a letter from Miss Cuthbert & she say's you promised to go to dinner but they did not see you so I suppose you were called out on Friday

I go to spend the day with Mrs Evan's & Saturday I am off for a week to Schnapper Point Let me hear from you on Friday morning love & then I will answer it & put in my address—on Saturday morning when I go to Ellen's to know it I shall have to leave here by nine oclock on Saturday morning & the post would not come in until 11 & then I should not get your dear letter so do write if it is only a line. The dinner bell has just rung so I must say Good bye for to night I will add a line presently—Brook Smith's sister[5] have sent me a lovely workbasket fitted up with such nice things as a present & the Father has sent you a book I have not seen it yet. It is getting quite dark so I must say Good bye to my own darling Walty God bless & protect you I have a sleeping draught to take so hope I will sleep & dream sweet dreams of you I do so long to see your dear face again I think it will be kissed all away. Good bye dearest with kisses many from| your loving wife

Mary

Do not forget to write

Wednesday morning [25 January 1860] I am so ill not able to move & easily sick 12 times already & it is not 12 oclock yet the sleeping draught had no affect. Graham[6] will post this besure & write to me darling—| Mary

Text: ALS NLA MS133/1/58

[1] On Thursday, 6 February 1851 (before MR or WLR arrived in the colony), a series of huge fires swept through Victoria to across the border of South Australia near Mount Gambier. At least ten people were killed and 10,000 square miles were burnt to ashes. The temperature in Melbourne reached 47° Celsius at 11 am.

[2] The temperatures were certainly very hot that weekend but MR's account is somewhat exaggerated. 'The following returns of the temperature of the atmosphere during Saturday and yesterday have been furnished to us by Professor Neumayer:—on Saturday the maximum temperature in the shade of 108.8 degrees, and did not change between 2 and 3 o'clock, the

wind blowing from N.N.W. shifting frequently to N.E. At six o'clock the thermometer showed 104 degrees slowly decreasing, the lowest during the night being 76.8. Yesterday, at 4 am, it rapidly rose. And at 2 pm, it was as high as 111 degrees, at which point it remained until 4.22 pm, when the wind slowly changed round to the south, it having during the day blown almost constantly from the north.' *The Argus*, 23 January 1860, p. 5.

3 Visiting Clara Agg.

4 Walter Powell, wholesale and retail ironmonger at 103 Flinders Street East and 60 Collins Street East. The auction, which took place at his home in Prince's Street, St Kilda, included the whole of his furniture and effects and also 'a pair of very handsome grey carriage horses, a splendid Brougham, nearly new by Kinder of Worcester', and an American buggy and a cab phaeton. *The Argus*, 24 January 1860, p.3. Walter Powell was born in London and brought to Victoria as a child. A strong supporter of the Wesleyan Church and education, he gave considerable financial assistance to found Wesley College. The school's inauguration (11 January 1866) occurred six years after his departure but his support was remembered and many years later the 'Walter Powell' Annual Dinner on his birthday (28 May) was instigated by the then headmaster in 1902.

5 Besides his three brothers, Alexander Brooke Smith had two sisters whom he mentioned in his will before he died in 1882: Caroline Smith of Orpington (spinster) and Emily Malden Alfrey, wife of Henry Alfrey of St Mary Cray, Kent, a surgeon (copy of ABS's Will in the Dorothy Green papers, ADFA).

6 Frederick Graham.

55   [From MR in Melbourne to WLR in Ballarat]

[Ellen Darling's home in Melbourne]
[Saturday, 28 January 1860]

[Page(s) missing]

if it was possible you might come down[1] by some Friday night mail & we could return on Monday morning I am sorry to hear about Poor Baby she never seem's to be well,[2] am glad Harry is such a good boy give my love & a kiss to both

Trotty never mentions or seem's to care about them she is very fat but perfectly well I think the change has done her good. I shall finish this in town & I then will enclose address. Goodbye so far dear darling

The address is Mr Jelfs

Tanti Hotel[3]

Schnapper Point

that is where the letter's are left & then I go there to enquire for them if you write on Monday I will get it Wednesday or Thursday & then I will write you again I feel very poorly & am behind time so Good bye darling Husband God bless you with all love & kisses from your loving wife

Mary R.

excuse this pen wont write| Goodbye dearest

Text: ALS NLA MS133/1/60

1 MR wrote this letter prior to taking the steamer to Schnapper Point, where she was hoping WLR would join her.

2 Edith Elizabeth Bailey died on 5 February 1860, aged one year eight months. On the death certificate the cause was 'Dentition and Effusion on Brain', having been treated for fourteen days by her uncle, WLR. MR may have received a telegram to return home but no letters have survived. 'On the 5th instant, of effusion of the brain, induced by teething and the excessive

heat of Tuesday, the 31st ultimo, the infant daughter of the Hon. J. R. Bailey.' *Star*, 6 February 1860.

3   The old Tanti Hotel was built in 1858 and the earliest recorded licensee was William Edwards. It was completely demolished many years ago but a new hotel exists on the same site, on the corner of the Nepean Highway and Tanti Avenue, Mornington.

56   **[From LC in Brighton, England, to WLR in Ballarat]**

17 Buckingham Place, West Cliff| Sussex| England.

April 10ᵗʰ 1860

My beloved Walter

If you received my former letters you would understand my condition, in regard to your father's state of suffering and my own[1]—I wrote in Dec^br and sent you "The Mount of Olives"[2] the reading of which had made a great impression on my own mind, unfortunately your father being deplorably ill at the time I did not register it and as you have never acknowledged the receipt of it, I conclude it never reached you, especially as the vessel it was to sail in "The White Star", mail ship, had to put back many times owing to the fearful severity of the gales, and she lay by for a long time.—The severe & increasing illness of your father so engrossed my every thought, causing besides such a demand on my bodily powers, as laid me at once prostrate; he has now <u>valvular</u> disease of the heart, and has been confined to the house since Dec^br until these last few days, when he has ventured to creep about a little, and come back in a carriage—very little exertion raises his pulse to 120—the complaint was going on for a long time without being suspected, all the attention being bestowed on the lungs,—the unusual severity of the winter precluded his going about for fear of adding to his bronchial affection,—We are now both of us so shattered and prostrate that Miss F— ever watchful insists on taking us to Tunbridge Wells[3] for awhile, to see what air will do for me, as I am in consequence of fatigue over exertion and anxiety, the worst by far of the two—an intermitting pulse, and frequent attacks of faintness, together with the loss of all muscular power, give me warning that my work is well nigh done, and the end of my life near. My old complaint continues, so that I grow weaker every day—I find writing difficult, as I sit up with effort, and am in pain while in an erect posture—my mind is mercifully spared, and I can yet pray and intercede for my children.

I had longed much to hear from you, when your last arrived, I grieve to learn that dear Mary is less well, and sorry to find dysentery threatening you again, do not leave off writing to me, I think you would be sorry to add to my many sorrows, and I prize your letters exceedingly—

I am desirous of knowing how your <u>soul</u> is. Are you growing in grace and knowledge of Him who is our life, our <u>all!</u> all else is emptyness and vanity The Holy Spirit is being poured out now in an extraordinary manner, the dead in trespasses and sins are being quickened and made alive, The Lord is working among all classes, He will soon return to rejoice His people and confound His enemies; the prospect is cheering comforting! Blessed!—

I shall think of you on your birthday especially, if I am in the body at the time, for every day, at early dawn, and 8 at night, you are remembered on other days, and my daughter Mary is not forgotten—I am glad Lucinda was with you, she does not write quite as fully as I could wish, but I am glad to hear from her in any way—Alick is here now, he is very tall, and very affectionate he says he will be what [h]is Uncle Walter is, and we speak of you frequently. Miss F. sends you her love, your Father love and blessing, Alick a great <u>many</u> loves, & remembrances of <u>old walks,</u> and with my best and warmest love & blessing| I am my dearly beloved Son| Yr fondly attached Mother

       Lucinda Cheyne
    Text: ALS NLA MS133/1/33

1   They still had not heard of the death of their son, John Cheyne, in Assam (15 December 1859).
2   *The Mount of Olives* (published in 1846, 12 mo.) was written by James Hamilton, DD (1814–1867), Presbyterian Minister. He was the son of William Hamilton, Minister of the Established Church of Scotland at Strathbane, Stirling. He graduated from Glasgow University in 1835. In 1838 he was licensed as Minister and inducted into the National Scotch Church, Regent Square, London, where he remained until his death on 24 November 1867. Throughout his ministry he continued to write extensively.
3   A fashionable spa in Kent.

57   [From MR in St Kilda to WLR in Ballarat]

    Westbourne Terrace [St Kilda][1]
    May 31st [1860, Thursday]

My dear dear Walter

I arrived safely per coach to Geelong where John met me it was very cold riding & so muddy until we got to Meredith—there, there had been no rain & dust was blowing. Melbourne's very like Ballaraat constant drizzle—M[rs] Patterson[2] is very kind & I am enjoying myself I stay here I think until Monday then I go to Turnham's for a few day's We went to the Ball[3] & enjoyed it very much you were invited as well—I wish you had been there—it was very gay the crowd was very great but upon the whole I think our Ballarat Balls compare very favorably with this there was such a very common vulgar appearance amongst the ladies present not thirty good-looking women out of about a thousand—

I was introduced to several gentlemen but not the governor[4]—we went in a carriage & pair & returned the same the building was well lighted & ornamented & every thing passed off well I saw M[rs] Reid[5] & M[r] & M[rs] Henderson[6] the latter will be up to-morrow-night. The ministry have resigned, the Land bill not being passed (as it was) in the Upper House[7]—John seems to think they will be asked again—He does not seem to care very much—I have not seen Harry[8] but am going to do so when I have posted this I called on M[rs] Wanliss[9] yesterday she return's home next week looking much better. She expected M[r] Wanliss[10] today My blister is still very bad constantly running & the smell from it hardly bearable nothing but matter & blood from it I am obliged to carry a bottle of scent for fear others should smell it I bathe it in cold water every morning but cannot get the lint off. I danced very little owing to it

I hope darling you are well & happy & do not miss me very much—I take you to bed with me every night I look at you the last thing at night & the first thing in the morning.—John gave me a white head dress composed of pearls & frosted leaves[11]—I hope to have a letter tomorrow & one on Monday morning before I go to Pentridge—

I hope Trotty is a good girl give my love & a kiss to her Is there any thing I can get for you in Melbourne? because I will do it if you send in time I am rather tired so shall say good bye & God bless you with all love & kisses| Ever your loving wife

Mary

Send the enclosed to Miss Cuthbert put it in an envelope—

Text: ALS NLA MS133/1/51

1   MR was staying with JRB who took her to the Governor's Ball, which was held each year on 24 May to celebrate the birthday of Queen Victoria (1819–1901). In 1860, the Queen celebrated her forty-first birthday. She became Queen at the age of eighteen, on the death of her Uncle, William IV (1765–1837), who died on 20 June 1837 with ten living children—but all were illegitimate.

2   Mrs Patterson was the wife of one of the partners of the drygoods (textiles, fabrics) firm, Patterson, Ray, Palmer and Co., which JRB joined when he left Parliament later in the year.

3   Queen Victoria's birthday ball. 'His Excellency, the Governor held as is customary, a full dress Levee at the Exhibition Building, which had been decorated & fitted up expressly for the occasion.' *The Age*, Friday, 25 May 1860. Among the names of those presented to the Governor and who stood with him on the dais (which was covered in crimson cloth and had crimson and gold hangings), were listed Lyttleton Bayley (Miss Fector's nephew), the Reverend Cooper Searle, Dr James G. Beaney, Professor Baron Ferdinand von Mueller, George Coppin and William Brooke Smith (perhaps a relative of Alexander Brooke Smith). Lyttleton Bayley's wife, Isabella, had died only a few weeks before (on 9 April 1860) of puerperal fever after the birth of her fourth child.

4   Sir Henry Barkly (1815–1898), Governor of Victoria from December 1856 to 1863 when he was transferred to the government of Mauritius. He married firstly Elizabeth Helen née Timms (c.1820–1857); they had four children, of whom two sons, Henry and James, were born in the West Indies (where Sir Henry Barkly had governed) and one son, Hubert Lee Pakington, in April 1857 a few months after the family's arrival in Melbourne. On 17 April 1857, shortly after the birth of Hubert, Lady Barkly was killed in a riding accident on Prince's Bridge. On 21 June 1860 at Christ Church, South Yarra, he married Ann, the twenty-two-year-old daughter of Major-General Sir Thomas Pratt, commander of the forces stationed in Victoria. In 1863 he was moved to the government of Mauritius for a term and then to the Cape of Good Hope in 1870, from whence he was recalled seven years later as it was considered that he had failed to carry out the British government's policy on South African union.

5   Jane Reid née Brown, wife of Alexander R. Reid, share broker, whose office was in 'The Corner', Ballarat. He became actuary of the Geelong Savings Bank. Withers, p. 236.

6   Mr and Mrs John Henderson; he was the Manager of the Colonial Bank of Australasia in Lydiard Street.

7   The Nicholson Land Bill had been introduced in November 1859 and was finally passed in a 'mutilated and almost unrecognisable form' in September 1860. The Bill had been forwarded from the Legislative Assembly to the Council where the squatter majority proposed so many amendments that Nicholson offered his resignation and suggested to Governor Barkly that J. B. Bennett, a lawyer who had 'led the hatchet-job' in the Council should form a ministry. The Governor, knowing that a viable government could not be formed from the Council, negotiated with Nicholson and he agreed to continue. Searle, pp. 290–297.

8   Harrie Elphinstone Bailey.

9   Eliza Wanliss née Henderson (1837–1918), daughter of Elizabeth née Hogg and John Henderson, a brewer in Flinders Lane, Melbourne. In 1859 she married Thomas Drummond Wanliss (see next endnote) and had given birth to her first baby, Elizabeth, on 2 March 1860, but the baby died four days later of 'Ileus & Diarrhoea'.

10 Thomas Drummond Wanliss (1830–1923), newspaper proprietor of *The Ballarat Star*, MLA. He was born in Abernethy, Scotland, the son of John Wanliss, a farmer, and Janet Drummond. He and Elizabeth née Henderson (see endnote above) had the following children: Elizabeth (1860–1860); John Newton Wellesley (1861–1950), who married Margaret Boyd; David Sydney (1864–1943) born in Perth, Scotland, and married first Jessie Guthrie and second Evelyn Muriel Bryant; Janet Drummond (1865–1866); Cecil (1866–1933); Agnes Somerville (b. 1867), who married Sir William Hill Irvine (1858–1943), Premier and Chief Justice of Victoria; Raleigh (1870–1871); Beatrice Mary (b. 1871), who married Archibald Fisken; Ewen (1873–1966), who married Rose Anderson; Neville (1876–1962); and Mabel Violet (b. 1878).

T. D. Wanliss owned 4490 acres in co. Rippon, Victoria. He retired to Edinburgh where he died in 1923. The *ADB* contains entries for several members of the Wanliss family. The eldest son, John Newton Wellesley, a solicitor, appears in the entry on his son, Harold Boyd Wanliss (1891–1917), who became a solicitor before he studied horticulture at Hawkesbury Agricultural College. In 1913, Harold took up 295 acres near Louttit Bay (Lorne) to plant an orchard, including hazlenut trees. Enlisting in 1915, he fought in France and was awarded the DSO before being killed on 26 September 1917. Harold's sister, Dr Marion Boyd Wanliss (1896–1984) graduated from the University of Melbourne (MB, BS, 1920; MD, 1929). After researching on cancer as a postgraduate in Vienna, she returned to Melbourne where she practised as a physician. She spent time at Louttit Bay on the farm purchased by her brother and was known as a conservationist. David Sydney Wanliss became an army officer of distinction and a judge. He led his battalion at the landing on Anzac and in the battle of Krithia on 8 May 1815. Wanliss Gully on Anzac was named after him. After the war he was appointed Chief Justice of the Mandated Territory of New Guinea. Ewen Wanliss, after serving as a Lieutenant in the South African War, became an associate to judges in the Supreme Court of Victoria (1903–1910 and 1922–1958). He spent ten years as a grazier before returning to public service (1910–1920). He also worked for two years (1920–1922) as private secretary to his brother-in-law, Irvine, who was then Lieutenant-Governor of Victoria. Both Cecil and Neville fought in World War I. Cecil, having graduated from Sandhurst in 1886, became a professional soldier with the South Lancashire Regiment. The first Australian officer in World War I to lead a battalion into battle (Mons), he was also the first to be wounded. He retired in 1920, having been appointed an OBE the previous year. Neville, the youngest of Thomas and Elizabeth's sons, was a jackeroo in Queensland and a clerk in New Zealand before enlisting as a private in 1915. He served at Gallipoli and, having been discharged in 1917, returned to Melbourne where he worked as a clerk.

[11]   See *FRM I*, p. 167.

58   [From WLR in Ballarat to MR in St Kilda]

Webster St. [Ballarat]

Saturday [2 June 1860]

My own Mary,

I expected a letter from you on Friday and was much disappointed however I suppose that you were better engaged: I am delighted that you are enjoying yourself and that M[rs] P. is kind. You say I was invited to the Ball I never received the invitation as you know!

I have made arrangements to have our names put down in the book at Government House so that we may get an invitation next year & go if we choose: You had better apply a bread poultice to the blister at bedtime that will remove all irritation it must be very distressing for you—Trotty is very good. Julia[1] takes her out often—King[2] has given Julia a stereoscope & Joe[3] a lovely Brooch of Ballt gold. Nothing doing—I was occupied all Thursday with M[rs] Gray,[4] was sent for 6 AM. baby not born till 7. PM—

It is fearfully cold today; Ther. while I write 3.30. 48° with rain clouds coming up over Warrenheip—No particular news—All well Johnson[5] was here last night & tried to operate on Harry[6] but failed owing to his laughing so—had better success with Mary[7] put her to sleep, a natural sleep only, after half an hour we are going to try again this evening & I have asked Irwin[8] to come up.

I hope you will stay away all next week & derive some benefit from it—Never mind us, we feel of course very lonely, but if it does you good as it may, that will counterbalance it. Brooke spent Tuesday night with me. He saw Julia—Wednesday night[9]—I was alone all evening reading, Thursday night I went to a lecture by one of "Greens"[10] freinds,[11] & last night I have told you of—I lunched one day up at the Cuthberts. Saw Bunce[12] today—Bitter against Creswick wretches, for I can call them by no other name, <u>ignorant deluded</u> beings: headed by Nicholson[13] of whom he speaks in bad terms: No sickness still—

I have discharged Harry he leaves next week If matters don't mend I will go to Snowy River you had better remain where you are—| Good bye dearest love| Your own husband

   Walter

Text: ALS NLA MS133/1/72

[1]   Julia Hoskins (stage name Julia Harland) née Wallack (1825–1872), daughter of American actor, Henry Wallack. She was an opera singer and actress. In 1850 she married William Hoskins (1816–1886), an actor who was born in Derbyshire, studied Law at Cambridge and then began acting in provincial companies in 1839. He was a pupil of Samuel Phelps at Saddler's Wells Theatre, London, where Charles Young had begun and ended his English acting career. Julia and William Hoskins arrived in Australia in 1856. He was Manager of the Theatre Royal, Ballarat, in 1860, the Theatre Royal, Melbourne, in 1863 and the Haymarket Theatre, Melbourne in the late 1860s. During 1864, Julia placed an advertisement in the *Star.* 'Mrs William Hoskins (pupil of Manuel Garcia and Signor Schira) gives instruction in the Art of singing and the Piano. Apply Errard St, Sturt St'. After Julia's death in 1872, William married actress Florence Colville and they moved to New Zealand in 1875. She died in 1881 and he returned to Melbourne and married Maude Bowman in 1882. He retired from the stage in 1884 and died in Melbourne in 1886.

[2]   Two possible Kings: Henry Newton John King appointed to the Victorian postal service on 19 March 1853; became postmaster at Ballarat in 1859 until 1867. Alexander Henry King had an ironmongery shop on Main Road, Ballarat.

[3]   Not identified.

[4]   *Case* 243, May 31 1860, Mrs Gray, shopkeepers' wife, aged twenty-three, first pregnancy, 'A slow labor, pains all week—gave ergot', son born 7 p.m.

[5]   Not identified.

[6]   WLR's groom.

[7]   Richardson's servant.

[8]   Samuel Irwin and Jabez Job Ham were the first editors of *The Ballarat Star* when the paper was launched on 22 September 1855. As the *Geelong Advertiser*'s correspondent in the 1850s, his eyewitness accounts from Ballarat of events leading up to the Eureka Stockade riot were adopted by the Governor, Sir Charles Hotham, as portions of his despatches to the English Secretary of the Colonies. Irwin was appointed a Justice of the Peace in July 1855 (at the same time as John Victor and William Bradshaw) and his name and those of Thomas Drummond Wanliss and Richard Belford appear on the Registration of the *Star* in December 1856 as Printers and Publishers. T. A. Darragh, *Printer and Newspaper Registration in Victoria: 1838–1924* (Wellington: Elibank Press, 1997).

[9]   On Wednesday, 30 May 1860, Julia Harland played Marianne in 'the laughable comedy' *Dumb Belle* with William Hoskins as Arthur Merton. But the main attraction for the evening was Miss Avonia Jones playing Camille in 'Alexander Dumas' great five Act Drama of *Camille or the Fate of a Coquette*', with Stuart O'Brien as Armand. *Star,* 30 May 1860, p. 3.

[10] Probably T. W. Green, the librarian at Ballarat.

[11] There were two lectures on in Ballarat that evening: the Reverend W. R. Lewis was in the Congregational Church at 7.30 p.m., lecturing on 'Incidents in the Life of the Apostle Paul' and the Reverend William Wilson delivered a lecture on 'The purpose of God toward Man' in the Church of England School House, Lydiard Streeet at 7 p.m. *Star,* 31 May 1860, p. 1.

[12] Dr Richard Bunce (1820–1885), surgeon, medical practitioner. He was born in Nantes, France, the son of a Captain in the Royal Navy. MRCS, England, 1842. He lived on the Continent for some years, marrying in Paris in September 1848 Blanche Defauche, who was born in 1831 in Ostend, Belgium. They emigrated from Plymouth to South Australia in 1851, moving to Victoria the following year. He was insolvent in 1856 and 1861. Noted for his treatment of diphtheria with carbolic acid.

[13] Nicholson not identified but the 'Creswick wretches' probably refers to the Ancient Order of Foresters, who organised the medical care of their members by electing doctors and paying fixed fees for consultations. The following year WLR wrote to MR that he was about to resign as their doctor. See Letter 74 and also endnote 2 of that letter.

59   [From MR in Pentridge, Melbourne, to WLR in Ballarat]

Pentridge Stockade
June 5th 1860 [Tuesday]¹

My darling Walter

Many thanks for your kind letter which I have only just received I thought you had forgotten me but your sending it to St Kilda made it a day later as I left them on Friday for here & shall remain at Pentridge till next Wednesday after that address my letters to John at the Post Office & he will forward them to me for Mrs Marsh wants me to stay a few day's with her & then I return to Mrs Patterson's until I come home. I feel much stronger & am very well blister healing at last but have a gathered finger John wishes Harry to return & live with us if you have no objection dear I said yes for I thought the money would come in useful because he will pay for both now. Harry has quite left school & will stay at Pentridge until I return He looks shockingly ill & John wants to have your advice about him his head is one mass of ringworms Uncle has got the Doctor here to come & see him he has had a bad cough for the last six weeks but that is a little better. I am glad Trotty's quite well & also yourself I hope you do not feel very lonely I had a good laugh at your sending Mary to sleep What did Brooke think of Julia? Why was he not at the Ball? Did he bring the Music?

I think John will perhap's pay my expenses up to Ballaraat I try to save though things are never very cheap in Melbourne Baker² the Bookseller is going to sell off is there any book or Medical book I could get for you if so send me word—

I had an unpleasant dream about you on Sunday night & woke up sobbing I have been quite uneasy about you darling until I got your letter Aunt & Uncle & [are] both delighted to see me we take a good walk every day—I hope you will write soon Shall I go to the Mesmerist³ in Collins street or not. Aunt would go with me.

Give my love to Julia⁴ M^{rs} H⁵—Anna Maria & Trotty & they all join me here in love to yourself & with kisses many| dear dear Walter| Ever your loving wife

Mary

God bless you too dark to write more

Text: ALS NLA MS133/1/70

---

¹   Envelope (MS133/1/46) addressed to 'Dr Richardson, Webster Street, Ballaraat' and postmarked 'Melb 7 JU 60' and 'Ballarat 8 JU 60'.

²   William Baker, 71 Swanston Street, Melbourne.

³   Caroline Dexter (1819–1884), feminist writer, born in Nottingham, the daughter of Richard Harper, watchmaker and jeweller, and Mary (née Simson). It is probable that Caroline Dexter was part of the model for the fictional Grace Marrine' in *FRM*. She was educated privately in England and in Paris, where she became friendly with the female novelist, George Sand (1804–1876). She married in Nottingham the painter William Dexter (1818–1860), of Melbourne, Derbyshire, who emigrated in 1852 to Sydney, where he taught at Lyndhurst College, Glebe. Although based in Sydney when Caroline joined him in 1855, he was in Bendigo in 1853, where he designed the diggers' banner and spoke at a protest meeting. In 1856 they moved to Gippsland, where he painted (including *Wood Ducks* and *Dead Birds*, both in the National Gallery of Victoria) and she wrote her *Ladies Almanack: The Southern Cross or Australian Album and New Years Gift* (Melbourne, 1858), the first ladies' almanac published in the colonies. The Dexters separated soon after the publication and William returned to Sydney, where he died in Redfern on 4 February 1860. Moving to Melbourne, the unconventional Caroline disturbed conservative society by opening an Institute of Hygiene and proclaiming support for such things as divided skirts and the abolition of corsets. She is listed as 'Medical Mesmerist' at 114 Collins Street East, in the Sands & Kenny *Directory* of 1860. In 1861 she married William Lynch (1839–1901), a former pupil from Lyndhurst and twenty years her junior. Lynch became a prosperous solicitor and his wealth enabled her to be a patron of the arts

from their fashionable home in Brighton. He was Mayor of Brighton in 1880–1881. After her death on 19 August 1884, he married Charlotte Mary Ochiltree (b. 1859), daughter of William Bertram Ochiltree (see Letter 80) and Annie, née Graham, both friends of WLR and MR. William Dexter's painting, *Lady's Pet*, 1855 (oil on canvas on cardboard, 60.8 x 84.4 cm in the Art Gallery of South Australia) is described as 'perhaps one of the most engaging portraits from mid-century Sydney'. It depicts Caroline's Blenheim miniature spaniel named Phocion holding Caroline's gloves in his mouth, with her white riding hat, veil and crop. 'The concept is based on the British animal painter Edwin Landseer's painting *The cavalier's pet* (Tate Gallery, London) ... In a sense it is a portrait of Caroline Dexter's absence.' See Ron Radford and Jane Hylton, *Australian Colonial Art: 1800–1900* (Adelaide: Art Gallery Board of South Australia, 1995), p. 44.

4 Julia Harland (Mrs William Hoskins).
5 Mrs John Henderson, wife of the bank manager.

60 [From WLR in Ballarat to MR in Melbourne]

[Webster Street, Ballarat]
Tuesday [5 June 1860]

My dear dear Mary

I did think I would have had a letter today in answer to mine written on Saturday. dear me you are very chary of your letters: Lucinda came down from Castlemaine yesterday & is off again tomorrow her machoir[1] was broken

We are all well: I have had to give her £3–0–0 & she wants a cheque for £5–0–0 as soon as you return–No practice–No money: do not think of asking me to come down for I could not do it

I have a dull time of it and sleepless nights, from excessive cold & mental anxiety: Will be glad to see your dear face again!

I am going to drive Lu. out this afternoon: Expect Smith tonight—No new[s] at all—

M[rs] H.[2] back, looking very delicate; had no word from you; did not see you except at the ball: Weather very, very cold: Letter from Ned this morning wh. I will keep for you—Nicholson[3] is sure to go in again & John as well tho' perhaps not as P. Master General—

Trotty suffers from the cold very much| Your affect
        Walter
Luc. sends kind love & regrets much not seeing you| WLR
        WLR
Text: ALS NLA MS133/1/73

1 A mâchoire is a mouthpiece. Lucinda had written to her mother in November 1858 (see Letter 40) about problems with gumboils. See also *FRM I*, 153.
2 Mrs John Henderson.
3 The ministry of William Nicholson (1816–1865) survived from October 1859 to November 1860. He was a merchant and politician; born on 27 February 1816 at Whitehaven, Cumberland, England, the son of a farmer, Miles Nicholson, and his wife, Hannah née Dalziel. He migrated to Port Phillip in 1842 and started a successful grocery business in Flinders Street, Melbourne. He was Mayor of Melbourne, 1850–1851; MLC, 1852–1856; MLA, 1859–1865; Chief Secretary, 1859–1860. He was one of the first six directors of the Bank of Victoria, which began trading on 3 January 1853. Elected President of the Melbourne Chamber of Commerce in 1858–1860, Nicholson helped to float the Hobson's Bay Railway Company (of which he was Chairman) in 1852, after deciding to establish his bonded warehouse in Flinders Street opposite

the projected city rail terminus. The Legislative Council passed an Act dated January 1853 granting free of charge a strip of land 100 yards wide from Melbourne to Port Melbourne railway pier. By 1856 the warehouse was one of Melbourne's biggest, with a capacity for 4500 tons of goods. Nicholson left most of the mercantile work to his partner Andrew Sutherland while continuing a successful political career. Nicholson died at St Kilda on 10 March 1865, leaving his wife, Sarah Burkitt née Fairclough, and four sons.

61   [From WLR in Ballarat to MR in Melbourne]

[Webster Street, Ballarat]
Friday [8 June 1860]

My own dear Mary

I only received yours of Tuesday this morning I thought it very negligent of you to keep me 10 days with only one letter from you feared you were ill, did not know what to think indeed! I have been very lonely indeed and longing for you every day got no sleep the first week: I have been away since 10 at a labor in the bush:[1] & have now been sent for to go to the Asylum[2] as D[r] Alison[3] is ill again.

I was so glad to get your letter I wrote one yesterday to Uncle about you, then one to yourself neither of wh. I sent—I have nothing worth telling you: weather cold:

Many enquiries when you are coming we did hope you would have been up today Friday but I suppose now we shall not see [you] until next week—Well perhaps it is all for the best as you are evidently enjoying yourself, made much of:

L. off on Wednesday morng Trotty well: M[r] & M[rs] Williamson[4] called & M[r] & M[rs] McQuie[5] Brook promised to see you today & drive you out he will be disappointed again he was at S. Kilda but you ran away one day before your time

Sorry to hear of Harry's illness, want of proper treatment doubtless: Does he wish to come back?—

You can easily telegraph up if you are coming suddenly: I will drive down to Corderoy to meet you let your box go on altho I dont know about Harry. I think I might manage it to Buninyong. Excuse haste my love as it is to catch the Post and believe me my dear dear Mary|
Your own loving
         Walty

Text: ALS NLA MS133/1/105

[1]   *Case* 244, 8 June 1860, Mrs Bredon, splitter's wife, aged twenty-four, first pregnancy, 'perineum lacerated by passage of head-put a stitch in per 2nd day'—female child born 1.30 p.m. The birth certificate states that Florence Bredon was born to James Bredon (aged thirty) and his wife Hermina Julian née Burns (aged twenty-one) at Mount Rowan, Ballarat. Both parents came from Ireland and they married in 1859 at Melbourne.
[2]   The Ballarat Benevolent Asylum, the foundation stone of which was laid on St Patrick's Day, 17 March 1859, with full Masonic honours. All Freemasons of Ballarat attended, headed by the Grand Master of Victoria, Worshipful Brother F. P. Gell. The first building was opened on 20 February 1860.
[3]   Dr Edward Dufferin Allison (*c.*1805–1861), medical practitioner; qualified at Aberdeen in 1829; FRCP, Edinburgh, 1830. Prior to his registration as a doctor in Victoria (sometime before July 1853), he was the Medical Officer at Newtown Dispensary in Edinburgh, and at Whitechapel, London. He was appointed Deputy Registrar for Births, Marriages and Deaths at Portland, Victoria in 1853. From there he moved to Bendigo, where he helped to establish the Presbyterian Church and the school in 1854. From 1856 he was living in Ballarat, based on

Bakery Hill Road. In 1858, he was appointed Camp doctor. He died at Ballarat on 27 October 1861. Bowden, p. 108.

4   Probably Mr and Mrs John Williamson. He was a bank manager at Ballarat.

5   James Blackmore McQuie (b. 1830), Manager of the Ballarat branch of the European Assurance Society, and his wife, Eleanor Hebden McQuie née Brodribb (b. 1833), who had married on 30 December 1857 at St Paul's Church of England, Geelong. She was the daughter of Edward Brodribb and Fanny née Hebden and cousin of William Adams Brodribb junior. The Brodribb family's first connection with Australia was through William Adams Brodribb senior (1789–1861), an attorney from a notable Somerset family. He was convicted at Gloucester Assizes of administering unlawful oaths and was transported in 1816 for seven years. He was sent from Sydney to Hobart Town in 1817 and was appointed clerk to the bench of magistrates and was pardoned conditionally the following year and fully in 1821. In 1819 he was permitted to practise privately as an attorney. Reunited with his wife and children, they lived on a farm near New Norfolk where three more sons were born. The respectability of this family was assured through the successful careers of William Adams Brodribb junior (1809–1886), pastoralist and politician, and his cousin, the educationist, Thomas Brodribb (1836–1923), who both appear in the *ADB*.

62   [From LC in Brighton, England, to WLR in Ballarat]

17 Buckingham Place West Cliff| Brighton Sussex| England.

June 8th /60

My beloved Walter

If you knew how much I suffer from your silence, I think you would write, more especially as my life is one unbroken round of suffering and of sorrow. I wrote you a few hasty lines before going to Tunbridge Wells, and gave them to Miss F. to post, begging you would tell me if the Mount of Olives by D[r] James Hamilton which I sent by a servant to the General post office, and had it registered, the registry receipt is now in my hands, this makes me most terribly uneasy, as I fear there is some calamity befallen either yourself or my dear daughter Mary; such fearful calamities are occurring now on every side, such awful judgments, devastations and horrors, that dread and terror stalk abroad daily—As nursing fatigue and grief had worn me so as to unfit me for every thing Miss Fector brought us off to Tunbridge Wells in March, the change was of great use to your father, he revived & became strong while I, having caught cold, on the Journey which proved too long for me in my then weak state, had to take to my bed, and after some weeks of no small suffering returned the worse for the experiment. we had not been long at home here when Influenza seized upon us all, the all including our one sole servant; this epidemic was of a peculiarly severe type, affecting chiefly the Bronchiae and larynx, cutting down strength at once, and producing such an amount of prostration as left the unhappy patients almost dead, ending in a multitude of cases in Typhus. I have not recovered any strength yet, nor has your father lost the severe fits of deep painful coughing so both are more invalids than ever, and the fearful weather has increased our ailments terrific storms, 2 vessels driven in our shore, & shattered to pieces within a few hundred yards of us.[1] 380 vessels wrecked on the eastern coast—an excursion vessel from Rotterdam containing 80 passengers went down with every soul on board another vessel from Antwerp bringing to us 15,000 sheep, and much cattle lost, with crew & cargo—a deadly disease amongst sheep & lambs here and in Ireland makes this a severe misfortune, mutton having risen here to 1/- per lb—there never was such severe weather known, there is even now scarcely a leaf on the trees, and no hay, nore any description of vegetable to be obtained—

The income tax is doubled, the times are indeed very trying for all classes, I trust they are better in your land

I am very anxious to hear how Mary is as well as yourself, there has been and is even now, so much sickness here of various kinds, and the Cholera is in Malaga (Spain) very near us. I tremble to think what would be the consequence of its coming to England, at such a trying time as this.

I had a letter last evening from Henry, they have been obliged to go to Dalkey for some months on poor Caroline's acct, she is much worse, and the opinion of the best skilled physicians of late is that she will never be better, there is too much internal disease to leave room to expect amendment, she is the victim in addition to this of neuralgia to such a degree as to allow no rest, until death releases her. Henry informs me of the death of John's eldest son Charles:[2] he had a place under government at Demarara, came home invalided to Liverpool one week ago, and died. his poor father's anguish is great, as Charles never expressed either sorrow or regret, at his monstrous conduct to his father, and now all is over for ever—"Walter[3] the son who is at home is going on well, and has been much softened under the revival movement at Kingstown and is" Henry hopes ["]a seeker at least after Salvation.'

My brother Harry ran down here to see me lately and staid a few hours, he is doing something in London as a Missionary, he is a changed man. Amelia[4] has gone over there to live with him, his wife is to join him soon, when his circumstances improve. Mrs Osborne lingers on, her disease a puerpural leg and thigh, I forget the name, but the case is hopeless. I suffer much from head ache, which unfit me for reading, writing, or needlework, my eyes too have given way again. Your Uncle George[5] and his wife are here now, he is somewhat better, and delighted with this locality, his wife is a pleasing sensible Scotch woman, and has taken quite a liking for me—Not a word from John these 3 months,[6] the cholera in India fearfully bad, I beseech you to write to me, I send you some myrtle seeds, I had to wait for them after bespeaking them, and I register this to secure their reaching you. Mrs Bailey would have sent them more securely perhaps, but when she was despatching a box or parcel, I was too ill to write or attend to any thing—Do not forget nor neglect in her old age her who watched over your cradle & spared not herself in her youth to tend and rear you. Your father sends love, he is low spirited and feeble, you are not forgotten in our prayers, both you & Mary are mentioned by name: May our God guard & bless you my dear son. Amen

L.C.

June 9th I am so unwell and so suffering you may not perhaps hear from me again. But while in this body of sin & death I am at all times your fond and anxious Mother

Lucinda Cheyne

I send you with this 8 Newspapers all of recent date see that you receive them 3 are Witnesses for the Scotch Minister[7]

Text: ALS NLA MS133/1/34

[1]   There were dreadful gales and many wrecks around the coast of England on 19–20 February 1860. The steamer *Ondine* was lost through a collision off Beachy Head near Brighton with the *Heroine* of Bideford; the captain and about fifty people drowned. *Haydn's Dictionary*, p. 875.
[2]   Charles Richardson (1830–1860), eldest son of John Richardson, Court of Probate in Dublin, and his first wife, Anna Bristow. He was educated at Dublin and admitted to King's Inns in the Trinity term of 1846.
[3]   Walter Richardson (b. 1842), youngest of seven children of John Richardson and his first wife, Anna Bristow.

4   Amelia Sirée (b. 1806) baptised 28 December 1806 at St Thomas's Parish Church, Dublin; daughter of Henry and Harriet Sirée; younger sister of Lucinda Cheyne.

5   George (1790–1869) and Grace Cheyne (1798–1871) were living at 2 Lansdowne Terrace, West Brighton.

6   He had been dead for six months.

7   The Reverend William Henderson (c.1827–1884) and his wife, Isabella née Thomson. They married in 1854 in Caithness, Scotland, and had eight children. He had been the Minister of St Andrew's Presbyterian Church, Ballarat, since 1858.

63   [From MR in Pentridge, Melbourne, to WLR in Ballarat]

New Prison| Pentridge
June 9th [1860]

My own dear Walter

I received your second letter on Thursday it was kind of you to write to me before you could get mine for if I did not get them posted before 1 oclock they do not leave Pentridge till next day You did surprise me about Lucinda being down I am sorry I was not at home to make her comfortable I hope that you are keeping well I want to come home very much & am only stopping because I feel so well & perhaps if I come home quite strong it might do me good in the sense we both wish[1]

You did not say whether I should go to the Clairvoyant[2] I should like to do so if I could afford it I have little news to tell you for all's so very quiet here.

We went into town on Wednesday but I did not see John he was to busy & we hurried home because it came on to rain & since then we have not been able to go outside it is so wet. I leave here on Wednesday evening & go to M\rs Marsh for a few day's & the week after I return to my own dear Walter & home My heart throbs while I wrote it I want to stay until something[3] is over but I have lost count of when it ought to be Can you send me word what day it was last month as soon as that is over I shall start I will not ask you to come for me dear as you wish besides I shall have Harry with me & I think I shall go to Geelong by the Afternoon train & sleep at Skarratts so as to get a good seat in the coach that leaves at 10 AM then if I do that I shall not put anyone about at St. Kilda by having to start from there early in the morning my blister is well & my finger getting better

I have a bad headache. Harry's very noisy I hope Trotty is a good girl & quite well I hope I shall get a letter from you today. I am to see John at 12 oclock on Wednesday so if there's to be a letter for me that day let it be addressed to John for I do not get any letter's here till afternoon I hope to see you looking well when I return. Till then God bless & prosper you is the prayer of| Your ever loving wife

Mary

Many kisses—

dear Walter I have just received another dear letter so I have opened this to tell you to send me down one of your visiting cards to leave at Toorak as all have to go & leave there cards I go on Monday week as that is the day M\rs Timmins[4] stay's at home to receive caller's

Next Sunday I am going with John to M\rs Francis's[5] I have not time for more darling as John takes this in Town to night so as to ensure your getting it on Tuesday he is very very kind god bless you dearest

Text: ALS NLA MS133/1/69

1   They were both hoping that MR would become pregnant.
2   The 'medical mesmerist', Caroline Dexter.
3   Her monthly period.
4   Not identified.
5   Mary Grant Francis née Ogilvie, wife of James Goodall Francis (1819–1884), who lived at
     149 Albert Street, East Melbourne. Originally a merchant, Francis became a politician and
     served as Commissioner of Public Works in the ministry of William Nicholson, and finally
     became Premier of Victoria from June 1872 to July 1874. He was a local director of the Bank of
     NSW; President of Chamber of Commerce; Director, Victoria Sugar Company; had pastoral
     runs in Victoria and Riverina; and owned a vineyard at Sunbury.

64   [From WLR in Ballarat to MR in Pentridge, Melbourne]

                                                          Webster Street [Ballarat]
                                                          Tuesday June 12. [18]60

My darling Mary
    Your letters are like Angels visits, few & far between! & in 14 days are not many. The
one I received this morning is dated June 9 Saturday. We are pretty well only—very solitary,
& having been very idle the last fortnight I feel it more.
    Nose bled twice yesterday once in the middle of the street on horseback when I was out
in the dark: Weather very cold & damp I am glad you are enjoying yourself I expect Brooke
up tonight which will amuse me a little—No news: I tea took tea once at Mrs Hendersons
Dr Stewart has gone down to get married to J. H. Taylor's sister[1] Holmes the lawyer[2] is
married: Dixie[3] kindly asked me to go & dine with him yesterday but as I was in riding
costume I declined—
    I am so delighted you appear to be better & enjoying yourself so much, there is nothing
like variety of scene & society: I made L. as comfortable as we could—
    Tuesday May 15th was the day[4] dear, so I suppose it is Monday this time & that you will
be here on Saturday next: Go to the Clairvoyant[5] if you wish certainly & ask her any questions
you choose you should however write down the answers—Kind love to Aunt & Uncle—I will
meet you at the Coach instead of coming to Bung.[Buninyong] I send you my card
    I do so long to kiss you once again do come on Saturday if you are at all able & if not
why make it next week I hope you will like Mrs Francis & give me a good acct of your doings
when you come back
    I am writing to L today I have paid her £7–0–0 since you were here–She got £5–0–0 of
goods from Thom & Gray down to me–so that we are square all but £5–0–0—
    Providence is wonderfully good & the money still comes in to keep house going: you
have never asked me for any! I understood from Johns letter that he would make it all
right—It was a farce to say I got an invitation to the Ball for I never did![6]
    I am suffering very much from cold feet & cold altogether—I am never warm—
    Good bye God bless you| I see the mail is in| Your loving husband
        Walter
Text: ALS NLA MS133/1/55

1   Anne Frances Taylor (b. 1828), born in Dublin, daughter of Samuel Taylor, gentleman, and
     Jane née Green. She married Dr James Stewart on 12 June 1860 at Christ Church, St Kilda. She
     was the sister of John Hamlet Taylor (1826–1882).

2   Robert William Holmes (b. 1826), solicitor; married Catherine Kain (b. 1849) on 9 June 1860 at St Alipius Roman Catholic Church, Ballarat. The bride and groom were both born in County Tyrone, Ireland. Keen on music and aquatic sports, he was Secretary of the Harmonic Society and at one time Vice-President of the Ballarat Rowing Club and time-keeper for the Ballarat Yacht Club. Withers, pp. 255–256.

3   John Morgan Dixie (1836–1865), gold broker at Ballarat; he was on the first committee of management of the Ballarat Hospital as a Trustee and also as the Treasurer. Withers, p. 258.

4   The day her period started. The inference is that her monthly cycles were twenty-seven days and that she would return after the June period had almost finished, i.e., Saturday, 16 June.

5   Caroline Dexter.

6   See *FRM I*, p. 172.

65   [From WLR in Ballarat to MR in Pentridge, Melbourne]

[Webster Street, Ballarat]
[Friday, 15 June 1860]

My darling Mary

I received letters last night from my mother[1] & sister[2] & your sister Lizzie[3] Nobody dead: I am so glad to hear you have at last fixed on a day to return, I have been so miserable—no sleep from cold I got last a better night as in addition to the bed cloths on the bed I put on Neds rug & four blankets & having found a night cap only awoke about ½ doz times which was decidedly better I have no end of a headache today I suffer much from the cold still:—

You will see or have seen Brooke by this: he does not expect to come here any more if he does next week send me latest intelligence as he says he will: Mr Bond & Mrs Farley[4] have been ill, both recovering—Dr Stewart sent me cards this morning—

Very bad news of "The Times" it is reported to have lost the Henderson £3000 & to be for sale: Julia as romping as ever I enclose you £1–0–0 in case you run short am going to send £5–0–0 to your mother for Sam[5] wh: ought to have been done last month, but which may perhaps be in time—Very fair but cold & frosty: you say my dear you answered all my letters but you let many days pass without giving me my first one—

Smith says Madam Carol was a Mrs Caroline Dexter the inventor of Bloomerism & is a decided humbug—

I send you two newspapers in one and have little else to say Trott is well but she should have pinafores to cover her arms & neck or she will most likely be carried off by croup or influenza this winter as she cannot be kept out of the kitchen & the door is always open

Good bye darling God bless you & restore you safe to the arms| of your fond husband
        Walter

I hope you keep my letters safely from the eyes of the public—
I keep Lizzies to us for the pleasure of your reading it here

    Text: ALS NLA MS133/1/101

1   Presumably letter MS133/1/33 dated 10 April 1860 from Lucinda Cheyne.

2   Caroline Richardson, living in Dublin with her husband, Henry Richardson, and their four children.

3   Elizabeth (Lizzie) Brett née Bailey, MR's older sister.

4   Possibly Mary Ann Farley née Whitaker who married Henry Farley, lamp seller, in 1857.

5   Samuel Bailey (1838–1911) arrived in Melbourne five months later in November on the *Result*.
     The money WLR sent to Elizabeth Bailey may have been to assist in the expenses of Sam's
     passage.

66   [From MR in St Kilda to WLR in Ballarat]

Westbourne Terrace [St Kilda]
Monday morning [18 June 1860]

My own darling Walter

I have just time to write & ask you to meet me on Wednesday evening I leave Geelong
by the 10 oclock Coach on Wednesday morning & I suppose will arrive at Ballaraat about 5 or
6 oclock

We are going to Toorak this afternoon & I want to Post this in Town I am much
obliged for the pound you enclosed I leave Melbourne by the last train on Tuesday afternoon
& sleep at Skarratts so as to get a good seat in the coach I need not write more as I can talk to
you dear so much better

I have seen nothing of Smith I hope I shall find you quite well & with all love & kisses
darling| I am Your loving wife
         Mary
    Text: ALS NLA MS133/1/50

67   [From LC in Brighton, England, to WLR in Ballarat]

[July 1860][1]

2nd Sheet

I have sent them to be <u>regilt</u>, as the gilding was rather worn off, altho I never have used
them since I left my country as I should have to pay the tax on arms if I did (coat of arms I
mean) they are a <u>small</u> present, but as a token of <u>Love</u> and remembrance you may possibly
value them—

I wish very much to <u>know</u> if you ever received "The Mount of Olives" a little work on
secret prayer by Dr James Hamilton of Regent's Square Church in London, I registered it for
you on the very day John received his death stroke, 15th December 1859 and posted it myself
and have the register, but you have never acknowledged it, I wrote your name in it and dated
it "New Years Day 1860"—it is a beautiful work, and I thought you would enjoy it—Your
father has not long since got into the habit of naming you and Mary and <u>all</u> our children in
prayer—we have been praying for the dead these 7 months, and now the omission of that <u>one</u>
name shakes me terribly,—I was nearly forgetting that I have two more deaths to record, the
first that of Charles Richardson, Albert's eldest brother, he returned from Demarara after an
attack of Paralysis, invalided landed at Liverpool, and <u>died</u> a few days afterwards leaving a
widow, and a little girl—& his poor father[2] to whom he behaved so shockingly having become
a devoted disciple of <u>our</u> blessed Master, has answered her petition for help (Charles having
lessened her income £100 per ann. by spending her capital) by telling her he will allow her £20
per ann. and either take her little girl to be educated by his wife Sophy,[3] or pay for her
education—

The 2nd death is that of M[rs] Hamilton your late father's eldest daughter[4] and first born child by Miss Bell an heiress, and the Surgeon General of Ireland's daughter: M[rs] Hamilton whose late husband was a relation of the Duke of that name died 3 years ago a christian at the age of 86! he walked 2 or 3 miles to see <u>me</u> when I was last on a visit to Caroline to tell me he was "now" at that time seeking Christ—he found him and rejoiced altho he became stone blind. I sent M[rs] H. books from time to time, and was always on good terms with them, visiting often when I was last over, she was also 85—and retained her senses to the last. Henry[5] visited her frequently in her last illness, and is satisfied that she has gone home to God—Your brother Alex[r6] is also a believer, walking <u>steadily</u> and lovingly in Christ Jesus—

[Page(s) missing]

Text: AL NLA MS133/1/35

1   Second sheet of a letter which presumably announced the death of WLR's half-brother, John Cheyne, in India on 15 December 1859.
2   John Richardson, WLR's cousin; lawyer in the Court of Probate, Dublin.
3   Sophy was John Richardson's second wife, therefore Charles's stepmother.
4   Mary Hamilton née Richardson (1775–1860), eldest child of Alexander Richardson (1758–1827) and his first wife; she married John Hamilton (1771–1857) in 1797. Marriage Licence listed in *Index to the Act or Grant Books, And to the Original Wills, of the Diocese of Dublin* [c.1638] *to the Year 1800 from the Appendix to the twenty-sixth Report of the Deputy Keeper of the Public Records and Keeper of the State Papers in Ireland* (originally published in Dublin, 1895) (Baltimore: Clearfield, 1997).
5   Henry Richardson, Caroline's husband.
6   Alexander Richardson (1803–1890), half-brother of WLR; son of Alexander Richardson and his third wife, Elizabeth née Smyth, whom he married in August 1800. Alexander would have been nearly thirteen when Lucinda Sirée married his father.

68   [From LC in Brighton, England, to WLR and MR in Ballarat]

17 Buckingham Place| West Cliff| Brighton Sussex| England.
Nov[br] 25th /60

My beloved Walter and Mary

I was indeed glad to hear from you once more, and to find you prospering & comfortable,—your father has completely recovered, but is not strong, yet he is wonderful after all the severe suffering he has endured. I also am much better since the water system was given up by D[r] Dill's orders and a full diet with a liberal use of wine and mild ale substituted—

We have had some further acct of John's last hours. M[rs] Loveday has returned to England <u>a widow</u> Cap[tn] Loveday into whose house John was so kindly received having survived him but <u>2</u> months—John was seized with fever and made for Cap[tn] L's station Suddyah in Upper Assam, accompanied with a young man named Preston[1]—They were taken into Cap[tn] Loveday's house, John having been known and liked, Cap[tn] L. went down to the boat to receive poor John who was ill of fever—he was tended with great care by both the Cap[tn] and his wife, she wrote me a full acc[t] his sufferings were <u>great,</u> and the poor sufferer's patience remarkable, at times delirium <u>was</u> present, he had no proper medical aid, and died about the termination of a week or ten days of extreme suffering.

Cap^{tn} L. and Preston laid him out & put him into the coffin, Cap^{tn} & Mrs L. went together and laid him in a retired spot, between <u>two</u> Lime trees, Captn L. reading the funeral service over him, there being neither Clergyman no[r] physician nearer than <u>80</u> miles!

What a life! and what an end!—no judgment can be pronounced on his spiritual state, that rests with God his Maker, and will never be known until the great day, let us submit humbly to the Sovereignty of Him without whose will not a sparrow can fall, I <u>can</u> say "I was dumb I opened not my mouth because <u>Thou</u> didst it"—

Be thankful for your day of grace, and seek to live near to God, be much in <u>secret</u> prayer—it is the only way to <u>grow,</u> you can enter into your closet and shut the door any where you find yourself <u>alone,</u> on horseback, in a buggy, at a sick bed side aye even in company! my prayers are frequent and fervent for you—I shall not touch on what I have suffered, it is now over, had I been certain of his being safe I would have <u>rejoiced,</u> the pang consists on the idea of <u>eternal</u> separation—

Did Lucinda lose her salary? by the insolvency of these people she has last been with, I was thankful to hear from her and am praying for a suitable place for her—

I have been very unwell again these last few days, more "purpura" and my gums ulcerated, cramp at night & diarr—I know the cause, it is the terrible struggle between heart breaking grief & perfect submission, I know <u>now</u> what Eleanor Kennedy[2] meant when <u>she said</u> "My dear friend submission <u>is hard</u>"!—I have been shut up perhaps too long, and been obliged to conceal my struggles too closely. I do not at any time like to reveal my inmost feelings to others none would understand them, but He who can <u>read</u> the heart to Him alone. I can pour out mine, and at times the outpouring exhausts the body.—I am comforted by thinking "the time is short"—and my work is done. No one would miss me, I can never be thankful enough for being ready!—

The poem was <u>not</u> in your letter, it contained a short one from Lucinda, perhaps she kept it out, by mistake, find out, should I send the spoons by post, or wait for an opportunity thro' Mary's Mother, say <u>which,</u> they are very pretty, too good to be lost

I am truly glad to hear that dear Mary is better. Tell her I should have been glad indeed to have seen her, and embraced her. Mrs George Cheyne is desperately grieved at having left Australia,[3] she has been ill Bronchitis, and George is very delicate our English Climate does not suit either of them. Miss Fector's health is deteriorating she is growing deaf, and her eyes not improving—Alick is here now; he is a <u>very fine</u> lad, and reminds me of <u>you,</u> he is loving but idle. The Mother is making desperate efforts to obtain him, we must hide him once more.

Your father's state of health is unsatisfactory, he cannot bear the least fatigue now, sleeps hardly any and suffers from depression. The temperature of the apartment <u>he</u> requires is destruction to <u>me,</u> but I must bear it—

You ought to get 3 Witnesses with this, do not omit <u>writing</u> nor fail to let me have the poem—tell L. I am anxious about her, & praying—God for ever bless you my dear Walter| With fond love to Mary and yourself & L. if with you ever | while in the body y^r affec^{te} Mother

   L.C.

  Text: ALS NLA MS133/1/36 [Black edged]

---

[1]   Jericho Preston (*c.*1835–1862), Lieutenant in the 60th (The King's Royal Rifle Corps), the 3rd Battallion of which had embarked for India on 7 July 1857. Preston became an Ensign on 14 September 1855 and a Lieutenant on 19 June 1857. He served in the campaign in Rohilcund 1858, including the actions of Bugawalla and Nugena and the relief of Mabundee.

H. G. Hart ed., *The New Annual Army List, and Militia List* (London: John Murray, 1859), p. 289. He never recovered from the hardships and illness endured in the campaigns and, returning home to England, he died very soon after at his father's home in Cambridge in 1862. See Letter 91.

2   Eleanor Kennedy not identified.

3   George and Grace Cheyne had left their adopted daughter, Emily Jane Moir (née Trimmer), in WA when they returned to Britain.

1861

69   [From LC in Brighton, England, to WLR in Ballarat]

17 Buckingham Place| Brighton| Sussex.

Feby 20th /61

My beloved Walter

The Australian Mail did not come in time to admit of my writing by that going outward, the unprecedented severity of the stormy weather may have been the cause, and fearful of bad news from your <u>long</u> silence I had not the heart to write, before I had some intelligence of you and my dear Mary, I thank my God for your prolonged life, and increasing practice how graciously He has vouchsafed to answer my prayer that he would pay you back <u>that</u> which <u>I</u> could not your kind assistance and money given to our poor John, you will I trust be still <u>more</u> paid, by increasing prosperity, in <u>spiritual</u> comfort, as well as with temporal abundance, the <u>chief</u> and only substantial happiness however is to be sought for in the light of God's countenance manifested to the soul and abiding with it, all else is as unreal as unsatisfying; I trust you grow in the experience of this—The hope of meeting you in the world where there is neither parting not sorrow, gives me unspeakable consolation, there we shall be better acquainted, and no <u>spy</u> shall interrupt ~~our~~ our peace: none of the garbled statements nor <u>unguest</u> like conduct to which you allude give <u>me</u> the least concern, such like matters are not <u>new,</u> they took place 25 years ago;[1] as far as I am concerned they cannot be carried on any more,—calumny and <u>backbiting</u> cannot consist with <u>any</u> measure of Religion, or knowledge of the Most High, and we have no inclination to keep up intercourse unless it proceeds from <u>true</u> love, not the interested semblance of it. I was <u>deeply</u> grieved, at the unworthy treatment I met with both from husband and wife, and that more on their account ~~that~~ than <u>my</u> own, <u>but</u> above all I was in anguish on your father's acc^t,[2] his well known respectability trampled on, his character assailed and this thro' a child nurtured, watched over helped continually by him, O—it <u>was</u> bitter. I am not careful to justify myself, I leave that to Him—whose unworthy servant I am let those who return evil for good, look to themselves, and what they may bring on their house—Your letter caused your father pain he cannot bear to think of the baseness and wickedness of the treatment I received at a time when my heart was overwhelmed and I was deprived of <u>his</u> sympathy & support. <u>No</u> trial that I ever endured was to be compared with Caroline's[3] conduct,—it appalls me even <u>now</u> to think of it.—I have a wretched pen more like a stick than any thing else, and your father is gone to bed, I fear it is a Bronchital attack, the writing these few lines to you, & the bringing to mind so many painful circumstances have brought on him illness that may prove very distressing—we have had fearful weather for this last year, such a winter I never remember, I had a sharp threatening of Rheumatism in the muscles of both arms they were nearly powerless for a time, I could and I could [sic] neither write nor hold a book They are better, but very weak & unable for much—I am just now recovering slowly from a severe bout of Influenza, the cough unusually hard and persisting, but I have mercies countless as the sands, and not the least is being ready and willing to depart when the messenger arrives, summoning me to another habitation—

I have at last forwarded the little salt spoons, to dear Mary's Mother who undertakes to convey them to you, they are a poor token, but love can be manifested in trifles as well as in larger gifts, when you look on them may they testify of mine for you, dearest daughter Mary, and any who may yet be yours. They are silver, gilt, they will tell you of my young days when your late father[4] placed me at the head of his house and table,—

March 15th

My beloved Walter, the night your father wrote his letter which I send he lay down in bed to undergo a long & severe illness, which is not ended yet—So severe an attack he has never experienced before, and the issue even now is doubtful,—I stay myself on Him, who has promised He will never leave me nor forsake me, and that every day my strength shall be if possible do not omit a line from yourself or dear Mary

Remember you and she are now my sole children; I have been nursing your father night and day, and yet all the while ill myself, I am greatly shaken therefore and cannot last long,—This Spring has set in with great severity, multitudes have already fallen victims, and multitudes dying now, sickness and death were never so prevalent here,—I fear I am too feeble to attempt a letter to Lucinda by this mail, tell her so with my sincere love and blessing, I use your Bible daily, and it speaks to my heart, do not grieve for me when you hear that the warfare is over, and the Celestial City entered, Christ is my All! I am a worthless worm but He has undertaken for me He is my surety, my God and my Redeemer, my Righteousness, my Salvation, He that performeth all for me. To Him I commend you and my dear daughter Mary may He be to you both what He has been to me these 37 years Give my tenderest love to Mary, and think of me ever as your fondly attached Mother

Lucinda Cheyne

Your father sends love and blessing to both. Amen.

Text: ALS NLA MS133/1/37

1   i.e., 1836, see endnote 3.
2   Dr Bayne Cheyne, WLR's stepfather.
3   If Lucinda Cheyne is indeed remembering events that took place twenty-five years before, i.e., 1836, Caroline and her cousin, Henry Richardson, were only in their fourteenth year. Dr Cheyne would probably have been away from home in February and March 1836, dealing with Cheyne family matters, as his brother, Dr John Cheyne, died on 31 January 1836 aged fifty-eight, at Sherrington, Buckinghamshire, followed less than a month later, on 24 February 1836, by their oldest sister, Mrs Elizabeth Wilkinson, who died aged fifty-seven. Caroline and Henry married in 1845, six years prior to Marmaduke Cheyne Richardson's birth in 1851.
4   Alexander Richardson.

70 [From MR in St Kilda to WLR in Ballarat]

Bull Street, [St Kilda][1]
May 23rd 1861 [Thursday]

My darling Walter

I write today so as to get John to post this in Town tomorrow morning. You will see I have arrived safely after the long journey & feeling very tired. John met us at the Station & was very glad to see me also Jeannie[2] I like her very much there house far surpasses our's in furniture it is most elegant you would be very pleased with every thing My boxes have not yet arrived it is very vexing I cannot go out until I do get them. Trotty[3] behaved very well though she is suffering very much today <u>no rest</u> day or night for coughing her face & eyes all inflamed quite a fright.

I forgot dearest to tell you that the day before I left Mrs Porter[4] called & told me to ask you to send a Nurse a temperance one you promised her, also send back the boots I had from Davis & pay 1/-.

Travelling in the coach was a party who knew you when at Smith's at Mary's Cray her name was Golding you attended her Mamma she knew you directly she saw you at the coach. She is married to Mrs Turnbull's Brother & lives far back in a paddock opposite the Turf Hotel[5]

I had to put this by last night so have got up early this Friday morning to finish it such a night I do not wish to pass again I have not had one hour's sleep since I left you Trotty sleeps with me & all night long she was either crying or ~~sleeping~~ coughing I struck a light & such an object as her face was like a spotted pink dress well I thought it very funny but said nothing Wrapt her up & made her perspire & at daylight I looked at her again & my suspicions were confirmed she has either Measles or Scarlet fever John & Jeannie are not up yet so they dont know—a pretty state of things she either caught them in the Coach where there was a sick boy or when in Skarrets Hotel he told me as we were driving to the Railway that all his children had been ill with measles though we did not see them I suppose John will send for a Dr It has quite put me about. No boxes have arrived & here I am & cannot get out

Jeannie has only been in the colony 7 months[6] has no relations whatever earned her own livelihood & is not ashamed of it say's she is thirty year's old a great deal to say for herself & will make John an excellent wife Very very different to Poor Susan she is anxious to return with me to see Ballaarat but John does not like that but she will come before three months are over you must come down a beautiful room for us both—I showed her your likeness & she thinks you very good looking & would so like to know you John say's the trip would do you all the good in the world

Bye the bye send down the prescription for Trotty cough mixture. We were to have gone to the Turnham's to spend tomorrow but we shall not be able to go on account of Harry.[7] I cannot tell you anything about Melbourne as I have not been out I feel very tired already & hope you will be down in about a fortnight for me I shall not stay the Governor's ball[8] I think. How do you & Sam[9] get on I hope Bridget[10] attend's to your wants & cooked the Sucking pig to your liking[11] I hope to get a dear <u>long long</u> letter from you on Monday & I will write again on Tuesday Give my love to Sam & accept many kisses with all my loves to yourself God Bless & prosper you darling is the prayer of| Your loving wife

Mary

Address M^rs R
   care of J. R. Bailey Esq
     S.E Corner of Bull St
      Alma Road East
       St Kilda
         Melbourne
Text: ALS NLA MS133/1/67

1   MR was visiting her brother John Robinson Bailey and his second wife, Jeannie, who had returned from their honeymoon.

2   Jane Bailey née Rainsford (1831–1866), second wife of John Robinson Bailey. They were married on 4 April 1861 by the Reverend David Seddon, at Christ Church, St Kilda, with Edward Harold (Ned) Bailey as one of the witnesses.

3   Emma Bailey (1856–1935), daughter of John Robinson Bailey and his first wife, Susannah. She had lived with MR and WLR since her mother's death in August 1859.

4   Two Porter families had babies born in 1861: William and Ann Porter had a daughter, Fanny, and William and Lydia Porter had a daughter, Emily.

5   Eliza Golding née Rodda (b. 1827) married William Golding, a miner, on 20 November 1856. She had a sister, Mary Rodda, who married James Turnbull, a builder, in 1857 and had seven children in Ballarat from 1858 to 1872. Their mother was Thomasina Rodda née Jones, married to James Rodda, a blacksmith. Originally from Marazion, Cornwall, where the two sisters were born, the family must have moved to Kent prior to 1851. Mrs Rodda may have been attended by WLR but not for a confinement, for her name is not included in the 120 cases in WLR's *Registry of Midwifery Cases* prior to his departure for Victoria. In her conversation in the coach MR had misunderstood the relationship, for Mrs Golding was the sister of Mr Turnbull's wife.

6   Jeannie Bailey arrived in September 1860 on board the *Wellesley*.

7   Harrie Elphinstone Bailey (b. 1853), son of John Robinson Bailey and his first wife, Susannah. He lived with MR and WLR for a time after the death of his mother prior to being sent to school in Melbourne.

8   The Governor's Ball was usually held on Queen Victoria's birthday, 24 May, but as Her Royal Highness the Duchess of Kent, the Queen's mother, had died on 16 March 1861, the Governor, Sir Henry Barkly, had postponed the Ball until Thursday, 20 June 1861, the anniversary of the accession of her Majesty to the British throne.

9   Samuel Bailey (1838–1911), brother of MR. Arriving in Melbourne the previous November (1860) on the *Result*, he had since lived with the Richardsons in Ballarat and worked in a bank.

10 The Richardsons' servant.

11 See *FRM I*, p. 294.

71   [Rrom WLR in Ballarat to MR in St Kilda]

[Webster Street, Ballarat]
Saturday 2.30 PM [25 May 1861]

My dear Mary

You have certainly not had a very nice time so far—I should advise a separate bed for you as sleeping with a feverish child is not good for you. I am glad you got down safely and hope you will enjoy yourself next week

You have escaped our miserable weather—wet & cold—

It is certainly very trying I shall not be able to write much now for I have to go again a long round and my hand is so cold I can hardly hold the pen

I was called out last night[1] & not in bed till one—Night mare both nights—first so tired that I could not catch my horse who walked away from me, & 2nd a large bone got into her foot & lamed her

You will understand these were my dreams—I have a case of broken jaw & I have to go every day 2 miles off—Queen's birthday wet spoiled everything[2] I send you "Times" of Friday

Sam well—Bridget doing well

Volunteers Ball[3] a great success—I enclose acct from Wanliss[4] which I will pay today—As to Trotty you will find a good article in the book I send to our new sister[5] I could not find your letter to Sarah—Kelly[6] has just been & we put in a vine at each end of the house & a few other plants & that has warmed me a little—I will write you a longer letter next time say on Monday evening and with kind & fond kisses to yourself & regards to Jack & Jean[7] I am Yours | ever

      W.L.R.

Text: ALS NLA MS133/1/157

[1]   *Case* 340, 24 May 1861, Mrs Scopie, second pregnancy, 'All normal'; child born at 10pm. Alice Amelia Scopie born to Charles Scopie and Margaret née Taylor. Alice Amelia survived and married twice: first in 1883 to Charles Woodrow Furmedge (from Cornwall) and second to Peter Bain McMaster in 1886. Charles Furmedge died in 1883 aged thirty and in 1884 Alice gave birth to Leslie Charles Furmedge in Ballarat. She had more children with her second husband.

[2]   A grand display of fireworks, which was to have taken place on the Copenhagen Grounds, had to be postponed until 29 May 1861, 'weather permitting.' *Star*, 28 May 1861, p. 2.

[3]   The Ballarat Volunteer Rifle Regiment was established in 1858, with the consent of the government, and consisted of four divisions of infantry and two of cavalry. The name was changed to 'Ballarat Rangers' but the locals referred to them as the 'Volunteers'. 'The Ballarat Rifle Rangers' Ball was held in the large hall of the Mechanics Institute last night, and certainly the room never presented a more brilliant and at the same time more crowded and animated appearance. From an early hour in the evening vehicles dashed up to the entrance to the Institute, and as night advanced, in rapid succession. In the streets the uniform of the rangers was to be seen escorting the better part of creation to the ball ... The room was tastefully decorated for the occasion. At the back of the orchestra was placed on a sort of ground-work an illuminated figure of the Queen, and a scroll on which was written "God Save Queen Victoria".' *The Ballarat Times*, 25 May 1861, p. 2.

[4]   Thomas Drummond Wanliss. During 1861 Elizabeth Wanliss gave birth to John Newton Wellesley (1861–1950). A year later she, Thomas and baby John took a trip back to Scotland, where their second son, David Sydney (1864–1943), was born in Perth on 20 February 1864. The four returned to Victoria later that year, arriving at Melbourne in the *Dover Castle* in September 1864. See Letter 57 for more details of the family.

[5]   Jane (Jeannie) Bailey.

[6]   John Kelly was a market gardener, the Swamp.

[7]   John Robinson Bailey and his second wife Jane (Jeannie) née Rainsford.

72   **[From MR in St Kilda to WLR in Ballarat]**

                                       Bull Street South [St Kilda]

                                       May 27th 1861 [Monday]

My dear Walter

    Your's I received this morning with the book to Jeannie & which she is much obliged for. Your letter was very short but I hope dearest you will let me have a long one on Wednesday morning. Trotty is a little better I think the rash seem's to be going in to day & she is not so feverish her cot came on Saturday so I put her in but it makes very little difference as I have to keep getting out of bed to her I am <u>nurse</u> & doctor both coughing constantly

I do hope dearest you will make up your mind to fetch me home as soon as you can. Harold was here yesterday he look's very well suffer's so much from cold he say's if it would not trouble you too much he would like to have his rug it is under one of the bed's marked E.H.B. if you can write a day or two before you come I am to write to him & he will come on purpose to see you. Jeannie is very anxious to return to Ballaraat with me & send Trotty to Pentridge[1] but I want her to let me come first & get the house in order & them to take Harry back—she does not believe in never going away & intends to begin as she likes very different to Poor Sue John not like the same man quite a pleasure to be in the house he say's he does hope you will come & Jeannie to so I said I knew you would. You will be so delighted with St Kilda if fine Jeannie & I are going to town tomorrow I wish you would send me word the exact width of the Drawing room window—from wood to wood I saw such a beautiful Gilt Cornice[2] for 25 shillings it measures 6 feet 4 inches they look better than poles & must fit just round the top wood work. I shall also get a set of new dish cover's for two pounds—I find my hat & cloak will not cost me quite so much as I thought for I shall have money enough to buy those if you dont object the cornice is very handsome. We have not been out anywhere nor anyone here all frightened at the measles so Jeannie & I walk about Seen nothing of Turnham's. The little book say's diarrhoea often sets in when the measles disappear send me word what to do in case such a thing occur's she wont eat anything I give her aniseed Tea to drink. I am glad to hear that Sam is well. You must tell me what you do all the Evening & how you amuse yourselves

Shall you bring the Buggy down mind you write good long letter's dear I forgive you the last one I hope you will sleep better I can sympathise with you for I am as bad myself—I will give John the Bill when he comes home there was such a row about the things the charge was 35 shillings & when they came here they wanted 5 shillings for fetching the things from our house John would not pay & there was a regular scuffle I do not know how it will end

I think I have told you all I can My head aches so I shall leave off—God Bless you darling with love & lots of kisses—ever your's

Mary

Do let me have a dear letter on <u>Wednesday</u>—

Text: ALS NLA MS133/1/65

[1] Harrie was at a school near Pentridge and staying with the Turnhams.
[2] See *FRM I*, p. 283.

73 [From WLR in Ballarat to MR in St Kilda]

[Webster Street, Ballarat]
Tuesday [28 May 1861]

My dearest Mary

I know my last was very short because I wanted to post it on Saturday and therefore I was prevented from writing more owing to my having to go out: There is no fear of Trotty if she does not take cold I would recommend a good large Mustard plaster between both shoulders if Cough continues. You say you want me to come but do not say when, if matters go go [sic] on as you describe your visit is made a punishment instead of a pleasure and sleepless nights will soon injure your health again & do away with any good that might arise from your trip—I think of going down on the 11th June so as to be present at the installation of the Grand Master[1] I have been asked to represent the Ballt Lodge: so if that is not too soon the ceremony takes place on the 12th I could stay until Saturday 15th that would make your stay under a month:

I do not think the gilt cornices would look nearly so well as poles: the width from wood to wood below is about 5 feet 6 but the cornice could easily be altered, up above it is about 6 feet 6 inches I should think—I have no new[s] to tell you on Saturday eveg. Sam went to theatre[2] & I staid at home Sunday I went to church. Monday played chess 3 games. Tuesday Bogle spent eveg with us—Tonight I am going to Hospital Committee meeting.

Have been & am fearfully busy the days are too short and I will either have to leave at 9 or stay out till 6 & 7—

M[rs] Henderson[3] gives a party tonight the Smiths[4] & O'Haras[5] Sam & I have been asked I told her I would not be able to go until late but I would be in time for supper I thought of her treatment of you: I cover myself up at night with your dress & I have managed very well, the last two nights—Weather fine yesterday & today but much dirt & sludge. Do you get the Star daily let me know. Bridget is behaving very well—I have not seen or heard of any of your freinds—& so have nothing to tell you of them.

Kind remembrances to all.

You will see by the Star if you get it that Vowles[6] has tendered per £1600 for Cuthberts house & has been accepted—

I have literally nothing more to add & so Farewell if I thought you burned my letters I would write much longer & fuller ones—| Your affect

     Walter

I have had a terrific cough & cold in consequence of getting wet twice daily for 4 days—I see rain coming on again tonight or tomorrow

Text: ALS NLA MS133/1/75

[1] WLR represented the Ballarat Freemasons at the installation of the Victorian Grand Master. See *FRM I*, p. 329.

[2] 'The Theatre Royal was well attended on Saturday night, when the old favourite piece of "The Green Bushes" was produced. Miss Julia Mathews played the gipsy girl, a character which afforded her an opportunity of singing several of her favourite ballads, which were rapturously encored.' *The Ballarat Times*, 27 May 1861, p. 2.

[3] Mrs John Henderson, wife of the Manager of the Colonial Bank of Australasia.

[4] Probably Mr and Mrs James Smith: he was a mining agent in Lydiard Street, Ballarat.

[5] Dr Henry O'Hara became a wealthy doctor in Melbourne, specialising in gynaecology. MRCS England 1837. He came out to Victoria with his family on board the *Northumbria*, arriving January 1853. He was practising in Warrnambool in 1859 and was in Ballarat during 1861. He was elected as a member of the Medical Society of Victoria at the same meeting on 7 May 1879 at which Dr Louis Hirsch Henry (*c.*1854–1924) was blackballed (see note 26 in Chapter 5: Illness and Death). O'Hara came to the attention of the medical profession in 1894 in the *Australian Medical Gazette* (no. 13, pp. 391–392), in which he was accused of performing illegal abortions; and then in 1900 the BMA committee voted thirteen to two for his expulsion from the society because of his alleged association with a company promoting a birth-control device. The committee's recommendation for expulsion failed to get the required support from the members, resulting in widespread resignation of members (including O'Hara). The new chairman of the BMA, Dr James Edward Neild, was elected on 11 April 1900. Love, pp. 184, 322.

[6] Dr James Vowles married to Priscilla née Rawlings. They had two surviving children: Lilla (b. 1857) and Emily (b. 1860).

74   [From WLR in Ballarat to MR in St Kilda]

[Webster Street, Ballarat]
Saturday morning: [1 June 1861]

My dearest Mary

I am still very busy, occupied every night until after dark, I cannot give you any particulars about my coming dearest yet for of course something may occur to prevent it even at the last moment: so do not be too sanguine my dear—Of course we are <u>very happy & not at all dull</u>: there was a fire this morning ½ past 5. Star Hotel & Binney & Broadbents both destroyed[1]—

Weather intensely cold—but anything rather than wet: No new[s] whatever of anybody

Sam went to Hendersons & I popped in at 10.30—~~but f~~ & had one Polka then just as we were sitting down to supper I was called away & did not go back again: D[r] Bunce is going thro the insolvent Court again! I will not keep the Forresters[2] longer than next Xmas & perhaps may not be reelected ~~next~~ this month or next month I am not sure which—No accouchements this week only two last week altho 24 down—

Gray[3] got in to the Hospital as Dispenser Sheppard[4] very nearly succeeded Gray 11 S—10[5]—

2.30[pm] I have just come in, quite knocked up & have to go all over the town again & up to Little Bendigo—I have determined to resign the Forresters they are a low mean set and my attention is too good for them besides which I feel I am killing myself I get no sleep now after 5 every morning & the worry & wear & tear is terrific

I have nothing more to add Good bye God bless you| Your own husband
        Walter

The sucking pig came this morning—I shall not get home tonight before 7—

Text: ALS NLA MS133/1/102

[1]   'The fire was believed to have been started by two grooms in the employment of Mr O'Connor, who ran a coach service with offices in the Star Hotel. When one of them was arrested, he was wearing a pair of trousers belonging to Mr [William] Irwin, the owner of the Hotel, but the money known to have been in the pockets of the apparel had been spent.' *Star,* 3 June 1861, p. 2.

[2]   Ancient Order of Forresters, one of the societies which by voluntary subscriptions provided for the relief or maintenance of its members in sickness, old age, etc., and elected a doctor for its members. The doctor was paid a set fee for each member, thus supposedly guaranteed a supply of patients, and the patients guaranteed stable medical costs. However, the fees generated often did not reflect the work provided by the doctors.

[3]   Douglas Mackie A. Gray (c.1831–1882), chemist in Sturt Street; married to Eleanor née Buckingham (c.1837–1888).

[4]   William Horder Sheppard, an old friend of WLR (see Letter 23).

[5]   'The election of a dispenser and house steward for the Ballarat hospital, took place yesterday evening, when the successful candidate was Mr Gray, who received eleven votes. Mr Sheppard stood next on the list—ten votes having been recorded in his favour. The other candidates were—Messrs Jackson, Elliston, Toole and Newman. Mr Hill, the gentleman who has just vacated the office, has done so in consequence of his intention shortly to proceed to England.' *The Ballarat Times,* 1 June 1861, p. 3.

75 [From MR in St Kilda to WLR in Ballarat]

Bull Street [St Kilda]
June 3rd 1861 [Monday]

My dear Walter

I am sorry to see by your letter that you are so put about resign the Forresters if you cannot give satisfaction besides your health is more important than any lodges at least to me altho you are so cool in your two last you have never sent me even your love or a kiss it seem's very hard but I suppose I am not missed very much no matter what my faults are I thought you would have had kind feelings toward's me. Your letter has destroyed what little enjoyment I might have had to day in Town & coming after my dreaming all night that you had your arm's round me was very chilling I must put it down to your being so busy but those two are the first really cool letter's I have had from you. Jeannie is going into Town to day for a new servant her's leave's tomorrow—will not stop to[o] much work it may be on account of the children I expect but so far she has had nothing extra to do for I have washed & dressed Trotty & done my own room & she has never done a single thing for me since here I've been. On Saturday we went to Pentridge they were glad to see us but more delighted to hear that you were coming down very anxious for us to stay there but John would not hear of it. I promised for one night

Yesterday we went to church & a walk on the Beach afterward's I saw Harris one day in Town but he did not see me I shall not stay for the Governor's Ball[1] I hope if possible dear you will come for me I feel dull. I hope you enjoyed the sucking pig & that Bridget cooked it to your liking

I think John intends taking us to the Theatre one night this week—

It was very vexing about the supper at Henderson's but your usual luck. I am not very much surprised at Bunce he is a man who will never do much good: I hope you will write me a little warmer dear next time my back aches today & head & perhaps I felt it more John's honeymoon is not over yet Give my love to Sam & God Bless you darling love & kisses| Ever your's

Mary

Text: ALS NLA MS133/1/64

[1] The Governor's Ball was held on Thursday, 20 June 1861, see Letter 70.

76 [From WLR in Ballarat to MR in St Kilda]

[Webster Street, Ballarat]
[Tuesday, 4 June 1861]

My own dear Poll

You never meant half you wrote to me—you must make some allowance I have never been so worried in my life I enclose you a list of my patients that I have seen today—On Saturday night was called out to Mrs Allen[1] home by 12. Called out again to Mrs Pearmain[2] at 2 Sunday morning, home by 4.—Sunday night called out at 11 to Mrs Rogers,[3] home by 3. as I got to my home found some person waiting to take me to another:[4] home by 7, as I got home found Mr Rogers back again, had to tear away there, home by 1. last night called out to sick child & called up to prescribe—

I was riding up Creswick road last night after dark & a dog flew out after the horse she shied stumbled & came down a <u>fearful smash,</u> I got clear providentially <u>without much injury</u> but she is done for—I have felt shaken all day & hands hurt: I had to walk all <u>morning</u> & hire a horse afternoon 10/- I fear this will stop my trip to you dear—as it is at least £10 or £15 out of my pocket—

I must say you do write punctually altho your letters are short & contain little news You must excuse the shortness of mine for I am aching, fitter for bed than anything else

I will give up the Forresters & then I will have a little peace—I am glad you saw the Turn[ham]s I should like to see them & to come down—

Sam is very well I asked him to write you—The Potters[5] called & Mrs Wayne[6] & Mr Walker[7] & the Adams[8]—

I am sorry to hear you feel dull my darling the reason I have not said anymore about ourselves is that we do not wish to make you duller or to hurry back until you have enjoyed yourself well:

Wednesday morning Called out again[9] 8 PM last night not home till 4.30 this morning & have got six new places to go to all wanting me first

Another confinement on hand[10] = 7 since Saturday night:

I will try & write a little more at lunch time I am going to try & walk this morning & go to a sale of horses at 12–2 P.M. went could not buy—an awful Catastrophe has occurred to me Puerperal inflammation of the worst kind has attacked 2 of my confinements[11] & I must be off at once very likely I will be down tomorrow or next day Good bye love till then|
Your own
       Walter

Text: ALS NLA MS133/1/74

[1] *Case* 341, 1 June 1861, Mrs Allen, second pregnancy. 'P.P. Haemorrhage—Cold to vulva, 1 child'. Elizabeth born to James Allen (miner) and Ellen née Wright, who resided in Grant Street. The baby died aged six weeks.

[2] *Case* 342, 1 June 1861, Mrs Pearmain, fourth pregnancy. 'All normal, 1 child'. William Fairbarn born to William Pearmain (boot maker) and Jane née Kirton, who resided in Bridge Street. The baby survived and was married in 1888 to Ellen Field.

[3] *Case* 343, 3 June 1861, Mrs Rogers, second pregnancy. 'P.P. Haemorrhage—Cold to vulva, 1 child'. Frederick William Rogers born to Thomas (draper) and Susan Hockings neé Bates, who resided in Dana Street. The baby survived and was married in 1885 to Bertha Binder.

[4] *Case* 344, 3 June 1861, Miss Thompson, first pregnancy. 'All normal, born before arrival'. Benjamin born to Laura Frances Thompson, aged nineteen, who was born in Finsbury, London, and was unmarried. In 1873 she married George Greig.

[5] The Reverend John Potter and his wife, Sarah Annie née Mathews. He became Minister in 1857 of Christ Church, in Lydiard Street, the oldest Anglican edifice in Ballarat.

[6] Probably Mrs Elizabeth Nicholas Wayne née Grigg, who had married Philip Wayne, the chemist on Main Street, Ballarat, in 1860.

[7] Possibly James Walker, a founding member of the Benevolent Asylum Committee. Withers, p. 262.

[8] Not identifiable.

[9] *Case* 345, dated 3 June 1861 in WLR's *Register*, Mrs Collis, second pregnancy. 'Placenta retained, born before arrival.' Edmund William born to Edmund Collis and Esther née Clarke.

[10] *Case* 346, 5 June 1861, Mrs Magor. 'Pregnancy all normal: Stillborn: Complained of pain all over body: after with symptoms of interusception—left her in hands of Drs Bunce &

Kenworthy: went to town—she died 2 days.' Constance Magor née Williams died aged thirty-nine. She was married to John Magor and they both came from Cornwall. She had three daughters in Ballarat: Mary Paul (b. 1853); Elizabeth Ann (b. 1856); Emily Jane (b. 1860). Her widower remarried in 1866 and he and his new wife, Eliza Maria Osborne, had a son (John, b. 1867) and a daughter (Eliza Maria, b. 1869). John Magor (spelt Mager by Withers) was one of the leading men in the mining industry and was director of the Sulieman and Indicator Company and the South Star Company. Withers, pp. 345, 354 and 357.

11   The first case WLR was referring to was Mrs Magor, see note above. His second case was *Case 347*, 7 June 1861, 'Mrs McMill[an], Attended for me by Dr O'Hara—died.' Catherine Mcmillan died, aged thirty-four.

77   [From LC in Brighton, England, to WLR in Ballarat]

17 Buckᵍ Place Brighton, Sussex. England.
August 26ᵗʰ /61 [Tuesday]

My beloved Walter,

I did not forget you on your birth day, your father remembered you also, I have only time for a very few lines the day is hot, and the air full of electricity which makes my head uneasy; the object of these few lines is to request you will give L.¹ £5–0–0 to purchase warm clothing, which I shall remit to you thro' the Bank at Ballarat, or by any other means you or Mʳˢ Bailey may point out—this is part payment of the money she lent to John, I shall I trust supply her with the remainder when she comes, but the danger will be great if she is not amply supplied with warm covering, I wish I could tell you to give her more, but at present this is all I can do, and your compliance will greatly oblige me, and you need not fear about the repayment

She tells me she has not enough yet for the expences of the voyage; neither does she consult me about it, I have invited her to come here first, and recruit, and when she has recovered, she can proceed; this place is cold too cold for her, George Cheyne has been in bad health ever since his return,—it is a dangerous experiment—I had a visit from dear Mary's Mother and Sister² on Sabbath 18ᵗʰ. Mʳˢ Bailey has been a beautiful woman, and is now very handsome, I would have known her anywhere from Mary's picture, she interests me greatly, and I felt quite drawn to love her, she is gentle, sorrowful & dignified with a countenance full of ~~benigncity~~ benignity and sweetness. I have time for no more and am very weak, worn down with Diarr. With best of loves to dear Mary and yourself| Ever my very dear Son| Your fondly attached Mother
        L.C.
I have sent 3 Witnesses this mail. |I was too late for the first.
   Text: ALS NLA MS133/1/38

¹   Lucinda Richardson, WLR's sister.
²   Possibly Sarah Bailey, who had returned to England from Australia, or Lizzie Brett, who may have been living near Brighton with the Rifle Brigade (her husband was Captain John Brett). Mary, Lizzie and their mother were supposed to be very alike.

1862

78   [From WLR in Ballarat to MR in Melbourne][1]

Webster St [Ballarat]
January 30—1862—Thursday

My dear Mary

In accordance with your wish I commence a letter to you this evening to be in time for tomorrow's post—I have been just as busy as usual, out all day to day, from 10 to ½ past 1. & from ½ to 2 to 6. Regatta[2] tomorrow, I have some remote idea of going, but of course will be prevented by some mewling & puking babies;[3] I hope you got down safely & that Lucinda did not laugh too much of a guffaw   I hope she is better, & that you too my own are better also—no pains or aches, but that the change of air & scene is enjoyed by you—

Did you breakfast on the road?

Did Ned meet you I suppose he did—

Fine weather since you left: I slept so well the first night: never waking: last night nearly as well, called up at ½ past 5[4]—

Bank holiday [Friday, 31 January 1862] I think Sam is going to the regatta: I could not lend him the mare; for I have work in plenty for both:[5] I send you newspaper with this: Mrs Haywood has another son[6]—Stewart was sent for to Creswick, to Lewers son,[7] and so Bunce attended her for him!

I got your letter this morning & hasten after lunch to finish this: <u>Oconnor has been in for an hour</u> 1 to 2 glad you got down pleasantly—take care & rest—

I see the Great Britain[8] is off

the Latona[9] in not advertised for any day so it may possibly be March

I have no news—very cross—Sarah[10] cant write the names of the people coming & confuses me very much:—I believe I have lost two private patients today[11]   Sam pretty well—Kind remembrances to Uncle Aunt & Ned—explain that I have no time to write to Ned

I shall expect a long letter about Tuesday| Ever Your affectionate
Walter

P.S. I see Shanklin has got todays "Star"[12]

Text: ALS NLA MS133/1/79

[1] MR went down to Melbourne to stay with her sister-in-law, Lucinda Richardson, to help her pack up and get ready for her trip back to England on the *Latona*.

[2] The Ballarat Regatta Club was formed on 20 November 1861 when several of the keen aquatic sportsmen in Ballarat decided to hold a regatta on Lake Burrumbeet on 31 January 1862. The club afterwards changed its name to the Ballarat Rowing Club.

[3] 'At first the infant| Mewling and puking in the nurse's arms.' Shakespeare, *As You Like It*, ii, 7, 143.

[4] *Case* 427, 29 January 1862, Mrs Strack, first pregnancy. 'Head shot rapidly thro & she jumped away Perineum lacerating up to but not thro the sphincter ... sutures on the 8th day left them in 10 days healed well.' Joseph Anton born to Anton Philipp Strack and Johanna née Ryan. The baby died nine months later.

[5] Sam was not alone in worrying about how to get to the regatta. 'The first Ballarat regatta will come off this day on Lake Burrumbeet, and all the sporting world is on the *qui vive* in

consequence. In every livery stable through the town eager enquiries are made for some sort of vehicle in which to perform the trip, and in most instances nothing at all can be obtained. Everything that runs on wheels seems to have been retained; and it is confidently expected that this will be the fore-runner of many successful gatherings on this fine sheet of water.' *The Ballarat Tribune*, 31 January 1862, p. 2.

6   Arthur Robert (1862–1945), second son of Robert and Charlotte Haywood, delivered by his great-uncle, Dr Richard Bunce. Their oldest son was William Bernhard (1861–1863).

7   Alexander John Lewers (1861–1862), the baby son of Alexander Lewers (1824–1886), the agent for the Bank of NSW at Creswick, and Rebecca née McFarland.

8   *Great Britain* (3,500 tons) sailed for Liverpool on 29 January 1862, Shipping Intelligence, *The Argus*. The *Great Britain*, designed by the engineer Isambard Kingdom Brunel (1806–1859), was the first ocean-going, iron-hulled screw steamer (322 feet long). It was launched by Prince Albert in 1843 at Bristol and owned by Gibbs, Bright & Co. It had originally been used for the Atlantic voyage from Liverpool to America, but on 21 August 1852 it changed from the America run to bring 650 passengers to the goldfields in Victoria and arrived in Melbourne in eighty-three days. In 1855 Gibbs, Bright & Co. built a companion vessel, the *Royal Charter*. The rotting hulk of the *Great Britain* was salvaged in 1970 from the Falkland Islands, and was towed back to the dry dock in Bristol where she was built and, restored, is now displayed as a permanent tribute to Brunel in the Bristol maritime museum.

9   The *Latona* (695 tons) was advertised in *The Argus* (29 January 1862) to sail on 4 February 1862 but as each deadline was reached the date was postponed until it finally sailed on Friday, 21 February 1862.

10 The Richardsons' servant.

11 Private patients provided doctors with a better income than those patients connected to a club or lodge, such as the Forresters. The club patients could only be charged the fee negotiated at the beginning of the contract.

12 Robert Shanklin (b. *c.*1820), a chemist at Ballarat. It is not clear what WLR means. He moved to Sale, Victoria, with his family.

79   [From WLR in Ballarat to MR in Melbourne]

Ballt. [Webster Street]
Monday. after lunch [3 February 1862]

My own dear wife

I am so grieved to hear about you, I declare your letter this morning filled my eyes with tears. It appears you are suffering a great deal for Lucindas sake and she ought to be very much obliged to you—I wish you had never gone. I do not see my dearest any chance of my going to you just yet, wait patiently

On Saturday I started at 10 & went over Ballt West & Hospital, home by one found of course several waiting & a confinement; started to Golden point, found I should not be wanted just yet & so went round by Specimen Hill, Eureka, Little Bendigo, Soldiers Hill, back to Golden point[1]—home by 9—dined, off again at 10 to another[2] home by 3. slept well. Sunday just as busy & another confinement[3] this morning—Could not sleep last night owing to sore throat—dreamed I was choking—called out at 2 home by 6—got no sleep, sent down for Chloroform—dosed from 8 to 9, up to a dozen people & out again in a broiling day till 1.30. Rain threatening: Confinement 1ˢᵗ do 2ⁿᵈ do 3ʳᵈ of this month & another likely to come off this evening—Bunce could not do ½ my practice so I do not see my own, how I am to leave just now.

Suppose you take Lodgings at Williamstown Sandridge or S. Kilda, away from bugs. Ned would see to it & I will send money down & try to come down at end of month—Let me ask Dʳ Tracy[4] to call & see you: I hear Mʳˢ W.[5] is coming back soon—There will be but little on in my coming down if you put off going to Dr Tracy till then because his treatment will require a week or two & I could not stay

I am so glad of Uncles rise—Capital![6] Remember me kindly to them both & thank them for their love of you—

Sarah is very good indeed—so sorry to hear of your illness

Hudson knocked up: Elliott[7] sun stroke—Rumour says that Mrs Dr H.[8] living on the Main Road who went home you remember some years ago before marriage had a child at home, & that H has found it out since & has kicked up a jolly row. Scott[9] told me & vouched for the truth of it

Sam went to the Pic nic came home brown as berry—No rise: Remember me to Ned & Lucinda

You have not said a word about John & family—| Ever your fond husband
   Walter

[WLR wrote across 2nd page: Mrs Ingoe, at Mr Chippendales, Dunhill Row, Finsbury]

Text: ALS NLA MS133/1/76

1 *Case* 428, 1 February 1862, Mrs Turner, Golden Point, first pregnancy. 'All normal: Colic after 2 days'; child born at 7 pm. Ann born to John Turner and Elizabeth née Morrison.
2 *Case* 429, 2 February 1862, Mrs Stratton, first pregnancy. 'All normal: Rigors 3rd days.' Ann born to David Stratton and Esther née Farrell.
3 *Case* 430, 3 February 1862, Mrs Longwill, third pregnancy. 'All normal.' William born to John Hercus Longwill and Catherine née McAllister (their fifth baby). William died aged six weeks.
4 Richard T. Tracy, MD, LRCSI (*c.*1826–1874), born at Limerick, Ireland, son of Thomas Tracy, gentleman, and his wife Elizabeth née Coglan. He studied at the Dublin School of Medicine and in 1848 graduated licentiate of the Royal College of Surgeons, Ireland. Appointed to the Cholera Hospital in Glasgow, he continued his studies at the University of Glasgow and in May 1849 was granted MD with honours. He subsequently practised in Ireland (King's County) and England (Reading, Berkshire). On 29 April 1851 he married his cousin, Fanny Louisa Sibthorpe, and seventeen days later they set sail on the *Ballangeich*, on which he was the surgeon. Landing in Melbourne, they immediately sailed for Adelaide where he practised until news of the discovery of gold in Victoria enticed him (and his friend James Bonwick) to Castlemaine and Bendigo in February 1852. He returned to his wife and daughter in Adelaide after four months and moved with them to Melbourne, where he first practised in Fitzroy and then Collins Street East. He was an original member of the Victorian Medical Association, then joined the rival Medico Chirurgical Society of Victoria and helped to unite these two bodies as the Medical Society of Victoria. He was on the original committee that published in 1856 the *Australian Medical Journal.* In August 1856, he and Englishman Dr John Maund (with the help of Frances Perry, wife of the Anglican Bishop of Melbourne) established the first maternity hospital for poor women in Albert Street, East Melbourne. He became physician to the new Lying-In Hospital, opened in 1858, on the site of the Royal Women's Hospital, and foundation lecturer and examiner in Obstetric Medicine and the diseases of women and children for the University of Melbourne. He performed the first successful ovariotomy in Victoria and, having established an international reputation as a pioneer gynaecological surgeon, was elected an Honorary Fellow of the Obstetrical Society of London in 1871. Visiting London in 1873, he returned to Melbourne in April 1874 in declining health. He died on 7 November 1874 from abdominal cancer, survived by his wife and six of his seven daughters.
5 Probably Mrs Elizabeth Wanliss.
6 Joseph Turnham, according to his employment records, did not get a rise in 1862. In line with all prison staff, his salary was reduced to Classification 3 under the Civil Service Act. There may have been a change to the allowances which included quarters, fuel and light (added in 1861).
7 Michael Elliot, the Manager of the Ballarat branch of the Bank of Australasia.
8 Probably Dr Richard James Hobson's wife, Annie née Bailey, whom he married in 1860. Richard James Hobson (*c.*1823–1865) arrived in Melbourne on the *British Queen*, 3 May 1853. His medical practice had been established on Main Road, Ballarat, since 1856. He was born in

Belfast, Ireland, studied medicine at Trinity College, Dublin (MB, 1846), and at the University of Cambridge. He was honorary surgeon at Ballarat Hospital 1856–1859. A member of the Freemason's and the AIOOF lodges, he died on 27 April 1865, aged forty-three.

9   Possibly William Scott who was Chairman of the Municipality of Ballarat in 1859 and President of the Asylum in 1865. Withers, pp. 254, 260.

80   [From WLR in Ballarat to MR in Melbourne]

[Webster Street, Ballarat]
Wednesday 1 to 2 [5 February 1862]

[No salutation]

I received yours my own love this morning I had been anxiously expecting it & was overjoyed to find you better at last; the change will be of benefit; do not talk of hurrying back just yet, theres a dear, I will try & come end of next week, or the beginning the week after, but I have so many bad cases that cannot be left, that I am unable to fix an earlier day:

"Abscence makes the heart grow fonder"[1] You know it is true love that dictates this advice, and not selfishness, for I feel your abscence every night, and want of rest makes me ill—

After an awful week, a cool breeze has set in & a cloudy day without rain—Still busy & likely to be, have ordered a new pair of wheels and when they are ready & on, so that I can lend Bunce the buggy, I may think of coming but I am certain that I cannot see Lucinda off, I am sure I regret it heartily, but I have a queer lot to deal with, & am but a poor man & can only hope to get on for your sake—L. ought to be content with your presence & the sacrifices we have made for her!

I send £1. in this & will send another in the next, so give her 30/- for your mother for the Ill News:[2]—I am surprised at Ned! poor chap I will buy a chair from the warehouse it will be a good chance. One with a bar—they asked me £7. here & £9–0–0

Sarah is very good! Sam has his salary raised to £150–0–0 & is Ledger Keeper: He is in good spirits about it. No news:—

I think I shall sleep in drawing room tonight or try to sleep—

Swamp going dry no rain—

Kind love to all: I send a newspaper with this & will expect another letter Saturday at latest

I was too busy to go to church last Sunday: went to bed Monday at 8. & last night at 10. Served them out; they kept coming to the Surgery & Sarah managed them: Her hieroglyphics on the slate are very amusing but very difficult to make out She misses your instructions & is going back!

Do not dissapoint me of a letter on Saturday dearest. & tell me how John & family are & if you have been boating since: the "Latino" was advertised for 4th. I do not believe she will sail punctually on the 8th. I may perchance be in time to see L. off yet!

Mrs Ocock[3] called I think that is the only one, Watson[4] is back. Bunce has got the Asylum—The people wont have him, so I intend giving up the Forresters as soon as I have paid Cuthbert:[5] Ochiltree[6] is in town,

Nothing else of interest but that I love you and will be so glad to fold you to the heart of your dearest on earth

Walter

There is some talk of your being <u>sub poenaed</u> in a case likely to come off soon—by that girl formerly of Mʳˢ Smith Melbourne Road who is commencing an action against her for defamation of character £200 damages! I said that whoever subpoenaed you would get the worst of it—I shall swear you are too ill to appear in a Court of Justice—

    Text: ALS NLA MS133/1/81

1   Thomas Haynes Bayley (1797–1839), *Isle of Beauty*, 12.

2   *The Illustrated London News*.

3   Rebecca Mary Ocock née Musgrave (1804–1882), daughter of William Musgrave and Elizabeth née Johnston; married to Richard Ocock (1804–1883), lawyer.

4   Albert Watson may have been WLR's shop assistant in early days (see Letters 94 and 96).

5   Possibly for the court case involving Jerry Luther, though Clark suggests that WLR had borrowed money from Cuthbert to build his house in Webster Street. Clark, p. 37.

6   William Bertram Ochiltree (*c.*1830–1898), the son of Matthew Ochiltree and Anna Bertram née Scott. He was the Manager of the Ballarat branch of the Bank of New South Wales; married to Anne née Graham (1831–1874), daughter of James Graham and Maria née Stratton. They emigrated to Melbourne on board the *John Knox*, which arrived in April 1853. Ochiltree was appointed Acting Manager of the Bank of NSW at Ballarat on 20 October 1854, to sort out the disorder created by George Dunmore Lang (son of the Reverend Dr John Dunmore Lang, Minister, republican member of NSW Legislative Council) and the accountant, Frederick Drake. Lang and Drake were brought to trial before the Chief Justice of Victoria, William á Beckett, for larceny and embezzlement and, despite the campaign and publicity brought to the case by Lang's father, each was sentenced respectively to five and four years of hard labour on the roads. In the late 1860s, Ochiltree was in trouble with the bank when it was discovered that there were losses incurred by lending to gold-mining companies in Ballarat. The advances had not been authorised, and only when enquiries were made about the losses was it found that the land was owned by Ochiltree, the bank manager. Fortunately for Ochiltree, the bank let the matter drop and he retired as a well-respected member of the Ballarat community. The Ochiltrees' first son, William Bertram, was born in Collingwood (1854–1884), educated at Ballarat College; the following ten children were born in Ballarat: Anna Maria (1856); Edward Graham (1857–1896) educated at Ballarat College and University of Melbourne, physician and surgeon in Ballarat; Charlotte Mary (b. 1859), who married William Lynch, the widower of Caroline Dexter (see Letter 59, endnote 3); Edith Florence (1861), enrolled on 19 April 1875 at Presbyterian Ladies College (PLC); Emma (1863), educated at Ballarat College and enrolled on 19 April 1875 at PLC; Alice Maude Marion (1865), enrolled on 19 April 1875 at PLC; Elizabeth Anne (1867); Henry Selwyn (1868–1893), attended Ballarat College in 1879, admitted as boarder to Geelong Grammar in February 1886, registered at University of Melbourne but died before he was able to start his course; Isabella (1870–1870); Walter George (1872–1873).

81   [From WLR in Ballarat to MR in Melbourne]

                                                 [Webster Street, Ballarat]

                                   Friday 1 to 3 [7 February 1862]

Dear dear Polly

    Your last cheered me up & was the best & longest you have written me: I have heard nothing more about the law case it is to come off on the 11ᵗʰ so I should have heard had there been any truth in it

    You are far from well yet my dear; <u>bath daily in cold</u> water drink plenty of beer & try & rise early: going to bed before 11. I have not much to say but I wish you not to have to wait over Sunday for a letter & so answer yours to day

    I received the newspaper

I was called at [out] at 7. this morning to go to a labor, found I could not manage & sent the case to Bunce.[1] He comes in to see me at 8 am I get up at 8.30 see half doz people swallow cup of tea & sent for at 9 to another labor & get <u>there too late</u>![2]

Bunce has had a charge preferred against him by the Governor Mc Gee[3] of <u>coarse & rude behaviour</u> & an investigation will take place before the Sheriff.[4]

Weather cool today, & not nearly so busy this afternoon!

M[rs] Bell & M[rs] Newman called.

Go on board my love & enjoy a little sea sickness & a fresh breeze, it must do you good. I met M[rs] Ochiltree she is thinking of going down to Queenscliffe she says—

If weather keeps cool & no sickness, you may see me <u>next week</u>! but dont be too glad or too delighted & wait quietly if I dont come until the week after

The house is very lonely especially midday—Sarah is very good all except the messages, those certainly she cannot manage

Nothing of interest except that I love you <u>still as ever</u> and that I want <u>20 kisses right off</u> & the remainder of the hundred as soon as possible If I dont squeeze you when I catch you! but try my pet & get stronger or you <u>wont bear my love,</u> and will be <u>too weak</u> to <u>return it;</u> for goodness sake <u>burn this letter,</u> or keep it out of sight

I must now conclude my own dear love it is very hard to have to wait until Tuesday morning to hear from you but I suppose there is nothing for it but patience—| Your loving husband

Walter

Kind love to Aunty Uncly Lucy & Neddy not forgetting Willy & Harrie

<u>Saturday</u> [8 February 1862] What can I do to make up for not sending this yesterday to my dear one—Why write another to be sure—Well dear I wrote it & stamped it & having to go out with Whitcombe[5] walked, intending to post it myself—You know my head for every thing <u>except my patients</u>—More Cholera today! I feel anything but right—bad cold from yarning last night at front door when wind from S. was blowing in—Was John kind? they did not ask you to stay there?

Very cold today fine—at breakfast—How I do long for you to come back & make breakfast for me & pour out my tea—it does not taste half as good now—

Does L behave more pleasantly to you now What a happy thing for her when she is alone in the wide ocean—I fear the Captains wife & she will not agree very well—

You will get this on Monday dont serve me as I did you but be sure & let me have one on Tuesday morning, and then I will write & tell you what day you may expect me—Meantime good bye dearest on earth—it is very cold at night now & I used the opossum rug & my [grey?] rug last night—

You will come to meet me at the station wont you Good bye again X| Your own

Walter

Text: ALS NLA MS133/1/77

1   *Case* 431, 7 February 1862, Mrs Dunne. 'Dr Bunce attended for me: Some flooding.' Frederick William born to Thomas Dunne and Susan née Harrison.

2   *Case* 432, 7 February 1862, Mrs Dobson, 'born before arrival'. Margaret Jane born to William Dobson and Priscilla née Hislop.

3   William Snell Magee was appointed the senior turnkey at the Ballarat Gaol in 1856. He arrived in Melbourne from Dublin on 6 February 1853, on the *Lorena*, on which he was listed as the

surgeon. He did not practice at Ballarat but may have given the inmates of the prison some
medical care.

4   It is not clear what happened about the charge. The only reference about Dr Bunce in the
newspapers concerned the Benevolent Asylum in November 1862, when it was reported that five
of the six honorary medical officers of the Benevolent Asylum had resigned in consequence of what
they considered 'harsh and ungentlemanly conduct of the committee towards Dr Bunce, the paid
medical attendant. It seems that Dr Bunce brought three specific charges of cruelty against the
master and matron of the institute, which the committee investigated without calling on Dr Bunce
to produce witnesses in support of the charge, and on the ex parte statements the committee found
that there was no truth in the complaints made by the doctor, and served him with notice that his
services would not be required after the present month ... Dr McFarlane is now the only honorary
medical officer connected with the institution.' *Star*, 12 November 1862, p. 2.

5   Dr William Philip Whitcombe (*c.*1809–1896), MRCS England 1853, born in Wolverhampton.
He arrived in Melbourne prior to 1854 when he married Annie Alderson. Registered as a doctor
in Victoria in 1855, he was practising at Horsham in 1856 before moving to Ballarat. President
of the Ballarat Acclimatisation Society, formed in 1870; Honorary Medical Officer of Ballarat
Benevolent Asylum; Assistant-Surgeon for the Ballarat Rangers; founding Chairman of the
Ballarat Rowing Club.

82   [From LC in Brighton, England, to WLR and MR in Ballarat]

17 Buckingham Place| Brighton, West Cliff| Sussex| England.

June 19th /62 [Thursday]

My beloved Walter and Mary

Lucinda[1] arrived at this house on Monday 16th Inst. at past 9 o/c P:M, completely worn
out by fatigue, long fasting and anxiety to attain her destination I suppose; her appearance
greatly shocked me, she is thin to emaciation, her face frightfully twitching, and working she
asked for some porter, here called stout we had none in the house, but we had bitter Ale my
drink and her fathers when he takes any thing of that sort, she would eat nothing but a few
cracknels, and went to bed—she slept well and looked much better the next morng, but
yesterday she wrote all day, letter after letter her difficulty of breathing set in about ½ past
6 P.M. and she went down to the garden, which relieved her; but this morng one eye looks
much congested I trust she will be willing to submit herself wholly to our management, for
your father is greatly interested in her and we love her, and have her well being at heart beyond
every thing—

My beloved Son your letter received the 16th per Mail moved me exceedingly the hope of
seeing you and my daughter Mary, before I go home revives me beyond what you can form
any idea of. I am not an advocate for advising any one to remove from a residence, from his
appointed place, but if circumstances such as failing health, or the life of those dear to us
render it expedient, I (as in my own case) would not hesitate to think it right. I came here by
Dr Williams's advice to save your father's life; he had one lung nearly <u>dead</u>, no other place
would do, the change <u>has</u> been for his good, his lung has recovered, his chest is strong, he can
walk and sing, and I have to be thankful & praise—I do not think I have derived benefit, but I
may be wrong, at all events I have learned to submit and to be content with such things as I
have—

Your father suffers much from Catarrh, and want of sleep one nostril is full, the
membrane thickened, he cannot bend forward to write without the nose swelling & growing
red, the color of his face becomes purple; the eyes suffused and uneasy, and evidence a

tendency of blood mounting to the head, he feels it needful therefore to abstain from writing as much as possible; he takes regular exercise in the open air and can walk well, and actively—

Alick[2] is not going to sea, merely for pleasure or health the profession of Midshipman is chosen however with a view to the improvement of the latter as he has a tendency to great delicacy of chest, and cannot live at Brighton even for a month without an attack of Bronchitis—he is a wayward youth, restless as the wind, perhaps has been too much tied up, a bad plan, which is never successful—he will explain to you the terms on which he goes to Sea, advise him to adhere to the profession, he is too fond of that of a gentlemen at large, doing nothing. Mrs Bailey has promised that Harold shall meet him he carries a parcel from Mrs Dickinson[3] to Mrs Turnham and will go to you as soon as he can he is very anxious to see you.

Mrs B. has been very kind to L. my state of health requires me to be stationary, and avoid the very smallest exertion or fatigue, I deeply regret that we can give no help in regard to seeking for an eligible locality for you to settle in, unfortunately this place is out of the question, it is so very dear, it would require a fortune to live here as a gentleman, we find it very difficult to make two ends meet, we live in seclusion, our food of the plainest, no company, mutton 91/2^d & 10^d, lamb 1/- veal 1/- pork 10^d butter 1/8 all winter & spring, Potatoes 1/- per gallon blue water called milk 4^d per qrt. coals £1–10–0 per Ton vegetables & fruit seldom attainable. Fowls 16/- per pair a Duck 4/6. The want of poultry tries me for mutton chops are unattainable at 1/- per lb! the half being fat. it is a lonely watering place, coming and going, and hurry and bustle, meeting and parting as soon as met, less christian love, and more scant social intercourse than any where in all the world beside—old trained afflicted Christians such as ourselves may be contented with the Great Supreme as our All, but the young & newly enlisted Soldier of the Cross might find it hurtful to health & spirits and long for something more of the human face Divine[4] than is to be found at Brighton. The medical men are very numerous, most of them have fortunes independently of their profession, these drive carriages and a pair of horses, the others demi fortunes, or cab and one horse.[5] Would you think of Scotland or Ireland.

June 20th I am obliged to write by scraps, my interruptions are so numerous, and I fear I may repeat myself. One point my beloved Walter I trust you will make in changing your residence in Australia a sine qui non[6] for Grt Britain, and that is not to settle where there is not an efficient Gospel Ministry; the proclamation of God's Love for lost man in giving His Son a Substitute for the guilty, the Just for the unjust that we might have the Righteousness of God, by faith in Christ Jesus!—The World passeth away! Oh how soon!—grandeur, fame, wealth all is vanity! vanity of vanities[7]—When we bade you that sorrowful farewell, and returned to our boat at Gravesend we had Lord and Lady Sydney Herbert[8] in our boat home to London;—Where is he now? in the grave, and a child in his place, and the happy wife, a lonely widow. Lord Canning[9] in the midst of the brightest career, he too is gone, Bronchitis seized him & a few hours pain laid him in the grave, "Love not the world", read that 2nd Ch. 1st Gen. Epistle John; pray over it, pray that you maybe enabled to set your affections on things above, on Christ, on Heaven and its joys!—to live for. Eternity! for God—if this is your choice He will guide, guard & provide for you, your life wherever it be passed will be happy, your end peace. What is our life, "a wind that passeth away"! & "cometh not again"[10]!!!

June 25th /62 You will perceive how long I have been about this letter; my feebleness increases in rapid strides and the little business of the house is latterly felt to be burdensome,—writing becomes more difficult daily, I suppose anxiety about L. has something to do with it, as she is an additional charge, perhaps too grief at parting with Alick may upset me, remembering <u>another</u> parting which was for <u>this</u> life[11]—and <u>yours,</u> which tried me exceedingly. I was always so happy when <u>you</u> were at home!—my nervous system is greatly shattered, I cannot bear the least emotion, this must be purely physical, as I am happy in mind, relative to my soul's concerns, willing to leave all my concerns in the hands of my Father in Heaven and have no will but His—

Your father sends best and kindest love and remembrances, with many thanks for the book you sent him; if writing did not injure him so much he would have sent you a few lines, but just now he is less well being rather pressed, for his brother's wife[12] has been ill, and the case was an anxious one, as it was an affection of the wind pipe,—and the patient a very large fat subject, George and she are very kind to us, and have great confidence in your father's skill besides his visits cost nothing!—[13]

We have had no Summer as yet, to day the N. East is bitterly cold, and makes me fearful for Lucinda; if the Lord will I shall write to you next month, and may have better acc^{ts} to give you. She shall visit Mrs Bunce's Mother[14] and children I do not visit since John's death, seclusion best suits my bad health and inclinations—L. requires some dress arrangements, when these are carried into effect, and she has recovered from her fatigue she shall go, they live a long way from her, in the Old Steine, and we cannot afford carriage hire now—

I am glad to tell you Caroline is better, a new Surgeon has established new treatment, the teetotal system was killing her; a poor creature worn down by disease, unable to eat food, forbidden to touch stimulants and sinking <u>hourly,</u> I heard from her yesterday—she wrote in high spirits, thankful to be relieved from Doctor H—it would not be right to give his name, therefore I withhold it—Tell dear Mary to accept my warmest thanks for all her care of and kindness to L.—say everything for me to M^r & Mrs Turnham, if my health permitted I would write; give my love to Sam! and Harold! and with <u>much</u> to dear Mary and yourself in which your father joins. I am whilst in the body my beloved Son| Yr tenderly attached Mother

> L:C:

Text: ALS NLA MS133/1/39 and MS133/1/40

1   Lucinda Richardson sailed from Melbourne on *Latona* (695 tons) which was advertised in *The Argus* (29 January 1862) to sail on 4 February 1862 but as each deadline was reached the date was postponed until it finally sailed on Friday, 21 February 1862.

2   Alexander Richardson (1845–1900), nephew of WLR; sailed on the *Great Australia* as midshipman, arriving in Melbourne in September 1862 for a short stay.

3   Possibly Emily Dickinson née Fector (b. 1792), christened on 1 November 1792 at St Mary the Virgin, Dover, Kent. Cousin of Caroline Fector; she was the daughter of Peter Fector and his wife Frances née Lane. She was married to William Rastall Dickinson on 25 October 1814 at St James the Apostle, Dover. Why she should be sending a parcel to Mrs Turnham is not known.

4   From William Blake, 'A Divine Image', *Songs of Innocence and of Experience* (1794): 'Cruelty has a Human Heart/ And Jealousy a Human Face/ Terror the Human Form Divine' (ll. 1–3).

5   *FRM II*, p. 60.

6   *Sina qua non*, something essential (Latin).

7   Ecclesiastes, 1, 2.

8   Sidney Herbert, Lord Herbert of Lea (1810–1861), statesman, son of George Augustus Herbert, 11th Earl of Pembroke by his second wife, Catherine, daughter of Count Simon Woronzow, Russian Ambassador in London. He was educated at Harrow and Oxford. In 1832 elected Conservative MP for South Wilts; was Peel's Secretary to the Admiralty from 1841 to 1845, when he became Secretary-at-War. In 1852 he was again Secretary-at-War for the Aberdeen Ministry and he was largely blamed for the sufferings of the army before Sebastopol. He was

Palmerston's Colonial Secretary for a few weeks in 1855, and his Secretary-at-War in 1859. After he resigned he was called in 1861 to the Upper House as Baron Herbert of Lea. He died on 2 August 1861. Lucinda Cheyne saw Lord and Lady Elizabeth Herbert (née à Court) in the boat at Gravesend in March 1852, when they were farewelling fifty-six needlewomen, who were emigrating to Australia on the *Roxburgh Castle*, and she was farewelling WLR. The scheme to send poor needlewomen to Australia had been raised by Lord Herbert in 1849 when he proposed the establishment of a society for promoting the emigration of these respectable women to Australia to alleviate their suffering and the loneliness of males in the colonies. (It was noted in *The Times* that in 1847 in NSW there were 83,572 males to 41,809 females.) This proposal became a reality with many philanthropists supporting the scheme and was assisted immediately by the editor of *The Times*, who wrote that the proposal was 'so good and so safe that it could hardly fail of a considerable success'. *The Times*, 7 December 1849, p. 4.

9   Charles John Canning, Earl Canning (1812–1862), statesman, third son of George Canning; educated at Eton and Oxford; in 1836 entered Parliament as Conservative MP for Warwick, but was raised to Upper House as Viscount Canning after death of mother, his older brothers having predeceased her. In 1841 became Under-Secretary in the Foreign Office; under Lord Aberdeen he was made Postmaster-General. In 1856 he became Governor-General of India. When in the following year the Indian Mutiny began, Canning's conduct was considered weak but now reassessed as moderate, judicious and courageous. In 1858 he became first Viceroy, and in 1859 raised to an earldom. His wife died in Calcutta in 1861 and he retired and returned to London, where he died on 17 June 1862. On hearing the news of her friend Canning's death, Queen Victoria, widowed so prematurely the previous December, wrote in her Journal on 17 June 1862: 'It is as if all that was best & greatest were to be taken away. Oh! how blessed to follow his wife so soon! He was only 49.' Longford, p. 428.

10   Psalm 78, 39.

11   She was probably remembering her parting from her son, John Cheyne, who sailed from England in 1853 and died in Assam on 15 December 1859.

12   Grace Cheyne née Melville.

13   See *FRM II*, p. 60.

14   Mary Defauche née Tomkison, mother of Blanche Emily Bunce (*c*.1832–1878), who was married to Dr Richard Bunce, friend and colleague of WLR.

83   [From LC in Brighton, England, to Elizabeth Bailey (EB) in Leicester, England]

17 Buckingham Place| Brighton| West Cliff [Sussex, England]
August 11th [1862]

My dear Mrs Bailey

Since the receipt of your kind notes, and the moss tree I have kept my bed for a fortnight with an attack of acute Rheumatism in my right knee, it has greatly reduced me, and left me weaker than I have ever been in my life—before—

My daughter[1] disliked Brighton <u>very much</u> all her complaints became worse, and she accepted an invitation from her Sister[2] in Ireland to proceed thither; Since her leaving us, she has lost one complaint that in her breathing and obstruction in her nostrils, but her sight is worse, she is about to consult an occulist of celebrity and hopes to derive benefit—

My dear husband is anxious and uneasy about me, and cannot leave me indeed I am wholly depending on his care—being perfectly helpless.—

I am happy to find you liked your expedition to Scarboro'[3] it is an agreeable and strengthening locality,—

The heat here has been <u>very</u> great, it tires me much; I have now a <u>small</u> bedroom at liberty, and shall look forward to seeing Walter and Mary, if I <u>live</u> until they reach England—

I shall not be able to write this month Give them my tenderest love—and with kindest regards to each member of your family and thanks for all your kindness, I am dear Mrs Bailey| Very Affec^{ly} Y^{rs}

      Lucinda Cheyne

Text: ALS NLA MS133/1/24

1   Lucinda Richardson.
2   Caroline Richardson.
3   Scarborough, North Yorkshire—a North Sea resort which became a stylish spa in the seventeenth century and continued to flourish as a retirement or holiday residence.

84   [From MR in St Kilda to WLR in Ballarat]

Bull Street [St Kilda]
Tuesday Morning [28 October 1862]

My dearly loved Walter

You see I have arrived safely at St Kilda Ned & Jeannie met us Alick^1 left me at the Station I fancy he was a little afraid of the Captain he began to tell me in the Railway a little of his affairs he said he had no idea he had spent all the money he had done he had quite mismanaged his affairs I told him if he had told you you would have helped him but he said he did not like for it was his own fault I felt quite sorry at parting with him he looked so lonely & unhappy we enjoyed the trip had the carriage to ourselves all the way did not do any reading talking all the time when we got to Melbourne it was raining very heavily so we came straight home found all well Trotty very thin Harry quite yellow neither improved in look's & according to all accounts very naughty Harry shocking taking improper liberties with Trotty Jeannie will not have him in the house after John comes home—my heart feels sad to think what is to become of them. Thank God we have none to be such a trouble. The baby^2 is such a fat fair little thing very like Jeannie & will be very pretty not very well on account of teething got a dreadful cold on its chest no trouble put to bed wide awake & never cries it is a really good child. Ned is looking very poorly though I have not seen much of him but shall see him to day as we go into Town this afternoon I have not seen any one else at present I shall have more to tell you in my next. I hope darling you are quite well & do not miss me very much though I do you particularly in bed I shall be glad when I get back. Jeannie just the same as ever talking all the time full of the children.—I shall go to Pentridge next week—I will write again on Thursday I send you to day's Argus to amuse you. It is a lovely day I hope Sarah^3 takes good care of you God bless you my own darling with all my love| & kisses ever your own| wifey

      Mary

Text: ALS NLA MS133/1/66

1   Alick Cook, step-cousin of WLR, returned to England on the *True Briton*, which sailed on 15 November 1862. The ship was moored alongside the Railway Pier at Sandridge. Built expressly for the Melbourne trade, it was about to embark on its second voyage. Advertised as a most commodious and comfortable ship, it included on board a milch cow for the Saloon passengers. *The Argus*, 10 November 1862, p. 1.
2   Gertrude Elizabeth Rainsford Bailey (1862–1939), born 11 February 1862; daughter of Jeannie and John Robinson Bailey. She is likely the model for the fictional Cousin Grace in *GW*, p. 26.
3   The Richardsons' servant.

85 [From WLR in Ballarat to MR in St Kilda]

[Webster Street, Ballarat]
Friday morning: [7 November 1862]

My dearest Polly

I have been a little more occupied since I last wrote. On ~~Wednesday~~ Tuesday night I told you I was called up to M[rs] Merry:[1] on Wednesday evening I went down to Hamburgher[2] & played whist till 12. found in the evening that John[3] had walked off; so put an advertisement in "Tribune"[4] & got up yesterday morng early to groom my horse myself; at 8 got a message to go off at once to M[rs] Blairs,[5] did not get home till 12.30 found several boys waiting & engaged one: last evening John walks up to the front door to know if I would give him the money I owed him: I told him he had left me without notice & I would not

I am delighted he is going, the new boy last night got up in his sleep & walked about the room kicking up a terrific rumpus talking & laughing I called out as loud as I could before I could awake him. There is a most disagreeable hot wind with clouds of dust blowing today: "Minton" is building a fine new brewery 80 feet by 24 which will shelter our house very much—Bunce came in last night & played "Ecarte" till 12.

I have just received yours and regret so much about your not sleeping try & take a sponge bath before you go to bed & drink a glass of wine. I am delighted you are enjoying the days I am sure I will be very happy to see Feldheim[6] when he comes up & there is no doubt it would do Ned good, remember me kindly to the old fellow—I see Mount & Harrison race[7] is talked off in the Herald about end of month at Melbourne

When your letter arrived OConnor was here, he came to ask me to put my name to a bill for £50–0–0 I declined most decidedly. M[rs] Heisse[8] is keeping very good H. took her out in buggy yesterday & walked out in eveg.

My face is very bad again: Agony all day—

Assisted Bunce at an operation—knocked up—fairly beaten: so you must excuse this short letter I will write you a longer one on Sunday.

Love to Jeannie| Your ever loving husband

Walter

Text: ALS NLA MS133/106

1   *Case* 495, 5 November 1862, 5.10 am, Mrs Merry, fourth pregnancy: '2nd I have attended her with pains in back: Born before arrival … Spina Bifida.' Sarah born to William Merry and Honora née Bowling (maiden name on marriage register but Dowlan on computerised birth register).
2   Simon Hamburger, pawnbroker in Ballarat, proprietor of the 'Cosmopolitan Credit Institute'; married to Elizabeth née Lazarus in 1860.
3   WLR's groom.
4   'Wanted a lad to groom a horse. Apply Dr Richardson, Webster Street.' *The Ballarat Tribune*, 6 November 1862.
5   *Case* 496, 6 November 1862, 12 noon, Mrs Blair, sixth pregnancy, 'slow, lingering labour'. Arthur David born to Lewis John Blair and Jessie née Hossack.
6   Probably Isaac Feldheim of Feldheim Brothers Wholesale Jewellers, 66 Little Collins Street, *Directory*.
7   Lampton Le Breton Mount (a Canadian from Montreal, accountant at the Oriental Bank in Ballarat) and Henry Colden Anthill Harrison, the amateur sprint champion of Victoria from 1859 to 1866. Harrison became Captain of the Melbourne team of Victoria Rules Football, a game for which he is credited with having written the rules with his brother-in-law, Thomas Wentworth Wills. Eighteen months earlier than this letter, on 15 June 1861, several Ballarat men (including

Dr Hobson and Henry Cuthbert) had gone down to Melbourne to watch Harrison and Mount race. The event attracted 5,000 persons and Harrison won by three lengths and the Ballarat men lost a great deal of money in bets. They collected a purse for Mount of £40.

8   Elizabeth Ellen née Kendrick Heise, wife of Dr William Augustus Heise, who lived in Webster Street.

86   [From WLR in Ballarat to MR in Melbourne]

[Webster Street, Ballarat]
Saturday 9. 1862 [Saturday, 8 November 1862]

My own dear Polly

I have been almost delirious all day with this blessed "Tic" I went out at 11 & felt it first coming on, hurried round home by 12.30 & never had a moments intermission from pain till about 6 when it abated a little. I took Chloroform for an hour & woke up ten times worse—20 drops of Chlorodyne! Fortunately no one at all came since morning—It has been a nasty dirty day I believe, but now the wind is round to the S—Kabat[1] looked in for half an hour & had a chat: says he saw you looking very well: glad to hear it hope you sleep better—I see nobody every thing is very dull & you will feel the house very lonely when you come back after Sam & Alick. I see the "True Briton" is postponed till the 15th inst: Kabat asked me to dine there tomorrow & so did Bunce but really I declined first because I dread another day such as this & 2nd because there may possibly be a lot of people about this place after me—

Sunday morning I was called out last night 10 PM to the Plank Road M[rs] Dunstan:[2] home by 2 pretty good night, but can feel my enemy coming on again—A nice cool day—I am writing to Alick by this same post—I am not certain whether to address it to the agents or to the ship Sandridge pier—I think I will do the latter.

Sunday night—I have not suffered so severely today but still have had it, but managed to sleep thro the worst of it from 3 to 5. I have been to Church tonight—M[r] P[3] preached a capital sermon—good night dear X

Monday morning I send you £1. in this & will enclose the other next time. Another fine day very little sickness. My face is paining me a little it is not toothache but genuine "Tic doloreaux": I believe there will be some good sport today at the Copenhagen[4] & I am going up to try & keep me from my usual sufferings every afternoon:—

William[5] is doing pretty well I have allowed him to get up on crutches—My new boy is a very good boy so far—

Kabat has asked me to go over tonight I do not know whether I shall be able or no—English mail I am glad to see just in: what a pity John was not at home or that you could not have gone to the "lawn party"—Kind love to Jeannie I hope Harry is behaving himself better:| Your affect husband

Walter

4 PM I have been up to the sports great fun—but I was obliged to leave my old enemy in full force: the tortures of the damned—a large fire somewhere about the Melbourne Road[6]

You will observe how much longer my letters are than yours so that if I do not write again till the end of the week it will [give] you the opportunity writing a long one in reply—You never said a word about the opera[7]—

Text: ALS NLA MS133/1/78

1   Captain Leopold Kabat (1832–1884), Inspector of Police. He and his wife Emily née Murchison (1840–1933) had one daughter, Antoinette Favorita Emily Kabat (1861–1940).

2   *Case* 497, 9 November 1862 at 12.30 am, Mrs Dunstan, 'All normal did not support Perineum': male child.

3   The Reverend James Melvin Paul.

4   There was a holiday on Monday, 10 November 1862 to celebrate the 21st birthday of Albert Edward, Prince of Wales, later King Edward VII (1841–1910). His birthday was actually on the Sunday but all good Victorians enjoyed a celebration and Ballarat closed its banks and shops on the Monday. 'To supply the requisite amount of sightseeing and pleasure taking, there will be at least two grand displays of sports for the holiday keepers. One display will be provided by the Volunteer Rifle Corps and the Cavalry, aided by the Western Fire Brigade, and the other by the Ballarat Cricket Club, their Smythesdale opponents, the Eastern Fire Brigade, and the other sporting people who may aid in the display. The Volunteer sports will come off at the Copenhagen Grounds, and will include running, leaping, sword exercise, hurdle race, steeplechase, jumping with pole, and other sports.' *Star*, 10 November 1862, p. 2.

5   Not identified.

6   The fire destroyed property to the value of about £1000. At first the people at the games (including members of the Ballarat West Fire Brigade at the Copenhagen Ground and the East Fire Brigade at the Cricket Ground) did not realise what was happening and thought that the smoke was from one of the mining claims. They all hurried from their sports using 'equestrian modes of reaching the fire' and after dousing the fire, the two brigades turned the hoses on each other 'in a most unfriendly mass. The men were completely drenched, and the officers had to interfere before the passage of arms was brought to a close.' *Star*, 11 November 1862, p. 2.

7   If MR had gone to the opera that week she would have seen the second subscription season of the company of William Saurin Lyster (1827–1880) at the Theatre Royal: on Wednesday, Mozart's *Le Nozze di Figaro*; Thursday, Auber's *Fra Diavolo*; Friday, Balfe's *The Rose of Castile*; and Saturday, Balfe's *Bohemian Girl*. His company included: Fred Lyster, Robert Farquharson, James E. Kitts, Frank Trevor, William Lloyd, Rosalie Durand, Georgia Hodson and Ada King. *The Argus*, 6 November 1862, p. 8.

87   **[From WLR in Ballarat to MR in Pentridge, Melbourne]**

[Webster Street, Ballarat]

<u>Wednesday</u> [12 November 1862]

My own dear Polly

Your nice long letter gave me greater pleasure this morning than any that you have written before—I am so pleased that you are enjoying yourself among freinds I hope the change to Pentridge will do you further good—I had ease yesterday thanks be to God and altho I feel it today it is not yet bad—

I have lost 3 pounds weight since you left for I weighed myself the same day—

I got a letter from Sandy[1] this morning tho not in answer to one I had sent him which I suppose he had not received you did not say if you had got the £1–0–0 safely so I conclude it must have been abstracted from the letter but I will not write the Post Master General[2] on the subject until I hear from you again—

Last night was the coldest night I think I have felt for many years I could not sleep for some hours—the night before I was so poorly, I went to Kabats & was better—A nice party: Sherard[3] <u>Burton</u>[4] <u>Robertson</u>[5] <u>Pooley</u>[6] <u>Mackay</u>[7]—Pooley & I won £6–0–0 each—Bob Cuthbert was almost the winner of the ladies cup—Willy Welch first Robert 2nd. What a low fellow that skipper of the "True Briton" must be[8]—

Remember me kindly to "Joe" & <u>Aunty</u> bring her back if you can & keep her till Xmas when "Joe" can come up for her—go out for a walk every day—go & see the gardens again—I am going to operate on the Hair [hare] lip this afternoon Not much sickness Sarah says she thinks the people are giving me a holiday—

I intended to have gone to hear Black[9] last night but prevented—I am going out tonight to the L.O.L.[10]

5 PM I have just come home & have to go to Specimen Hill & Main Road so must cut this short—

I send you a newspaper acct of sports & fire poor Trevor[11] burnt out

Ever| Your own dear

Walter

I shall be so glad to see you again—

Text: ALS NLA MS133/1/107

[1]   Probably a nickname for Alick Cook.

[2]   i.e., his brother-in-law, John Robinson Bailey.

[3]   Charles Wale Sherard (1820–1889), Warden of the Ballarat Goldfield; married on 6 May 1856 to Isabella Morrison Sherard née Welsh (b. 1834), daughter of Patricus W. Welsh; the ceremony was conducted by Theodore Stretch, who travelled to Ballarat from Geelong to perform the ceremony. Charles Wale Sherard was the second son of the Reverend Robert Sherard, a descendant of the third son of the first Lord Sherard (created 1627). Charles was a cousin of the 9th Baron Sherard, who inherited minor title from 6th Earl of Harborough. Arthur William (1861–1931), the third son of Charles and Isabella Sherard, became the 12th and last Lord Sherard in 1924. At his death in 1931 the barony became extinct. See de Serville, p. 514.

[4]   Evan Burton, a neighbour in Webster Street.

[5]   William Robertson, Manager of the Ballarat branch of the Bank of Victoria since November 1854, was the oldest banker in Ballarat when he retired in 1886. Back in October 1854, three or four bushrangers had tied up and gagged the previous Manager, John Buckley, and stole £18,000. A new stone house, the first in Ballarat, was built for the bank and during the Eureka Stockade crisis, it was closed to customers while the military used the building as a garrison. Withers, p. 122.

[6]   William Thomas Pooley (1813–1872), born in Ramsey, Huntingdonshire, the son of Thomas and Roseanna Pooley. He became Deputy Registrar for Ballarat. The first actuary for the Ballarat Savings Bank, founded November 1857, he continued in that role until 1870, when he was succeeded by Charles Wale Sherard. He died on 29 July 1872 aged fifty-nine after suffering from heart disease for six months and Anasärca (dropsy) for six weeks.

[7]   George Gordon Mackay, Manager of the London Chartered Bank of Australia at Ballarat; Treasurer of the Ballarat Mechanics Institute when it was set up in 1859. He was in correspondence with WLR over monetary matters during their trip to England. See Letters 122 and 128.

[8]   G. H. Bawn was the Commander of the *True Briton*, but what he had done to warrant WLR's comment is not clear.

[9]   Dr Joseph Black (*c.*1812–1879), physician, born Antigua; MRCS; president and founder of the Medical Society of Victoria.

[10] Loyal Orange Lodge, a Protestant Irish order formed in Ireland in September 1795 after competition for land in Ulster led to rural rioting between Catholics and Protestants, which culminated in the 'Battle of the Diamond', near Loughgall, County Armagh.

[11] Joseph Robinson Trevor (1826–1898), Professor of Music. The fire had started at the rear of a two-storeyed wooden building occupied by a manufacturer of upholstery and mattresses and the cottages (including Trevor's) on either side of this building were burnt out. Mrs Sarah Crucifise Trevor née Gunnell (1832–1911) raised the alarm.

88   [From MR in Pentridge, Melbourne, to WLR in Ballarat]

Pentridge
Thursday night [13 November 1862]

My own darling Walter

I am sure you would feel disappointed at not receiving a letter from me in the morning but I did not get your's until 7 o clock this evening I came here on Tuesday afternoon & Uncle then asked for three day's leave & got Thursday Friday & Saturday so he went into Town & hired a nice four seated buggy to take us about in so we set off this morning before the post came in & drove to St Kilda for Jeannie & baby took lunch there & then drove right along the beach to Brighton & got back here at 7 oclock very tired tomorrow we start at nine in the morning for the Yan Yean[1] & on Saturday for Heidleburgh[2] so you see I am having a fine time of it I am dreadfully tired & am writing this instead of going to bed—I have Jeannie & baby for bedfellows how I wish it were you darling You did not say in your's whether you had any English letter's for me. I saw one from Mother to John She is in great trouble again Sarah was in the train at the time of that frightful collision on the Midland Railway[3] had been in bed a fortnight & lost the situation she was to have gone to: no bones broken but a shock to the whole of the body & nerves will be a long time before will expect to get compensation alway's something happening

Ned had a letter from Lucinda had you one? also from Lizzie.[4] I am so glad to hear that you are better you want me at home to fatten you I know I did not make you thin I wish you could get a change ever so little would do you good—I think of coming back next Wednesday night could you not afford out of your winnings to come down by the 6 oclock train in the evening & return with me by the seven train in the evening you could have a bathe darling & it would only be a single fare for return ticket Oh do come darling it would do you good & you would see the line so nicely I hope you will send an answer you could leave your patients for one day I leave here on Monday afternoon so be sure & let me have a letter written Saturday or Monday telling me to meet you I got the 1£ all right thought I told you so. I wish you would come darling it seem's ages since I have seen your dear smiling face I long to kiss it again & again I expect to see Alick tomorrow to say good-bye as I believe they sail on Saturday

I hope darling you will forgive me for writing so short a letter this time but I am so tired I can scarcely hold my pen God Bless you dear dear Walty with love & kisses| Good night Ever your own loving
        Polly
Absence makes the heart grow fonder.
    Text: ALS NLA MS133/1/71

[1]   Yan Yean, about twenty kilometres north of Melbourne, was a favourite spot for picnics. The water supply to Melbourne from the reservoir was connected on 31 December 1857.
[2]   Heidelberg, about fifteen kilometres north-west of Melbourne.
[3]   A collision at Market Harborough on 28 August 1862; one person killed and fifty injured. Listed in 'Memorable Railway Accidents' in *Haydn's Dictionary*, p. 659.
[4]   Elizabeth Brett (b. 1830), MR's sister. On 7 June 1859 she married Captain John Brett, of the 2nd Battalion, Prince Consort's Own Rifle Brigade.

89   [From MR in St Kilda (before driving back to Pentridge)
to WLR in Ballarat]

[St Kilda]
November 15th 1862 [Saturday]

My own dear Walter

This is only a scrap to say I got the second 1£ all right also English letters many thanks
for your sending them. I am looking forward to Wednesday to see your dear face once more. I
hope you will be able to come for me it would do you much good. I am very tired & have just
come in from a long drive to Heidleburg & when we have had tea to drive back to Pentridge. I
shall not tell you now where we have been to but leave it until I can talk to you & describe the
scenery I am so glad to learn you are better—

I have not seen Alick & I hear they are going to day I should like to have seen him once
more. That was a sad accident[1] Sarah not written

I went to the agents with Mr Marsh on Tuesday for W. P. White & Co.[2]—so shall be
able to tell you some news there is so much talk going on around I hardly know whether I am
on my head or my heels—send the enclosed to Miss Cuthbert as it saves fourpence I have not
seen M[rs] Haywood[3] twice I started & it came on so wet besure & not write to me after
Monday morning at Pentridge

Will you also ask M[rs] Kabat the names of the New Waltzes I was to bring for Miss
Cuthbert I have quite forgotten no news of John yet: I wish I was home again I feel lonely
now—Give my love to all friends & excuse more as I wait an answer from you I shall only
have to write once more

Tell Sarah to have the Carpet up & now Good bye my own dearie & with all love &
kisses ever| Your loving wife

Polly

I am longing for some kisses

Text: ALS NLA MS133/1/68

---

[1]   Railway collision at Market Harborough, 28 August 1862.
[2]   W. P. White and Co. owned by William Pomeroy White; he was an agent for the Australian
Steam Navigation Company.
[3]   Charlotte and Robert Haywood, a civil servant, moved to Emerald Hill from Ballarat with their
two boys, William Bernhard and Arthur Robert. They subsequently had five daughters in
Emerald Hill, three of whom survived infancy.

1863

90 [From LC in Brighton, England, to WLR and MR in Ballarat]
17 Buckingham Place| Brighton Sussex| England.
New Years Day 1863 [Thursday]

My beloved Walter

Last night I received yours dated October 23rd, it was forwarded from the wreck of the Colombo,[1] sealed up by the post master in a <u>new</u> envelope, the one in which you had enclosed it having been destroyed. Illness of a severe kind has caused my silence and brought me very low, I was greatly grieved at not hearing from you for such a lengthened period as since June I have received no letter from you nor dear Mary. I was confined to bed <u>for six weeks</u> at one time, and again for 3, you wrote to L. and I had to forward the letter without knowing how you might be, she had gone weeks before—left me in very declining health, and in a helpless condition, but believing that Brighton did not agree with her as she stated, I could not object, the nose & chest suffering increased so much that she was miserable. Dr Dill agreed that the climate in Ireland would be more suitable & so it has turned out, for she has experienced a complete remission of that affection since she left this—she is now I understand quite strong and well.—

Jany 3rd 1863 I am exceedingly weak and feeble my beloved Son, and have been wholly unable to write even a note, for these six months past, so had to leave off, before I offered my earnest and warmest wishes for your health happiness and advancement in the spiritual life for the year which is now commencing May <u>my</u> God be your guide, your councellor your help in every place in every trouble, may His will be your object in every proposed removal His presence your sole desire—

In my long illness I thought of you incessantly I prayed for you, I longed for you—O my beloved Son I should like to see you again to hear your voice once more, —to bless you before I die—To please you I endured half dying in a photography sky light a few days ago, that I might at least send you a stupid likeness, for these likenesses have no mind, and are scarce shadows of those we love; I suffered a good deal, from crowd, heat, and exhaustion, but in doing this for you, I thought it brought you <u>nearer,</u> and I bore it!—Miss F—was with me to watch me & encourage me, but the heat, and fatigue made me ill many days!

This year has been emphatically a year of death! Such a mowing down of all ranks has never before been recorded—a vast deal of sickness here, dipththeria, fever of the typhoid kind, and other fevers such as have never before been known, and a great number of <u>sudden</u> deaths—if I were able to write I would tell you startling things,—but sitting up and holding a pen is a great effort, and I must be brief read the iii chapt 1st Gen. Ep. of John 15th verse[2] and onwards, and ł you will discover my objection to Crinoline[3]—and in the Gen. Epistle of Peter and Timothy, the directions for my dressing myself. I dare not wear the garb of this world, while professing to be a follower of Jesus, I rank not with the daughters of the Land but with Him who took the form of a servant;—"who said "I am not of the world", but I have chosen you out of the world.

My beloved Walter, there are two <u>grand</u> divisions of the people dwelling on this earth I beseech you make sure to which of the two you belong, a mistake of your company may be fatal—as they must not unite, separation must be strictly adhered to—lest we be drawn from our allegiance,—I have not expressed myself as I could wish but you will understand my meaning,—one part of your letter gave me pleasure & it was that in your motives for returning, you had a desire to see us once more, O how I should rejoice to see you!—I am not surprised at your health waning, such practise in such a climate must be destructive—the voyage would restore you at once, if you came at a proper time of the year; we have had awful weather, a wet summer, a hot autumn, and now a hot winter with deluges of rain, and incessant hurricanes, the heat makes me so faint and feeble, that I am able for nothing,—however I am better since I began to take Lemonjuice. I take about two or 3 wine glasses in the day, the bowels are much improved by it, the appetite restored the secretions more natural, I eat Oranges also and drink London Porter—my illness began at the Sacrament[4] in March, and I have never been in Church since, I have a ganglion in my right knee, which troubles me at times very much, and prevents my walking, I am thankful when I can go downstairs as little children do, and creep up in a similar way—I grieve that you are tried with sleepless nights, and face pain, O that you may understand these warnings, and seek God more earnestly what would millions a year profit you if you missed Salvation what would the anguish of my soul be if I could not expect to have you beside me in Heaven!—Return home that you may be saved Colony life is ruinous,[5] return if to be a beggar while while[6] I have a habitation you shall not want a shelter, nor your wife a corner if she can be content to want fashion and fashionable entertainments, and partake of humble fare & unworldly ways we dare not be conformed to this world if we had 10,000 a year,—"we have food and raiment" and peace which the world of fashion knows not—neither can understand, this is the true riches.

My dear Caroline growing worse, Henry set off with her and their two eldest boys[7] to Glasgow to proceed to Edinbro to consult Simpson,[8] they had a favorable passage, introductions to Dr Guthrie and others. D^r G—s was given to Simpson, and he was very kind "The uterus is quite out of its place, glued to the back bone and lying on the bowel,"!—he performed an operation the first day, she suffered much; but her sufferings from exhaustion have been such that he said she would not have lasted any time being fearfully low—They have thro' friends got a respectable lodging at a cheap rate compared to this babylon, good kind people, Caroline is to stay in Edinbro' under Simpson, so Henry returned home yesterday leaving Cheyne with his Mother, and as he is a most wise and peculiarly loving child, and the people of the house tender christian people she will be well cared for—Henry has behaved admirably with true tenderness, he is now an elder of a new Church built thro' his efforts, with an excellent and devoted Minister of great piety and ability, and is much esteemed and in an enlarged sphere of doing good, he will be a credit to you when you return So will his brother John,[9] and your brother Alex^r[10]—in both of whom I take a deep interest—Character is precious and Alexr has established a good one and is now a servant of our Saviour, married to a sensible useful woman,[11] who is a good mother to his little Sarah,[12] Tommy[13] is in the Army I believe.

Jany 8th I had a letter today from Mary's Mother, Sarah is still suffering still under medical treatment, from the accident (so called) of an excursion train in which she was a passenger—so much for pleasure excursions would not young women be better at home? If you had any idea of the numbers who are burned to death from their clothes catching fire owing to crinoline you would not approve so much of its being worn, it is really painful to read of the victims to this most unnatural ungraceful and unwomanly fashion, which converts a woman who ought to be <u>graceful</u> into a mass of mis-shapen deformity—The Empress of France[14] has thrown off <u>hers,</u> and the fashion will not last another year as our Aristocracy will follow <u>her.</u> She has introduced <u>large</u> bonnets—

Miss Fector's brother[15] is breaking up, some affection of the sight which indicates either brain disease or coming blindness, he has taken a furnished house here for 1 month to try change of air & I think to be near her. Henry Handel[16] comes to us next month, happily I have a little Iron bed stead I bought for Lucinda, it has no curtains, and yet it cost £4 odd, we have only an attic for a spare room, our house consisting of only 4 rooms and this attic—and a small dressing closet, made into a store room. Our rent is high for a house so incommodious, and the taxes and poor rates heavy, and we purpose leaving it, there are houses near us less expensive with more rooms and larger, but in a less fashionable street, with no view such as this has, and no garden, our garden costs a good deal, for this last year or two I have not been able to do any thing in it, and shall be less I apprehend, I have to day an attack of Rheumatism in my left and well knee, and am suffering so much, that I find I must go to bed, and can therefore add no more to this feeble attempt at letter writing, but to intreat you will not manifest such an indifference to me as your leaving off writing indicates, for I do not deserve it at your hands and I find it hard to bear, you know well I never neglected <u>you</u>—and if you could not spare time, surely your wife could manage to scribble a few lines to <u>your</u> Mother—I <u>trust</u> I shall be able to tie up a few newspapers this mail, hitherto my right wrist precluded my doing it,—and your father has a weak hand also, owing to a sprained thumb and wrist overlooked in his last fall—

Jany 14th I have only to day got out of bed, where I have been since I wrote last, unable to turn or get out of it, and suffering much pain, I applied the lint wetted & oiled silk over which gave relief, & used a Liniment comp. opii, chloroform comp. ammon, &c without benefit—old age & debility admit <u>no</u> cure, <u>death</u> begins before we die, it makes dying easier, and makes it welcome too—

A letter this moment from L,[17] your brother Alex has lost his son-in-law,[18] a fine well disposed young man cut off in Typhus fever, took ill died & was buried in <u>one</u> short week, leaving 2 infants[19] one of them 7 months old—Jany 16th I am sitting up to day, but grieved and disappointed at being told there is a mail in. George[20] has had letters and I have none. The wreck of the Colombo has deprived us of any news of dear Alick,[21] and Miss Fector is sad about him, I regret to say she will leave Brighton at the end of this month, I shall miss her very much, and perhaps never see her again, Low Gout & Rheumatism are pronounced to be <u>now</u> my temperament, an endeavour has been made to bring on a fit regular of the former of these diseases, but ineffectually, while the latter is flying about me—Miss F.— also suffers from Rheumatism, and is far from strong, she is sorry to leave us but Alick cannot be brought hither, as Bronchitis immediately attacks and prostrates him, if he were to choose a sea life Miss F. would settle here again as her love for me is as strong as ever stronger I think as she sees the rapidity with which I decline, she shewed me the Cartes de visites[22] you sent her, yours is pretty well, but Mary is disfigured, so unlike her picture, it is all clothes, so stiff & old. You will receive your father's carte with <u>this,</u> it is very like I made myself <u>ill</u> by going and sitting for mine 2 months ago, but cannot get it out of the Photographer's hands, you shall have one when I can obtain it—As I have written with difficulty and not been able to say what I would have wished about our meeting in the Celestial City, I send you a Book just published, which if you have any love left for me I ask you to read thro' for <u>my sake;</u>—my prayers follow you,

you are now my all!! do not forget or neglect me for your <u>own</u> sake; give my very tenderest love to Mary, and believe me with true and never varying Love your fond & anxious Mother

        Lucinda Cheyne

excuse bad writing the cold is intense, N.E. wind, most bitter

    Text: ALS NLA MS133/1/41 and MS133/1/43

[1]   On 19 November 1862, the *Colombo*, East India mail steamer, was wrecked in thick weather on Minicoy Island, 440 miles from Point de Galle, Ceylon. No lives were lost for the crew and passengers were taken off by the *Ottawa* from Bombay, on 30 November 1862.

[2]   'Love not the world, neither the things that are in the world. If any man love the world, the love of the Father is not in him. For all that is in the world, the lust of the flesh, and the lust of the eyes, and the pride of life, is not of the Father, but is of the world.' *The Bible, Authorized Version*, The First Epistle General of John, verses 15 and 16.

[3]   Originally a stiff fabric of horse-hair and flax used to distend the skirts of women; this was developed into a hooped petticoat or skirt made to project all round by means of whale-bones or steel wire.

[4]   Easter.

[5]   '"My beloved son, colony life is disastrous. It ruins the body … as it ruins the soul."' *FRM II*, p. 58.

[6]   Repeated in the transition to the next page.

[7]   Marmaduke Cheyne Richardson (1851–1925) and Lindesay Richardson (b. 1853).

[8]   James Young Simpson (1811–1870), physician. He was a baker's son who studied medicine at Edinburgh, taking his MD in 1832. In 1837 he became Assistant to the Professor of Pathology. Becoming Professor of Midwifery in 1839, he taught WLR during his studies at the University of Edinburgh. Simpson is chiefly remembered as having popularised the anaesthetic virtues of chloroform (1847), which was used very successfully for the birth of Queen Victoria's eighth child, Prince Leopold, on 7 April 1853 by Dr John Snow, anaesthetist from Edinburgh, invited by the Royal Physician, Sir James Clark. In obstetrics Simpson's improvements in practice were numerous and valuable. He was created a baronet in 1866. He died on 6 May 1870.

[9]   John Richardson, son of Marmaduke Jenny Richardson and brother of Henry, who was married to Caroline Richardson, WLR's sister.

[10]   Alexander Richardson (1803–1890), half-brother of WLR; son of Alexander Richardson and his second wife, Elizabeth née Smyth (1778–1815).

[11]   Jane née Pyke, Alexander Richardson's second wife, the daughter of Captain William Pyke, Royal Navy, Devon, England. His first wife, Elizabeth Richardson was also his cousin, the daughter of his youngest uncle Marmaduke Jenny Richardson, and the sister of Henry, Caroline's husband. After bearing him twelve children, Elizabeth had died. Jane and Alexander did not have any children.

[12]   Sarah Louise Richardson (b. 1848), the youngest child of Alexander Richardson, jnr, and his first wife, Elizabeth Richardson.

[13]   Thomas Richardson (b. *c.*1838), ninth son of Alexander and Elizabeth Richardson.

[14]   Eugénie (née de Montijo) (1826–1920), daughter of the Spanish Count Don Cipriano of Montijo and the Countess Manuela of Montijo née Kirkpatrick. She was the wife of the Emperor of the French, Napoleon III (Louis-Napoleon Bonaparte) (1808–1873) and she accompanied her husband on a state visit to Britain in April 1855. She was very tall and beautiful, in contrast to Napoleon who was extremely short, with a large head and long waxed moustaches. She not only entranced the Royal family, but the British population with her elegance, fashion and beauty. She brought the first crinoline to England—grey with black lace and pink bows and the Queen 'was charmed to learn that Prince Albert admired Eugénie's toilette excessively'. Elizabeth Longford, *Victoria R.I.* (London: Pan Books, 1966), p. 314.

[15]   John Minet Fector (b. 1812), only son and fourth child of John Minet Fector and Ann Wortley Montagu; christened on 7 April 1812 at St Mary the Virgin, Dover, Kent.

[16]   Henry Handel Richardson (b. *c.*1842), grandson of Lucinda Cheyne, older brother of Alick and nephew of WLR. He was the son of Henry Downing Richardson, Lucinda and Alexander Richardson's eldest son.

[17]   Lucinda Richardson, WLR's sister.

[18]   Effingham Lindesay Richardson (1829–1863), died 4 January 1863 leaving a widow and two small sons. He was the son of Robert Richardson (1775–1842) and Jane Elizabeth née Cooper (1803–1871); and the nephew of Alexander Richardson (1758–1827). His widow was Harriett

Amelia Richardson (1840–1916), the daughter of his cousin (and WLR's half-brother), Alexander Richardson (1803–1890). She remarried in 1868 to George Nugent (1822–1902) and they had six daughters.

19   Effingham Lysart Richardson (b. 1860) and Alexander Lindesay Richardson (1862–1942).

20   George Cheyne, who was still living in Brighton. He and Grace moved to Lochmaben later in the year.

21   Her grandson, Alick (Alexander) Richardson (1845–1900), a midshipman on board the *Great Britain*. He finally emigrated to Australia in 1866, arriving in Melbourne on the *Yorkshire* on 22 March 1866.

22   Small photographic portraits called 'Cartes des Visite' were first taken at Nice, France, by M. Ferrier in 1857. The Duke of Parma had his portrait placed upon his visiting cards, and his example was followed by Paris and London society. The Parisian portrait photographer, André Adolphe Eugène Disdéri (1819–1890) had patented in 1854 a camera with four lenses, which could make eight photographs on a single full-sized glass plate. The relative cheapness of this new portraiture enabled all classes to enjoy the technology.

91   [From LC in Brighton, England, to WLR in Ballarat]

17 Buckingham Place Brighton| Sussex, England
Nov^br 17th /63

My beloved Son

Do not judge of my love by the frequency or absence of my communications my feeble frame and breaking up constitution render it very difficult to get thro' the duties which I am compelled to perform without help. Your father since I last wrote has been so unwell I feared I might have had distressing news for you by this mail; he was seized one morn^g with faintness and asked for <u>wine</u>, on following him to his room, I found him extended on the bed, with an intermitting and fluttering pulse, quite sunk wine was freely administered, but finding at the end of some hours no improvement in the pulse I sent off for Dr Dill,—and he has continued to visit from time to time. The faintness has occurred at different times since, he can hardly mount the stairs without its recurrence in a slighter degree—he is ordered to be kept very quiet, to keep the house and avoid exertion A few days after this seizure a Telegram arrived in the Ev^g from Lochmaben[1] Dumfriesshire stating that his brother George was dangerously ill, and required his presence immediately, we were greatly distressed, but your father could not go even the length of the Street—medical aid from the Town of Dumfries was obtained for George, he and his wife had on removing to Lochmaben joined the Free Church[2] there, your father wrote at once to the Minister, Revd B. Hill,[3] requesting to know the complaint, medical opinion and other particulars which could not be learned by Telegraphic messages, and the anxiety of his wife would not allow of her giving—The disease inflammation of the Kidneys was serious, and altho' the Dumfries Physician was skilful, Mr Hill rode to Locherbie and sent off a Telegram for Dr Chrisiston,[4] who has written on that disease he came, says the danger is over for the <u>present</u> and we learn that he is going on since very favorably—George had just settled himself in an excellent house[5] in Lochmaben standing in a large garden, surrounded by land enough for cows, horses, & poultry he has been in infirm health since his return from Australia, and had longed and languished for a country dwelling, and disliking Brighton on acc^t of its excessive dearness,—and the impossibility of getting even a flower plot in the South of England he chose Scotland, where he could procure what would suit him—

I find it very difficult to write my dearest Walter your father being unable to go out and order in all the various requirements of a household, every thing devolves upon me, I have to plan and to order, to write letters, and answer others, to soothe and amuse your father mend his stockings, and in short to be Chef du Ménage, and oftentimes am more worn out, than is desirable.—I miss Miss Fector. Now and then she runs down for a few hours, she came lately because I was worse than I had been for a long time, she looks worn and overworked, but says she is well,—

Your sister Caroline is declining rapidly, her husband is better, and the remaining boys in good health now, but she mourns still for your name sake,[6]—

By one of those events we are apt to think strange, Mrs Loveday, widow of Cap^{tn} Loveday in whose house our poor John died came to Brighton lately with her Mother, widow of General Simpson[7] and hearing of my infirm state of health, came to visit me, to tell me of John, whom she nursed on his dying bed, he excited in her and Cap^{tn} L. the deepest interest, and affection. Their care of him was wonderful, he spoke much of me, was patient and grateful for all the attention they bestowed upon him, he arrived worn out from want and privation, accompanied by a friend of the name of Preston who was devotedly attached to him. This friend came home to his father in Cambridge and died a year ago, he had a lock of hair he cut off John's head before he was laid in the coffin, and this hair was lately sent to me by Mrs Preston—young Preston never recovered the affect of the famine and hardship John & he had undergone, he was an only son, & his father calls himself heartbroken in consequence of his death—I think your father is better, he had a few lines from George yesterday, & was cheered. My state however keeps him low, since I began this miserable attempt at a letter, I have suffered from severe diarr. which not even opium can keep under—so you must excuse brief notices instead of letters, as I sit up with difficulty. I trust you are recovered long since from the effects of the wetting and able to resume your practice. & that Mary is well.

Ever my beloved Son with fondest remembrance and anxious affection| Your attached| Mother

     L. Cheyne

Mrs Bailey never writes to me now. Since L—[8] returned our correspondence has ceased. I fancy there has been false statements and misrepresentations, I cannot help it; the tongue is a little member, but it does much evil| with love, much love to Mary & yourself

    Text: ALS NLA MS133/1/42

[1]   Lochmaben, a small town in Dumfrieeshire, was once the site of the castle of the Bruce family, visited by Mary Queen of Scots and Lord Darnley in 1565. The site and the lordship of Annandale were conferred on Robert de Brus by David I in about 1124 and it was around Lochmaben that the future Robert I spent much of his childhood. Where once was the castle moat, now is the green swathe of the fourteenth tee of Lochmaben's golf course.

[2]   Lochmaben had two churches in addition to the parish Church of Scotland. The Barras Church (1813–1920) was set up by the Burgher Associate Congregation in protest against the *Patronage Act of 1712*. The Victoria United Free Church (1843–1920), to which the Cheynes belonged, was set up after the disruption of the Church of Scotland in 1843 (see Letter 40, endnote 9). In 1920, the Barras and Victoria Churches were united to form the congregation of St Margaret's Church (1920–1954). In 1955, St Margaret's was reunited with the parish church. John B. Wilson, *The Royal Burgh of Lochmaben: Its History, Its Castles and Its Churches* (Dumfries: Dinwiddie Grieve, 1987), p. 122.

[3]   The Reverend Ebenezer B. Hill, Minister of Victoria United Free Church until 1884.

[4]   Dr Robert Christison from Edinburgh had been the doctor of Bayne Cheyne's brother, Captain Charles Cheyne (1786–1857), who died on 23 February 1857 (see Letters 26 and 28).

[5]   'Bank House', Bruce Street, Lochmaben is now lived in by an architect and his family. It is the oldest house in Lochmaben, originally built about 1703. In 1778, it was bought by Dr Robert Clapperton (1728–1802) who remodelled it. It is double-fronted with pillars at each corner and appears to be a single storey from the street but is in fact built on three levels and has a Palladian

window at the rear. It is deceptively large, with an attached coach house set back from the street. From 1847 to 1852 it was used by the National Bank of Scotland. In late 1864 or early 1865 Bayne and Lucinda Cheyne moved from their Brighton home to live with Grace and George Cheyne at 'Bank House', where Lucinda Cheyne died on 20 June 1866. Bayne continued to live there with his brother and sister-in-law, until his death on 2 August 1868.

6   Walter Lindesay Richardson must have died between January and November 1863. Presumably Lucinda or WLR's brother-in-law, Henry Richardson, would have sent a letter to WLR and Mary reporting his death, but none has survived.

7   General Sir James Simpson GCB (*c.*1791–1869), Colonel of 29th Regiment of Foot from 27 July 1863 until his death. He began his career as an Ensign in 87th Regiment of Foot (Royal Irish Fusiliers) on 3 April 1811. He was appointed Captain on 25 December 1813, Lieutenant-Colonel on 28 April 1825, Colonel on 28 June 1838, Major-General on 11 November 1851, Lieutenant-General on 29 June 1855 and General on 8 September 1855. H. G. Hart, *The New Annual Army List, Militia List and Indian Civil Service List for 1870* (London: John Murray, 1870), p. 584.

8   Lucinda Richardson.

1864

92   [From MR at 'Glen Ayr House', Kilmore,[1] to WLR in Ballarat]

Glen Air House [Kilmore]

Monday April [18, 1864]

My own darling Walter

I thought I had better write this morning as it may be a week before you get another letter from me & I have had no letter as yet from you & cannot now get one before Thursday so you need never say again what a time elapses before you get one from me for it will be 9 days before I get your's as to day we start for the Station[2] & there is only a post every two day's I hope dear you are keeping well & do not miss me too much that Mary[3] is taking good care of you I am enjoying myself very much every one seems so kind & hospitable M[rs] M[c]Kenzie[4] is such a nice person & although there are 9 children[5] I never saw any so obedient & well behaved it is a pleasure to be with them. There is a M[rs] Gibbons[6] close here used to live on Ballaraat he an Engineer you attended her once for D[r] Holthouse[7] & on the Melbourne Road rather fond of Pale Brandy

We had a drive in the carriage to Broadford 10 miles from here such a nice macadimised Road & Magnificent scenery all hills & valley's every thing so picturesque The trees are quite different from those about us & so thick Close to the Garden here there is one tree with I should think a 100 Magpies on it quite covered. Yesterday we went to church[8] a much handsomer building than any on Ballaraat but a very poor clergyman[9] not 80 people in the building in the afternoon we had a long walk thro' the Police Paddock[10] & to the Rèsovoir[11] we have no walks so pretty with us When you write will you send some simple thing for Dilly[12] They think she has got worms she starts in her sleep & her hand alway's at her nose. Mrs Kabats brother[13] is very like Mr Kossack[14] but much taller & finer looking altogether so dark with bushy Black beard & Moustache not like any of the other's

The Ohara's[15] left here long ago D[r] Bingley[16] has all the practice something like Hudson[17] he has just built himself a large Brick & Stone House with Verandah all round both Stories one of the best houses here[18]—The weather is very pleasant cold mornings & evening's but very nice during the day. How is M[rs] Cuthbert[19] getting on & baby[20] I hope the Nurse continues to give satisfaction Give my love to them Have you seen any thing of Leopold[21] Mary must have the Spare Bed Room Dusted when I come back because they will stay a day or two with us before going to Hamilton if they can Has Felix[22] gone yet. I shall be able to tell you how I like the Station in my next I received two paper's I was dreaming about you last night & felt very lonely when I awoke & found you were not beside me

I have a bad cold in my head change of air make [may] take it away

I hope your cough has not come back take care of yourself darling you are all I have to love in this world & it would break my heart were any thing to happen [to] you I suppose I shall get home letter's in your next. Send me word how much you weighed direct the letter's as follows until I write again M[rs] Richardson care of J Murchison Esq[23]—Kerisdale Broadford I can perhaps tell you in my next when we shall be likely to return Mrs Kabat is waiting to hear from Leopold Good bye darling with love & kisses as ever| Your loving wife

      Polly

Text: ALS NLA MS133/1/47

1   MR and Mrs Emily Kabat (née Murchison) were staying with Emily's sister, Martha MacKenzie and her husband, Farquhar MacKenzie, at Kilmore on their way to Kerrisdale, near Broadford. The MacKenzies had moved from Kerrisdale to Kilmore in 1863. Kilmore was a 'bustling Borough' with a population in 1865 of 2000. It was an important regional centre, servicing the area of Lancefield, Pyalong, Broadford, Wallan, Beveridge and Darraweit Guim, and, as a popular place for travellers to stop on their way north, boasting nine hotels, five wine and spirit merchants, five grocers, two brewers, four lodging houses and four butchers. Maya Tucker, *Kilmore on the Sydney Road* (Kilmore: Shire of Kilmore, 1988), p. 1. At the time of MR's visit, Andrew Murison McCrae (1800–1874), husband of Georgiana Gordon, illegitimate daughter of 5th Duke of Gordon, was the Police Magistrate at Kilmore, a post he occupied from 1857 to 1867, living on Camp Hill overlooking the town.

2   Kerrisdale, near Broadford, home of Captain John Murchison (1797–1882), who was the cousin of Sir Robert Impey Murchison (1792–1871), the first geologist to be created a baronet. John was the son of Kenneth Murchison, an officer in the British army, and Martha née Urquhart. Both cousins had served in the British Army but Robert had returned from the Napoleonic War in 1814 and began his study of geology, whereas John, who was commissioned in the Royal Scots Regiment in 1813, remained in the army and joined the Scots Fusiliers in 1818. After serving as quartermaster of the 96th Regiment from 1828 to 1832, he emigrated to NSW in 1833. He and his family lived for eleven years in NSW and then in 1844 he became a pioneer overlander to Victoria with Farquhar MacKenzie, and took up a pastoral run, Kerrisdale, adjacent to the King Parrot Creek. In 1825, while stationed in Nova Scotia, he had married Mary Ann née Roberts (1806–1872), born in Ireland, daughter of John Roberts and Mary Ann née Rankin. They had seven children: Martha (married Farquhar MacKenzie) b. 1828 in Bermuda; Janette Violet b. 1830; Kenneth b. 1832 (deceased); Robert Impey b. 1834 (married Julia Urqhart); Marianna MacKenzie (married William MacKenzie) b. 1836; Emily Bradley (married Leopold Kabat) b. 1838; and Flora Agnes (married Cuthbert Fetherstonhaugh) b. 1844. John Murchison died on 20 June 1882 of senile decay and bronchitis.

3   Mary, the Richardsons' servant.

4   Martha MacKenzie née Murchison (b. 1828), sister of Mrs Kabat, married to Farquhar MacKenzie (1811–1874), the grandson of Sir Alexander Mackenzie of Gairloch, 3rd Bart. He was born in Ross-shire, the son of army Captain Kenneth MacKenzie and his wife, Flora Emily (née McRae). He was described as a 'settler' on his son's death certificate (Herbert Douglas) in 1865, but since 1862 he had been appointed as a Sheep Inspector—first for the district known as Benalla and then for Kilmore district and finally in 1868, for the Echuca area. His job was to administer the Pastoral Scab Act. He was also a Justice of the Peace. According to a neighbour of

the Murchisons and the MacKenzies, John Cotton of Doogallook, who was not an admirer of John Murchison: 'His son-in-law [i.e., Farquar], who lives with them, is a better-principled man, and is much esteemed by most persons.' Cotton's letter (held in the State Library of Victoria) is quoted in W. C. Bossence, *Murchison: The J.G. Memorial History* (Melbourne: The Hawthorn Press, 1965), p. 50. See also note on Harry Power in Letter 156, about Farquar MacKenzie's encounter with the bushranger.

5   By the time of this visit, the MacKenzies had nine children: Hector Roderick (b. 1849), Catherine Violet (b. 1850); Mary Anne (b. 1852); Kenneth Murchison (b. 1854); Farquhar (b. 1856); John (b. 1858); Flora Emily (b. 1860); Charles Edward (b. 1862): Herbert Douglas (b. 1864). Herbert Douglas died in 1865 and then on 28 February 1866, Josie was born but she died later that year. Stuart Leopold was born in 1869 and Ada in 1871.

6   Mrs Gibbons, wife of William Gibbons, Kilmore's civil engineer. They lived on Mitchell Street.

7   Dr Thomas Le Gay Holthouse (1819–1901) born in Edmonston, Middlesex. He emigrated on the *Charles*, arriving in Melbourne in October 1853. First President of the Ballarat Medical Society, he was the paid medical officer of the Benevolent Asylum for thirty years.

8   The first stone of Christ Church, Kilmore, was laid on 19 November 1857 by Bishop Charles Perry and was completed, except for the tower (still incomplete), by 1864. The chief architect was James Fleury (1817–1868). It is of bluestone in the Early English Gothic style, measuring inside approximately 38 metres by 14 metres, with the height of the nave nearly 16 metres.

9   The Reverend William Jones Singleton, MA (1804–1875), son of William Singleton, a prosperous merchant in Dublin, and his wife Mary née Lewis; he emigrated to Victoria in 1849 and was given the incumbency of Kilmore and remained there for nineteen years. He was married to Frances and they had nine sons and two daughters. He was the elder brother of John Singleton (1808–1891; see *ADB*), physician, philanthropist, who followed William to Victoria with his family in 1851. John Singleton's welfare work included gaol visiting, establishing shelters for the destitute and a mission to the blind. His interest in Aboriginal welfare lead to the establishment of the Framlingham Reserve near Warrnambool. He established the Collingwood Free Medical Dispensary (now the Singleton Medical Welfare Centre).

10 The Police Paddock was fenced in 1850 by the government at a cost of £40 and was finally sold in 1925 for £520 (£80 an acre). Tucker, pp. 54 and 205.

11 The town's first water supply was connected by the government in 1862, and the old reservoir continued to be used until it became a health hazard through pollution. The reticulated water system was begun in 1895.

12 Antoinette Favorita Emily Kabat (1861–1940), born 30 June 1861, daughter of Leopold and Emily Kabat.

13 Robert Impey Murchison (b. 1833), son of John Murchison and Mary Ann née Roberts and named after his father's cousin, Sir Robert Impey Murchison. On 11 April 1860, he married his sixteen-year-old cousin, Julia Rose Urquhart (1844–1875), daughter of Captain John Urquhart and Jane née Roberts. They had four children: John Henry born 1861 at Kerrisdale; Edith Jane (1864–1874); Julia (b. 1867); Philip Douglas (1871–1888).

14 Ladislaus Sylvester Kossak (1828–1918), Police Inspector, arrived with Leopold Kabat in Melbourne in May 1852 aboard the steamer *Chusan*. He was born in Wisnicz, South Poland, and in 1848, when the revolution against Austria broke out in Hungary, left the university to join the regiment of lancers in the Polish Legion. In 1849 he was interned with Kabat in Turkey after the capitulation of the Hungarian army. When released in 1851, they first travelled to England and then to Melbourne where they both joined the Victorian police force. Kossak was one of the four sub-inspectors in charge of the seventy mounted police at the Eureka Stockade, although many years later he was publicly named as one of the few officials in sympathy with the miners.

15 Dr Henry O'Hara had been based at Ballarat in 1861 and was a friend of WLR. See endnote to Letter 73.

16 Dr Frank Lane Bindley (1830–1870) arrived in Kilmore about 1856 after four years as resident surgeon at the County Hospital in Kent. He was the MacKenzie's doctor and attended Herbert Douglas at his death on 25 January 1865 and delivered Martha's last child, Josie, on 28 February 1866.

17 Dr Robert Fawell Hudson (1834–1898). See endnote to Letter 43.

18 'Bindley House', Powlett Street, designed by local architect James Fleury, still survives and is listed on the National Estate Register, the Heritage Victoria Register and is classified by the National Trust.

19   Emma Wilmer Cuthbert formerly Hepburn née Kirby (1835–1877), born in Woodend near
     Blakesley, Northamptonshire, daughter of William Kirby and his wife Emma née Wilmer. She
     married Thomas Hepburn, eldest son of Captain John Hepburn of Smeaton Park in 1857.
     When Thomas died on 21 July 1859 aged twenty-three, she was left with an infant son, Thomas
     John Hepburn, who was born at Smeaton in April 1859. On 28 May 1863 she married Henry
     Cuthbert and gave birth to John Headen Cuthbert on 11 April 1864 with WLR as the
     accoucheur. (*Case* 623, 'Mrs H. Cuthbert Solicitors wife, third pregnancy … face towards left
     thigh'.) WLR noted in his record that this was her third pregnancy as she had had a son who
     died aged six months in 1858. (That baby's birth and death at Smeaton were not registered.) On
     16 December 1865, the Cuthbert's second son, Henry Herbert, was born; he died on 27 April
     1866. On 18 May 1868 their daughter, Annie Wilmer Cuthbert, who was a childhood friend of
     HHR, was born. Thomas John Hepburn, Emma's second child by her first husband, died on
     11 February 1879 aged nineteen, of 'fatty heart'.
20   John Headen Cuthbert (1864–1934), son of Henry Cuthbert and Emma Wilmer Hepburn,
     who was born on 11 April 1864. He married Mabel Julia Costin (1870–1975) on 10 December
     1890 at Ballarat and they had two sons: Henry Headen (1891–1957), a solicitor; and John
     Bryan (1894-1918), Lieutenant in 13th Squadron RAF, who was killed in action on 28 August
     1918 in France.
21   Captain Leopold Kabat (1832–1884), Inspector of Police, married to Emily née Murchison.
22   Felix Kabat (1835–1904), broker, who had followed his brother Leopold to Victoria in 1862.
     He married Gail Adams in 1871 and had two sons, Ernst (1872–1949) and Felix (1874–1957).
     He died in Fitzroy South on 17 March 1904.
23   John Murchison (1797–1882).

93   [From WLR in Ballarat to MR in Kerrisdale]

[Webster Street, Ballarat]
Wednesday morning [20 April 1864]

My own dear P:

It was very good of you to write without waiting to receive my reply to your first letter. I
was very glad indeed to hear you were well—There appears to be some awkwardness about the
postal arrangements of the neighbourhood in which you are now: I have been very busy since
you left—I posted the last to you on Saturday morning well I had a busy day and dined with
Hudson went back & spent evening

Too busy on Sunday to go to Church dined with Cuthberts: Monday night labor[1] &
called out to another case Tuesday out all day & 5 miles on the road past the
Cuthberts—Rubber at my house from 8 to 11.30 bed by 12—called up to a case of very
protracted labor at 3.30 on Plank Road where I now am & likely to be for some hours.[2] It is
very annoying because it will upset my days work & cause me to neglect my patients: & as I
promised to go to the country patient the first thing I see nothing for it but running home at
8: & breakfasting & finishing this to you—

Do not be in too great a bustle to return—you may not get away again this year. M^rs C.
& baby all well. She came down to dinner with us on Sunday & played a chant—

Just had a letter from Ned[3] about the box he says he may send it up to day: Bills[4] Carte
de V. very good

No home letters for you Enclosed from Sam.[5] Not seen Leop. since you left I am too
busy I see Felix loafing about—

Nobody has called—

Weather wet this morning I send Star—

and now I will either have to close this or put it off till the afternoon I think you wd. not like the latter| Your affect husband

        W—

I will give you a longer one next time

    Text: ALS NLA MS133/1/104

1   *Case* 624, Monday, 18 April 1864: Mrs J. H. Hill, third pregnancy. 'Been married 6 months: premature ... dead several days.'
2   *Case* 625, Wednesday, 20 April 1864: Mrs Joe Powell, aged thirty-five, seventh pregnancy. 'Always hard times—Head detained at brim for hours—Born whilst absent. 9.30 am: male.' Charles Rigney born to Joseph Powell and Ann née Rigney.
3   Edward Harold Bailey.
4   Possibly William Bailey's *carte de visite*. He was in India.
5   Samuel Bailey.

94   [From WLR in Ballarat to MR in Kerrisdale]

[Webster Street, Ballarat]
Friday evening [22 April 1864]

My own darling Polly

I have just come in & got your letter—I am sorry you thought my last so short but really I had nothing to interest you no news—and moreover I always found such a difficulty in getting the time even by staying up at night—I wrote you the day before yesterday—Yesterday morning I got up at 7.30 breakfasted & started off 4½ miles & busy all day till dark—This ~~out~~ morning out at 6 to Mrs Loney[1] who kept me till 12—Hudson dines with me to night. He went down to Breens[2] wedding—I asked H. Cuthbert but of course he couldnt come—She (Mrs H.[3]) looks so pretty that he could not leave her: the old gent[4] threatened to bring her out today but fortunately it has been raining very heavily & so they are prevented—I told you I dined there on Sunday. I am delighted you admire the scenery & that it is so charming I wish I were with you—Mary is doing very well—I hope she wont burn the dinner tho'—No sign of the box altho Ned has passed it & wrote to me Wednesday—

I sleep pretty well—of course you do not—You must not abuse Hudson about promises if it was any ones fault it was mine. I do not see the use of giving Flora's[5] love if she accepts Mr Pooleys[6] lock of hair!! however we will have a talk about you all this evening—

No news—Letter from Watson[7] he has been to Woods Point I will keep them all till you come—no I will send that

No parties—I have never yet seen Leopold—I do not know where to find him but I suppose Mrs Kabats letters are filled with details of auctions & removals & meetings of creditors[8]—what does Flora say of it all Is she looking as well as she did—You ask me for a prescription for the little boy[9] from your description I make out that the fits are caused by a <u>determination of blood</u> to the <u>head</u>, & that they are apoplectic a good smart purge of <u>salts</u> wd. be better than oil—preventing the overloading the stomach by heavy food as puddings the treatment adopted was good

I enclose a prescription if there is heat of head, redness of eyes, pain in head or loss of power in any limbs for any one of these the medicine will be useful as directed—Heavy storm last night & today. Hope you will get rid of your cold & come back quite well—weight day you left 10 st. 7.

Remember me kindly to M^rs M[10] M^rs K & Flora—I hope Dilly is improved & does not cry "uppy Mamma" quite as often—Saty= [Saturday] Leopold, Felix & a stranger came last night & we had a lot of rubbers they stayed till 12—

Leopold says you are not coming home next week that he shall be at Smythes[11] until Saty & then he's going down to Geelong—May 1st. He said why shd they hurry back let them enjoy themselves

Very bitterly cold this morning—Rain Winter in fact—

No box yet—S.[12] has not come up—I hope you are still enjoying yourselves and that it is doing you good—Ned wrote to say that Aunty[13] had been very ill—Two doctors About the illness he did not say a word—No news—and now my dear wife—may God give you his blessing & may you come back safe & well to the arms of your own dear husband when I shall make up for the abscence of kisses during the past fortnight by taking you on my knee all the evening—I suppose you will come back by the 11 P.M. train As ever Your| own

W

Sam has just turned up by this mornings 10 oclock train he says he has nothing to [add] looks very smart

Text: ALS NLA MS133/1/87

1   *Case* 626, 22 April 1864, Mrs Loney, Market Square, aged forty-one, fifth pregnancy. 'Lingering—gave Ergot, 1 dose of Brandy'—male child. James William born to James and Eliza Loney; the baby died aged two years.

2   On 18 April 1864, at the Roman Catholic Church at Sandhurst, Thomas Breen, a miner from Baywood, married Mary Naylor, a domestic servant.

3   Emma, Mrs Henry Cuthbert.

4   John Cuthbert (1793–1878), father of Henry Cuthbert.

5   Flora Agnes Murchison (1844–1931), youngest daughter of John Murchison, squatter, Kerrisdale, near Broadford; sister of Mrs Emily Kabat. In 1876 Flora married Cuthbert Fetherstonhaugh (1837–1925), pastoralist, clergyman and journalist.

6   William Thomas Pooley (1813–1872), Deputy Registrar at Ballarat.

7   Albert Watson.

8   Leopold Kabat had money troubles through some ill-advised mining speculations. See Sadleir, p. 116.

9   It is likely to be one of the older sons—Hector Roderick (b. 1849), Kenneth Murchison (b. 1854); Farquhar (b. 1856); John (b. 1858); Charles Edward (b. 1862). The youngest son, Herbert Douglas, was only two months old and would be too young to be eating solids. He died nine months later aged eleven months, on 25 January 1865.

10 Martha (Patty) MacKenzie.

11 Smythes not identifiable.

12 Samuel Bailey.

13 Elizabeth Turnham.

95   [From WLR in Ballarat to MR in Kerrisdale]

[Webster Street] Ballt.

Friday evening [29 April 1864]

My darling Polly

I received yours this evening & I was sent for hurriedly out just as I met postman. I was not therefore able to write you by return. I am glad to hear that you arrived safely after your long & tedious journey—how singular that Mrs Kabats letter was never got what became of it?

On the morn of your departure[1] I was sent for to the Springs 6 miles at 7 oclock back by 10 to breakfast: House full Mr Cummins[2] called on you—told him I cd. not afford anything

Busy day—to Essex meeting.[3] home by 11. Yesterday Busy also. Paid late visit to Cuthbert & dined there—Whist—Nixon[4] there—I am glad to say that Mrs C. is doing as well as could be wished—The baby is admired more daily—Leopold is away. We will have no whist party this week—Mary is doing very well she is becoming more particular about the messages & the addresses I have sent you a Star every day

Letter today from Lucinda[5] another from Alick:[6] nothing of interest in either so will keep them until you come—none from your mother—

I hope you slept well & that you are pretty well: make up your mind to enjoy yourself & try & come back with roses in your cheeks & with your lips red & ready for kissing—I cannot deny that I sleep well—never awaking

No news of any interest: xcept that Bunten[7] has <u>been dismissed & suspended</u>, & has cut & left his wife & family. It seems he has been a <u>regular scamp,</u> & Elliott[8] got him away from this so that nothing might occur here: Nurse Millar[9] says the trip will do you a great deal of good "and it will do you good too, Doctor" she said—I was on the point of saying none of your impudence!

I am at home this evening—Mary gets me every thing very nicely & I make myself eat—

I have not seen Hudson since you left

Saturday morning [30 April 1864]

Very cold—did not sleep owing to the cold—must have more blankets—I have told Mary

Good bye dear| Your affect| & loving husband

W—

Love to Mrs Kabat & Flora Kind regards to Mrs M.[10]

Text: ALS NLA MS133/1/93

1   Probably means departure from Kerrisdale back to Melbourne.
2   The Reverend Robert Turner Cummins, Minister of St Paul's Church (Anglican), in Humffray Street, probably collecting for charity.
3   Essex Gold Mining Company, Swamp Lead, Ballarat. The Manager of the mine was Thomas Broadbent. Presumably WLR was a shareholder.
4   William Nixon (1833–1905), a broker in mining shares. He married Henry Cuthbert's sister, Anna Maria Cuthbert, on 8 September 1864. He arrived in Melbourne aboard the *Nepaul* in October 1852.
5   Lucinda Richardson, WLR's sister. She would have written the letter three or four months before and by the time WLR received it, she would probably have been planning her trip back to Australia. She sailed from Liverpool aboard the *Marco Polo* and arrived in Melbourne on 6 October 1864.
6   Either Alick Cook or Alick Richardson. Alick (Alexander) Richardson (1845–1900), nephew of WLR; sailed on the *Great Australia* as midshipman, arriving in Melbourne in September 1862 for a short stay. He eventually returned to Australia on board the *Yorkshire*, arriving in Melbourne on 22 March 1866 and settled in NSW where WLR visited him in 1870 (see Letter 156).
7   Robert Clark Bunten, a bank clerk, married to Mary Ellen née Clark in 1856. They had four children in Ballarat between 1857 and 1862 and their last child was born in Melbourne in 1864.
8   Michael Elliot, Manager of the Bank of Australasia, was married to Margaret McKenzie in 1857. They had two sons born 1858 and 1865.
9   Nurse Millar was probably a midwife. Not identifiable.
10   Mary Ann Murchison née Roberts (1806–1872), mother of Emily Kabat.

1865

96   [From WLR in Ballarat to MR in East Melbourne[1]]

[Webster Street, Ballarat]
Monday Evening [6 March 1865]

My dear own Polly

You need not be cross because you did not get a letter in the morning, as I was prevented from replying by return post: I am glad you arrived safely and that the journey was a pleasant one—I hope the whole trip[2] may be as pleasant: you must not talk so soon of returning but make up your mind for the entire month of March—Leopold went down Sunday afternoon—I dined at the Saddlers,[3] we had a very pleasant dinner

I found it very cold last night & told Maria to put on some more blankets.

Jim called me at 7 & we had a bath—I have been pretty busy to day and as I was at tea in walked Albert[4] from Woods Point—The account of his life is like a romance—sleeping out in the open air for weeks, no covering from rain or snow, wading in rivers & swimming them night & morning—he says he is better off than he has ever been since he has left home. I am glad all are well—I will finish this in the morning

Tuesday morning

Another cold night: Had a bath this morning—the weather is pleasant, not too hot: No news of any interest.

All going on well in your abscence   Enjoy yourself as much as you can—go to Abbotsford & Pentridge & the Murchisons—and on board the G. Britain[5] & try & come back fat.

Ask Turnham for my acct.[6] Remember me to them & to Jeannie[7]—I think I will not write to Ned this time as I have nothing to say

If any English letters come I will send them to you. Hudson did not come back yesterday—I am much obliged to Ned & Jeannie for their invitations but must for the present decline altho' I may run down to Geelong to meet you & stay for one day—& have a bathe—migt we might arrange it so as to meet on Saturday & stay till Monday—

Jim has just called to ask me up this evening for a rubber—

Good bye dear says| Your affect Husband

W.L.R.

Text: ALS NLA MS133/1/103

---

[1]   MR was staying with her sister-in-law, Jeannie, whose husband, JRB, was away on business. They lived at Hotham Street, East Melbourne.

[2]   MR was not only in Melbourne to visit her relatives, but also to farewell three members of the Murchison family (Flora and her parents, Captain John and Mary Ann Murchison), who were sailing to Liverpool on the *Great Britain* for a visit to England. The Murchisons returned from England at the end of the year arriving on board the *Royal Standard* in December 1865.

[3]   James (Jim) Saddler (b. *c.*1837), son of Joseph Saddler and Sarah née Parr. He married Emily Caroline Eliza née Hodgson (b. *c.*1841) on 2 January 1862. In June 1864, James was appointed as clerk in a bank in Ballarat, where they set up home with their son, Edwin Harold (b. 1863). They became close friends of the Richardsons. Prior to their move, they were living in Powlett Street, East Melbourne, where they advertised 'Superior Board & Residence.' *The Argus,*

25 April 1863, p. 1. Annie Baxter Dawbin stayed with them after her husband, Robert, returned to England. Mrs Dawbin wrote an amusing eye-witness account of Emily Saddler's love affair with Dr James Edward Neild in her Journal. *Dawbin*, pp. 389–395, 410–414. Emily Saddler's second baby, Walter Augustus (named, perhaps, after WLR who delivered him), was born on 8 February 1865 in Ballarat, nine months after the affair with Dr Neild. There is another earlier connection between Emily Saddler and Mrs Dawbin, for in 1845 when Annie was living with her first husband, Andrew Baxter, in Yambuck in the Western District of Victoria, she met Evelyn Pitfield Shirley Sturt (1816–1885), the very much younger brother of the explorer Charles Sturt (1795–1869). They were sons of Thomas Sturt, a judge in Bengal under the East India Company. E. P. S. Sturt was then an unmarried squatter living further west in Victoria on the border with South Australia, and he travelled to Port Fairy for the races and social gatherings. He fell in love with Annie Baxter (as many men did) and she adored him but did not discover until 1862 how much he had loved her. See *Dawbin*, pp. xxvi and 289. E. P. S. Sturt was Emily Saddler's legal guardian (revealed on her marriage certificate on which it is noted that he gave consent to the marriage because she was only nineteen). Sturt, the quintessential gentleman, came from a landed gentry family in Dorset. He migrated to NSW in 1836, and was appointed Commissioner of Crown Lands (Yass, NSW). He resigned in 1839 to overland sheep and cattle from Bathurst to Adelaide and took up Compton Station in Mount Gambier district in 1844. Appointed as Police Magistrate in Melbourne in 1849, the next year he became Superintendent of Melbourne Police. In 1854, Sturt was appointed to the commission of inquiry into the Bentley Hotel affair at Ballarat. In 1861 was a member of the royal commission on the Burke and Wills expedition. He was President of the Melbourne Club. He married Mary, the daughter of the Reverend John Couch Grylls, Melbourne's first Anglican clergyman. de Serville, 1991, pp. 8–9, 341, 531.

4   Albert Watson.
5   The projected sailing date for the *Great Britain* was 15 March 1865 but she sailed a day later, bound for Liverpool.
6   Joseph Turnham had sent WLR a new brass doorplate.
7   Jane Bailey née Rainsford, wife of John Robinson Bailey.

97   [From WLR in Ballarat to MR in East Melbourne]

[Webster Street, Ballarat]
[Friday, 10 March 1865]

My dear dear Polly

I know you will like to hear from me altho I have no news to interest you—I am exceedingly busy It is very strange that the letters are not delivered at Toorak—I am writing this on Friday evening & I will post it myself before 6 so that you should get it Saturday morning—I spent Tuesday at the Saddlers & met Mrs Dawbin[1]—a wonderful woman plays & sings correctly & offered to ride any horse we could bring her—her rings[2] are a sight

Wednesday dined at the Mitchells a bachelor dinner & whist party—Thursday my chess club. Tonight O'Connor has asked me over—but as I dread Miss Mooney[3] & the musical box, I am doubtful whether I will go—

Hot morning. shower of rain about 1 cool since—

Hudson not back yet—I am sure the Saddlers can not go down—I enclose letter from Sam—

You did not say anything of the Turnhams or Leopold—or Ned! or the children[4]—

Be sure & stay away this month—I have nothing else to say as I am very tired—Pooley I saw this morning, he was going off by this morning's train to say good bye to the Murchisons but was taken suddenly ill—

Maria is very good, cleaning up putting up clean curtains &c & takes messages very correctly—

And now dearest you must excuse this, but really I am not able to write any more. English mail as you know has not yet been heard of—| Kind love to all & believe me| Your affect Husband

       W. Lindesay Richardson

      Text: ALS NLA MS133/1/88

[1]   Annie Baxter Dawbin (1816–1905) 'Drove to Ballaarat this morning; and just as I got there, in turning the street the horse slipped, & the driver thrown from the car, and hurt his ankle, but not seriously. I got the man to drive me to Drummond Street and found Mrs James [Saddler] ready to start down to meet me at the station: so we went instead, to call on Mrs Sherrard and Mr Rutter. In the evening Dr Richardson, Mrs Sherrard & her sister, Miss Welsh; were at Mrs James': we had some music, and quantities of scandal.', *Dawbin*, pp. 519–520.

[2]   Annie Baxter Dawbin had a fine collection of jewellery, including heirlooms. In a marriage settlement of 2 September 1857 (registered 24 July 1859), her jewellery and plate were transferred to William Rutledge and Horace Flower as trustees, to ensure that her assets were separated from those of her husband, Robert Dawbin. She often lent her jewellery to friends attending balls and commented in her Journal on 31 May 1863 that Lady Fleming 'had the bad taste to sew my exquisite sapphire ring on to the front of her dress, and placed a gold brooch over it! She had a crimson velvet wreath on her head, and my diamond brooch sewn on to it. Well, it is not my taste, and I like my friend better in her morning dress, than of an evening' *Dawbin*, p. 324.

[3]   Miss Mooney, a teacher of music, Sturt Street, Ballarat.

[4]   John Robinson Bailey's children: Harrie Elphinstone (aged eleven years three months), Emma (eight years six months), Gertrude Elizabeth (three) and Ida Beatrice (one year nine months).

98   [From WLR in Ballarat to MR in East Melbourne]

                                      [Webster Street, Ballarat]

                                Monday morning [13 March 1865]

My own dear Polly

    Yours written on the 10th & posted on 11th came to me this morning most unexpectedly at breakfast of course you have received before this, one I wrote & posted on Friday evening—I like your photograph very much—the one with the head on one side full face in the dress with the white border at the bottom is the best, and I should be very well with this even if he gives us no better. I send them back but should like to have kept it

    I think I will go down to Schnapper Point[1] for a fortnight as I do not feel at all equal to my work I went to church last night—but was obliged to <u>leave before the sermon</u>

    On Friday evening I went to O'Connors Saturday to chess club.

    Hudson arrived Saturday last train pressed me very much to go to dinner yesterday but as the Saddlers had given me an equally kind invitation for same hour and I did not feel good enough company I remained at home—There is every probability of rain today yesterday was one of [illegible word]—prayers were offered up in church last night for rain & altogether ruin is impending from drought—Black Hill works are about to be stopped—one squatter at Echuca lost 5000 sheep—I am so delighted you are enjoying yourself, it quite makes up for my suffering. I hope you remember my advice about the bathing not to stay in but just go in & then come out. I think by your feeling sleepy after it you stay in <u>too long</u> & if so you are better without it—

If you go giving away my likenesses there will be none left

To one of your questions I say Yes: you know which it is—

Jim says he cannot manage to go down—I am sure I cannot, <u>it would be quite impossible for me to bathe</u> at present.

1 PM I have just come in from my morning round, such a day <u>equal to Black Monday</u> only not so hot I am so pleased with your likenesses I should like <u>six of each</u> for my own self—but especially do I love thee in the <u>front picture </u>with that elegant dress—

Maria is behaving very well & making every thing as comfortable as possible for me—she does better than any other for she never bothers me to know what I'll <u>have</u>

I feel in a little better spirits today after seeing your dear face—still dont hurry home—you can do no good—I do get some sleep—

Send me up one of the other likenesses you get done—

Mrs Saddler & Jim kindly came down to see me last night about 8—very kind was it not?—

You cannot see the Turkish Baths. I dread going out this afternoon

Say good bye to Flora for me

I have seen none of the Cuthberts since you left—I or Nixon

Good bye dearest—God bless you |says your affect

     Walter

Text: ALS NLA MS133/1/108

---

1   Schnapper Point was where Thomas and Anne Jelfs had a property.

99   [From WLR in Ballarat to MR in East Melbourne]

            [Webster Street, Ballarat]

            Wednesday [15 March 1865]

[No salutation]

Your letter dated 14th reached me my own dear Polly this morning, with one from Ned—I was much pleased to receive your dear picture again, and can now make you happy by saying that since my last I <u>am better </u>so you need not be in a hurry back but can stay and derive the full benefit of your trip—Monday was a second edition of black Monday without the fires towards evening heavy rain set in & fell in torrents most of the night—

The Saddlers had arranged for a whist party but in consequence of the rain it did not come off: Yesterday Tuesday, I took tea at Hudsons, & found them very happy & pleased with the house, which is indeed very nice, I afterwards went to the Saddlers, & met M^r & Mrs Sturt,[1] & Welsh[2] & we had a rubber—they had asked me up to dinner to eat a goose, but I <u>quite forgot all</u> about it till 8 oclock. Today was showery & very unfavorable for the review[3] & the show[4]

I hope you are still enjoying yourself—Mrs S. says she misses you very much—

You will have to do without me for I do not see how the house could be left without one of us: other reasons also prevent me from accepting <u>Neds invitation</u>

9 P.M. Jim has just popped in to borrow a pair of white kids[5] fortunately I found a new pair—they are going to the Volunteer Ball[6] both of them. The Wynnes[7] called & took them to the show & review—

16 [Thursday]. I got a letter from Brighton[8] this morning there are none for you as yet. I presume you will get them by Ned—Henry Caroline's Husband has been appointed Registrar to the Court of Probate Cork a very good billet & they have left Dublin—

It is a fine pleasant morning after the rain—Sickness has somewhat abated—The ball was not very crowded last night—the old set were there. Sherards[9] of course

I suppose I may expect the Kabats up by the ½ past 8 train on Friday. I will have dinner ready by 4 the second week of my bachelorhood is nearly over—

I do not think of any more news to interest you I will send you down the £5–0–0 in my next weeks letter—I send you the Star with the acct. of the doings yesterday—

It was very cold last night, I could not get to sleep for some hours—Good bye dearest says| Your lonely husband

WLR

Text: ALS NLA MS133/1/83

[1] Henry Onslow Sturt (b. 1828), a law clerk in Ballarat, born in Kensington, London, the son of George Sturt, a banker, and Jane née Ward; probably a nephew of E. P. S. Sturt. "Mr G. Sturt, from Ballaarat, brought his intended to see Mrs Saddler; she is a sister of Mrs Coppin', and there is some queer story of her sister' marriage with the actor." *Dawbin*, p. 481. Mr Sturt may have used a nickname but his initial was not 'G'. He married Harriette Sarah Hillsden in 1865, the daughter of Harriette Coppin, formerly Hillsden née Bray, who had died in 1859 aged thirty-eight, leaving two daughters by her first marriage and three by her second to George Selth Coppin (1819–1906), the actor and theatrical entrepreneur and elected member of the Legislative Council (1858). In 1861, Lucy Hillsden married her stepfather George Selth Coppin, and baby Ada Lucy was born seven months later, followed by two sons and four more daughters. Harriette Sturt née Hillsden died aged thirty-one in 1876.

[2] Patricus William Welsh, head of a large merchant-house in early Melbourne; bankrupted in the economic depression in the 1840s, he resurfaced in Ballarat as an estate agent. Paul de Serville, *Port Phillip Gentlemen*, pp. 58–9, 153, 156. Welsh was a neighbour of the Richardsons on Webster Street and the father of Isabella Sherard.

[3] The Governor, Sir Charles H. Darling and his wife and daughter visited Ballarat for a review of the Ballarat Rangers but the rain was so heavy that instead of arriving on the Tuesday evening, they had to arrive by a special train on Wednesday at noon. The Ballarat Volunteer Rangers were drawn up at the platform and the Ballarat Troop of Cavalry were drawn up outside to greet the official party. The previous week a deputation from the Ballarat Agricultural Society had travelled to Melbourne to meet with the Governor's aide to negotiate the visit's schedule so that the National Grain Show, which was scheduled for the same day, would not be injured by the counter attraction. The Ballarat Volunteer Rangers accompanied His Excellency from Craig's Royal Hotel to the National Grain Show at the show yards, with the procession headed by Captain Sherard's troop of light horse.

[4] The National Grain Show.

[5] Gloves made out of the skin of baby goat.

[6] 'A grand volunteer ball was held in the evening in the hall of the Mechanics Institute, and was very numerously attended. Although the hall was not decorated at all the ball did not lack in brilliancy of appearance. The officers of the Volunteer staff and the officers of the several corps in town were in attendance, and their uniforms and those of the several members of the different corps present lent a pleasing variety to the picture ... Dancing began soon after 10 p.m., and was kept up with brief intermissions until this morning had nearly dawned. A new polka was composed by Mr Austin T. Turner, the well-known music maker and conductor of the Vocal Union, "The Ballarat Review Polka".' *Star*, 16 March 1865, p. 4.

[7] Edward Agar Wynne (b. 1827) and his first wife, Sarah Maria née Palmer; she died in 1882 aged fifty-five and he remarried in 1884 to Rebecca Maude née Samuel. He was a squatter and involved as a company director in the mining industry. By the time of this letter, the Wynnes had six children born in Ballarat, two of whom had died as infants. His son Agar Wynne was a solicitor and friend of Henry Cuthbert with whom he became a partner in 1877. In WLR's Probate of Will dated 2 October 1879 by the Supreme Court of the Colony of Victoria, there is

a note signed on the front by Cuthbert and Wynne indicating that they were paid £18–10–0 on 14 October 1879 for their services. NLA MS133/1/272.

8 Presumably from his mother. The letter has not survived. The Cheynes moved from Brighton to Lochmaben (Scotland) in late 1864 or early 1865.

9 Isabella Morrison Sherard née Welsh (b. 1834) and Charles Wale Sherard (1820–1889), Warden of the Ballarat Goldfield.

100 [From WLR in Ballarat to MR in Pentridge, Melbourne][1]

[Webster Street, Ballarat]
Monday [20 March 1865]

My own dear Polly

I was very dissapointed at there being no letter on Saturday and again this morning Yours of 18th reached me however this afternoon, you are always going to write a long one next time but that next time never seems to arrive—Yes, the Kabats came on Friday & Maria had a nice dinner a few freinds dropped in during evening & we amused ourselves M[rs] S.[2] keeping saying how strange it appears that there is no M[rs] R. They remained on Saturday & left Sunday morning. I was glad to see them to relieve the fearful dullness & monotony of a silent house even Dilly's[3] screaming was some relief—M[rs] K wrote the enclosed & put it in an envelope I did not see why I should send an envelope—so I read it

And so you really think you will be ready to come to my arms this week—I shall have forgotten how to kiss having been so out of practice

Forbes[4] has left but I may go down to Geelong on Saturday to meet you—I do not intend to go to Melbourne Hudson never told me he had a letter from you—He certainly offered to see my patients but theres sure to be some rows if I go away I am far from well yet in fact I have been very very poorly since you left I thought last Sunday week that I should have to keep in bed—and altho I would dearly love to have you back yet I do not want to spoil your trip—I miss your nice little dishes

Yesterday Sunday I dined at the Saddlers very pleasantly: tomorrow evening I have a few bachelors for a rubber I am not busy now—

Ask Turnham how much I am indebted for the door plate and I will send him a crossed cheque

No letters for you from home Weather is pleasant—

We lunched at Pooleys on Saturday so well that we could eat no dinner—I suppose you enjoyed Neds party[5] altho you do not say one word about it—

I was up at ½ past six this morning to M[rs] W. M. Brown[6] got it over by 8 I went & took a bath I have been too ill to have any since you left—

I have lost about 10 lbs weight

Kind regards to Joe & Aunty & ask when they are coming up again—I suppose your next will be your last—I enclose a crossed cheque for £5–1–0—to be paid thro Neds acct—

God bless you dearest & bring you safely back to your own| dear & fond husband

Walter

Text: ALS NLA MS133/1/91

1 MR was staying with the Turnhams at Pentridge.
2 Mrs Emily Saddler.

³   Antoinette Kabat then aged almost four.
⁴   A. J. Forbes, mining manager, or Charles Forbes, veterinary surgeon. Was the plan that WLR
    would travel with him?
⁵   Presumably Ned's thirty-seventh birthday party.
⁶   Margaret Brown née McGuckin (married to William Maxwell Brown) gave birth to Rosa Ada
    Brown. William Maxwell Brown was the Manager of the Theatre Royal, Ballarat, in the 1860s.
    WLR's midwifery cases for 1865 were in a new record book, which has not survived.

1866

101 [From WLR in Ballarat to MR in East Melbourne¹]

[Webster Street, Ballarat]

Tuesday evening [23 January 1866]

My dear Polly

I have been too busy to write before and have had nothing to say

No news of any sort to interest you. All well ~~An open~~ I have been so busy with
Influenza & I have had to perform Tracheotomy both yesterday & today two different
children diptheria in the wind wipe [pipe]²

Kind regards to all—| Your affect | Husband

WLR

I am a little better this morning but still very poorly—Wednesday morning

Text: ALS NLA MS133/1/97

¹   MR had gone down to stay at Hotham Street, East Melbourne, with her brother John Robinson
    Bailey, whose second wife, Jeannie, was expecting her third baby, Mary Jane.
²   Diphtheria causes the development of a false membrane on the mucous membrane connected
    with the throat.

102 [From WLR in Ballarat to MR in East Melbourne]¹

[Webster Street, Ballarat]

Thursday [25 January 1866]

My dear Polly

I have been very ill with this confounded Infl[uenza]: for two or three days—I had made
up my mind to telegraph to you this morning if not better; but I am happy to say I am—

I had to refuse to go out to several cases yesterday evening & had to send Bunce to a
confinement in the night—I was just able to crawl down stairs with the shawl over my
head—I had a letter from Ned this morning he tells you you have had the same: I hope you
went to bed and that you are now better also that you were not so bad as I was: Tell John²
North Clunes were sold yesterday here at £7–0–0—Holthouse³ was offered 6–10–0—It is a
certain fortune: I have seen the stone & by no means the best specimen—There is ten years

work to get out the stone between where we have struck it & the Victoria <u>without opening</u> <u>any more ground</u>

John might get <u>some cheap in Melb</u>: to bring down the price of his: mine do not stand me more than £12–0–0 with this call pair—The old shaft is right over it—& where the Victoria are crushing from yields 10 dwts to the ton: No news to interest you—No sign of the Yorkshire[4] 81 days from Plymouth on Sunday—I shall not be sorry to see the notice of her arrival

I suppose I feel your absence more because I am so poorly. Nights are fearful

If you were to see a nice small scarf necktie—

No home letters for you

Two for me—

A little better today: You had as bad an attack as I had

Much love| Your affect Hubby

W.

Text: ALS NLA MS133/1/96

1 Writing paper has the Richardson family crest.
2 John Robinson Bailey.
3 Dr Thomas Le Gay Holthouse (*c.*1819–1901).
4 The *Yorkshire* finally arrived on 22 March 1866 after taking 140 days to make the passage from Plymouth. WLR's anxiety was because on board as a passenger was his nephew, Alexander Richardson, who was emigrating to Australia.

103 [From WLR in Ballarat to MR in East Melbourne]

[Webster Street] Ballt:

Feby: 22. 66 Thursday morning[1]

My dear Polly

I received your letter <u>only this morning</u> It was posted in Ballt. <u>yesterday afternoon</u>—so the postman says—Who was entrusted with it?—

Of course I was much shocked to receive Ned's telegram about ½ past 10 and feel deeply for John: Your letter this morning fills me again with grief—What an unfortunate thing ~~that~~

I hope Tracy will see you every day—

I had intended to have gone down to the funeral but as it took place <u>yesterday</u> of course it was <u>out of the question</u>

Leopold left—All are well—

I enclose crossed cheque for £5–0–0   Ned will cash it for you—do not hurry back—what about taking the baby?[2]

Ask Ned to write me about your hand—Kind remembrances to all| Your

Walter

Text: ALS NLA MS133/1/110

1 John Robinson Bailey's second wife Jeannie (Jane Rainsford) died on 21 February 1866 aged thirty-five, of puerperal fever. Their address was Hotham Street, East Melbourne. (Death Reg. no. 2466). She was buried in Boroondara Cemetery on 21 February. Dr Richard T. Tracy had attended her.
2 Mary Jane Bailey (b. 12 February 1866) was just nine days old when her mother, Jeannie, died. John had two living children by his first wife and two others (excluding the new baby) by

Jeannie. They were: Harrie Elphinstone Bailey, aged twelve when his stepmother died (he was sent to Scotch College where he remained for the year); Emma aged nine-and-a-half; Gertrude Elizabeth aged four; and Ida Beatrice aged two years nine months.

104 [From WLR in Ballarat to MR in Streatham[1]]

[Webster Street, Ballarat]
Friday [23 March 1866]

My dear Polly

I got your note yesterday & was glad to find you had reached Streatham safely. I have not seen Mackay[2] yet but Pooley[3] told me last evening that he had reached Carngham & spent the night at Russells[4] coming on here yesterday Thursday.

I hope you will enjoy your trip—I enclose you letters from Flora,[5] John Neds is here there is nothing in it—

The day ~~of~~ necessary for me to go to Melbourne has been altered to the 24th April[6] so that you will have plenty of time to enjoy yourself

Sickness thank God has slacked off—

It rained nicely last evening & this morning showery & heavy rain I applied for your Newington scrip—I cannot get it without the receipt paper you got from Wynn[7]—They are down to £1–17–6 Nixon[8] bought some at that price—No more news—kind regards to M[r] & M[rs] K—and remain| Your aff. H.
                W.

Text: ALS NLA MS133/1/92

[1]   MR had set off on Tuesday, 20 March 1866 to visit Emily and Leopold Kabat, who were living in Hamilton.
[2]   George Gordon Mackay.
[3]   William Thomas Pooley (1813–1872), the Deputy Registrar.
[4]   Phillip Russell (c.1822–1892), pastoralist, MLC. Born in Fifeshire, he was the son of James Russell, farmer, and his wife Elizabeth Couper. The Russell family and twelve other families held some million and a half acres across Victoria. Philip Russell held 22,285 acres at Carngham (where he lived and died) and 18,088 acres at Langi Willi. de Serville, 1991, pp. 149, 333, 487.
[5]   Flora Agnes Fetherstonhaugh née Murchison (1844–1931).
[6]   It is not clear why WLR had to go to Melbourne but 24 April was the day that WLR said he had seen the four-month-old baby, Henry Herbert Cuthbert, three days before he died of 'muco enteritis'. If he had indeed gone to Melbourne, WLR was certainly back in Ballarat on 27 April when he certified the baby's death. Whether WLR certified the real cause of death still remains a mystery. See Chapter 4.
[7]   Edward Agar Wynne.
[8]   William Nixon (1833–1905), Henry Cuthbert's brother-in-law, was the informant of Henry Herbert Cuthbert's death to William Pooley (the Deputy Registrar) and was a witness at his burial on 29 April 1866.

105 [From WLR in Ballarat to MR in Hamilton]

[Webster Street, Ballarat]

<u>Tuesday afternoon</u> [27 March 1866]

My dearest P:

Yours reached me this morning—Hope Leopold[1] has not Scarlatina or Diptheria—but that you are all well—& enjoying the change: Jane[2] is doing very well—I dined with Mrs Saddler[3] on Sunday & at Hudsons last evening, met the Emblings[4] rubber and some good fun He sang & accomp himself <u>Maid of Judah in German</u> Bridegroom[5] &c.

<u>I saw no conceit</u> or very little certainly no bumptiousness—Mrs E. very plain—

I was out all the hrs last night: & have now a bad case of Placenta Praevia on—

Invitation to party at Morrisons[6] for Tuesday April 2nd[7]—

You must sign the enclosed & get it witnessed—

Newingtons had a run on them yesterday sold at £4–0–0 then back to 3–10–0 Dons up to <u>£5–0–0</u> I send todays Star with this—No other news—

Kind regards to the Kabats| Your affect H

W—

Text: ALS NLA MS133/1/95

[1] Captain Leopold Kabat (1832–1884), Inspector of Police at Hamilton.

[2] Jane was the Richardsons' servant.

[3] Emily Caroline Elizabeth Saddler née Hodgson, married to Jim Saddler.

[4] Dr William Henry Embling (1840–1912) was the son of Dr Thomas Embling and Jane Webb Embling neé Chinnock. He married Elizabeth Harding Austin in 1866. On 23 September 1866, their first son, Austin Henry, was born prematurely and died that day. They had seven more children (four born in Ballarat) who all survived infancy. His father, Dr Thomas Embling (1814–1893), medical practitioner and parliamentarian, was born on 26 August 1814 at Oxford, England, son of John Embling, a breechesmaker, and his wife Sarah née Edwards. Apprenticed at the age of sixteen to an apothecary, he then studied medicine in London. He married Jane Webb née Chinnock (1820–1887), daughter of an upholsterer; they had three sons (including Dr William Henry Embling) and four daughters. In 1851 the family emigrated to Melbourne because of 'pulmonary infections' in Thomas and Jane. In 1852 Embling became the first resident medical officer to Yarra Bend Lunatic Asylum but his reforms (such as removing manacles from inmates) angered the Colonial Surgeon and his position became untenable. He resigned and returned to private practice in Gore Street, Fitzroy. He supported the popular movement at Eureka in December 1854 and won the seat of North Bourke in the Victorian Legislative Assembly in 1855. A keen supporter of the Eight Hours Work reform, he is credited with coining the phrase: 'Eight hours labour, eight hours recreation, eight hours rest'. He was defeated in the 1861 election and, after being re-elected in 1866, he left politics and returned to private practice. He died of senile debility on 17 January 1893.

[5] Possibly the Scottish air, 'The Bridegroom grat when the sun went down'.

[6] Malcolm McNeil Morison and his wife, Emily née Newcomen. He was the Manager of the Commercial Bank of Australia.

[7] Tuesday was 3 April 1866. The only Tuesday 2 April would have been in 1861 and the context of this letter is clearly 1866.

106 [From WLR in Ballarat to MR in Hamilton]

[Webster Street, Ballarat]

Friday afternoon [6 April 1866]

My own dear Polly

Yours dated April 3rd reached me last night at 12 oclock—it had been brought down by
the coach & not posted—I had been out all day & taken away to a confinement at 5 oclock
kept there till 12 a case of twins[1]—

I am glad to see you are enjoying yourself & that the thumb is better—You will have
seen what sort of a place Portland is—it would take us 3 months to clear out of this—but I
should [missing words] the change & [especially the] sea-side—it would [missing words] up to
I am sure [missing words]

I dined at Hudsons[2] [missing word] evening—on the Turkey [missing words] went to
see "Arrah na pogue"[3] on Tuesday very much pleased I am going to Melbourne tomorrow
morning Saturday,[4] will be back on Monday—so that when you get this I will most likely be
at home again I am very busy & hardly know how to manage leaving—

. Mrs Saddler promised to write you yesterday—of course I shall go to Johns he wrote me
a letter & asked me—Ned also wrote one of his epistles, about being determined to "protect
her" "innocent creature"[5] &c.—the spooney[6]—

You will have been away 3 weeks next Tuesday—

[Missing corner] for some poor [missing words] You will be glad to hear that
Newingtons were sold at [£]4–12–6 on Thursday—going down with the shaft well—about 40
feet on Saturday night—Jane is doing as well as she can: I see she has washed the things but
stupid like she has put them up again—

You will not get this before Monday—Remember me kindly to the Kabats—Very cold
here

Mrs Cuth[7] & Mrs O.[8] called today   Mrs Stewart D^r[9] asked us to her house last
Thursday—| Good bye Your loving| Hubby

WLR

X [kiss]

Text: ALS NLA MS133/1/94 [Damaged]

1 Unfortunately all WLR's cases for 1866 were recorded in a second Registry of Cases, which did
not survive.
2 Dr Robert Fawell Hudson and his wife Elizabeth Ann who married in 1865.
3 *Arrah-na-Pogue* was an operetta by Dion Boucicault (1822–1890), an Irish dramatist and actor.
It was first performed in 1864 in London. Boucicault was born in Dublin on 26 December
1822, the illegitimate son of the sister of George Darley (1795–1846), mathematician and poet,
and Dr Dionysius Lardner (1793–1859), who wrote works on algebraic geometry (1823) and
the calculus (1825), and was best known as the originator and editor of *Lardner's Cyclopædia*
(132 vols 1830–1844). Dion Boucicault lived in France, then England, and then moved to the
USA in the 1850s. His most famous work was the comedy *London Assurance* (1841). The
production seen by WLR had opened at the Theatre Royal, Ballarat, on Saturday, 31 March
1866 and was advertised as having 'entirely new scenery, under the personal superintendence of
Mr John Hennings of the Theatre Royal, Melbourne' and starred the celebrated American
tragedian, Mr J. H. Allen. *Star*, 31 March 1866, p. 1.
4 WLR's name appeared in the list of graduates at the Conferring Ceremony at the University of
Melbourne held on Saturday, 7 April 1866. He was admitted to the degree of Doctor of
Medicine (*ad eundem gradum* Edinburgh). A dinner was held in the evening at the University.
The Argus, 7 April 1866, p. 2. The name immediately above WLR's in the list of graduates
published in *The Argus* was that of Charles Kernot (1845–1909) who graduated with a BA (first
class in civil engineering) and became the first Professor of Engineering at the University.

Kernot's younger brother, Percy White Kernot (1866–1943) was to marry Mary Amelia Robertson (1866–1954), who was HHR's schoolfriend at the PLC. The two women renewed their friendship after the publication of *GW* in 1910 and continued their correspondence until HHR's death on 20 March 1946.

5   Ned (Edward Harold) Bailey married Agnes Eleanor Hablethwaite on 1 May 1866 at her home, 28 Brunswick Street, Fitzroy, Melbourne. The ceremony was performed by William Potter, Pastor of the Howe Crescent Baptist Church. Samuel Bailey, the groom's brother, and Jessie Hablethwaite, the bride's sister, were the witnesses.

6   Foolishly or sentimentally amorous.

7   Emma Wilmer Cuthbert née Kirby (c.1836–1877), married to Henry Cuthbert. Their second son, Henry Herbert, who had been born on 15 December 1865, died three weeks later on 27 April 1866.

8   Anne Ochiltree née Graham (1831–1874) was married to William Bertram Ochiltree (c.1830–1898), the Manager of the Ballarat branch of the Bank of NSW. See endnotes to Letter 80 for short biography..

9   Anne Francis Stewart née Taylor, married to Dr James Stewart.

107 [From WLR in Ballarat to MR in Melbourne]

[Webster Street, Ballarat]

Thursday morning [11 May 1866[1]]

My dear Polly

    I am very much dissappointed at your not coming up today: There may be a great deal of difficulty about Alicks[2] bill of exchange: & it may not be payable except to himself personally—You had better not delay any longer <u>but come at once.</u> I should prefer your [coming] by this evengs train—

    But I shall excuse you if you will go <u>now</u> with John—either to Tracy or Dougan Bird[3]—this afternoon—bring up the prescription or get it made up & begin taking the remedies at once—I am sorry that Alick has made so bad a commencement by getting into debt—I had made all arrangements for your coming up this afternoon & think I had better not make any more as I do not know when to expect you now—

    <u>I have nothing</u> to do & if you were at home could take you out nicely & enjoy ourselves when I want to do so I suppose I shall be busy again & prevented—| Your affect Hubby

       W

Text: ALS NLA MS133/1/82

1   This is a tentative date for there is not much information in the letter to be accurate. However Alexander Richardson, WLR's nephew, arrived on 22 March 1866. MR was away at the end of March and early April visiting the Kabats in Hamilton. She and WLR very probably would have attended Ned Bailey's wedding on 1 May 1866. It is very likely that WLR would have returned to Ballarat after the celebrations and that she would have stayed on with her recently widowed brother, JRB, and his children.

2   Alexander Richardson (1845–1900), nephew of WLR, emigrated on the *Yorkshire*, which arrived on 22 March 1866.

3   Samuel Dougan Bird (1832–1904), physician and university lecturer; born in Lichfield, Staffordshire; educated at Kings College Hospital (LRCP, 1851 and MRCSE, 1854) and University of St Andrews (MD, 1859). He worked at the Hospital for Consumption, Brompton, and in private practice in Richmond, England; spent 1854–55 as a divisional surgeon and served at Sebastopol. In 1860, discovering that he had tuberculosis, he and his family took a sea-trip and visited Melbourne; he returned with his wife and son in February 1862 and became physician to the Benevolent Asylum & Immigrants Aid Society. Although a leading physician in Victoria, he failed in 1865 to be elected as an honorary physician for

Melbourne Hospital but succeeded in election as the first honorary physician elected to the
Alfred Hospital when it opened in 1871. He was President of the Medical Society of Victoria in
1869 and became a lecturer in the medical faculty at the University of Melbourne the same year.
He married first, in 1856, Catherine Tate who died in 1869; second, in 1872, Susan Brown
who died in 1882; third, in 1883, Eleanor Rossiter.

108 [From Dr Bayne Cheyne in Lochmaben, Scotland, to WLR in Ballarat]

Bank House| Lochmaben| Dumfriesshire| N.B.[1]

[20 June 1866]

My Dear Walter

It now becomes my duty a sad & painful one to acquaint you with the fatal termination
of your mother's illness. She died calmly this morning about 10 minutes before 11.
Dr Macullochs[2] practice seemed to be endeavouring to produce reaction through the Bowels,
but none took place. I had small hopes of any, & I dare say D^r M's were not much greater
I cannot enter more into details respecting the complaint now.[3]

It has been settled that your ever dear Mother will be interred in the Church yard of this
town in a place where no other grave has been yet made. The funeral will take place on the
25th Inst.

I believe that your mother's faith in the Lord & her love of Him was genuine & stedfast
and if so we must infer that she has made a happy change

I am glad that your health is so far established as to permit you to continue your
profession The risk however to all of us is, that our secular work may overbear the work of our
salvation which although gratuitous on God's part, requires on ours much careful & earnest
study much self denial much perseverance, which after all will only be effectual by God's
working in us & for us but this is promised by Him who is the true & the faithful one| Yours
My Dear Walter| affectionately

B.C.

Text: ALS NLA MS133/1/44

[1]   The home of George and Grace Cheyne. See endnote 5 to Letter 91 for description of the
      house. 'N.B.' means 'North Britain'.
[2]   Dr James M. McCulloch, a physician from Dumfries.
[3]   The Lochmaben Parish Register of Deaths records that Lucinda Cheyne, married to Bayne
      Cheyne, MD, died on 20 June 1866 at 10.55 a.m. at Bruce Street, Lochmaben. She was aged
      seventy, the daughter of Henry and Harriet Sirée; it incorrectly records her mother's maiden
      name as 'Macascle' (McCausland). The cause of her death, which was certified by
      Dr McCulloch, was 'Apoplexy', after an illness of about three days. Dr Cheyne, the informant
      of her death at which he was present, registered her death on 25 June 1866 with Hugh B.
      Currie, the Registrar.

1867–1868

Sojourn in England

1867

109 [From WLR in London, England, to MR in Brighton, England][1]

7 Victoria Gardens [London][2]

Monday Evening [13 May 1867]

My dear "Marie"

Sarah[3] tells me that you will not get this until tomorrow afternoon—If I had known this I would have written this morning—On Saturday I went over the Surgical Home[4] and then out to Hanwell

Sunday with Sarah to the Catholic Apostolic Central Church Gordon Square[5] morning & to Westminster Abbey[6] Evening—We arrived there at ¼ past 6 (service commenced at 7) & found the old Abbey nearly full—I estimated the number about 1800

Today I went to Cooks,[7] Fleet St. & then to see Harrie[8] at Tottenham—He is pretty well & getting on nicely no complaint against him—I dined with M[r] White[9] & his family—& came home very tired to write this—We were glad to hear that you had arrived safely

What a blessing that the little Indian[10] is behaving herself at last! Sarah will write some other time she is worried to death about that good for nothing hussy of hers—It is difficult to know what to decide upon as to our Paris trip—A month will cost us £40–0–0 but for that we will see Paris & Exhibition[11] go right across France from Paris to Switzerland see Lake Lucerne & Lake of Geneva & return to Paris & home—

I suppose I had better come down[12] to see you all, as you are not coming up to me; you may expect me then by the 3.40 train on Tuesday—I suppose I shall see your face this time and with love to all

I am my dear wife| Your faithful & true

W.L.R.

Text: ALS NLA 133/1/148

1   The writing paper with Richardson family crest.

2   WLR and MR set sail for England on 3 January 1867 on the triple-masted clipper, the *Red Jacket*, which arrived in London on Sunday, 7 April 1867. Harrie Elphinstone Bailey, John Robinson Bailey's eldest son, aged thirteen, travelled with them and was enrolled in a school in Tottenham, London.

3   Sarah Ann Bailey (1829–1911), eldest daughter of John Bailey and Elizabeth Bailey née Robinson.

4   The Surgical Home was a private hospital at Notting Hill, where two large houses had been 'thrown together' and where Mr Baker Brown was successfully operating on *prolapsus uteri*. WLR refers to a visit to this hospital in 'A Letter from Home', *The Australian Medical Journal*, vol. XII, December 1867. He wrote four letters from home which were published as follows: August 1867, in which he describes the voyage on the *Red Jacket*, visits to London, Cork, Dublin and Sussex; September 1867, written in the first week of July in Edinburgh, describing hospitals and asylums in Dublin, Edinburgh and Leicester; December 1867, written in September in London after their trip to Paris, describing visits to hospitals and treatments in Paris and London; and February 1868, written from Manchester (Eccles) in November 1867, in which he included a reference to a recent conversation with Dr Bayne Cheyne, 'a name well known in medical literature, in connection with the early reports of typhus, and the pathology of croup'—but did not reveal that Cheyne was his stepfather, although presumably his friends in the medical profession would have known his relationship.

5   The cathedral of the Catholic and Apostolic, or Irvingite, body in Gordon Square had been built by followers of the Scottish preacher, Edward Irving (1792–1834). He was born on 2 August 1792 in Annan, enrolled at the University of Edinburgh when thirteen, and became first a schoolmaster and then gained a licence to preach in 1815. In 1819 he was appointed assistant to Dr Thomas Chalmers (1780–1847), who founded the Free Church of Scotland in 1843. Irving was called to the Caledonian Church, Hatton Garden, London, in 1822, where his success as a preacher was unprecedented. In 1825 he began to preach on the imminent second advent of Christ and followed this three years later by asserting Christ's oneness with us all in the attributes of humanity. At the same time he became deeply involved in prophecies and in 1830 he believed in extraordinary manifestations of prophetic power, occurring in Dunbartonshire. He was arraigned before the Presbytery of London in 1830 and convicted of heresy; he was ejected from his new church in Regent's Square in 1832. His followers stuck by his views and a new community, the Catholic Apostolic, was developed, commonly known as Irvingite, though Irving had little to do with its development. His health failed and he died in Glasgow of consumption on 8 December 1834. *Chambers*, pp. 196, 521.

6   Westminster Abbey was probably on the site of a pagan temple and the first abbey was erected in the seventh century. It was rebuilt by Edward the Confessor (reigned 1055–1065), and consecrated on 28 December 1065. It was rebuilt in magnificent style by Henry III in 1220–1269 and periodically added to, with cloisters, windows and chapels, over the following centuries. The 800th anniversary of the foundation was celebrated on 28 December 1865 (Mary Richardson's thirtieth birthday).

7   Travel Agency run by Thomas Cook (1808–1892), railway excursion and tourist pioneer. Cook was born in Melbourne, Derbyshire, and his first organised railway trip (a temperance one) was from Leicester to Loughborough in 1841. *Chambers*, pp. 243–244.

8   Harrie Elphinstone Bailey (b. 1853), son of John Robinson Bailey and his first wife Susannah Tyler née Nicholson. Harrie was soon removed from that school and placed in Mr Craig's school in Fairfield, near Eccles, where WLR was locum from October to December 1867 before they moved to Rawcliffe, Yorkshire.

9   Probably George White, principal of the English and Foreign Collegiate School, 152 Kentish Town Road, N. W. London. J. S. C. Morris, *The Business Directory of London* (London: Morris, 1867).

10   Probably referring to Grace Bailey, MR's sister. It was suggested by Axel Clark that this letter was circa 1874 but for several reasons (i.e., references to Harrie, to the Paris Exhibition, the style of salutation and ending) it should be dated 1867 and thus the phrase 'little Indian' cannot refer to Ethel Florence Lindesay Richardson (HHR), who was not born until 3 January 1870.

11   The French government and the city of Paris sponsored l'Exposition Universelle de 1867 which took place on the Champ de Mars, the military parade ground on the left bank of the River Seine; about 43,000 exhibitions were shown, and more than 6.8 million visitors attended, including Queen Victoria's second daughter, Princess Alice, the Grand Duchess of Hesse.

Emperor and Empress of France, Napoléon III and Eugénie, entertained almost all the crowned heads of Europe during that summer.

12   MR was probably staying with her sister Lizzie Brett whose husband, Captain John Brett, was in the Rifle Brigade and stationed in Brighton before they moved to Devonport some months later.

110 [From WLR in Edinburgh, Scotland, to MR in Leicester, England]

[Edinburgh]
Friday Evening [5 July 1867]

My dear Marie

Your nice long letter with enclosures from Mother and Grace[1] was very welcome. I am obliged to them for thinking of me—I hope your mother keeps well—

Edinburgh is too cold a place for me[2] and it will not be advisable for me to stay out the fortnight the wind is always East or North—You will have the pleasure of seeing me then on Monday or Tuesday. I want The North British[3] is the line and the train leaves about 9 am & gets to Leicester 7.30 or so—

Give my love to all—I suppose you wrote to Bayne[4] What an extraordinary letter about the lady!

I hope your budget of Australian letters amused you—They want us back you see: Leopold must have been pretty well "cocked" when he wrote that—

I like the people here very well, but the climate!

I cannot get what I want in lodging. No milk or dried fish—and as I do not see much advancement in physick,[5] I hardly think I need run any risk but may at once go South, for it seems there is no summer going to be here at all

With love, again—I may write again but as you would not get it before Monday night why you may see me same time, or Tuesday if I do not write again| Yours faithfully,

Walter

Text: ALS NLA MS133/1/158

1   MR's youngest sister, Grace Bailey (1839–1934).
2   'I write this in Edinburgh where in June, last week, the daily heat was about 65º in the shade and the nightly cold about 45º.' WLR, 'Another Letter from Home', *AMJ*, vol. XXII, September 1867, p. 274.
3   North British Railway Company, Head Office, Canal Street, Edinburgh.
4   Dr Bayne Cheyne (1785–1868), stepfather of WLR.
5   See *FRM II*, pp. 62–63.

111 [From WLR in Edinburgh, Scotland, to MR in Leicester, England]

[Edinburgh]
Monday morning [7 July 1867]

My dear Wifey

I thought I should have had a letter from you this morning but perhaps you did not get mine early on Saturday I start from this tomorrow morning Tuesday by the train that leaves this on the North British Line at 9.45 am and gets in to Leicester at 7.45 PM. We had a warm day on Sunday but the East wind is at it again today—I enclose you another letter from Bayne

Have you written? You see the distress you have unwittingly created—I think by that he is fond of you—

Of course I shall look out for your dear face at the station and shall see you a long way off—Have a little nice supper ready, of something you know I like, with a cup of coffee—Kind love to your ma and Gracy I hope you enjoyed your visit to "the Gorse"[1]—Good bye and God bless you| Your faithful and true

    W

Text: ALS NLA MS133/1/159

[1]   MR had been staying in Scotland with WLR, visiting his stepfather, Dr Bayne Cheyne, in Lochmaben but she departed for Leicester leaving WLR to spend more time visiting the hospitals and the university in Edinburgh.

112 [From WLR in Eccles, England, to MR in Leicester, England]

[Eccles, Manchester, Lancashire][1]
Saturday 6 PM: [28 September 1867][2]

My dear dear M.

I am afraid you have been overdoing it—You should keep in bed & apply hot fomentations around the seat of pain—Dont hurry back if you are not better on Monday, of course it is dull but come back well—

M[r] & M[rs] Beech called on Thursday <u>nice people,</u> he is something like General Yorke[3] Yesterday I was out walking & met the clergyman, M[r] Sayers & wife, I lifted my hat & he spoke & we walked some distance together He is an Irishman and of a better class than we have accustomed to meet abroad—

They said they hoped to have the pleasure of seeing you when you return. We shall have lots of visitors next week I am sure.

I'll get the carpet down on Monday in case Carries[4] sister[5] I told you has arrived they expect M[rs] Fisher[6] this evening—William[7] returned Friday evening—The oak chest & chest of drawers arrived this morning <u>all</u> the <u>drawers except one open,</u> but apparently not meddled with—Annie[8] is behaving very well indeed she cooks capitally and is getting every thing cleaned up

<u>Do keep quiet Sunday</u> and rest yourself Your mother ought to be able to nurse you

Bradshaw[9] I enclose 11.23 & 12.0. one the shortest 3 hours & 48 minutes—The nights & days are <u>very cold</u>—we shall feel this winter very much

I had a newspaper from H.H[10] in America today—Give my kind love to Mother to Grace & lots to some body else—You know dear my letters are never burnt so must be careful—If you are not better send for D[r] Barclay tomorrow he knows me—I do not like the stump business in pens; Yours and Graces very much alike but especially Graces!—I have no more news so what can I write—I am going to dine tomorrow Sunday at Swiss Cottage[11]—

<u>Lizzy[12] cannot care about getting well</u>; the medicine cannot be good, I am mending at last but it has only been by perseverance & <u>pushing the medicine</u> I do not believe any thing else will ever cure her—Camphor & pepper & spice the <u>Platypus</u>[13] if they are moth eaten—

Good bye dearest I hope to have better news on Monday morning—if I do not hear from you I will conclude you come by the twelve oclock Train from Leicester on Monday—I will meet you—If you have much luggage leave it at the station Manchester for the carrier &

address it by carrier before leaving Leicester—I only paid 6/2 for the two & 2/- from Manchester by carrier—

God bless you till we meet & ever after

Tell your Mother we will soon have a room ready for her—

If you borrow £15–0–0 you can repay it in the middle of November when my bill of exchange is cashed Good bye Dearest says| Your faithful & true

W

X [kiss]

Read the enclosed dont laugh when you read it! be sure & save it for me

Let your mother see it but <u>on no account any one else</u>

Text: ALS NLA MS133/1/161

1   WLR was engaged for a short period in a medical practice in Eccles (end of September to December 1867). Eccles, Lancashire, was a small town, with a population in 1867 of about 53,000, four miles west of Manchester. It is now part of greater Manchester.
2   Envelope addressed to: Leicester, 58 Rutland Street, Mrs Lindesay Richardson with the postmark: L OC 3 1867 Manchester (MS133/1/156).
3   General Sir Charles Yorke, GCB (Knight Grand Cross of the Order of the Bath) (1789–1879), Field-Marshal, Commander of the Rifle Brigade (John Brett's Brigade) from 1 April 1863. He was the son of Col. John Yorke (who was the Deputy-Lieutenant of the Tower of London from 1795 to his death on 26 January 1826) and his wife Juliana, daughter of John Dodd. General Yorke served in the Peninsula with the 52nd Foot Regiment and was present at the battles of Vimiera, Fuentes d'Oñoro, Salamanca, Vittoria, Pyrenees, Nivelie (wounded), and Orthes (severely wounded), and at the sieges of Ciudad Rodrigo, and Badajoz (wounded), for which he received the War Medal with Ten Clasps. He served also in the Waterloo Campaign. On 5 April 1875 he was appointed Constable of the Tower of London. On 2 June 1877 he was made a Field-Marshal.
4   Caroline Richardson née Fisher (b. 1832), daughter of William Henry Fisher and his wife Ellen Ryley. She was married to WLR's cousin, William Duke Richardson. They had a baby son called Robert Lindesay, who was christened at the cathedral, Manchester, on 18 July 1867.
5   Sarah Ellen Fisher, sister of Carrie Richardson; christened 4 May 1842 at the cathedral, Manchester.
6   Ellen Fisher née Ryley (b. December 1807), oldest daughter of John and Ann Ryley. She married William Henry Fisher on 30 August 1832 at the cathedral, Manchester.
7   William Duke Richardson, son of Robert Richardson, who was a younger brother of Alexander Richardson, WLR's father.
8   The Richardsons' servant.
9   The *Bradshaw Railway Guide* was first issued in December 1841 by George Bradshaw (1801–1853). WLR and MR each had copies.
10   Henry Handel Richardson (b. *c.*1842) was WLR's nephew; son of Henry Downing Richardson (1816–1849).
11   The home of Carrie and William Duke Richardson.
12   Lizzie Brett née Bailey (b. 1830), MR's sister.
13   The skin of a platypus, a favourite souvenir from Australia.

113 [From MR in Eccles, England, to WLR in Yorkshire, England][1]

[Eccles, Manchester, Lancashire]

Wednesday evening [11 December 1867]

My dear old man

   John's[2] reply to hand this morning I was so glad you were all safe & so well pleased Of course nothing can be done until you come back. Two letter's came for you one from Devon saying he was in treaty with some one & the other from Mrs Dunne at Brixton[3] they have sold the practise to a young man so I suppose fate intends us for one of the two you are after. I have just had a letter from Mother enclosing one from John[4] but I am to return it by tonights post Captain Pope[5] had arrived safely John had a dinner party for him asked Ned[6] Turnham[7] & Brooke Smith just half an hour before dinner the Captain sent word that he had a bad cold so John was vexed—John was at the Levèe Ball & all sorts of pleasure No time to write to any one but Mother, Ned sent his baby's likeness[8] that I shall keep for you to see. I hope darling you will be home on Thursday I could not sleep without you We have been in Manchester all day We went to see a grand wedding at Eccles old Church such a grand affair. I am writing to Mother by this post I hope you have had the same fine day as we have had it was lovely Mrs Sayer's called but of course I was out with Carrie & William

Come home soon darling I hope to have a letter from you in the Morning Good Night God Bless you ever| Your own

Marie

Dr Richardson

Eccles, N^r Manchester in case my letter does not reach you

Text: ALS NLA MS133/1/152

[1]   WLR was looking for a practice to buy in Yorkshire. Alfred Joseph Hodgson (1808–1867), MRCS, the surgeon in Snaith and Rawcliffe, had died on 8 May 1867 and a practice had been advertised for Rawcliffe.

[2]   Captain John Brett, MR's brother-in-law, was looking out for a medical practice for WLR in Stoke, Devon, where his Brigade was stationed. Note that in *FRM* it is Devon where Richard Mahony works for a time.

[3]   A London suburb.

[4]   John Robinson Bailey (1826–1871), residing in Melbourne.

[5]   Captain A. K. Pope (d. 1869) was the master of the clipper *Red Jacket*, which had returned to Melbourne after the voyage to London with the Richardsons. WLR called him 'an excellent sailor' in 'A Letter from Home', *AMJ*, 12, 1867, p. 236. Presumably Pope was carrying messages from the Richardsons for their family. A year later he and his ship returned to Melbourne with Joseph Connolly, an American, on board, who wrote an account of this voyage. He said of Captain Pope: 'This particular Captain was a gentleman—a trait which no train of circumstances can alter.' On this trip in 1869, the *Red Jacket* sailed from Melbourne to Bombay and then on to Aden and back to Bombay where Captain Pope, visiting friends, caught a fever and died. 'He was a good man a Gentleman—without any bad habits—and a Christian, too—he lays alone far from kindred in Colaba Cemetery there to await the trump, that calls together, from East to West.' Joseph Connolly, *A Cruise of the Red Jacket around the world in the Sixties. Reminiscences of a Voyage to Australia in the clipper Red Jacket 1866–8*. Filmed 27 July 1976 by Old Dartmouth Whaling Museums, New Bedford, New England, USA. ALS NLA PMB 699.

[6]   Edward Harold Bailey, her brother.

[7]   Joseph Turnham.

[8]   James Harold, born 22 August 1867 in Melbourne; the first child for Edward Harold (Ned) Bailey and Agnes Eleanor née Hablethwaite, delivered by Dr James Edward Neild. They had married the previous year, on 1 May 1866, and lived in Palmerston House, Palmerston Street, Carlton, Melbourne. Ned was working as an accountant.

1868

114 [From WLR in Rawcliffe,[1] England, to MR in Eccles,[2] England]

Rawcliffe [Yorkshire]

Sunday after Church [26 January 1868]

My dear M.

I arrived here safely yesterday about 3. P.M. Harrie[3] will have told you that he saw me safely & comfortably esconced with a foot warmer—In consequence however of the guard putting me into a wrong carriage I had to change over before I came to Wakefield then at Wakefield for ½ an hour, and more, we got there 20 minutes to 1. & the train came up for us at ¼ past 1—We then started for Knottingley, reaching it ~~at~~ a little before two—left it ¼ past—There is a <u>first class ladies waiting</u> room both at Wakefield & Knottingley—Be sure & ask the porter for it as the stations are cold. Macauley[4] met me at the station here & I had the traps brought on—after a chop we went out & I saw two patients—He introduced me to four families—comfortable houses, & well to do people one family very pleased, the father[5] clerk of the court (County) or some such thing said they were very pleased indeed to have a gentleman of my experience as they were getting a little anxious & feared they sho[d] get some very young man.[6] His sons are in one of the Banks of Goole, nice gentlemanly young fellows—eldest about 20—This morning went to Church[7]—not bad. ~~clerg~~ parson[8] an elderly man about 60 service well read, singing fair, "Hymns antient & modern[9] used"—Capital Sermon—A lovely day bright sky, more sun than I have seen since we left Brighton—

I send you the measure of the parlor 10 feet by 19 feet 20 inches without the projection of the fireplace which is small—the surgery is 12 by 14 about but if you send me word what you want I will measure them—Milk 2[d]—a quart fresh eggs 10 for a shilling—Coals 13/- no shops—Butchers three—a small drapers, ditto Grocers—a little P.O. I got your Standard[10] this morning by ½ past 8—& hope all are well. How is Mothers cold? & did you sleep?—Harrie got home all safe? & How is Gracy? Have you been up to Carrie, did you write to Mary Yorke.[11] I have not coughed much—the air is so delightful—We had a walk before Church & we are going out again now so that I will not close this till we come back—Be sure and let me have a long letter from all of you on Tuesday morning

4.P.M. Just returned from a walk—Have seen three patients today & been engaged for my first Accouchement[12]—Have seen primroses & wallflowers in flower & the birds have been singing in the groves at the back of the house—

Am going to Church again this evening—

Good bye and God bless you.| Love to Mother Grace & H[arrie]—| Be sure & tell me of your visit to Fairfield| Two large cupboards in my room.| Your faithful & true

Walter

Text: ALS NLA MS133/1/125

[1]   In January 1868, WLR established himself in a practice in Rawcliffe, south-east Yorkshire, for what was intended to be a long-term appointment. Rawcliffe was in those days a small village in the West Riding of Yorkshire with a population of about 1600 people. Surrounded by good farming land, it had a flaxmill, two breweries and a mineral water factory. It stands on the River Aire, near the Goole railway, about five miles west of Goole, three miles north-east of Snaith.

[2]   Elizabeth and Grace Bailey were staying with MR at Eccles.

3   Harrie Bailey, now aged fourteen, had been placed in another school, run by Mr Craig, in Fairfield, Manchester.
4   WLR stayed with Dr and Mrs Macauley and bought the practice from them. The house, in which the Macauleys and then the Richardsons lived, was rented from the Creykes, owners of the manor and Rawcliffe Hall. The squire, Ralph Creyke (3rd) (1849–1908), was only eighteen years old and had inherited the estate on the death of his father, also Ralph Creyke (2nd), who died on 7 February 1858, aged forty-four. Ralph Creyke (2nd) (1813–1858), was the eldest surviving son of Ralph Creyke (1st) and Frances née Denison (married 14 November 1807 in Leeds) and was born on 5 September 1813 in Marton, Yorkshire. From his siblings' baptismal records, the family appears to have moved to Rawcliffe and taken over the estate prior to June 1816. Ralph Creyke (2nd) was married on 27 August 1841 to Louisa Frances née Croft (c.1825–1890), daughter of Colonel Harry Croft of Stillington; and they had six children christened at Rawcliffe: Ralph (3rd) (born 5 September 1849), Ersalda Elizabeth (christened 10 June 1851), Katherine Harriet (christened 10 August 1852), Blanche Priscilla (christened 21 July 1854), Walter Richard (christened 14 April 1856), and Louisa (christened 29 July 1857). Ralph Creyke (3rd) became the best known of all the Creyke family when he was elected Member of Parliament for York in 1880. On 28 December 1882, he married Frances Elizabeth Bacon, daughter of Sir Hickman Bacon of Gainsborough, Premier Baronet of England and granddaughter of Sir Thomas Beckett Bart.
5   Edward Hernshaw (1826–1904).
6   See *FRM II*, p. 65.
7   St James's Parish Church of Rawcliffe, which stands in the centre of a large village green, was built in 1842, in Early English style with a chancel, nave, aisles and tower with spire. The cost of building the church had been borne mainly by Ralph Creyke (2nd).
8   The Reverend Robert Turner (1804–1880), vicar at St James's Parish Church, Rawcliffe, from 1860 to 1879. His wife, Jane, died on 13 February 1873, aged fifty-seven.
9   *Hymns Ancient and Modern*, a collection promoted and edited by the Reverend Sir Henry Williams Baker (1821–1877), vicar of Monkland, near Leominster, who contributed to it many original hymns and translations from the Latin. The collection first appeared in 1863.
10 *The Standard* was one of the principal London daily newspapers, established in 1857, of conservative party persuasion.
11 Mary Yorke was possibly the daughter of General Sir Charles Yorke (Rifle Brigade); or Bayne Cheyne's sister's grand-daughter. Elizabeth Cheyne (b. 1778) married William Wilkinson in 1803 and their daughter, Elizabeth Wilkinson, married Lieutenant Frederick Augustus Yorke in 1842.
12 Between January and 26 May 1868, WLR attended fifteen births in Rawcliffe: 28 January, 9 February, 11 February, 12 February, 14 February, 17 February, 20 February, 28 February, 9 March, 12 March, 14 March, 10 April, 19 April, 21 April and 26 May.

115 [From WLR in Rawcliffe, England, to MR in Eccles, England]

Rawcliffe Selby [Yorkshire]
Tuesday—[28 January 1868]

My d. d. M.

Yesterday Monday was wet nearly all day—We called on several more nice plain homely people, one a brewer[1] with a pretty daughter;[2] another farmer who lives in a capital house—dining room I should think 25 X 15—Drawing room like our Ballt one—His wife a nice body We talked about servants they are paying £12–0–0 for a bad one Thinks you may get a bad one for £10 at Hull, but advises us not to engage one in the village—I can see this will be a difficulty—

Was called up last night at 11 to see a child & called up this morning at 8 to Accouchement[3] it will be on all day—

I saw the Station Master[4] & he shewed me the rate of furniture from Manchester here direct 40/- per ton Insurance about a few shillings extra—luggage 28/4 per ton—he advises all the good things to be sent as furniture & insured all the common things as kitchen utensils &c to be packed in cases or casks & sent as luggage—

You had better write to Gibson & ask the charge for a man to come & pack all I should think one man would do all in three days—I hardly would entrust Palmer altho' you might ask him—

The House is the worst part of it the big room never will be dry for the house is on Brick foundations & the damp creeps up—we must just hope to get another if we stay in a year or so—There is just a chance of the one I was in last night but there is no stable & the rent would be about £30–0–0—

The place that is the village looks worse than it really is, for I can see there are plenty of well to do people about—

My cough is quite gone I am so sorry to hear that you are dull you ought not to be so with Mother & Grace!—

I do hope Mothers cough is better put the feet & legs into hot water every night & mustard to the chest—Glad you liked Mrs C.[5] You did not say how much the Van held? but I think you might get the whole done under ten pounds—

I sleep on a nice feather bed wh. I shall try & buy—Where did you put the tape measure I have not found it yet—

There is a capital cupboard in the kitchen a pantry about 8 feet square with a guaze over the window like a safe—

In fact excepting the damp walls of the big room I consider it a more convenient house than yours—

When you tell me where the tape measure is I will measure every room—Any sort of felt stuff will do for my surgery & the bedrooms—there are no bugs nor mice—Glad to hear Carrie is better, it was a lovely day for her—

I do not know how long the house will take to do but I will see the agent some day this week—

Am I happy & comfortable? pretty well—I eat well, 2 fresh laid eggs every morning ditto for tea—plenty of ham bacon & Yorkshire pudding—

I hope dear Grace will make you sleep—you will quite miss her Do you think you can do with the quiet of a Village life—I believe there is as good an opening as at Cray[6] except that there are not ~~quite as many~~ swells of [or] noblemen—Be sure & say before I pay the first installment altho' of course we can move in two years but then the expense will be great—

I weighed on Sunday without any great coat 10st. 12lb. very good—Macauley is going in for getting me 11st. 6. before you come—The Station Master—there is an opening for me "against the world"—that is his phrase. Dr Robertson has a very pretty daughter—there are said to be several good pianists—& we are likely to have a penny reading room[7] at which of course I shall go in—

Give your Mother my kind love how glad I am that you have got her with you—think seriously of taking Anne with us—I shall have to keep a man servant soon & that will relieve her of the boots & knives—I have just seen 6 nice sticks of celery & about a dozen small curly cabbages bought by Macauley from the garden at the Hall[8] for sixpence Is not that splendid—we can get early potatoes & green peas, asparagus, & every delicacy there—as soon as they are up for a nominal charge—of course Mother will read this—They are no relations of the Leicester family[9]—I declare to you that the day is quite warm the kitchen door is open & the birds are singing around the House—I will give you full particulars of the sale & send you a list   dont fret about being without me—cheer up take walks & let me have some roses on your cheeks to kiss when you come—until when dear Polly Adieu from your| loving & true

W

Text: ALS NLA MS133/1/129, MS133/1/138 and MS133/1/147

[1] John Helliwell married to Eliza Anne; they had at least four children: Frederick Ernest (christened 11 April 1857), Guy Percy (christened 27 March 1858), John Storr (christened 11 January 1863), and Theodora Elizabeth (christened 22 May 1864). The first two children were christened in Goole and the other two at Rawcliffe.

[2] Theodora Elizabeth Helliwell, whose nickname was 'Minnie'.

[3] *Case* 1 Rawcliffe, Mrs Rusby, aged twenty-eight, fourth pregnancy: 'Hooping cough in the House': one male born, 28 January 1868. The baby appears to have survived but three weeks later his two-year-old brother, Charles W. Hill Rusby, died on 21 February 1868, perhaps of whooping cough, and was buried in the graveyeard of St James's, Rawcliffe. Sarah Ann Rusby née Hill (1839–1900) was married to Robert Rusby (1841–1902). She was the daughter of Richard Hill, the Stationmaster at Rawcliffe.

[4] Richard Hill (1811–1877) died on 17 December 1877. His gravestone in the parish church of St James's, Rawcliffe, reveals that he had been the Stationmaster at Rawcliffe for twenty-seven years. He was married to Sarah (1815–1885), who died on 17 May 1885.

[5] Mrs Craig, the wife of Harrie's school principal.

[6] St Mary Cray, Kent, where WLR had worked prior to emigrating to Victoria. WLR had been looking at possible practices in the area in 1867.

[7] Subscription library. See *FRM II*, p. 65. The Rawcliffe Public Reading Rooms building was finally opened in 1883 and still remains as a small library on the corner of the village green.

[8] Rawcliffe Hall was built in 1660 by Sir John Boynton whose family bought the estate after the death of the Abbot of Selby (the early owner of most of the land in the area). The Creykes inherited some of the estate in 1772 by marriage and purchased adjoining land. The Hall was badly burned in 1897 and was rebuilt. After World War I, the Creyke family sold the estate north of the River Don to West Riding Council and the Hall was converted into an institution for 150 mentally handicapped patients. The land was divided into small farms. In the 1990s, the Hall was pulled down for a housing development plan. Dorian Bingham ed., *Rawcliffe 'The Queen of Villages': A Brief History* (Goole: Rawcliffe History Group, 1989) pp. 14–17.

[9] WLR might be referring to the other doctor in the area, Dr Robinson (Elizabeth Bailey's maiden name).

116 [From WLR in Rawcliffe, England, to MR in Eccles, England]

Rawcliffe Selby [Yorkshire]

Thursday morng [30 January 1868]

My V. d. Marie

I got my first confinement[1] over at 11 PM. on Tuesday night—All well M[rs] Macauley remained with her all the time—Yesterday Wednesday I saw two or three patients & we went to Goole: It is about 5 miles off by rail—a small sea port or rather river port for it is on the Humber. There are several docks & I saw some fine steamers & small craft—There is a trade with Hull & the continent. Pop some 5 or 6000—Tidy shops Ironmongers, Drapers, Chemists—Hotels—&c. We came home & spent the evening at a M[r] Hernshaws—where we played a rubber of whist, <u>of course for nothing</u>—M[rs] H.[2] enquired kindly how you were & if you were very anxious to know what sort of a place Rawcliffe was? Did you play? Were you a good sailor—She was a clergyman's daughter—the boys are going out hunting this morning, as the hounds meet about 8 miles off & they keep a lot of horses & two traps—What a pity you started off on Tuesday before getting my letter. It is the Lancashire & Yorkshire Railway in the same station as the Victoria—They forward it direct here for as I told you 40/- per ton for furniture with a shilling or two for insurance & 28/4 for luggage! I think I wrote this on Tuesday—Then of course it must be packed at the house & forwarded to the station, as they direct—I am afraid you applied first at the wrong station—I am sure you must have had a troublesome job—48/- a ton is too much for luggage they are imposing on us—The Station Master here turned up his book and shewed me the charges printed—

You must not decide on a fixed day my dear nor engage people or lorries yet, for I cannot say about the house—I certainly cannot bring you into it as it is! For goodness sake dont forward them on the 12th of F^{by} or any other day until I decide. I am delighted Mother is coming with you—The accounts are not glowing my dear—plain people and a dull place is all it is but our happiness must not depend on others—I know there will be pretty walks in Summer—and is ten times pleasanter than dirty Eccles—

There are other doctors attending in the Village now from Goole, so it will be some time before I expect to do any thing—I must get a horse soon—Lie in bed for your influenza—the weather is mild here, we have not had one cold day yet—My surgery has a fireplace & is 12 feet by 11½—thus [small sketch:]

I think this will do for the two lower rooms—but it does seem a pity to get good carpets for such a den—Mine will only be dirtied by the boots

Front windows for poles 5̶4̶ 43½ inches from extreme wood to wood

Back one 54 inches for pole—

windows down stairs two front & one back

| 2 front blinds | 32 inchs wide |
| | 49—long |

| Back window | 52— " |
| | 41—wide |

Carpet of big room [small sketch] fireplace comes out 30 inches & the cut out of carpet is 60 inches

My room is 12 feet by 11½ a cut out for fender & hearthrug of 43 inches long & 18 to 20 inches

Had we taken a £60–0–0 house how much worse it would have been—

Beg Mother when she writes to Australia not to say anything of our plans, as I do not wish it to be known yet that we are not going back—as we might have to do so yet and it wd. look very foolish—We may tell them at the end of the year, and it will be quite time enough then—The afternoon has cleared up and the wind has got round to the north W. I have taken the Evening Standard & so get it every morning at breakfast, you know how fond I am of a newspaper in my hand with you opposite me making my coffee too sweet, reading you bits of the news. My room is a much warmer one than that at Eccles, no draught at all; and all it wants is you and mother—They do not give me good dinners—I shall give Mrs M. the first installment tomorrow & shall then enquire the day of the sale—

Be sure and call at the P.O and write down my address as several Australian mails will be delivered there yet—I will write to the Lancet,[3] Constitution, & Edin Med Journal[4] and have my address altered in their books—How does Mother like the smoke Be sure & tell me all about Harrie & Fairfield & what class he is in & what Mother thinks of Mrs C. No letter from

Dr C.[5] or Mr Hill[6]—Good bye dearest and with love to Mother and many [kisses?] to yourself|
I am as ever| Your own
                    Walter
Dont bring any more 6^d paper but some better sort with cross lines and thin yellow or mauve
Blackbirds singing at the grove at the back
          Text: ALS NLA MS133/1/130, MS133/1/140 and MS133/1/200

1   See endnote 3 to Letter 115.
2   Ellen Hernshaw (1831–1903), wife of Edward Hernshaw, Clerk of the Court.
3   *The Lancet* medical journal, established in 1823.
4   *Edinburgh Medical Journal*, established in 1855.
5   Dr Bayne Cheyne.
6   The Reverend Ebenezer B. Hill, Minister at Lochmaben, Dumfriesshire.

117 [From WLR in Rawcliffe, England, to MR in Eccles, England]

Rawcliffe [Yorkshire]
Saturday [1 February 1868]

My dear Mary
     We had a severe storm all night from the West wh. rattled against the windows with rain
all night—when I came down I found no letter and was very disapointed—However they
arrived soon after—I am glad you think "it cannot be a worse place than this" I like it better
every day—
     About the sketch of the carpet [Small diagram of oblong room and fireplace in centre on
north long wall and door to left side on south wall] this is it. There must have been some other
sketch of the passage perhaps near it in my last, for the wall opposite the fire is quite straight &
even as I have drawn it above. Mr Lake the agent for the estate called yesterday—they do the
room and passage next Monday & will have it finished in the week The time will soon pass
and you will soon see me again & come to our humble tho' I hope happy little home—The
rates are paid by the estate, so we shall [not] be bothered by that expense—Mrs Macauley says
there are good enough servants to be got in the village & she is looking one out for us or she
was yesterday—I will not stop her, but will see what they can do—She says they can <u>all</u>
<u>bake</u>—You can have two if you like by & bye—I must have a man after hearing this of course
I am somewhat sorry you concluded with Anne without consulting me further as I only said
"<u>I would think seriously of taking Anne with you</u>"—
     If you have to slave & worry as you have done it will be a pity—I am glad you bought
more forks from Simmonds we can easily send to them from this, get a list from him before
you leave—Buy me a dozen box of paper collars no. 16. as the last I bought in Deansgate[1] and
a pair of driving gloves, small one leather fingers—you know—
     You have managed very cleverly about the carpet & taxes—
     What did Annie mean by it—from what M^{rs} M[acauley] says I should think we could
get a good active girl here for about £9. to 10. so do not bring her, if she does not want to
come but a month will not hurt—
     I am so delighted to hear mother is better—
     <u>The two front bedroom</u> windows 41 inches long & 37 inches wide—for the blinds—I
hope Fleming will make these better than the last—

We are having a regular gale—It was as much as I could do to walk out this morning—Give my kind love to Mother & Grace—The Clergyman[2] called this morning. He is a quiet elderly man. Asked when you were coming. I will be able to say next week when the sale is going to take place Have got nothing more to say except that I do hope you will get well & strong before you come. I will be just as glad to see you as you can be to come for I miss your good dinners!—So good bye from Your loving| & true

> W—

Text: ALS NLA MS133/1/123 and MS133/1/145

1   Manchester's premier shopping area.
2   The Reverend Robert Turner.

118   [From WLR in Rawcliffe, England, to MR in Eccles, England]

Rawcliffe [Yorkshire]
Monday [3 February 1868]

My dearest

For you know I have only one of that name, Your last does not tend to make me happy—If Grace says you are looking thin how sad it will look to me—I fear you did not get to Fairfield today as it has been blowing and snowing and raining here all night & day—

However we must get some wintry weather and the sooner it comes the sooner it will be over—I do not sleep very well myself—

The workmen commenced this morning & will have done this week and I have been asking Macauley when the sale is to take place—I can see my way to £200 at least this year, this ought to cheer you up—

Miss Fector[1] 19 Lowndes St Belgravia London W.

I will write to Jack[2]—There are rollers for the blinds but I do not know if they are sold with the house, or if they go with the blinds—There is a small table in the lobby that I shall bid for—I should like you to be here at the time of the sale but we will see—

I am too busy to send a line to Bill[3]

Did I tell you the parson called on me on Saturday? I suppose you will call & say Good bye to Mrs Brett[4]—

I was at Church twice yesterday—The girls that is Bessie[5] & Grace will see much more of the country & have a better chance of enchancing young men here than in Leicester dont say this to them however we must have them both down next Midsummer Bessie shall never go to Rutland St again unless she likes

I think we shall be as happy here as anywhere and there will always be two spare bedrooms—we can write to Gibson for any furniture we want Do try and get strong & bonny for my sake—You will miss dear Grace—I got the two Newspapers this morning—I shall be glad when I can name the day for you to come, you will arrive here at ¼ to 3. wont it be jolly? Anything will be better than that lonely spot in that damp dirty street, still we must be pleased we did not do worse.

4. PM

We have been driving out all morning from 11 to 3—& have been round to see the Farmers—a high west wind we came home & I ate a capital dinner not of course as good as if you were here—I cannot say when the sale takes place—they talk of beginning to do the place tomorrow—I have a fire in my bedroom every night & they do their best to make me comfortable—I think a year or two here will make us both fat—You need not address at Mrs Macauleys

Dr Lindesay Richardson
Rawcliffe
Selby

is quite enough—

My kind love to Grace, you will be more lonely than ever when she goes—

If any body is writing to Sarah—Be sure & tell her to send on letters & papers here—If you are not writing I will do it—Your mother can write & you can put a stamp on—I got the Standards this morning—I wrote to Dr Cheyne & Mr Hill & have had no answer from either

I got the tape measure, where is the sponge? The passage is 26 feet 8 inches long 39 inches wide with a recess for a table 6 feet 4 inches in & 8 feet 4 inches long [Small diagram of kitchen and passage]

Adieu Your loving &|true

W

Text: ALS NLA MS133/1/127 and MS133/1/144

1   Caroline Fector (b. 1804) had moved to London to be with her brother, John Minet Fector.
2   Jack Brett married to MR's sister, Lizzie.
3   Probably William Duke Richardson.
4   A relation of Jack Brett's, perhaps his grandmother, lived near them in Manchester.
5   Elizabeth Turnham (b. 1838), MR's cousin. She was the daughter of William Henry Turnham and Sarah née Robinson, and sister of William Henry Turnham, who was living in Melbourne.

119 [From WLR in Rawcliffe, England, to MR in Eccles, England]

Rawcliffe [Yorkshire]
Wednesday [5 February 1868]

My dearest

I am sorry to hear that your cold continues, you will soon get better here, my room is as warm and cosy as any one I ever sat in, no draughts at all, altho' the wind has been high enough all the time—The House will strike you as being small & poky at first, but you will soon get used to it and I am sure we shall be very happy & comfortable; I feared you would not be able to go to Fairfield and am sorry that mother has not seen the place and Mrs Craig, for it is all so different from that unprincipled man's place[1] at Tottenham—The afternoon was fine here—Poor Grace was in low spirits was she—She has had a long holiday at all events—I think the best way will be to pay Jones up £14–0–0 and have done with it I will send you a P.O. order next week you will want some for yourself if I make it £20–0–0 will that do? I am sorry William[2] should behave so cooly to you—I expect nothing else from his wife—However never mind be sure & dont ask them to come here for I do not want them—If you say anything, regret that you cannot ask them as the bedrooms will not be furnished—I wish to have done with them for ever—His radical principles do not suit me I do not approve of the way he talks about the Queen, and their treatment of poor Miss Fisher[3] shews what they are to their friends—No, Let us drop the acquaintance Dont go near them anymore I dont want them coming here & spying out the place so try & not give them the address. <u>It is near Selby</u> that is enough—

The House stood the gale very well—~~so~~ tiles & chimney pots fell in the village but none off this house—I think you will like the paper I have selected—

I think Mothers pains in her bones are only the effect of cold—Have W. & C.[4] been down to see her—What does she think of them?—

I am glad you are beginning to take down & wash—our bedroom is a very airy one it will require carpet of some sort, the size is 11½ by 14 about—the small one 10 by 12 ~~& the other two~~ & the other irregular shape, two have fire places <u>The rollers of the blinds go with the House</u>—

Twelve or thirteen stair rods—but those you have are ours—The eyes of M[rs] Macauley screw in so that I think I would leave yours—The parlor is <u>on the right</u> hand side of the passage near the back window I <u>marked it</u> my room; door left hand

Price a set of dish covers, so that if you have to buy them at Goole you may know the price—I have been obliged to <u>order a horse,</u> and have written to Jack[5] to buy me saddle & Bridle & whip at Leicester—I am already called out to the country 3 miles off yesterday & day before—& shall soon have as much as I care to do—Why not come before the luggage Bring some bedding for Anne[6] & things for her food & we can stay at an Inn here—

Lucindas[7] letter is amusing she talks of <u>all heart</u> what stuff! Do not write to her till you come here—

Fancy rabbitts 9[d] each here! The keepers sell them at 1/- & Macauley says that the skins are readily bought by dealers at 3[d] each—We cannot get groceries here—no good tea or coffee every such thing dearer than in Leeds so the Macauleys get theirs from Leeds you must do the same & get a months supply in every month—bring some good tea & coffee with you to go on with—

There is a good opening here for an Iron mongers, Stationer & grocer & Chemist all in one a general store in fact—Of course those here in little bits of shops have made fortunes & are very independent—What a pity Tom[8] is not in business—

Dont forget the Thermometer outside the surgery window—I have asked M[rs] Macauley when the sale is to be, she cannot say just yet—

A showery afternoon—I slept better last night did not wake till day light—All are anxious to see you—The evenings are tedious—Make arrangements to come at the end of next week if possible but I will be able to say definitely by Saturday next. Kind love to Mother, lots of X to yourself from

   Walter

I beg you will <u>not</u> stay at Williams. I do not wish to be under any obligation to them now what is to prevent your employing M[r] Palmer to pack the things, <u>& see them</u> off taking all responsibility off you; you must come <u>before</u> the things so as to let Ann get the rooms ready one by one. I can easily get rooms at one of the Inns here for a trifle, & <u>it will do me no harm</u>—This way you can come before the sale & buy what you want I should bring all the bedding with you as <u>luggage</u>—My cough is all right—

  Preserve the enclosed [Lucinda's letter]

  Text: ALS NLA MS133/1/128 and MS133/1/139

---

[1] The school run by Mr White, see Letter 109.

[2] WLR is referring to William Duke Richardson and not MR's brother, William Bailey (see Clark, p. 57). William Bailey had not yet returned from India where he was working for the Civil Service. Despite WLR's unfavourable comments about his cousin, in the next letter he suggested that MR should give him their old Hymn Books and in December that year WLR stayed at 'Swiss Cottage' (see Letter 139).

[3] Sarah Ellen Fisher, sister of Carrie Richardson.

[4] William Duke Richardson and his wife Carrie.

[5] John Brett must have been visiting Leicester.

[6] Annie, the Richardsons' servant.

[7] His sister, Lucinda Richardson, who was working as a governess in Mt Jeffcott, Victoria. F. Baillière, *The Official Post Office Directory of Victoria for 1868* (Melbourne: F. Baillière, 1868).

[8] Thomas Robinson Burton Bailey (b. 1833), christened 9 January 1833 at St George's Parish Church, Leicester; fifth child and third son of John Bailey and Elizabeth née Robinson. It is not clear what he did for a living (except that he spent time and money in the West End of London). He was a terrible worry to his mother, borrowing money from her and WLR.

120 [From WLR in Rawcliffe, England, to MR in Eccles, England]

Rawcliffe [Yorkshire]
Sunday [9 February 1868]

My dearest

I am so sorry that you keep poorly—That nasty damp house cannot agree with you England itself does not agree with you as you were far better in Australia. If you do not get strong & well here, it will distress me greatly—I fear you fidgett & worry too much—when will you be easy? What does Mother say to you—you ought to take a lesson from her—

Friday will do very nicely to send the things off—They will not be here before Monday I think, but I will make arrangements for them whenever they come—

Macauleys sale takes place in the yard. I shall expect you then by the 11.15 train on Saturday but how are you going to do on Friday night you did not say—

There is a very nice Inn on the Eccles old Road "The White Horse Inn"—You had better take two rooms there—What is Mothers objection to Inns? If you would follow my plans dear better, your health would be better! It is a nice clean place. I will send you £23. on Wednesday or Thursday. Pay Jones £14 & I will send a notice & form of receipt in my next—

Of course you will come first class. You can buy the dish covers if you like them. The Marseilles mail will be delivered in London Feb[y] 13th. I suppose Mothers will come on here I had a letter from M[r] Hill this morning—he says Bayne is pretty well[1]—hopes we may like our new spot;—Poor Caroline[2] Cork is too damp & relaxing for both H & her—We will be able to ask her over here when we get settled—I am sure you will get better here. This is a lovely bright bracing sunny day—

You must cheer up—you will see me before this day week if we are spared—The gas fitting bill you will find on the file & the cost of putting them in I think together they came to near three pounds—

I think I would give W[m][3] our old Hymn books—& should like one of the "Hymns Ancient & Modern" with the Music & red edged leaves like Graces—

I have booked over £9-0-0 in the two first weeks without a horse—I think that ought to make you better—you see I have a very comfortable & certain income & we can put by all our Australian Dividends & buy Water works Shares—or Victorian Six per cent Government

Stock or <u>Three per cent</u> Consols—or leave in the Bank at 2½ per cent—We will be just as well off as ever we were—

An old woman came yesterday about her daughter—who is leaving her last place because it is <u>term time.</u> It seems they all leave here <u>every year</u>—She was getting £10–0–0 at a farm house & hearing I wanted a servant thought to better herself—I told her mother we ~~were~~ always used to keep our servants two or three years & ~~we~~ thought it very unwise of her daughter to leave a good place, just because it <u>was term time!</u> <u>This beats Victoria!</u> I can see servants here will be the great bother—We must just give the best wages & get the best servants—I know I shall have to give £16–0–0 for a groom <u>at least</u>—

But what does a few pounds matter when I am doing well—we must not be mean & stingy here. I wrote to Jack Brett yesterday—No more news but hope you will try & get well—I should send you X X X but you know you never burn my letters & I dont like them kept—You shall have them when you come| Y— h—

    W

Text: ALS NLA MS133/1/124 and MS1133/1/131

1   Dr Bayne Cheyne died at Lochmaben on 2 August 1868.
2   Caroline Richardson, WLR's older sister.
3   William Duke Richardson.

121 [From WLR in Rawcliffe, England, to EB in Eccles, England]

[Sunday, 9 February 1868]

My dear Mother

I suppose you too will not be sorry when you start for Yorkshire—It is a flat country, but the farmers are well to do and an independant class. I shall look anxiously for Saturday to come—I have directed Mary to come first class & shall be very angry if she does not as cold feet in a second class carriage will only lay her up again when she arrives—the best way is always the cheapest way—You will have two foot warmers & give the man twopence

Be sure & ask for a Wakefield carriage before starting—

Go there into the refreshment room & have two cups of hot coffee & two buns—

Wait till the train comes up at ½ past 1—Go on to Knottingley—ask the porter for the ladies first class-waiting room & wait there till the train comes at ¼ past Two—Get in & the next move is at Rawcliffe station <u>next to Snaith</u>[1]—

You get a pretty view of the village if you sit on the <u>near</u> side of the carriage & face the engine that is the side you get in at from Wakefield—

Good bye & make Polly give up fidgetting & get her well by Friday—| Your affect Son

    W

Text: ALS NLA MS1133/1/131 [On reverse of second sheet of letter to MR]

1   Snaith, a small town with a population of about 13,000, is situated five kilometres from Rawcliffe. It has a beautiful twelfth-century prior church, St Laurence Priory, in the centre of the town.

122 [From MR in Leicester, England, to WLR in Rawcliffe, England]

[58 Rutland Street, Leicester]

June 15th 1868 [Monday]

My own darling

This is to say that I shall be home at a ¼ to 6 o'clock on Tuesday the train leaves here at 2-10 & arrives at Wakefield at 4-50 I shall only have time to get out of one train & pop into the other I don't believe I shall have time to get a ticket but M[r] Hill[1] know's me so I must do the best I can Mother is keeping all right we are going out shopping this afternoon

I don't believe you want me back but I am coming just to torment you—every day you say stay on Mother won't hear of our not going to Devon say's Lizzie will not be there another year & she would like us to go—

The weather fearfully hot I hardly know what to do with myself—I am going to see for a hat or bonnet today I hope your cold is quite gone—If I do miss the Train it will be 9-15 before I can arrive—Mother sends love & hoping soon to feel your arm's round me. I am your loving| wife

Mary

lots of kisses

Text: ALS NLA MS133/1/155

[1]   Richard Hill, the Stationmaster at Rawcliffe.

123 [From WLR in Rawcliffe, England, to MR in Devon, England][1]

Rawcliffe [Yorkshire]

Tuesday [29 September 1868]

My dearest

I was glad to learn by yours of Sunday evening that you had arrived safely at Havelock Terrace—The Baby will die and the sooner it is relieved from its suffering the better—It is unfortunate that you have not decided about the ball—surely you will go with Jack if it lives over Friday—it may linger some week or two—I am glad Edith[2] is so pretty—Give her Uncle Walters love & a Kiss—I saw her donkey yesterday[3]—Get a new dress if you feel you want it my dear. We can afford a fiver! I have just had old Bramley & his wife in they have <u>decided to take the house</u> if I would give it up—by Saturday December 5th. I have agreed to do so—I shall borrow £100 from Mother so as not to let us run short & to take out plenty of nice things which are always better than what every body else has—

Give my kind love to Jack & Lizzy—I am sorry for the poor baby—a drop or two of Chlorodyne would soothe it when moans are bad—I was over at Helliwells—had supper with them—did not get home till 11-30—Wale[4] is doing very well—cooks every thing very nicely This is a wet day—I see by the "Argus" that Kabat is going to take charge at Beechworth for a time—

J. H. Peebles has a son[5]—I shall speak to Ellis & Nunn about making cases for the furniture

The Bramleys seem inclined to buy—altho' I see they are mean screws—I hardly see how to run down to you: we must be packing up: if I leave this on the 1st Nov[r] & we are back Nov[r] 14—it will give us three whole weeks to get off—& I ought to go to Liverpool to see

Ismay & Co[6]—I dont believe I can do it, arrange about sale, see to the packing &c—Wherever I go now I hear regrets at my leaving—

I had a letter & Argus from Mother this morning—one from Lucinda[7] with photograph which I shall not send but keep for you to see when you return—

Mother writes in better spirits & is not worse—No line from Grace—nice sister that perhaps I will write to her again in a hurry—dont she wish it—No letter from Mackay[8]—|
Your faithful & true

    W

Text: ALS NLA MS133/1/137 and MS133/1/142

1   MR left Rawcliffe on 28 September 1868 to stay with her sister Lizzie and Captain Jack Brett at 7 Havelock Terrace, Stoke, Devon, where John Walter Brett, their six-week-old baby son, was fatally ill.
2   Edith Brett, young daughter of Lizzie and Jack Brett. She kept in touch with the Richardsons all through her life. She never married and her address in Cornwall was in HHR's old address book, now in the HHR Collection in NLA MS133/8/8.
3   This indicates that the Bretts had stayed with the Richardsons at Rawcliffe.
4   The Richardsons' servant in Rawcliffe. Note that WLR had picked up the English habit of referring to the servant by her surname.
5   Frank Montgomerie Peebles, son of John Home Peebles (Bank of New South Wales Manager) and his wife, Anna Maria née Jennings. Peebles and his brother Charles (both bank clerks) had lived in Webster Street in 1858.
6   Ismay & Co. were agents for the White Line Company, based at Liverpool, later to gain notoriety through the *Titanic* disaster.
7   Lucinda Richardson.
8   George Gordon Mackay, WLR's sharebroker in Ballarat.

124   [From WLR in Rawcliffe, England, to MR in Devon, England]

[Rawcliffe, Yorkshire]
Tuesday Evening [6 October 1868]

My dear M.

I have just had Nunn in looking at the furniture & asking him as to the probable cost of making cases for it—He seemed completely bamboozled at it—says the legs will not come off the tables; the cheapest stuff he could get for the job would cost ½[d] the running foot will think it over & will try to let me know if it will cost under or over £10–0–0. I fear that we shall have to pack it all off to a Manchester Broker.

if it cost £15–0–0 to pack I know it will cost £15–0–0 more for freight & insurance that is [£]30–0–0 we could surely get [£]22–0–0 for the lot & replace all in Melbourne for £50–0–0 however we will see what he says next week—

Wednesday morning. [7 October] Your letter dated 6th just come. Poor little sufferer eased from pain[1] Liz. ought to be rejoiced that the moans have ceased—Truly unfortunate for you: I got your Sunday letter & wrote you Monday & Tuesday. Mother wished me to send "The Argus" to Harrie[2] so will send you some via Southampton No news of interest beyond what I told you. Agnes expecting another about end of August:[3] Poor Ned. or as she calls him P.B.[4] His troubles are beginning

You rather surprise me about the style There can be no want of money then! I am glad to hear you walk, your mourning will come in handy now.[5]

Did you see "The Galatea" or has she left?[6] I wrote again yesterday to Wigram—Yesterday Tuesday was a pouring day which was very hard on me—Today is fine so I must walk double—A letter from Harry—I paid my life money & saddler—Wale is doing very well is washing today. I am pretty sure M[rs] Fleeman[7] had the small pox—She was at the Helliwells the other night & I saw her face is marked tho slightly—the child I attended altho' the face was covered has not a sign—I am afraid I will not be able to run down to you but we will see. I do not see how we can spare the time if we have to be out by Dec[r] 5 Saturday—it would be better for me to do it afterwards when you are at Mothers—I would not be so hurried & would enjoy it more—I told you old Bramley had taken the house I saw Lake[8] yesterday it is all right I give up the key to him & am "shut" of it as they say in Leicester—

I told you also of the first div. of the N.N. Clunes £75–0–0 for August 1st & sent you Sams letter. I will enclose him one & you must write him next week—He is a good fellow, tho' laiky[9]—

The best thing for Lizzy's breasts is a piece of sticking plaster about 8 inches square <u>with a hole cut in the middle</u> warmed at the fire & put on each breast & left on—for two or three weeks there will be no fear of abscess if this is done at once—

Lucinda has left the Simons, she could not put up with their anti-Christian conduct does not intend coming home—She seems quite independent & in good spirits. I expect we will have some letters via Southampton—They are due in London on the 10th Saturday but will probably be delivered here on that day—If there are any I will forward them with a newspaper. I got your letter of October 6 that was Tuesday this morning Wednesday—so if the letters are posted early it is only one days post from you—Did you take a copy of my Jour[10] for Jack?

Your attached

W

Text: ALS NLA MS133/1/143 and MS133/1/146

---

[1] John Walter Brett died aged seven weeks on 6 October 1868.

[2] Harrie Bailey at school in Fairfield, Manchester.

[3] The letters from Melbourne were of course full of old 'news', for Walter Robinson Bailey (1868–1877) had been born on 26 September 1868 to Agnes and Edward Harold (Ned) Bailey, their second son.

[4] Probably 'poor boy'.

[5] MR would have bought mourning clothes after the death of Dr Bayne Cheyne who died on 2 August 1868 aged eighty, at Bank House, High Street, Lochmaben, Dumfriesshire. His death certificate states that he died of 'Apoplexy' and that he had been ill for two weeks. Elizabeth Yorke, his niece, was the informant of his death for the Registrar but she was not present at his death.

[6] The *Galatea* (named after a Greek legend in which an ivory statue of a maiden was brought to life by Aphrodite in response to the prayers of the sculptor Pygmalion, who had fallen in love with his work) was a 3,500-ton steam frigate, commanded since 1866 by Prince Alfred Arthur George, Earl of Ulster, Duke of Kent, Prince of Saxe-Coburg-Gotha, fifth child and second son of Queen Victoria. Launched at Woolwich in 1859, she was one of the fastest and best equipped ships of her time, with an auxiliary steam engine of 800 horse-power, giving a top speed of 13 knots. Prince Alfred, recently created Duke of Edinburgh, was the first member of the Royal Family to tour Australia. He sailed to Adelaide (arriving on 30 October 1867), Melbourne (from 23 November 1867 to 4 January 1868, including trips to Ballarat and the Western District), Tasmania (arriving 6 January for two weeks), and Sydney (arriving 21 January 1868). From Sydney he sailed by HMS *Challenger* to Brisbane in order that the *Galatea* be dry-docked. The tour of Queensland was for only a few days and, leaving Brisbane on 29 February, he returned to Sydney, where he planned to stay until April before sailing to New Zealand. A picnic was arranged on the harbour at Clontarf on 12 March 1868 and a deranged Irishman,

James O'Farrell, drew a double-barrelled pistol from his coat pocket and shot the Prince. The bullet entered his back, fortunately deflected by his leather braces, and lodged in his abdomen. He recovered after a successful operation. News of this attempted assassination and the Prince's recovery reached England in June. The Prince sailed from Sydney straight to England on 4 April 1868 and embarked at Greenwich in early August. WLR and MR had missed all the excitement of the Prince's visit to Melbourne and Ballarat but no doubt had received many letters regaling stories of the visit and the attempted murder, which had devastated the people in Ballarat. The Richardsons may even have known O'Farrell as his father, a prosperous immigrant butcher, had set him up in a small mixed-business in Ballarat. His older brother had been a solicitor in Ballarat and had absconded with trust funds and fled to Hong Kong and India. Brian McKinley, *The First Royal Tour 1867–1868* (Adelaide: Rigby Ltd, 1970), pp. 3, 5, 173.

[7] Mrs Fleeman was the wife of Mr S. Fleeman who owned the flax mill and was Chairman of the Rawcliffe School Board.

[8] The agent for the Creyke's estate.

[9] An expression from northern England meaning 'playful'.

[10] Probably one of the *Australian Medical Journals* containing an article by WLR.

125 [From WLR in Rawcliffe, England, to his brother-in-law, John Brett, in Devon, England]

Rawcliffe [Yorkshire]
Wednesday [7 October 1868]

My dear Jack

I trust Time the great softener of affliction has shown Lizzie that Baby's removal is a happy release for him, and a cause for thankfulness for her. I do not know whether I may have the pleasure of seeing you to say "Good bye" to you before we sail or not! but I suppose if I cant run down Lizz: can be spared to come up to Leicester or London—

I hope when the funeral is over you will make Polly go out every day for she is a sad stick-in-the-house, and consequently often off her food I hope the change will do her good—Devonshire cream is good & Gloucester cheese-apples & pears are the only abundant stores here. Polly will have given you all the news—

Make Lizz exert herself and help Polly to make herself a new dress in half mourning Give the darling[1] a kiss for Uncle Walter and believe me with affectionate love to Lizz—| Your affect. Brother

W: Lindsay Richardson:
Text: ALS NLA MS133/1/136

[1] Edith Brett.

126 [From Ismay & Co. in Liverpool, England, to WLR
in Rawcliffe, England]

White Star Line of Ex-Royal Mail Packets| 10 Water Street| Liverpool
9 October 1868 [Friday]

W L Richardson Esq'
Rawcliffe Yorkshire

Dear Sir

We are in receipt of your favor and beg to inform you that we allow to Saloon passengers
40 Cubic Feet of Luggage and our charge for Freight is 40/- p[er] Ton of 40 Cubic feet, you
can address anything you may have for shipment to our Care and every attention shall be paid
to it, you had better have it consigned to our Agent Mess'' Lorimer Marwood & Rome
Melbourne who would store it until you arrive there or we shall be glad to have it stored here
until you sail, which you can decide when you call upon us here to arrange

We are|Yours truly

J. H. Ismay & Co.

Text: ALS NLA MS133/1/141

127 [From WLR in Rawcliffe, England, to MR in Devon, England][1]

[Rawcliffe, Yorkshire]
[Sunday, 11 October 1868]

[Page(s) missing]

without the bother of being Surgeon at all, there is the difference however between £45 &
£105. I know I can get no better offer than Ismays—

Ellis has promised to come in next week & give me some idea of what it will cost to case
the lot. I have measured the table it is 5 x 4 x 2½ cost of freight [£]2–5–0 without expense to
Liverpool or case or insurance

The sofa 7 x 2½ x 3 = 53 feet—freight [£]2–12–6– my table [£]1–5–0 & so on

It is difficult to decide—I had a letter from Grace this morning—Sarah is
there—Mother is evidently getting worse—I am very gl[a]d you saw the Review;[2] who is
D' Clino? They[3] cannot decide to buy any thing till you return—M'' B.[4] wishes to see you—I
cannot leave this possibly before Nov' 1 and then I do not see how we are to manage to pack
up & get off by Dec' 5—

Wale is doing very nicely—cooks capitally—This is a fine day. Yesterday pouring wet all
day—No newspapers or letters yet via Southampton

Kind remembrances & love to J & L[5]—

It will be necessary for me to go to Liverpool to see the owners before we leave this—I
can then arrange about the furniture &c—& we can go on to Leicester & London & wait
there till we hear from them about Hry[6]—With fond love & hoping you will come back well
fat & rosy I am as ever| Your attached

W

Text: ALS NLA MS133/1/141 [On reverse of Letter 126]

1. The second part of a letter written on the reverse of Letter 126 from Ismay. Presumably there had been two letters from the shipping agents and the second letter from Ismay, which has been preserved, had this part of WLR's letter to MR.
2. *The Times*, in its column headed 'Military and Naval Intelligence', reported in detail about the review of the troops quartered at Plymouth district by His Royal Highness the Duke of Cambridge, Commander-in-Chief (b. 1819). He was a cousin of Queen Victoria, served in the Crimea and was appointed Commander-in-Chief in 1856 until 1895. The review was held on Rosborough Downs on Wednesday, 7 October 1867, the day after baby John Walter Brett died. All the troops gathered on the ground by 10.30 a.m. and were then posted to the various positions they had to occupy to receive an imaginary enemy, who were supposed to be advancing from Tavistock. After inspection of the troops in position in different parts of the Down, the battle commenced. 'Despite the heavy showers which fell at times the proceedings were watched by a considerable number of spectators in carriages and on foot.' There were 2718 troops in total, including the 2nd Battalion Rifle Brigade, with twenty-nine officers, twenty-two sergeants, forty-four band, fifteen drummers, eleven pioneers and 397 rank and file (518 total); Field Battery; 13th Brigade; 2nd Brigade—3rd Regiment; 1st Brigade—12th Regiment; and the Royal Marines Light Infantry. *The Times*, 9 October 1868, p. 10.
3. Mr and Mrs Bramley were negotiating about the Richardsons' house at Rawcliffe.
4. Mrs Bramley.
5. Jack and Lizzie Brett.
6. Harrie Bailey: they were waiting to hear if JRB would agree to Harrie remaining in school while WLR and MR returned to Australia.

128 [From EB in Leicester, England, to MR in Devon, England]

58 Rutland St, Leicester
11th Oct^r [1868, Sunday]

My dear Mary

The enclosed letter came this morning not any Newspapers for Walter Sarah left orders and stamps for her maid to forward all to Rawcliffe we have none by this Mail at present Grace returns to morrow I hope you keep well and Lizzie is more reconciled to her loss poor little thing tis far better off than a sufferer here no doubt you have been fully occupied and I hope now will take rest whilst you can Walter tells me in a letter this morning he wishes you were at home for there will be so much packing as he has Let the house to leave the first week in Decr why you can do all in a fortnight and why bother stay whilst you can there will be time enough to store them away the last week in Novr they are dry where they are and why should Walter <u>Hurry off</u> until a Ship is fixed upon he seems to prefer Liverpool to sail from

You can come home here any time and bring all you need Walter also but so long and expensive a journey to Devon had not ought to be cut short this is the fruits of separating Man & Wife I want you to be with Lizzy awhile so John must try and persuade Walter four weeks will be as long as you wish at Rawcliffe I fancy I shall persuade Sarah to stay as long as she can she looks stout and well has a bad cold so has Grace tis time to put on winter clothing our Room very hot to me when the Gas is lighted I have been very unwell it seems as if I could not go on long without medicine "Oh such a size and so hard Grace & Sarah sent off for Mr Lankaster[1] for I got that sore the skin was in blisters like skin dipped in milk in the lower part of the Abdomen I quite thought I was ruptured and all would burst through so was Examined M^r L said the water had accumulated there was more than the Body would hold so it had stretched the skin to its extremity and was also in my legs I was parched with fever I have medicine twice a day and a pill at night tis not so difficult to pass the water now altho'

like Neddles [needles] and I am better thank God tho obliged at times to carry my Burden on my hands I must move about or there would be no action   Sarah brought me some fine Ostend Rabbits M^r L said Rabbits were not good for me (Game <u>was</u>) or Mutton or fish no Beef nor Pork nor pickles all simple and pure and supporting) dont tell but we had Eels for dinner I enjoyed it with Grace when I began to swell I thought the fish were swimming in the water instead of which I was as hard as a brick bat) I must keep up to good support I cannot take Brandy & water nor Whiskey and the Gin tastes queer have had a glass of Port to day and keep to one cup of tea Grace wrote to Walter we got letters from him this morning am better to day only a size—I don't want to see any one—callers put me about I shall be better in time I think my good constitution will bear me through with Gods help and He has never forsaken me in my hour of need—give my love and a kiss to dear Edith I want <u>your</u> Affida<u>v</u>it have got all the others [this] morning why dont Walter or you send it Mr Williams[2] has all del^d [delivered] to him but yours says tis nothing but correct that he should file them I am responsible for Edith[3] She cannot sell until 21 bless her she may get another by then do write dear Mary it seems so long Sarah and Grace join me in love ever your| Affectionate Mother
>   Elizabeth Bailey
>   *Text:* ALS NLA MS133/1/119

[1]   Dr Henry Lankestor, Surgeon, 63 High Street, Leicester, was a witness to Elizabeth Bailey's will
         dated 16 October 1868 and to the codicil dated 17 May 1869. She died on 8 July 1869 (cause
         of death stated as 'Morbis Cordis'), aged sixty-seven.
[2]   EB's solicitor in Leicester.
[3]   Edith Brett, her granddaughter.

129 **[From EB in Leicester, England, to LB in Devon, England]**

>   58 Rutland St, Leicester
>   [Sunday, 11 October 1868]

My dear Lizzie

Just a line of love in Mary's Sarah & Grace gone to Church I hope all has passed away with resignation and remember the dear one is not lost but gone before I hope Walter will not hasten Mary from you as you will be a comfort to each other I sent John a Leicester paper did I do right by the Obituary it will save you some writing about how is your bosom do not take much liquid for a month or it will fly to your head and you will find the milk springs more abundant Kiss dear Edith and give my love to John all alive and <u>looking well</u> at 62[1] | God bless you all accept the love of Sarah Grace and your affectionate Mother
>   Elizabeth Bailey
write me soon and tell me all
>   *Text:* ALS NLA MS133/1/119 [Reverse of Letter 128]

[1]   Mrs Sarah Brett lived at 62 Rutland Street, Leicester. Probably Jack Brett's mother or aunt.

130 [From WLR in Rawcliffe, England, to MR in Devon, England]

[Rawcliffe, Yorkshire]
Sunday Evening [18 October 1868]

My dear Poll:

I got yours of Friday this morning—I sent you an "Illustrated Australian Post" today—You will see Adolphus Sïeveright[1] died of consumption   I enclose with this a letter from John—You will see he says he misses us and is glad to hear of our return—I had also one from Mackay with draft for £60–0–0—He is nearly sure to send another £60. this month October wh I will get end of November—as he say the div. on N-Clunes[2] has been paid in to my acct.

I am glad you are being taken care of so well by Liz.—It is impossible for me to leave before the last day of October—I walked to Snaith Church[3] today was much pleased—small congregation—Sermon for half an hour without any notes and very excellent[4]—almost as good as Marchmont—also Choral service. ~~I send you a paper with this~~—& write to your mother—If I do come down it must positively be only for a week as it will take us all our time to pack and arrange about the Sale—I send money for Piano to morrow and enquire cost of same—I dreamed about you last night our usual three week absence is nearly up—I hope you sleep well without anyone to trouble you night or morning I suppose you begin to want me badly—No letters for you. Ned sent you that paper I posted to day—Send Johns letter on to mother in your next to her. My correspondence is awful—Wale does very well. her great weakness is being out at night. I wish she'd do her courting in the kitchen!

I paid Mrs Ibbetson for the Ham [£]1–3–0.—[e]xpenses of House meal &c so far 8.10½—No Star Times yet, will post it when it comes

Have had Ellis to measure how much the cases will come to, he says he can do it in a fortnight—

Took Porter children present of apples today—

Minnie H off to school—

With kind love to the Rifles[5] | I am my dear Poll| Your affect. cousin

Walter

Text: ALS NLA MS133/1/126

[1] Adolphus Sïeveright (1835–1868) born in Malta, son of Charles Whightman Sïeveright, a captain in British army, and Christina née Watt. The family arrived in Port Phillip in 1839. A civil servant, Adolphus was appointed by Governor La Trobe in 1850 to handle foreign mails. See Michael Cannon, *Old Melbourne Town Before the Gold Rush* (Main Ridge, Victoria: Loch Haven Books, 1991) p. 239. Married to Mary Augusta Campbell in 1864, Sïeveright left her with two children (Ada aged three years and Henry, sixteen months) when he died on 27 July 1868.

[2] New North Clunes gold mine shares.

[3] St Laurence Priory Church at Snaith is a large and beautiful church with several chapels, including: the Guild Chapel of the Holy Trinity; Daurney Chapel of the 1st Viscount Downe, Baron Daurney of Cowick; the Stapleton Chapel. Its tower is the oldest part of the church, being Early English (*c.*1215).

[4] The minister was the Reverend Henry R. Rees, who was Vicar for fifteen years and died on 9 June 1877.

[5] John Brett was a Captain in the Prince Consort's Own Rifle Brigade, 2nd Battalion.

131 [From WLR in Rawcliffe, England, to EB in Leicester, England]

[Rawcliffe, Yorkshire]
Monday [19 October 1868]

My dear Mother

I send the enclosed which I only received on Sunday. Mary appears to be enjoying herself amid plenty of hares, grouse, & partridges, good living & sea air—I had a letter from John[1] which I send on to M she will forward it to you He is glad we are going back I trust you are no worse and that Sarah will stay for some days—I walked three miles to church on Sunday and was well rewarded by choral service and an extemporaneous sermon. It is awfully dull here all day. I have got over the first fortnight but the next will be "a tryer"—Harrie is getting on well. He is too young yet for business.[2] John must try & let him have six months at least (after Xmas) more at Fairfield—Wale is very attentive & cooks capitally she wants to go to Australia badly—Minnie Helliwell goes to Nottinghill tomorrow. Love to Sarah & yourself from|Your affect Son

Walter

Text: ALS NLA MS133/1/132

---

[1]   John Robinson Bailey in Melbourne; father of Harrie.
[2]   Harrie Bailey was only fifteen on 7 December 1868. His father relented and Harrie remained at school in Manchester. He did not return to Melbourne until March 1871 on the *Superb*, less than two months before his father's death.

132 [From EB in Leicester, England, to LB in Devon, England]

58 Rutland St, Leicester
19th Oct[r] [1868, Monday]

My dear Lizzie

You will think I might answer more quickly our last just on the way when I am not well I have not spirit to use my pen all last week has been one of suffering the medicine has been more effectual in removing the waters, but it weakens me M[r] Lankaster has been very attentive—seems to alter it as the case requires, he says he can only watch me but cannot cure—Thanks for all your good wishes there is no need for you to come—some bright day "please God" I may improve—then I can come to you and John and Edith I hope you will gain strength and be all happy again in the future—are your nails better dont be making a lot of black for three months mourning dont allow Mary to be at the sewing Machine so long she will without you watch her and tis not good for her. it is an alias for Stocking makers, I dont admire them for Ladies only finishing off let those who have to toil take their full benefit—you would have spurned them when a Girl I know and Mary will repent when she gets the pain in her side. Grace did not manage it so got nothing done—Sarah is a good nurse is talking of leaving for home her maid so far has manag[d] well with her House full and respectable one is a Doctor in a Noblemans Family close by, a Lady and Gent in the dining room and a Lady of good Family at the Top quite full for the winter but Let for less so she will do as well as if for less with uncertainty dear Grace left me last Monday with a full "heart" have a letter to day from her has full duties on and but little leisure says she has not rec[d] a letter from any one since her return M[rs] Wilson the same poor creature Sarah has seen M[rs] Lloyd also Miss Bearington who is an invalid and not able yet to resume her daily Engagement at

Mr Haxbys as Governess all about Graces wishes are made known to her if she is not able to continue at Xmas then Miss B will name it about Grace to Mrs Haxby this for the present is to be kept quiet I am best for the present very quiet even talking is too much for me and I do not get down much before Dinner my appetite has been bad and sickly have had four Oysters at a time they have refreshed me but I soon get tired and choked a Fowl yesterday but I did not care for it feeling so sickly with drink the same, I do not want for any thing thank you am wearing Marys warm red worsted on my Shoulders not too large and being without stays I need a Paletot[1] or scarlet flannel Jacket loose and large not long ones any black one that will wash and wear without ornaments for lying down

Sarah sends love to all is busy stitching Old man[2] better wants Walter to prescribe for him love to John am glad he enjoys the Stilton[3] (mostly bad this fair) Kiss dear Edith is she busy with her Dollys I ought to have sent this last night but did not get all done and was expecting a line from some one—how have you managed your bosom dont drink too much beer I never taste a drop and whilst this nausea is on me the smell of wine or spirits, Lemonade or lemon juice to oysters I have not yet ventured upon Game 3/6 a small brace I fear I should soon be sick so rest up and I want for nothing with love to all and every blessing believe me my dear Children your affectionate| Mother

    Elizabeth Bailey

Full of worth at 62 apparently Hawkins[4] has been there a fortnight to and fro

   Text: ALS NLA MS133/1/120

[1] A paletot was a three-caped mantle with arm-slits.
[2] Samuel Hester (1784–1871), the fourth son of John Hester (1751–1826) and his first wife, Sarah (1747–1798). His older brother, William Hester (1783–1835), had been married to Ann née Robinson, who was EB's deceased older sister. Ann had married William Hester on 17 March 1813 and on her death, Elizabeth inherited 60 Rutland Street (the next door house). Samuel Hester was given free rental of this house (under Ann's will and Elizabeth's will) until his demise. Samuel had been a victualler, like his father and brother William, and ran the New Inn in Leicester. He was also an inspector of weights and in 1849 was described as 'County Inspector of Weight and Measures, Rutland St'. *Cook's Annual Guide to Leicester*, 1849. He became a Freeman of the City of Leicester on 7 May 1807, the same day as his brother William.
[3] Cheese.
[4] Hawkins not identified.

133 [From EB in Leicester, England, to MR in Devon, England]

    58 Rutland St Leicester
    Monday [19 October 1868]

My dear Mary

I was looking for a letter from you to day or else Walter, so did not complete mine last night, I will return Johns[1] letter when next I write Walter, there is none to day only from Grace desires her love to all, is very much engaged now with so many at the commencement of the Quarter am glad John[2] is able to take you about I read of the ball[3] in the paper you are all just as well off if you can only think so "the Almighty appoints all for the best" and I hope dear Lizzie sees it so

dont buy a lot of dresses wear out what you have all will get crushed in packing get a bit of wash leather and stitch it with the yellows in the safest place you will want so many things for your favored land all are pretty they went to Grace but Sarah forgot to tell her who they were for

you will read dear Lizzies and know all for I do not feel up to letter writing it makes me nervous I got Williams[4] paper and sent it to him from Walter all that business is done right I believe Sarah took it the past week has been one of much suffering occasionally I got so large—happily Mr Lankaster has removed it by medicine—the water flows freely but my strength seems to go with it occasionally to day am quite flexible and not so sickly as yesterday when I can take better support it will be better am fanciful as yet I want for nothing and Sarah is a good nurse I have had bad restless nights am better to day and do not rise before 12 or one the blisters of the Skin tight are down

Mr Lankaster has been very anxious and attentive—it is not from medicine I dont know what and a fill water in large quantities and clear no swollen legs to day the heart easier comparatively quiet lying down occasionally suits it best I need not report all this to Walter) he says he will patch me up and do his best but cannot cure and I must keep as gentle as I can in all my movements (he also Mr Toone[5] signed all Testamentary effects last week for me when I asked him about it he said let it be done at once to day if you can but I could not complete all for their signatures before Friday evening when they came and attested all "so that you will know I have given, devised, and bequeathed all I die possessed of or am likely to have from any source now or hereafter to my ten dear Children share & share alike. House Property, yard Coach house 3 cottages &c also all monies out at use Water works Bank &c after all just Debts Funeral Expenses and Testamentary Documents &c shall be satisfied by my Sole Executrix Grace Bailey her Administrating & assigns leaving my youngest daughter Sole Executrix some little spot of Earth must be selected here for my remains whilst I can pay for it the rest will satisfy all for Mothers anxious care forgive more now I am tired

Sarah's love—when will you be coming through here she wants to see you before she leaves me—says your last letter was so long (short) she had scarcely time to read it dear When will be all-right for Harry stay we shall hear 2nd Nov^r

I send Walters last let me have your latest views God bless you dear Mary does Edith remember you Sarah joins in love from your affectionate Mother
        Elizabeth Bailey
I could not collect myself to write this properly
Any letter from Lucinda yet
    Text: ALS NLA MS133/1/120 [On reverse of Letter 132]

1   John Robinson Bailey.
2   John Brett.
3   The ball was held in honour of the visit by His Royal Highness, the Duke of Cambridge, Commander-in-Chief.
4   EB's solicitor.
5   John Hamlet Toone, Chemist, 82 Granby Street, Leicester, a signatory to EB's will.

134 [From WLR in Rawcliffe, England, to MR in Devon, England]

[Rawcliffe, Yorkshire]
Tuesday morning [20 October 1868]

My dear Poll.

Yours of Sunday morning just received—You forgot me on Saturday so I shall see how you like it by not posting this till Wednesday. I shall most likely start from this on Friday week go on to Wakefield & from that to Birmingham that night, then on next morning—You say you are home sick, you cannot want to come back to this dull hole. No No! You want me to teaze you. We are jogging on quietly no news—I am <u>not</u> going to have any open waistcoats, they dont agree with my chest, and I have already got a little cough and must grow my beard under my chin I believe! Medical men are never expected to dress in the height of fashion, and I have always had an aversion to three yards of shirt front being worn in the street. I have been obliged to put on one of the lambs wool undershirts from Scotland they are very cosy.

You did not send the key. I asked you how mother was you said "never heard since Tuesday"—<u>but how was she then</u> We have frosty nights, and I fear she will feel the cold, I suppose by my having no word she is keeping better. Is Grace going to remain at home after Xmas?

I hope your likeness will be a pleasing one, you ought to have a smile on now, nobody to worry you. Be sure and save Holthouses[1] letter as I want to shew it to his brother when I go to London:

Wednesday. A dull wet day. 10 days after this reaches you I will follow it and give you fits. It is now 23 days since you left. I have got on pretty well so far but begin to feel precious dull—My case is better altho' not out of danger yet. One of Robinsons[2] patients came last evening for me to attend his wife—they had not bespoken me—I declined to go—

I will attend to your dressing case. I think when in London I will get a better lock put on it. The piano case has arrived

Love to Lizz. Tell Jack he must issue a new "carte" when I arrive that bill of fare wont shoot this child[3]—

How is Edith? I see that by leaving Birmingham 7. morning, we reach Plym[outh] 20 minutes past 5. you can tell me where they stop long enough for lunch or breakfast. Did you get your likeness taken?[4] I suppose you will send Sam[5] one, wont the others be jealous? I must write & tell Mother to send "The Argus" on to Stoke, & not here.

Lake tells me Mrs Creyke[6] comes here next week—I am glad we shall be away. Wale busy as usual washing, cleaning, scrubbing; I did not sleep well last night at all—Did you? What was the matter—you know, awoke several times—

I suppose you will meet me at Plymouth—Wont it be jolly—|Your affect H
                    W

Text: ALS NLA MS133/1/134

---

[1]   Dr Thomas Le Gay Holthouse (*c.*1819–1901), physician at Ballarat.
[2]   Dr Robinson was the other doctor in the area. Note HHR's use of his name for the fashionable and drunken 'bottle-nosed surgeon' in Buddlecombe with whom Richard Mahony feuds. See *FRM II*, pp. 67–94.
[3]   'To shoot one's fry', to lose the good opinion of others which one once possessed. It seems an unfortunate turn of phrase, since Jack's son had died only two weeks previously.
[4]   One of the photos (showing MR reading) taken by Blake Brothers Photographers, 93 Fore Street, Devonport, has survived in the MoU Richardson Collection.
[5]   MR's favourite brother, Samuel Bailey.

⁶   Louisa Frances Creyke née Croft (*c.*1825–1890), widow of Ralph Creyke (2nd) and mother of
the present young squire Ralph Creyke (3rd).

135   [From WLR in Rawcliffe, England, to MR in Devon, England]

Rawcliffe

Thursday morning [22 October 1868]

My dear Poll:

Yours of 20th. Your Bradshaw is different from the old one I have I can however make it
nearly all out except the fares, and those we must leave to the clerks. I think I will start Friday
morning 6.45. & get to Leicester about 2 as my getting there at 11. night & leaving so early
would give me no time to see Mother & might upset her.

Can then leave for Birmingham you say 10 minutes to 7. My old Bradshaw says 7. I
suppose the latest is correct that is yours—

This is a charming day but the nights & mornings are getting cold. I am sorry the time
passes slowly with you that is a bad sign—10 days today one week only when you get this. I
suppose the letters are delivered about 4 or 5 PM—I shall enjoy the run down & the smell of
the sea once more before we embark on "the Briny"—Not a word from Leicester so conclude
all is not well—My bad case is better and on the road to recovery. I shall be able to leave him.
Be sure & dont miss the Australian mail by putting off: Remember your letter must be posted
on the 29 at the latest that is Thursday next. Wale says you have locked up your bonnett. Do
you remember a double breasted silk vest I had, where is it? or did I dispose of it? Shall I bring
Lizz down a few pots of jam & keep the chickens for mother. I see one of the hens is
missing—There is only the Cock & one old hen now—I had better bring you apples, pears,
Artichokes, Jam & keep the fowls for mother as they are not looking well just now & they will
get over their moulting by December 5.

Friday morning: I have just got yours of Wednesday with the Photos. I am very much
pleased indeed—they are both very nice. I shall have half a dozen of the reading & smiling
beauty for myself. The other is nice too but it is a leetle bit too much of the "Regal"—Wale
likes it best Which does Liz prefer? I will write to mother Your acct. is almost what I feared.
The action of the heart was so fluttering as to alarm me several times when she was here, and
the dropsy also a bad sign and one announcing the approach of the end. I trust she is prepared
for the great change, I think she is for altho' not a demonstrative woman she read much and
Grace gave her some nice books. Tell me of some clergyman I could ask to visit her. I will start
on Friday this day week & spend the evening with her. I am greatly pleased she has in some
measure settled her affairs. I think she ought to have a young person entirely to wait on her,
for when once she goes to bed she will not get down stairs again, & Selena¹ is unable for both
& Grace seems to be unable to remain at home! We must be thankful we came home to see
for the last time Poor old Dr C.² your mother and our other relatives—

Wale says your black lace bonnett is locked up in the trunk in the box room—

See and get all your sewing done before I come to you—Yes I do think these Photos the
best you have ever had done & especially the reading one—You naughty thing to give me
quite the thrill of the heart when I look at you—The Helliwells came over last evening & took

supper with me sitting for two hours—She says she feels quite lonely in your abcence—I got the enclosed letter from Cork this morning with a likeness of Cheyne[3] which I keep—

I paid willingly the <u>extra twopence</u> on yours this morning—They have done the correct thing with Lindesay[4] to send him away from wretched Ireland, to wealthy Manchester—

This is a damp muggy day. I hope to get another letter on Sunday at the latest—Remember I leave Friday morning—No letters after Wednesday from me here <u>Oh!</u> <u>Yes I will post one on Thursday</u> so you will get it Friday afternoon.

Love to Lizzy & Jack & trust they are fattening you up for the show for I mean to have a look <u>at your legs</u>—

The day has cleared up & got quite warm—

I cant say I admire the new envelopes much—Good bye old woman with much love & many kisses from Your| Affect Cousin

      Wa R.

That gabby woman M^{rs} H[5] is pestering me to go over there—I have refused half a dozen times

    Text: ALS NLA MS133/1/134A

1   Selena Sanders (b. 1814), daughter of Thomas Sanders and his wife Elizabeth; she was christened on 12 September 1814 at All Saints Church, Loughborough, Leicestershire. She was Elizabeth Bailey's servant and was present at her death (witness on EB's death certificate).
2   Dr Bayne Cheyne died on 2 August 1868.
3   Marmaduke Cheyne Richardson (1851–1925), son of Caroline and Henry Richardson.
4   Lindesay Richardson, the younger brother of Marmaduke Cheyne.
5   Eliza Anne Helliwell, the brewer's wife.

136 [From WLR in Rawcliffe, England, to MR in Devon, England]

Rawcliffe
Sunday—[25 October 1868]

My deary

We had a heavy gale last evening—I had to get Wale to shut the shutters. I thought at one time the windows would have been blown in. It abated before 11—I had a wretched bad night—Called out to a confinement <u>the last</u> this morning & did not get lunch—I have just seen the Helliwells they like the reading picture & Mrs H has bespoken one—She presented me with the enclosed for you—of course her head was a guy—I think she is a little touched! She admires the white dress amazingly & there is no doubt you should never be taken in black again—Photographers are as a rule asses & dont know their business! I hope all are well & that you are enjoying yourself & working away. I shall soon start for you now. Don't be afraid I shall not be tired! I shall have some oysters at Leicester & a good breakfast before starting. You take a hot bath every morning that is a new dodge, however it is good for you I am sure & you look ever so much plumper in your Photo <u>but I must see</u> & judge for myself—I still take my cold bath & shall miss it fearfully on ship board. I must start for Liverpool as soon as we get back here so Lizz must not xpect me to stay more than a week or at most 10 days. Monday week after I arrive

Monday—I hear two pieces of news one that Mrs Creyke returns on Thursday the other that Turner[1] leaves Rawcliffe my informant added "<u>there wont be many sorry at that</u>". I am beginning to pack up—was rather dissapointed this morg. no letter Sunday no letter

Monday—Mrs H.[2] is without a servant again. H. has taken a lease of the Brewery for 7 years—a charming morning but turned very cold in the afternoon with showers

You wont get many more letters nor write many more before I come to you now—

Tuesday I have just got yours of Sunday—a mere scrap[1]. I suppose you got my other of Saturday Monday morning when you didn't expect it

Get as many photos as you like 1 doz. Reading—& 1 doz of the last that Jack likes—I dont believe you want me a bit, all gammon! you wont hug me will you? We'll have a row the first night—You'll want to put on my trousers. This is the last letter then but one—I'll attend about the jam—the apples &c.

This is a cloudless day I wrote to mother and told her when I shd. arrive, & not to have anything but a small tender beef steak & a mealy potatoe. Of course Lancaster[3] knows as I do that she is only likely to last a very short time—any week may be her last or she may live on with perfect rest & ease of mind for some months This is a frequent termination of such cases—The bonnett in my hat box is a black Tuile[4] one not lace—it is one I never saw you wear not the pretty one you had last winter with the Red Rose & long lace strings Wale says that is put away in my box & I've not the key—However I will bring it

The Creykes come on Thursday—I'll write on Thursday

Love to all—I suppose I'll get another tomorrow morg. Shall I bring Edith a doll from Leicester—| Ever your bullying & kissing Hubby

W

I do [hope] Grace has told Miss Wilson she must leave—She will be so sorry afterwards that she did not remain with her.[5] She cannot say she has not been told. I think if she does not intend doing so—you ought to engage a little girl to remain with her & to do nothing else as it is quite possible that a sudden seizure of syncope[6] or fainting may come on & if no one is near she may fall & never rise again—

Text: ALS NLA MS133/1/135

1   The Reverend Robert Turner (1804–1880), Vicar at St James's until 1879.
2   Mrs Helliwell.
3   Dr Lankestor.
4   Tulle, a delicate thin silk fabric.
5   Elizabeth Bailey.
6   Brief loss of consciousness associated with transient cerebral anaemia, as in heart block, sudden lowering of the blood pressure. MD, p. 1773.

137 [From EB in Leicester, England, to MR in Devon, England]

58 Rutland St Leicester
26th Oct^r [1868, Monday]

My dear Marie

I was glad to see your dear face this morning altho' I do not like white as a dress for Photogram the features are good I will return by Walter whom I got a letter from yesterday he will be here on Friday and will not write again you will here from Sarah she left me last Friday after my slight dinner of Leverett I felt sick and the vomit gave me great relief as the swimming feeling had been on me some days I was upset but greatly relieved Tom[1] came next night and I have slept relieved from choking sensation and phlegm better I do not rise until nr [near] Dinner time and take my medicine once a day a Cup of bran & milk for breakfast no relish

for Tea or Coffee nor wine or spirits is it not a strange change M[r] Lankastor thinks me better
to day will meet Walter here on Friday afternoon [illegible word] I do not need any thing
from Rawcliffe you are very thoughtful for me—I will see to your Engraving at Grays Grace
could not get them done for less so here they are as you left them it has been raining poor
weather had a nice Pheasant yesterday but I feel sick to day my stomach will not take all at
once—The water keeps off I am all in Wrinkles and shaking I think the change may be for the
better only I wish have time—"Gods Will be done"—He will do "what seemeth best for me"
do not reproach yourself for not remaining with me tis wrong" I appreciate all your goodness
also Walters I want for nothing either small loose jacket or Gown that will be useful over my
dress tis only the arms and back I feel the draught but even this is not expedient I have white
I hope you keep up your walks and keep well never mind the work

you will note what I say about the Chinese Robes of Toms better sold and his few debts
honorably paid let me know your wishes he will then be able to pay what he borr[d] of Walter
and I shall feel relieved he has given up his W W[2] I have to pay so far his feet are very bad he is
good and quiet here

write me by return post will attend to all you say Kiss Edith for me and forgive me not
sending this yesterday is there any thing else I can send you would you like a Pork Pie[3] letters
from Sarah who left me with heavy heart she was very thoughtful Grace Bessie and others
I am not dull if I can get this bile off shall feel relief God bless you dear Marie with love ever
your affect Mother
> Eliz Bailey

if I have not send all ask me again This is for 2 days Toms love to all

> *Text:* ALS NLA MS133/1/121

---

1   Thomas Bailey.
2   Wild Ways, or Wicked Ways or Wild West?
3   The pork pies of Mowbray, Leicestershire, are still considered a special treat. See *FRM II*,
     pp. 34, 47.

138 [From WLR in Rawcliffe, England, to MR in Devon, England]

Rawcliffe
Wednesday—[28 October 1868]

My own old "gal"

I know you dont want to see me at all & wont be glad to know in [I'm] coming—I am
tho' and when you get this will be at Leicester as I started Thursday morning instead of
Friday—Your letters will miss me serves you right you should have written sooner—

I have been packing up & getting all ready Hip! Hip!

Friday. 5.20—at Plymouth instead of Saturday[1] The fact is I couldn't go on dream
dreaming all night—and want to punch you so bad and to give it you—

Wont I just diddy iddy I do—Youll have much to put up with—Your affect friend|
Sincerely yours &c

> W.

> *Text:* ALS NLA MS133/1/133

¹ While he was visiting MR and the Bretts in Stoke, WLR received an invitation from Lt-Col. Hercules Walker: 'Lieutenant Colonel Walker and the Officers, 2nd Batt. Rifle Brig., request the pleasure of Dr Richardson's Company at Dinner on Thursday next the 5th Inst at 7.30 o'clock. Devonport, November 3rd.' NLA MS133/1/247.

139 [From WLR in Eccles, England, to MR at Leicester, England]

Swiss Cottage Eccles [Manchester]¹

Sunday [29 November 1868]

Dear M—

I arrived safely about 11 & after seeing W.D.² at his office went to Fairfield I found Harrie all well & had an excellent character of him from M^r C³—I took him out a walk & as he was fond of oranges gave him a treat⁴—I told him of Mrs Helliwells kind invitation—He is at the top of the first Geography class: there are several bigger boys than he is in the school

I found W.D. & Carrie very well & glad to see me—I brought with me a little rabbitt skin dog which has given intense delight to little Lindesay⁵—They were pleased with the rug—Mrs Johnson & two other rather nice people spent the eveg. with us & a splendid supper was served at 10—Some rich trifle knocked me up & I have not eaten any breakfast or dinner yet altho' roast goose was very tempting—

We had arranged to go to the Cathedral this morning but I was not able, however I have had a glass of beer & a bit of toast & am coming round—I hope to have a line from you tomorrow at Ismay's and to find that you go on as nicely as I did. Manchester was as usual, cold slippery & dirty! Eccles has improved—I hope Wale saw to all the luggage & that you have been resting yourself and not obliged to resume nursing Grace

Give her my love and let me know if she enjoyed the chickens and mother the tea—W.D. says we can buy in Liverpool just as well as here or in London—Both he and Carrie send love & a kiss from Lindesay—he toddles about & eats at Table not spoiled a bit! he is sent off when he cries! & so know to be good is best—

Your next will be to Rathgar Road⁶ if you write Monday I will get it Wednesday or Thursday morg—Hoping you feel rested & slept better than I did, with much love & kisses| I am my dear Mary| Your fond & true

W.L.R.

Text: ALS NLA MS133/1/160

¹ The home of his 'radical' cousin, William Duke Richardson and his wife Caroline née Fisher. WLR was *en route* to Liverpool to make the final arrangements for their trip back to Melbourne and then on to Dublin to visit his cousin. The Rawcliffe house had been sold and their belongings packed for shipment and their servant, Wale, was staying in Leicester with MR, helping with final preparations.

² William Duke Richardson.

³ Mr Craig, principal of Harrie's school.

⁴ It was Harrie's fifteenth birthday a week later (7 December).

⁵ Robert Lindesay Richardson, christened 18 July 1867 in the cathedral, Manchester, son of WLR's cousin, William and Carrie.

⁶ The Dublin home of WLR's cousin, John Richardson and his second wife, Sophy née Wood.

140   [From WLR in Dublin, Ireland, to MR in Leicester, England]

23 Rathgar Road [Rathgar, Dublin][1]

Wednesday [2 December 1868]

My dearest Polly

I arrived safely in Dublin yesterday morning about 11 & came out here direct—Sophy was very glad to see me & I went into Dublin to meet John—

We had a roughish passage & you would not have liked it at all—Miserable small bunks I got yours & Argus safely, they were here on my arrival—so you see letters do not take 3 days—

I also got yours & mothers this morg. You will get this some time Thursday Sophy wants to know if you would like the stockings white or grey—I should think you could get them as well in Leicester to tell you the truth I am as near full as possible—However I will bring you half a doz pair of the best I can get—NNC.[2] are looking amazingly well—I have not had time to read my Argus yet I can see nothing of Langleys dismissal[3] but I see the Revd Seddon & two other ministers[4] have had to resign in consequence of improprieties—of course S. & J. are full of regrets because you are not with me

I am sorry mother does not improve. I hope you will get a nice dress & will not think <u>of the price</u> get a 30/- one <u>not</u> grey! <u>Claret</u> or half mourning

You must forgive me not writing yesterday—send on letters to me when they arrive—

Fine mild weather here—Is Lancaster visiting Mother

Sophy chose the reading one[5] & John the straight one—

We are going to see M[rs] Os.[6] this morng & then I am going to buy a guineas worth of groceries to send to an old stepbrother[7] who is out of a billett—& who is supported by his wife.—

We must do some good with the dividends entrusted to us—I sent off Lucindas parcel—Love to Grace

Have not decided about going to Cork[8] yet—Am glad to have a line from mother I will write her next time—Get all you want dont think of prices—There is <u>already</u> £325 safe for us when we land in Melbourne Money laid out here in <u>good</u> things really good things will be doubled when we get to Australia by their increased value—I intend to buy a 20 guinea gold watch at Bennetts in London—Get three new pair of boots at Selenas freind, also your underlinen let it be the best—see if you can buy it ready made—I intend to make you a present of a writing desk[9] for your birthday[10] so dont buy one. I think I shall buy one here or in Liverpool I am using one of Sophys that I like not a little one like we saw but a good one—

I am quite well again & hope you will soon be rid of your cold—I went to hear Bellew[11] read—It was acting, recitation, dramatic I counted 30 priests there—the most magnificent Hall I have <u>ever</u> been in You will be delighted with Liverpool—The Southampton letters will be delivered Saturday or Sunday I will write again tomorrow—I have bought some photos of Ireland 6[d] each—I could not find my kid gloves I bought 2 pair of calves skin 8¼ 2/6 each—in Sackville Street—Write & let me know when the cleaning takes place tell mother—That would get the fever out of the neighbourhood—fumigate with sulphur every day in the kitchen until you feel the fumes up stairs—Good bye God bless you dearest—get out as soon as the weather gets fair & try & get well for Your Attached Husband

Walter

Text: ALS NLA MS133/1/114

1   The home of Sophia née Wood and John Richardson, son of Sarah and Marmaduke Jenny Richardson of the Rothsay and Caithness Regiment of Fencibles, who was the brother of WLR's father. John, an Attorney in the Court of Probate, Dublin, had seven children (all by his first wife, Anna née Bristow whom he had married in 1829): Charles (who died aged thirty in 1860, leaving a widow and small daughter), Marmaduke, Mervyn (who had travelled to Australia with John Cheyne in 1853), Albert, Sarah, Alexander, and Walter. John Richardson married Sophia Wood (the daughter of Edward Bell Wood) in 1854.

2   New North Clunes Gold Mining Company started in 1859, with James W. Esmond, the gold discoverer, being one of the shareholders. The mine became one of the best in the district and contributed to WLR's increasing prosperity. The first gold was obtained on 5 October 1867 and up to the end of May 1867 424,461 tons of quartz had been crushed yielding 2,411,802 ounces of gold—value at £4 per ounce, £967,208. Withers, p. 225.

3   Thomas E. Langley was discharged from the Victorian Police Force on 2 October 1868. He had entered the force on 1 March 1852.

4   Three scandals from ecclesiastical circles were reported in *The Argus*. The first concerned the Minister at Christ Church, St Kilda, the Reverend David Seddon. Seddon was well known to the Richardsons. He had performed the marriage ceremony for John Robinson Bailey and his second wife Jane Rainsford on 4 April 1861, and was the cousin of Elizabeth Searle née Cooper (married to the Reverend Cooper Searle in 1856), one of two cousins whom he had brought with him when he emigrated in 1852. Seddon had to relinquish his position two months before in consequence of an 'accusation which he was unable to refute, of having been guilty of a serious impropriety'. The second concerned the Reverend Joseph Beer, a Congregational Minister, whose resignation from the Church was refused by the Congregational Association, which instead expelled him because he had seduced a young woman in his employment. On top of these two scandals came another involving the Reverend James Taylor, a leading Baptist Minister and late Pastor of the Collins Street Church, Melbourne. 'The charge, which originally was that he had kissed a lady member of his congregation, has subsequently assumed a much more serious aspect, though in consequence of the unwise reticence of the committee who were appointed to investigate the matter, the precise nature of the misconduct complained of has not been indicated.' *The Argus*, 12 October 1868, Supplement, p. 2.

5   The *cartes de visite* made in Devonport.

6   Caroline Osborne née Sirée (b. 1808), the sister of WLR's mother, Lucinda Cheyne. Mrs Osborne lived at 21 Wellington Road, Dublin.

7   Most likely to be Alexander Richardson (1803–1890), the eldest son of WLR's father, Lieutenant-Colonel Alexander Richardson by his third wife, Elizabeth née Smyth. Alexander had retired from his position as an Inspector of the Dublin and Kingston Railway Company. He was living with his second wife, Jane, the daughter of Captain William Pyke, RN, Devon, England.

8   His sister, Caroline and her husband, Henry Richardson lived in Cork, where Henry was Registrar of the Court of Probate.

9   A portable case holding writing material, which when opened out had a surface for writing upon.

10 MR's thirty-third birthday was on 28 December 1868.

11 John Chippendall Montesquieu Bellew (1823–1874), born at Lancaster; from 1848 to 1868 was an Anglican clergyman in England and Calcutta, for twelve years a most popular London preacher; then turning Catholic, devoted himself to public readings. His younger son, Harold Kyrle Bellew (1857–1911), became a famous actor, whose career started in the early 1870s on the goldfields in NSW. He returned to England, joining the Henry Irving Company at the London Lyceum. Later he toured the world, twice visiting Australia, and joined the Yorick Club in Melbourne. Eric Irvin, *Dictionary of the Australian Theatre 1788–1914* (Sydney: Hale & Iremonger, 1985), p. 45.

141 [From MR in Leicester, England, to WLR in Dublin, Ireland]

[58 Rutland Street, Leicester]

Thursday afternoon, Decr 3nd [1868]

My dear Walter

I have been in a regular fright thinking you had not arrived safe I have only just received your's I really think if it had not come I should have telegraphed to Sophie I sent to the Post Office & they told me if I posted before 7 at night you would get next morning so I made sure you were ill at Liverpool I am a little more composed now but it quite upset me this morning when none came. I was very glad darling you are better & I hope you will keep so—Be sure & don't bring Grey stockings they are my aversion besides they are for evening wear & must be white but never mind them I can get them here—You are very good to buy me a desk but don't burden yourself with it I would not wish a prettier than Grace's—& her's cost a guinea Walnut inlaid—I could not carry a larger one about. I have just found out I am writing on two sheets of paper—My usual trick—I am glad you are seeing all old friends remember me kindly to them—Lanley's [Langley's] dismissal was in the gazette news—I suppose you will be telling me one of these fine day's when to come & meet you. My cold is a trifle better but my mouth all broken out, the cleaning is nearly finished—Grace talk's of returning to Wansford on Tuesday. She is quite well. Mother a little better We went in to see Uncle[1] yesterday he is as well as ever—Mother had a present sent her of a couple of Rabbits & a Pheasant which she is going to keep (if she can) until you come—

The weather is so wet that we cant go out—I went to Gray's about the Silver & ordered it for I was afraid if I waited longer they would be sold for the small fork's had gone so I have 6 <u>new</u> small ones & they are doing the crests for 6^d each that is reasonable—Mother has bought you such a pretty present of course I chose it a handsome Fish Knife & Fork. Shall I have the Crest put on it You are quite right to make a present of groceries gladden some hearts for Xmas—

I had a letter from Bessie[2] & one from Sarah the former will be home next Tuesday fortnight. Send me word if you go to Cork—I am sure John & Sophy will make you very happy.

Besure you see the Phoenix Park[3] this time. I shall not buy my under linen until we go to London. I find it difficult to fill the paper for I have no news to interest you—I shall be very delighted to see you again What day will it be. If you tell me in time I will have a letter at Ismay's for you

I have renumbered the sheets so I hope you will make it out Love to your host & hostess—& now my own Good bye dont be so long in writing again God bless & keep you is ever the prayer of your| loving wife

Marie

lots of love & kisses from us all

Text: ALS NLA MS133/1/154 and MS133/1/162

---

[1]   Samuel Hester.

[2]   Elizabeth Turnham, MR's cousin.

[3]   Phoenix Park was designed and walled by the Duke of Ormonde (1610–1688) in 1671, and opened to the public by Lord Chesterfield (Philip Dormer Stanhope, 1694–1773), Lord-Lieutenant of Ireland, in 1747. The park has a circumference of about seven miles and the total area in about 1750 acres. The name 'Phoenix' is a corruption of the Irish words *fionn uisce*, meaning 'pale or clear water', which referred to the spring (once a noted spa) in the grounds. Adrian MacLoughlin, *Guide to Historic Dublin* (Dublin: Gill and Macmillan, 1979), p. 127.

142 [From WLR in Dublin, Ireland, to MR in Leicester, England]

23 Rathgar Road Dublin
Thursday [3 December 1868]

My dearest

I posted a letter to you last eveng which I hope reached you this morng. The air here is delightfully warm equal to Rawcliffe in Octr. Yesterday Sophy & I went to a morg lecture by a very eloquent man at one of the churches: the place was full—Then we went to see Mrs Osborne & her daughter & right glad they were to see us I have promised them our photos—Nelson[1] has left Dublin & gone to Sligo to be one of the brethren—We then went & ordered the little hamper of groceries I mentioned in my last & I came home & wrote a letter. Spent the eveng quietly at home with them. I found time to read "The Argus" & saw Langley's dismissal rather a good thing for Kabat, I suppose he was sent to Beechworth to supersede Langley. I have not decided yet what day I leave this or where I go but think I will stay over Sunday; they are most kind! I hope you are better & have chosen a pretty and good material for your dress. Tell Wale to go to Mr Cox at the "Advertiser" office & ascertain how & on what terms, she can get out to Australia Melbourne

Friday [4 December]—Yours of Thursday just come—An unnecessary fright my dearest Yesterday we went over the Phoenix Park & I then took leave of Sophy & applied at the Castle for an order to go over Mountjoy prison.[2] I presented my order & was shewn by the assistant superintendent over the womens prison I did not tell her who I was for some time. You remember she is Alicks mother my brothers widow[3] She has still the vestiges of beauty and a subdued quiet manner. I went to her little house & saw her daughter Lucinda & was of course much affected. They are R. Catholics—I am going out with Sophy this morng to buy her a new dress—also your stocks & John & I purpose going this eveng to see Charles Mathews[4]—in two of his celebrated characters

I am delighted you are better & only regret you are not with me altho our roads are very sloppy & without strong boots or goloshes you would most probably get constant colds going about with me—And so Grace is really well & going back. I think at this moment of starting on Monday but do not write to Ismays as I do not return via Liverpool but Holyhead getting home to you perhaps same night—Kind love to Grace & mother—glad the old gentleman[5] is better. It rains here at night but the days have all been fair—get the crest on all you like. If I decide to go to Cork I will tell you before I start Tremendous number of carriages in Dublin & many pretty girls—The streets filthy the prisons empty—Mr Disraeli[6] has resigned & the poor Queen obliged to send for that turncoat Gladstone[7]—The Roman Catholics here rule every thing & no Protestant any chance of any help or support from them—I hope you are getting on with your work—Any letters via Southampton you may I think send them here to me if you get them so as to post them Saturday—I will then get them Sunday—Most likely I will write again tomorrow to you however as you are so fidgetty—John & Sophy desire their kind loves—They talk of moving to the seaside next summer or spring rather—

You need not post all the Australian newspapers—They will amuse me when I come to you I have been obliged to take off my linen shirt the climate is so mild & wear my light coat—

Good bye dearest; get well and tell me when you would like me to come so as not to incommode Mother with much love & kisses ever Your Attached| Husband

Walter

You did not tell me the color of your new dress!

Text: ALS NLA MS133/1/115

1   Probably Horatio Nelson Sirée (b. *c.*1844), WLR's cousin, son of Henry Sirée, who was Lucinda Cheyne's brother.

2   Mountjoy Prison, named after Lord Mountjoy (d. 1798), was erected in the 1850s to the plan of London's Pentonville. Over the years it not only housed many political prisoners, but was where many executions took place, and as such was an emotive place in Ireland for decades during the bitter struggles between the Irish and the British government. Adrian MacLoughlin, p. 53.

3   Ellen née O'Connor, the widow of Henry Downing Richardson.

4   Charles James Mathews (1803–1878), described as a 'delightfully light comedian, of charming grace and delicacy' (*Chambers*, p. 642). Son of comedian Charles Mathews (1776–1835) who became immensely successful in the profession of 'entertainer', visiting America twice. In 1838, Charles James Matthews married Madame Vestris, née Lucia Elizabeth Bartozzi (1797–1856), actress and theatre manager. He performed in Melbourne during the 1870 season and Dr James Neild arranged for the Yorick Club to welcome him with a dinner at Scott's Hotel on 28 March 1870 (Love, p. 238). As a new member of the club, WLR may well have attended.

5   Samuel Hester.

6   Benjamin Disraeli (1804–1881) had become Prime Minister on 27 February 1868. Some months later, a vote of confidence defeated Disraeli and the Queen decided not to accept his resignation (as she was an ardent and life-long supporter of her new PM) but opted instead for a later dissolution of Parliament, hoping that the Tories would win the election. However in November 1868, the Tories were beaten and the Queen had to ask the Liberal Party leader, William Gladstone, to form a ministry. '"Mr. Disraeli threatens to resign. The poor Queen will be forced to send for that turncoat Gladstone.'" *FRM II*, p. 18.

7   William Ewart Gladstone (1809–1898) had originally been elected to Parliament as a Conservative in 1832; had become a 'Peelite', a supporter of the Conservative Prime Minister, Sir Robert Peel, during the 1845 machinations of the repeal of the Corn Laws, when Lord Stanley (afterwards Earl of Derby), Disraeli and others formed a 'no surrender' Tory party; and finally moved over to join the Liberal Party in 1859.

143 [From MR in Leicester, England, to WLR in Dublin, Ireland]

[58 Rutland Street, Leicester]

Saturday noon, Dec' 5ᵗʰ 1868

My own darling

    I am so pleased to hear that I shall so soon see you. I do so long for you again but still I do not wish to hurry you for this place will be duller than ever after such going's about as you seem to be having—Sophy is very kind I am sure. Today I have a bad headache only when I move just as though small stones were rattling about but I think it is from lying awake so long in a morning My cold is nearly gone & the sight of you will quite restore me, we really can't get out here except in pouring rain all the week we have not had a fine day so you are fav'or'd

    The enclosed came from Lucinda yesterday—I could not post in time—I half hope you wont go to Cork.

    You can come whenever you like as I have the Top room all to myself & I'll guarantee to make room for you—I have had no other letter's so after this shall keep all until you come—

Besure & tell me when you leave Dublin. I shall like to come & meet you. I have bought
3 nice prs of Boots from Selina's brother 1 at 7/6 1-6/6 1-5/9—very good indeed.

My new dress is the same as the one you used to admire so much on Lizzie only trimmed
with Blue instead of Black. I am glad you are leaving a good Name with your poor relatives
I hope you will enjoy the Theatre—he[1] is a good "actor"—My work is nearly done—Wale is
still with me—

Grace wont go back until you come her old plan putting off till the last but she is
company for me so I don't mind

Besure & remember <u>White stockings</u> I should love to have been with my darling but I
think the rest here has done me good If you would like to spend another week pray do—I will
do without you We are going to make you some "Brawn" on Tuesday—I dont forget what
you like, Mother better, sends her love also Grace. God bless & keep you my own darling all
love & kisses| from your wife

      Mary

Wrap up well it will be cold travelling Goodbye XXXXXX

You need not ask me when I would <u>like you to come</u> you know quite <u>well—you teaze</u>

    Text: ALS NLA MS133/1/153

[1]   Charles James Mathews.

144 [From WLR in Dublin, Ireland, to MR in Leicester, England]

              23 Rathgar Road [Rathgar, Dublin]

              Saturday 4. PM [5 December 1868]

My dearest

This is to let you know that I purpose starting for you on Monday morning at ¼ past
6—from Dublin and shall, all being well, be with you the same evening about 6 to ½ past—

Do not post any letters ~~after~~ on Sunday—

We have just returned from Dalkey[1]—yesterday we went to the Irish Academy[2]—

John recommends me to say that a pressing invitation from Cork may alter my plans but
I do not think so—if I decide at all on going to Cork I will telegraph Monday morning—I
hope ~~we~~ I will not put you about if so I can easily get a bed at Cooks—

The weather is wet & fearfully muddy—

I am writing in the dark

Love to every body—I expect a letter from you Sunday morning| Your affect Husband

    Walter

    Text: ALS NLA MS133/1/116

[1]   Although Dalkey was a popular seaside jaunt for Dubliners—south of the Dublin City and
connected by railway through Kingston (Dun Laoghaire)—it was for family reasons that WLR
would have gone there. His uncle, Dr Horatio Nelson Sirée, brother of Lucinda Cheyne, resided
at Rhoda Cottage, Kent Road, Dalkey.

[2]   First meeting of the Irish Academy was held on 3 May 1785. Its title was changed to 'Royal
Irish Academy' by charter, 28 January 1786.

145 [From EB in Leicester, England, to MR in Liverpool, England][1]

58 Rutland St [Leicester]

Thursday Morning 9 o'clock [26 December 1868]

My dear Mary

Am glad you and Walter are well I thought much of you all day but tis best to try and imagine this is one of your pop visits[2] and I shall see you both again after the Trip—

Grace has written you on board I enclose a letter for Walter have sent Allen to the Package Office he knows the man who took the Packages I found them on the file he has taken it to shew them

28th Dec[r] it is part of your Drawing Room Furniture Selena remembers running after the Man for a receipt

I'm so afraid Allen will not be back for me to post it with the result of his Enquiries

I keep about as usual had bad Cough with Bronchitis last night relieved by a large mustard plaister Thank God feel better

Mind dont take cold above all keep your feet warm tis bitterly keen here fine to day am writing my Australian letters The Grave was not large enough for Mr Boyers Coffin after all was read it had to be taken care of until [it] was built larger Mr Nicholson[3] and Whyman both came in God bless you and give you & dear Walter health and Strength with every blessing and the love of your Affectionate Mother

Elizabeth Bailey

I will post this as Allen has not returned tis ½ past 9 God prosper you and protect until we |meet again |my Children dear

Roberts is the Draymans name

28 Dec[r]

Text: ALS NLA MS133/1/117

[1]   MR and WLR were about to sail from Liverpool to Melbourne on board the *British Prince*, which arrived in Melbourne on 26 May 1869.
[2]   A visit at an odd time, casual visit.
[3]   Possibly a relative of Susannah Tyler Bailey née Nicholson (1833–1859), who was the first wife of Elizabeth's eldest son, John Robinson Bailey (1826–1871). Her father Henry Nicholson, a professor of music, and her brother Henry Tyler Nicholson (who married Matilda Clarke on 13 April 1852) both lived near to Mrs Bailey.

1869–1875

Melbourne, Parenthood and Holidays

1869

146   [From EB in Leicester, England, to MR and WLR in Melbourne][1]

58 Rutland St, Leicester
15th April 1869 [Thursday]

My dear Mary & Walter

Your last letter by Tug Boat reached safely was pleased to know you left the Shores of old England with good heart and spirits I got the last I wrote you back from the agents stating "Ship had sailed" I trust when this meets you all will be in health & safety as regards my self I have done all I can to humour this trying malady but cannot obliterate the Ravages time has made have suffered more from my legs which have been an enormous size and hard as marble no Bathing or rubbing will soften them the tendons are so tight that tis quite unsafe to walk without support still I get about the Bed & dressing Room have been down stairs but had great difficulty in getting up again the effort is too much for my weak state it brings on the difficulty in breathing which takes time to recover my body is as large as ever and at times is as hard as the legs yet rubbing will at times disperse the swelling which comes on when I eat or drink my appetite is better now I do not take medicine only aperient pills[2] occasionally have got over an attack of Bronchitis used mustard plaisters, my Cough almost left me dont scold when I tell you I have not sent for Mr Lankester he has not called to say how d'ye do, was glad to hear of your getting out of Port safely, I sent Selena to tell them that's all"

I think I hear you say naughty Mother to be so self willed I need not pay & suffer too the advice might be acceptable but the Physic I wont have The little food I can take without it will keep me up Gods time I am too worn down now my spirits are good and I never feel alone often think of you and fancy you by my bed cannot realize you are gone only on a Trip and coming again as dear Edith says

Lizzie tells me John[3] does not gain strength have had another Doctor who says there is something on his mind which retards him making progress we know that so do not hint a word They are still tiresome at <u>62</u>[4] Edith[5] suffers with her decay[d] teeth I tell Lizzy to give her a small jar of Honey and put some Borex in it and let her help herself the Standard says the 2 Bat[n] Rifle Brig[de] is ordered to Aldershott[6] have waited to hear but no letter come shall have more for May Mail Sarah & Tom are well the latter has not answ[d] my last of course you will hear from him I told him of Walters gift <u>to him</u> £2 but did not send it, has he had sent to borrow of me a larger sum than <u>was convenient,</u> <u>then</u> however I sent him goodness knows when I shall get it I also gave him a lecture and told him to quit the expensive West End[7] he has been on for several appointments <u>all unsuccessful</u> please dont hint "a word".

I would not encourage him to Emigrate he could not do a Labourers work and has no idea of Agriculture he has no means nor yet to get an outfit for voyage "and to hook on others, it would not be right but all keep free of each other" and I trust something yet may turn up I will ever do a Mothers part but told him I could not continue to find cash as I had invested my capital to bring in an income for <u>my wants</u> but these are Mothers cares and I ought not to trouble you I could not explain without I will not contract debts I cannot meet neither will I live beyond my income which you have so liberally helped with I wish to be quiet, am truly contented and happy God giving me sustaining strength dear Grace was over at Easter for 9 days will write you the Siamese Twins are here <u>Giantess</u> &c at the Temperance Hall.[8] Whyman & Selena desire to be remembered (old Fellow[9] treated Whyman to see them[10] the Bridal Party are expected from Paris (Nelly Gill and you will recollect Felix Gill[11] the Cousin being married to Miss Hardy she giving him 700 the remainder fortune being tied upon her well I prognosticate Albert from America will now pop the question to another sister all have near 3000 each, but ill health M[rs] Holland[12] came to see me all well provided for) dear Walter Sharp of Goole has not remitted so I have wrote him as he put some into the Court. I suppose poor M[rs] Smith died (your next neighbour) before <u>you left Liverpool</u> <u>your House not Let</u> a new D[r] wont have Robinson[13] Rawcliffe has been giving several parties & dances Wale has left M[rs] Helliwell wrote me hoped to have had a farewell line from <u>you</u> at last tell me dear Mary if <u>you</u> found <u>your cambric</u> Handkys best mark[d] Richardson in full also <u>your fine new white</u> stockings that you were telling me of did <u>you give them away?</u> <u>answer</u> <u>me</u> <u>correctly</u> I have reasons for asking!! I hope your Cargo will arrive without damage—we use the Tea pot & think of you

Surely Harold will not be gone[14] from Melbourne before you arrive all transits are so sudden tell me all about Turnhams and their prospects[15] Miss Turnham[16] is to undergo operation next month in her own Room the D[r] from the Ophthalmic[17] operates her own will administer Chloroform I hope she will do well not a letter from Pentridge—love to all I will write Sam in yours then it will be doubly dear to him. I shall live in hopes of getting letter from you God bless you with love ever dear Walter & Mary your affect[te] mother

    Eliz[th] Bailey

The key I sent you to Liverpool is one Piano key a small one

    Text: ALS NLA MS133/1/118

[1]   EB wrote this letter when MR and WLR were still on board the *British Prince, en route* to Melbourne, where they arrived on 26 May 1869.

[2]   Laxatives.

[3]   Captain John Brett.

[4]   Sarah Brett, 62 Rutland Street.

[5]   Her grand daughter, Edith Brett.

[6]   Aldershot Camp, situated on a moor near Farnham, thirty-five miles from London, was created as a permanent camp for the army after the purchase of 4000 acres of land in April 1854.

Barracks were erected and more land purchased in 1856. The troops returning from the
Crimean War, including Captain Jack Brett and his Rifle Brigade, were reviewed by Queen
Victoria in a series of military days at Aldershot in June and July 1856. Her costume worn on
those occasions (a scarlet military tunic with gold braid, brass buttons and a gold and crimson
sash; a navy skirt piped with white; and a round felt hat with a scarlet and white plume, crimson
and gold hatband and golden tassels) may still be seen, somewhat faded, in the London
Museum. Elizabeth Longford, *Victoria R.I.* (London: Pan Books, 1966) [first published by
Weidenfeld & Nicholson, 1964] p. 320.

7   The fashionable and expensive part of London.
8   'Temperance Hall, Leicester: Positively for three days only, Monday, Tuesday and Wednesday,
    April 12, 13 and 14. Wonderful Combination of the Greatest Living Curiosities the World has
    ever saw, The Renowned SIAMESE TWINS! Miss Anna Swan the Nova Scotia Giantess! Eight feet
    high, weighs thirty-one stone, and is only twenty years of age, and is undoubtedly the largest
    Woman in the World! ... Admission: one shilling.' On the same page, the Theatre Royal
    advertised its current productions with the addition of 'a piece of absurdity, entitled the SIAMESE
    TWINS. The Twins, Messrs Harry Windley and A. McLean.' *The Leicester Chronicle and
    Leicestershire Mercury United*, 10 April 1869, p. 5.
9   Samuel Hester.
10 Presumably she means the Siamese twins and the Giantess.
11 Felix Gill listed as a Freeman (8 July 1859) in Henry Hartopp, *Register of Freemen of Leicester,
    1770–1930* (Leicester: Corporation of City of Leicester, 1933) with the profession of
    Woolstapler.
12 Possibly the wife of Thomas Holland, an auctioneer, who lived near to Rutland Street at
    44 Humberstone Gate, where Elizabeth and John Bailey had lived prior to his death in 1846.
13 See note on Dr Robinson (Letter 133).
14 Edward Harold Bailey and his wife, Agnes, were still living at 'Palmerston House', Palmerston
    Street, Carlton, until after the birth of their third child, Mabel Elizabeth, on 18 December
    1871. In 1872, they moved to 163 Albert Road, Emerald Hill (now South Melbourne), where
    Edgar Charles was born (7 December 1872) and Celia Agnes (3 November 1874).
15 Elizabeth Turnham, wife of Joseph Turnham, had died on 30 November 1868 in Pentridge.
16 Elizabeth Turnham (Aunt Bessie), sister of William Henry (deceased) and Joseph Turnham.
17 Leicester Eye Infirmary.

147 [From EB in Leicester, England, to MR and WLR in Victoria]

58 Rutland St, Leicester
May 12 to 14 [18]69

My dear Mary & Walter

You will be sorry to hear I have had a suffering time since you left I got on pretty well in
quiet and managed to get up my appetite without much medicine but Hemmorage began and
I had Mr Lankaster who thinks it was a rupture of a vessel of the Kidneys so black it ceased the
third day water came freely but no stone or Grit could be found. Since then I have lost
strength appetite gone and a torpid feeling is ever upon me rest broken am always cold and
frigid I take what I can Mustard Plaisters relieve my Cough as the Easterly winds have tried
so here I am like a log of wood cannot always turn my self in bed rubbing relieves me now and
again I often see dear Mary by my bed side I trust you will arrive safely think of me in
Affliction and accept Mothers Blessing Sharp from Goole wrote to say all were in the Court
some time since so he will have to wait for his money. love to dear Sam I dont forget him tho
unable to write him when Sarah comes Mr Lankaster will talk to her of puncturing the legs &
thighs so have <u>not consented to Tapping</u> He desires to be remember^d to each of you Aunt
Bessie operated on yesterday so far all going on well done without Chloroform I know no

more bore it well the D[r] from Ophthalmic attended there—God bless you with love ever my dear| Children| Your affectionate Mother

      Eliz Bailey

Grace nervous & poorly

Toms feet bad again he wrote you last mail he told me

[Written in WLR's handwriting: 'Return this in next letter', which indicates that he sent it to MR while she was visiting friends in Ballarat.]

    Text: ALS NLA MS133/1/122

148 [From WLR in Ballarat to MR in Melbourne][1]

                     Ballt

          Friday Eveng at Hudsons[2] [11 June 1869]

Dear M—

    I have been about all day seeing old freinds all sorry that you are not with me—Nixons[3] very warm. Wanliss ditto. Saddlers, Hudson ditto Wanliss has invited us for 3 weeks—I think matters are [at] the Bank are pretty right—All shares are but I do not get my pass book till tomorrow morning—I am to go to Reids office[4] "Saturday morng" to get some information about Newingtons, so that I may be delayed leaving this till Monday as I have not got the mining maps for John[5]—Nixons have asked us to stay there:

    Old Cuthbert[6] says he knows there is a room there waiting for us—Lots of news Saddlers bills all right—Love to all| Your affect H.

      W.L.R.

    Text: ALS NLA MS133/1/90

[1] The Richardsons returned to Melbourne from England on 26 May 1869, leaving Harrie Elphinstone Bailey at school in Fairfield, Manchester. MR would have discovered that she was pregnant soon after their return. MR's mother, Elizabeth Bailey, died on 8 July 1869. While WLR visited Ballarat to sort out their finances and shares, MR probably stayed with her brother (John Robinson Bailey) and the children. John remarried a few weeks later for the third time (24 July 1869). His bride was Mary Ringrose Atkins.

[2] Dr Robert Fawell Hudson (1834–1898). See note to Letter 43.

[3] William Nixon (1833–1905), a broker in mining shares, married Anna Maria Cuthbert in 1864. Anna Maria had given birth to her third child and second daughter, Helen Lillian, on 28 January 1869. Their older children were Elizabeth (three years six months) and William (two years); and the Nixons' final child was Emma Florence (1871–1950).

[4] A. R. Reid, sharebroker, whose office was in 'The Corner', Ballarat. He became actuary of the Geelong Savings Bank. Withers, p. 236.

[5] John Robinson Bailey.

[6] John Cuthbert (1793–1878), formerly landowner and Excise Officer at Parsonstown, Ireland; father of Anna Maria Nixon, Henry, Thomas Headen, John, Kingston and Robert (and three babies who died as infants). He followed Henry and Kingston to Victoria in 1857 with the remainder of his children, his wife, Elizabeth née Headen, having died in 1842.

149 [From WLR in Melbourne to MR at the Cuthberts
('Beaufort House') in Ballarat]

139 V[ictoria] Parade [Blanche Terrace, East Melbourne]
Friday [24 September 1869]

My dear M:

I was glad to hear that you arrived safely. I have no recollection of ever mentioning the fact to Hudson[1]—He must have inferred it from some indirect remark about you I suppose—

I hope you slept better last night—I went to see Bandman[2] last night—met Ochiltree[3] there & saw Montgomery[4] in the dress circle—using his handkerchief to his eyes! as the people did when we saw East Lynn[5]—I saw Bandman in Liverpool & did not like him then nor do I indeed now much—The piece was well put on however & is worth seeing—They never could play it at Ballt for the dresses, scenery, & get up are too complex.

Sands[6] has been in bed all day Thursday & must stay there today—a threatening of Rheumatic fever, with inflammation of the heart

N. N. Clunes[7] have had another rise and were sold yesterday at £159: If you see Wanliss find out if the reefs are making again.

Give my kind regards to M[rs] C: Henry, father, & all the boys[8]—I got yours yesterday evening—

Have seen no one since you left—Emma[9] has just been over & with a note from Mary[10] asking me to dine with them on Sunday—

Weather fine not too warm

Ever Your attached| Husband
W.

Text: ALS NLA MS133/1/151 [Black edged]

[1] WLR had probably revealed to Dr Hudson that MR was pregnant.
[2] Daniel Bandmann, the German tragedian. See *FRM II*, p. 157. His Melbourne season at the Theatre Royal opened on 18 September 1869 and he was performing the character Narcisse in a play of the same name. 'The great German and English Actor Herr Bandmann who is nightly received with acclamations of the highest approval and delight by all classes of our enlightened and generous public.' *The Age*, 23 September 1869, p. 3.
[3] William Bertram Ochiltree (c.1830–1898).
[4] Walter Montgomery (1827–1871), Shakespearian actor, trained by Charles Albert Fechter (1824–1879), he was famous for his Hamlet; born Richard Tomlinson, Long Island, USA. He performed in Melbourne between 1867 and 1869, with his debut as Hamlet at the Theatre Royal on 20 July 1867 (*The Argus*, 22 July 1867). He became a member of the Athenaeum and Yorick clubs; married an American actress, Laleah Burpee Bigelow, in London and shot himself two days after his marriage. 'His restrained stage manner was a discipline imposed on a personality that in its off-stage manifestations was intensely excitable ... His public behaviour became increasingly flamboyant and his professional relationships strained.' Love, p. 233.
[5] *East Lynne*, written by Ellen Wood (Mrs Henry Wood) (1814–1887) in 1861. The plot concerns a woman who is disgraced by having abandoned her husband and children to run away with her lover. Her return, disfigured, to act as governess to her own children, but unable to reveal herself and claim their affection, was thought by Victorians to be unbelievably pathetic. By the time the actress uttered the famous line from the stage adaptation, 'Dead. Dead. And never called me mother,' the audience was already in tears.
[6] Elizabeth Charlotte Sands (c.1847–1885) was the Richardsons' domestic servant, who had arrived in Melbourne on the Lightning in September 1866. She came from Middlesex, the daughter of Jonathan Sands, a farmer, and Emma née White. On 8 November 1871, she married a baker, Thomas Silvester Cooper, by whom she had five children: Helen Douglas (b. 1873), Mary Ann Sarah (b. 1875), Alfred John (born and died one day old in 1878), Thomas Silvester (b. 1880), and Alfred John (b. 1884). It was after the birth of this fifth child

that she became ill again with heart disease, dying at her home in Bellerine Street, Geelong, on 7 November 1885, aged thirty-eight years.

7   Shares in the gold mine, New North Clunes, 'have been asked for up to £155 but are held at £159', *The Age*, 23 September 1869, p. 2.

8   Emma Cuthbert, her husband Henry Cuthbert, her father-in-law John Cuthbert, and her son by her first marriage, Thomas John Hepburn, aged nine, and Emma and Henry Cuthbert's son, John Headen, aged five. Their second son, Henry Herbert, had died aged four months on 27 April 1866. WLR does not mention their daughter, Annie, who was born the previous year on 18 May 1868 and became a childhood friend of HHR.

9   Emma Bailey (Trotty) (1856–1935), the thirteen-year-old daughter of John Robinson Bailey and his first wife, Susannah Tyler (née Nicholson). She was living with her father, her new stepmother and three half-sisters, Gertrude (aged seven), Ida (aged six) and Mary Jane (Jeannie) (aged three) at Vaucluse, Richmond. Her brother, Harrie Elphinstone Bailey, was still at school in Manchester.

10   Mary Ringrose Bailey née Atkins (b. 1843), third wife of JRB, whom she married on 24 July 1869.

150   [From WLR in Melbourne to MR at 'Beaufort House', Ballarat]

139 Vict[oria] Terrace [Blanche Terrace, East Melbourne]

Monday Evening [27 September 1869]

My dearest M.

Received yours this evening and am very glad you are enjoying your visit—it is very unfortunate about the tongue   write a note to Hudson or call & see M[rs] H. & him. M[rs] Saddler is of course proud of her daughter[1] as someone else[2] will be next year—Did M[rs] Colvin[3] know you were there. I suppose M[rs] Macdermott[4] is as vulgar as ever—try & walk a little it will do you good—You have a number of visitors

Sands is better today for the first time she has been very ill with a sharp attack of endocarditis, inflam. of the inside of the heart in bed since Thursday morning—

I have dined in middle of day to save Cook: I went to hear Ernani[5] again on Saturday Eveng. Yesterday Sunday dined at Vaucluse[6] & tomorrow dine with the Kabats

Weather mild today rather cool—I have no news so that I do not know how to fill the paper

John Mary & I took a long walk after dinner up past the convent & Mary was very much interested about the Nuns[7]—The mail has again arrived before its time & I expect the letters will be delivered tomorrow morning.

I will go to the Warehouse[8] the first thing & slip any for you inside this—I suppose you will get them tomorrow afternoon.

My kind regards to all at Beaufort House| from Your affect. H.

WLR

Thursday Oct 7 is appointed a day of special prayer for rain—all are getting very apprehensive—

I sold 2 N.N.C. one at £157 & one thro' Nixon at £158–10—as Wanliss talked so depreciatingly about 7 pennyweights & ⅓ profits &c & this being the last [£]3–0–0 dividend–

Mrs Kabat[9] sends her love & says she misses you very much—I was at the football match[10] on Sat. & saw Captain Ross & 2 other officers of the 14th playing with their men, stripped & begrimed & knocked down & shouting "now 14th"—

Text: ALS NLA MS133/1/150 [Black edged]

[1]   James and Emily Saddler's third child (first daughter) Emily Sarah was born in Ballarat in 1869; she died the following year.

[2]   i.e., MR for she was pregnant with HHR.

[3]   Grace Elizabeth Colvin née Hocking. She married Robert Colvin (1826–1883) in 1858 and they had four children born between 1859 and 1867.

[4]   Mildred Lavinia Freeman MacDermott née Glover, wife of Townsend MacDermott (1818–1907), barrister and politician; they were born and married in Dublin. Townsend MacDermott was elected to represent Ballarat East in April 1874 but lost the election in May 1877. He served in the Kerford Ministry (July 1874 to August 1875).

[5]   Victor-Marie Hugo (1802–1885) wrote the play *Hernani* in 1830. Guiseppe Verdi (1813–1901) wrote the opera *Ernani* in 1844 based on Hugo's drama. The story concerns Count Hernani, in love with Elvira and about to marry her, who kills himself when he hears the blast of a horn sounded by his enemy, Don Ruy Gomez, to fulfil the pledge he has given. WLR attended the Duke of Edinburgh Theatre, where *Ernani* was performed by the Melbourne Philharmonic Society. Advertised in *The Age*, 25 September 1869, p. 3.

[6]   Home of John Robinson Bailey, off Church Street, Richmond.

[7]   Sisters of the Good Shepherd Order came to Australia from Scotland in 1863 and, taking over a colonial villa home set in a garden on the River Yarra, they set up a women's refuge, the Magdalen Asylum. A number of buildings were subsequently erected including dormitories, a chapel and a laundry. The convent still stands at the corner of St Heliers Street and Clarke Street, Abbotsford, but it ceased to be a convent in 1973 when the nuns left. The site and buildings were bought by the State Government in 1975, with the Catholic Church keeping one hospice and a chapel. In 1989 La Trobe University bought the site and moved the faculty of Health Sciences temporarily. However, after a very short time, the university abandoned its plans and, by the mid-1990s, the site was placed in the hands of a developer.

[8]   English mail.

[9]   The Kabats were living in Melbourne at this time as Leopold was in charge until 1874 of Russell Street, the headquarters of the Metropolitan Division of Police.

[10] The Melbourne Football Club was formed in 1859 to play Australian Rules football. 'On the Metropolitan ground this afternoon, the 14th Regiment and Melbourne Club try conclusions. The match will probably attract a large number of spectators, to keep whom off the playing ground a number of police will be in attendance.' *The Age*, 25 September 1869, p. 3.

151   [From WLR in Melbourne to MR in Ballarat]

Blanche Terrace [Victoria Parade, East Melbourne]

Thursday morng. [30 September 1869]

My dearest Marie

I am sorry the tongue keeps so bad—see Hudson as soon as he comes back and do try & eat some vegetables—a change of food from bread & meat is most necessary. I have not read the letters I sent you I just glanced thro them to see that all were well You should insist on going to Mrs Wanliss as she is sure to feel hurt if you do not—

I went out to Pentridge yesterday. It rained hard for some hours—lunched with Joe[.][1] Sands is a little better just able to sit up for a few hours—It seems she has been a sufferer from Rheumatic fever at Home—I am afraid she will never be fit for hard work again—I dine at

Kabats again tonight to meet some doctor from home. Friday eveng. <u>at the Atkins</u>[2] I cannot leave at present as Sands is so poorly—there will be no cleaning done no washing this week—Cook has to answer the door—I am not going to have any party in fact it would be impossible—Grace[3] ought to have sent out <u>the Transfer for you to sign</u>—write & tell her to do this in your next—or she should have found out & said what it was she wanted—the share is not losing money by being there—You had better tell M[rs] Cuthbert that I regret I am not able to leave home & then you must make your arrangements about your other visits—I am sorry M[rs] Nixon is poorly—

You had better write a scrap to John[4] for his letters if you want to see them as it is no business of mine and he has not offered them to me and you know his disposition—

Ever Your affect. Husband
W.

Text: ALS NLA MS133/1/165 [Black edged]

1   Joseph Turnham, now a widower, Elizabeth Mary Turnham having died on 30 November 1868, while MR and WLR were in England. They would not have known about her death until they arrived in Melbourne in May 1869.

2   John Robert Atkins and his wife, Mary Agnes née Campion, were the parents of Mary Ringrose Bailey, the new and third wife of John Robinson Bailey. Atkins was a barrister.

3   Grace and Sarah Bailey, as the executors of EB's will, were having problems with Samuel Hester, who wanted the house in which he lived rent free (60 Rutland Street, Leicester), to be given to him. The house had been left to Elizabeth Bailey by her sister, Ann, who had married William Hester in March 1813.

4   MR wanted to see the letter received by her brother John so she would have a better understanding of the legal position of her mother's will.

152 [From WLR in Melbourne to MR in Ballarat]

Victoria Parade [East Melbourne]
Saturday morg. [2 October 1869]

My dear Marie

<u>If I knew my letters were destroyed I would write differently</u> but you <u>will</u> keep them & I dislike the idea of any other having the chance of reading them—You know my wishes and have known them for years—Sands is a little better, I am really grieved for the girl—yet I am not without hope that she may be pretty well again, but doubt if she will ever be strong I am sorry your mouth continues so bad—<u>I write Hudson by this mail</u>—

I am glad you are going to M[rs] Wanliss. I am afraid your ideas of the people wanting to see me is a myth—they did not shew me much kindness when I was among them—I hope you will remain & enjoy yourself—We spent a very pleasant evening at Williams Road[1] and had plenty of laughter[2]—I am not going to Johns on Sunday but on Monday evening for practice[3] with Mary—

M[rs] Kabat sends her love. M[rs] Murchison[4] is still there

We had heavy rain here & the weather is now pleasantly cool. M[r] D[r] & M[rs] Blair[5] left cards yesterday I think they are nice people from all, I hear—also the Spragues[6] & M[rs] Nield[7] called—I am afraid Grace will make a great mess of affairs—John tells me that in one of the letters they said that old Hester[8] would give them no peace <u>until they</u> had given him possession of the House</u>—Can it be possible they have been idiots enough to give up House & land!—

I have really nothing more to tell you| With love & kisses| I am Your attached| Husband
            W

Mrs Kabat wants to know if we still write every day—

Text: ALS NLA MS133/1/166 [Black edged]

1   The Atkins' home.
2   One of the Atkins' children was John Ringrose Atkins (1851–1908) who became a theatrical
     manager and was a musician and actor. At the time of this letter he would have been eighteen
     and may have been in his final year at Melbourne Church of England Grammar School, which
     he entered in 1862. After a short but spectacular journalistic career, he adopted the name 'Dan
     Barry' (his father was a friend of Sir Redmond Barry) and became a performer and manager,
     particularly in country areas and was best known as Australia's leading outback manager. He was
     also known for his practical jokes. WLR enjoyed the Atkins' family musical entertainment and
     fun. See *ADB.*
3   Singing practice.
4   Emily Kabat's mother, Mary Ann Murchison née Roberts (1806–1872) born in Ireland,
     daughter of John Roberts and Mary Ann née Rankin.
5   Dr John Blair (d. 1887) and his wife, Mary née Hunter, may have been 'nice people from all
     I hear' in 1869, but Dr Blair's reputation took a tumble in 1878. Blair, a prominent member of
     the Medical Association of Victoria, became a close friend of the populist surgeon Dr James
     Beaney, who made an enormous fortune through his medical practice, and, according to the
     more sober medical fraternity, through some unethical and questionable methods. Eyebrows
     were raised when in 1866 Blair put his name to James Beaney's defence committee, formed at
     the time of his trial for the murder of Mary Lewis. (See Letter 225, WLR to MR.) Then in
     1878, Blair took over Beaney's practice when the latter went to Britain and the Medical Society
     of Victoria was given evidence about one of the ways Beaney had made his fortune. Dr James
     Edward Neild received a bundle of correspondence between Blair and a supposed patient from
     New Zealand, a sheep farmer, who had written describing symptoms of spermatorrhoea, a
     specialty of Beaney. Following Beaney's normal practice, Blair wrote requesting a sample of
     urine to be tested and three guineas; the payment and the urine arrived but the latter was in fact
     from an old lady. The next letter from Blair confirmed the diagnosis and requested £65 to be
     sent in advance of receiving medication. Blair was confronted with this correspondence and
     resigned from the Medical Society of Victoria, after some pressure. See Love, pp. 157, 190.
6   Edgar Toby Sprague (1835–1893), a stockbroker, and his wife, Amy Elizabeth née Govett.
     They lived in Hawthorn and by 1869 they had four of their six children.
7   Susannah Neild née Long (1831–1918), daughter of David Rutter Long, chemist and druggist.
     She was married on 26 March 1857 to Dr James Edward Neild (1824–1906).
8   Samuel Hester.
9   Grace and Sarah Bailey.

153 [From WLR in Melbourne to MR in Ballarat]

139 Vict[oria] Parade [Blanche Terrace, East Melbourne]

Tuesday Evening [5 October 1869]

My dear Marie

        I am glad you are enjoying yourself, I may run down on Friday but it must only be for a
day or two—Sands is still too ill—I fear it will be necessary to get another house maid as soon
as you return If I leave on Friday, I must return the following Wednesday at furthest; there
will be no cleaning done during your abscence—She is only able to sit on a chair—I got

Dougan Bird[1] to see her last Saturday. I am glad your tongue is better I wrote to Hudson about you but he has never answered my letter—We had fine rain all last night—

I dont feel very well myself today—I cant get a decent cup of tea at home, it is so different to what I get out—It must be the 2/- trash[2]—~~I have told Cook to take 3/- in future~~—

I was over at Vaucluse last evening & got a very nice enjoyable one there—I shall go out & buy some at 3/6 & try that—

You say nothing about Sam[3] & he has never written to me saying whether he went to see Day[4] or not—I have got nothing to tell you—I see nobody & have no news. I must see how Sands is before I decide about leaving on Friday—Cook is such a deaf old stupid I cannot trust her, she stands & talks to the people at the door & lets them talk to her

I find that this will not catch the post this evening so I must post it in the morning—I posted my last Saturday morning—

Wednesday

Rain all morning I could not go to the general P.O.

Hope you keep better and am so glad you feel the movement[5] I suppose Mrs C. Mrs N. Mrs O.[6] are all delighted. I think I will leave Friday morning ½ past 11 train weather is not favorable for the boat we shall have floods on the Yarra I will write again tomorrow Thursday With love & kisses Ever Your Attached Husband

W

Text: ALS NLA MS133/1/149 [Black edged]

1   Dr Samuel Dougan Bird (1832–1904).
2   Price per pound, equivalent to 453.6 grams in the metric system.
3   Sam Bailey (1838–1911).
4   Dr John Day (*c.*1817–1881), son of George Day and his wife Jane née Hall. He died in Geelong aged sixty-four. *MJA* 1881, p. 78.
5   The baby (HHR).
6   Mrs Emma Cuthbert, Mrs Anna Maria Nixon, Mrs Annie Ochiltree.

154 [From MR in Ballarat to WLR at East Melbourne]

Bank N S Wales [Ballarat][1]
Thursday [7 October 1869]

My dear Walter

I was very glad to get your letter this Morning & I shall be sure to be at the Train to meet you at ½ past 3-o-clock. I do hope Sands will get better I am afraid I shall have a difficulty in getting another to do as well I am going back to Mrs Wanlis's to night as she is giving a party on purpose for me but if you only stay such a short time we shall have to go to the Cuthberts on Saturday & the Saddler's on Monday as I have put off going there until you come for I thought you would enjoy that best. I am writing to Sam to meet you at the Station he has seen Dr Day & he say's its liver & indigestion. You had better make no promises about when you will be back for I think you will enjoy yourself & I am so pleased you are coming. Mrs Ochiltree has given me three new dresses & three petticoats for the little one[2] when it comes every body seem's delighted:

It has rained here for the last 4 day's it seem's to be pretty general I want to catch the morning post so will be sure to be waiting your arrival to morrow—

　　　Good bye till then with love & kisses from your| own wife

　　　　　Marie

I shall wait here till the post comes in to night—

It is very cold here so put on Flannel I have a cotton suit if it gets warmer

　　　Text: ALS NLA MS133/1/46

1　　MR was staying at the Bank of New South Wales where William Bertram Ochiltree was Manager.
2　　HHR born 3 January 1870.

1870

155　[From WLR in Sydney to MR in Melbourne][1]

Royal Hotel Sydney

Sunday—[5 June 1870]

My dearest M.

You see we arrived safely.[2] After you saw the last of us it was very cold and I felt the benefit of wraps. On going down the Yarra we came on "The City of Hobart" steamer ashore. She had been stuck for 2 hours: a lady came off her in a boat as pass[enger]. to Sydney—we passed out of the heads about 7 or 8 oclock: Had a fine day Friday with fair wind She is what I call a steady boat altho' the ladies never appeared after the first meal at table. We sighted land on Saturday morg. & kept it in view all day sailing along shore about 6 miles off. The scenery is very charming & we kept one big mountain named by Cap[tn] Cook[3] "The Dromedary" in sight all day. We got into Sydney heads about midnight or a little later & soon brought up along the wharf—our table was pretty fair and of course I ate like a hunter. We got up a rubber every evening & the Cap.[4] turned out to be a jolly little fellow—

My cabin was very comfortable & altho' I dosed only the first night I slept well afterwards with the window open of course—I had no one else with me—I am at The Royal[5]—I find no mail leaves today so you will not get this before Thursday. I hope you & the darling of our hearts[6] are both well—

I am going to Church[7] this morning and will close this in the afternoon. The weather is delightful & I have had to leave off my flannels already—Monday morng [6 June] I went to church yesterday morg. & to the Cathedral[8] at 3½. A great many pretty girls in Melb. Sydney. The table here is all that could be wished—This is a lovely morg. & there seem to be good shops—Address to Post Office as I shall go to "The Oxford" Hotel[9] most likely before long It is prettier situated than this & any change is good—

I will be very anxious to hear from you. I see the Agamemnon[10] now arrived—You will be getting your home letters tomorrow—We lunch at 1—dine at ½ past 6 I have just made a fine breakfast—first two pork sausages & potatoes, then Ham & eggs—I am now going out 9 am. to post this & will commence another letter as soon as I have seen Alec[11]—

I see The City of Adelaide[12] made a fair voyage of under 48 hours, 45½ from heads to heads—Good bye dear from Your own

      W.

Text: ALS NLA MS133/1/173

[1] The Richardsons were still living at 139 Blanche Terrace, Victoria Parade, East Melbourne, where Ethel Florence Lindesay Richardson (HHR), called Ettie by her father, was born on 3 January 1870. Six months later, WLR set off for a trip, leaving Melbourne on Thursday, 2 June 1870, to recuperate from an illness. His destinations were Sydney and Parramatta to visit his nephew Alec Richardson and his wife, Fanny. It is questionable whether Alec and Fanny were married at that time, for there is no record of any marriage prior to WLR's visit and on 23 March 1875 Alec and Elizabeth Frances Watson were married by the Presbyterian Minister, Arthur Davidson, in Carlton, Melbourne. Both bride and groom claimed to be single and both gave the same address as Ross Street, Glebe Point, Sydney. If Fanny was Elizabeth Frances Watson and they had begun their 'married' life together without proper sanction, it would explain why they chose to marry in Melbourne and why one of the witnesses was the Minister's wife rather than WLR or MR, whom they visited during their stay in Melbourne.

[2] WLR sailed on the *Dandenong*, 575 tons, and arrived early Sunday morning, 5 June 1870. *Sydney Morning Herald*, 6 June 1870, p. 4.

[3] Captain James Cook (1728–1779), English navigator who explored and mapped the east coast of Australia in the *Endeavour* in 1770.

[4] Captain John Pain.

[5] The Royal Hotel, 438 George Street, Sydney. The hotel keeper was Charles Carleton Skarratt, who had previously kept the Royal Mail Hotel at 70 Bourke Street and at 105 Victoria Parade, Melbourne.

[6] HHR.

[7] Probably St James's Church, the oldest ecclesiastical structure in Sydney, which opened for worship in 1824. Its architect was Francis Greenway (1777–1837), a convict transported for life to NSW where he resumed his profession as an architect under the patronage of Governor Macquarie for whom he designed many buildings.

[8] St Andrew's Cathedral.

[9] The Oxford Hotel, King Street, Sydney; the hotel keeper was William Gannon.

[10] The *Agamemnon*'s arrival in Melbourne announced in *Sydney Morning Herald*, 6 June 1870, p. 4.

[11] Alexander Richardson, Walter's nephew. At the time of WLR's visit, Alec and Fanny, resided in Parramatta while he worked as a travelling auditor for the railways. HHR recollected a visit by Alec and Fanny in March 1875 (after the marriage ceremony, presumably) to her family in their house in Sydney Terrace, Fitzroy Gardens, East Melbourne. They brought HHR and her sister Lil a beautiful bride doll and a 'sumptuous' volume of *Fairy Tales* illustrated by Gustave Doré. *MWY*, p. 11.

[12] *City of Adelaide*, 615 tons (Captain D. Walker).

156 [**From WLR in Sydney/Parramatta to MR in Melbourne**]

                            [Royal Hotel, Sydney[1]]
                            [Tuesday, 7 June 1870]

My dearest M

Skarratts Hotel, Tuesday

    I wrote yesterday & posted it to go by City of Adelaide by advice at the G.P.O. I am going to send this overland. I see by this mornings telegr[m] that "Power" is captured by Nicholson & Hare[2]—You will also have your English letters wh. will cheer your tedium, altho' I suppose you do not miss me as much having Baby. Bless her I hope she is well. I enjoyed

Monday amazingly. I went to Wooloomooloo bay by omnibus 3ᵈ there I found two steamers just starting to go down the Harbor I got into one & we went down among the Islands to a place called "Watson bay" most lovely scenery, the bay wooded along its shores in most places to its edge—Villas dotting the shores here & there & the sun bright & warm. I then returned to my hotel for lunch at 1. Out again in the afternoon to the Botanic gardens wh. you will enjoy amazingly. They are smaller but much more charming than those of Melb. there is more lawn and finer trees, the grass plots presenting such a relief to the eyes and the flowers most luxuriant—In there is a fine collection of birds &c. wh. is very creditable indeed—

The more I see of Sydney the more I like it. There seems to be more business doing than in Melb. and the weather is set fair wh. is a great thing—You will enjoy it. It reminds me of Devonport & Plymouth—altho' much finer

I have not seen Alec yet—The table here is all that can be desired—I hope you and dear Bab. are well & sleep a little better—How nice it will be when we are able to travel about—I am going to the P.O. & will not post this till evening—

Wednesday morning I went to the P.O. yesterday & found nothing not even an Argus—Perhaps I may have better luck next time—I went out to "Botany Bay" yesterday a pretty drive of seven miles by omnibus there I strolled about for an hour at "The Sir Joseph Banks Hotel" a charming & truly rural spot. The landlady said she wd. charge us two & servant £6–6–0 per week to include servants—on returning strange to say I saw Alec. crossing the street, & he saw me on the top of the bus—We had lunch together & I went out to Paramatta 14 miles from Sydney—where I am now this morning. I am much pleased with Fanny—She is plain but engaging and has charming manners and is evidently a dear good girl—You will like her much—We are going out this morning to see the orange groves for which this place is famous³—

I was fearfully attacked by mosquitoes all night—the bedroom swarming with them—I am writing to the P. Master Sydney this morning for any letters to be forwarded to me here—I think I am better—I will return by the boat at the beg. of next week as I am uneasy at not hearing from you for so long—

We will take apartments at Paramatta also if you like—No change in the weather every day since I left has been fair with me—

Kiss baby for me| & believe me| Your affect. H.

    W.L.R

Text: ALS NLA MS133/1/172

¹   The writing paper is from the Royal Hotel C.C. Skarratt, Sydney.
²   Harry Power, alias Henry Johnstone (or Johnson) (1819–1891), born in Waterford, Ireland. He was transported to Van Diemen's Land in 1842, after being sentenced to seven years imprisonment at Lancaster Assizes for stealing a pair of shoes. Receiving his ticket of leave in 1847, he worked in Geelong as a horse dealer in the early 1850s. In 1855 he was sentenced to eight years and five years accumulative at Maryborough District Court for horse stealing, even though the receipt he produced from Dr Farrell and sons proved to be genuine. He later said that the wrongful imprisonment and the ill-treatment he received in the prison hulk caused his subsequent life as a bushranger. His capture had been telegraphed to *The Age* by Inspector Leopold Kabat and the news was printed under the heading, 'Capture of Power—The Police Vindicated. The police had been embarrassed for years by the exploits of this man, who had been waylaying unwary travellers, especially in the north-east of Victoria, and who was reputed to have educated Ned Kelly in the art of bushranging. One of Power's victims was Farquhar MacKenzie, bailed up on 25 February 1870 at 7 p.m. on the Yea road close to King Parrot Creek; Power stole his horse, saddle and bridle. He was finally captured by Superintendents Charles Hope Nicholson (from Kyneton) and Francis Hare (from Melbourne), and Sergeant

W. B. Montford. (from Melbourne), in the King's River Ranges, near Beechworth. Montford had been based at Wangaratta previously and, with his local knowledge and the assistance of a black tracker and guide, Power was caught 'by the energy and perseverance of three officers of the Victorian police, who have thus cleared away the odium so long hanging over the force through the numerous unsuccessful efforts to capture this marauder'. When they found his 'gunyah' (humpy), Nicholson crept in and pounced on Power before he could reach for his guns. (Nicholson was close friend of the Kabats and one of their witnesses at their marriage.) *The Age*, 6 June 1870, p. 2. WLR would have read of Power's capture in the *Sydney Morning Herald*, 7 June 1870, p. 5. John Sadleir, *Recollections of a Victorian Police Officer* (Melbourne: George Robertson & Co., 1913; facsim. repr. Ringwood, Vic.: Penguin, 1973), pp. 155–164. Kevin Passey and Gary Dean, *The Bushranger Harry Power: Tutor of Ned Kelly* (Wodonga: Victorian Bushrangers Enterprises, 1991), p. 41.

3   Orange groves were established on the hills north of Parramatta by the 1820s with James Pye (1801–1884) the leading orchardist.

157 [From WLR in Parramatta to MR in Melbourne]

Paramatta
Wednesday afternoon [8 June 1870]

My dear M.

I dont think you can say I do not write often to you. I posted my second letter to you this morning <u>overland,</u> and I begin this the 3rd: I told you how I arrived here last evening, and how pleased I was with Fanny I got a carriage this morning and we drove out to an "Orangery" about 3 miles out of Paramatta. There the scenery is magnificent and we saw the orange groves; trees 35 feet high, laden from top to bottom with oranges and lemons. The estate is situated very romantically in a glen, & belongs to one man,[1] the trees grow best in sandy soil and they are planted in terraces along the sides of a steep ravine—[Small sketch of three terraces of orange trees] Fanny had never been there before, & so she enjoyed it as well as I did. She is a very nice girl & improves on acquaintance. Alec is very much altered, so quiet & thin: got quite steady—& has lost all his absurd notions. I believe he will get on. He writes to, & hears from, Miss F.[2] every mail—There has never been any family and so Mrs Saddler must have been misinformed.[3] I shall make up a box of books and other things useful to young house keepers when I get home: They are commencing just as we did, & furnishing by degrees—living very properly <u>within</u> their means—

I have written this morning to the P.O. Sydney to forward my letters & papers here so if there are any I will get them tomorrow. This is Wednesday & I have had as yet no "Argus" altho' I called yesterday after the overland mail was in—However I saw Fridays "Argus" in Sydney on Monday—Paramatta is a considerable town 4 churches:[4] jail[5] lunatic Asylum[6] & the old government House[7] where the governor used to live when Paramatta was <u>the Capital,</u> the town is 2 full miles long. I do not think I will stay much longer away. You will not get this letter before Monday, if I post it tomorrow Thursday as it seems, the mail takes nearly a week between posting & delivery—I will find out tomorrow if "<u>The You Yangs</u>" sails on Tuesday & if so will start. This is awkward being so far from Sydney. So you had better not write any more after receipt of news when I sail. The climate is certainly much more enjoyable than Melb. barring the confounded Mosquitoes—I think I had a better appetite on board the steamer than on shore. I saw an old Ballt. man at "Skaratts" named Warner[8] who lived in Webster St. He is going to "Figi"—he knows Frazer[9] very well—Alec is engaged as travelling auditor of accounts on the railway and is from home all day and nine nights a month—Fanny thinks this very hard how would you have liked it when we were 2 years married?

Friday. We were in Sydney all yesterday and so I cd. not finish this. I got Friday & Saturdays Argus & saw by your initials[10] that all was well up to Saturday The "You Yangs" sails about Friday June 17 that is the boat I will return by. Holroyd has got me made an Honorary member of The Sydney Club.[11] We are going over to his place "The Scrubs"[12] to spend Sunday—Tonight we are going out to tea & talk to a freind of Alecs: The weather is still most lovely I have not had one really winters day since I left home—yesterday was the worst and that was only very dusty—Tomorrow Saturday I am going into Sydney by boat along the river to see if there is any letter from you—as I cannot get them here somehow. This is the place to winter—

A letter from Miss F. arrived by the mail containing an agreeable draft for [£]35–0–0. They are spending this on furniture so that by & bye they will have all they desire—they make his pay cover all expenses, & are perfectly free from debt. She is evidently a capital manager—Today I am going over the jail & in the afternoon I take Fanny over the Asylum & tonight we are going out to a little whist at the station masters—

I did not see Mrs Kabats name in the list by mail to Sydney. I do hope & trust that you and the dear baby are well & that the house has been safe at night—I wrote by City of Adelaide & she put off sailing till Wednesday then I posted one here overland on Wednesday & now this goes overland.

I think Thursday is the day The You Yangs leaves not Friday If so I will get in by Sunday—I have got some photos of Sydney—God bless you & baby says Your affect. H.

    W.L.R.

Text: ALS NLA MS133/1/171

1   Arthur Todd Holroyd (1806–1887), born in London, son of Joseph Holroyd, a gentleman. He married first Sophie Abbs and had a daughter, Emily Sophie. He acquired his MD, but turned to law and was called to the Bar in 1841. He travelled extensively in Europe and the Middle East, and from 1843 spent two years in New Zealand. Arriving in NSW in 1845, he was admitted to the Bar and built up a lucrative practice. He was elected to the Legislative Assembly, representing the Western Boroughs between 1851 and 1858, and was the member for Parramatta from 1861. He was Minister for Public Works in 1863, but resigned the following year as a result of charges of abusing the position in various ways. (He was later cleared of all these charges.) Between 1866 and 1885 he was Master in Equity and from 1879 was Acting Supreme Court Judge. His first wife having died, he remarried in 1865 to Elizabeth Armstrong. Western Sydney's Holroyd was named after him. Grace Karskens, *Holroyd: A Social History of Western Sydney* (Kensington, NSW: NSW University Press, 1991), p. 70.

2   Caroline Fector (b. 1804).

3   It is not known what Emily Saddler had heard about Alec and Fanny. Considering Emily's own behaviour with Dr James Edward Neild in 1864, as revealed in Mrs Dawbin's Journal, she probably took delight in spreading gossip about others. *Dawbin*, pp. 389–416.

4   There were at least five churches: St John's Anglican Church (1820), St Patrick's Roman Catholic Church (1839), Centenary Methodist Church (1839), All Saints' Church (1847), and St Andrew's Scots Church (first service 1849).

5   The original wooden gaol was destroyed by fire and the new Parramatta Gaol was commenced in 1834 and used from 1842.

6   In February 1821, a building, designed by Francis Greenway but built very shoddily, was opened for unmarried women convicts. It was christened the Female Factory and although it was intended to house 300, there were generally 200 additional women and 100 children on top. The women wove and spun wool. Because of its terrible environment, by 1846 it was used predominantly for female lunatics. In 1850 it was turned into the Parramatta Lunatic Asylum.

7   The original Government House at Parramatta was a small plaster cottage built in 1790 by Governor Arthur Phillip (1738–1814), Australia's founding Governor. It deteriorated quickly so

that when Governor John Hunter (1738–1821) became the second Governor of NSW in 1799, he commissioned a new two-storey structure which still remains as the central block of the present Government House. In 1816, Governor Lachlan Macquarie (1762–1824) commissioned Francis Greenway to carry out repairs and add a front porch and fanlight. Five years before WLR visited Parramatta, it had been leased by the Legislative Assembly, becoming first a boarding house and then a grammar school. Later the National Trust, having restored it, opened it to the public in 1970.

8   William Warner, a coach proprietor, lived in Webster Street. F. M. Dicker, compiler, *Ballarat and Ballarat District Directory 1865–66* (Ballarat: James Curtis, 1865).

9   Possibly Samuel Fraser, draper, Webster Street, or J. Frazer, engine driver, off Webster Street.

10   MR put her initials on each newspaper prior to sending to WLR as a pre-arranged signal that there were no problems at home.

11   The Union Club: WLR used that club's writing paper for the next letter to MR. The Sydney Club was not formed until 1912. Holroyd was President of the Australian Freemasons' Orphan and Destitute Children's Society, which had its headquarters at 55 Pitt Street, Sydney.

12   'Sherwood Scrubs' was built on land bought by Holroyd in 1855 from William Sherwin. The brick building had a long, low symmetrical façade, shuttered French windows opening onto a tiled verandah with some cast iron detailing. The rooms were arranged around a central glass-covered conservatory, possibly with a fountain, and stables and servants' wing formed a rear courtyard. The estate included orchards and vineyards. Holroyd also established a tile works at the north-western part of his property. Grace Karskens, *Holroyd*, p. 70.

158   [From WLR in Parramatta to MR in Melbourne][1]

[Parramatta, NSW]
Saturday [11 June 1870]

My dearest Marie

I cannot tell you how pleased I was to hear from you this morning only for the first time. You have I hope got my three letters—posted Monday, Wednesday and Friday—I am still at Alecs but intend starting for home next Thursday or Friday by the You Yangs—I will tell you in my next the exact day—Friday we all went to Sydney to buy furniture—Saturday I went alone by steamer down the river "Paramatta" and a real lovely sail it is—I returned the same way. The weather has been all that could be desired since I left Melbourne. Not a single wet day—We went out on Friday evening to a little musical party & a rubber: Did not get home till 12—I bought them a little clock for the dining room—

Sunday morning [12 June]—I was glad to hear baby was keeping well & that you were not obliged to get out of bed so often. I think I am better as I certainly am eating better, & the doors are always open the air is so mild. This will be the place for our next winter quarters. We can stay at a very nice quiet family hotel and I cut the enclosed out of a Sydney newspaper—

Monday morning [13 June]—Still glorious weather—Yesterday we went to Holroyds and spent the day there, he got us horses and we went over his Orangery and rode & walked about for hours—Had a capital dinner with the door wide open all the time, so you may imagine the weathe—& he sent his coachman & trap to drive us home—

I suppose Sam[2] got safely to Sandhurst and that he has written to you—I am going in to Sydney this morng. by the Steamer again and hope to get if not a second letter at least Wednesdays "Argus" initialled—I got Monday & Tuesdays all right—I shall be glad to see you once more—We did the voyage to this in 58 hours from wharf to wharf. If I arrive at the Melb. wharf during the night, I shall wait quietly in my berth till daylight & then take a cab, this will be better than disturbing the house—It was my mistake about 72 shares. It was

52—of course Saddler[3] never called—I hope dear Etty gets her gruel regularly—You did not say how the goat[4] was so I conclude she is not dead—

I hope you have not written after today Monday if you have of course we can write & get the letters returned to Melb.

Good bye dear Marie, try & be quite well when I come back—Baby will soon now be 6 months old, & I expect to see a great change in her—I trust the bad weather will have passed away—I will write tomorrow Tuesday for <u>the last time</u> just to say when the boat starts on Thursday or Friday. With lots of kisses for yourself & the wee pet| from Your fond husband

        Walter

Text: ALS NLA MS133/1/170

[1]   The letter was written on Union Club Sydney paper and the envelope has also survived, addressed to 'Dr Richardson 139 Vict. Parade, Fitzroy, Melbourne, Mrs R'. The word 'Overland' in WLR's handwriting at the left-hand corner (postage stamp has been removed). The envelope has been stamped by the PO at Parramatta 13 June 1870 on the front, and on the rear by PO at Albury 16 June 1870, by PO at Melbourne 18 June 1870 and PO at Collingwood 18 June 1870.

[2]   Sam Bailey had been appointed to the position of bank clerk at the Sandhurst branch of the Bank of New South Wales. He eventually became the Manager.

[3]   James Saddler.

[4]   'As she could not nurse me, I was brought up on goat's milk ... I think I can safely put my abhorrence of milk in any shape or form to that goat. (Why it could not have been a cow I can't imagine.)' *MWY*, p. 5.

159 [From WLR in Parramatta to MR in Melbourne]

                                      Paramatta N.S.W.
                                 Tuesday [14 June 1870]

My dearest Marie

You would not get my first letter until yesterday Monday owing to the unfortunate weather "The City of Adelaide" steamer encountered. I have written & posted three since namely Wednesday Friday & Monday—four altogether this making 5—I post this to say I have only had as yet one from you written the Saturday after I left June 4—& 4 Argus—I only hope & trust all is well. I am still at Alecs: I leave tomorrow for Hotel in Sydney—The You Yangs is advertised to leave on Thursday but it will be Friday or Saturday before she sails—so do not expect me before Monday eveng[1]—

Weather still delightful—English mail closes here tomorrow Wednesday—I am sure I am better, fatter, & stronger—doors open all day weather positively warm—no fires required except in the mornings & at night & if I had not been anxious about you & the pet I should have done better even still. From the wretched postal arrangements I do not suppose you will get this before Monday morning—but it will let you know I am coming—Fanny sends her love & will like to see you very much   We can spend a fortnight at Paramatta very pleasantly—next winter & a fortnight at Sydney—ditto at Manly Beach—I enclose advertisement that I omitted in my last—I am going to the Post <u>again</u>—I have got nothing since Saturday. Kiss the Baby and believe me| Your ever loving Husband

        Walter

I have posted by steamer as I have just got your letter & the home ones & Thursday & Friday Argus all together The overland takes 7 days

>   *Text:* ALS NLA MS133/1/164

[1]   *You Yangs* departed on Friday, 17 June 1870. *Sydney Morning Herald*, 18 June 1870, p. 4.

1871

160 **[From WLR in Sandhurst to MR in St Kilda]**[1]

Sandhurst [Victoria][2]
Monday. 8 am [13 November 1871][3]

My dear Marie

Arrived in due course found all well. Heavy rain Sunday morng. wh. I suppose you had also. Saw splendid cake from Ext H.[4] 90/- oz. top of the list once more—Div. 1/6.

Am going down the shaft today—Emily L[5] is staying with Polly[6]—I enclose photo of Grace which is the best we have—

I hope M.[7] from Va[u]cluse is with you and that the dear bairnies are all right—I think I will start on Wednes[da]y midday, as I am going out to Eaglehawk Tuesday. The weather is most delightful, and every one appears in good spirits

Kiss the kids for Papa and take a few for yourself| from Your affect.| Husband

W. Lindesay Richardson

I will have to bring the photo it wont go into the envelope |WLR

>   *Text:* ALS NLA MS133/1/167

[1]   The Richardsons had moved to 'Springfield', Chapel Street, St Kilda, Melbourne, on 6 October 1870. Ada Lillian Lindesay Richardson (ALR) was born on 28 April 1871. The announcement of her birth was on page 4 of *The Argus* on Monday, 1 May 1871. One week later, the announcement of the death of John Robinson Bailey, JP, which had occurred on 6 May 1871, appeared in *The Argus*. Harrie Elphinstone Bailey had returned from school in England aboard the *Superb* in March 1871 and was present at his father's death.

[2]   WLR went to Sandhurst and stayed with his brother-in-law, Sam Bailey, and his wife Polly (Frances Mary Louisa Lascelles).

[3]   WLR's accounts show that he went to Sandhurst in November 1871 ('6. Self to Sandhurst. P.O. order Home 7.4 & self £23–0–0'). He probably took money from his account on Monday, 6 November 1871 and travelled a few days later to Sandhurst. (NLA MS133/1/295)

[4]   Extended Hustlers gold mine.

[5]   Emily Sophia Lascelles (1857–1946), sister of Polly (Frances Mary Louisa Bailey née Lascelles). Polly had two other siblings: Emma Mary (born in 1860) and Thomas Allen (born in 1863).

[6]   Polly (Frances Mary Louisa Bailey née Lascelles) (1854–1934) was the daughter of Thomas Allen Lascelles, a land and stock auctioneer, and his wife, Sarah Emma Atkinson. Polly and Sam were married on 22 December 1870 at All Saints Church of England, Geelong. The bride was only sixteen years of age, half the age of the groom. Her guardian, C. J. Dennys, gave his consent to the marriage. Polly and Samuel had four children: Leila Maud (1874–1936), Frank Lascelles (b. 1879), Guy Robinson (1886–1950). When HHR came back for her trip to Victoria in 1912, she visited her Aunt Polly and cousin Leila in Geelong. Thirty years later, on

27 January 1942, she wrote to her sister, Lil Neill: 'In Geelong N. [John George Robertson] & I stayed the night with Aunt Pollie & Emilie Lascelles, who had a very nice little house with an indoor lavatory! With water laid on, too. Very different from those up country. Yes, we had tea with Leila [Sam and Polly's daughter], & you may remember that we didn't care at all for her house, which she thought so much of.'

7   Mary Ringrose Bailey (b. *c.*1843), widow of John Robinson Bailey, who had died on 6 May 1871. Their son Edgar Atkins Bailey, born 15 October 1870, died on 11 December 1871. After the death of her only son, Mary was left with five stepchildren: Harrie (aged eighteen) and Emma (aged fifteen), children of John and his first wife Susannah Tyler Nicholson, and Gertrude (aged nine), Ida (aged eight) and Jeannie (aged five), daughters of John's second marriage to Jane Rainsford.

1874

161   [From HHR (and MR) in London, England, to WLR in Melbourne][1]

[London][2]

[August 1874]

my dear papa

i love you very ~~mae~~ much, lilly is very fat i carried a large parcel for dear mama

[MR continues]

Ettie too tired to finish

Sends lots of hugs & kisses & Lilly also & say she loves you 40 lbs—& loves to her frends friends Ettie say's she will write next time—she wrote to Lucy[3]

Text: AL NLA MS133/2/1

1   WLR and MR and their two daughters left Melbourne on the steamship *Atrato* on 18 April 1873. They arrived in England on 11 July 1873 and stayed with relatives in England and Ireland. MR and WLR travelled to the Continent, leaving HHR and ALR with relatives in Cork, and it was while they were away that WLR heard disastrous news about their finances (probably from Sam Bailey). He returned overland from Italy to India, sailing from Bombay on the steamship *Nubia* arriving in Melbourne 21 August 1874. MR, the children, her sister, Sarah Bailey, and the nurse sailed from Plymouth on 17 September 1874 on the sailing ship *Sobraon*, arriving in Melbourne on 12 December 1874. They lived in a furnished house in Sydney Terrace, Fitzroy Gardens, East Melbourne, and then moved to a newly built house in Burwood Road, Hawthorn, in August 1875. It was on the *Sobraon* trip that Sarah met the Reverend James Laughton and the shipboard romance resulted in their marriage on 22 March 1875. Ill with consumption, he died less than six months later, on 11 September 1875.

2   Endorsed 'London 1874' in MR's handwriting.

3   Lucinda Richardson (b. 22 April 1857), HHR's cousin, daughter of Henry and Caroline Richardson. Her two older brothers, Marmaduke Cheyne Richardson, aged twenty-three, and Lindesay Richardson, aged twenty-one, may have been home in Cork on holiday from their university studies in Dublin during HHR and ALR's visit.

1875

162 [From WLR in Hawthorn, Melbourne, to MR in Blairgowrie]

Hawthorn [Melbourne]
Tuesday Eveng [9 November 1875]

My dear Mary

I have just received yours of Sunday—I was beginning to get uneasy—Am glad to hear all is well & that you had a nice passage[1] Sunday was cold with us but only a few drops of rain—More today—So glad they like the beach I suppose they will take a dip when the weather gets warmer Do encourage them—about an hour before dinner is the best time—

Delighted to hear that Sydney[2] is so nice—They must be happy—Kiss them for Papa—All is well here. Cook going out tomorrow—Was awoke at 5. Sunday by the blessed ducks & cock—& this morning ¼ to 5 by the sparrows[3] that are getting under the eaves—I have sent to Davidson[4] to get the holes covered—as I dont like to put down poison on acct. of the neighbours pigeons—

Some callers—

Am in better spirits—Fancy another dividend of 9^d on Kneebones[5]—£30 in the month—I bought another 100 have got 500 now—the next div. will be for Xmas—

We expect good news from the Newingtons every day & when that happens I am happy! & safe, & if it occurs before Sat week I will come down

I enclose 6 stamps—

I see O'Connor has had a success at the Magdala[6] & the manager speaks most favorably of his powder His fortune is safe—

Remember me to Mrs G| Your loving husband

W.L.R

Wednesday morng.

Am afraid you wont get this till Saturday—Heavy gale all night. Awoke at daylight by the sparrows—am going to put poison in the verandah—Love to all| W.

Text: ALS NLA MS133/1/163

[1] MR, HHR and ALR had travelled down to Blairgowrie to the seaside holiday home of Dr George Graham (1829–1893) and his wife, Sydney Boyd Graham (1835–1923). When the Grahams first came to live in Victoria from Adelaide in 1861, Dr Graham set up his medical practice in Richmond. They lived in Swan Street and then Church Street. The Grahams had seven children: George Robert Moore (b. 1860), Margaret Elizabeth Frances (b. 1862), Emily Josephine (b. 1863), Luduvina Marion (b. 1864), James Sidney Boyd (1866–1938), William Archibald (1872–1944), and Edgar Gerald Hastings (1873–1932). During the 1860s, Sorrento (with the back beach at Blairgowrie) was being promoted as a holiday resort by the entrepreneur George Selth Coppin, who resided near to the Grahams at Pine Grove, Richmond. Coppin had owned the Cremorne Gardens, Richmond, until 1862, when he sold them to Dr James Harcourt, who converted them into a lunatic asylum, the Cremorne Private Hospital, where Graham was the visiting medical officer. Coppin also was a part-owner in the Sorrento and Queenscliff Steam Navigation Company, which owned the *Golden Crown* (renamed as the *Silver Crown* in *FRM II*, p. 147 and the *Silver Star* in *GW*, p. 168). John Gower Ritchie, 'Reminisces of the Back Beach, Blairgowrie', held in the Dorothy Green Papers (Folio W) at the Archives of the ADFA, states: 'Travelling to Sorrento must have been quite an undertaking in the 1870s. Dr Graham used to speak of taking a vessel called the *Golden Crown* to Dromana and then driving by horse and trap along the beach.' In the 1876 *Guide to Sorrento*, Dr Graham

extolled the virtues of his choice for a holiday home: 'I know no other place in Victoria equal to it, more particularly on account of the water holding lime in solution in such quantities as renders it most beneficial to children whose bones are soft.' Andrea Inglis, *Beside the Seaside: Victorian Resorts in the Nineteenth Century* (Carlton South: Melbourne Press, 1999), p. 37.

[2] Sydney Graham née Boyd.

[3] Compare *FRM III*, p. 12.

[4] Davidson, building contractor, Boundary Road, Richmond.

[5] Kneebone mining shares.

[6] During spring of 1875, there was considerable excitement about the discovery of some of the richest stone raised from deep shafts. 'In the Magdala mine at Stawell, auriferous quartz has been found, at a depth of about 1,700 ft, which is far below the level at which gold had previously been found in this colony.' *The Argus*, 6 October 1876, p. 2.

1876

Flight to Chiltern

1876

163 [From WLR in Chiltern to MR in Hawthorn, Melbourne]

Chiltern[1]

Thursday [15 June 1876]

My dear wife

I arrived here safely last night—without any other misadventure than leaving my hat box behind me in the Saloon carriage wh I did not discover until this morning—The place looks much better today the morning is fine & sky clear—Rohner[2] & Lloyd[3] met me at the station Rohner is a very handsome man and a gentleman I shall have great difficulty in coming after him.

I hope & trust Ettie is better as I got no telegram from you—I look anxiously for a line tomorrow morning—

I have got a nice room at the hotel & they say they will find me a private parlor if I require one 30/- a week—

Thank God I had a good night & only awoke by the train ½ past 6. I heard a cough & I thought it was my darlings Ettie or Lilly—& woke to find me alone. I have been over to Arrowsmiths[4] house I find the _front_ about 33 feet. did not see him—out—all say he is not going away—that would give 15 feet for each room & 3 feet for door but will be more particular some other time—

I enjoyed the sandwiches & sherry very much—& was not at all cold—Be sure <u>if you come</u> to buy the 1^d Railway guide as it gives you all the names of the stations as you come along You must break the journey at Seymour—it would be too long otherwise—If you post every morning I get it next morning. I will write again tomorrow—Dont send the letter to James Bonwick[5] as we need not tell the people I am gone for good as I may not like it.

Give papas dear love to my darlings—he will write tomorrow

Tell Sarah[6] how sorry I was not to see her & that ~~she~~ I hope she will come & stay with you.| Your loving husband

       Walter

I have just heard that Mr Arrowsmith is <u>not</u> going away—

    Text: ALS NLA 133/1/175

[1] WLR had left his family and practice in Burwood Road, Hawthorn, while he stayed in Chiltern in order to take over the practice of Dr Rohner, who was about to leave for Hamilton. From this letter it is clear that he had been in correspondence with Dr Rohner and had heard about the possibility of renting Robert Arrowsmith's house. Until he found a house, WLR stayed at the Star Hotel, Chiltern. In *FRM III*, HHR called the hotel 'The Sun Hotel' and the place 'Barambogie'. Many of the following letters were used by HHR as a source. See *FRM III*, pp. 52–65.

[2] Dr Charles William Rohner (c.1830–1890), medical practitioner at Chiltern. Like Richardson, he was a staunch supporter of spiritualism and, having contributed greatly to the cultural and social life of Chiltern, was immensely popular. 'An offer, we understand, has been made to Dr Rohner to succeed an extensive practice in Hamilton. He intends leaving Chiltern on Monday next to arrange matters, and will possibly leave Chiltern for good at the end of the current month. The Dr is one of the oldest residents, and we part with him with great regret. It will be difficult to find an eligible successor.' *FS*, Saturday, 3 June 1876. His death in 1890 was surrounded in mystery. Depressed after the death of his eldest living son from typhoid the previous year, he disappeared from his home one morning in January and was presumed drowned at San Remo, Victoria, where he had officiated as health officer. He had been estranged for some time from his wife, Margaret, who was living in Melbourne. My attention was drawn to this mystery by Robert Ashley. His fictional counterpart is Dr Rummel in *FRM III*.

[3] Charles James Lloyd (1838–1881), a chemist in Chiltern since 1868; born in London, the son of John Lloyd and his wife Christian Ann née Tetsell. WLR may have known Lloyd previously for he and his family lived in Ballarat in 1866–1868. Lloyd married Elizabeth Garrett (1840–1884) on 1 January 1862 at Morses Creek, Victoria. The daughter of William Garrett, she was born in the Isle of Man. They had five living children (and one deceased) at the time of this letter and three more subsequently: Fanny Elizabeth (b. 1863), Charles Henry (b. 1865), John Garrett (1867–1873), William Tetsell (b. 1869), Amy Christian (b. 1872), Lillian Ellen (b. 1875), Isabel Jones (b. 2 October 1877), Margaret Louise (1880–1881), and Harry Clifton James (1881–1882). Charles James Lloyd was only forty-one years old when he died on 27 January 1881 in Chiltern of apoplexy (thrombosis). His youngest daughter, Margaret, who was aged two months at her father's death, died shortly after. The last child, Harry, conceived shortly before his father's death, died aged six months on 4 March 1882.

[4] Robert Todd Arrowsmith (d. 1911), engineer and surveyor of Shire of Chiltern; appointed Mining Surveyor and Registrar for the Indigo Mining District on 2 May 1862; he was the first surveyor for the Rutherglen Municipal Council and the first engineer for the Rutherglen Road Board; he retired in 1908. Ashley, pp. 38–64.

[5] James Bonwick (1817–1906) born on 8 July 1817 at Lingfield, Surrey, England, the eldest son of James Bonwick, carpenter, and his second wife Mary née Preston. He began his teaching career in 1833 and while at Liverpool in 1837 became converted to Noncomformism and was pledged to the temperance cause. He married Esther Anne, daughter of the Reverend Barnabas Beddow, Baptist Minister at Exeter, in 1840. A year later, he and his wife were selected to manage a new school in Hobart Town, set up by Governor Sir John Franklin's new Board of Education. The conditions in the school were so poor that he resigned after two years and opened his own boarding school. While in Hobart he came under the influence of George Washington Walker (1800–1859) in his studies of Aboriginals, and Henry Melville (1799–1873) in his studies in occult philosophy, astronomy and Freemasonry. In 1850, after failing to secure the position of Inspector of Schools, he left for Adelaide where he remained until the discovery of gold in Victoria. After a brief stint on the goldfields in 1852, he returned to Melbourne and worked as a lecturer and then proprietor of the *Australian Gold Digger's Monthly Magazine, and Colonial Family Visitor*. Publication ceased in 1853 and he opened a land agency and lectured around Victoria for the Colonial Reform Association, which was pledged to 'unlocking the lands'. He was appointed an Inspector for the Denominational Schools Board in 1856 and, after extensive tours of Victoria, was forced to retire after a serious

coach accident in 1859. After a trip back to England he opened a successful school in St Kilda in 1862 and continued his historical and anthropological studies and writing. In 1871 he arranged a lease for his school and returned to England. In 1875 he returned to Melbourne to arrange the final sale of his St Kilda property. For further details see *ADB*. WLR knew both James and his younger brother, Walter Bonwick (see Letter 179).

6   MR's sister, Sarah Laughton, the widow of the Reverend James Laughton, was about to leave Melbourne for London.

164 [From WLR in Chiltern to MR in Hawthorn, Melbourne]

Chiltern
Friday [16 June 1876]

My dearest M

I have just had your telegram—Your post card received this morning made me very anxious I am so glad to know there is no danger—the white patch must be follicular inflammation which I cured in London by Guaiacum lozenges[1]—get 3ᵈ from Rawle[2] & give her half a one three times daily if there are any white spots on receipt of this—Give the darlings Papas best love & kisses

Brooke Smith[3] & judge Hackett[4] have been here yesterday & today so we have been lively—They are off today—The Hotel is full good table—Rohner being here still, I am not doing anything but getting known   one patient yesterday—Revd Mʳ Green[5] English Clergyman called ~~yesterda~~ this morning nice little man—3 children[6] grown up—lost his wife[7]—Says he is likely to leave his cottage & to move out a mile off—Cottage is of brick he thinks it is as good as Arrowsmith's only no ground. Said he was very glad to see me coming—as there must be a good practice in the district. Brooke sends his love says I am to tell you he is looking after me—he admits now there is a fine opening here altho he thinks it would be almost better to run off to Corowa a nicer place & he says only one doctor. However I think I will remain here for 6 weeks after Rohner has gone & see what results—

Be sure & drop me a line every morning before ½ pass nine or send letter in to town if you have a chance before 5. so then I will get it always ~~get it~~ next afternoon about 2. Yesterday was a pleasant day & Brooke & I took long walk—today is cold but not out of the way there are lots of flies about & blow flies—I had my cold bath & 2 eggs for breakfast: meat lunch at one & tea dinner at 6 Turkey Bacon: Roast beef pudding—Cheese—God bless you all dear M.

I hope M.B.[8] was with you of course the wet kept her from seeing me off, even if she had got my letter| Your affect Husband
        Walter
Text: ALS NLA 133/1/176

1   A tropical American genus of trees, yeilding *lignum vitae* (extremely hard wood): their greenish brown resin, formerly used for rheumatism, cutaneous eruptions and even as a laxative. See *MD*, p. 779: and J. Haggar, *Australian Colonial Medicine* (Adelaide: Rigby, 1979).
2   William Rawle (1807–1886), pharmaceutical chemist in Melbourne; born in Cornwall, the son of William Rawle, a barrister, and his wife, Mary Elizabeth née Kingston. He married Harriet Raggett in Exeter, Devon, in 1835 and they emigrated to Australia in 1861 with six children.
3   Alexander Brooke Smith had been working in north-east Victoria since 1861, when he became a Sub-Inspector at Wangaratta. In February 1863 he was stationed at Chiltern for about a year before leaving for Wood's Point. He was an Inspector at Wangaratta between August 1870 and

June 1874. At the time of this letter he was Inspector at Beechworth (until 1880) and 'Officer in Charge of the Ovens District' between February 1876 and February 1878.

4   Charles Prendergast Hackett (1818–1889), judge, whom WLR met through the Victorian Lodge of Freemasons which he joined in the early 1850s. He was the oldest son of John Prendergast Hackett, a barrister, of Stratford Place, Middlesex. He was sent to Dublin and educated at Trinity College and was admitted to Lincoln's Inn on 15 April 1840, aged twenty-two. *The Records of the Honorable Society of Lincoln's Inn, vol. II Admissions 1800–1893 and Chapel Registers* (London: Lincoln's Inn, 1896). He was married to Frances Ann née Day. He was a member of the Melbourne and the Yorick clubs, the latter to which WLR also belonged.

5   The Reverend Samuel Dutton Green (1830–1879) born in Hertfordshire, son of Job Green and his wife Martha née Dutton.

6   By his first wife Green had in fact five children: Agnes Maria (b. 1855) who lived in a convent in Wiltshire, England; two daughters (Edith Lizzie and Mabel Dutton) died in infancy; and two children were with him in Victoria—Arthur Vincent (1857–1944), studying in order to matriculate at the University of Melbourne and also taking services from Benalla to Yarrawonga, based at Wangaratta and occasionally visiting Chiltern; and Florence Emily (1862–1926) at school in South Yarra.

7   Eliza Green née Dutton (*c.*1830–1872) died in Oamaru, New Zealand. At the time of this letter, Samuel Dutton Green was engaged to be married to Harriet Amy Sheppard (1837–1923), who became his second wife on 6 February 1877 in East Melbourne, Victoria.

8   MR's sister-in-law, Mary Ringrose Bayles née Atkins (formerly Bailey) (b. 1843), widow of John Robinson Bailey, whom she had married in 1869. She married William Bayles on 18 November 1875.

165 [From WLR in Chiltern to MR in Hawthorn, Melbourne]

Chiltern

Saturday 12 noon [17 June 1876]

My dearest Mary

Your post card made me very uneasy, then your telegram gave me comfort & finally your letter describing your anxiety all night was grievous—Not having had any telegram this morning I conclude that they are better.

It is just possible that they may have had a mild attack & it will be necessary to be very careful about cold & to watch the water they pass. If it looks thick cloudy, smoky like porter you may be sure it has been scarlet fever & this cannot be known for some weeks—I am no further advanced about a house. Mr Arrowsmith does not know & will not know if he is going until the 6th of July—Every one says he will be retained here—The clergyman's cottage is brick about <u>20 by 18</u> with four rooms in that space. Rohner has no house at Hamilton so Mrs R.[1] will stay here—he tells me his sheds cost him £500. I was half determined to return to Mel. [Melbourne] today disgusted, but Lloyd chemist says that Rohner is going over to Beechworth tomorrow & Monday, & Albury next week, so that there may be some patients for me. It is very dull now Brooke is gone. It was very cold this morning but it is clearing up now at noon—

2 PM—Just got yours of Friday—Glad to find things are no worse

Mrs Graham[2] is indeed a real friend—how shall we repay her.

No chance of a house here I fear—two offering but very small cabins—I am glad Sara is with you I hope she will stay

If ~~you~~ we could get a house she should not leave. Loves to my darlings & same to yourself from| Your Affect| Husband

Walter

Text: ALS NLA MS133/1/182

---

1   Margaret Emmeline Rohner née Edmonds (1841–1918) married Charles William Rohner in 1862 in Albury, NSW. They had the following children: Charles Armin (1864–1889), William Abelard (1865–1901), Ferdinand Charles (died at Chiltern aged six months in 1868), Hypatia Irene (b. 1869), Corinna Dolores (b. 1874), Laura Beatrice (b. 1877), Emmanuel (1879–1940), and Ania Mara (died at Chiltern aged twenty-one days in 1883). When WLR met the Rohners they had four children living. Laura Beatrice was born in Hamilton after they moved there.

2   Mrs Sydney Boyd Graham.

166 [From WLR in Chiltern to MR in Hawthorn, Melbourne]

Chiltern

Monday morning [19 June 1876]

My dearest Mary

Since writing on Saturday I had two patients Saturday night, & one last night. 4 miles drive into the country for which I will charge £3–3–0. Rohner has not been a favorite with everybody as these people told me that if I had not been here they would have gone to Rutherglen 8 miles from them—I am sure I shall have a good practice by & bye—& there seems to be money in the district & no clubs a great mercy. The worst thing is ~~h~~ about a house

I hear now that Arrowsmith is likely to go—He told me himself that his staying depends entirely on his being re-appointed a shire engineer which will be decided July 6—The Post Master says he will <u>not</u> be appointed, that the shire council will <u>not</u> have him—His is the only decent shed to be got—we can <u>just</u> live in it—as it is about the size of our wooden cottage in Webster St. I went to church yesterday morning the clergymans cottage is brick but very small—He thinks he was fortunate to get that We have two or three nice fellows staying at the Hotel & I shall be very lonely next week We had Green[1] Sams[2] bank inspector Saturday but he left suddenly this morning before I thought to ask if Sam had left Corowa. This is a lovely morning. There is Paterson[3] an old clerk of the bench of Ballt. East who is only relieving officer—A nice young fellow in the bank also relieving some one. The Station master & commercial men in & out every day—some ½ doz. coaches stop at the house.[4]

<u>Monday. 3 PM.</u> I get yours every day at 2. I am so glad they keep better—But one is never safe—you must examine the skin carefully & if you see any signs of peeling, of scurf you may expect Dropsy. I think I should give them a good warm bath <u>occasionally</u> & if you see any scurf about them oil them all over after their bath at night—

I was very delighted to get their letters—Rohner leaves next Monday—

Nothing further. Love to Sarah & the darlings—will write to them tomorrow—Ask M.B. for the book I lent her father[5]—Your affect| Husband

Walter

Text: ALS NLA MS133/1/180

---

1   George Frederick Green (b. 1833), an accountant, married on 14 February 1860 to Catherine née Gloster (b. 1842).

2   Samuel Bailey.

3   George W. T. Paterson, Clerk of the Petty Sessions, Ballarat.

[4]   The Star Hotel.
[5]   John Roberts Atkins (1809–1878), barrister; born in County Cork, son of Captain Ringrose Atkins, 10th Hussars. He was married to Mary Agnes, daughter of William Campion, and they had six children including Mary Ringrose and John Ringrose.

167   **[From WLR in Chiltern to MR in Hawthorn, Melbourne]**

Star Hotel Chiltern

June 19 1876 [Monday—though WLR says

he is writing on Tuesday, 20 June]

My dearest Mary

I got yours of Sunday evening this morning Tuesday. I am glad to hear that the little ones are recovering, but very grieved you do not sleep Try & take a cold sponging before going to bed & a stroll if ever so little in the afternoon. Do think a little of your own health. it will be dreadful if the chicks lose you & your constitution must break down if you do not get rest—

You must do the best you can with the house—I fear you will not get the rent you asked—It cost close upon £1800. & there is £400 due on it—I think we might get £1500 for it & invest £1000 at 7 per cent for the chicks An extra room put up in the shed would not cost more than £30 & with new shed £40 to £50. I am glad Sarah is with you I have done nothing further about a house. I would much rather you did not come for a m two or three months as it is a horridly dull place Mʳ Greens house is a wretched brick cottage. I have not yet seen the one 1 mile away as Mʳ Lloyd thought it would be nonsense to go there.

I had very bad nights at first but better now I do not know what I should have done without the opossᵐ rug—The food is excellent but my bedroom is small & cold at night. I get my bath—I have suffered from bad diarrhoea Saturday & Sunday but am better this morning I cannot acct for it unless the water. It is tank water from the roof & excellent but a change often affects me—I shall go & see Sergeant Ellis[1] this morng about the house—Give my love to Sarah: I am surprised at M.[2] never being over Mʳ A.[3] could not have got my letter at the Yorick

You had better send for Davidson & ask him to give estimate of the alterations his address is Mʳ Davidson Contractor Boundary Road Richmond—

The darlings are improving wonderfully in their letter writing Ettie has a sore mouth Lilly says this is a sign of bad cold—altho the lips are often cracked & the gums bleeding & sore after S.F.[4]

The house in the country is too far away quite a mile off I walked half way to it since beginning this letter, but find it wont do—

As long as Rohner remains here of course the people will go to him—I have just examined a lunatic—I am glad I shall get your letters in the morning instead of afternoon.

Kiss the darlings for Papa| Your affect. Husband

Walter

Text: ALS NLA 133/1/183

[1]   Sergeant George Ellis was appointed to the Police Force on 28 January 1854 and pensioned on 31 December 1895. He was based in the Chiltern area. He married Fanny Girling in 1858 and

they had six children. 'Sergeant George Ellis, afterward Superintendent, ... one of the reliable
sort.' Sadleir, p. 281.
2   Mary Ringrose Bayles.
3   John Roberts Atkins.
4   Scarlet fever.

168   [From WLR in Chiltern to MR in Hawthorn, Melbourne]

Star Hotel Chiltern
June 21st 1876 [Wednesday]

My dear Mary

I get your letters every morning now—Rohner is certainly going Monday—I have not
been so cheerful because I have not been so well. I cannot make out what has upset me unless
it is my cold hole of a bedroom & my regret that you should have to come to such a place. I
have written to answer the advertisement of Kiesser[1] as it appears in yesterdays Argus[2]—the
climate will be better & the house may be decent & we should not be so out of the world as
this—You would be near the Cuthberts—I have been thinking it would be very unpleasant for
me to be all alone here—In the event of your illness or the chicks or my own. So I will not
hurridly decide about this especially as at present there is no place to bring you to—

You can get another bottle of San mora if you see it does Lily good or an injection of salt
& water or lard rubbed around every night.

You had better see Russel[3] about the house—I am not sanguine that it will let. See what
rent he advises & what reserve we should put upon it—

I am glad Sara is with you still—I have just been over the cottage where M[r] Green
clergyman lives—It is brick—Iron roof—two front rooms about 12 x 12. & two back rooms
the same—snug little kitchen Col oven[4] & stable—It seems a warmer house than
Arrowsmiths: & being in the town would be more convenient

I see a fresh patient every day altho there is no scarlatina—I hope you have had better
nights—No news of Sam

Give Papas dear love to my darlings & I hope they are not teasing & worrying dear
Mama—

The mornings here are intensely cold. Rohner says he has 100 confinements a year &
I see several women in that way—They are giving him a supper at this hotel tomorrow eveng.[5]
The people still run after him in the streets—

Nothing more| Your affectionate Husband
Walter

Text: ALS NLA MS133/1/184

1   Caesar Kieser (*c.*1815–1885), MD (Wurzburg, Germany, 1841; the University of Wurzburg
was famed for its medical faculty). He was registered as a doctor in Victoria in 1856 and worked
first at Casterton and then at Mt Blackwood in 1856 as the vaccinator. At Buninyong in 1862,
he was insolvent in Ballarat in 1867. Bowden, p. 114.
2   'To Medical Men—Good OPENING in Country district. Residence always occupied by
physician. Address Medicus, Carngham.' *The Argus*, Tuesday, 20 June 1876, p. 1.
3   Thomas Russell, Burwood Road, Hawthorn, listed under heading 'Brokers, Agents &
Commission Agents specialising in Land, House & Estate', Sands, 1876, p. 693.
4   Colonial oven: an iron oven, usually bricked in, and heated from above and below. *MD*, p. 357.

5   Reported under heading 'Telegraphic Despatches: Chiltern', the article stated: 'Dr Rohner, who
     is leaving this district after a residence of 17 years, was entertained at a banquet at the Star Hotel
     today. An illuminated address, handsomely framed, was presented to him. About 40 gentlemen
     were present. Mr B. J. Barkley, president of the shire council, presided.' *The Argus*, 24 June
     1876.

169 [From WLR in Chiltern to MR in Hawthorn, Melbourne]

Chiltern

Thursday [22 June 1876]

My dear Mary

This is certainly a lovely winter climate every day since I arrived has been fine—mostly
clear blue sky sunshine with cool bracing wind from South. I am glad the darlings are well &
able to go out & that Maria[1] is kind. She must be good if they like her better than nurse—

The landlady[2] tells me servants are very difficult to be got here. Dr Rohner's only has
one—there is only one at the bank opposite who gets 10/- week She gives hers 15/- I suppose
M: would not care to leave Melbourne—I am sorry to hear M:B: is ill & in bed[3]—I may be
able to say something definite next week—after Rohner is gone—

Every one tells me that Mr Greens house will be the best for me as it is in the town &
Arrowsmiths is nearly ½ mile off—Greens kitchen is best—it is a brick house & must be
warmer in winter

I am certainly not well completely off my food & a headache on rising—I fear that my
bedroom is damp—I have nothing further to say except my love to the dear ones & yourself &
Sara| Ever your affect| Husband

Walter

Text: ALS NLA 133/1/185

1   The Richardsons' servant.
2   Catherine Peel née Jordan, landlady of the Star Hotel. She was married to Henry William Peel
     and had two children who had both died in 1873: Emily (aged two years) and Henry Joseph
     (aged six months). An advertisement stated: 'Henry W. Peel, Star Hotel (Late agent at
     Beechworth for Messrs Robertson & Co. coach proprietors) Having taken the above Hotel, begs
     to inform his friends and the public generally that he will spare no pains to make it one of the
     most complete and comfortable houses in the colony.' Sands, 1875.
3   Mary Bayles was three months pregnant at the time and may not have disclosed that
     information.

170 [From WLR in Chiltern to MR in Hawthorn, Melbourne]

Chiltern

Friday evening [23 June 1876]

My dear Marie

I was prevented from posting this in time today by one or two people I got yours of this
morng. & again this afternoon.

I would have remained at Hawthorn if I had thought there was a chance of my getting
any clubs even. I confess I feel the extreme discomfort of my horrid bedroom so cold & damp
always—It gave me Rheumatism—I am a little better today thank God

My great grief & sorrow is that you & the dear ones have to give up the comforts of our fine house & put up with cottage life—I spent an evening with Mr Green they keep no servant because they have no bedroom! for her! I wrote to Mrs Kiesser[1] because I thought their house might be habitable at least—but we will say no more about it—I wish I had not hurried up here before the place was properly vacant altho Rohner has now discontinued going out—

It is not nice being here all alone from the profession but perhaps I may get used to it—I am a little The dear chicks letters improve each day Etties & Lillys are both very very good—I have more than paid all my expenses Railway & hotel since I came already. I have put an advertisement in the local paper for a month

> Dr Richardson
> Temporary Residence
> Star Hotel
> Chiltern

I will hire a saddle horse or a buggy as I require them at first—

Call & get the likenesses from Hibling & send me one also get mine at Hiblings[2] or Botterells[3] enlarged for the children; which you like; I should also like another of yours taken for enlargement.

If you should decide on coming nearly every thing will have to be packed away & stored—I dont know when you will get this perhaps Saturday night God bless you

We have gone up the hill of life together & now it seems we have to go down—|Your loving husband
> Walter

Text: ALS NLA 133/1/202

[1] Temperance Kieser née Gibbons, who married Dr Caesar Kieser in 1857.
[2] Hibling and Fields, 7 Collins Street East, Melbourne; the photograph of WLR has survived (Monash Richardson Achives). On the reverse of an earlier photograph of MR in the Monash Richardson Archives taken by E. E. Hibling, there is a description of the photographer as 'formerly principal operator to G. W. Wilson of Aberdeen and R. W. Thrupp of Birmingham, both Photographers to Her Majesty the Queen; & late from Johnstone, O'Shannessy & Co.'
[3] J. Botterill, 'Portrait Painter and Photographer', 19 Collins Street East, Melbourne.

171 [From WLR in Chiltern to MR in Hawthorn, Melbourne]

Chiltern
Saturday afternoon [24 June 1876]

My own dear Mary

I missed the post yesterday but sent 2 letters last night wh. ought to have reached you Saturday night. I wrote to Slatterie[1] asking for particulars of specifications I intend to apply & if I do not get it I must make the best of this for a time—I was called out this morng 2 to 4 [a.m.] 5 miles for wh. I charge have been paid £4. buggy will cost me about 15/- I told you I had more than covered all expenses since here—Mr Green is very ill today & I have been busy with other patients of Rohner who declines to see people now—

I am much better thank God & have had a good lunch of cold fowl—

Your letters cheer me up & fill me with hope—I never felt the cold so intensely as I did in my drive this morg. In spite of my wraps.

Give my love to the dears & Sara & Sam   Poor George Walker[2] of Sams bank died 22nd—sorry M:B: is ill. Kind regards to the Grahams, thank them for all their kindness—

Good bye dearest| Your ever loving

    Walter

Text: ALS NLA MS133/1/204

[1]   Apollos Slatterie (1830–1917), Town Clerk of Hawthorn, lived next door to the Richardsons in Burwood Road. Sands, 1876, pp. 143, 589. He married Elizabeth Jane Cook (1839–1918) in 1859 and they had thirteen children.

[2]   George Walker was the accountant for the Bank of New South Wales, Melbourne branch. 'The funeral of the late George Walker will move from No. 6 Simpson Street, East Melbourne, THIS DAY, at 3 o'clock & will proceed to place of interment at Melbourne General Cemetery. Alf. Aug. Sleight, undertaker.' *The Argus*, 23 June 1876, p. 8.

172   [From WLR in Chiltern to MR in Hawthorn, Melbourne]

Chiltern

Sunday [25 June 1876]

My dearest Mary

    I am anxious not to let a post pass without a line—I told you I had been called out Saturday morning 2 to 4. I got buggy at the hotel stables—I had a busy day owing to the parson being <u>as he is still</u> dangerously ill I was called out 5 PM. 5 miles in another direction so that there is a good prospect here of £700 a year to £1000—when Rohner is off—I see there are two doctors at Corowa & three banks but that is a rising place & this is a falling place—people are leaving this every day—no mining—Still there must always be some, & the farming district is good—I think you

    I am not able to say anything more definite about the house & hope to know soon if we may get Greens, meanwhile my dear you must be patient for it is best that you and the darlings should not hurry away from comforts. If I get Greens house I shall only take it for a term as I have a scheme in view of taking an old oddfellows hall[1] brick like a chapel about 60 feet long & 20 front & converting it into a dwelling house it would make 6 rooms It is just away from the town ¼ mile opposite the p.o. & Telegraph office & I hear it can be had cheap to buy, or to rent

    I am happy to say I am much better again & can enjoy my food—of course altho I wrote to Slat. I do not expect to get the lodge—and indeed after yesterdays sample of work I hardly think it would be wise <u>This</u> appears a certainty the other only a <u>chance.</u> I will move about Greens house as soon as he is out of danger—Give Papas dear love to our darlings he does not forget them I should not be at all astonished if some other doctor came here—What a sad thing about Sams freind Sawell[2] absconded with £6000. & poor George Walker dead—

    The clerk of the bank here is very astonished—

    The nights are cold Ice ¼ inch thick on all the tanks—& the streets & fields covered with white frost—the days are warm the sun hot I can hardly bear my flannels. I hope you are sleeping better my darling

    Is Sara still with you?—

    I sent my life premium to the Melb. office yesterday—

    Be sure & let me have a photo:—also get dear Ettie taken again & have Lilly enlarged I am really obliged to bank some money taken as fees—

We ought to be in better spirits—take the savings bank book to the bank after July 1st. I will send you a cheque—Let me know if you want money which you must do if no one has paid—

If you come you & the chicks can run down to Sorrento[3] in February—

I have not been to church today—I have two bad cases of inflam of the lungs one case of Rohners neglected not seen for 5 days: It is a great thing that our letters are sent off by the early train that leaves this 6.30 am Monday—

The people seem to take to me very kindly & all are very civil & want me to drink with them| Your loving husband

      Walter

Text: ALS NLA MS133/1/192 and MS133/1/252

1   The Oddfellows Hall was situated on the west side of Main Street and was a simply constructed brick building completed in 1864 to the design of architect Thomas Dalziel, with arched windows and door openings. It was built and owned by the Manchester Unity Independent Order of Oddfellows, and was reputed to be the earliest Lodge building constructed outside Melbourne. In the Chiltern Conservation Study, commissioned in 1981 by the Shire of Chiltern and the Australian Heritage Commission (prepared by Heather Sutherland and Elizabeth Vines, assisted by Robert Ashley), it was noted that the Hall was in 'a seriously deteriorated condition'. The Hall was later demolished. See *FRM III*, p. 54.

2   John Greig Sawell, a paying teller for the Bank of New South Wales, was well known in rowing circles and at a race held on 10 June 1876, he was the coxswain of the bank's boat. He was also a gambler and had lost money on the boat race as well as at the Sydney races. On the Monday following the boat race, he had requested a week's leave because he claimed he was not feeling well and during his absence his defalcations were discovered. A warrant for his arrest was issued and it was discovered that he, his mother and all their furniture had departed for Adelaide aboard the steamer, *Tartarus*. Before Sawell could catch a boat to Europe, however, he was caught in Adelaide and returned to Melbourne. The story as it unfolded was reported in the *Federal Standard*. 'James Greig Sawell, the late paying teller in the Bank of New South Wales, in whose accounts deficiencies to the extent of nearly £6000 have been discovered, who arrived by the steamer *Tartarus* from Adelaide, on Friday afternoon, was brought before the City Court on Saturday. In the dock he presented a sad picture of humiliation and distress, and appeared to feel the position into which he had brought himself very keenly, as a large number of bank clerks and others with whom he was acquainted were in court … He was committed for trial at the main sittings of the Central Criminal Court to be held on the 17th Inst.' *FS*, Wednesday, 12 July 1876, p. 3.

3   He was probably referring to a standing invitation to the Grahams' holiday home in Blairgowrie, near Sorrento, on the Mornington Peninsula.

173 [From WLR in Chiltern to MR in Hawthorn, Melbourne]

Chiltern
Monday [26 June 1876]

My dear Mary

I am so sorry about your fingers—you must poultice them & take a few drops of Tinct. of Arnica[1] say 5 in water three times daily leaving off the Iron meantime—

I am so glad M.[2] is good & kind & that the darlings take to her. You would see by my last that I was better & getting more used to the place I think dear I will decide on remaining here as there is a good practice to be done You must be patient however about the house as nothing can be done immediately You had better see Russel & let him get a tenant if he can at what rent he thinks fair—

I hope M.[3] went to you Sunday & that you sleep better. Lovely weather here such days—but the mornings cold. ice ½ inch thick—I get your letters regularly. I got your last on Sunday by favor of the Post Master just after I had posted mine to you—The people are ~~beginning~~ all very pleasant & civil. Some are very pleased to get rid of Rohner

The parson is not safe yet it has been a most troublesome case of obstruction of the bowels—I have a child with a broken arm at the elbow—Two cases of Inf: [inflammation] of the lungs—& cases from the country every day—Every one tells me I shall do well   The Roman Catholic priest stayed at the hotel one evening & told his people they would be lucky if they kept me—It will be very dull & quiet but there are no lodges & a pop[n] in the shire of 2000

Rohner is not going until tomorrow he told me yesterday he should never come back—~~I write~~—I met two doctors yesterday from the neighbourhood ~~the~~ Yackandandah they were very pleasant they came to drink a last bottle with Rohner—

2 PM Monday

Just got your two letters & one from Slatterie wh. I will reply to tomorrow—

I have decided to remain here!—

If I had got the other offer a month ago I would have remained & not broken up my house but I think this is too good a chance to throw up—I will decide about M[r] Greens house as soon as I can that is as soon as he recovers, he is still in a critical state & I hope you will arrange with Russel to let the house

Much love to my darlings. I will write them tomorrow| Your own husband

Walter

Text: ALS NLA MS133/1/177

1   Tincture of Arnica (any plant of the genus *Arnica*) was commonly applied for sprains and
    bruises.
2   Maria, the Richardsons' servant.
3   Probably Mary Bayles visiting.

174 [From WLR in Chiltern to MR in Hawthorn, Melbourne]

Chiltern
Tuesday morning [27 June 1876]

My dear Mary

I dont know that I have anything fresh to say. I thought it more prudent to accept this certain opening with all its discomforts, than to ~~at~~ take the uncertain chance of Hawthorn with two paltry lodges & the expenses of horse necessary—The bank manager Cameron[1] came in to the hotel last night & we had a chat he was queer had been taking nobblers[2]—~~he~~ I hear he always does so—We spoke about Sam he said he could get Sam manager to Beechworth if S. liked it—Capital quarters the manager there not a fixture. He seems to be quite independent has been here 17 years or 20—Says there is plenty of money about Chiltern. I saw about Sawell & Walker last Friday—very sad.

M[r] Green is a bit better today. Rohner not gone yet—

The weather has changed & rain has come at last.

I hope your fingers are better.

2 P.M. Post in & no letter—I fear the fingers are worse   see Dr Graham about them—Nothing new| Much love Yours ever

      W.L.R.

I will not expect you in future to write so often if all is well every 2nd day will do   same from me unless I have something particular to say—

    Text: ALS NLA MS133/1/178

1   Archibald Cameron (b. 1826) born in Scotland, the son of Alexander Cameron, a farmer, and his wife Christy. The Manager of the Bank of New South Wales at Chiltern, he was also the Treasurer of the Shire of Chiltern. He retired in January 1877 after eighteen years of service at Chiltern. *FS*, 27 January 1877, p. 3.

2   Glass of spirits. 'Nor was it feasible to ask the old couple over of an evening, for cards or music; for, by then, old Cameron was as a rule so fuddled that he couldn't tell a knave from a king.' *FRM III*, p. 73. HHR changed his occupation to 'Clerk of the Court' but his drinking habits were consistent with Cameron, the Bank Manager.

175 [From WLR in Chiltern to MR in Hawthorn, Melbourne]

                                     Chiltern

                          Wednesday 28 [June 1876]

My dear Mary

I have just been over a decent house.[1] 6 rooms kitchen stable fowl house pigstye & fine garden with fruit trees—it is the best house in Chiltern   the owner[2] wants £80 per year & to be taken for 4 years—the verandah is not floored—it is not papered—built about 18 mo[nths]—high & dry. Water tank—earth closets—small range oven & boiler wash house & boiler built in

    In fact it is a comfortable place. Of course it is a venture as if I were to die before 4 years! but after all it is only like paying 100 or 200 for the practice

    He refuses to do anything is quite careless about letting—He is the leading draper here—Of course if our house at Hawthorn can be let or sold—we might decide on this—& be really very comfortable & the possibility makes me quite happy—

    I should be inclined to sell Hawthorn if we could, as the expense of repairs is constant see Russel at once—

    I have also seen another 4 rooms & 2 smaller rooms for servant & me. Kitchen Col. oven. not near so nice garden indeed only orchard—He[3] wants £75 & 3 years will floor verandah   I am inclined to the first as we could be comfortable & the chicks have fine nursery &-p & a room for me with splendid garden & orchard   I would keep a man to garden or at least a boy. he says I can get one for 3 or 4/- a week with keep—I wish you were here to decide but the distance is too great & the journey too weary but you can see what to do with Russel.

    The freight on luggage is £4–4–6 per ton weight   Keep your eyes about for some man to pack if we take this house we can manage nearly all our furniture—No fresh patients: the parson a little better gastric fever—

    Any news of Sam. Tell him about Beechworth—I saw Brooke Smith passing thro he sent me word by court [?] & I went to the train & had a chat—He introduced me to some lady of

a squatter great swell in these parts. She said we would [be] quite an acquisition—have just
been engaged to a confinement Rohner gone at last today

    Love to darlings same to you from Your| Affect Husband

      Walter

Glad your fingers are better

    Text: ALS NLA MS133/1/188

[1]   'Lake View', constructed of brick with a corrugated iron roof. It has four well-detailed chimneys
and french doors opening to the verandah from all rooms. The cottage was restored by the
National Trust of Australia (Victoria) and remains open to the public.

[2]   John Hancock owned a drapery business in Conness Street, Chiltern. He was the widower of
Mary Ann Kinnear and it was she who had purchased the allotment in 1872 on which they then
built 'Lake View'. They had four children born in Richmond, Melbourne and South Yarra prior
to moving to Chiltern in about 1870. They subsequently had four more children between 1871
to 1875, all born in the Chiltern area. Mary Ann Hancock died aged thirty-five in 1875 after
the birth of their last son, George. The Hancock family occupied 'Lake View' immediately
before Dr Richardson moved in on 29 July 1876.

[3]   Alexander McCleery, see Letter 176.

176 [From WLR in Chiltern to MR in Hawthorn, Melbourne]

Star Hotel, Chiltern
June 28 1876 [Wednesday]

My dear Mary

    I have made an offer to Mr Hancock to pay the first year's rent in advance provided he
floor the verandah. Mr Lloyd thinks this most liberal on my part & that his demand about
4 years lease is excessive. Brooke Smith has just sent a telegram saying he has fallen from his
horse & requesting me to go to Wangaratta to see him this evening—I do hope we may get
the house: I told you I think it was brick with verandah all round—6 fair sized rooms good
height—not papered, walls soiled. detached kitchen—& washhouse bath shed with shower
bath. Water tank—large garden fruit kitchen & flower—We can be quite happy &
comfortable if we get it I will send you the dimensions of the rooms if I get a favorable answer
which he has promised today—

    I am afraid my darling that the journey would knock you up It is dreadful
8 hours—Still I leave it to yourself—

    I wish you would go & see [illegible word crossed out] Miss Armstrong[1] about your state
generally—I will write to her by this post—It would give me great comfort—follow her
advice. I am very anxious about you—She lives in Russell S^t near Dr Campbells[2] & next the
detective office—

    dont forget about the photog. I would m Was called out again last evening 5 miles—

    Mr Greens case has gone on to Fever & Infl. of the liver—

    I am glad M: is so kind to the darlings—

    Fine day but foggy morning. My appetite is good & I enjoy the good fare. Wild fowl.
Turkeys, Fowls, Eggs & good butter—Cold bath every morning—

    I have written to Miss Armstrong & have asked her to go & take a cup of tea with you &
prescribe for you.

Kind love to Mary B. hope she is better—

Much love to Ettie & Lilly Papa will jump them & give them swings every day when they come to their new home| Your affect Husband

      Walter

Text: ALS NLA MS133/1/186

1   Elizabeth Armstrong was a medium and a member of the Progressive Spiritualists. She was the niece of the Archbishop of Dublin and WLR wrote in his article 'Spiritualism in Australia' that he was proud to be able to call her 'his dear friend'. Clark, p. 58. Clark also suggests she might be the model for the character Grace Marriner in *FRM* but Grace Marriner's personal situation reflects much more closely Mrs Caroline Dexter. Grace was introduced to Richard Mahony as 'a youngish widow', however it is revealed later that her husband has left her, just as William Dexter left Caroline and returned to Sydney, where he subsequently died. In common with many of the characters in *FRM*, Grace Marriner appears to be an amalgam of HHR's imagination and two women who were of interest to WLR and MR. (See Letter 59, endnote 3.) In WLR's notebook there is an entry about a seance with Miss Armstrong: 'We had a manifestation from my brother, John Cheyne, he said God bless you, & told us where he died wh. we did not know until we looked at his mother's letter ... we asked what he died of ... jungle fever.' NLA MS133/1/292.

2   William Henry Campbell (1814–1888), surgeon; member of the Melbourne Club. He arrived in Melbourne in December 1841.

177 [From WLR in Chiltern to MR in Hawthorn, Melbourne]

                                      Chiltern

                            June 30 [Friday 1876]

My dear Mary

I have not seen Mr Hancock since & he has made no approval of my offer. I was out again last ~~nig~~ evening 5 miles, up all night with a confinement that is not off yet, & out this forenoon 10 miles to see a patient of Dr Peeles of Corowa[1] that he has neglected—So that I cannot complain of want of success at starting—If Hancock accepts I will telegraph at once—Cameron the bank manager wishes me to take Mc learys[2] £75 per an 3 years—4 decent rooms & 2 small ones with detached kitchen orchard—not any thing so nice as Hancocks.

I think I shall be obliged to accept his conditions 4 years—but will wait until you say what you think or come up to see it—Thank God I am keeping well—I hope Miss A. will go & see you

    Love to Sara & 100 kisses to each of the pets from| Your afft Husband

      Walter

It was quite impossible to go & see Brooke as I had the confinement on hand & the journey 5 miles into country—

    Text: ALS NLA MS133/1/187

1   John Richard Peele (1849–1916), born in Lincolnshire, married in 1872 to Isabella Anna née Johnstone.

2   Alexander McCleery (c.1833–1900) described himself in advertisements in *The Federal Standard* as an auctioneer and cattle salesman, commissions and insurance agent. He married Anne Robinson Heppell in 1858 and had eleven children between 1859 and 1880, three of whom died at birth and one at four months.

178 [From WLR in Chiltern to MR in Hawthorn, Melbourne]

Chiltern
Sunday [2 July 1876]

My dear Mary

I was too busy to write Saturday—so I telegraphed to you—Mʳ Lloyd tells me that he has arranged with Hancock about the house & that I may consider it as settled that I am to have it for 2 years £80. per an. Rent of year paid in advance. I am sure you will be pleased with it when you see <u>the choice I had</u>—I did not give you all the details—It is brick. 6 rooms & kitchen & washhouse with built in boiler splendid cellar where you can sit in the very hot days—stable 2 pig styes. fine garden & orchard full of fruit trees Of course the rooms are not as large as ours—the house is high & dry. I am told there are not many mosquitoes—I <u>certainly</u> have seen none. I hope you may succeed in letting our house—Ham¹ is certainly the best. I am afraid there will be a difficulty, perhaps Ham might get a purchaser more readily than a tenant

I am sorry about Jos. Graham² the medicine is evidently losing its affect [part of a sentence scribbled out] but I had a letter from Miss Armstrong & she promised me to see you so like a good creature be entirely guided by her & tell me what she says—

I did not say much about your coming here because the journey is so terrific—The house is one story—no gas—no coals The picture rods ought I think to be left—I am so sorry you dont feel well but I shall be much easier if I know Miss A. has charge of you

This is a splendid winter climate—the change will I am confident do you & the darlings much good & by & bye I shall have a trap of my own—The Coach Co treat me very well I only pay 7/6 for a horse & buggy each trip—This is owing to Brooke Smith speaking to them—

I ~~had~~ never had my clothes off for two nights & I have had a 10 mile journey for the last 4 days—I have been paid over £15 & have booked over £30 since I arrived & Rohner has only been away this week—

We can enjoy ourselves very well here & you & the chicks can run to Melb. in the summer. We can ask freinds to come & stay & we will I am sure save money. Should you really come bring a box or two—I can store them at the hotel & my Thermometer & more books—

I am sure Graham will be glad to hear of my good luck—If I not popped in here quick as I did there would have been others & indeed I am not sure there may not [be] another settling—Every one is pleasant & civil & the place is no doubt healthy—Do not forget to tell Sam what Cameron³ said about Beechworth as it would be pleasant for you—Let Sam write to me about it if he cares for it & I will shew the letter to Cameron—Lots of love & kisses to my darlings—there is a nice stable for the pony & lots of pear & apple trees, plenty of fruit & splendid grapes oranges 1/6 per doz |Your loving husband

Walter

Text: ALS NLA MS133/1/190 and MS133/1/191

¹   Cornelius Job Ham (1837–1909) and his brother, Theophilus Job Ham (1828–1892), were land agents; they were born in Birmingham and came to Victoria with their parents and siblings in 1842. Cornelius worked as clerk to Henry and John Cook who owned *The Age* newspaper. Henry Cook married Amelia Ham (Cornelius's sister). CJH was a member of the Victorian Legislative Council (1882–1904) and a Minister (1890–1892).

2   Emily Josephine Graham (b. 1863), the Grahams' thirteen-year-old daughter, remained a semi-invalid all her life. She was brought down for HHR's wedding breakfast in Dublin on 30 December 1895 (*MWY*, p. 103) so she survived into her thirties.

3   The Manager of the Bank of New South Wales at Chiltern.

179 [From WLR in Chiltern to MR in Hawthorn, Melbourne]

Chiltern

Monday [3 July 1876]

My dear Mary

    I enclose open cheque for £5–0–0 which M[r] Rawle or Smith will cash for you. I hope you are better & that Miss A. has seen you. M[rs] Bresnan[1] lives next house to the Terminus Hotel.[2] at the back. I also enclose Bonwicks[3]—

    I have closed with Hancock about the house—2 years rent in advance with the option of 2 years after—wood[4] at a valuation—These were the best terms I could make & it is like paying Rohner for the practice I am going over the place tomorrow & will pay him deposit of £10. on account

    I am sure the change will do all of you good—So far I have done very well. I hope it may continue—Kind love to Sara & lots of kisses for my darlings—I will get possession of the house in about 3 weeks.

    See Ham about our house & offer it for sale £1500 would satisfy me. it cost £1800—

    I will enclose cheque for building society tomorrow I hope M. will come with you for there are none to be had here—You may begin to pack up so as to have the things ready for Waddingham[5] You had better see if Slatterie knows a decent man to pack the furniture in cases—as Effey[6] cannot be had—

    Your own Husband

        Walter

Text: ALS NLA MS133/1/181

1   Miriam Bresnan née Riddle, married in 1866 to Patrick Pembroke Bresnan. They had five children but two daughters died as infants, including Lucy who was born in Richmond in 1875 and died in 1876.

2   Terminus Hotel still stands on Victoria Street, corner of Flockhart Street, Abbotsford.

3   Walter Bonwick (1824–1883), born on 21 November 1824 at Southwark, London; son of James Bonwick, carpenter, and his second wife Mary née Preston, and younger brother of James Bonwick (see Letter 163). He was educated at the Borough Road School where he also trained as a teacher. While teaching in provincial schools he developed his talent for teaching music. He was admitted as a sizar at St John's College, Cambridge, in 1852. Two years later, before taking out his degree, he left England for Victoria, joining his elder brother, James, who had by that time opened a land agency in Melbourne. The Commissioners of National Education appointed him one of the first singing masters. He worked for the Education Department until his death in 1883. He published several collections of popular songs and *The Australian School Song Book* (*c.*1871). He married Mary Britton in 1856; they had eight children between 1857 and 1874, two of whom died as infants. They lived in Weinberg Road, Hawthorn. Sands, 1876, p. 266. See also entry on James Bonwick, *ADB*.

4   Fuel for kitchen oven and fireplaces.

5   Samuel Waddingham, a carrier, married to Phoebe née Franklin (1828–1884). They had four children born in Hawthorn.

6   Charles J. Effey, cabinet maker, 16 Little Collins Street, Melbourne.

180 [From WLR in Chiltern to MR in Hawthorn, Melbourne]

Chiltern
Tuesday eveng [4 July 1876]

My dear Marie

I paid M^r H £10. on acct of the house & went over it with him today—

1{The best room is 13 feet 3 inches by 14 feet. the fireplace comes out of the 14 feet width &
{is 57 inches long by 23 inches—

2{The next best room is 14 feet 1 or 2 inches by 11 feet 6 inches.

3{The next best a bedroom is 13 feet 3—by 12 feet 9 inches

the other three are nearly the same or a little smaller   The passage right thro is 38 feet
6 inches—long by 46 inches wide

There are outside venetians which he has consented to let stand on condition that I
took—the following at my own prices—a book case in a corner of the sitting room painted
deal glass doors £3–10–0 he declares this cost him this for labor alone—Two curtain poles
25/- fireguard 15/-   Mangle £4–0–0—clothes horse 12/6—a capital one—Hencoops 5/-:
2 pig troughs 10/- & about 40 fowls at 1/3 each amounting to some 14 pounds then there is a
quantity of wood to be taken & measured at 15/- a cord some 20 or 30 pounds worth he
says—

He was quite independent & I could not do better—He is to floor the verandah I am
afraid your wardrobe will not go into the best bedroom I think I would sell the large dining
room bookcase—I hope you will put the house for sale into Hams hands reserve £1650—as if
it remains empty it will not improve—& there is the £10–5–0 per month going on I enclose
cheque for amount which must be paid to Mr Bradley[1] at the office next door to the
Atheneum reading room Collins St—Thursday next before 3.PM.

I hope you got my cheque for £5 safely. I think I will write to those owing asking them
to settle with you—You had better write to Mr Box[2] or send Maria they live in Pakington St
Kew—It will be a pity to lose £25–0–0—You had better sell or kill off your fowls as we shall
have plenty here—I will send you the dimensions of the other bedrooms if you need them

Dont forget the garden tools, 1 spade 1 fork 1 rake—I think you had better get the front
garden done up by Ludlow[3] I enclose 3 accounts—You can send them by post—

He will give per possession in about 3 weeks but it will take you more time to arrange &
get packed—I intend to have one bedroom white washed—Give the dear chicks my love their
letters are splendid & they are improving each time| Your loving Husband

Walter

Text: ALS NLA MS133/1/189

---

[1]   Mr Bradley may have been the clerk but C. Ferdinand was the accountant and Manager,
     Australasian Building Society, 81 Collins Street East.

[2]   Henry Box junior lived at Pakington Street, Hawthorn, and was married to Rebecca née
     Armstrong. They had six children including their last child, Henry, born in 1875. His father,
     Henry Box (*c.*1800–1882), a merchant, lived in Power Street, Hawthorn. He was married to
     Ann née Strongitharm.

[3]   John Ludlow (*c.*1827–1896), Hill Street, Hawthorn, Sands, 1876, p. 466. Ludlow was married
     to Mary Ann née Underhill and they had two daughters in Hawthorn who both died as small
     infants: Maria Jane (1861–1862) and Sarah Ann (1864–1864).

181 [From WLR in Chiltern to MR in Hawthorn, Melbourne]

Chiltern
Wednesday Eveng. [5 July 1876]

My dear Mary

M[r] H has given orders to have the verandah floored & also he leaves the venetian blinds which are <u>outside</u> the principal windows which are French casements. I do not think these will require blinds, with curtains inside ~~In case howeve~~ There are no blinds up now—no rollers & as these are always a bother I think you might dispense with them <u>for the present</u> as the verandah is wide & protects the windows from all but the West or setting sun. I think there are two bedroom windows without venetians facing the South—but I will let you know this particularly tomorrow—

M[rs] Lloyd[1] & M[rs] Peel[2] the landlady strongly urge you bringing your servant if she is at all good—you cannot get supplied here ~~save~~ xcept with some slipshod dollop at 10/- a week who wont do the washing—I should recommend your bringing M. there is a nice detached kitchen ~~with~~ brick—better than ours, a washhouse with built in boiler & chimney, a splendid cellar—You will perceive that the rooms are small ~~the fireplace~~ but there are six—

I hope you will let Ham get rid of the house or try to for it will <u>take some months.</u> The furniture must all be packed in cases & ~~labelled~~ my name painted on each case or well labelled—You can fill the drawers & have them packed & sent first. also the carpets—I hope the weather will be fine or else it will be damaged—Get some one in to help you—I am glad you are better—and sorry that my darling eldest has got a sore finger. I have had a rest today & I am not sorry for it—The people are all very pleased to hear that you are coming—Archdeacon Tucker[3] of Wangaratta came today & made quite a fuss with me—I hope some more people have paid—I said the best room is 14 feet x 13. 3—& the fireplace is 23 inches out by 57 inches wide projecting out on the 14 feet side of the room—

The 2nd best is 14 feet 1 or 2 inches by 11½ feet & the fireplace is on the 14 foot side—fireplace in every room but one—the two passage doors are about same width 46 inches so you can see if the piano can get in I think so—I expect the move will cost £100—The Station master thinks Permewan & Co[4] will do it as they have Lorries & men who can go to Hawthorn & load at Spencer St.| Your loving Husband

Walter

I dont think you can get the full length of me enlarged it was done at Manchester & is not so good as Botterells or Heblings—Love to Sara, Mary & Mrs Graham—The house is on the outskirts of Chiltern about ¼ mile from the Town Hall—& my hotel—

Text: ALS NLA MS133/1/198

1   Elizabeth Lloyd née Garrett (see endnote to Letter 163).

2   Catherine Peel née Jordan, married to Henry William Peel.

3   Joseph K. Tucker, Archdeacon of Beechworth; his daughter, Matilda, married Arthur Vincent Green on 28 December 1880 at Avenel.

4   Permewan & Hunt Co. (railway and general carriers, 120 Collins Street West) was owned by John Permewan (*c.*1837–1904), based at Ballarat, and Ebenezer Hunt (*c.*1831–1911), who lived at Williams Road, Prahran. Sands, 1876, p. 420. John Permewan married Isabella Towers in 1858 and they had two children. Ebenezer Hunt married Mary McMichael in 1860 and had one son (Ebenezer Alfred) who was born in 1875 and lived for only twenty weeks.

182 [From WLR in Chiltern to MR in Hawthorn, Melbourne]

Chiltern

Thursday Evg. [6 July 1876]

My dear Marie

I am sorry to hear about dear Lilly—She must have <u>more</u> salt sprinkled over her food—Injections—greasing her at night; if these things do not do I will give her some Iron when you join me. The season is splendid I am always hungry—I have been very slack the last two days—What a sad affair about Sam. Surely there must have been something very remiss when they allowed defalcations of £6000 to exist without discovery—I should think Slyly & Millidge[1] would catch it hot—

There are two french casement windows & one door on the front of the house—Three ditto on the east side—one window & one door West & two windows & one door south—I shall go over the house more particularly by & by & tell you all details—

The inhabitants are endeavouring to reorganise a mine only partly worked but which by bad management fell thro—They are very sanguine of its paying well & it will employ some 150 men—My patients are all well—Every one says I have got the best house in the district & I shall advertise when we get into it—You had better kill off or sell your fowls as we shall have lots when you come—Surely the gas bill was not 16/. The butter here is very bad—milk good—all things I have bought are same price as Melbourne—

I dont think you will get a tenant or any one to give £1600 we shall I fear have it on our hands—I hope some more accts will come in for you—They describe the summer as something awful—

I hope you will induce Maria to come as there are no decent servants here—

I am engaged for 3 confinements.

Rohners sale takes place on the 18th I am told there will be great bargains—Can you tell me anything to buy—

They are going to bid for the house for the parson[2]—

Lovely days—I get my bath every morning—I shall be glad to have you again as my nights are very broken noises up to 12 & ½ past & servants about at ½ past 6—Love to the dears—& same to yourself| from Your fond Husband

Walter

Text: ALS NLA MS133/1/199

[1]   Frederick Millidge, accountant of the Bank of New South Wales; lived at Weinberg Road, Hawthorn, and was married to Jane Powell. They had four children in Victoria but only Catherine Elizabeth, born 1868, survived childhood.
[2]   Reverend Samuel Dutton Green.

183 [From WLR in Chiltern to MR in Hawthorn, Melbourne]

Chiltern

Friday Evening [7 July 1876]

My darling Marie

I am so sorry to find by your Wednesday's letter that you are were in very low spirits. The rooms are certainly smaller than ours but they are better than any ones in this place, parsons or doctors. If you only knew the choice I had or the holes I had offered to me at first you would not wonder at <u>my</u> being in bad spirits or at my wanting to try elsewhere & writing about Carngham[1] All the windows have venetian blinds some outside some in—no rollers to any—I do not think you need blinds with venetians—the verandah is 6½ feet wide—<u>The best</u> sitting room has 2 windows with good curtain poles up—& fireplace <u>&</u> venetians.

The 2nd best sitting room has one window & venetians & one glass door ½ window leading out to the yard—

Bedroom No 1 has one window ~~window~~ is 13 feet 3, by 10 ft. 9. Fireplace & venetians—

Bedroom No 2 has window with venetians fireplace & is 12 ft by 13 feet—

Bedroom No 3 has inside venets. is 10ft 8 by 10.9.

Bedroom No 4 has no fireplace window with inside venetians & is 10 ft. 8 by 11.3. I am sure I hardly know what to advise about the furniture we can get most of the things in—You must dispose of the large bookcase & drawing room glass <u>certainly</u> the wardrobe might stand in one of the bedrooms perhaps in the nursery. or spare bedroom—for No 1. would do for us No 2. for the children No 4. for servants & No 3. for the wardrobe—I should have to see my patients either in the drawing or dining room whichever was disengaged Many would go to Lloyds[2] & send for me there—

It is no use fretting over sacrificing the things—they are not worth more than they will bring & Steinfield[3] will do the fairest—

~~You~~ There are no furniture shops here—the cornices would be out of place in a cottage or if they come the poles will do for some other rooms—It was a choice with me to take the few things or have the Venetian blinds taken down—

I am afraid you wont get the house off—Times are so bad in Melbourne. It is very unfortunate that we had to break up our home but it was folly to build the house & now I am punished for it—

I am certain there is a practice here that will keep us from want & our wants are not walls. I hope Sara will have a pleasant voyage. The ship[4] she is going in is a very fine one altho very old—am sorry I did not get yours soon enough to send prescription for podop. pills[5]—

I fear if your coming depends on your <u>letting</u> the house that I will have to live alone a long time—However I dont grumble I am earning money ~~&~~ & keep well—

Kiss the darlings for Papa & accept love from| Your loving husband

Walter

Text: ALS NLA MS133/1/193 and MS133/1/222

[1] See Letter 168.
[2] The chemist's shop.
[3] Emanuel Steinfield owned a furniture warehouse at Ballarat East; Mayor of Ballarat East township from 1866 to 1869; first President of the Ballarat Public Library (established 1862); Vice-President of the first committee of the District Orphan Asylum (established in 1865). Withers, pp. 183, 248, 261, 286, 333.
[4] *Agamemnon* on which Sarah was about to depart for England. She returned to Australia aboard the *Ellora* in 1881. It may be that in *FRM III*, pp. 320–321, HHR was recollecting her mother's request to Sarah to return to assist her in Koroit in the last months of WLR's life.
[5] Podophylline was a resin obtained from the dried rhizome of the May apple (*Podophyllum peltatum*), used as a purgative and in the treatment of some skin diseases. WLR wrote, 'Podophylline is not quite so much a favorite as it is with you in Victoria, owing, I believe, to fewer cases of functional liver disorder occurring here [in England], the general complaint against it being its uncertainty.' 'Another Letter from Home', *AMJ*, vol. XXII, September 1867, p. 277.

184 [From WLR in Chiltern to HHR and ALR in Hawthorn, Melbourne]

[Star Hotel, Chiltern]

[Friday, 7 July 1876]

My darling Pets

Bring Maria[1] with you—I am glad you like her and that she is good to you—The railway[2] is near our new house and the summer house is splendid—

Have you written to Annie Cuthbert[3] you did not say what old Nurse[4] said in her letter|
Your affect

        Papa

Text: ALS NLA 133/1/222 [On reverse of Letter 183]

[1]   Maria, their servant at Hawthorn, travelled to Chiltern and remained with them until the family moved to Queenscliff in September 1877.

[2]   The opening of the North-Eastern Railway was on Wednesday, 19 November 1873. The line was constructed in three sections, the first from Melbourne to Seymour, the second from Seymour to Benalla and the third from Benalla to Wodonga. W.C. Busse, *The History of Chiltern*, Chapter XIV, published in the Chiltern *Federal Standard* in 1922. The Goods Shed was built in 1874 and the Railway Passenger Station was completed in 1876. It is recorded by the National Trust for the ornate brick work and the cast iron work.

[3]   Annie Wilmer Cuthbert (1868–1901), daughter of Sir Henry Cuthbert and Emma Wilmer née Kirby. She was born on 18 May 1868 and became a childhood playmate of HHR when they met for holidays in the Cuthbert's holiday home in Queenscliff. On 1 October 1890, Annie married Captain (later Major) John Wilberforce Stanley-Low (1865–1902), member of the Australian Club, and they had a son, Cuthbert John Stanley-Low, in 1891. She died on 22 February 1901, aged thirty-two.

[4]   Not identified.

185 [From WLR in Chiltern to MR in Hawthorn, Melbourne]

Chiltern

Saturday Evening [8 July 1876]

My dearest Marie—

I have been rather busy again today & had not time to go up to the house to see if the ~~book~~ large bookcase would fit into the parlor. The wardrobe as I said can stand in the spare bedroom & I should think it would take to pieces I sent you particulars of windows in my last—There is plenty of room in the garden & a summer house—fine large yard behind. I should think there is about twice as much land as we have at Hawthorn—The verandah will be a splendid place for them as it extends around the front & one side of the house—The station master[1] now advises to pack all the furniture possible without cases. 98/6 a ton—Tables & chairs packed with Straw he says will come very well We cannot engage trucks but the department will fill as many trucks as our furniture will require for Chiltern & it will never be disturbed—piano will require case—

Dear Mrs Cuthbert perhaps she will ask you some other time! Give my last love to Sara—You will be lonely indeed—

I hope you are better I am very hearty & feel the benefit of this splendid winter climate I like your photo tho not as well as Botterells—

The station master is leaving & a married man[2] with family coming—I have not heard of Brooke—

Give lots of love & kisses to papa's darlings

The summer house is large enough for tea parties & we will have birthday parties there with a table—I have got my eye on a swing that I think will be for sale—They can have their own gardens—

I have nothing more to say—Good bye|God bless you says|Your affect Husband

Walter

Sunday Eveng [9 July 1876]

I am afraid Russell & Ham will run up long bills for advertising I dont think anything would do so well as a notice board—"To let" Dont let the chicks eat any colored lollies I see by todays Argus that an analysis gives lead & other poisons in them[3]—

Text: ALS NLA MS133/1/203

[1]   Not identified.
[2]   Arthur William Maude (b. 1849), born in Watton, Suffolk. On 2 July 1873 at Elsternwick, Victoria, he married Annie Richards (1854–1944), the daughter of James Richards and his wife, Elizabeth née Pack.
[3]   A long report (almost two columns) under the title, 'Confectionery Analysis', explained that Mr Frederick Dunn of the Technological Laboratory had been engaged for some time in analysing samples of sugar confectionery. 'Of 69 samples coloured yellow, and orange red, 64 were found to contain considerable quantities of chromate of lead, and 10 blue samples were found to contain ultramarine, which is a double silicate of alumina and soda, with sulphate of sodium. The green specimens also contained lead.' *The Argus*, 8 July 1876, p. 9.

186 [From WLR in Chiltern to MR in Hawthorn, Melbourne]

Chiltern

Tuesday Eveng [11 July 1876]

My dear Marie

This is a sketch of the 2nd best sitting room [Sketch of room]

Mr Hancock says he will be out about this day fortnight. I should take the house out of Hams hands if he does not find a purchaser in 10 days—There are no buyers for things here—I am sorry to say many people are leaving—as they have failed to reorganize a great mine[1] that they were sanguine of doing when I came here—I still think it would be wise to sell the pier glass[2] & the sideboard & the drawing room Cheffonier & the large bookcase—There is an old dresser in the kitchen that I dont suppose he will take but it is not so good as ours & you had better leave yours if the people take the house & we can get an additional one put up there are tables but of course he will take them—There is no room to store furniture in the cellar—I hope you will not think of storing things in Melbourne—The repairs to the house will be a constant worry & any agent will expend what he likes without our control being absent

Best to get rid of things It is unfortunate that times are so dull in Melbourne but it cannot be helped—

I hope you had a pleasant day to see Sara off—Magnificent weather here Strange about poor Mrs Bright[3]—she has her troubles We are not the only ones—

It is very annoying the people do not pay you—It is very rude of the Boxes after my sending in my acct twice—Mr Utber[4]

Mrs Shaw[5]

Mr Jordan[6]

Mr Box[7]—
W. Bonwick[8]
Mrs Rutherford [9]
Mrs Bresnan[10]—.

If you do not write you will have to leave them—I hope you are better I conclude you are as you say nothing of yourself—With much love |Your loving husband
    Walter
Text: ALS NLA MS133/1/194

[1] From April 1876 there had been reports in Chiltern that a new company would be formed to work the ground held by the Doma Mungi and Chiltern Sons of Freedom Mining Company. See *FS*, Wednesday, 12 April 1876, p. 2. In June, the editor was critical of the 'supineness and want of energy on the part of the inhabitants'. *FS*, Saturday, 3 June 1876, p. 2. In July, the editor was full of praise for the Bendigo miners and the support of their community. 'There were also public prospecting associations to which the community subscribed for a similar purpose, that of prospecting and opening up ground upon which the miner could afterwards work. The work done at Bendigo was enormous. Compared with it the feeble attempts that have been made in the same direction in the North Eastern districts are like a drop in an ocean of water.' *FS*, Saturday, 8 July 1876, p. 2.
[2] A tall mirror; a mirror hung between windows.
[3] Josephine Bright née Bertrand, first wife of Charles Bright (1832–1903), journalist, lecturer and insurance secretary. He was an editor (*My Note Book*, the *Examiner*, *Melbourne Punch*) and a lecturer on spiritualism and free thought. Member of the Yorick Club. One of Melbourne's chief cultural critics. de Serville, pp. 358, 376–377, 519.
[4] Arthur Goddard Utber (*c.*1828–1894), married Betsy Bird in 1859. Between 1860 and 1884 they had twelve children, four of whom died in infancy.
[5] Sarah Shaw née Thatcher who was married to Thomas Shaw (*c.*1828–1907). They had nine children between 1855 and 1870, two of whom died in infancy.
[6] William Norris Jordan (*c.*1833–1877), born in Cambridge; married to Harriet Reeves; they had three children born in Victoria between 1866 and 1878. They lived in Liddiard Street, Hawthorn. Sands, 1876, p. 435.
[7] See Letter 180.
[8] See Letter 179.
[9] Elizabeth Rutherford née Register, married to Thomas Rutherford (*c.*1832–1912). They had twelve children between 1855 and 1878. Their eleventh child, George Henry, was born in Richmond in 1875 and their second child, Edward, died in 1875 aged sixteen.
[10] See Letter 179.

187 [From the Reverend Samuel Dutton Green in
Chiltern to WLR in Chiltern]

Chiltern, 13 July 1876:
Dear Dr Richardson,

Now that I am able to get about again, I cannot but thank you most cordially for the great kindness & attention which you shewed me during my recent illness: I shall always remember with gratitude your treatment of me, and I trust you will accept of my sincere good wishes for your happiness & prosperity in this your new sphere of professional labours.

With kind regards| Believe me to be| Very sincerely yours
    S. D. Green
Text: ALS NLA MS133/1/174

188 [From WLR in Chiltern to MR in Hawthorn, Melbourne]

Star Hotel Chiltern
July 14 187[6, Friday]

My dear Marie

I fear I did make the powders rather strong but I hope they brought away the worms, you did not say—They ought to have been given before breakfast <u>not</u> over night—You did not say how you were yourself—Agnes[1] wrote a kind sensible letter she has had experience about moving—our house is not 200 yards from the railway station & I can get a man & a dray to load, & get them over—The drawing room is 13 feet 4—by 14 feet 1. with the fireplace————₄₄————|[23] in the ~~longest~~ 13 feet length two french casement doors or windows & one entrance door-

~~I am not sure~~ I find I can get a man to whitewash & make the carpets he is a mattress maker—& very handy he will hang the glasses & pictures—I suppose they will leave the dirty little dresser in the kitchen but the tables are good & will be taken away as I declined them at 30/.-

If Miss A[2] did not go into house I would not give much for her medicine—however you may try she only uses simples[3]—

I will look after the lamps at Rohners sale 18th of this month, & any cheap things I will pick up—

I have not been so busy this week—It comes in rushes—I received the enclosed from the parson[4]—The new Station Master is married man one little boy[5] nice play fellow for our—about 2 years old & she is a very nice ladylike little woman has engaged me to attend her—

The bank manager's wife[6] is pretty & stylish & her sister also I am rather uneasy about the house not letting—It will have to be shut up & the keys left with Russell—I hope the windows wont be broken—the gates must be fastened securely the front one with a chain—I hope Davidson has been if not let me know & I will write him letter

I am writing to Ellis[7] about the scandalous work—our Ballt house never came down about our ears altho we lived in it for 4 years after being built.

Much love to the chicks & yourself & the Grahams| from your affect| husband
       Walter
Will write again Sunday night—

   Text: ALS NLA MS133/1/196

[1]   Agnes Bailey née Hablethwaite (b. *c.*1840) married to Edward Harold Bailey; they had moved from Carlton to Emerald Hill in 1872 and then to Wodonga in 1876.
[2]   Elizabeth Armstrong.
[3]   A medicinal herb.
[4]   See Letter 187.
[5]   Arthur William Maude, aged two, was born at The Loddon in 1874, son of Annie and Arthur William Maude.
[6]   Elizabeth Cameron formerly Flockhart née Easdown (b. *c.*1842), daughter of William Easdown, a farmer, and Ann née Barnes. She was a widow with one child when she married Archibald Cameron on 19 May 1875.
[7]   Possibly William Ellis, brickmaker, Riversdale Road, Hawthorn.

189 [From WLR in Chiltern to MR in Hawthorn, Melbourne]

Star Hotel Chiltern
Sunday 1876 [16 July]

My dear Marie

I write according to promise altho' I have nothing to say—Have been rather idle the last few days—Have mislaid your last letter & so forget what you said—shall postpone writing this until I get yours tomorrow morning—

I want you to call at the tobacconist[1] corner of Collins & Swanston St, by the pillar box & ask for a meershaum pipe[2] I left there to be mended before I came away—It will be a shilling or two

Monday morning [17 June]

Just received yours of Friday night—So glad the dear ones are well you say nothing of yourself—I have been better ever since—You must not forget the filters. I do not know what to do about Box—They have behaved scandalously & I have no redress but summoning them which I cannot do as I am away—Could you not give Russell the accounts to collect—he would send his boy—I write to Davidson by this post—

There will be no packing at the station if we have enough—the things will be put into one or two waggons for Chiltern by themselves—

I am afraid the house will not be let—Take it out of Hams hands—put up a board & leave it entirely with Russell—ask him his terms for the agency—You will have to take £120—& the tenant pay the rates—There will be three or four nice families for you Cameron the Bank—Martins[3] Clerk of the Court—the parsons, the station masters—

I went to the Scots Church yesterday morning—good attendance of well dressed people—

With much love| Your affect Husband
Walter

Take the pass book to the Savings Bank & get it made up—& let me know amount

Text: ALS NLA MS133/1/179

1 Gustave, Damman & Co. Sands, 1876, p. 780.
2 Ornamentally carved pipe with a bowl made of a fine light whitish clay mineral, hydrous magnesium silicate; originated from Vienna and very popular in the nineteenth century.
3 A. L'Espinasse Martin, previously Clerk of the Court at Bright. He remained in Chiltern until 1889 and was President of the Athenaeum from 1886 to 1889.

190 [From WLR in Chiltern to HHR and ALR in Hawthorn, Melbourne]

[Star Hotel Chiltern]
[Monday, 17 July 1876]

My dear Ettie and Lilly

Your letters are better each time—I know one little girl[1] and one little boy[2] to come to a party in the summer house We will not wait for the birthday but will have it as soon as we get settled—& we will have plenty of fowls & eggs here—and I think you will be happier| Your affect

papa

Text: ALS NLA MS133/1/179 [Reverse of Letter 188]

1   Probably Florence Cordelia Portch (1873–1949), daughter of George Portch and his wife, Marianne née Rowe. Her father, a well-to-do miner, bought the Flour Mill next to 'Lake View' in November 1876.
2   Arthur William Maude, son of the stationmaster.

191 [From WLR in Chiltern to MR in Hawthorn, Melbourne]

Chiltern
Tuesday Eveng [18 July 1876]

My dear Marie

I was so glad to get your telegram that the H[ouse] was let.[1] Hancock has promised to turn out early next week so as to let the whitewashing be done on Monday. I have told him I will not want the curtain poles the cases can lie in the goods sheds if we are not ready for them by Wednesday or if they come earlier—

Wednesday morng. [19 July 1876]

Just got yours—you have done well. You may send the things up as early as you like the station master says they may come on the day after, or they may be a week. So send them off as soon as you can get a load on Saturday if possible carpets & some beds—

The drayman who is constantly receiving & carting all sorts of things says they come much better loose & unpacked & if he was sending a piano he says he would send it unpacked—I enclose cheque for £5-0-0—

Rohners sale came off & the things realised well a good crowd of farmers in from the country the worst things sold best

I only bought one lamp. I have written to M. Bayles her father[2] has a book of mine—You had better accept M[rs] Grahams invitation & stay there until Saturday or till I telegraph you things are a bit in If you can forward some things on Saturday I will most likely get them Wednesday & can begin—If you put them off till Tuesday or Wednesday we should have them that week—You can stay at the Hotel with the chicks—but if I could put up the servant a bed she[3] could come up first & help me

You may bring all you can for I see things sell well here. Love to the dear ones we shall soon meet now—I count the days| Your loving Husband

Walter

Text: ALS NLA MS133/1/197

1   The house was rented by Walter Tully (1829–1912) and his wife Elizabeth née Sutherland. See Letter 197.
2   John Roberts Atkins.
3   Maria, the Richardsons' servant.

192 [From WLR in Chiltern to MR in Hawthorn, Melbourne]

Chiltern
Wednesday [19 July 1876]

My dear Mary

You have done splendidly to let the house & to dispose of the furniture so well—all I say
is send up some as fast as you can without waiting for the whole—If I could have 2 or 3 beds
& some carpeting early in the week—as the delay on the road may be great—I will have all the
chimneys swept & the place ready by Wednesday or Thursday I hope but you had better stay
at the Grahams & send M. on 2nd class—to help me—as soon as you leave the house.—You
must indeed be tired with no one to help you amid all your excitement—I told you that the
goods would be safe & could stand for 2 or 3 days in the goods shed if we had not the rooms
ready—I do not know what to do about Box Can you not get Russell to try—all have paid
except Box—Jordan—Utber—Mrs Shaw—Mrs Bresnan

I shall be so glad to have you for my rest is sadly broken here—noises to ½ past 12—&
begin again. 6.30 or at daylight, small damp bedroom—

I have not been quite so busy since—There appears to have been an unusual rush of
sickness at first—

What shall we do about the ~~pa~~ oil cloth for the passage? I will price it tomorrow there are
two large drapers & 2 small—Rohners cottage—with 2 acres of land sold for £195—

We have never lived in such a hovel. Dont trouble about writing again until you send off
something I will send another cheq[u]e Saturday.

I suppose Hams terms are 5 per cent—He had better receive rent & pay same into my
credit at City Bank quarterly—forwarding me bank slip deposit receipt

I hope there are no children & that they will take care of the house—explain the
venetian blinds—of course I would ~~either pay~~ take the additions at end of lease ~~subject to~~ &
allow for them if done by Davidson| Your affect Husband

Walter

Text: ALS NLA MS133/1/201

193 [From WLR in Chiltern to MR in Hawthorn, Melbourne]

Star Hotel, Chiltern
Sunday 187[6, 23 July][1]

Dear Marie

I am sorry you sold your wardrobe for I am sure you will miss it—There is no oil cloth
to be had here suitable therefore order piece 38 feet long by 45 inches wide—Could it be sent
to Permewans & Hunt to be forwarded with the rest addressed to me—I send blank cheque
for it & another ~~blank~~ £10. for you ~~for £5-0-0~~—Hancock gives me possession on Monday &
I have got man to whitewash & sweep all the chimneys—You must tell me dear positively the
day you mean to arrive. There is only one room in the hotel that you & the chicks can occupy
only one double bed—Dont you think it would be better to stay at Grahams until Friday
afternoon. You will find the Saloon carriage most comfortable—there is a good hotel at
Seymour "Gills Hotel" if you like to break the journey & come on on Saturday morning you
will do it more comfortably 8 hours is long & you do not get in here until 10.15.

Telegraph to me when you start—If you write Tuesday night I will get it Thursday morning—Mrs Cuthbert's[2] visit must have tried you sadly amid all your packing still she is a good freind & we will have a room for her here—

How I long to see you all once more—

I shall have 3 men to unpack the things as soon as ever they arrive—I hope the weather will keep fine | Love to the darlings & yourself from |Your loving husband

       [No signature]

Text: AL NLA MS133/1/195

[1]   Later that day (23 July 1876), WLR delivered Florence Evelyn Maude, the second child of Annie and Arthur Maude. The nurse who assisted at the birth was Margaret Slocum née O'Leary, who was married to John Slocum (1823–1884), a miner. The Slocums had one daughter, Agnes Ellen, born in Chiltern in 1869.

[2]   It is possible that Emma Cuthbert had a drinking problem as did her fictional counterpart 'Agnes Ocock'. See *FRM III*, pp. 30–36. Emma Cuthbert died on 1 August 1877, the following year, and on her death certificate, the cause and duration of illness are stated as 'Hepatitis—some months; Pulmonary congestion—a fortnight'. See Chapter 4.

194 [From WLR in Chiltern to MR in Hawthorn, Melbourne]

Chiltern
Tuesday Eveng [25 July 1876]

My dear Marie

I expect another letter but not getting it I will have the room ready Thursday night & will meet you—with a man to take your packages into the house which is close by & what you need for the night to the hotel—There will be a comfortable bed & parlour for you & the chicks & I will have tea ready at ½ past 10—

Do I hope you thought of the wine & the thermometer outside my window—

You will not forget to get a 1^d time table at the station Spencer St as it will show you all the stations along the line—Tea & coffee at Seymour & Benalla Ladies rooms at both places stopping 15 minutes at each.

You must indeed have had a trying time surely you got a man to pack—Telegraph to me about the luggage & yourse[l]f Thursday morning from Spencer St before you start—

Give my kindest regards to D^r & M^rs G: & thanks for all their kindnesses—You will want wraps & possum rug for the nights here are bitterly & intensely cold—Wrap the chicks up well—They can sleep in the saloon carriage "The Springs" is the station before Chiltern—about ½ one hour—I have got a man in today sweeping chimneys & whitewashing 3 rooms—another one cleaning out the outhouse & tomorrow to scrub out the house—I will keep the luggage untouched until you arrive. I will get them into the yard

Good bye| & God bless you|Your affect husband

    Walter

Text: ALS NLA MS133/1/206

1877

A Chiltern Summer and a Queenscliff Winter

1877

195 [From WLR in Chiltern to MR in Richmond, Melbourne][1]

Chiltern
Sunday [28 January 1877]

Dear Marie

As I expect a letter from you by tomorrows midday post I begin this today so as to be able to post it tomorrow Monday afternoon. Friday & Saturday were delightfully <u>cool</u> with South wind—Ida[2] stayed ~~me~~ with me till Saturday & went home by afternoon train—She is a dear good girl—I saw that she was so lonely sitting reading by herself when I was out that I thought she would be better among her sisters. She took the chickens, plums, honey, & three books I gave her for herself Gertrude[3] & ~~Ida~~ Jeannie[4]—I had a telegram from Sam[5] asking for the prescription I gave Leila[6] last xmas at Hawthorn so I suppose she is worse & dangerously ill:

M[rs] Porch was taken ill early this morning & I went 10. am. baby[7] born about 3, nice easy time all well, & <u>all</u> much pleased. They are really nice people what a fool Rohner must have been to have alienated them. They said if I had not been here they would have sent to Wangaratta—I wish to God there were more people like them—Mary[8] has done very well so far. ~~She~~

Monday morning. Just got yours. Am so glad you got there safely & well. We have had no change here yet. There is a strong North wind today with clouds but it will all blow away—I got the papers does D[r] G. want them back? Am sorry about poor Mary.[9] Do not feel very well myself today—not a soul coming near the house—Give my kind love to M[rs] Graham & thank her for being so thoughtful as to write me the letter which I got Saturday morning also thank D[r] G for the papers

Give Papas fond love to Ada & Florence & I hope they are good & obedient—I hope to have another letter before you leave for Sorrento.

3 PM We have had a tremendous Storm of wind from all quarters with great heat but no rain| Your affect Husband

    W.L.R.

Text: ALS NLA MS133/1/205

1.   Mary Richardson, Ettie and Lil left Chiltern on 26 January 1877 to spend two months with friends. They stayed first at the Grahams' house in Richmond and then travelled with Mrs Graham to their seaside home at Blairgowrie, Sorrento. Then they sailed to Queenscliff to stay with Mrs Cuthbert at the Cuthberts' seaside home.

2.   Ida Beatrice Bailey (1863–1940), daughter of John Robinson Bailey (1826–1871) and his second wife, Jane Rainsford (1831–1866). She married and lived in Victoria, Canada.

3.   Gertrude Elizabeth Bailey (1862–1939), daughter of John Robinson Bailey and his second wife, Jane Rainsford. She never married and worked as a postmistress at Romsey (1883–1886), Wedderburn (1886–1888), Abbotsford (1888–1900+). She died at Sandringham on 20 May 1939, aged seventy-seven. HHR wrote about her as the seventeen-year-old cousin who accompanied MR and the children to Koroit. *MWY*, p. 22.

4.   Mary Jane Bailey (1866–1909), daughter of John Robinson Bailey and his second wife, Jane Rainsford.

5.   Samuel Bailey, MR's brother.

6.   Leila Maud Bailey (1874–1936), born on 1 June 1874, the first child of Samuel Bailey and Polly (Frances Mary Louise) née Lascelles. At the age of twenty-three, on 5 October 1897, she married Tom Henry Southam Hawkes (1867–1923), a merchant, who died in a major earthquake on 1 September 1923 in Yokohama, Japan. They had two sons born in Geelong: Tom Bailey (b. 1898) and John Bailey (b. 1899). John Bailey Hawkes was an exceptional tennis player and a member of the Davis Cup team representing Australia in 1921, 1923 and 1925. He won the Australian Singles Championship of 1926; the Men's Doubles (with G. L. Patterson) in 1922; Mixed Doubles (with Miss E. Boyd) in 1922, 1926 and 1927; American Mixed Doubles (with Miss K. McKane of England) in 1925; and American Mixed Doubles (with Miss Helen Wills of America) in 1928. HHR was a keen tennis player and spectator. She was unfortunately prevented by rain from seeing Helen Wills play at Wimbledon in July 1929, but watched the Australian team win the Davis Cup on 27 July 1936. Letters to Mary Kernot, 4 July 1929 and 28 July 1936, ALS ML MSS 45. Leila remained in touch with her cousin HHR all her life and her address ('Llanberis', Western Beach, Geelong) is in HHR's address book (NLA MS133/8/9) crossed out with the word 'Dead' written in HHR's handwriting.

7.   Charles William Portch (1877–1902), son of Marianne (née Rowe) and George Portch (c.1830–1902), who married on 13 December 1867. He was delivered by WLR on 28 January 1877. His birth certificate reveals that Charles was their seventh child but that only Florence Cordelia (four years) and George Richard (twenty-one months) were alive at his birth, as the Portchs had lost four children at very young ages from the various epidemics which swept through the Chiltern area. Marianne bore George a further five children up to 1886, three of whom survived their infancy. George bought the flour mill next to 'Lake View' at Chiltern after the insolvency of the first owner, William Tucker Pyke. At the time of the purchase of the mill, for which he paid £1550, George was working as a miner and was described as 'of the Magenta Reef'. (*FS*, 18 November 1876, p. 1.) The mill recommenced operation in January 1877. George Portch bought the lease of 'Lake View' from the Richardsons when they vacated the house in September 1877.

8.   Mary or Maria, the Richardsons' servant.

9.   Mary Bayles was probably not well after the birth of a daughter, Josephine Agnes Cassie Bayles on 29 December 1876 at Toorak. This baby survived and HHR taught her piano before she left for Leipzig in 1887 (HHR's Diary Ms133/8/7). Mary and William Bayles subsequently had two sons, both of whom died as infants: Hadzley Caldicot Bayles (b. 1880) and William John Cam Bayles (b. 1882).

196 [From WLR in Chiltern to MR in Richmond, Melbourne]

Chiltern

Wednesday [31 January 1877][1]

Dear Marie

I got your two letters and am glad you are all enjoying yourselves & that the weather is cool & pleasant. Of course I have nothing to write about so you must not expect many letters—There are no patients & I am doing nothing & the practice has gone—It will be

It is not a very pleasant look out for the future, so I advise you to value your money as it is likely to be scarce—Sam wrote asking me to telegraph again about the baby—I wrote Hancocks[2] eldest son died of Diptheria at Brighton a few days since & I hear that he has brought all the children back to Chiltern. Mary is doing very well indeed. She does every thing as I like it—She had a freind in on Monday all day, helping her with the wash—it was a very heavy one for she was at it again on Tuesday. The weather this week has been trying Ther[mometer] 90 to 100 I am glad you are out of it—

Kind love to the Grahams & 100 kisses to the little ones—I hope they are good

They are going to alter the trains next month. They are to start an hour earlier from each end & to do the journey in one hour less—

one patient in yesterday and two today—

3 PM. Just got yours of Tuesday with dear Etties so good—We have had a terrific dust storm this afternoon—The town could not be seen from our house but only a drop or two of rain

I think you will enjoy Queenscliffe better than Ballt & it will save the fares—

Glad you are getting bargains—I am better today but very little sleep—I hope you sleep well| Your attached husband

      W.L.R.

I will return the papers

    Text: ALS NLA MS133/1/209

[1]   Upside-down on the back page WLR had written in 'Chiltern Jan.ʸ 19 1877'. He had crossed out 'Dear Graham'. Careful not to waste paper, he recycled an unfinished letter for MR's.

[2]   John Hancock (born in 1869 in South Yarra) died of diphtheria aged seven on 29 January 1877 at New Street, Brighton, after an illness of five days. He was buried the same day at the Brighton Cemetery, the service being conducted by the Presbyterian Minister, the Reverend T. H. Ballantyne. He had three older sisters and was the fourth of eight children of John Hancock and Mary Ann Kinear (deceased). They had moved to Chiltern after John's birth in South Yarra. Two of their infants had died in Chiltern: Henry Noble in 1873, aged one, and Emma Georgina in 1875, also aged one.

197 [From WLR in Chiltern to MR in Richmond, Melbourne]

Chiltern

Friday Evening [2 February 1877]

My dear Marie

I am so glad you are all enjoying yourselves how fortunate to have a wealthy freind in M.ʳˢ Graham—

I hope none of the rest of you have been attacked I have been so myself but I put it down to a plum pie as they were not ripe but acid. Sam has not written again about Leila so I fear she is worse. You are quite right to pick up bargains as you cannot get any here. I got a letter from Arthur Green today A married man named Rhodda[1] is appointed as clergyman. The new parsonage is nearly finished & the fencing of the church is really begun—

Mary is still doing excellently she has cleaned out every room since you left, & my dinners are excellent—

No news of any kind at all. The Revd Ewing[2] lectures here on this day week & I have offered him a bed again—No rain & all are now getting anxious as the Barrambogie[3] supply is to be turned off except at certain times. Thank dear Lilly for her pretty letter I hope she is better & that dear Ettie will come back with a rosy cheek. The weather is bearable & still no sickness & no patients. Are you going to have a look at the house if you do & see M[r] Tully[4] you might ask him if he is willing in the event of a purchaser coming forward to give up his tenancy before the full term or not—

Of course I have no idea that Russel[5] would find one, but he might—I told him to offer the house at £1700. Kind regards to all & love to the darlings with same from your attached

     W.

Wain[6] has sent in milk bill 8/3 I suppose it is correct.

    Text: ALS NLA MS133/1/214

[1]   It had been reported in December in *The Federal Standard* that the Reverend Green would be leaving St Paul's Church, Chiltern due to ill health. At first it was suggested that he would be going to New Zealand and would be replaced by the Reverend Pickering, from Eltham (*FS*, 30 December 1876); and then it was revealed that Green was to go to Colac. 'It is hoped he will regain his good health in his new field of usefulness, and that he will be as thoroughly appreciated there as at Chiltern and neighbourhood.' *FS*, 10 January 1877, p. 2. It was announced that the Reverend Rhodda would be the new incumbent. *FS*, 3 February 1877, p. 2. On 6 February 1877, the Reverend Samuel Dutton Green married his second wife, Harriet Amy Sheppard, in East Melbourne, and then they moved to Colac where their son, Stanley Dutton, was born in July 1878.

[2]   The Reverend Robert Kirkwood Ewing (1823–1899), the Presbyterian Minister at Beechworth. WLR, who had been elected as Vice-President of the Athenaeum in July 1876 shortly after his arrival in Chiltern, chaired the lecture in aid of the Athenaeum on the poets Thomas Moore (1779–1852) and Thomas Campbell (1777–1844). The lecture was held at the Star Hotel, Chiltern. Ewing was born in Glasgow, the son of John and Elizabeth Ewing née Young. A Presbyterian, he had been the subject of much publicity in *The Argus* and Chiltern's newspaper, *The Federal Standard*, during 1875 and 1876. The dispute with the Presbyterian General Assembly of Victoria, which dragged on for months, was initially concerned with the illegal induction of Ewing to the pastorate of the Presbyterian congregation at Beechworth. His story began in Tasmania where he was an influential minister in St Andrew's Church, Launceston from 1848 to 1867. Having discovered by chance that his wife's first husband might not be dead, he separated from her and left the ministry to become headmaster of South Yarra College in Melbourne in 1868. In South Yarra he lived with a young woman and her widowed sister. He married the young woman, Frances Sanden, on 13 January 1873, thirteen days after he heard of the death of his first wife. He was forty-nine and she twenty-eight. In 1873, Ewing had been recovering from an illness in Bright when he accepted a call from the Presbyterian churches in Beechworth and Stanley to become their Minister. After being called to the Bar of the General Assembly in November 1875, however, his application to be placed on the roll of Ministers of the Victorian Presbyterian Church was refused. In May 1876, the whole story was revealed to the community through its publication by Ewing and the subsequent final appeal to the Presbyterian Assembly. The story included an assault on a professor of music at the Launceston Mechanics Institute over a dispute concerning a room (which resulted in a court appearance and a fine of 40 shillings), and his acceptance of the office of Provincial Grand Master of the Tasmanian Masonic Lodge, when the Presbyterian Church was opposed to Freemasonry. As the Chiltern editor wrote: 'On the one hand we have presented to us sacerdotal charity with its envy, vanity and malice, while on the other there is the spectacle of an unruly servant of the church objecting to submit to its laws and regulations and in a somewhat

unhandsome manner taking the public into his confidence in order that the church's interest shall participate in his fall. An independent and self-reliant man would have shaken the dust from his shoes, and walked out proudly from the presbyterian portico.' *FS*, 6 May 1876, p. 2. The Beechworth congregation staunchly stood by Ewing, who remained there until 1878 when he left to become an Anglican minister at Inverell, NSW. He and his wife, Frances, stayed with WLR at 'Lake View', the Richardson's home in Chiltern, on 9 February 1876, when he gave a lecture on the poets Moore and Campbell at the Star Hotel in aid of the Athenaeum, with WLR in the chair. His second wife, Frances (1843–1910), was the daughter of Edward Sanden and Lavinia née Pennel. She was born in Goulburn, NSW, and christened in the Goulburn Church of England. R. K. Ewing died in Lismore, NSW, in 1899. His widow, Frances, died in 1910 in Woollahra, NSW. As a further link between the Reverend Ewing and WLR, when Ewing was in Tasmania, Captain Alexander Cheyne knew him well. The Scotch Church in Hobart opened on Thursday, 11 May 1848 and Alexander Cheyne wrote in his diary on Sunday, 21 May 1848: 'Mr Ewing, who has left the Independents and joined the Scotch Church, preached today. I was very much pleased with him. He is evidently a man of considerable talent, eloquent, and a fine imagination.'

3   Constructed by the Railways Department in 1873, the Barambogie Reservoir supplied water to Chiltern and its environs. Note: Barambogie is the fictional name given to Chiltern in *FRM III*.

4   Walter Tully (1829–1912) and his wife, Elizabeth née Sutherland, rented the Richardsons' house at Burwood Road, Hawthorn. Walter Tully was the second son of David Tully (1798–1855), a shepherd to the Duke of Sutherland on the Borrobool Estate in Northumberland, and his wife, Beatrice Pringle née Robson (d. 1894 at Woodend, Victoria). Walter Tully first came to Australia on the *Star of the East*, arriving on 24 September 1853. Returning home to marry Elizabeth Sutherland, they sailed back to Australia aboard the *Mermaid* (arriving on 20 October 1856). He managed various stations in NSW and Victoria and then bought an interest in stations, including Mountside at Winchelsea. Walter and Elizabeth had six children: David (m. Ada Constance Armstrong), Jane, Walter, William (m. Ada, daughter of a Melbourne solicitor, William Riggall), Annie, and Beatrice (m. Archibald Craig). Two sisters, Margaret and Nancy, followed Walter to Australia in 1857, followed by three brothers, William Mark and Robert, in 1861. A year later, Walter's mother, Beatrice, emigrated to Victoria with her eldest son, Henry, and two youngest daughters, Jane and Beatrice, arriving in Melbourne aboard the *Great Britain* on 15 August 1862. Only one married sister remained in Northumberland.

5   Thomas Russell, agent at Burwood Road, Hawthorn.

6   T. Wain purchased two allotments in Main Street, Chiltern, in 1870. Lands Department Map, *Township of Chiltern*. In the 1902 Chiltern Rate book, a Thomas Wain at the same location was described as a carrier by occupation. H. Sutherland and E. Vines, *Chiltern Conservation Study* (Chiltern: Shire of Chiltern and the Australian Heritage Commission, 1981) p. 205.

198   [From WLR in Chiltern to MR in Blairgowrie]

Chiltern
Wednesday Eveng [7 February 1877]

Dear Marie

I suppose you will be comfortably settled by the sea when this reaches you. I think the weather here this week is the most trying we have yet had, there is no wind and the heat is so continuous, so persistently dry—there are great outcries about water & the Barnawatha people are getting alarmed & declare it will have to be carted: there are still 10 feet in our tank—

I have no news to write about—I saw Arthur Green passing homeward on Monday: he knew nothing about his family[1]—Am glad you & chicks are well, how sad about Josephine[2]—

Thank Mrs Graham very much for the book.

I have heard nothing from Sam—I am surprised at his not writing—

Mary is still doing well. I think she is the best servant we have had. She is certainly the most tidy: & every meal is well served her pastry & puddings are excellent—

The Revd. Ewing lectures on Friday Evening.

There is still no sickness—

Kind regards to D^r & M^{rs} G & love to the chicks.| Your affect Husband

W.

Text: ALS NLA MS133/1/213

[1]   When Arthur Green was going 'home ward', he was probably about to catch the train to Melbourne, for his father, the Reverend Samuel Dutton Green, was married the next day (Tuesday, 6 February 1877) to Harriet Amy Sheppard at the Trinity Church, East Melbourne.

[2]   Emily Josephine Graham, aged thirteen, the invalid daughter of Dr and Mrs George Graham.

199 [From WLR in Chiltern to MR in Blairgowrie]

Chiltern

Monday [12 February 1877]

My dearest Marie

I was glad to get yours of Thursday on which day I also wrote you. We have it awfully hot here also & so continuous a month of it & no change & no rain The country is being ruined & all will suffer, hundreds of cattle are driven thro Chiltern to go to the Murray—Yet no sickness—

Ewing came on Friday with 3 ladies[1] we had the Star Theatre nearly full & only got £8-15 ~~without &~~ total—I took the chair. I made them come home as the ladies seemed much afraid of driving back in the dark. Mary got hot coffee & eggs & they turned in about ½ past 12 off next morning by ½ past 5—

Mary is all that could be wished & I think she is the best servant we have ever had. She is doing the washing better. Lloyd took tea with me last evening Sunday—I do not like your lined paper. Go to Purtons, I am sure he will serve you better I detest common paper & envelopes. You can see all kinds there & get them cheaper than any other shop—it is nearly opposite McEwen's Ironmongery—

The tank is getting low & dirty—we shall have no rain worth speaking of until probably April. I am glad the darlings are happy & thriving & without lessons. Sam has never written a line. Have you heard if Lela [Leila] is dead!—

I see that Wanliss family has had scarlet fever at Loutit Bay.[2]

Hydnman[3] was acquitted. I suppose you get the Argus—I send an Age with this—

I sleep in the nursery as I can have the window open all night—I am sorry to say there is still no sickness or patients. I go in for tea—three times a day—I find that is best: Business throughout Chiltern is frightfully bad & every one admits the place is done & will never recover. No sign of Mr Rhodda

A tremendous storm appears to have been raging all round us but we have not had a drop—Kind love to all & the darlings from| Your attached Husband

W.L.R.

Text: ALS NLA MS133/1/215

[1] One lady may have been Mrs Frances Ewing née Sanden. Two ladies from Beechworth were identified in the newspaper report of the forthcoming event as Mrs Kaye and Miss Waite. The former was to sing 'Oft in the Stilly Night' and 'She is Far From the Land' and the latter was to sing 'The Last Rose of Summer' and 'The Harp that Once Through Tara's Halls'. *FS*, 3 February 1877, p. 2. 'The Beechworth ladies sang most sweetly, so sweetly indeed, that it is hoped on some early date they will favour the Chiltonese with another specimen of their vocal abilities ... Mr Ewing was frequently applauded during the delivery of his lecture, his reading of several extracts from the poets being received with great favor. At the conclusion of the lecture, Dr Richardson, who was in the chair, moved a vote of thanks to Rev. R. K. Ewing and to those who had assisted him for the very excellent entertainment they had given them.' *FS*, 14 February 1877, p. 2.

[2] Thomas Drummond Wanliss and his family spent their summer at Louttit Bay, originally named for Captain James Louttit (*c*.1788–1865), who had reported on the bay having a good anchorage and shelter from north-west and westerly winds. It was renamed Lorne in honour of the marriage of Queen Victoria's daughter, Princess Louise, to the Marquis of Lorne in 1869. Situated on Victoria's south-west coast, it became a popular resort for Victorians. K. L. Cecil, *Lorne: The Founding Years (To 1888)* (Lorne: Historical Society, 1989), pp. 5–43. See endnote to Letter 57, regarding Harold Boyd Wanliss and his sister, Marion, the grandchildren of T. D. Wanliss, and their connection with Louttit Bay.

[3] WLR meant 'Hyndman' not 'Hydnman'. The previous week, it was reported in *The Federal Standard* that William Moody Hyndman, the Manager of the Sandhurst branch of the Oriental Bank, was going to take a year's leave of absence and it noted, 'It will be a matter of gratification to the many friends that Mr Hyndman has in the Ovens District to know that the charge now laid against him is considered by the Oriental Bank authorities to be both "unfounded" and "malicious".' *FS*, 3 February 1877, p. 2. 'Mr W. M. Hyndman, manager of the Oriental Bank Corporation, was brought up last week at the Assizes before Mr Justice Stephen charged with perjury. After hearing the evidence for the prosecution, His Honor directed an acquittal, remarking that the accused had been most unfairly treated.' *FS*, 17 February, 1877, p. 2. William Hyndman had been based at Beechworth where he and his wife, Matilda née Johnstone, had three daughters: May Verena (b. 1864), Kath Fanny (b. 1866), and an unnamed girl (b. 1884). It is most likely that he would have been a friend of ABS. His brother was Robert Hyndman, the Bank Manager of Kyneton's branch of the Bank of Victoria. Robert was married to Georgiana Lucia McCrae (1881–1908), the daughter of Andrew and Georgiana McCrae.

200 [From WLR in Chiltern to MR in Blairgowrie]

['Lake View', Chiltern]

[12 February 1877]

My dear little loves

Papa has not been well or he would have answered your nice letters sooner

I am so glad you are happy and like the sea I wish we could live near the sea. Perhaps Mamma may like Queenscliffe and we might move there—

Mary is very good

The bees are still hard at work and the chickens are all getting big—I sleep in the nursery and last week three ladies slept in one room and a gentleman[1] slept in yours, and they went away in the morning while I was asleep.

Your fond

Papa

with much love—

Text: ALS NLA MS133/1/221

[1] The Reverend R. K. Ewing, Mrs Frances Ewing, Mrs Kaye and Miss Waite.

201 [From WLR in Chiltern to MR in Blairgowrie]

Chiltern
Wednesday [14 February 1877]

My dearest M.

Yours of Saturday received Tuesday. The heat has reached Sorrento at last. It has been roasting here but as far as I can perceive our thermometers have not been as high as Melb. We had an hour or two rain Monday night but not enough to do more than lay the dust. I hear Mr Rhodda is curate from St. Judes Melb. & is to be here Saturday next alone. He is married & has family. The Bishop[1] visits Beechworth April 28 & so will be here about that time. You need not do any thing if you do not feel disposed for I am sure we will not & cannot remain here, the practice is gone, & is now a farce there is <u>no money</u>, & <u>no sickness!</u> Time hangs very heavily & it is very trying—I never could have believed things could have so collapsed from £70 a month to almost nothing—There is a good deal of sickness in Beechworth & Wangaratta; I hear & the traffic superintendent whom I spoke to since you went, died a few days ago of Dysentery there—We have a few mosquitoes about—the peaches are getting soft. plenty of grapes 4 lb: they tell me there will be no butter soon—M. is saving & buttering a nice lot of eggs for you: She is really the best girl we have had, so careful & clean, always scrubbing—I let her go out as often as she likes—Greens[2] buggy & harness sold for £16.

I feel very poorly again and hope it wont be long before you come back. I am very anxious & uneasy about you & the dear ones & am wretched <u>about the future</u>—I dont think I shall ever be an old man for I feel myself getting more feeble—every year, and the worry & anxieties of life make me very anxious to go.

Thursday. We had a fine drop of rain last evening & the weather is pleasanter this morning—I am writing to Brooke Smith to see if the place he talked about is still open—It was a bad days work that ever I came here—I should have gone back to our house & waited with the offer of the clubs.

I am really very distressed at the idea of your having to move again & to undergo the packing but there is nothing else for it apparently for this is done

Love to all & my darlings| Your affect Husband
W.L.R.

It will kill me if I dont get out of this soon—I would go away at once only I cant leave Mary

Text: ALS NLA MS133/1/212

---

[1] James Moorhouse (1826–1915), the second Church of England Bishop of Melbourne; born in Sheffield, England, the son of James Moorhouse, a master-cutler, and his wife Jane Frances née Bowman. Educated at a private school, he then studied at St John's College, Cambridge (BA 1853, MA 1860, DD 1876). He had a distinguished career in the Church in England, culminating in the position of Chaplain in Ordinary to the Queen (1867–1876) and Prebendary Canon of St Paul's in 1874–1876. When the first Bishop of Melbourne, Charles Perry (1807–1891), retired to England in 1876, Moorhouse was offered the appointment. Consecrated as Bishop at Westminster Abbey, he arrived in Melbourne on 22 October 1876 and was installed at St James's Cathedral, Melbourne, on 11 January 1877. See endnote to Letter 211 for details on the visit to Chiltern.

[2] The Reverend Samuel Dutton Green and his new wife, Harriet Amy née Sheppard.

202 [From WLR in Chiltern to MR in Blairgowrie]

['Lake View', Chiltern]

[Thursday, 15 February 1877]

[Page(s) missing]

Have just got yours of the 13th I wrote & posted letter Monday. Am so pleased you are all well.

Not a soul ever comes near the house—It is very heartbreaking—

I am too low spirited to write to the darlings & the continued heat is upsetting me—

A man called Mein[1] who was Bath man & Mc leeries clerk is appointed clerk of court Martin remains as paymaster—

~~The~~ I will not decide on another place until you have seen it.

I will attend to Dr Grahams order about the wine. I think it is the best Slocum[2] has no more. The carriage on 4 dozen will be 8/- I think but will enquire—1 doz case costs 4/- & 2 doz cases cost only 4/—I think the bottled will be best as giving least trouble

[Page(s) missing]

   Text: AL NLA MS133/1/261

1   'We have it on good authority that Mr. T. K. Mein has been appointed Clerk of Petty Sessions at Chiltern, in consequence of the retirement from the service of Mr. L'E[spinasse] Martin. We have to congratulate Mr. Mein. He will make a good officer.' *FS*, 3 February 1877, p. 2.
2   John Slocum (1823–1884), see Letter 193, endnote 1.

203 [From WLR in Chiltern to MR in Blairgowrie]

Chiltern

Saturday [17 February 1877]

My dear Marie

I was very poorly when I wrote last, am a little better today—We had some fine showers of rain Thursday night with such a storm of hail rain & thunder that I never saw equalled. I have really had. [repeated] I have really had six patients this week but this is very dull—The clergyman "Rhodda" is not coming after all.[1] What a lucky get off for him if he only knew it—

We have had no butter for days. We have pleasanter weather & the woman has called to day.

I was just up at Maudes[2] posting a letter & I found myself unable to articulate[3]—I could not say what I wanted, I am very uneasy about myself I lay down—I said I thought it was a faint & said I had been out in the sun—I am afraid it is something worse—I have been so distressed about the practice I fear it has upset me—I am going in to lie down & must let M post this letter—

Love to my dear loves| I will write or telegraph Monday morning early| Yours

        WLR

   Text: ALS NLA MS133/1/210

1   'It appears as if the church of England at Chiltern, is to be fooled by the bigwigs of the Church. We learn that Mr. Rhodda, who had been appointed to the parish, preached his farewell sermon to his old congregation, but influence had been brought to bear on the Bishop to make him

stay, and he has allowed this. A telegram now says that Mr. Rhodda must not be uprooted.'
FS, 17 February 1877, p. 2.

2   Richard Mahony experienced the same aphasia while attending the stationmaster who had hurt
his foot. *FRM III*, pp. 154–156. Dorothy Green (Green, 1986, p. 351) was not aware that
HHR interpreted her father's letter to MR rather more accurately than was supposed, for he was
visiting the stationmaster, Arthur Maude, who often took the post to catch the Melbourne train.

3   WLR was suffering from the tertiary stage of syphilis, which usually appears some fifteen to
twenty years after the primary infection. The syphilitic organism attacks the structure of the
brain and spinal cord causing speech defects including aphasia, disorders of handwriting,
convulsions and difficulties in walking.

204 [From WLR in Chiltern to MR in Blairgowrie]

Chiltern
Tuesday [20 February 1877]

My dearest Marie

I dont want to say much about my attack on Saturday I will tell you all about it when I
see you: I suppose it must have been mental depression & the intense & protracted heat—It
seems settled that Rhodda is not to come and it seems pretty certain that there is to be a new
bank[1] The new mine expects to be on gold next Monday. The weather is still hot tho' of
course not so bad as last month or the beginning of this—I am glad Lela got better Sam
might have written—I shall think twice before I expend 2/8 on a telegram for him again—I
got your letter of Friday—glad to hear you are all well—no news from this—very few patients
indeed.[2] Scots bazaar[3] opened today—

Two persons owing me accounts have become insolvent since I came here
Wednesday [21 February]
Got yours of Saturday this morning & your papers still very hot here—

Mary cleaning up every day. Practice completely gone. I bought a case of apples for 5/-
for you & put them in the cellar but I see the case is not full—

Lloyd had not got one person in his shop the whole of last Sunday—Thomas the
Wesleyan Minister has left—gone to Rutherglen. Am sorry you do not sleep better. I could
not sleep for long after you left I always woke at or before daylight—I do a little better now I
take some wine during the day & at night. I hope D^r G: got his wine or if not he will I
ordered it—

Kind love to M^rs G and lots of kisses to the pets happy darlings—

The drought & heat still continue—the mutton is very lean—We have a fowl twice a
week as I am sick of tough steak

Good bye dearest, I suppose you will be off to Queenscliffe[4] next week—I dont feel
strong enough to travel just at present| Your affect Husband
             W.L.R.
        Text: ALS NLA MS133/1/211

1   The Bank of Australasia opened on 1 March 1877 under the management of Robert Owen.
FS, 3 March 1877, p. 2.

2   WLR had delivered the Wakefield twins at 5 a.m. that very morning. The eldest twin, Edward,
died that day and his brother survived only twelve days. Their French mother, Leontine Celina
Wakefield née Tourbour, aged forty-two, also died after the birth, leaving her husband, George
Wakefield, a miner, with four living children aged fifteen, thirteen, nine and seven.

³   A Bazaar and Bruce Auction were held on Tuesday, 20 February 1877, at the St Andrew's
     Presbyterian Church in aid of the Manse Building Fund. *FS*, 21 February 1877, p. 2. A Bruce
     Auction is one of donated goods, designed as a fund-raising activity for some charitable cause
     (from John Vans Agnew Bruce (1822–1863), construction contractor and philanthropist). *MD*,
     p. 230.
⁴   MR and the girls were going to stay with Mrs Emma Cuthbert on holiday in Queenscliff.

205   [From WLR in Chiltern to MR in Blairgowrie]

Chiltern
Thursday [22 February 1877]

My dearest Marie

Do not hurry back I am much better now. The trip to Queenscliffe will benefit you. I
would not have written on Saturday only I was afraid I was going to be ill <u>all alone.</u> Stay on
until the weather improves for it is still unbearable. I am so sorry about your being ill
yourself—My going first would be bad but <u>your</u> leaving the darlings would be much worse, let
us pray you may be spared. I have got one or two patients—It is my writing that has upset you
I should have kept my complaints to myself. It was all my anxiety about you & the darlings.
You did not say what side the pain is in I suppose it is the left—the old pain the heart always
brought on by worry & care <u>about others:</u> poor dear: I hope this will reach you before leaving
Sorrento—I am so sorry I wrote as I did, ~~but I was~~

You will be easier now dear wont you, & try & get strong for my sake & for the darlings
sake think what they would do without you—I shall expect you back the week after next I
think by that time you will have enjoyed Queenscliffe. We will make up our minds until that
time & altho' I am afraid the hot weather will not have gone it must be going—

Thank dear Mrs Graham for all her love & kindness to me & mine they will never be
forgotten. I will Telegraph if anything occurs and I have jotted down particulars of affairs in
my box to make things easy—

What with life assurance	545
& House	1550
Bank—Chiltern	270
Yourself	150
Savings bank	35
Debts due here	100
Shares—about	<u>450</u>
	3000
My acct city Bank	<u>35</u>
	3035

Due on House about 300

Affairs will not be so hopeless or so complicated as many other persons leave them

This was a <u>frightful</u> morning but a change seems imminent, could eat no dinner—but
am going to try a little cold fowl 4 PM—

Fond love to my darlings I hope they will bring back rosy faces

[No signature]

Text: AL NLA MS133/1/220

206 [From WLR in Chiltern to MR in Queenscliff]

Chiltern
Saturday [24 February 1877]

My dearest Marie

I got yours of Wednesday this morning. I did not feel well enough to write until Wednesday, as I had frequent fits of giddiness which made me reel like a drunken man, & I had to hold on to fences when out walking. There must be something wrong inside my head—You know I have complained of head ache for some years ever since that sun stroke at Ballt. I hope I am better now however. Judge Hackett[1] called Friday, & asked me to dinner at the Star. Shortly after Espinass Martin[2] came up & apologising for the shortness of the invitation said he had asked the judge to dinner that day, & would I go down to meet him: of course I thought Martin has arranged with the judge & went—judge of my astonishment when 7 oclock arrived & no Hackett Martin sent off to the Star & found that he <u>had dined</u> alone, ~~no~~ Martin not making the case out clearly to him. He came sat at table would eat nothing & I thought ~~thot~~ treated them with great rudeness at all events with want of politeness. Every thing was splendid Fish, lamb capital pudding splendid desert & all for nothing as it were! There is something behind the Martins

In the midst of dinner in comes a note from Brooke Smith who arrives at the Star—we soon joined him & his language of the Martins was something dreadful. He said he <u>was a liar</u> & worse! but would give no explanations. I thought of going on to Beechworth today but am afraid of my giddiness & must keep quiet until you come back—one or two patients but poor people. The weather is sensibly cooler we had fine rain Thursday all night. no fear of the tank now. nights & morning are cold. Mary is still all that can be desired she has mended my socks for me. I hope this will find you in Queenscliffe & that my last will have comforted you & that you ~~ha~~ will have a better week with dear Mrs C.[3] Give her my kind love & say I hope her health ~~is~~ keeps good—How happy she & Mrs Graham ought to be with no cares on their minds for the future. The Archdeacon[4] preaches March 11th morning & evening: but the place is gone so <u>completely</u> to <u>the bad</u> that I do not believe any other clergyman will get a living. Brooke does not speak hopefully of any other place at present. He is nearly quite bald & lame still & denounces the world & things in general as usual. He seems to be harder worked than ever. I do not think I could stand the 16 miles jolting in the coach

Love to my darlings & much to your own dear self from| Your loving

WLR

Text: ALS NLA MS133/1/217

[1] Charles Prendergast Hackett (1818–1889). The Court was in session in Chiltern on 24 February 1877. (See Letter 164, endnote 4 for biographical details).
[2] A. L'Espinasse Martin was formerly Clerk of the Petty Sessions at Chiltern and had been appointed in February 1877 as Receiver and Paymaster at the Receipt and Pay Office, Chiltern.
[3] Emma Wilmer Cuthbert (formerly Hepburn née Kirby) (1835–1877), wife of Henry Cuthbert. She died on 1 August 1877, less than six months later.
[4] Joseph K. Tucker, Archdeacon of Beechworth.

207 [From WLR in Chiltern to MR in Queenscliff]

Chiltern

Tuesday [27 February 1877]

My dearest Marie

Yours of Saturday came this morning. The weather is still awful Ther 90° to 100°. Hope you will enjoy your Queenscliffe trip. Am thankful to say I am better. Hope you will get stronger before you return to this wretched place. I shall not even if we stay put in another Feby here. It would be as much as my life is worth I hope you got my letter posted here Thursday for Sorrento & one to Queenscliffe posted Saturday It was well I did not go to Beechworth as B.S.[1] did not get home until Sunday night & I had a confinement Sunday night

You must use your own judgment about a nursery governess—if you wish it I shall not oppose it—only do not make a long engagement for the practice is altogether gone—& will never return. Not You will see the state when you come back—Of course if we moved she could go with us—The last tea was splendid & is still & I think another box would be good—I think a few pair of merino socks—& a pair of driving gloves or two with some paper & envelopes from Purtons & a light

Mary is still all that could be desired She cooks & washes well—makes me stews & curries & pastys

It has been threatening rain all day but the wind changes around & carries all away—

Kind love to Mrs C. & 100 to the darlings—How nice to have cold weather, it seems to be giving you Rheumatism No news from this vile place—not a soul ever comes near the house & I see no one but Lloyd.

Your affect & attached | Husband

W.

Text: ALS NLA MS133/1/219

[1]   Alexander Brooke Smith.

208 [From WLR in Chiltern to MR in Queenscliff]

[Chiltern]

[Saturday, 3 March 1877]

My dearest M.

Just as if we had not got enough troubles, I have received notice from Mr Flower[1] of Toorak who was joint security for Brooke Smith with me & Rutledge[2] in 1871 that there is a sum of £60 still due—that he has forfeited his life Policy & that we are looked to for payment

I have of course written & telegraphed to Brooke. Is it not scandalous?—

I do not see that we can incur xpense of governess as my practice has quite gone—

A few poor people with no money

Then the mine is flooded & will require pumps & machinery & delay for 6 months.

I hope you will come home soon before I go quite mad for what with solitude & misfortunes I am very very put about—|Your affect Husband

 Walter

I thought you had done all your shopping before you went to Sorrento. Dont buy anything for me

 Text: ALS NLA MS133/1/207

1   Horace Flower (1818–1899), merchant and pastoralist, was trustee, with William Rutledge, for Annie Baxter Dawbin (see Letter 97). Born in London, he emigrated in 1838 to Sydney and then moved to Portland, Victoria, finally settling in Port Fairy in 1847, where he became a partner in William Rutledge & Co. The company was very successful until 1862 when it went bankrupt through heavy losses in grain transactions and depreciation of landed securities. His own company (Flower, Salting and Co.) and the Bank of Australasia were the two largest creditors and he was declared bankrupt. He successfully fought for an honourable discharge which he achieved in 1866, paying his creditors 20/- in the £1. Early in 1869, Flower sold his house in Port Fairy and moved to Melbourne, living in Carlton and then Toorak. He worked for a time for the auctioneering firm of Samuel Macgregor & Co. As William Rutledge had died on 1 June 1876, Flower must have been ensuring that all the outstanding debts were paid.

2   William Rutledge (1806–1876), merchant, banker, pastoralist and early settler; born in County Cavan, Ireland. He originally settled in Sydney in 1829 and then in 1838 he took sheep overland to Port Phillip and bought several lots at early Melbourne land sales. He moved back and forth between Sydney and Melbourne until he bought a mercantile firm at Port Fairy in 1843. In partnership with Horace Flower and Francis Forster, he founded the firm William Rutledge & Co., shipping wool, tallow, and later, gold to England. At the firm's collapse in 1862, he was made bankrupt with £117,000 in debts. He moved to Farnham, near Koroit, and made another fortune through his land and farming activities. He was a member of the first Victorian Legislative Council in 1851 and a representative of the first Victorian Legislative Assembly from 1856 to 1859.

209   [From WLR in Chiltern to MR in Richmond, Melbourne, with the Grahams]

 Chiltern
 Sunday [11 March 1877]

My dearest Marie

 The weather is now delightful & the nights & the water cold. I wrote in great annoyance in consequence of the rascality of that unprincipled fellow B[rooke].S[mith]. I suppose I will have to pay it. I have received no reply to 2 letters & suppose he is as usual away from his home—I am still doing literally nothing—the Newingtons are going up & it is thought they will get the reef struck by the Patricks which has given 1 oz-18-dwt to the ton for the first crushing—

 If you like to venture on a governess you <u>can</u> try for 6 months & a year—I think you might buy a nice reading lamp or a drawing one like M[rs] Martins[1] Also you had better get some paper & envelopes a[t] Purtons for I use a great deal—

 I have a case of apples I told you I bought but I am afraid they wont last till you come back as they are too ripe. I cannot measure the collar of the shirt—you had better leave it—I have plenty to last me another 6 months

 Your boat sickness seems to have done you good, it is a pity you did not take more fishing excursions—

 Arthur Green passed thro to Wodonga & dined & took tea with me on Saturday. He is much improved[2]—

Love to the Grahams—& to the darlings & write & say what day we are to expect you.|
Your affect Husband
> W.
I think it will be wet Wednesday
> *Text:* ALS NLA MS133/1/208

1   Wife of A. L'Espinasse Martin.
2   Why WLR made this comment about Arthur Green is not known but he may have been trying
>   to rehabilitate Arthur in MR's eyes. When HHR wrote in *FRM III* about the escapade of
>   'Cousin Emmy' and the curate 'Mr Angus', was she remembering a flirtation between her cousin
>   Emma Bailey and Arthur Green?

210   [From WLR in Chiltern to MR in Richmond, Melbourne]

> ['Lake View', Chiltern]
> [Saturday, 17 March 1877]

My dearest Marie
>   I enclose Sarahs[1]
>   Thank dear M[rs] Graham for her kind invitation. I must however think of the money &
coming back first class with you—I am sorry you found the sea too bleak—
>   No news here whatever The weather is pleasant & the nights cold—
>   You will see Sarah has got quite a lot of things & boots—I am afraid your new dresses &
bonnett will be lost at Chiltern—The place is deserted & the streets empty—
>   Tell D[r] G. that I found that rascal Gueria[2] had sent me wine that was fermenting in the
bottles[3] & bursting—I wrote him at once & countermanded D[r] Grahams order—I do not
know if I was in time to stop it or not | Your affect | Husband
> W.
Be sure if you buy a lamp to get one of Rowatts[4] without wide chimney.
Just heard from B.S. He says he is asking for time & will settle it by April 11—
>   *Text:* ALS NLA MS133/1/218

1   Letter from Sarah Ann Laughton née Bailey.
2   Not identifiable.
3   A letter from WLR was published in *The Federal Standard*, 2 May 1877: '*To the Editor of the
>   Federal Standard* SIR—I have for some 10 years been a friend of the native wines. I have had
>   them on my table daily and I have promoted their use in every way as a medicinal agent.
>   Coming to this district where wine making is general, I certainly expected to find more matured
>   wines easily procurable. The prejudice of the public in Melbourne is still strong against their
>   use, and one would imagine that the vignerons would be desirous of assisting in removing this
>   prejudice. I visited a vineyard some months ago; I tasted two wines, and I ordered five dozen, on
>   its arriving at my house it was placed in a capital cool cellar. Thinking I had got a sound wine
>   that would improve by keeping I recommended the same to a friend [Dr George Graham] in
>   town, who also ordered five dozen. In a few weeks on opening my wine (which by the way I had
>   paid for) I found that the honest man had sold me not wine but vinegar. I wrote, but the honest
>   man took no notice of two letters and the vinegar charged as wine is bursting in my cellar. I am
>   happy to say the vendor in this transaction is not an Englishman. My friend in town found his
>   wine also turned to vinegar, and by my advice packed it back to the vendor, fortunately, not
>   having paid for it. Now this conduct, putting aside the immorality of it, can have but one effect,
>   that of further disgusting the public with the article in question, and of bringing at some time
>   retribution on the perpetrator of such scurvy conduct. I am Sir, Yours, W.L.R.'

4   Rowatt's Patent Safety Kerosene Lamps were being advertised weekly in *The Federal Standard* from February 1877 under the banner: 'No more Smoke or Smell! No Breakages of Chimney!!'

211 [From WLR in Chiltern to MR in Richmond, Melbourne]

['Lake View', Chiltern]
Saturday [14 April 1877][1]

Dʳ Marie

I received the enclosed this morning. Poor Jack[2] has like ourselves been unfortunate—His Russian bonds have gone down fearfully—He evidently enjoys our letters. I will write again this mail. The weather is getting pleasanter & such cold nights—Lespinasse Martin[3] has retired on his pension—The people are petioning [petitioning] to get up a new bank—I think they will succeed as the farmers declare New S. Wales is not liberal enough to them. The Bishops visit is postponed until after the 28th[4]—evidently done by the Archdeacon because you are not here. A few more patients since—I had to go to the Springs & to Gooramadda & was engaged today for a confinement—Things are however awfully dull.

Mary is still all that could be desired. Every thing she cooks is excellent & she is always scrubbing & cleaning. Thank Dʳ G. for his papers I enjoy them. Love to all, kisses to my darlings same to yourself from your attached Husband

W.

Text: ALS NLA MS133/1/216

1   The previous letter was written on 17 March 1877 and in the gap between these letters Walter Robinson Bailey, the son of Ned and Agnes Bailey, had died aged eight years, at Wodonga, on 20 March 1877. It is not known whether WLR went down to Melbourne for the burial at Melbourne General Cemetery on 21 March 1877, but it is very likely that he did. It is also probable that he then visited Queenscliff (perhaps persuaded by MR that the sea trip and sea air would do him good), for in the sequence of letters written in August and September by WLR in Queenscliff to MR in Chiltern, it is clear that he had spoken to Dr David John Williams in March about taking over his medical practice (see Letter 225). MR, HHR and ALR returned to Chiltern shortly after this letter.
2   The husband of Mary's sister Lizzie, Jack Brett. He retired from the service as Lieutenant-Colonel on full-pay in 1877. It is possible that Lizzie had died prior to this letter and hence the 'poor' Jack.
3   'Mr. A. L'E Martin, late Clerk of Courts and Land Officer of Chiltern and Rutherglen, notifies in our advertising columns that, as he has retired from the civil service, he will be happy to transact any business entrusted to him in connection with the Lands and Survey Department.' *FS*, 14 April 1877, p. 2.
4   It was reported that the Bishop of Melbourne, the Right Reverend Dr James Moorhouse, would be arriving in Chiltern on 3 May 1877 to consecrate St Paul's Church. Whether he and his wife stayed with the Richardsons at 'Lake View' is not known. He was on a tour visiting his parishes in the north-east of the State with his wife and Archdeacon Tucker, *FS*, 14 April 1877, p. 2. The Bishop's party duly arrived on Thursday, 3 May to consecrate the new Church of St Paul's. His text for his sermon was Matthew 21, 13: 'It is written, My house shall be called the house of prayer; but ye have made it a den of thieves.' 'It was a most able discourse, entirely extempore, an appropriate to the occasion. His Lordship after describing the holiness of Solomon's temple, spoke in severe terms of the want of reverence which he had observed in the churches of Victoria forming a striking contrast to the conduct of congregations in the mother country, and enjoined on his hearers the solemn obligation to shew that devotion and reverence due to God's house.' *FS*, 5 May 1877, p. 3.

212 **[From WLR in Richmond, Melbourne, to MR in Chiltern]**[1]

Melb ['Lyndoch', Richmond][2]

Monday [27 August 1877]

Dear Marie

I arrived safely after a long & weary journey as you know—I fell asleep—the carriage was full. I enjoyed your good things very much: As I am convinced the wine does not agree with me I am going to make D[r] G. accept it: as it acts very injuriously on me and I am sure I am better without it—I left that book on the Port wine wrack [rack]. I put it away carefully in my book case, so that I might have it in my hand & read it going but I forgot it. I think it fell down behind the books on the 2nd shelf I also forgot my testimonials addressed to M[r] Shill.[3] I think you might have it posted at Chiltern

I hope all are well, & that Josephine keeps better

I have not seen any one as yet but post this early so that you have [will] get it Tuesday midday—Love to M[rs] G. & all as well as to your own dear good self from| Your affect |Hub

WLR

Text: ALS NLA MS133/1/242

[1]   WLR left Chiltern to seek a practice in Queenscliff. Mrs Sydney Graham and her daughter Josephine went up to Chiltern to stay with MR and the girls and to help her pack up the house. Miss Fenton, the governess and Mary, the servant, were also at 'Lake View'. The letter is written on Yorick Club paper with embossed logo (see Letter 214, endnote 1).

[2]   WLR stayed with Dr Graham for a few nights prior to travelling to Queenscliff.

[3]   Probably Robert Shill (*c*.1829–1902), married to Mary Ann née Snart (*c*.1828–1877).

213 **[From WLR in Richmond, Melbourne, to MR in Chiltern]**

Melb. ['Lyndoch', Richmond]

Tuesday [28 August 1877]

Dearest wifey

I am not going to Queenscliffe before <u>Thursday</u> as I find I have matters to detain me here, & Graham is pressing that I should not hurry. I feel better already, and had better night: what I suffered from the last night at <u>home</u> did not affect me thank God. I drank nothing but milk since I left you & there is splendid milk at D[r] G's: I have written to M[r] Johnson[1] telling him I wd not be there until Thursday. D[r] G prescribed some med[e]. for me this morning which I must get made up. I hope you are all well & that M[rs] G is getting good nights still—I saw Ham,[2] he has asked £1700 to a M[r] Simmonds who went to look after it—Now Graham tells me he thinks D[r] Alsop[3] may become a purchaser—Tell M[rs] G. I found Griffiths most obliging, & convenient In fact I do not know what I should have done without his kind services in allowing my pile of luggage to remain there—Tell M[rs] G. that Miss Rivers[4] says all are well & good, & the way in which the youngsters play into a <u>huge</u> heaped plate of porridge shews that—

Of course the birds awoke me at daylight but I felt so well that I did not mind—I hope things will enable you to leave that horrid place before Nov[r]. I will soon be strong as ever. D[r] G. tells me that M[rs] G has £300 in city Bank. He thinks Jacques Martin[5] not so safe—as he has been <u>once</u> an inmate of Cremorne[6]—So I will <u>not</u> risk it, but will lodge the 3 hundred in the City Bank & when you draw the hundred at Chiltern Oct 31ˢᵗ you can lodge the £105. in Melbourne as well—

I am going out a drive with Dʳ G. this afternoon & will go round by the house.

Kindest love to Mʳˢ G. to Josephine—to dear Ettie & my own Lillie—tell them Willy & his brother[7] want to go to Chiltern & beg me to take them & Miss Rivers| Your own hubby

WLR

Text: ALS NLA MS133/1/241

1 Possibly the father of Fanny Maria Admans. See Letter 216.
2 C. J. & T. Ham, auctioneers and agent for the leasing and selling of the Richardson's Hawthorn house. See Letter 178.
3 Dr George Charles Alsop, medical practitioner, married to Grace née Hatherly (1834–1909).
4 Miss Rivers was the nursery governess of Dr and Mrs Graham's younger children, Willy (aged five) and Edgar (aged four). Their older siblings, George Robert Moore (aged sixteen), Margaret Elizabeth Frances (aged fifteen), Luduvina Marion (aged nearly thirteen) and James (aged eleven) were at school. Emily Josephine (Josie) (aged fourteen) was an invalid and did not attend school. Margaret was in the first cohort of girls enrolled at the Presbyterian Ladies College in 1875 (enrolment number 122), Luduvina joining her sister the following April 1876 (enrolment number 235).
5 Thomas Jacques Martin (1839–1896), businessman; Manager, Australasian Insurance Co.; founder, Mutual Life Association of Australasia, and of Colonial Mutual Life Association; died in St Kilda; unmarried. WLR had been discussing with Dr Graham whether he should purchase more life insurance.
6 Formerly the site of the Cremorne Gardens and Zoo, Cremorne Private Hospital, Richmond, was where Dr Graham was the Medical Officer and where WLR was admitted on 11 September 1878 after his mental deterioration. From there WLR was transferred to the government asylum at Yarra Bend on 18 November 1878.
7 William Archibald Graham (aged five) and younger brother Edgar Gerald Hastings Graham (aged four).

214 [From WLR in Richmond, Melbourne, to MR in Chiltern][1]

Melbourne ['Lyndoch', Richmond]
Augt. 29 [Wednesday, 1877]

Dear Marie

I leave for Queenscliffe tomorrow morg at 10.30. I am told we shall not get in before 5 or 6 oclock—so you need not expect any letter that day—I drove round with Dʳ G. yesterday & called at our house. Mʳˢ Tully insisted on g my going all over & shewed me the improvements. They have distempered all the rooms & the lower ones green the upper blue & certainly it has added very much to the appearance; they have put up a little crib of a servants room off the kitchen & she said I had allowed £15 & it had cost £18. She had my letter. She evidently indulges, for her face was like a peony & she was very pressing that I should have some ale or wine. Mʳ Tully was away but she said she had sent the acct. The house does not appear to have deteriorated on the outside—but the garden is untidy & the Camelias are gone—stolen G. says. they always are!

I hope you are all keeping well & that I will get a letter at Queenscliffe. I got no sleep last night owing to the carriages coming home from the fancy ball,[2] & the birds at daylight—I send Newspaper Argus with this & Dʳ G. says he sent a Warder with an interesting case of breach of promise Dʳ G. says he makes £500 a year bad debts.

I do not feel quite so well to day. I suppose it is the want of sleep—I see the Clunes are still advertising Dr G. says it will be too hard work for me

I hope to get better by that time—Give my love to Mrs G. & to the darlings & write & tell me all the news if there is any which I dont expect. I am going to the picture gallery this day. & shall leave tomorrow.

All well at Lyndoch—| Your affect husband

Walter

We came in last evening to the Georgian minstrels,[3] but I was too poorly to enjoy it

Text: ALS NLA MS133/1/240

[1]   The letter is written on Yorick Club paper with embossed logo.
[2]   The Mayor's Fancy Dress Ball held on 28 August 1877 and described in detail in *The Argus* the
       following day. It was held in the Town Hall, which had been opened in 1870. The ball was
       attended by His Excellency the Governor Sir George Bowen and Lady Diamantina Bowen who
       were welcomed at the start of the Ball at 9.30 p.m. by his worship the Mayor, Alderman Smith.
       In his afternoon reply to a toast to him and his family, the Governor noted that it was forty-two
       years to the day that 'six white men rowed up the River Yarra'. *Argus*, Wednesday, 29 August
       1877.
[3]   Advertised in *The Argus* as 'The American Slave Troupe (organised 1865) who are recognised
       exponents of the Negro songs, Choruses, Dances, Eccentricities & Peculiarities of the Natives of
       the Sunny South.' *Argus*, 24 August 1877, p. 1. The very complicated history of this troupe, and
       its black entrepreneur, Charles B. Hicks, is given in Richard Waterhouse, *From Minstrel Show to
       Vaudeville: The Australian Popular Stage 1788–1914* (Kensington, NSW: NSW University
       Press, 1990), pp. 47–97.

215   [From WLR en route to Queenscliff to MR in Chiltern]

Off Queenscliffe

Thursday Eveng [30 August 1877]

My darling Wifey

I came off in the steamer[1] this morning & judge of my surprise when a nice looking gentleman came up & spoke to me. It seems he is a Dr Tovell[2] who used to be in Geelong he has been unfortunate like myself & has had to resume practice. He said he had been staying at Queenscliffe all the week & had quite decided to settle there, but that as I had made arrangements to go there, he would make way for me and if I did not like it after a fair trial say of a month he would fulfil it himself. I told him of Chiltern & mentioned the house & Sale of furniture & told him there was a practice ready at hand—rather quiet just now but certain to improve. I told him my income for the year was over £600 & I stated that I was certain that he would do £400 & if so all I asked was a cheque for £30 at end of the year—He must make terms with you about the house: perhaps you could accommodate him with a room as he is a perfect gentleman. The only thing is he is too good for the people. I told him that loneliness & the climate drove us away—I am keeping pretty well but get very little sleep. I am sorry you sent the accts to Ham he has nothing to do with them & will only charge us for anything he does with them. I authorized Tully by letter for a joint expense of £15. each & I am very pleased with the improvements he has made. I have written to Ham to send them to me—I found I could not sell a single share—there was a perfect panic on all the time I was in Melb. All were sellers—no buyers I therefore paid £50 only to your name which makes £250 & will put in the other £50 as soon as ever things mend—

Kindest love to Mrs G. & so glad Josephine keeps well. Beg of Mrs G. to stay. Dr G. will be so pleased & is so thankful to have quiet nights for Mrs G. Unfortunately I forgot to bring a hat from the Yorick Club[3]—It was an old wide awake[4] that I had sent there when I got a new one. I must try & get it down here—Lots of love & kisses to all—& kind regards to Miss Fenton[5] You will get this unexpectedly on Friday

I am glad the people miss me they will perhaps know better in future how to treat a gentleman & not to injure him because he does not drink with them in every pub. Love to the darlings. I do not think there will be enough to do here & Graham does not think I could overtake the work at Clunes. I told Tovell about Clunes he said he would prefer Queenscliffe

I do not know what to do for stamps this big portmanteau costs 1/- every time a man looks at it[6] I had a capital dinner on board—Soup, two joints, two vegetables, p capital plum puddings & tarts, & cheese & biscuits & all for 2/-. Of course my appetite is ravenous as soon as I smell the sea air

And now good bye. I hope the troubles of the house & furniture will not be too much for you & that the bills will come in—I am very thankful to get away from the bark huts & the 10 Publicans & the everlasting lake[7] & the mill whistle[8]

So good bye Sweetheart. We shall soon meet again, both stronger to renew the battle of life| Yours affect Hubby

      W.

Text: ALS NLA MS133/1/238

[1] There was a daily steamer passenger service from Melbourne to Queenscliff. The railway line between Geelong and Queenscliff was not completed until 1879.

[2] Dr Charles Joshua Tovell (1826–1897), MRCS (England, 1851), was married on 12 May 1855 at St Mark's Church, Collingwood, to Eliza Spencer née Lee (1824–1888). They had eight children born in Brighton, Victoria: Mary Eliza (b. 1856), Charles Edward (b. 1858), William Raymond (b. 1859), Alfred Spencer (1862–1878), Ernest Walter (b. 1863), Lillian Constance (b. 1864), Henry Herbert (1866–1872), Frank Gerald (1869–1873). His descendant, Ann Tovell, was the librarian and archivist of the Australian Medical Association and 'The Ann Tovell Collection', comprising her extensive collection of nineteenth-century material and indexes on medical matters, is now in the Brownless Library, the University of Melbourne.

[3] The Yorick Club arose from informal gatherings held by F. W. Haddon, the editor of *The Australian* and *The Argus*. These 'at home' parties, attended by journalists, freelance writers, artists and poets outgrew Haddon's home and so they met at Nissen's Café until the group decided on a room at the *Melbourne Punch* office, next door to *The Argus*. The first meeting of the club took place in early May 1868. WLR joined when he returned from England in 1869. If the Melbourne Club reflected the strata of men in Victoria representing the aristocracy or 'birth', then, de Serville suggests, the Yorick Club represented 'worth', and the Union Club 'wealth'. de Serville, pp. 360–363.

[4] Broad-brimmed soft-felt hat, popular in the colonies.

[5] Governess for Ettie and Lil.

[6] i.e., that the porters expect a shilling tip to carry his large suitcase.

[7] The Chiltern Lake was developed in 1875 as part of a public park area and a boating channel was created. The first trees were planted in the park in June 1876. It was named 'Lake Anderson' early in January 1876, after George Anderson who was the editor of *The Federal Standard* from 1859 and a leader in the community.

[8] The flour mill began operation in March 1876. 'It is a handsome and substantial three storied structure, and will be supplied with powerful machinery and the newest designs in mill work.' *FS*, 9 February 1877, p. 2. 'The Victorian Steam Flour Mills at Chiltern are now completed, and it is announced by the proprietors, Messrs W.T. Pyke and Co., that they are prepared to purchase good milling wheat at once. The mill in question stands on a piece of ground close to the Chiltern Railway Station, and consequently is admirably situated for receiving and forwarding all goods by rail.' *FS*, 1 March 1876, p. 2. By August 1876, William Tucker Pyke

had become bankrupt and the mill closed until it was purchased and refurbished by the new owner, George Portch, in March 1877.

216   [From WLR in Queenscliff to MR in Chiltern]

Queenscliffe
August 30 [1877, Thursday]

My darling Marie

Just arrived, got yours at Grahams this morning & at this place at 8 PM. We had a nice run down. I told you about Tovell. I explained to Mr Johnson[1] who came to meet me & who before I explained, was full of apologies—& regrets that I had not come sooner, however I think it is all right now. I was obliged to come to Admans[2] until I can get apartments as Mrs Richardson where Johnsons stay could not accommodate me—

It is very kind\ of Mrs Martin[3] & Mrs G. to interest themselves so much. If you send Miss F. she can post the testimonials & they will think it music besides the Post mistress does not gossip like Stevenson—please dont send them here

There are a lot of unpaid bills Riley[4] is a scoundrel & uncertificate insolvent. Your only chance would be to see Mrs R. but I am afraid you will be insulted Grundman[5] is a contractor under the Council & engaged now making the Barnawartha Road he lives close to the Wesleyan Chapel near Les. Martin.

Smith has gone away, been long from work—injured the bones of his foot, could not possibly pay as he was off work for weeks. Boyd Doma Mungi must only be charged 10/-. Letchmere[6] Farmers wife Indigo must be posted—Soule[7] has been insolvent. Tomkins[8] never pays any I got a pound out of him. Richards up near Williams on the Hill 7/6 You can try & get the enclosed accts. They live up on the hill behind us I think I am better my darling. Father Bleasdale[9] came in to the hotel & we had a long chat about Clunes. I got a tremendous fright on arriving I went up to my room & washed face & hands for tea—After I wanted to open my portmanteau, & put my hands into my pockets for my keys. Gone! Oh the state I was in—I went out & asked for a blacksmith thinking I wd. have to have them burst open. As I was asking the way a sudden light struck me that I had taken them out of my pocket in my bedroom—I came back—no light or servant visible felt my way up to room & in the dark got them on the dressing table with my knife wh I had taken out of my pocket, I certainly thought it was a great misfortune prevented You will of course make a charge if Tovell wants accommodation He is a perfect gentleman I have known him for years. I only hope he will go altho a jolly sight too good for the place—do not put him against it. He will want a nice table & the charge at the Star is 30/- a week. He is living at present in 4 Victoria Parade in apartments next to Mrs Waters—I will wait patiently here for a month without grumbling or until October 9th when as you know I must be off to Beechworth—I dont think I have much to grumble about unpaid bills. Grahams loss is ¼ or 25 per cent of all—mine was nothing like that—certainly not more than one twentieth or 5 per cent in the year—about £30 out of £650.

I never expect to do any thing like that here or elsewhere—so Tovell ought to know that they pay up—if they are looked after—I enclose acct for £5–18–0 You must put in the date 7.18 [July 18] Mc Coms of Shamrock Hotel ~~from~~ his wife promised me repeatedly & he is earning good wages at the Doma.[10]

[Page(s) missing?]

Text: AL NLA MS133/1/239

[1]   As noted previously, possibly a relative of Mrs Admans.

[2]   George Admans (c.1832–1918), hotel keeper. Probably too expensive for WLR, the advertising for Adman's Hotel boasted that the clientele included: 'Governors, Judges and the Gentry of Victoria.' Andrea Inglis, *Beside the Seaside: Victorian Resorts in the Nineteenth Century* (Carlton South: Melbourne University Press, 1999), p. 75. Admans was elected Mayor of Queenscliff nine times in 1876, 1877, 1878, 1879 and 1888. Drosken, pp. 2–3. He was married in 1854 to Fanny Maria Johnson and they had one daughter, Frances Elizabeth, born in Queenscliff in 1858. Admans had settled in the Queenscliff area as a young man and was originally a building contractor. He successfully tendered in 1857 to build quarters for Captain John Preston, the Signalmaster appointed in 1852 to the Point Lonsdale lighthouse. E. T. Raison, *Lighthouses at Port Phillip Heads* (Point Lonsdale: Queenscliff Historical Publications, 1997), p. 12.

[3]   Wife of A. L'Espinasse Martin, Receiver and Paymaster at the Receipt and Pay Office, Chiltern.

[4]   Charles Riley, a carrier at Chiltern, married Elizabeth née Horrigan in 1861.

[5]   Probably Conrad Grundmann.

[6]   Catherine Lechmere née McGill, married to Henry Lechmere.

[7]   'The insolvency of Jean Francis Soule, farmer and miner, Chiltern—debts, £350 8s 4d; assets £95; deficiency £255 8s 6d. Causes of insolvency: Losses in mining as an operative miner and losses in mining speculation; also want of water to carry on his business as a tanner in consequence of the drought.', *FS*, 17 February, 1877, p. 2. Jean Francois Soule married to Louise née Dorrotte (c.1828–1904). They had five children between 1858 and 1878.

[8]   Henry Arthur Tomkins was described by a correspondent as 'a mining shark'. 'H. A. Tomkins & the Golden Bar Affair', *FS*, 16 April, 1877, p. 2.

[9]   Dr John Ignatius Bleasdale (1822–1884), Catholic clergyman, born in Lancashire; emigrated to Victoria in 1851 when he was appointed to the Geelong and Colac mission; transferred to St Francis's Seminary; seminary moved to Eastern Hill at St Patrick's College in 1855. His interest in and contribution to scientific studies in Victoria was considerable; he was a founder member of the Melbourne Microscopical Society, Fellow of Geographical and Linnean Societies, honorary member of the Medical Society of Victoria, member of the Royal Society of Victoria. His public appointments included the boards of the Melbourne Public Library, Museum and National Gallery, Denominational Schools Board, and the Central Board of Health. As Inspector-General of schools and orphanages, he was influential in the development of the Education Bill of 1867 and the Act of 1872. He served a term as Private Secretary to Bishop James Alipius Goold (1812–1886) in the 1870s and was appointed Chancellor of the Archdiocese of Melbourne in 1874. A connoisseur of colonial wines, he wrote extensively about the health benefits of moderate imbibing. His health having deteriorated in 1877, he retired and was recuperating in Queenscliff when WLR met him in August. They would have known each other through their membership of the Yorick Club. Bleasdale left Victoria later in 1877 for San Francisco, where he died in 1884.

[10] Doma Mungi Mine.

217 [From WLR in Queenscliff to MR in Chiltern]

Queenscliffe

Friday Eveng [31 August 1877]

My dearest Love

You cannot get this before Monday morning & I hope to get one from you before that. I sent you this morning a letter containing a lot of bills that I never could get in. I want you to copy out on rough paper John Tanners[1] acct & I will make it out, & send it, he is earning wages now, & will doubtless pay. Can you give any news about the reef at Lamberts? ask Mr Piper[2] about Hornes reef—I hope you may get in the bad bills. With Rileys they would make another £12—I put up at Admans last night & went about this morning to look for apartments the first 3 or 4 asked £2–2–0 but after a while I found one at 25/- including my washing. The rooms were small & poorly furnished–but M[r] Johnson came & took me to a M[rs] Keans where Father Bleasedale is staying–nice rooms clean & sweet & only 30/- per week including washing. So you see I am favored so far; lovely situation looking out on the Sea near the lighthouse.

We had WC Smith[3] here today opening the public school & a feast for 280 children buns, sausage rolls, oranges £20 collected: Wilkinson[4] & the Scots parson[5] spoke. Most people are introduced to me & they say they are glad to see me. Wilkinson says if I keep a horse & ride round the district & go over to Sorrento two or three times weekly there is about £400 a year to be done. Others tell me D[r] Barker[6] will not go out at night. He has the clubs & they must give him 3 mo[nth]s notice. There certainly are no poor people about, but there does not appear to be any sickness. about I suppose by waiting 6 mos. matters would arrange themselves so as to give me a little settled income. Of course it would be an easy life, & we could take a house here, & perhaps fill it with boarders—that is to say if we could get a house which I doubt. I will look about next week & see how the land lies, & tell you more.

Of course we would decide on nothing hastily or before October end—Most medicos who come here, end by getting muddled with liquor, & one D[r] Roberts[7] not only got drunk & neglected his patients but left heavily in debt paying no one. I suppose it is the solitude that compels drives them to alcohol. Dont forget to send me the Port wine book by post. Lee[8] has gone to Bethanga

You need not be afraid of the people knowing I am here. I never got a wink of sleep till early morn—from taking a cup of tea at Admans late on arrival—I have just opened the tin box, my darling & I have shewed the cakes to my landlady. I enjoyed your sandwiches going to Melb. & now shall think of you at dinner. Will still hope to get a letter Saturday. D[r] Bleasdale is a most interesting companion—

W.C. Smith made a most wretched ungrammatical speech   Love to all I hope the darlings are well & that Josephine keeps free—we only get our letters 5 P.M. & the mail leaves 9 A.M. —God bless you & keep you safe for| Your affect Husband
        WLR
Send down the book by M[rs] Graham. Also get from M[r] Wendt tobacconist 2 long sticks of D[r] Richardson own tobacco. I cannot get it anywhere else & it suits me as it is so mild it is 2/- a stick & the two will last me 6 months—put them both in one parcel & Graham will leave them at the Yorick for me
        Text: ALS NLA MS133/1/237

[1]   John Tanner was the proprietor and licensee of the Hotel de Paris, Conness Street East, Chiltern.
[2]   Charles Godfrey Piper who married Bessie Selina Francis in 1879. They had a son born in Chiltern in 1881 (Boyd Winsborrow Piper) and a daughter (Vera Tutty Piper) born in Melbourne in 1886.
[3]   William Collard Smith (1830–1894), appointed Minister of Public Instruction twice: from 21 May 1877 to 5 May 1880 and from 3 August 1880 to 9 July 1881 (when he was also Minister of Mines). He was appointed Treasurer on 27 December 1878. Born in 1838 at Bollington, Cheshire, England, he emigrated to Victoria in 1852 and died 20 October 1894 in Brunswick, Melbourne. He would have been well known to WLR and MR as he settled in Ballarat in 1855, after a short period as gold miner, as a land agent and auctioneer. He was a member of West Ballarat Council from 1856 and Chairman of the borough in 1860 and 1861. During his period as Minister, Collard Smith dictated building policy. Between the years 1877

and 1879, ten country schools were established by the Minister without recommendations of the departmental officials and seven other schools were built contrary to recommendations. His and other Ministers' use of political patronage led to the Public Service Act 1883.

4   The Reverend Henry John Wilkinson, Anglican parish priest at Queenscliff for thirty-six years from 1863, father of Edwin Stanley (b. 1865), with whom HHR became friends and whom she visited in 1889 at St Catharine's College, Cambridge, where he was studying prior to taking Holy Orders. See *MWY*, p. 71.

5   The Presbyterian church was opened in 1862 and the first resident clergyman was the Reverend Donald Smith Brunton. He married his first wife, Margaret Lang née Nicholson, in 1871. She died in 1875, aged twenty-one, after the birth of her third baby, who died aged twelve days. Her two previous babies had also died when they were only weeks old. In 1877, Brunton married his second wife, Johanna Paterson née Barnet. They had three sons and one daughter who all survived their infancy.

6   Dr Thomas Barker (1804–1894) was vaccinator at Queenscliff in 1877. MD (Edinburgh, 1829). *AMJ*, 1877, p. 223. He died at Lorne aged eighty-nine, on 7 April 1894. *AMJ*, 1894, no. 13, p. 217. See *FRM III*, p. 267.

7   Dr William Robert Roberts (*c.*1840–1877) was Health Officer at Queenscliff and also vaccinator in 1876. *AMJ*, 1876, p. 308.

8   Daniel Lees, a miner, who became prominent in community and mining issues in Bethanga from 1878. June Philipp, *A Poor Man's Diggings: Mining and Community at Bethanga, Victoria 1875–1912* (Melbourne: Hyland House, 1987), pp. 58, 67, 120–121.

218   [From WLR in Queenscliff to MR in Chiltern]

Queenscliffe

Monday [3 September 1877]

My darling Marie

My telegrams doubtlessly surprised you I have taken a splendid house in a fine, high, dry, situation. It contains 8 rooms, kitchen, boiler, & washhouse. S̶u̶ with surgery, & side door It belongs to Dʳ Williams[1] he lived there—Every one tells me I shall do £300 a year; our house money will give £100 & we can get £2–2. to £2–10 for boarders per week in the season. we can let three rooms & have a common table. Try & induce Mary to come & offer a rise of wages, say 15/- a week. Mʳˢ Keane tells me they are difficult to be got. Of course we will require new carpets so you can arrange about the old <u>worn</u> ones. The drawing room about 18 x 15: the dining room about 16 x 15 & bedrooms of <u>tremendous</u> size. I must either have taken this, or smaller ones at <u>same price</u> & not near so good. I am told there is a tremendous rush here & I feared I could not get any house at all—This was the <u>only</u> one unfurnished.

Dʳ Bleasedale has taken a great fancy to me, & he & Keane my landlord have been <u>running about</u> looking for a house, & I closed this morning from the 1ˢᵗ of October or <u>sooner</u> if the house is ready & <u>you</u> are ready—The garden back & front is to be done up & other things done—It is in excellent repair inside marble piece in drawing room tank, boiler & wash house safe old—lawn in front & facing the East. I called on the parson & asked him if he knew anything <u>against</u> the house. He said I had got an excellent bargain This will make a freind of Dʳ Williams & we will once more be among civilization, & away from bark huts. <u>Thank God</u>! every thing happens for the best & our fortune may improve, & this be the turning point. Of course you will bring as much as you can with you—Try & get Ned[2] to arrange, or McCulloch's[3] agent at Chiltern unfortunately that is "Fred Nickless"[4]—but he will do if you cannot find another; you had better send for Peter[5] at the German carpenters as Maclachlan[6] is never at Chiltern: ask Frederickson[7] his charge & you had better get them both father & son. I am sure If you are satisfied of course that our good things <u>which are worn</u> would fetch a <u>fair</u> price we might let them go. You could put a reserve on them, & if they did not bring that from which the expense of carriage should be added deducted they should come. Say a reserve of £20 on the dining room, carriage & packing £4—If they dont bring £16–0–0 they should not go—No furniture can be bought here. All must come down in the steamer—

The Piano of course you will put a reserve of £60–0–0 carriage £5–0–0. If it does not bring £60 or £55 you can bring it. Mrs G. will say if you can replace it in Melb. or get an "Aucher Freres" for £60 which the tuner told me is much <u>better suited for the</u> climate so I should put a reserve on it of only £55. £60 guineas Auchers stands the heat better.

I enclose letter from Tovell D^r this decided me I should hardly think he will come <u>now:</u> I was delighted to hear of Dear Josephine. How nice it will to have them here & for you to go to Sorrento. Send <u>immediately</u> about the accounts, for if the Chiltern people get wind about the auction, they will <u>never pay a</u> farthing—What terms with Porch?[8]

I am much better since I came here—Eyes <u>quite right,</u> the other thing <u>gone,</u> free & open from pills; appetite good & yet no bathroom. Mrs Keane gives me a tub every morning & of course in summer I shall jump in to the sea & the darlings can bathe. I have heard them say "they love it." I am sure all this will be better than Clunes a place of dust & dirt & poverty—there is no dust here, & <u>no</u> poor persons—Splendid turn out of children on Friday 289 stuffed with buns sausage rolls, & tea & oranges. It was the opening of the new State School by WC Smith, & a mess he made of his speech. Excuse the scribble but I am late for the post, & I am anxious you should get this Tuesday afternoon

Love to M^{rs} G to the darlings, to Josephine, kind regards to Miss Fenton, & a thousand kisses to your dear self

Wont you all be delighted to get away from that hole & its back-biting people—This good news ought to make you <u>strong & well</u> before you meet me; I know the change will tell on the darlings & yourself when you get peace of mind—

I returned the spectacles & paid in £2–10 to make up the £50. Did the Bank send you deposit receipt—

You had better sell the pig at <u>once</u> I suppose the wood will be sold & all the things I got from Hancock Pig trough, hen coop rabbit hutch

There is an old large Col. [colonial] oven in the kitchen here—you must get the range in, or get Porch to agree exchange when he leaves—Give my kind love to Mrs Porch. Thank her for all her attention to you—

Find about Hornes Reef from Piper—I must forfeit my shares if no shew—write him a note & get a written answer or ask Mrs Horne—If you can bring the wine do so; drink the Brandy with the red seal <u>badly corked</u>—but save the other if any

It is raining now, Monday and

It has been wet & cold all yesterday, gales but inclined to clear. Old Bleasedale is a fine old man an enthusiast in all sciences, can preach a sermon on every thing.

Wont the darlings enjoy the Cliff.

I left a pamphlet on wines—try & save it if you can—Also find my card plate & send it by Post to Purtons. <u>This is important</u> as I want to put it in the Sorrento Hotels & Portsea & other places|Your affect Husband

    W.L.R.

Text: ALS NLA MS133/1/228 and MS 133/1/258

1   Dr David John Williams (1819–1902) may have met WLR in Ballarat in the early 1850s. Born in Glamorganshire, Wales, he studied medicine in England and Scotland: MRCS (England, 1841); FRCS (1861); LSA (London, 1845); MD (St Andrews, 1848). He first visited Sydney in August 1844 as Surgeon-Superintendent aboard the *Templar*. Joining the Russian service, he became medical attendant to the Czar Nicholas on summer cruises aboard the yacht *Victoria*, and in the winter months was attached to the hospital at St Petersburg. The Czar presented him with the Order of St Anne, when Williams left his service. Arriving in Victoria as Surgeon-Superintendent on the *Bride* in May 1853, he was posted in September 1853 to the Quarantine Station at Point Nepean. After Dr Heise's resignation in 1854, Williams was appointed District Surgeon and transferred to Ballarat. During that eventful year, Williams conducted the inquest into James Scobie's death in October 1854 and he tended the wounded from the Eureka Stockade uprising in December. The position of District Surgeon being abolished in December 1854, Williams remained as Coroner until 23 March 1855, when he resigned and took a trip to England. On his return, he settled in Queenscliff where he became the Health Officer at the Heads until his retirement. Bowden, pp. 76–77, 119. The house, which WLR leased from Dr Williams, was a single-storey timber dwelling with a slate and iron roof and nine rooms, on a large block of land in Mercer Street (now numbered 26). When the Queenscliff Borough was created on 12 May 1863, elections for the first Municipal Council were held. Dr Williams was elected with four others (Messrs Craig, Pagan, Wright and Dr Alexander Robertson) and at the council's first meeting it was Dr Williams who was elected Mayor of Queenscliff. (Dr Alexander Philadelphia Lamb Robertson, who died in 1878 aged forty-seven, was the uncle of HHR's school and lifelong friend, Mary Kernot née Robertson. Robertson, the first Health Officer in Queenscliff, built his house at 28 Mercer Street, next-door to Dr Williams.)

2   Edward Harold Bailey (1828–1893), MR's brother, who was living at Wodonga. He must have offered to assist MR in the move.

3   William McCulloch & Co., carriers based at Melbourne, Ballarat and Sandhurst.

4   Frederick Edward Nickless (*c.*1849–1908), son of Enoch Nickless and Elizabeth née Pardoe. Fred married Margaret McLaren Hood in 1870 and they had six children between 1870 and 1888. His brother, Henry Nickless, was an important man in Chiltern. Henry, a miner and one of the first settlers in the Chiltern area, was elected a councillor in the first Municipal Council of Chiltern in 1862. He was the manager of two important Chiltern Mining Companies: Doma Consoles Company and the Doma Mungi Tribute Company. During 1877, the miners of Chiltern gave Nickless a memorable tribute when they drew his buggy from the railway station to the Commercial Hotel and presented him with an address and expressed their highest confidence in him, despite recent troubles in the mine.

5   Peter Fredericks, son of Heinrich Fredericks. See endnote 7.

6   Robert McLachlan, carpenter at Chiltern; was married to Elizabeth née Smith. They had seven children born between 1857 and 1870, the last five of whom were born in the Chiltern area.

7   Heinrich Fredericks (*c.*1801–1883) and his son described themselves as carpenters, builders and cabinet makers and their business was in Conness Street West, next to the Albion Hotel, Chiltern. 'Beg to inform the Public of the above township that they are prepared to execute orders for ... all articles manufactured by the carpenter & cabinet maker, at MODERATE PRICES, and with QUICK DESPATCH.' *FS*, 8 July 1876, p. 1.

8   George Portch (*c.*1830–1902), owner of the Chiltern Flour Mill, who was negotiating with MR about the lease of 'Lake View'.

219   [From WLR in Queenscliff to MR in Chiltern]

Queenscliffe

Septr 4. 1877 [Tuesday]

My dear Marie

You did well with the dining room suite. You had better sell every thing if you can get such prices The dining table ought to go it is not an oval table & it cost £9. at Harrisons,[1] look on the file. Then my book case cost £5–5. I should get the Fredericksons father & son & let them varnish the drawing room sofa.

Copy out John Tanners acct <u>the whole page</u> & I will select his acct unpaid and I will recopy it & send it to you, he ought to pay as he is in work–The weather here is bleak and cold. Do not forget about my card plate and I also want my gate plate–

The earth closet nuisance is likely to turn up again a man asked 5/- a week. I hear that Jakins[2] of Ballt is coming. A Wesleyan who preaches on Sunday—

This is rather hard after my taking the house, but I hardly believe it. I have been obliged to put an advertisement[3] in the Argus—

I wrote to Towle.[4] The mining market is in a fearful state. I cannot get some scrip from Nixon. Thank God I cleared out of Patricks[5] they are down to £2–1–0 Every thing unsaleable!

The chemist says he will arrange about the closet for 2/6 a week—This & every thing will be right if we can only get our house furnished: the season & the rush begins on the 1st October. and with 3 large Rooms & 4 middling ones it will be hard if you cannot get £10 a week during the season: for if another doctor comes no dependance can be placed on practice.

I hope you are sending out the accounts and that they are coming in better. You had better put an advertisement in the Standard I think—I find it very difficult to get to sleep I hope you do not lie awake: You had better pack me a box with my books—only send Braithwait from 1869. leave the others. Also splints, bandages & instruments

No word from Ham. I am afraid he will charge for his interference I agreed for alterations up to £15. & I consider the house to be £50 better by them. Send my books & brass door plate & my card plate, as soon as you can with comfort.

I will tell you when the house is ready to receive anything of course there will have to be new carpets, but they need <u>not </u>be the <u>best </u>as the rooms are so huge. druggetting or matting at the sides—Another reason for selling the table is that it is not large enough if we take boarders—and it cost £9 at Harrisons I should let my bookcase go—You never told me what you got from Porch for the 10 months to run—You had better arrange to stay at M^{rs} Gr^s a week & you can send on the furniture as you buy it in small lots. I believe the freight by steamer is 8/- per ton so you see you save packing & the railway charges to Melbourne besides the wear & tear ~~& p~~ & get new furniture. Every one takes boarders here & there is no disgrace

Milk is a 6^{d} quart

The out mail from this closes 9 am & 5 PM.: only one comes in at 5.30 PM: just after the the [sic] Melb. mail leaves by the Steamer. I do not think I have any thing else to say except that I hope Josephine keeps well & still does without medicine that the darlings are well & that you are not killing yourself with hard work

Your letters posted by the afternoon mail reach me by the steamer next eveng & mine posted 5PM get to you 2.30 PM—|With much love to all| Your loving | Hubby

W

Text: ALS NLA MS133/1/236 and MS133/1/254

1   Harrisons & Sons, furniture dealers, 8 Little Collins Street East.
2   William Vosper Jakins, MRCS (England, 1858), LSA (London, 1859), from Ballarat, was registered by the Medical Board in 1867. He was married to Charlotte née Arthur and they had six children between 1877 and 1887, one of whom died as an infant.
3   See Letter 228, endnote 1.
4   Dr Frederick William Towle (1818–1892), MRCS (England, 1840), married on 3 January 1850 in the Wesleyan Church, Geelong, to Maria Kirkpatrick née White. They had three sons born in Geelong: Charles Frederick (b. 1851), Edward Percival (b. 1855) and William Bentley (b. 1857).
5   Prince Patricks Mine at Stawell.

220 [From WLR in Queenscliff to MR in Chiltern]

[Queenscliff]
[Wednesday, 5 September 1877]

[Pages 7 and 8 of a letter]

 It has been bitterly cold Sunday & Monday I had a good night for the first time

 D^r G was to pay in £20 & £17 last week I paid in the £2–10 for the glasses & made it up to £50 I thought as we were making a fresh start that I had better keep a little ready money in the Bank until we saw an income.

 Of course there is nothing yet, but I expect to get the clubs by Xmas & the acting health officers billet after young Macfarlane[1] leaves then there is sure to be sickness when the visitors arrive. I have not seen Dr Williams yet. I called on Mrs W.[2] but the house appears to be shut up. I told you milk was 6^d Butter 1/4 Beef 7^d & 8^d Mutton by the side 3/- Bread 8^d.

 Where did you put my ring with the stone loose I cannot find it—

 Give my best love to all I suppose the weather is getting hot and you ought to be getting some peas & beans & cabbages soon.

 Are the hens laying better? The mirror as it is now is valueless but if repaired will be good as ever| Your loving Husband

  W.

I have got a little giddiness come over me to day

 Text: ALS NLA MS133/1/256

1 Dr William Henry Macfarlane, MD (Edinburgh), had worked in Ballarat after his registration as a medical practitioner in 1855. He had been Honorary Medical Officer at the Ballarat Hospital from 1860 to 1862. He returned to London in 1879, leaving his father, Dr John Macfarlane (*c.*1807–1880), who died in Queenscliff on 11 July 1880.
2 Jane Walters Williams née Voss (*c.*1836–1890).

221 [From WLR in Queenscliff to MR in Chiltern]

[Queenscliff]
Thursday morning [6 September 1877]

[No salutation]

 I had written the letter Sept 4 before I got yours: of course I have declined to sign the agree as you seemed to wish it! I again think that I am not able for Clunes Graham said so. My poor head wd soon give way & having to provide for a substitute after 4 hours would simply be ruin—The attending on 400 men & half the number of women besides the average of 3 or 4 children, the night work the exposure to the heat, the having to keep horse man & buggy—are all serious questions. It is very easy to go there & attempt it & if I break down there will be no saving money. I cannot do impossibilities, & I feel that I am an old broken down man. Of course all were surprised. Dr Bleasedale said I was wrong It was not the Cliff that would support me it was the entire district; that a competent man had never settled here before & that it would soon become known; Revd Wilkinson says there is a good population at Drysdale 5 or 6 miles off. Mrs Keane said I need have no fear, that members of Lodge would much prefer a private family that there was sure to be sickness when the visitors came & would pay what you liked that they never had a sober med.^{l} man & that I had only to wait a few months & I would find she was right".

There is no doubt that Towle will be here now & will <u>jump at it</u> & I consider your decision most unfortunate

I have not [been] well at all for the few days the old pain & swelling & your letters keep me from sleeping. You must excuse my writing for some days as I dont feel able & my old <u>head</u> ache & giddiness. I feel that I should not have left home to fall sick among strangers—

I generally have to write my letters twice over owing to the mistakes, so do not expect so many. It was your writing that Porch wanted the house by the <u>24</u>th that misled me, & to find now that nothing is going to come of it. I thought it better to have a place for you & the furniture & children at once & I made sure that Porch would have given you nearly the rent of the house here! I will reply to my little darlings letters in a few days I had written all about the Cliff & the sea to Ettie, but it is no use now.| Yours.

      W.

I'll take no other house until you come yourself—Am sorry you did not see to the bad debts before—there will be little chance now if the good ones come in so slowly. I put an advertisement in the Argus by the advice of my landlord which you will see Thursday & 3 succeeding Saturdays. I thought it better to lose no time. It will be a quiet practice & there would be no risk of breaking down by over work as at Clunes: the one would lead to strength the other to the Benevolent asylum—

Why dont you ask Mrs Graham

I am getting quite stiff after sitting a little while—my old enemy seems come back pain in one knee—after the late rain—Another reason against Clunes is that I am <u>not</u> well up in Surgery: I know no one there to <u>consult</u> with & that I should be all alone & have to pay for any consultations

You had better telegraph on receipt of this if you wish this place sacrificed or not. If you want the house given up or not <u>Yes or No</u>

    Text: ALS NLA MS133/1/232

222   [From WLR in Queenscliff to MR in Chiltern]

Queenscliffe

Sept 6. [1877, Thursday]

Dear Marie

I have concluded that in spite of my debility I had better not conclude about this place until I see if I get Clunes. If I do I had better ~~to~~ go there alone for 3 months & if I find I cannot overtake the work I must give it up. This will be the best thing to do & we then can but come to Queenscliffe—

When did the Secretary say the election would take place? There are six lodges I see, he could not say how many members—

I have just been offered one lodge of 48 members 30/- each out of wh 8/- goes to the druggist—This would just pay the rent. Embling[1] told me he made in ~~the~~ one season £40. Old Macfarlane & his son[2] are still here & old Dr Barker—I have not succeeded in meeting Dr Williams. The Clunes is not so good for we could get no boarders & our expenses would therefore be much higher. Two horses man & buggy—

However I will say no more ~~We~~

I have not got Clunes yet & shall not build on it—but can only try it alone for 3 months & then give it up if I find things not to answer.

I shall have to go to Beechworth Oct 10 & if Porch is <u>not</u> going to take your house I think it is a pity that you should have the Sale so soon. I did not know this when I telegraphed—I concluded by your letter that you had an <u>immediate offer.</u> Do not write so again. It would have been better if you had remained quiet till Oct 10 as we decided at first I should not have rushed away I see no chance <u>now</u> of <u>our meeting</u> again, nor indeed of <u>our saving any money</u>—I do not consider this as the main object of life—comfort & ease & a moderate income are better fitted to induce happiness—I had written letter to Ettie about this place I cannot send it now.

On thinking the matter over carefully it appears best that I should try Clunes <u>if I get it.</u> Therefore do not telegraph

I will try Sea bathing as soon as ever the weather gets warmer Love to all| Your own
    W.

Text: ALS NLA MS133/1/234

¹   Dr William Henry Embling (1840–1912).
²   Dr John Macfarlane and Dr William Henry Macfarlane.

223 [From WLR in Queenscliff to MR in Chiltern]

Queenscliffe
Septr. 7. 1877 [Friday]

My darling Wifey

I am now quite reconciled to try Clunes; & if I do <u>not</u> get it will think it very hard after waiting so long. There is a small living to be made here if what every one says is true £50 from the lodges £40 or £50 from the office of acting health officer & some sickness in the season, besides Sorrento Portsea & Drysdale. Of course it would be supplemented by boarders & freinds would have to be told that we did <u>not</u> keep open house but could not pay our rent unless it was shared by visitors—I telegraphed this morning as I felt & indeed do feel now pretty bad with the old pain & swelling. If it does mend next week I certainly must go & see Graham again & perhaps come home. I wish I had not come but stayed until 10ᵗʰ October. The applications are to be sent in by 15 of this month—do you remember <u>when</u> the election is to take place. My head is bad. I am quite stupid at times. Young Macfarlane who has been acting health officer for 6 weeks, tells me he took during that time £2–2–0 & his father £4–4–0 of course there is nothing doing except in the season.

Give my kindest love to Mʳˢ Graham. I hope some of the accounts are coming in.

Dʳ Bleasdale is still here & as full of anecdote as ever. A young fisherman was drowned crossing Swan bay & leaves wife & family He says I am certain to do well if I can only wait six months. I will therefore tell them I am coming back. Dʳ Towle has declined to come now & I do not suppose anyone will, & with young Macfarlane away I shall hope to get the acting health officers billet—if we come here.

Give my dear love to the darlings| Your afft | Husband
    WLR

Text: ALS NLA MS133/1/233

224   [From WLR in Queenscliff to MR in Chiltern]

Queenscliffe
Saturday morng [8 September 1877]

My dear Wifey

I think under the circumstances it will be the wisest thing for us to do to come here.
I shall not sign the agreement until I have seen Dr Williams & have his opinion. He is
expected from quar^e on Monday. Our income will be small but you and dear ones will be
much more comfortable even with a small income. Every thing is not dearer. I told you I had
written to Solomon about the mirror—Tell me when it is packed & sent off Solomon & Co
Furniture dealers Swanston St. I suppose I must wait patiently here I am a little better this
morng I am going to take nothing but porridge until the pain & swelling abate & go away.
When is the sale to be. Has Porch taken the house. I am sorry the accts have not come in
better dont hurry away until you are compelled. Towle is not coming now. This will be a
comfortable home for you & the children if the income be small—

Everyone cannot be wrong & every[one] says there is a living to be made Dr Barker is an
awfully ignorant old man he doses the people with Calomel[1] & orders most expensive
medicines

Young Macfarlane the assistant health officer is going away & his father is not much

Love to all. You will I suppose stay in Melbourne for a week or two & arrange about the
furniture coming if I decide after seeing Williams. You will I suppose ~~store~~ get Ned to forward
the things ~~& stor~~

I will have the house ready as soon after I decide as I can.| Your affect Hub.
    W.L.R.

I have told the people I shall not decide until after October 10th

    Text: ALS NLA MS133/1/249 and MS133/1/257

---

[1]   Calomel, a purgative, derived from a compound of mercury, sulphuric acid, and chloride of
    sodium, first mentioned by Crollius in the seventeenth century; the first directions for its
    preparation were given in 1600s by the Beguines, a congregation of nuns, who were first
    established in Liège and tended the sick in Belguim and Germany.

225   [From WLR in Queenscliff to MR in Chiltern]

Queenscliffe
Sunday [9 September 1877]

My dearest M.

I am so grieved that you should be so annoyed & worried. What a good thing it is that
Mrs Graham is with you. You will have to write to the people in the country if they do not pay.
Drop a line to OBrien schoolmaster Barnawartha Hunter. I should post a note to one every
day. There will be a lot left behind if you dont.

I am sorry about the Porchs I dont believe they want the house after all You are quite
right to sell all the furniture you can & save Railway fare. I can replace them in Melbourne I
hope it will be as good a sale as our two last.

I think this will be better than Clunes as more comfortable for all of us. D^r W comes
ashore tomorrow & I shall see him & get his opinion. I have accepted the Club £55. They

give a monthly notice. Every body says I will do well, that there has never been a sober man here before. Time will shew.

I am very sorry to hear about poor Josephine I thought her recovery was only temporary. I am very grieved to hear of Miss Fenton It is a poor return for our selecting her from 20 others Of course a little slap will not hurt anybody but it will only make them dislike her She is too young & too well paid & has no control over them—She should not tell lies to her mother. Six months engagement is too long. One months notice is quite ~~noti~~ enough.

The most beautiful church in Victoria[1] & capital choir here

Please put on 2^d stamp & post the City bank book. You had better get the door plate cleaned & taken down. I know the darlings will be delighted with the place if I can only make a living

No word from Ham. I was very poorly indeed Thursday but am thankful to say better in every respect today. I am certain I would not be able for hard lodge work & night work. I hope dear you will not mind taking boarders; old Mr Johnson says he will be changing soon, & gave a hint that he would like to be in a family I think he pays 30/- a week but then he is permanent. Thank Mcleery[2] from me for his attention. I will not leave this my darling do not be uneasy. I must have been wrong in my head when I telegraphed. I did not telegraph on receipt as I knew my letters would reach you & it would cause excitement I will have the house thro^{ly} cleaned & washed out.

Did the N. N. Clunes[3] div. come. If so send the cheque to me here. The city Bank is only one we have two others—I keep that for the Building Societys acct. I think Dr Bleasedale might come & live with us too He pays 35/- & has been here some months.

Rain again last night & today. Have you had much: Make M. take off the upper part of the water pipe—I must see Dr Williams as soon as he arrives & find out if he recommends the cliff as much as he did six months ago. If he does I think I may venture to sign the agreement—

Be very careful to pack <u>all</u> my instruments. I have left my Hypodermic Syringe & speculum behind me Bring the inkstands & ornaments & my card board & pasteboard

Dr Bleasedale enjoys my wine very much. He tells a nice story about the Baron.[4] It seems that some years ago a German under gardener named Wilhemi[5] ~~your to~~ sent home to England for a complete & expensive work on Botany & Horticulture. When it arrived the Baron insisted either that poor Wilhemi should sell the book to the Baron or leave the service. ~~Wil~~ He would not have his under gardener studying science Ultimately the book was sold to the government & poor Wilhemi got rid of—Dr Bleasdales stories of the old Melb. identities would fill a volume—He has given me receipts for drivg bugs & fleas out of the house The whole history of the Aspinal[6] & Beaney case[7] & LL Smiths[8] trial for murder—He has taught how to list wine & there is no subject except Med^e on which he cannot deliver a lecture

Frightful gales here.

It is a cold place in winter altho there is no frost. They will want all their warm things if this continues

Love to all. It is blowing so hard that I do not think Dr W. will be able to come across to day—I am keeping better thank God.

Good bye dearest. do not be so worried, all will I hope be well yet.| Your loving Hubby

W

Rowe should be written to

Text: ALS NLA MS133/1/223, MS133/1/224 and MS133/1/225

[1] St George the Martyr Anglican Church, Queenscliff, built of limestone, locally quarried, and opened for worship on Sunday, 7 February 1864. Bishop Charles Perry dedicated the church on 3 October 1867 and consecrated it on 7 January 1868. The cost of the building was £1800 without the chancel and tower, both of which were added later. It is a perfect example of Early English Gothic architecture with special features of comparative lightness, long narrow, lancet-shaped windows, pointed arches, supported on slender and lofty pillars and (externally) boldly projecting buttresses and an acutely pitch roof. The first priest in charge of the church as a separate parish was the Reverend Henry John Wilkinson, who remained the parish priest for thirty-six years.

[2] Alec McCleery, Chiltern auctioneer, organised the sale of the Richardsons' furniture on 22 September 1877 at 'Lake View'.

[3] New North Clunes mining shares.

[4] Baron Sir Ferdinand Jakob Heinrich von Mueller (1825–1896), Government Botanist, who was known personally to WLR. He was born on 30 June 1825 in Rostock, Mecklenburg-Schwerin, the only son of Frederick Mueller, Commissioner of Customs, and his wife, Louise née Mertens. Having been awarded a PhD in 1847 for his extensive research and impressive herbarium by the University of Kiel, his ill-health required that he should live in a warmer climate. He and his two sisters set sail for Adelaide, arriving on 15 December 1847. While working as an assistant chemist, he continued his botanical studies, including writing papers for the Linnean Society in London. In 1852 Mueller went to Melbourne and the following year Lieutenant-Governor La Trobe appointed him Government Botanist. His research on Victorian vegetation was extensive and he sent duplicate specimens of all species to Kew. He was appointed Commissioner for the Melbourne Exhibition in 1854 and botanist to the North-West Australia Expedition in July 1855, exploring country between Sydney to Moreton Bay. Returning to Melbourne in January 1857, he was appointed Director of the Botanical Gardens. He published *Fragmenta Phytographiae Australiae* in twelve parts over 1858–1882. Criticism of his directorship of the Gardens emerged in the late 1860s, and in 1873 he was replaced as director by William Robert Guilfoyle (1840–1912), who was a member of the Yorick Club. Mueller remained as Government Botanist without loss of salary but the injustice he felt at the dismissal was so great that he never entered the Gardens again. In 1871 he was appointed a hereditary Baron by the King of Württemberg, although he was a naturalised Australian. He died on 10 October 1896 in South Yarra. His fictional counterpart is Baron von Krause in *FRM*.

[5] In WLR's Scrapbook there is a letter to the Editor of *The Argus* on Australian plants from Carl Wilhelms, Botanical Gardens, Melbourne, dated April 1857. NLA MS133/1/293.

[6] Butler Cole Aspinall (1830–1875), barrister, journalist, politician and wit. Son of the Reverend James Aspinall and sister of Clara Aspinall who wrote *Three Years in Melbourne* (1862). See next endnote for case.

[7] James George Beaney (1828–1891), surgeon, politician and philanthropist; born in Canterbury, England; while studying medicine in 1852 in Edinburgh decided to migrate to Victoria because of his poor health (possibly tuberculosis); lived with John Hood, MLC, and worked in his chemist shop; returned to England 1853 as surgeon on the *Barrackpore*; qualified at Edinburgh (MRCS, 1855); assistant surgeon to the 3rd Regiment, serving in Gibraltar, and at the Crimean War—these appointments were the subject of satirical comment and a libel case (not the case referred to by WLR) *Beaney v. Fitzgerald* in 1863. After the war, he returned to Europe, studied venereology in Paris, visited America and finally returned to Melbourne in 1857 and acquired the practice of Dr John Maund who died in 1858. He was elected an Honorary Surgeon to the Melbourne Hospital in 1860. His skills as a surgeon led him to perform hazardous operations. In four inquests on patients dying after surgery, he faced criticism of his competence. In three of these in 1875, the verdict was in his favour, but following an earlier inquest in 1866, he was charged with the murder of a barmaid, Mary Lewis, after an allegedly illegal operation. In this case (referred to by WLR), the first jury failed to agree but in the second trial, his counsel, Butler Cole Aspinall, successfully defended him. Beaney was a member of the Legislative Council for the North Yarra Province from 1883 to 1891. He was known for his flamboyant appearance (bedecked with diamond and ruby rings, studs and watch) and his personal habits (drinking champagne and port with staff and students and lavish hospitality). Love, pp. 127, 148–151, 188–190.

[8] Dr Louis Lawrence Smith (1830–1910), medical practitioner and politician. Migrating as ship's surgeon in the *Oriental*, he arrived in Melbourne in December 1852. After a brief time on the goldfields, he set up his practice in Bourke Street, Melbourne, in 1853 and by 1862 had expanded to include a museum of anatomy and the Polytechnic Hall. He advertised profusely,

spending £3000 a year by 1863. He became one of the leading disreputable and rich members of the medical fraternity with his friend Beaney and was regarded as Melbourne's leading abortionist (he was acquitted in 1858 of procuring an abortion). Elected as a representative in the Legislative Assembly (1859–1865) representing South Bourke; won Richmond in 1871, but defeated in 1874 when he opposed J. G. Francis's reform proposals. He continued to win and lose elections, as well as maintaining his medical practice, running model farms with pigs and sheep, a racehorse stable at Emerald Hill and becoming an expert wine-maker with grapes from his own vines. His first wife, Sarah Ann Taylor by whom he had ten children, died in 1882. By his second wife, Marion Jane Higgins, he had four children, one of whom, Louise (1884–1962), a pianist, founded the Lyre-bird Press in 1932 and was at PLC. HHR and Mary Kernot commented about her in their correspondence. Love, pp. 80, 149–151, 188–190.

226 [From WLR in Queenscliff to MR in Chiltern]

Queenscliffe
Monday [10 September 1877]

My darling Marie

I have seen D\u02b3 Williams.[1] I said I thought of taking his house if I could make a living here. He said I could do £500 a year that he was glad I had come—that I had lost £60– by not coming when he recommended me 4 months ago. The assistant health officer gets £2–2 a day—I am going to sign the agreement as I am now perfectly satisfied that we shall be comfortable & happy & as I said our luck is about to turn. I posted letter this morning to you the mail leaves every morng at 9. The house is to be throughly cleaned, the garden done up & the kitchen range built anew—

D\u02b3 Williams has lived on the cliff for 20 years & he likes it better than other place & would not exchange it. He asked after you. I am so happy & relieved of ~~the~~ a great anxiety which has pressed on me since I came here. You will cheer up now, with our little we need have no fear, & we will add to them by degrees living among nice people and once more within the bounds of civilization; what a blessing for our darlings too to have associates of refined manners—You can send me down my box the first opportunity & the glass to Solomons. You will want another large Mirror & some looking glasses for the bedrooms & get the best of every thing; its cheapest in the long run. Try Harrisons he is the best in Melb. You can take his word he always treated us well

I will write to the Steamer as soon as you are able to tell me what you are going to bring. Anything by weight. Harrison must take the furniture to pieces & send a man here to put it together again—that will be the best way—but I will inquire if there is anyone here who will undertake it—The boat leaves now at 7 in the morning. I am going to buy a goat ~~1 each~~ as we have a splendid paddock & back orchard with grass 1 foot high. I see Ham is advertising the house in Saturdays Argus.[2] it is to be put up by auction Septr I shall chain the goat up & perhaps have 2.

We are getting fearful gales here| Your affect Hubby
         WLR

If you can do with £50 from me for the expenses of moving & new furniture. I think I can man[a]ge but if you get £35 from Porch & the sale brings £100 you wont want much
Monday evening

I have just got yours my darling—do not be so anxious or worry so much. Things will all be right if you do not make yourself ill—Offer the house to Porch for £35 for the remaining

10 months—That will be better than leaving it—Do not be in a hurry with the sale, it will be better for me here to <u>pay the October rent</u> for the house £4–4–0 than for you to leave £20 or <u>£30 of debts</u> behind you. You ought to be pleased that our prospects are brighter & that I am better do not mar our pleasure by making yourself ill—I have written to Graham altho I had nothing to write about

How could I answer chicks letters better when I was ill & could say nothing definite about this place I hope you are satisfied with what I recommend about Porch & the sale & the debts write to them the best of them if not paid this week

Love to all and for Gods sake cheer up Your affect |Hubby

Walter

Text: ALS NLA MS133/1/235 and MS133/1/250

[1]   'Queenscliff, Monday: Dr Williams returned from the Quarantine Station yesterday, and has relieved Dr W. H. Macfarlane, the acting health officer.' *Argus*, 11 September 1877, p. 2.

[2]   'C. J. & T. Ham received instructions from the owner to sell by PUBLIC AUCTION, at their rooms 45 Swanston-street on Thursday 27 Sept at twelve o'clock All that piece of land, having a frontage of 66ft to Burwood-road, Hawthorn, by a depth of 290ft, to a right of way off Glenferrie-road, on which is erected that well-built, commodious, and elegant FAMILY RESIDENCE containing on ground floor hall 7ft 6in wide, drawing 23 x 15.6, dining room 18 x 15.6, breakfast room 13 x 12, storeroom 12 x 6, kitchen & scullery & on 1st floor best bedroom 18 x 15.6 & four bedrooms 15.6 x 11.6 & two smaller bedrooms, bathroom, & dressing room with spacious balcony & verandah at front.' *Argus*, 8 September 1877, p. 2.

227 [From WLR in Queenscliff to MR in Chiltern]

Queenscliffe

Thursday morg [13 September 1877]

My darling Polly

You will have had mine telling you that I had arranged to take the house from the 1st of October You will have lots of time between your auction & the 9th of October when I must be off to Beechworth.

I enclose the form of endorsement I have every confidence in Mr Sammonds[1] but I fear he will never get the accounts in. I hope you will be easier in your mind now dear & will not fret so much

It is all past & done & you will soon be here now. Ham is offering on Thursday the 27 inst our house by auction. He told me he would put it up at £1700 & as he said £50 would cover all expenses I said I was prepared to take £1650. I hope you will sell all the furniture at good prices—I want a box packed with all my things as the books in a box by themselves, clothes & instruments &c door plate, card plate old ribbon box—

Drapers "Physiology". the Comic book,[2] the wine book the little science books on astronomy Physiology I never found my ring.

Mrs Keane brought in an old servant of hers to recommend her. Fancy she was in the family way a widow. Mrs K. never noticed he it until I told her of it afterwards

Get Ned to manage the giving up the keys after you are ready to go.

I shall not get the man to put things right until the last week of this month I still intend to get a goat or two as there is splendid feed in this orchard & Dr Bleasedale advises me to get it cut into Hay—I am much better & can eat again without pain. Thank Mʳˢ Graham for her Kindness. I hope & trust she wont desert you until you are clear of the place.

Hadnt Dʳ Bleasdale & I a laugh about the event recorded on the preceding page.[3] You had better order a lot of matting for the bedrooms & some of the sitting rooms as they are of immense size, we have it in the room I am sitting in. It can be taken up occasionally—If we get a house full we will require more than one. 10/- a week is the regular thing—The Russians have had their first victories and a great & final battle is impending—I am afraid poor Turkey is going to be conquered at last and the great flag will have to be bought[4]

Did you read an account of the loss of the great Queensland ship that left Engla[nd] in 1876 with 2 tons of OConnors powder on board 33 passengers & 16 crew, OConnors name by [was] mentioned[5]—It seems there was ignorance & villainy in the manufacture of it & it was liable to explode at any moment owing to its being bad. There is no doubt that the ship exploded Poor OConnor the firm has smashed & is ruined. We had fine rain. I hope we will get into the house soon & that you will have a house full.[6] We can try & get another servant

I hope you will try & get better & not lie awake all night that does no good. There are very nice neighbours next to us One takes boarders & the other family is highly spoken of by Dʳ Bleasdale who describes them as very nice—Does Mcleerie think it is going to be a good sale—

I sent that letter to Melb by private hands on Saturday as there was no mail from this before Monday—

The Sandhurst lottery off tomorrow 13ᵗʰ—We have a bank here[7]

Love to all try to get better—| Your affect Hubby

    W.L.R.

Text: ALS NLA MS133/1/230

[1]   Joseph Edward Sammons (*c.*1834–1896) married to Charlotte née Brockwell. They had seven children between 1861 and 1882.

[2]   See Letter 14: WLR was probably referring to Gilbert Abbott A'Beckett, *The Comic History of England: with 20 Coloured Etchings and 200 Woodcuts* by John Leech (London: Bradbury, Evans & Co., 1848).

[3]   i.e. that the servant was pregnant and Mrs Keane did not realise it.

[4]   Russo-Turkish War continued from 24 April 1877 to 3 March 1878, during which Britain was supposed to be neutral. The Turkish Empire until 1878 included principalities of Moldavia and Wallachia, Servia, and Montenegro, the hereditary vice-royalty of Egypt, and Tunis. The population of the Empire in 1877 was 47,660,000. The population of Russia in 1877 was 86,952,347. The Turkish Sultan visited Queen Victoria in July 1867 and she, like WLR, was a supporter of the Turks against Russia. The Turks were defeated at Taghir, Armenia, on 16 June 1877 and then victors on 20 June at Zewin Dooz, Eshek-Khalian, Delibaba with the Russian forces retreating. The victories continued to see-saw between the two powers with the loss of many lives on both sides. During January 1878 the Russians advanced towards Constantinople, causing great panic and part of the British fleet was ordered to Constantinople to protect British lives and property. In February 1878, the British fleet entered the Dardanelles without permission from the Sultan. Treaty of peace was signed at San Stefano 3 March 1878 and ratified at St Petersburg on 17 March 1878.

[5]   An inquiry before Mr H. C. Rothery, the British Wreck Commissioner, had delivered its judgment on Saturday, 21 July 1877 on the disappearance of the *Great Queensland*, last heard from a few days after she set sail from an English port on 5 August 1876 bound for Melbourne. It was carrying impure patent gunpowder, ordinary gunpowder, and 569 persons on board; supposed to have exploded (pieces of the wreck were found), near Finisterre, after 12 August 1876. The verdict of the Wreck Commission was against the owners. (The Wreck Commission, a new court established to enquire into the causes of shipwrecks, first sat on 26 October 1876 and this was its first case.) Some of the gunpowder was for Mr O'Connor who was a friend of

MR and WLR from their Ballarat days. Report of the inquiry was in *The Argus*, 11 September 1877, p. 4.

6   i.e. a house full of boarders.

7   The first branch of the Bank of Victoria was established in Hesse Street, Queenscliff, in 1873.

228   [From WLR in Queenscliff to MR in Chiltern]

Queenscliffe
Friday [14 September 1877]

My Dear Mary

Send Drapers Physiology & put it on the top of the box so that I can get at it easily. On talking over the matter alluded to in my last with Mrs Keane I am inclined to think that I was wrong because M^{rs} K noticed it when she was in her service 6 mos. ago & 2^{ndly} because she rode in on horseback from Drysdale Dr Bleasdale moreover gives her such an excellent character that I have written to her & asked her to call & see you the first week in October. Mrs Keane says she expects to get out often when her work is done. Wages 10/- a week I suppose if we get boarders & she stays you would raise it in 6 months.

I thought of going over to Sorrento & Portsea but the weather is too rough It has been frightful all the ~~weather~~ time—This paper seems to be very greasy it will not carry the ink—Call at Purtons & get some ruled like this but better & 250 better envelopes better that this but not square

The people still blow about the fine practice I will get but I had not a single patient except old Johnson which was gratuitous—Mrs Martin should not be allowed to blow & Im afraid Williams is another However I tell the people I came here for a rest[1]—

Young Macfarlane does not go before Monday—I am leaving my apartments. The man has been drinking for nearly a fortnight & his wife in spite of all my remonstrances will send out for drink for him I told her today I could stand it no longer & I have moved to a place where there will be nothing of that sort—I never in all my life felt anything like the continued blow of the equinoctial gales all the week. The food here has been excellent but she only washed one shirt & that was dreadful do you remember how many shirts you put in. I hope truly this weather will not last for I had a twinge of my old enemy Rheum. today I put on 2 flannel shirts my red one & 2 pairs of flannel drawers I hope it will be warmer before you come or you will all be laid up—It blows all day & all night—No fishing a wreck off the jetty—& rainy constantly.

Love to all| Your loving hubby

W.L.R.

Text: ALS NLA MS133/1/231

1   WLR had inserted an advertisement in *The Argus*, which was printed on Saturday, 15 September 1877, under the heading 'Medical': 'QUEENSCLIFF—DR RICHARDSON having commenced practise, may be CONSULTED at his temporary residence, Gellibrand-street.'

229 [From WLR in Queenscliff to MR in Chiltern]

Queenscliffe
Wednesday [19 September 1877]

My darling Marie

Yours of Sunday came tonight. Have you got the medicine. I have cured many cases with it & among the rest my sister Lucinda who was very bad if you remember and who got relief—very soon she was delighted. It has no taste & should be continued until looseness & pain come then & then <u>one</u> drop a dose ought to be stopped—& 4 drops taken gradually dosing down to one drop but the case will be sure to be cured before that generally the 2nd week does it—Of course Mr Wain paid I wrote it before. I did not put down accounts opposite the names in the day book but on the days they were paid you may be certain I would have put down Wains name if it had not been paid. All right you had better let the box go with the rest, I do not see that it will cost less however. I know nothing of the plates they may turn up in some corner perhaps when the house is cleaned. I must get a new one at Purtons—Saturday is the best day for the country beg of him to put up a flag & to have the bell man.[1]

You will be too worried to see about the glass you had better get it packed as I wish & forwarded to Solomon & I will tell him to call at Spencer St. unless you are going with the luggage which you cannot do

You know the luggage & all the things are likely to be 4 days or a week on the road unless they are all put into one van: the freight for packages across in the Steamer is 10/- per 40 feet cubic measure. it was £2. coming from England. You had better come over after sending the chicks to Mrs Graham. The boat leaves ½ past 10

I think you might send me a box with the splints bandages, paste board & card board [illegible word] instruments & some books, any warm socks or flannels that I did not take with me as it is very cold here—Dr Williams has recommended me to open a little surgery at Sorrento & says it will be worth £200 a year. Try & send my card plate & door in the box. I will go over to Sorrento & Portsea the first fine day but we have had such frightful weather you might send me my very old greatcoat for if I have to board ships I am told we generally get wet thro. I am going to get an oil skin coat—I hope you are keeping better & that the <u>pain in</u> the heart is better if you can pack all bottles I left on my chimney piece they will be of great use if I am to dispense medicine| Your loving Hubby

W.

Let Mr Sammonds see the enclosed—this was passed by the Chiltern Council in the Standard you sent me The scoundrel owes us £1–0–0 for about 6 attendances on his wife & when I asked him he declared he could not pay—

Freer[2] owes a guinea. I see Wheat is down & flour at Chiltern—this is what made Porch so savage

Text: ALS NLA MS133/1/229 and MS133/1/251

[1]   Refers to the auctioneer, Alex McCleery, putting up a flag to indicate an auction was to take place and engaging the town crier to ring his bell up and down the main street on the morning and announce the furniture sale at 'Lake View'. See *FRM III*, p. 230.

[2]   Freer not identified.

230 [From WLR in Queenscliff to MR in Chiltern]

Queenscliffe

Thursday [20 September 1877]

My dear Marie

I find that my room is 11 feet x 8 Passage 4 feet—1ˢᵗ bedroom 10 x 8 2ⁿᵈ bedroom 10 x 11. 3ʳᵈ bedroom 14 x 13. Cupboard 4 feet in with shelves 5 rows all round. Dining room 18½ x 14½. 4ᵗʰ bedroom 18 x 12—Drawing room 18 x 14. They are all newly papered. The lady next door takes boarders & teaches children & I am told that a lady next behind is from Ballarat & has opened a ladies school a month ago. I hope you are better & take your medicine.

Thursday the 27. is the day of the sale of the house at Hams. If you think of coming here to see the house you had [better] wait at Mʳˢ G. until over that & go H̶ to the sale or not just as you like. I may go—I have written to Ham to know if there have [been] any enquiries or likely buyers. We are getting the house done up & Dʳ Williams says we can go in whenever we like. I hope the auction will not be too much for you. I hope you will drop me the enclosed postal card the last thing to say if the sale was good or bad or middling—We could try boarders for one season & get a young person to help the cook—I want you to send me the £20 I deposited in your name. I do not want to spend it, but I want to make up a cheque that I have to place in the auctioneers hands at Stawell ~~to replace~~ which will be returned to me when those 15 Newingtons are put up to auction—I have been trying to sell New North Clunes but cannot. I have got 40 Newingtons & they have gone up 10/- a share since I bought—the only bit of luck I have had for some time. They are likely to go very much higher & if I can hold them without selling I will make a good pile as they will get the great cross reef, but not until after Xmas—Ned & the children[1] will have their fortune made. When you [he] told you to buy they were only £2. now they are £3–10. Send me the cheque like good girl by Fridays afternoon post. Love to all we shall meet soon again

I hope Josephine keeps better| Your loving Hubby

W.

Sign the cheque <u>yourself</u> & make it payable ~~dont~~ scratch out a bearer ~~but draw your fo~~ & write over or order. that is the safest way to send it nobody can draw but me.

Text: ALS NLA MS133/1/227

[1] MR's brother, Edward Harold Bailey (1828–1893), and his wife, Agnes, had three living children at this time, Walter Robinson, having died, aged eight, on 20 March 1877, twelve months after his younger sister, Mabel Elizabeth, died aged four. Their last child, Percy François was born on 23 September 1879 in Wodonga.

231 [From WLR in Queenscliff to MR in Chiltern]

Queenscliffe

Friday morng [21 September 1877]

My dearest Wife

Your nice letter made me much happier How clever of you to polish up the furniture. It ought to bring good prices. I have written to Flower & asked him if it is true that he committed the breach of confidence to show my private letter to ABS[1] I dont believe it! You are very clever, and Mary is invaluable. I shook hands with her when I left—we shall never see her like again—so good and simple so kind to the wee ones & such a capital learner from you; I hope Sammond went to the people who had received such sums & who pleaded poverty to me. I had a 2nd patient to day—The man & myself have been at work in the garden all day & Williams spent an hour superintending—He tells me that if I must be made a P.M.[2] & said that nobody but good men sit on the bench at the Cliff—I had a most pleasant letter from Blair[3] saying the Sorrento people had long been crying out for a doctor that he had indeed been looking out for one to settle there but now that I had come he would give me all his influence. "I shall be very glad to advance your interests in Sorrento in every way in my power I had an application since I received your note about getting a medical man for the Sorrento side but now that I know you to be there my influence if any will be in your favor" so you see I <u>must </u>go over there & stay a day at Portsea & another at Sorrento—I have now some nice cards by Purton

Dr Richardson

Queenscliff.

I must spend a day or two at each hotel & ask them to put my placard in the window. Certainly buy the wine. I can get splendid & magnificent 7 year old here for 24/- doz but I am not taking anything but I hope you will go in with M^rs [Graham] & that she will get it bottled—The Bank Manager[4] called & the Scotch parson.[5] Every body is so nice & pleasant & so agreable. The bank manager has got a splendid little place with a tiny bit of garden behind where he has the choicest flowers I got some cutting of magnificen[t] geraniums from him—His family are in Tasmania. I took a season ticket for bathing to day. The place is much improved by the garden being done up—The old man who is a capital gardener & has worked for Williams for 20 years agrees to come every month for 5/-. ~~To my surprise the secretary of the Forresters~~ To my surprise the secretary of the Forresters came to see me & told me that tho they had been paying Dr Barker 30/- a year to include medicine they had to pay 5/- a year out of their own pocket & could not afford & offered me 25/-. I told them I would not accept it & they had better keep Dr Barker—He said he was going away I said apply Dr Macfarlane:—He would not attend anybody but his own personal freinds—The man seemed uneasy—I said it would pay you better to give me £2. than Dr Barker 30/-. We had a long talk & finally he begged me <u>not to mention it to any</u> one till after their next meeting—I took a firm stand & I know that I will get. Fancy them trying such a trick—love to all & Mrs G. & good luck for the Sale| Your loving husband

WLR

Remember I had promised not to speak about it to any person

It will serve them right if in a year Barker gone & Mcfarlane still determined not to practice for me to raise my terms. That would be a good joke—

He said they had never given more than 24/- & 20/- before Dr Barker The accounts seem to come in a little better. Our tank here is down to 4 feet from the bottom Dr W. says the water has been stolen that before he got in quarantine he measured it & it was 4 feet from the top & tho October rains will fill it he says I hope so

Thank dear Mrs G. for the socks. I hope they will fit—I hope dear Ettie has not been reading too much & no London journals or novels

~~Ys~~

Text: ALS NLA MS133/1/246 and MS 133/1/260

[1]   Alexander Brooke Smith.
[2]   Police Magistrate. Dr Williams had been appointed Territorial Magistrate of the Geelong
       Sessions District on 9 June 1859. Drosken, p. 5.
[3]   Dr John Blair, see endnote to Letter 152.
[4]   George Benjamin H. Cathcart had been the Manager of the Bank of Victoria since it was
       established in 1873. He was married in 1863 to Margaret Eleanor née Gatliff and they had five
       daughters born between 1863 and 1872.
[5]   The Reverend Donald Smith Brunton.

Note on Equivalences

Currency

The British pound (£) was the currency in use in the Australasian colonies during the nineteenth century. The pound divided into 20 shillings (20s or 20/-), each of 12 pennies or pence (d). A half-crown was equivalent to 2s 6d. A sixpence and a threepence were small silver coins; the penny, halfpenny and farthing (one quarter of a penny) were copper.

Length and area

Length was measured according to the Imperial system, in which the foot (ft) is divided into 12 inches (in.). A foot is equivalent to 0.3048 metres on the metric scale. Three feet make a yard (equal to 0.9144 metres); 5280 feet make a mile (equal to 1609.34 metres). Land was measured in acres or square miles. One acre equals 4840 square yards or 0.405 hectares; one square mile equals 2.58 square kilometres.

Temperature

Temperature was measured on the Fahrenheit scale (°F), in which the freezing point of water is 32° and the boiling point 212°. The relation of the degree Fahrenheit to the degree Celsius (°C) is expressed by the formula °F = 5/9 °C + 32.

Weight and volume

Weight and volume were measured according to the Imperial system. The pound (lb), equivalent to 453.6 grams in the metric system, is divided into 16 ounces. A pint, equivalent to 568 millilitres, is divided into 20 fluid ounces; 2 pints make a quart, and 8 pints a gallon (4.55 litres). The stone was the unit of mass in the imperial system and used to measure the weight of a person or large animal. A stone (equivalent to approximately 6.35 kilograms) is divided into 14 pounds. A hundredweight (cwt) was equal to 112 pounds (equivalent to approximately 45.36 kilograms). Doctors and apothecaries, working on a smaller scale within the Imperial system, divided their weights into the dram, equal to 1/16 of an ounce.

Bibliography

Manuscript Sources

Henry Handel Richardson Collection held in the National Library of Australia, Canberra. Most of the items of correspondence relating to Richardson's parents were purchased from Richardson's nephew, Dr Walter Neustatter of London, in 1971. MS133, Series 1 and 2

Alexander Cheyne's Diary (February 1848 – December 1851) and personal papers held at the University of Tasmania, Archives

Transcripts of Alexander Cheyne's Diaries (14 November 1834 to 11 December 1835, 30 January 1847 to 31 December 1847, 29 April 1852 to 22 March 1855) held at the Battye Library, Perth, Western Australia

Graham Papers: Microfilm of papers relating to the Cheyne and Graham families (loaned by Colin Graham to University of Tasmania Archives)

Letter to T. L. Symers from George Cheyne (26 December 1837) and Indenture between George Cheyne and Andrew Moir (March 1858) held at the Battye Library, Perth, Western Australia

Unpublished typescript by John Gower Ritchie, 'Reminiscences of the Back Beach, Blairgowrie', held in the Dorothy Green Papers (Folio W) in the Archives of the Australian Defence Force Academy Library, Canberra.

Official Sources and Public Archives

The Ann Tovell Collection, Brownless Library, University of Melbourne

Australian Institute of Genealogical Studies, Blackburn, Victoria

Records of Deaths in England and Wales, St Catherine's House, London, England

Family History Centres of the Church of Jesus Christ of Latter-day Saints, Blackburn, Braeside, Knox

Irish Public Record Office, *Index to the Act or Grant Books, And to the Original Wills, of the Diocese of Dublin [c.1638] to the Year 1800 from the Appendix to the twenty-sixth Report of the Deputy Keeper of the Public Records and Keeper of the State Papers in Ireland* (Baltimore: Clearfield, 1997) (first published in Dublin, 1895)

Irish Public Record Office, *Index to the Act or Grant Books, And to the Original Wills, of the Diocese of Dublin 1800–1853 from the Appendix to the Thirtieth Report of the Deputy Keeper of the Public Records and Keeper of the State Papers in Ireland* (Dublin: 1899)

Register of Officers in Victorian Penal Service and Staff Appointments 1854–1873, Laverton: Public Record Office of Victoria

Registry of Births, Marriages and Deaths, in Victoria, New South Wales, South Australia, Tasmania, Western Australia

Books and Articles

à Beckett, Gilbert Abbott, *The Comic History of England: with 20 Coloured Etchings and 200 Woodcuts by John Leech* (London: Bradbury, Evans, 1848)

Aronson, Theo, *Queen Victoria and the Bonapartes* (London: Cassell, 1972)

Ashley, Robert W. P., *History of the Shire of Chiltern* (Ballarat: The Author, 1974)

Aspinall, Clara, *Three Years in Melbourne* (London: L. Booth, 1862)

Bagot, Alec, *Coppin the Great: Father of the Australian Theatre* (Carlton: Melbourne University Press, 1965)

Baillière, F., *The Official Post Office Directory of Victoria for 1868* (Melbourne: F. Baillière, 1868)

Baillière, F., *The Official Post Office Directory of Victoria for 1875* (Melbourne: F. Baillière, 1875)

Barry, Jonathan and Kenneth Morgan, eds, *Reformation and Revival in Eighteenth Century Bristol* (Bristol: Alan Sutton (Bristol Record Society), 1994)

Bassett, Marnie, *The Hentys: An Australian Colonial Tapestry* (London: Oxford University Press, 1954)

Bate, Weston, *Lucky City: The First Generation at Ballarat 1851–1901* (Carlton: Melbourne University Press, 1978)

Bennet, Bruce and Jennifer Strauss, eds, with Chris Wallace Crabbe, assoc. ed., *The Oxford Literary History of Australia* (South Melbourne: Oxford University Press, 1998)

Billis, R. V. and A. S. Kenyon, *Pastoral Pioneers of Port Phillip*, 2nd edn (Melbourne: Stockland Press, 1974) (1st edn, 1932)

Bingham, Dorian, ed., *Rawcliffe 'The Queen of Villages': A Brief History* (Goole: Rawcliffe History Group, 1989)

Blainey, Geoffrey, James Morrissey and S.E.K. Hume, *Wesley College: The First Hundred Years* (Melbourne: Wesley College, 1967)

Blake, L. J. ed., *Vision and Realisation: A Centenary History of State Education in Victoria* (Melbourne: Government Printers, 1973)

Blunt, Reginald, ed., *Mrs Montagu 'Queen of the Blues': Her Letters and Friendships From 1762 to 1800*, 2 vols (London: Constable, n.d.)

Boldrewood, Rolf, *Old Melbourne Memories* (Melbourne: George Robertson, 1884)

Bossence, W. H., *Murchison: The J.G. Memorial History* (Melbourne: The Hawthorn Press, 1965)

Bowden, Keith Macrea, *Goldrush Doctors at Ballaarat* (Mulgrave: the Author, 1977)

Brabner, J. H. F. ed., *The Comprehensive Gazetteer of England and Wales* (London: Mackenzie, 1893)

Bradfield, Raymond, *Castlemaine A Golden Harvest* (Kilmore: Lowden Publishing, 1972)

Briggs, Asa, *The Age of Improvement: 1783–1867* (London: Longmans, Green, 1959)

Brothers, C. R. D., *Early Victorian Psychiatry: 1835–1905* (Melbourne: Cheshire, n.d.)

Brown-May, Andrew, *Melbourne Street Life: The Itinerary of Our Days* (Kew: Australian Scholarly Publishing, 1998)

Brownshill, Walter Randolph, *History of Geelong and Corio Bay* (Melbourne: Wilke and Co., 1955) with Postscript 1955–1990 by Ian Wynd, (Geelong: *Geelong Advertiser*, 1990)

Broxam, Graeme and Ian Nicholson, *Shipping Arrivals and Departures Sydney 1841–1844* (Canberra: Roebuck Society, Publication No. 34, 1988)

Buckley, Vincent, *Henry Handel Richardson* (Melbourne: Lansdowne Press, 1962). In the series, Australian Writers and their Work, ed. Geoffrey Dutton

Busse, Wilfred C., 'The History of Chiltern', *The Chiltern Federal Standard* (16 chapters written in weekly parts from December 1922)

Castlemaine Association of Pioneers and Old Residents, *Records of the Castlemaine Pioneers* (Adelaide: Rigby, 1972)

Cannon, Michael, *The Land Boomers* (Carlton: Melbourne University Press, 1966)

Cannon, Michael, *Old Melbourne Town Before the Gold Rush* (Main Ridge, Victoria: Loch Haven Books, 1991)

Cannon, Michael, *Melbourne After the Gold Rush* (Main Ridge, Victoria: Loch Haven Books, 1993)

Cantlon, Michael, *Homesteads of Victoria: 1836–1900* (Adelaide: The Griffin Press, 1967)

Carboni, Raffaello, *The Eureka Stockade* (Carlton: Melbourne University Press, 1980) (first published by the author, 1855)

Castlemaine Association of Pioneers and Old Residents, *Records of Castlemaine Pioneers* (Adelaide: Rigby, 1972)

Cecil, K. L., *Lorne: The Founding Years (To 1888)* (Lorne: Historical Society, 1989)

Charles, Michael, *Pictorial Memories: Old Parramatta* (Alexandria: Atrand Pty, 1986)

Clark, Axel, *Henry Handel Richardson: Fiction in the Making* (Brookvale, NSW: Simon Schuster, 1990)

Clutton-Brock, M. A., 'The Melancholy Optimist: An Account of Walter Lindesay Richardson and his Family', *Meanjin Quarterly*, 2 (1970), 192–208

Combe, T., *The Leicester Directory* (Leicester: T. Combe and Son, 1827)

Comrie, John D., *History of Scottish Medicine*, vol. II (London: Baillère Tindall and Cox, 1932)

Cook, T., compiler, *The Annual Guide to Leicester* (Leicester: T. Cook, 1867)

Cooper, John Butler, *The History of St Kilda: From its First Settlement to a City*, 2 vols (Melbourne: Printers Proprietary Ltd, 1931)

Corfield, Justin J. and Michael Collins Persse, *Geelong Grammarians: A Biographical Register: Volume One 1855–1913* (Corio, Victoria: Geelong Grammar School, 1996)

Crockford's Clerical Directory: 1921–1922, 52nd edn (London: Oxford University Press, 1921)

Dalton, Charles, *The Waterloo Roll Call* (London: Arms and Armour Press, 1971)

Darragh, Thomas A., *Printer and Newspaper Registration in Victoria: 1838–1924* (Wellington: Elibank Press, 1997)

Davies, Alan and Peter Stanbury (with assistance from Con Tanre), *The Mechanical Eye in Australia: Photography 1841–1900* (Melbourne: Oxford University Press, 1985)

Davison, Graeme, John Hirst and Stuart Macintyre, eds, *The Oxford Companion to Australian History* (South Melbourne: Oxford University Press, 1998)

de Serville, Paul, *Port Phillip Gentlemen: And Good Society in Melbourne Before the Gold Rush* (South Melbourne: Oxford University Press, 1980)

de Serville, Paul, *Pounds and Pedigrees: The Upper Class in Victoria 1859–80* (South Melbourne: Oxford University Press, 1991)

De Vries, Susanna, *Strength of Spirit: Pioneering Women of Achievement From First Fleet to Federation* (Alexandria, NSW: Millennium Books, 1995)

Dicker, F. M., compiler, *Ballarat and Ballarat District Directory: 1865–66* (Ballarat: James Curtis, 1865)

Drake, E. S., *Commercial Directory of Leicestershire* (Leicester: J. T. Spencer, 1861)

Drosken, G. W. ed., *Historical Record of Queenscliffe Borough: 1863–1933* (Queenscliff: Queenscliff Council, 1933)

Dunlop, A. Ian, *The Kirks of Edinburgh: The Congregations, Churches, and Ministers of the Presbytery of Edinburgh Church of Scotland* (Edinburgh: Scottish Record Society, 1988)

Ebsworth, Rev. Walter, *Pioneer Catholic Victoria* (Melbourne: The Polding Press, 1973)

Erikson, Rita, compiler, *The Bicentennial Dictionary of Western Australians: Pre 1829–1888* (Nedlands, WA: University of Western Australia Press, 1987)

Eureka Reminiscences, ed. Ballarat Heritage Services (Ballarat: Ballarat Heritage Services, 1998)

Eustace, P. Beryl, 'Index of Will Abstracts in the Genealogical Office, Dublin', *The Guide to the Genealogical Office Dublin* (Dublin: Irish Manuscripts Commission, 1998), 80–282

Falley, Margaret Dickson, *Irish and Scotch-Irish Ancestral Research: A Guide to the Genealogical Records, Methods and Sources in Ireland*, 2 vols (Baltimore: Genealogical Publishing, 1984)

Farrar, Henry, *Irish Marriages: Being an Index to the Marriages in Walker's Hiberian Magazine 1771 to 1812* (Baltimore: Genealogical Publishing, 1972)

Flanagan, Martin, *The Call* (St Leonards: Allen and Unwin, 1998)

Fowler, J., *Directory of Leicester* (Leicester: J. Fowler, 1815)

Forster, Frank M. C., 'Walter Lindesay Richardson, 1826–1879, As Obstetrician: His Case-book and Midwifery practice in Early Ballarat', *Festschrift for Kenneth Fitzpatrick Russell* (Melbourne: Queensberry Hill Press, 1978), 140–158

Fraser, Rod, *The Champion of the Seas* (Glen Waverley: Pilgrim Printing Services, 1999)

Frost, Leonore, *Dating Family Photos 1850–1920* (Essendon: the Author, 1992)

Frost, Lucy, ed., *The Journal of Annie Baxter Dawbin: July 1858 – May 1868* (St Lucia: University of Queensland Press, 1998)

Garden, Donald S., *Albany: A Panorama of the Sound from 1827* (West Melbourne: Nelson, 1977)

Gaskell, Philip, *From Writer to Reader: Studies in Editorial Method* (Oxford: Clarendon Press, 1978)

Geddie, Wm, and J. Liddell Geddie, eds, *Chambers' Biographical Dictionary*, 2nd edn (London: W. and R. Chambers, 1945) (first edn 1897)

General Post Office Directory for Edinburgh, Leith, and Their Environs 1845–46 (Edinburgh: Ballantyne and Hughes, 1845)

Graham, John A., *Early Creswick: The First Century*, facsim. repr. (Creswick: Creswick Historical Museum, 1987)

Green, Dorothy, *Henry Handel Richardson and Her Fiction* (North Sydney: Allen and Unwin, 1986) (first published as *Ulysses Bound: Henry Handel Richardson and her Fiction*, Canberra: ANU Press, 1973)

Green, Dorothy, 'Walter Lindesay Richardson: The Man, the Portrait, and the Artist', *Meanjin Quarterly*, 1 (1970), 5–20

Greer, Germaine, 'The Getting of Wisdom', *Scripsi*, 1 (1982), 4–12

Hagar and Co., *Commercial Directory of the County of Leicester* (Nottingham: Stevensons, 1849)

Haggar, Jennifer, *Australian Colonial Medicine* (Adelaide: Rigby, 1979)

Ham, C. J. and T. Ham, *Register of Properties for Sale* (Melbourne: Central Land Office, 1878)

Harrod, J. G., *Postal and Commercial Directory of Leicestershire and Rutland* (London and Norwich: J. G. Harrod, 1870)

Hart, Colonel H. G., ed., *The New Annual Army List, and Militia List* (London: John Murray, 1856 to 1868)

Hart, Colonel H. G., ed., *The New Annual Army List, Militia List and Indian Civil Service List for 1870* (London: John Murray, 1870)

Hartopp, Henry, *Register of Freemen of Leicester, 1770–1930* (Leicester: Corporation of City of Leicester, 1933)

Harvey, Ivor L., *125 Year History of the Ballarat Fire Brigade* (Ballarat: R. Fletcher and Sons, 1981)

Harvey, Sir Paul, ed., *The Oxford Companion to English Literature*, 3rd edn (Oxford: Clarendon Press, 1946) (first edn 1932)

Holden's Directory: Hinckley, Leicester and Market Harborough (Leicester: Holden, 1805–1811)

Holder, R. F., *Bank of New South Wales: A History: Volume 1: 1817–1893* (Sydney: Angus and Robertson, 1970)

Inglis, Andrea, *Beside the Seaside: Victorian Resorts in the Nineteenth Century* (Carlton South: Melbourne Press, 1999)

Irvin, Eric, *Dictionary of the Australian Theatre 1788–1914* (Marrickville, NSW: Hale and Iremonger, 1985)

Karskens, Grace, *Holroyd: A Social History of Western Sydney* (Kensington: NSW University Press, 1991)

Keane, Edward, P., Beryl Phair, and Thomas U. Sadleir, eds, *King's Inns Admissions Papers 1607–1867* (Dublin: Stationery Office of the Irish Manuscript Commission, 1982)

Keay, John and Julie Keay, eds, *Collins Encyclopaedia of Scotland* (London: Harper Collins, 1994)

Kelly and Co., *Post Office Directory of Leicestershire and Rutland* (London: Kelly and Co., 1855)

Kelly, William, *Life in Victoria or Victoria in 1853 and Victoria in 1858*, 2 vols (London: Chapman and Hall, 1860)

Kimberly, W. B., *Ballarat and Vicinity* (Ballarat: F. W. Niven, n.d., c1895)

King, D. and N. Dooley, *The Golden Steam of Ballarat* (Kilmore: Lowden Publishing, 1973)

Kramer, Leonie, *Henry Handel Richardson* (South Melbourne: Oxford University Press, 1967)

Kramer, Leonie, *A Companion to Australia Felix* (Melbourne: William Heinemann, 1962)

Loney, Jack, *Bay Steamers and Coastal Ferries* (Frenchs Forest, NSW: A. H. and A. W. Reed, 1982)

Longford, Elizabeth, *Victoria R.I.* (London: Pan Books, 1966) (1st published by Weidenfeld and Nicholson, 1964)

Love, Harold, *James Edward Neild: Victorian Virtuoso* (Carlton: Melbourne University Press, 1989)

Love, Harold, *The Golden Age of Australian Opera: W. S. Lyster and His Companies 1861–1880* (Sydney: Currency Press, 1981)

MacLoughlin, Adrian, *Guide to Historic Dublin* (Dublin: Gill and Macmillan, 1979)

McCalman, Janet, *Sex and Suffering: Women's Health and a Women's Hospital: The Royal Women's Hospital, Melbourne 1856–1996* (Carlton: Melbourne University Press, 1998)

McCorkell, H.A., *A Green and Pleasant Land or The Story of Koroit, 1836–1970* (Koroit: Borough Council, 1970)

McCrae, Hugh, ed., *Georgiana's Journal: Melbourne A Hundred Years Ago* (Sydney: Angus and Robertson, 1934)

McFarlane, Brian, 'Power in Dark Places: The Fortunes of Richard Mahony', *Southerly*, 2 (1977), 211–228

McKinley, Brian, *The First Royal Tour 1867–1868* (Adelaide: Rigby, 1970)

Maddicks, Henry T. (assisted by K. H. Butler), *100 Years of Daylesford Gold Mining History 1851–1951* (Daylesford: Daylesford Historical Society, 1951)

Mein, W. Gordon, *History of Ballarat College 1864–1964* (Ballarat: Ballarat College Council, 1964)

Miller, E. Morris, 'Richard Mahony's Grave', *Meanjin Quarterly*, 8, 3 (1949), 177–180

Miller, E. Morris, 'Richard Mahony's Euphoria: A Psychological Note', *Meanjin*, 51, 4 (1952), 397–401

Montgomery-Massingberd, Hugh, ed., *Burke's Irish Family Records* (London: Burke's Peerage, 1976)

Moody, T. W. and F. X. Martin, eds, *The Course of Irish History*, 2nd rev. edn (Cork: Mercier Press, 1984) (first edn 1967)

Morehead, Leslie M., *Mornington in the Wake of Flinders* (Elsternwick: Shire of Mornington, 1971)

Morgan, Henry, compiler, *Huxtable's Ballarat Commercial Directory, Embracing the Eastern and Western Municipalities* (Ballarat: Huxtable, 1857, 1858, 1862)

Morris, J. S. C., *The Business Directory of London* (London: Morris, 1867, 1868, 1869)

Murphy, Brian, *Dictionary of Australian History* (Sydney: McGraw-Hill, 1982)

Murray, Robert and Kate White, *State of Fire: A History of Volunteer Firefighting and the Country Fire Authority in Victoria* (North Melbourne: Hargreen Publishing, 1995)

National Trust of Australia, 'Fitzroy's Blanche Terrace Saved', *Trust Newsletter*, I, 21 (1972), 1, 6

Niall, Brenda, *Martin Boyd: A Life* (Carlton: Melbourne University Press, 1988)

Niall, Brenda, *Georgiana: A Biography of Georgiana McCrae Painter, Diarist, Pioneer* (Carlton: Melbourne University Press at the Miegunyah Press, 1994)

Niall, Brenda and John Thompson, eds, *The Oxford Book of Australian Letters* (South Melbourne: Oxford University Press, 1998)

Nobbs, Raymond, *Norfolk Island and its Second Settlement 1825–1855* (North Sydney: Library of Australian History, 1991)

O'Byrne, William R., *A Naval Biographical Dictionary Comprising The Life and Services of Every Living Officer in Her Majesty's Navy, from the Rank of Admiral of the Fleet to that of Lieutenant, inclusive* (London: John Murray, 1849)

O'Hart, John, *Irish Pedigrees or the Origin and Stem of the Irish Nation*, 2 vols, 5th edn (Baltimore: Genealogical Publishing, 1989) (first published Dublin 1892)

Osborn, Betty and Trenear DuBorg, *Maryborough: A Social History 1854–1904* (Maryborough: Maryborough City Council, 1985)

Palmer, Nettie, *Henry Handel Richardson: A Study* (Sydney: Angus and Robertson, 1950)

Parsons, Philip, ed., with Victoria Chance, *Companion to Theatre in Australia* (Sydney: Currency Press, 1995)

Passey, Kevin and Gary Dean, *The Bushranger Harry Power: Tutor of Ned Kelly* (Wodonga: Victorian Bushrangers Enterprises, 1991)

Pearson, Hesketh, *The Smith of Smiths: Being the Life, Wit and Humour of Sydney Smith* (Harmondswoth: Penguin Books, 1948) (first edn 1934)

Perkins, Roger, *Regiments: Regiments and Corps of the British Empire and Commonwealth 1758–1993: A Critical Bibliography of Their Published Histories* (Newton Abbot, Devon: The Author, 1994)

Peterkin, A. and William Johnston, *Commissioned Officers in the Medical Services of the British Army 1660–1960*, 2 vols, (London: The Wellcome Historical Medical Library, 1968)

Petrie, Sir Charles, *The Victorians* (London: Eyre and Spottiswoode, 1961)

Philipp, June, *A Poor Man's Diggings: Mining and Community at Bethanga, Victoria 1875–1912* (Melbourne: Hyland House, 1987)

Pigott's Directory of Gloucestershire for 1830 (Bristol: J. Pigott, 1830)

Pigott's City of Dublin and Hibernian Provincial Directory for 1824 (London: J. Pigott, 1824)

Pike, Douglas, Bede Nairn and Geoffrey Serle, *Australian Dictionary of Biography* (Carlton: Melbourne University Press, 1966–93)

Radford, Ron and Jane Hylton, *Australian Colonial Art: 1800–1900* (Adelaide: Art Gallery Board of South Australia, 1995)

Records of the Honorable Society of Lincoln's Inn, vol. II Admissions 1800–1893 and Chapel Registers (London: Lincoln's Inn, 1896)

Refaussé, Raymond, *Register of the Parish of St Thomas, Dublin: 1750–1791* (Dublin: Representative Church Body Library, 1994)

Refaussé, Raymond, with Colm Lennon, eds, *The Registers of Christ Church Cathedral, Dublin* (Dublin: Four Courts Press, 1998)

Reid, M. O., *The Ladies Came to Stay: A Study of the Education of Girls at the Presbyterian Ladies' College Melbourne 1875–1960* (Melbourne: Brown Prior Anderson, 1960)

Reynolds, Henry, *This Whispering in Our Hearts* (St Leonards: Allen and Unwin, 1998)

Richardson, Henry Handel, *The Fortunes of Richard Mahony, Vol. I, Australia Felix* (London: William Heinemann, 1917)

Richardson, Henry Handel, *The Fortunes of Richard Mahony, Vol. II, The Way Home* (London: William Heinemann, 1925)

Richardson, Henry Handel, *The Fortunes of Richard Mahony, Vol. III, Ultima Thule* (London: William Heinemann, 1929)

Richardson, Henry Handel, *The Getting of Wisdom* (London: William Heinemann, 1910)

Richardson, Henry Handel, *Myself When Young* (Kingswood, Surrey: Windmill Press, 1948)

Richardson, Walter Lindesay, 'On hydatis of the uterus', *Australian Medical Journal*, 7 (1862), 9–11

Richardson, Walter Lindesay, 'On flooding after delivery', *Australian Medical Journal*, 3 (1863), 1–3

Richardson, Walter Lindesay, 'A fatal case of cholera', *Australian Medical Journal*, 9 (1864), 199

Richardson, Walter Lindesay, 'A contribution to the statistics of midwifery: being 630 cases of pregnancy', *Medical Surgical Review* (Australasian), 3 (1864), 37

Richardson, Walter Lindesay, 'A letter from home', *Australian Medical Journal*, 12 (1867), 236–243

Richardson, Walter Lindesay, 'Another letter from home', *Australian Medical Journal*, 12 (1867), 274–278

Richardson, Walter Lindesay, 'A letter from home', *Australian Medical Journal*, 13 (1868), 178

Robin, A. de Q., ed., *Australian Sketches: The Journals and Letters of Frances Perry* (Carlton, Victoria: Queensberry Hill Press, 1984)

Ryan, James G., ed., *Irish Church Records: Their History, Availability and Use in Family and Local History Research* (Glenageary: Flyleaf Press, 1992)

Sadleir, John, *Recollections of a Victorian Police Officer* (Melbourne: George Robertson, 1913; facsim. repr. Ringwood, Vic.: Penguin, 1973)

Sands, Kenny and Co., *Commercial and General Melbourne Directory* (Melbourne: Sands, Kenny and Co., 1858 to 1861)

Sands and McDougall, *Commercial and General Melbourne Directory* (Melbourne: Sands and McDougall, 1862)

Sands and McDougall, *Melbourne and Suburban Street Directory* (Melbourne: Sands and McDougall, 1863 to 1877)

Serle, Geoffrey, *The Golden Age: A History of the Colony of Victoria 1851–1861* (Carlton: Melbourne University Press, 1963)

Sexton, R.T., *Shipping Arrivals and Departures in South Australia: 1687–1850* (Adelaide: Gould Books, 1990)

Shaw, A. G. L., *Convicts and the Colonies: A Study of Penal Transportation from Great Britain and Ireland to Australia and Other Parts of the British Empire* (London: Faber and Faber, 1966)

Shaw, Henry, *Dublin Pictorial Guide and Directory of 1850* (Belfast: The Friar's Bush Press, 1988) (first edn 1850, Dublin)

Smyth, Brigadier, The Rt Hon. Sir John, *The Story of the Victoria Cross* (London: Frederick Muller, 1963)

Somerville-Large, Peter, *Dublin: The Fair City*, rev. edn (Dublin: Hamish Hamilton, 1996) (first edn 1979)

Southerwood, W. T., *Planting a Faith in Melbourne* (Sydney: Opus Books, 1973)

Stancombe, G. Hawley, *Highway in Van Diemen's Land* (Glendessy, Western Junction: Author, 1968)

Stevens, R., 'Builders of Albany: George Macartney Cheyne', *Journal and Proceedings of the Western Australian Historical Society*, IV, 3 (1951), 68–80.

Stewart, D. Macrae, *The Presbyterian Church of Victoria: Growth in Fifty Years 1859–1909* (Melbourne: D. W. Paterson, 1909)

Stewart, John Watson, *Gentleman's and Citizen's Almanack* (Dublin: John Watson Stewart and Thomas Stewart, 1795)

Stoller, Alan and R. H. Emmerson, 'Richard Mahony, Walter Lindesay Richardson and the Spirochaete', *Papers presented at a Centenary Seminar on Henry Handel Richardson 1870–1946* (Canberra: National Library of Australia, 1972), 9–22

Stoller, Alan and R. H. Emmerson, 'The Fortunes of Walter Lindesay Richardson', *Meanjin Quarterly*, 1 (1970), 21–32

Strange, A. W., *Ballarat: A Brief History* (Kilmore: Lowden Publishing, 1971)

Summons, Elizabeth, 'Ethel and Florence and Arthur and Mattie', *Overland*, 72 (1978), 24–30

Sutherland, H. and E. Vines, *Chiltern Conservation Study*, (Chiltern: Shire of Chiltern and the Australian Heritage Commission, 1981)

Syrett, David and R. L. DiNardo, *The Commissioned Sea Officers of the Royal Navy 1660–1815* (Aldershot: Scholar Press, 1994)

Tait, J., *A History of Fort Queenscliff 1882–1982: In the Context of Port Philip Defences* (Queenscliff: The Author, 1982)

Thom, A., *Thom's Irish Almanac and Official Directory with the Post Office Dublin City and County Directory* (Dublin: Alexander Thom, 1849)

Thomson, Kathleen and Geoffrey Searle, *A Biographical Register of the Victorian Legislature: 1851–1900* (Canberra: Australian National University Press, 1972)

Thornton, P. T., *The History of Freemasonry in Victoria* (Melbourne: United Grand Lodge of Ancient Free and Accepted Masons of Victoria, 1978)

Todd, James H., compiler, *A Catalogue of Graduates who have proceeded to degrees in the University of Dublin from the Earliest Recorded Commencement to July 1866 with Supplement to December 16, 1868* (Dublin: Hodges, Smith and Foster, 1869)

Trevelyan, G. M., *Illustrated English Social History: Volume Four: The Nineteenth Century* (London: Longmans, Green, 1952)

Tucker, Maya V., *Kilmore on the Sydney Road* (Kilmore: Shire of Kilmore, 1988)

Turner, Henry Gyles, *Spiritualism: a paper read before the Eclectic Association of Melbourne, on September 2nd, 1869* (Melbourne: George Robertson, 1869)

Venn, J. A., compiler, *Alumni Cantabrigienses: Part II from 1752 to 1900* (Cambridge: University Press, 1953)

Vicars, Sir Arthur, ed., *Index to the Prerogative Wills of Ireland: 1536–1810* (Dublin: Edward Ponsonby, 1897)

Vincent, Benjamin, *Haydn's Dictionary of Dates and Universal Information Relating to all Ages and Nations*, 17th edn (London: Ward, Lock, 1881) (first edn 1841)

W., S. G., *Spiritual communication, &c. through the mediumship of Elizabeth Armstrong* (Melbourne: Robert Bell, 1869)

Waghorn, John F., *Index of Victoria's Postmasters and Postmistresses: 1839 to 1901* (Thomastown, Victoria: the Author, 1987)

Waghorn, John F., *Index of Victoria Postal and Telegraph Department Staff Who Commenced Duty Between 1839 and 1901* (Thomastown, Victoria: the Author, 1989)

Watson, Samuel, *The Gentleman's and Citizen's Almanack* (Dublin: Watson and Stewart, 1736 to 1775)

West, John, *The History of Tasmania, Vol. 1* (Launceston: Henry Dowling, 1852; facsim. repr. 1966)

Weston, Richard, *Leicester Directory for 1791–94* (Leicester: Richard Weston, 1794)

White, William, *History, Gazetteer and Directory of the Counties of Leicester and Rutland* (London and Sheffield: Simpkin and Marshall, 1868)

Willis, Arthur J., ed., *Canterbury Marriage Licences: 1810–1837* (Chichester, Sussex: Phillimore, 1971)

Wilson, John B., *The Royal Burgh of Lochmaben: Its History, Its Castles and Its Churches* (Dumfries: Dinwiddie Grieve, 1987)

Wilson, William, *Wilson's Dublin Directory* (Dublin: William Wilson, 1775)

Windle, John, compiler, *The Ballarat Directory 1869* (Ballarat: James Curtis, 1869)

Withers, William Bramwell, *The History of Ballarat from the First Pastoral Settlement to the Present Time*, 2nd edn (Ballarat: F. W. Niven, 1887; facsim. repr. with Index by Frank Cusack, Carlton: Queensberry Hill Press, 1980) (first edn 1870)

Woods, Carole, *Beechworth: A Titan's Field* (North Melbourne: Hargreen Publishing, 1985)

Wynd, Ian, *Geelong—The Pivot* (Melbourne: Cypress Books, 1971)

Newspapers

Payne's Leicester and Midland Counties Advertizer

Kilmore Free Press

The Age

The Argus

The Ballarat Courier

The Ballarat Star

The Ballarat Times

The Brunswick and Pentridge Press

The Chiltern Federal Standard

The Freeman's Journal, Dublin

The Geelong Advertiser and Intelligencer

The Herald

The Leicester Chronicle and Leicestershire Mercury United

The Sydney Morning Herald

Register of Letters

LETTER	DATE WRITTEN	SENDER	RECIPIENT	SOURCE
1	22 April 1854	FROM MR (Bell Post Hill)	TO WLR (Ballarat)	MS133/1/4
2	7 June 1855	FROM WLR (Ballarat)	TO MR (Bell Post Hill)	MS133/1/14 (b)
3	11 June 1855	FROM MR (Bell Post Hill)	TO WLR (Ballarat)	MS133/1/2
4	7–11 June 1855	FROM WLR (Ballarat)	TO MR (Bell Post Hill)	MS133/1/13
5	17 June 1855	FROM MR (Bell Post Hill)	TO WLR (Ballarat)	MS133/1/3 & MS133/1/10
6	12–17 June 1855	FROM WLR (Ballarat)	TO MR (Bell Post Hill)	MS133/1/11 & MS133/1/12
7	24 June 1855	FROM MR (Bell Post Hill)	TO WLR (Ballarat)	MS133/1/1
8	19–25 June 1855	FROM WLR (Ballarat)	TO MR (Bell Post Hill)	MS133/1/15 & MS133/1/16
9	5 July 1855	FROM MR (Bell Post Hill)	TO WLR (Ballarat)	MS133/1/9
10	8 July 1855	FROM MR (Bell Post Hill)	TO WLR (Ballarat)	MS133/1/8
11	10 July 1855	FROM WLR (Ballarat)	TO MR (Bell Post Hill)	MS133/1/21 & MS133/1/22
12	15 July 1855	FROM MR (Bell Post Hill)	TO WLR (Ballarat)	MS133/1/7
13	17 July 1855	FROM WLR (Ballarat)	TO MR (Bell Post Hill)	MS133/1/17 & MS133/1/18
14	22 July 1855	FROM MR (Bell Post Hill)	TO WLR (Ballarat)	MS133/1/6
15	23–26 July 1855	FROM WLR (Ballarat)	TO MR (Bell Post Hill)	MS133/1/19 & MS133/1/20
16	28 July 1855	FROM WLR (Ballarat)	TO MR (Bell Post Hill)	MS133/1/111
17	2 August 1855	FROM WLR (Ballarat)	TO MR (Bell Post Hill)	MS133/1/112 & MS133/1/113
18	12 August 1855	FROM MR (Bell Post Hill)	TO WLR (Ballarat)	MS133/1/5

19	December 1855	FROM MR (Ballarat)	TO GB (Leicester, England)	MS133/1/266
20	3 February 1856	FROM MR (Bell Post Hill)	TO WLR (Ballarat)	MS133/1/49
21	7–9 February 1856	FROM WLR (Ballarat)	TO MR (Bell Post Hill)	MS133/1/99 & MS133/1/100
22	15 February 1856	FROM MR (Bell Post Hill)	TO WLR (Ballarat)	MS133/1/53
23	November 1856	FROM WLR (Ballarat)	TO MR (Collingwood)	MS133/1/14 (a)
24	November 1856	FROM WLR (Ballarat)	TO MR (Collingwood)	MS133/1/56
25	Late 1856	FROM JC (Melbourne)	TO WLR (Ballarat)	MS133/1/263 & MS133/1/264
26	9 September 1857	FROM LC (Brighton, England)	TO WLR (Ballarat)	MS133/1/25
27	2 October 1857	FROM LC (Brighton, England)	TO WLR (Ballarat)	MS133/1/26
28	10 July 1858	FROM LC (Brighton, England)	TO WLR/MR (Ballarat)	MS133/1/27
29	18 July 1858	FROM JC (Gorruckpore, India)	TO WLR (Ballarat)	MS133/1/243 & MS133/1/253
30	11 August 1858	FROM WLR (Ballarat)	TO MR (Melbourne)	MS133/1/84
31	14 August 1858	FROM WLR (Ballarat)	TO MR (Melbourne)	MS133/1/85
32	16 August 1858	FROM WLR (Ballarat)	TO MR (Melbourne)	MS133/1/98
33	19 August 1858	FROM WLR (Ballarat)	TO MR (Melbourne)	MS133/1/86
34	23 August 1858	FROM WLR (Ballarat)	TO MR (Melbourne)	MS133/1/80
35	25 August 1858	FROM MR (Melbourne)	TO WLR (Ballarat)	MS133/1/48
36	25 August 1858	FROM WLR (Ballarat)	TO MR (Geelong)	MS133/1/89
37	27 August 1858	FROM WLR (Ballarat)	TO MR (Geelong)	MS133/1/109
38	28 August 1858	FROM MR (Geelong)	TO WLR (Ballarat)	MS133/1/52
39	30 August 1858	FROM WLR (Ballarat)	TO MR (Geelong)	MS133/1/31
40	6–13 January 1859	FROM LC (Brighton, England)	TO LR (Kyneton)	MS133/1/28

41	15 April 1859	FROM Masonic (Buninyong)	TO WLR (Ballarat)	MS133/1/248
42	21 April 1859	FROM WLR (Geelong)	TO MR (Ballarat)	MS133/1/168
43	27 April 1859	FROM WLR (Queenscliff)	TO MR (Ballarat)	MS133/1/226
44	30 April 1859	FROM WLR (Collingwood)	TO MR (Ballarat)	MS133/1/169
45	19–20 October 1859	FROM LC (Brighton, England)	TO WLR/MR (Ballarat)	MS133/1/29
46	9 November 1859	FROM LC (Brighton, England)	TO WLR (Ballarat)	MS133/1/30
47	7–14 December 1859	FROM LC (Brighton, England)	TO WLR (Ballarat)	MS133/1/32
48	6 January 1860	FROM MR (St Kilda)	TO WLR (Ballarat)	MS133/1/61
49	8 January 1860	FROM MR (St Kilda)	TO WLR (Ballarat)	MS133/1/62
50	11 January 1860	FROM MR (St Kilda)	TO WLR (Ballarat)	MS133/1/63
51	16 January 1860	FROM MR (St Kilda)	TO WLR (Ballarat)	MS133/1/59
52	19 January 1860	FROM MR (St Kilda)	TO WLR (Ballarat)	MS133/1/57
53	21 January 1860	FROM WLR (Ballarat)	TO MR (St Kilda)	MS133/1/54
54	24–25 January 1860	FROM MR (St Kilda)	TO WLR (Ballarat)	MS133/1/58
55	28 January 1860	FROM MR (Melbourne)	TO WLR (Ballarat)	MS133/1/60
56	10 April 1860	FROM LC (Brighton, England)	TO WLR (Ballarat)	MS133/1/33
57	31 May 1860	FROM MR (St Kilda)	TO WLR (Ballarat)	MS133/1/51
58	2 June 1860	FROM WLR (Ballarat)	TO MR (St Kilda)	MS133/1/72
59	5 June 1860	FROM MR (Pentridge)	TO WLR (Ballarat)	MS133/1/70
60	5 June 1860	FROM WLR (Ballarat)	TO MR (Pentridge)	MS133/1/73
61	8 June 1860	FROM WLR (Ballarat)	TO MR (Pentridge)	MS133/1/105
62	8–9 June 1860	FROM LC (Brighton, England)	TO WLR (Ballarat)	MS133/1/34
63	9 June 1860	FROM MR (Pentridge)	TO WLR (Ballarat)	MS133/1/69

64	12 June 1860	FROM WLR (Ballarat)	TO MR (Pentridge)	MS133/1/55
65	15 June 1860	FROM WLR (Ballarat)	TO MR (Pentridge)	MS133/1/101
66	18 June 1860	FROM MR (St Kilda)	TO WLR (Ballarat)	MS133/1/50
67	July 1860	FROM LC (Brighton, England)	TO WLR (Ballarat)	MS133/1/35
68	25 November 1860	FROM LC (Brighton, England)	TO WLR/MR (Ballarat)	MS133/1/36
69	20 February 1861	FROM LC (Brighton, England)	TO WLR (Ballarat)	MS133/1/37
70	23 May 1861	FROM MR (St Kilda)	TO WLR (Ballarat)	MS133/1/67
71	25 May 1861	FROM WLR (Ballarat)	TO MR (St Kilda)	MS133/1/157
72	27 May 1861	FROM MR (St Kilda)	TO WLR (Ballarat)	MS133/1/65
73	28 May 1861	FROM WLR (Ballarat)	TO MR (St Kilda)	MS133/1/75
74	1 June 1861	FROM WLR (Ballarat)	TO MR (St Kilda)	MS133/1/102
75	3 June 1861	FROM MR (St Kilda)	TO WLR (Ballarat)	MS133/1/64
76	4 June 1861	FROM WLR (Ballarat)	TO MR (St Kilda)	MS133/1/74
77	26 August 1861	FROM LC (Brighton, England)	TO WLR (Ballarat)	MS133/1/38
78	30 January 1862	FROM WLR (Ballarat)	TO MR (Melbourne)	MS133/1/79
79	3 February 1862	FROM WLR (Ballarat)	TO MR (Melbourne)	MS133/1/76
80	5 February 1862	FROM WLR (Ballarat)	TO MR (Melbourne)	MS133/1/81
81	7–8 February 1862	FROM WLR (Ballarat)	TO MR (Melbourne)	MS133/1/77
82	19–25 June 1862	FROM LC (Brighton, England)	TO WLR/MR (Ballarat)	MS133/1/39 & MS133/1/40
83	11 August 1862	FROM LC (Brighton, England)	TO EB (Leicester, England)	MS133/1/24
84	28 October 1862	FROM MR (St Kilda)	TO WLR (Ballarat)	MS133/1/66
85	7 November 1862	FROM WLR (Ballarat)	TO MR (St Kilda)	MS133/1/106
86	8–11 November 1862	FROM WLR (Ballarat)	TO MR (St Kilda)	MS133/1/78

87	12 November 1862	FROM WLR (Ballarat)	TO MR (Pentridge)	MS133/1/107
88	13 November 1862	FROM MR (Pentridge)	TO WLR (Ballarat)	MS133/1/71
89	15 November 1862	FROM MR (St Kilda/ Pentridge)	TO WLR (Ballarat)	MS133/1/68
90	1–14 January 1863	FROM LC (Brighton, England)	TO WLR/MR (Ballarat)	MS133/1/41 & MS133/1/43
91	17 November 1863	FROM LC (Brighton, England)	TO WLR (Ballarat)	MS133/1/42
92	18 April 1864	FROM MR (Kilmore)	TO WLR (Ballarat)	MS133/1/47
93	20 April 1864	FROM WLR (Ballarat)	TO MR (Kerrisdale)	MS133/1/104
94	22 April 1864	FROM WLR (Ballarat)	TO MR (Kerrisdale)	MS133/1/87
95	29–30 April 1864	FROM WLR (Ballarat)	TO MR (Kerrisdale)	MS133/1/93
96	6 March 1865	FROM WLR (Ballarat)	TO MR (East Melbourne)	MS133/1/103
97	10 March 1865	FROM WLR (Ballarat)	TO MR (East Melbourne)	MS133/1/88
98	13 March 1865	FROM WLR (Ballarat)	TO MR (East Melbourne)	MS133/1/108
99	15 March 1865	FROM WLR (Ballarat)	TO MR (East Melbourne)	MS133/1/83
100	20 March 1865	FROM WLR (Ballarat)	TO MR (Pentridge)	MS133/1/91
101	23 January 1866	FROM WLR (Ballarat)	TO MR (East Melbourne)	MS133/1/97
102	25 January 1866	FROM WLR (Ballarat)	TO MR (East Melbourne)	MS133/1/96
103	22 February 1866	FROM WLR (Ballarat)	TO MR (East Melbourne)	MS133/1/110
104	23 March 1866	FROM WLR (Ballarat)	TO MR (Streatham)	MS133/1/92
105	27 March 1866	FROM WLR (Ballarat)	TO MR (Hamilton)	MS133/1/95
106	6 April 1866	FROM WLR (Ballarat)	TO MR (Hamilton)	MS133/1/94
107	11 May 1866	FROM WLR (Ballarat)	TO MR (Melbourne)	MS133/1/82

108	20 June 1866	FROM BC (Lochmaben, Scotland)	TO WLR (Ballarat)	MS133/1/44
109	13 May 1867	FROM WLR (London, England)	TO MR (Brighton, England)	MS133/1/148
110	5 July 1867	FROM WLR (Edinburgh, Scotland)	TO MR (Leicester, England)	MS133/1/158
111	7 July 1867	FROM WLR (Edinburgh, Scotland)	TO MR (Leicester, England)	MS133/1/159
112	28 September 1867	FROM WLR (Eccles, England)	TO MR (Leicester, England)	MS133/1/161
113	11 December 1867	FROM MR (Eccles, England)	TO WLR (Rawcliffe, England)	MS133/1/152
114	26 January 1868	FROM WLR (Rawcliffe, England)	TO MR (Eccles, England)	MS133/1/125
115	28 January 1868	FROM WLR (Rawcliffe, England)	TO MR (Eccles, England)	MS133/1/129, MS133/1/138 & MS133/1/147
116	30 January 1868	FROM WLR (Rawcliffe, England)	TO MR (Eccles, England)	MS133/1/130, MS133/1/140 & MS133/1/200
117	1 February 1868	FROM WLR (Rawcliffe, England)	TO MR (Eccles, England)	MS133/1/123 & MS133/1/145
118	3 February 1868	FROM WLR (Rawcliffe, England)	TO MR (Eccles, England)	MS133/1/127 & MS133/1/144
119	5 February 1868	FROM WLR (Rawcliffe, England)	TO MR (Eccles, England)	MS133/1/128 & MS133/1/139
120	9 February 1868	FROM WLR (Rawcliffe, England)	TO MR (Eccles, England)	MS133/1/124 & MS133/1/131
121	9 February 1868	FROM WLR (Rawcliffe, England)	TO EB (Eccles, England)	MS133/1/131 (verso)
122	15 June 1868	FROM MR (Leicester, England)	TO WLR (Rawcliffe, England)	MS133/1/155
123	29 September 1868	FROM WLR (Rawcliffe, England)	TO MR (Stoke, England)	MS133/1/137 & MS133/1/142
124	6–7 October 1868	FROM WLR (Rawcliffe, England)	TO MR (Stoke, England)	MS133/1/143 & MS133/1/146

125	7 October 1868	FROM WLR (Rawcliffe, England)	TO JB (Stoke, England)	MS133/1/136
126	9 October 1868	FROM Ismay & Co. (Liverpool)	TO WLR (Rawcliffe, England)	MS133/1/141
127	11 October 1868	FROM WLR (Rawcliffe, England)	TO MR (Stoke, England)	MS133/1/141 (verso)
128	11 October 1868	FROM EB (Leicester, England)	TO MR (Stoke, England)	MS133/1/119
129	11 October 1868	FROM EB (Leicester, England)	TO LB (Stoke, England)	MS133/1/119 (verso)
130	18 October 1868	FROM WLR (Rawcliffe, England)	TO MR (Stoke, England)	MS133/1/126
131	19 October 1868	FROM WLR (Rawcliffe, England)	TO EB (Leicester, England)	MS133/1/132
132	19 October 1868	FROM EB (Leicester, England)	TO LB (Stoke, England)	MS133/1/120
133	19 October 1868	FROM EB (Leicester, England)	TO MR (Stoke, England)	MS133/1/120 (verso)
134	20 October 1868	FROM WLR (Rawcliffe, England)	TO MR (Stoke, England)	MS133/1/134
135	22 October 1868	FROM WLR (Rawcliffe, England)	TO MR (Stoke, England)	MS133/1/134A
136	25–27 October 1868	FROM WLR (Rawcliffe, England)	TO MR (Stoke, England)	MS133/1/135
137	26 October 1868	FROM EB (Leicester, England)	TO MR (Stoke, England)	MS133/1/121
138	28 October 1868	FROM WLR (Rawcliffe, England)	TO MR (Stoke, England)	MS133/1/133
139	29 November 1868	FROM WLR (Eccles, England)	TO MR (Leicester, England)	MS133/1/160
140	2 December 1868	FROM WLR (Dublin, Ireland)	TO MR (Leicester, England)	MS133/1/114
141	3 December 1868	FROM MR (Leicester, England)	TO WLR (Dublin, Ireland)	MS133/1/154 & MS133/1/162

142	3–4 December 1868	FROM WLR (Dublin, Ireland)	TO MR (Leicester, England)	MS133/1/115
143	5 December 1868	FROM MR (Leicester, England)	TO WLR (Dublin, Ireland)	MS133/1/153
144	5 December 1868	FROM WLR (Dublin, Ireland)	TO MR (Leicester, England)	MS133/1/116
145	26 December 1868	FROM EB (Leicester, England)	TO MR (Liverpool, England)	MS133/1/117
146	15 April 1869	FROM EB (Leicester, England)	TO MR/WLR (Melbourne)	MS133/1/118
147	12–14 May 1869	FROM EB (Leicester, England)	TO MR/WLR (Melbourne)	MS133/1/122
148	11 June 1869	FROM WLR (Ballarat)	TO MR (Melbourne)	MS133/1/90
149	24 September 1869	FROM WLR (Melbourne)	TO MR (Ballarat)	MS133/1/151
150	27 September 1869	FROM WLR (Melbourne)	TO MR (Ballarat)	MS133/1/150
151	30 September 1869	FROM WLR (Melbourne)	TO MR (Ballarat)	MS133/1/165
152	2 October 1869	FROM WLR (Melbourne)	TO MR (Ballarat)	MS133/1/166
153	5–6 October 1869	FROM WLR (Melbourne)	TO MR (Ballarat)	MS133/1/149
154	7 October 1869	FROM MR (Ballarat)	TO WLR (Melbourne)	MS133/1/46
155	5 June 1870	FROM WLR (Sydney)	TO MR (Melbourne)	MS133/1/173
156	7–8 June 1870	FROM WLR (Sydney)	TO MR (Melbourne)	MS133/1/172
157	8–10 June 1870	FROM WLR (Parramatta)	TO MR (Melbourne)	MS133/1/171
158	11–13 June 1870	FROM WLR (Parramatta)	TO MR (Melbourne)	MS133/1/170
159	14 June 1870	FROM WLR (Parramatta)	TO MR (Melbourne)	MS133/1/164
160	13 November 1871	FROM WLR (Sandhurst)	TO MR (St Kilda)	MS133/1/167
161	August 1874	FROM HHR & MR (London, England)	TO WLR (Melbourne)	MS133/2/1
162	9 November 1875	FROM WLR (Hawthorn)	TO MR (Blairgowrie)	MS133/1/163
163	15 June 1876	FROM WLR (Chiltern)	TO MR (Hawthorn)	MS133/1/175

164	16 June 1876	FROM WLR (Chiltern)	TO MR (Hawthorn)	MS133/1/176
165	17 June 1876	FROM WLR (Chiltern)	TO MR (Hawthorn)	MS133/1/182
166	19 June 1876	FROM WLR (Chiltern)	TO MR (Hawthorn)	MS133/1/180
167	20 June 1876	FROM WLR (Chiltern)	TO MR (Hawthorn)	MS133/1/183
168	21 June 1876	FROM WLR (Chiltern)	TO MR (Hawthorn)	MS133/1/184
169	22 June 1876	FROM WLR (Chiltern)	TO MR (Hawthorn)	MS133/1/185
170	23 June 1876	FROM WLR (Chiltern)	TO MR (Hawthorn)	MS133/1/202
171	24 June 1876	FROM WLR (Chiltern)	TO MR (Hawthorn)	MS133/1/204
172	25 June 1876	FROM WLR (Chiltern)	TO MR (Hawthorn)	MS133/1/192 & MS133/1/252
173	26 June 1876	FROM WLR (Chiltern)	TO MR (Hawthorn)	MS133/1/177
174	27 June 1876	FROM WLR (Chiltern)	TO MR (Hawthorn)	MS133/1/178
175	28 June 1876	FROM WLR (Chiltern)	TO MR (Hawthorn)	MS133/1/188
176	28 June 1876	FROM WLR (Chiltern)	TO MR (Hawthorn)	MS133/1/186
177	30 June 1876	FROM WLR (Chiltern)	TO MR (Hawthorn)	MS133/1/187
178	2 July 1876	FROM WLR (Chiltern)	TO MR (Hawthorn)	MS133/1/190 & MS133/1/191
179	3 July 1876	FROM WLR (Chiltern)	TO MR (Hawthorn)	MS133/1/181
180	4 July 1876	FROM WLR (Chiltern)	TO MR (Hawthorn)	MS133/1/189
181	5 July 1876	FROM WLR (Chiltern)	TO MR (Hawthorn)	MS133/1/198
182	6 July 1876	FROM WLR (Chiltern)	TO MR (Hawthorn)	MS133/1/199
183	7 July 1876	FROM WLR (Chiltern)	TO MR (Hawthorn)	MS133/1/193 & MS133/1/222
184	7 July 1876	FROM WLR (Chiltern)	TO HHR/ALR (Hawthorn)	MS133/1/222 (verso)
185	8–9 July 1876	FROM WLR (Chiltern)	TO MR (Hawthorn)	MS133/1/203
186	11 July 1876	FROM WLR (Chiltern)	TO MR (Hawthorn)	MS133/1/194
187	13 July 1876	FROM SDG (Chiltern)	TO WLR (Chiltern)	MS133/1/174
188	14 July 1876	FROM WLR (Chiltern)	TO MR (Hawthorn)	MS133/1/196
189	16 July 1876	FROM WLR (Chiltern)	TO MR (Hawthorn)	MS133/1/179

190	17 July 1876	FROM WLR (Chiltern)	TO HHR/ALR (Hawthorn)	MS133/1/179 (verso)
191	18 July 1876	FROM WLR (Chiltern)	TO MR (Hawthorn)	MS133/1/197
192	19 July 1876	FROM WLR (Chiltern)	TO MR (Hawthorn)	MS133/1/201
193	23 July 1876	FROM WLR (Chiltern)	TO MR (Hawthorn)	MS133/1/195
194	25 July 1876	FROM WLR (Chiltern)	TO MR (Hawthorn)	MS133/1/206
195	28–29 January 1877	FROM WLR (Chiltern)	TO MR (Richmond)	MS133/1/205
196	31 January 1877	FROM WLR (Chiltern)	TO MR (Richmond)	MS133/1/209
197	2 February 1877	FROM WLR (Chiltern)	TO MR (Richmond)	MS133/1/214
198	7 February 1877	FROM WLR (Chiltern)	TO MR (Blairgowrie)	MS133/1/213
199	12 February 1877	FROM WLR (Chiltern)	TO MR (Blairgowrie)	MS133/1/215
200	12 February 1877	FROM WLR (Chiltern)	TO HHR/ALR (Blairgowrie)	MS133/1/221
201	14–15 February 1877	FROM WLR (Chiltern)	TO MR (Blairgowrie)	MS133/1/212
202	15 February 1877	FROM WLR (Chiltern)	TO MR (Blairgowrie)	MS133/1/261
203	17 February 1877	FROM WLR (Chiltern)	TO MR (Blairgowrie)	MS133/1/210
204	20–21 February 1877	FROM WLR (Chiltern)	TO MR (Blairgowrie)	MS133/1/211
205	22 February 1877	FROM WLR (Chiltern)	TO MR (Blairgowrie)	MS133/1/220
206	24 February 1877	FROM WLR (Chiltern)	TO MR (Queenscliff)	MS133/1/217
207	27 February 1877	FROM WLR (Chiltern)	TO MR (Queenscliff)	MS133/1/219
208	3 March 1877	FROM WLR (Chiltern)	TO MR (Queenscliff)	MS133/1/207
209	11 March 1877	FROM WLR (Chiltern)	TO MR (Richmond)	MS133/1/208
210	17 March 1877	FROM WLR (Chiltern)	TO MR (Richmond)	MS133/1/218
211	14 April 1877	FROM WLR (Chiltern)	TO MR (Richmond)	MS133/1/216
212	27 August 1877	FROM WLR (Richmond)	TO MR (Chiltern)	MS133/1/242
213	28 August 1877	FROM WLR (Richmond)	TO MR (Chiltern)	MS133/1/241
214	29 August 1877	FROM WLR (Richmond)	TO MR (Chiltern)	MS133/1/240
215	30 August 1877	FROM WLR (Off Queenscliff)	TO MR (Chiltern)	MS133/1/238

216	30 August 1877	FROM WLR (Queenscliff)	TO MR (Chiltern)	MS133/1/239
217	31 August 1877	FROM WLR (Queenscliff)	TO MR (Chiltern)	MS133/1/237
218	3 September 1877	FROM WLR (Queenscliff)	TO MR (Chiltern)	MS133/1/228 & MS133/1/258
219	4 September 1877	FROM WLR (Queenscliff)	TO MR (Chiltern)	MS133/1/236 & MS133/1/254
220	5 September 1877	FROM WLR (Queenscliff)	TO MR (Chiltern)	MS133/1/256
221	6 September 1877	FROM WLR (Queenscliff)	TO MR (Chiltern)	MS133/1/232
222	6 September 1877	FROM WLR (Queenscliff)	TO MR (Chiltern)	MS133/1/234
223	7 September 1877	FROM WLR (Queenscliff)	TO MR (Chiltern)	MS133/1/233
224	8 September 1877	FROM WLR (Queenscliff)	TO MR (Chiltern)	MS133/1/249 & MS133/1/257
225	9 September 1877	FROM WLR (Queenscliff)	TO MR (Chiltern)	MS133/1/223, MS133/1/224 & MS133/1/225
226	10 September 1877	FROM WLR (Queenscliff)	TO MR (Chiltern)	MS133/1/235 & MS133/1/250
227	13 September 1877	FROM WLR (Queenscliff)	TO MR (Chiltern)	MS133/1/230
228	14 September 1877	FROM WLR (Queenscliff)	TO MR (Chiltern)	MS133/1/231
229	19 September 1877	FROM WLR (Queenscliff)	TO MR (Chiltern)	MS133/1/229 & MS133/1/251
230	20 September 1877	FROM WLR (Queenscliff)	TO MR (Chiltern)	MS133/1/227
231	21 September 1877	FROM WLR (Queenscliff)	TO MR (Chiltern)	MS133/1/246 & MS133/1/260

Index to Part I
Biographical Background

The index includes all persons and vessels referred to in Part I by *page number*. If the person or vessel appears in the notes only, the page number is followed by *n*.

Index to Part II
The Letters

The index includes all persons and vessels referred to in the letters (and endnotes) by *letter number* not page number. If the person or vessel appears in the notes only, the letter number is followed by *n*. Where there is a significant biographical note, the letter number is in bold.

83, 88, 90–91, 95, 109n, 110–124,
127–130, 132–137, 139–143, 145–146,
148n, 151n
Bailey, Elizabeth (Lizzie) see Elizabeth Brett
Bailey, Emma (Trotty), 31n, 45n, 48n, 49, 53,
55, 57, 59–61, 63, 65, 70–73, 75, 84, 97,
103n, 149, 160n
Bailey, Frances Mary Louise (Polly) née
Lascelles, 44n, **160**, 195n
Bailey, Frank Lascelles, 160n
Bailey, Gertrude Elizabeth, 84, 88, 97, 103n,
149n, 160n, **195**
Bailey, Grace, 19, 109n, 110–112, 114–115,
117–120, 123, 127–129, 132–137,
139–143, 145–147, 151–152, 160
Bailey, Guy Robinson, 160n
Bailey, Harrie Elphinstone, 31n, 34, 45n, 48,
50–53, 55, 57, 59, 61, 63, 70, 72, 81, 84,
86, 97, 103n, 109, 114, 116, 124, 127,
131, 133, 139, 148n, 149n, 160n
Bailey, Ida Beatrice, 97, 103n, 149n, 160n,
195
Bailey, James Harold, 3n, 113
Bailey, Jane (Jeannie) née Rainsford, 70–72,
75, 84–86, 88, 96, 101n, 103n, 148n,
160n, 195n
Bailey, John senior, 3n, 8, 33n, 109n, 119n,
146n
Bailey, John Robinson, 3n, 5, 13n, 20–21, 23,
31–34, 36–39, 42–44, 45n, 47n, 48–53,
55n, 57, 59–60, 63–64, 70–72, 75,
79–81, 84, 86–89, 96n, 97n, 101n,
102–104, 106–107, 109n, 113, 127n,
130–131, 133, 140n, 145n, 148, 149n,
150–152, 160n, 164n, 195n
Bailey, Leila Maud, 160n, 195–197, 199, 204
Bailey, Mabel Elizabeth, 3n, 146n, 230n
Bailey, Mary Jane (Jeannie), 101n, 103, 149n,
160n, 195
Bailey, Mary (dau. of Polly and Samuel), 160n
Bailey, Mary Ringrose (see also Mary Bayles
post-1875), 148n, 149–150, 151n, 152,
160
Bailey, Percy François, 3n, 230n
Bailey, Samuel, 34n, 65, 70–71, 73–76,
78–80, 82, 86, 93–94, 97, 106n, 124,
134, 146–147, 153–154, 158, 160n,
161n, 166, 168, 171–172, 174–175, 178,
182, 195–199, 204
Bailey, Sarah Ann (see Sarah Ann Laughton)
Bailey, Susannah Tyler née Nicholson, 31,
33–36, 39, 43–44, 45n, 47n, 49n, 70, 72,
103n, 109n, 145n, 149n, 160n
Bailey, Thomas Robinson Burton, 34n, 119,
137, 146, 147
Bailey, Walter Robinson, 3n, 124n, 211n,
230n
Bailey, William, 3–7, 9–13, 16–18, 21, 30n,
32, 39, 93, 119n
Baillieu, Emma Lawrence née Pow, 44n
Baillieu, James George, 44n

Baillieu, James Lambert, 44n
Baillieu, Norman Horace, 44n
Baillieu, William Lawrence, 44n
Baker, Sir Henry, 114n
Baker, William (bookseller), 59
Baker Brown, Dr, 109n
Balfe, Michael, 86n
Ballangeich, 79n
Ballantyne, Reverend T. H., 196n
Bandmann, Daniel, 149
Bannester, Benjamin, 4n
Bannester, Tilly (Harriet Matilda) née
Bradshaw, 1, 2n, 3–12, 14–18, 20–21,
22n
Bannester, Henry Fisher, 4, 7, 21, 22n
Barclay, Dr, 112
Barker, Dr Thomas, 217, 222, 224, 231
Barkly, Ann née Pratt, 57n
Barkley, Benjamin Jackson, 168n
Barkly, Elizabeth Helen née Timms, 57n
Barkly, Henry, 57n
Barkly, Sir Henry, 48n, 57, 70n
Barkly, Hubert Lee, 57n
Barkly, James, 57n
Barrackpore, 225n
Barry, Mr, 30
Barry, Sir Redmond, 152n
Barry, Mrs, 32, 35, 39
Barton, Sir Edmund, 49n
Bath, Elizabeth née Bews, 43n
Bath, Malachi, 43n
Bawn, G. H., 86
Baxter, Andrew, 96n
Bayles, Hadzley Caldicot, 195n
Bayles, Josephine, 195n
Bayles, Mary Ringrose formerly Bailey, née
Atkins, 164, 166–167, 169, 171, 173,
176, 181, 191, 195
Bayles, William, 164n, 195n
Bayles, William John Cam junior, 195n
Bayley, Ella, 40n
Bayley, Isabella Constance, 40n
Bayley, Isabella née Mactier, 40n, 57n
Bayley, Sir John, 26n, 40n
Bayley, (Sir) Lyttleton Holyoake, 26n, 40, 45,
57n
Bayley, Stanhope Lyttleton Fector, 40n
Bayley, Thomas, 80n
Bayley, Vernon Batthyring Fector, 40n
Beaney, Dr James George, 57n, 152n, **225**
Bearington, Miss, 132
Beckett, Sir Thomas, 114n
Beech, Mr and Mrs, 112
Beer, Reverend Joseph, 140n
Belford, Richard, 58n
Bell, Mrs, 81
Bellew, Harold Kyrle, 140n
Bellew, John Chippendall Montesquieu, 140
Bennett Brothers, 3n, 31
Bennetts (London), 140
Bennett, J. B., 57n